INVESTMENTS

An Introduction · *Second Edition*

INVESTMENTS

An Introduction • *Second Edition*

Herbert B. Mayo
Trenton State College

The Dryden Press
Chicago · New York · San Francisco · Philadelphia
Montreal · Toronto · London · Sydney · Tokyo

Acquisitions Editor: Ann Heath
Editorial Assistant: Betsy Webster
Project Editor: Diane Tenzi
Design Director: Alan Wendt
Production Manager: Mary Jarvis
Permissions Editor: Cindy Lombardo
Director of Editing, Design, and Production: Jane Perkins

Text and Cover Designer: C. J. Petlick, Hunter Graphics
Copy Editor: Judith Lary
Compositor: G&S Typesetters, Inc.
Text Type: 10/12 Berkeley Oldstyle Book

Library of Congress Cataloging-in-Publication Data

Mayo, Herbert B.
  Investments : an introduction.

  Includes bibliographies and index.
  1. Investments. 2. Investment analysis. I. Title.
HG4521.M37 1988   332.6′78   86-29129
ISBN 0-03-009769-X

Printed in the United States of America
789-016-987654321

Address orders:
111 Fifth Avenue
New York, NY 10003

Address editorial correspondence:
One Salt Creek Lane
Hinsdale, IL 60521-2902

The Dryden Press
Holt, Rinehart and Winston
Saunders College Publishing

Cover Source: Courtesy of Salomon Brothers Inc.

For
E. B. M. C. S. R. B. E.

The Dryden Press Series in Finance

Preface

Many textbooks on investments are written for students with considerable background (and in some cases extensive background) in accounting, finance, and economics. However, not every student who takes an investments course has such an extensive background, and these students cannot cope with (or be expected to cope with) the material in fine, but advanced, textbooks on investments. This text is aimed at these students. The book covers the basics of investing, ranging from descriptive material on how securities are bought and sold to theoretical material on how securities are valued in an efficient financial market.

The text does assume that the student has a desire to tackle a fascinating subject that may have real impact on his or her well-being. Thus, while the presentation may be at an elementary level, in some cases the concepts are very sophisticated. No attempt is made to make the material unnecessarily difficult, but the very nature of evaluating investments and choosing among competing uses for the saver's funds is not easy, nor should it be.

Investing also requires an ability to forecast future events, or at least to anticipate the future. If one knew what was going to happen, investing would be easy. But the future can only be expected, and these expectations in many cases are not fulfilled. During the 1960s few individuals anticipated the inflation of the 1970s. The economy experienced a long period of stable economic growth in the 1960s, and economists believed that the problem of the business cycle had been overcome. They thought that by careful manipulation of fiscal and monetary policy, an era of continuous growth and prosperity would be upon us. That expectation certainly was not fulfilled!

If professional economists and others trained in forecasting have problems anticipating the future, one can imagine the problems besetting the typical saver who seeks to invest a modest sum to help fulfill some future financial goal, such as putting a child through college. For the vast majority of individuals, investing is by its very nature a difficult problem. The security world is one of special jargon and terms, sophisticated professionals, and an almost limitless number of possible alternative investments. It is a primary aim of this text to make investing a little less difficult by explaining the terms and jargon, by elucidating the possible investments available to the individual investor, and by explaining many of the techniques used by the professionals to value an asset.

This text uses a substantial number of examples and illustrations employing data that are generally available to the investing public. It is believed that this information

is accurate; however, the reader should not assume that any mention of a specific firm and its securities is a recommendation to buy or sell those securities. The examples have been chosen to illustrate specific points and not to pass judgment on individual investments.

CHANGES FROM THE PREVIOUS EDITION

This book is a revision of an existing text, and the thrust, structure, and tone of the previous edition have been retained. However, there have been major changes in the material covered. Besides updating illustrations and improving the prose, the following major changes and additions have been made:

• The introductory chapter has been expanded to include more material on risk to better establish the trade-off between risk and return that is crucial to all investments.

• The material on short-term investments in Chapter 2 has been expanded, especially the discussion of financial intermediaries and deregulation of the banking system, and the material on money market mutual funds has been moved from the chapter on mutual funds to this chapter.

• Chapter 4 on sources of information has been expanded to include data bases and on-line investing, as well as more extensive coverage of financial literature.

• Chapter 5 on taxes includes the extensive changes in the federal income tax laws enacted in 1986.

• Chapter 6 on the time value of money has been rewritten to differentiate between ordinary annuities and annuities due.

• Chapter 7 on financial statements now starts with material on general accounting principles.

• Chapter 8 on risk and efficient markets has been extensively revised. The theoretical material (e.g., beta coefficients and the portfolio's dispersion) has been expanded and better illustrated. A section on portfolio construction and the efficient market hypothesis has been added so that the analysis of risk is perceived in a portfolio context.

• Chapter 9 on debt instruments has new material on variable-interest-rate bonds, zero coupon bonds, and junk bonds. An appendix on the explanations of the term structure of interest rates has been added.

• Chapter 10 now includes a description, as well as an example, of how to use the concept of "duration."

• Chapter 11 on preferred stock has new material on adjustable-rate preferred stocks and the disadvantages associated with investing in preferred stock.

• Chapter 12 on government securities has been expanded to include zero coupon securities based on federal government securities (e.g., CATS). A special section on Ginnie Maes and mortgage-backed securities and an appendix on riding the yield curve using treasury bills have been added.

• Chapter 13 on measures of stock prices and rates of return has additional material on the various measures of security prices.

• The material in Chapter 14 on required rates of return, expected rates of return,

and valuation has been clarified. The relationship between the use of the dividend-growth model and the use of P/E ratios to value securities has been included.

• Chapters 16 and 17 on fundamental analysis have been significantly expanded to include additional material on the growth in the money supply and monetary growth targets, the anticipated economic environment and different investment strategies, the use of ratio analysis by specific investors, weaknesses in industry average statistics, and alternative methods of valuation for selecting stocks.

• Chapters 19 and 20 on options have been reorganized. The material on warrants has been shifted to Chapter 19, which permits expansion of the coverage of puts and calls in Chapter 20. Additional material on stock index options and their use in hedge positions and an appendix on protective puts have been added.

• Chapter 21 on convertible securities now includes a section on selecting convertibles, and coverage of put bonds has been added.

• Chapter 22 on investment companies has been extensively expanded to include material on selecting mutual funds, hidden capital gains and losses, old versus new and large versus small funds, expenses (exit fees and 12b-1 plans), and risk adjustments to facilitate comparisons of funds.

• Chapter 25 on real estate has been expanded to illustrate the determination of cash flow from rental properties and the special risks associated with investing in these properties.

• Chapter 26 on international investments is an entirely new chapter. It includes material on foreign stock exchanges, American Depository Receipts (ADRs), exchange rates, Euro-bonds, risk management through hedging, advantages offered by foreign securities, and American mutual funds with foreign investments.

• Chapter 27 has expanded coverage of the forms of the efficient market hypothesis and anomalies in the empirical evidence that seeks to verify the hypothesis. The chapter ends with a totally revised section devoted to financial planning that includes a review of the assets covered in the text, the construction of the individual's pro forma balance sheet and cash budget, and the role of professional money managers and financial planners.

PEDAGOGICAL FEATURES

This text has a variety of features designed to assist the learning process. Each chapter starts with a set of **learning objectives**. These objectives point out topics to look for as the chapter develops. Each objective is stated using an action verb, such as "differentiate," "define," or "describe." The choice of the verb also gives the reader a clue as to how the material should be learned. For example, the objective "differentiate preferred stock from long-term bonds" requires the student to learn the features that are common to both instruments and how they differ.

Running alongside the text material are **marginal notes** which highlight what is being discussed. Students who have used the previous edition found these notes to be the single most helpful pedagogical feature employed in the book. These marginal notes also serve as a guide for notetaking.

There are many interesting sidelight points that may not fit neatly into a particular chapter. To include these, I have added boxed **Points of Interest** to many of the chapters. These boxes may amplify the text material or present new material to supplement the coverage in the text. The tone of the points of interest is somewhat lighter than the text and is designed to increase reader interest in the chapter as a whole.

At the end of each chapter there is a list of **terms to remember**. Care has been taken to present the terms in the order of their appearance in the chapter. These terms reappear fully defined in the **glossary** at the end of the text; the glossary in turn gives the chapter number in which each term first appears.

Each chapter also includes **questions** and, where appropriate, **problems**. The questions and problems are straightforward and are designed primarily to review the material. The *Instructor's Manual* includes points to consider when answering these questions as well as the solutions to the problems. A *Test Bank* with questions for each chapter is included in the *Instructor's Manual*.

The chapters end with **suggested readings** intended to give the student a brief description of selected sources of further information. These are drawn from a cross-section of the literature on finance and investments. They include academic publications (e.g., *Financial Management*), the professional literature (e.g., *Financial Analysts Journal*), and general business publications (e.g., *Forbes*). This literature and the books cited should be readily available in many libraries. The suggested readings are generally not technical, and while they may require serious reading, they should be accessible to the student using this text.

This text also has several **short case studies** which cover the material presented in several chapters and usually appear at the end of each of the book's parts. These cases serve both as a review and a means to tie the chapters together. They may be used as a basis for class discussions or homework assignments.

POSSIBLE ORGANIZATIONS OF INVESTMENT COURSES

The text has 27 chapters, but few instructors may be able to complete the entire book in a semester course. Many of the chapters are self-contained units, so individual chapters may be omitted (or transposed) without loss of continuity. There are, however, exceptions. For example, the valuation of preferred stock uses the same model as the valuation of bonds. The ratio analysis of a firm's financial statements in Chapter 17 assumes the student knows the material in Chapter 7.

Part I covers the environment of investing. It includes the role of brokers and financial intermediaries such as commercial banks, as well as how securities come into existence. This is essential material on investments that many students may not have had. These chapters are not easily omitted. Part II, however, covers material that students may already know (such as financial statements), in which case the omission of any particular chapter should release time for other chapters.

The bread and butter of investing in financial assets is the analysis and selection of fixed-income securities (Part III) and common stock (Part IV). Like Part I, Parts III and IV should be assigned and covered in class, with the possible exception of the chapter on technical analysis. Parts V and VI on options and alternative investments leave the

instructor considerable choice. Since each instructor has personal preferences, any of these chapters is easily omitted or included depending on the availability of time. I do, however, believe that Part VII, on financial planning in an efficient financial market, *should* be included, as it may serve as a means to summarize the material presented in the course.

ACKNOWLEDGMENTS

A textbook requires the input and assistance of many individuals in addition to the author. I would like to acknowledge the following individuals who contributed their time and thoughts to this text: Robert J. Hartwig, Worcester State College; Neil Gaston, Trenton State College; James P. Kuttner, College for Financial Planning; Donald W. Johnson, College for Financial Planning; Christian Guvernator III, Scott and Stringfellow; and Steven Stern, Trust Department—United Jersey Banks.

At this point in the text, it is traditional for the author to thank members of the production staff for their help in bringing the book to fruition. I wish to thank Ann Heath, Betsy Webster, Alan Wendt, C. J. Petlick, and Joe Pesce for their support. Their efforts are appreciated. In addition, a special bouquet of long-stemmed roses or a king-sized box of designer chocolates is due Diane Tenzi, whose frequent memos, letters, and phone calls shamed me into maintaining the production schedule.

I encourage readers to contact me with suggestions and comments. Please feel free to write me at RD 2, Box 529, Ringoes, New Jersey 08551.

Herbert B. Mayo
April 1987

Contents

INVESTMENTS
An Introduction   •   *Second Edition*

I The Environment of Investing

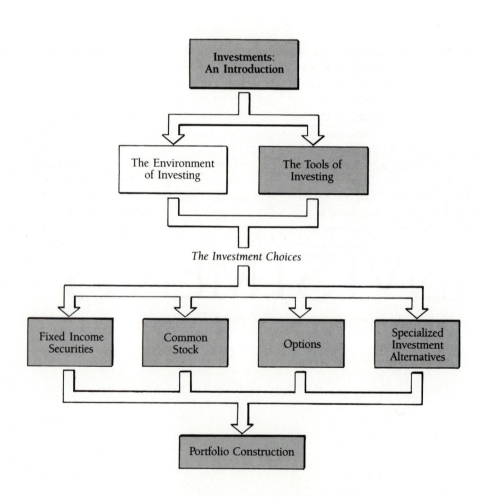

Investments:
An Introduction

The Environment
of Investing

The Tools of
Investing

The Investment Choices

Fixed Income
Securities

Common
Stock

Options

Specialized
Investment
Alternatives

Portfolio Construction

To enhance the learning process, this text has been divided into distinct sections. The first considers the environment in which investment decisions are made, since it can have considerable impact on which assets the investor chooses to include in his or her portfolio.

The investor should start by specifying his or her goals of investing. Investing is a means to an end, such as financial security during retirement or the ability to make the down payment on a house. These ends should be specified before the individual acquires a portfolio, because not all assets will serve to meet the particular financial goals.

Once these goals are established, the investor should be aware of the environment and the mechanics of investing, including the process by which securities are issued and subsequently bought and sold, the regulations and tax laws that have been established by the various levels of government, and the sources of information available to investors. An understanding of this environment, along with the tools discussed in Part Two, lays the foundation for the process of analyzing specific assets for possible inclusion in one's portfolio.

1

An Introduction to Investments

LEARNING OBJECTIVES

After completing this chapter you should be able to

1. Explain why individuals should specify investment goals.
2. Differentiate between liquidity and marketability.
3. Distinguish between primary and secondary markets.
4. Identify the sources of risk.
5. Understand why financial markets are considered efficient.

In 1972, the common stock of Xerox reached an all-time high of $171⅞ per share. Fourteen years later, Xerox's common stock was trading for $60—65 percent below its historic high. In 1970, Federal Express did not exist, but if an investor had bought Federal Express shares when they were initially sold for $3 to the general public on April 12, 1978, that investor would have watched the shares appreciate over 1800 percent within eight years. It was not until 1975 that Americans could legally own gold bullion. At that time gold traded for about $200 an ounce; its price rose to more than $800 an ounce during 1980. Prior to 1975, individuals deposited funds in savings accounts at commercial banks because one of today's most popular investments, shares in money market mutual funds, was not available.

What a dynamic subject investments has been! Over the years some investments have produced extraordinary gains, while others have produced only mediocre returns and some have generated substantial losses. Today the field of investments is even more dynamic than it was only a decade ago. The individual has so many assets to choose among. Events occur so rapidly—events that can and do alter the value of specific assets. The amount of information available to the investor is staggering and continually growing. The development of home computers will increase individuals' ability to track their investments and perform invest-ment analysis. Furthermore, the inflation of the 1970s has made virtually everyone more aware of the importance of financial planning and wise investing.

PORTFOLIO CONSTRUCTION

Once an individual receives income, there are two choices: to spend it or to save it. If the individual chooses to save, an additional decision must be made: What is to be done with the savings? This is an extremely important question because in 1985, Americans' personal income was $3,294.2 billion and they saved $172.5 billion.[1] The saver must decide where to invest this command over goods and services that is currently not being used. This is an important decision for the individual because these assets are the means by which today's purchasing power is transferred to the future. In effect, the saver must decide on a **portfolio** of assets to own. A portfolio is a combination of assets designed to serve as a store of value. Poor management of these assets may destroy the portfolio's value, and the individual will not achieve his or her investment goals.

There are many assets that the investor may include in the portfolio, and this book will discuss many of them. The stress, however, will be on long-term financial assets. While the saver may hold a portion of the portfolio in short-term assets, such as savings accounts, these assets do not seem to present the problem of valuation and choice that accompanies the decision to purchase a stock or a bond. Understanding the nature of long-term assets, i.e., how they are bought and sold, how they are valued, and how they may be used in portfolio construction, is the primary thrust of this text.

Several factors affect the construction of a portfolio. These include the goals of the investor, the risks involved, the taxes that will be imposed on any gain, and a knowledge of the available opportunities and alternative investments. This text will cover the range of these alternative investments, their use in a portfolio, the risks associated with owning them, and their valuation.   *Investment goals*

The investor's goals should largely determine the construction and management of the portfolio. Investing must have a purpose, for without a goal a portfolio is like a boat without a rudder. There must be some objective that offers a guide to the composition of the portfolio.

There are many reasons for saving and accumulating assets. Planning for retirement and preparing for the education of one's children are only two of the many reasons for saving. Other motives include the desire to meet financial emergencies, to leave a sizable estate, or even to accumulate wealth for the sake of accumulating. For these reasons, people acquire a portfolio of assets rather than spend all of their current income.

These motives for saving should dictate, or at least affect, the composition of the portfolio. Savings that are held to meet emergencies should not be invested in assets whose potential return involves substantial risk; instead, emphasis should be placed on assets on which the return is assured and which may be readily converted to cash, such as savings accounts. A portfolio that is designed to help finance retirement can stress long-term assets, such as bonds that will mature many years in the future or stocks that offer potential growth in value.   *Their effect on the portfolio*

---

[1]Source: *Survey of Current Business* (January 1986): 11.

Willingness to bear risk

In addition to the individual's goals, his or her capacity or willingness to bear risk plays an important role in constructing the portfolio. Some individuals are more willing and able to bear risk, and these persons will tend to select assets on which the return involves greater risk to obtain the specified investment goals. For example, if the saver wants to build a retirement fund, he or she can choose from a variety of possible investments. However, not all investments are equal with regard to risk and potential return. Those investors who are more willing to accept risk may construct portfolios with assets involving greater risk that may earn higher returns. Although conservative investors may select securities issued by the more financially stable firms, investors who are less averse to taking risk may select stocks issued by younger, less seasoned firms that may offer better opportunities for growth over a period of years.

Taxes

Taxes also help to decide the composition of an individual's portfolio. Investments are subject to a variety of different taxes. The income that is generated is taxed, as is the capital appreciation that is realized. Some states levy personal property taxes on one's securities. When a person dies, the federal government taxes the value of the estate, which includes the portfolio. In addition to the federal estate tax, several states tax the distribution of the wealth (i.e., they levy a tax on an individual's inheritance). Such taxes and the desire to reduce them affect the composition of each person's portfolio.

The purchase of an asset

Although decisions regarding the portfolio's construction and management as a whole are certainly important, the investor's primary decisions center around the acquisition of one asset at a time. The selection of a specific asset is the domain of security analysis. Security analysis considers the merits of the specific asset, while portfolio management determines the effect that the individual asset has on the whole portfolio.

A large portion of this text is devoted to security analysis, because it is impossible to know an asset's effect on the portfolio as a whole without first knowing its characteristics. Stock and bonds differ greatly with regard to risk, potential return, and valuation. Even within a single type of asset such as bonds, there can be considerable variation. For example, a corporate bond is different from a municipal bond, and a convertible bond differs from a straight bond that lacks the conversion feature. The investor needs to know and to understand these differences as well as the relative merits and risks associated with each of the assets. After understanding how individual assets are valued, the investor may then construct a portfolio that will aid in the realization of his or her financial goals.

SOME PRELIMINARY DEFINITIONS

The economic definition of investment

The term **investment** can have more than one meaning. In economics it refers to the purchase of a physical asset, such as a firm's purchase of a plant, equipment, or inventory, or an individual's purchase of a house. To the lay person the word denotes buying stock or bonds (or maybe even a house), but it probably does not mean purchasing a plant, equipment, or inventory.

Primary and secondary markets

From the viewpoint of the aggregate economy, an individual's buying stocks or bonds is not an investment. For every investment by the buyer there is an equal *disin-*

vestment by the seller. These buyers and sellers are trading one asset for another: The seller trades the security for cash, and the buyer trades cash for the security. These transactions occur in secondhand markets, and for that reason security markets are often referred to as **secondary markets.** Only when the securities are initially issued and sold in the **primary market** is there an investment in an economic sense. Then and only then does the firm receive the money that it, in turn, may use to purchase a plant, equipment, or inventory.

In this text, the word *investment* is used in the lay person's sense. Purchases of an asset for the purpose of storing value (and, hopefully, increasing that value over time) will be called an investment, even if in the aggregate there is only a transfer of ownership from a seller to a buyer. The purchases of stocks, bonds, speculative options, commodity contracts, and even antiques, stamps, and real estate are all considered to be investments if the individual's intent is to transfer purchasing power to the future. If these assets are acting as stores of value, they are investments for that individual. *The lay person's definition of investment*

Assets have **value** because of the future benefits they offer. The process of determining what an asset is worth is called **valuation.** An investor appraises the asset and assigns a current value to it based on the belief that the asset will generate income or a flow of services or will appreciate in price. After computing this value, the individual compares it with the current market price to determine if the asset is currently overpriced or underpriced. *Present value depends on future benefits*

In some cases this valuation is relatively easy. For example, the bonds of the federal government pay a fixed amount of interest each year and mature at a specified date. Thus, the future benefits are known. However, the future benefits of other assets are not so readily identified. For example, while the investor may anticipate future dividends, neither their payment nor their amount can be known with certainty. Forecasting future benefits may be very difficult, but forecasts are still crucial to the process of valuation. Without them and an evaluation of the asset, the investor cannot know if the asset should be purchased or sold.

The valuation of some assets is complicated, and two people may have different estimates of the future benefits. It is therefore easy to understand why two people may have completely divergent views on the worth of a particular asset. One person may believe that an asset is overvalued and hence seek to sell it, while another may seek to buy it in the belief that it is undervalued. Valuation may be very subjective, which leads to such inconsistencies as one person's buying while the other is selling. That does not mean that one person is necessarily irrational or incompetent. People's goals and perceptions (or estimates) of an asset's potential may change, affecting their valuation of the specific asset. *Different goals and forecasts produce different valuations*

An investment is made because the investor anticipates a **return.** The return on an investment is what the investor earns. This may be in the form of **income,** such as dividends and interest, or in the form of **capital gains** or appreciation if the asset's price rises. Not all assets offer both income and capital appreciation. Some stocks pay no current dividends but may appreciate in value. Other assets, including savings accounts, do not appreciate in value, and the return is solely the interest income. *The return: income and price appreciation*

Return is frequently expressed in percentages. It is then referred to as the **rate of return,** which is the return that is earned by the investment relative to its cost. Before purchasing an asset, the investor anticipates that the rate of return will be greater than that of other assets of similar risk. Without this anticipation, the purchase would not

be made. The realized rate of return may, of course, be quite different from the anticipated rate of return. That is the element of risk.

All investments involve risk

Risk is the uncertainty that the anticipated return will be achieved. As is discussed in the next section, there are many sources of risk. The investor must be willing to bear this risk to achieve the expected return. Even relatively safe investments involve some risk; there is no completely safe investment. For example, savings accounts that are insured still involve some element of risk of loss. If the rate of inflation exceeds the rate of interest that is earned on these insured accounts, the investor suffers a loss of purchasing power.

While the term *risk* often has a negative connotation, there is both positive and negative risk. Risk is uncertainty regarding the expected return, and this uncertainty works both ways. For example, events may occur that cause the value of an asset to rise more than anticipated. Certainly the stockholders of Signal Corp., SCM, or Richardson-Vicks reaped returns that were larger than had been anticipated. All three firms were taken over, and the prices paid for their stock were considerably higher than the prices these securities commanded before the announcements of the takeovers.

Bearing risk is not speculating

A term that is frequently used in conjunction with risk is **speculation**. Many years ago virtually all investments were called speculations. Today the word implies only a high degree of risk. However, risk is not synonymous with speculation. Speculation has the connotation of gambling in which the odds are against the player. Many securities are risky, but over a period of years the investor will reap a positive return. The odds are not really against the investor, and such investments are not speculations.

The term *speculation* is rarely used in this text, and when it is employed, the implication is that the investor runs a good chance of losing the funds invested in the speculative asset. Although a particular speculation may pay off handsomely, the investor should not expect that many such gambles will reap large returns. After the investor adjusts for the larger amount of risk that must be borne to own such speculative investments, the anticipated return may not justify the risk involved.

Marketability and liquidity

Besides involving risk and offering an expected return, stores of value have marketability or liquidity or both. **Marketability** means that the asset can readily be bought and sold. Frequently this is confused with **liquidity,** which is ease of converting the asset into cash *without significant loss*. An asset, such as stock that is traded on the New York Stock Exchange, may be very marketable but not very liquid, since its price could decline. Other assets may be very liquid but not marketable. A savings account in a commercial bank is liquid because it may be readily converted into cash, but it is not a marketable asset. Instead the saver withdraws the funds from the account.

Matching goals and assets

Recognizing the difference between liquidity and marketability is important when selecting assets to meet specific investment goals. If the goal is safety of principal or the need for funds to meet financial emergencies, then the investor should acquire liquid assets. Liquidity implies safety of principal and applies to assets that may be readily converted into cash with little risk of loss of the funds invested. It is the safety and accessibility of the funds and not the marketability of the asset that is the important consideration. Of course, the investor may acquire a liquid asset that is also marketable (e.g., a U.S. Treasury bill), but the emphasis is placed on the asset's liquidity.

In other cases marketability may be more important than liquidity. Suppose an investor seeks to accumulate funds to finance a child's college education. This goal

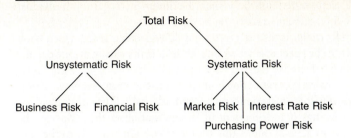

Exhibit 1.1
The Sources of Risk

does not require that the asset be immediately convertible into cash with little risk of loss. Instead the investor wants an asset that offers safety of principal and the potential for growth over time through the compounding of interest or through price appreciation. However, the asset must ultimately be converted into cash at the specified time in the future. For most assets to meet this requirement, there must exist a market in which the asset may be sold. Without such a market, the investor may be unable to convert the asset back into cash when the funds are needed.

All assets that serve as potential stores of value possess some combination of marketability, liquidity, and the potential to generate income and/or appreciate in price.[2] These features, along with the risk associated with each asset, are considered when including the asset in the individual's portfolio. Since assets differ with regard to their features, it is important for the investor to know the characteristics of each asset. Much of the balance of this text considers each asset's features as well as the sources of its risk and return. In the last chapter, Exhibit 27.1 gives a summary of the various assets' characteristics—their liquidity, marketability, sources of return, and risk exposure.

Characteristics common to all assets

SOURCES OF RISK

As was mentioned previously, risk refers to the uncertainty that the actual return the investor realizes will differ from the expected return. As is illustrated in Exhibit 1.1, this variability in returns is often differentiated into two types of risk: systematic and unsystematic risk. **Systematic risk** refers to those factors that affect the returns on all comparable investments. For example, when the market as a whole rises, the prices of most individual securities also rise. There is a systematic relationship between the return on a specific asset and the return on all other assets in its class (i.e., all other comparable assets). Since this systematic relationship exists, diversifying the portfolio by acquiring other comparable assets does not reduce this source of risk; thus, systematic risk is often referred to as "non-diversifiable risk." The individual investor must ultimately decide on how much systematic risk he or she is willing to bear.

Systematic risk

---

[2] The investor must realize that investments are made to transfer purchasing power to the future (i.e., to store value). However, some investments that may not be successful generate losses and thus do not transfer purchasing power to the future.

(How systematic risk is measured and how such measurement helps the individual determine the amount of systematic risk being borne is discussed in Chapter 8.)

Unsystematic risk

Unsystematic risk, which is also referred to as "diversifiable risk," depends on factors that are unique to the specific asset. For example, a firm's earnings may decline because of a strike. Other firms in the industry may not experience the same labor problem, and thus their earnings may not be hurt or may even rise as customers divert purchases from the firm whose operations are temporarily halted. In either case, the change in the firm's earnings is independent of factors that affect the industry, the market, or the economy in general. Since this source of risk applies only to the specific firm, it may be reduced through the construction of a diversified portfolio.

The total risk the investor bears therefore consists of unsystematic and systematic risk. The sources of unsystematic risk may be subdivided into two general classifications—business risk and financial risk. The sources of systematic risk may be subdivided into market risk, interest rate risk, and purchasing power risk.

Sources of unsystematic risk
1. Business risk

Business risk is the risk associated with the nature of the enterprise itself. Not all businesses are equally risky. Drilling for new oil deposits is considerably more risky than running a commercial bank. The chances of finding oil may be slim, and only one of many new wells may actually produce oil and earn a positive return. Commercial banks, however, can make loans that are secured by particular assets, such as residences or inventories. While these loans are not risk-free, they may be relatively safe because even if the debtor defaults, the creditor (the bank) can seize the security to meet its claims. Some businesses are by their very nature riskier than others, and, therefore, investing in them is inherently riskier.

2. Financial risk

All assets must be financed. Either creditors or owners or both provide the funds to start and to sustain the business. The second major source of risk is **financial risk.** Borrowing funds to finance a business may increase the element of risk, because creditors require that the borrower meet certain terms to obtain the funds. The most common of these requirements is the paying of interest and the repayment of principal. The creditor can (and usually does) demand other terms, such as collateral or restrictions on dividend payments, that the borrower must meet. These restrictions mean that the firm that uses debt financing bears more risk because it must meet these obligations in addition to its other obligations. When sales and earnings are rising, these constraints may not be burdensome, but during periods of financial stress the firm must meet the obligations required by its debt financing. Failure of the firm to meet these terms may result in financial ruin and bankruptcy. A firm that does not use borrowed funds to acquire its assets does not have these additional responsibilities and does not have the element of financial risk.

Sources of systematic risk
1. Market risk

Market risk refers to the tendency of security prices to move together. While it may be frustrating to invest in a firm that appears to have a minimum amount of business risk and financial risk and then to watch the price of its securities fall as the market as a whole declines, that is the nature of market risk. Security prices do fluctuate, and the investor must either accept the risk associated with those fluctuations or not participate in the market.

While market risk is generally applied to stocks, the concept also applies to other assets, such as stamps, art objects, and real estate. The prices of each of these assets fluctuate. If the value of houses were to rise in general, then the value of a particular

house would also tend to increase. But the converse is also true because the prices of houses could decline, causing the value of a specific house to fall. Market risk cannot be avoided if the individual acquires assets whose prices may fluctuate.

Interest rate risk refers to the tendency of security prices, especially fixed-income securities, to move inversely with changes in the rate of interest. As is explained in detail in Chapters 10 and 11, the prices of bonds and preferred stock depend in part on the current rate of interest. Rising interest rates decrease the current price of fixed-income securities because current purchasers require a competitive yield. The investor who acquires these securities must face the fact that interest rates can and do fluctuate, thus causing the price of these fixed-income securities to fluctuate. The source of this risk depends on the demand and supply of credit. Thus, diversification can not affect interest rate risk because it applies to all securities. Instead the investor may alter the term (i.e., length of time to maturity) of the securities acquired to reduce the impact of interest rate fluctuations.

2. Interest rate risk

In addition to the previously mentioned risks, the investor must also bear the risk associated with inflation. Inflation is the loss of purchasing power through a general rise in prices. If prices of goods and services increase, the real purchasing power of the investor's assets and the income generated by them is reduced. Thus **purchasing power risk** is the risk that inflation will erode the buying power of the investor's assets and income.[3]

3. Purchasing power risk

Investors will naturally seek to protect themselves from loss of purchasing power by constructing a portfolio of assets with an anticipated return that is higher than the anticipated rate of inflation. It is important to note the word *anticipated,* because it influences the selection of particular assets. If inflation is expected to be 4 percent, a savings account offering 6 percent will produce a gain and thereby "beat" inflation. In this illustration the real rate of return is 2 percent (at least before taxes). However, if the inflation rate were to increase unexpectedly to 7 percent, the savings account would result in a loss of purchasing power. The real rate of return is negative. If the higher rate of inflation had been expected, the investor might not have chosen the savings account but might have purchased some other asset with a higher potential return.

Real rate of return

Higher yields, however, may be achieved by bearing more risk. This is an essential trade-off that all investors must face. Federally insured savings accounts offer lower yields but are less risky than bonds issued by AT&T, and AT&T bonds are less risky than the stock of a small, emerging firm whose securities are traded over the counter.

Higher yields are associated with additional risk

The investor may select riskier assets in anticipation of a higher return, but this higher return is not necessarily superior to a lower return. The investor must decide if the anticipated additional return is worth the additional risk that he or she must bear. The aim, then, is for the investor to optimize the risk/return trade-off and to construct a portfolio that offers the highest expected return for the individual's willingness to bear risk.

---

[3] The opposite of inflation is deflation, which is a general decline in prices. During a period of deflation, the real purchasing power of the investor's assets and income is increased (unless the value of the assets or the total amount of income is also declining).

*The investor cannot
avoid risk*

By now it should be obvious that all investors bear risk. Even an investor who does nothing cannot avoid risk. By "doing nothing" and holding cash or placing the funds in a savings account, the investor is still making an investment and is bearing some element of risk. The very nature of transferring purchasing power from today to tomorrow requires accepting some risk, because the future is uncertain. Risk simply cannot be avoided, as any choice will involve at least one of the sources of risk: business risk, financial risk, market risk, interest rate risk, and purchasing power risk.

EFFICIENT AND COMPETITIVE MARKETS

In addition to bearing risk, investors participate in very efficient and competitive financial markets. Economics teaches that markets with many participants (i.e., buyers and sellers) who may enter and exit freely will be competitive. That certainly describes financial markets. Investors may participate freely in the purchase and sale of stocks and bonds. Virtually anyone, from a child to a grandmother, may own a financial asset, even if it is just a savings account. Many firms, including banks, insurance companies, and mutual funds, compete for the funds of investors. The financial markets are among the most (and perhaps *the* most) competitive of all markets.

*Prices reflect known
information*

Financial markets tend to be very efficient. As is explained throughout this text, security prices depend on future cash flows such as interest or dividend payments. If new information suggests that these flows will be altered, the market rapidly adjusts the asset's price. Thus, an efficient financial market implies that a security's current price embodies all the known information concerning the potential return and risk associated with the particular asset. If an asset such as a stock were "undervalued" and offered an "excessive" return, investors would seek to buy it, which would drive the price up and reduce the return that subsequent investors would earn. Conversely, if the asset were "overvalued" and offered an "inferior" return, investors would seek to sell it, which would drive down its price and increase the return to subsequent investors. The fact that there are sufficient investors who are informed means that a security's price will reflect the investment community's consensus regarding the asset's true value and also that the expected return will be consistent with the amount of risk the investor must bear to earn the return.

*Hard to outperform the
market consistently*

The concept of an efficient financial market has an important and sobering corollary. Efficient markets imply that investors (or at least the vast majority of investors) cannot expect on the average to beat the market *consistently*. Of course, that does not mean an individual will never select an asset that does exceedingly well. Individuals can earn large returns on particular assets, as the stockholders of many firms know. Certainly the investor who bought Magic Chef for $53 in December 1985 and sold it for $75 in June 1986 when the firm was acquired by Maytag made a large return on that investment. What the concept of efficient markets implies is that this investor will not consistently select those individual securities that earn abnormally large returns.

If investors cannot expect to outperform the market consistently, they also should not consistently underperform the market. Of course, some securities may decline in price and inflict large losses on their owners, but efficient markets imply that the individual will not always select the stocks and bonds of firms that fail. If such individuals

do exist, they will soon lose their resources and will no longer be able to participate in the financial markets.

Thus, efficient financial markets imply that investors should, over an extended period of time, earn neither excessively positive nor excessively negative returns. Instead the returns should mirror the returns earned by the financial markets as a whole and the risk the investor bears. While security prices and returns are ultimately determined by the interactions of buyers and sellers, there is little that the typical investor can do to affect a security's price. Instead, the individual investor selects among the various alternatives to build a portfolio that is consistent with that individual's financial goals and willingness to bear risk.

THE PLAN AND PURPOSE OF THIS TEXT

Since the individual participates in efficient financial markets and competes with informed investors, including professional security analysts and financial managers, each individual investor needs fundamental information concerning investments. This text seeks to help those investors, especially individuals with little knowledge and understanding of investments, to increase their knowledge of the risks and returns from various investment alternatives. Perhaps because investing deals with the individual's money and the potential for large gains or losses, it has a mystery about it that is not justified. By introducing the various investments and the methods of their acquisition, analysis, and valuation, the text seeks to remove the mystery associated with investing.

While investments is sometimes treated as a complex subject, the approach here will be to describe the various assets, the risks associated with them, and the advantages and disadvantages they offer. This is essential information that all investors need, whether they have large or small portfolios.

This text is divided into several parts, the first two of which lay the foundation on which security selection is based. Part One covers the environment of security selection. This encompasses how securities come into existence (Chapter 2), the mechanics of buying and selling stocks and bonds (Chapter 3), sources of information (Chapter 4), and the tax environment (Chapter 5). Part Two discusses basic tools and information necessary to make investment decisions. These include an explanation of the processes of compounding and discounting (Chapter 6), the construction of financial statements (Chapter 7), and the analysis of risk (Chapter 8).

Parts Three and Four of the text are devoted to valuation and analysis of more traditional investments: bonds and stocks. Chapter 9 describes the features common to all debt instruments, and Chapter 10 discusses the pricing of debt. Chapter 11 deals with preferred stock, and Chapter 12 is devoted to government securities. Chapter 13 examines the past performance of investments in common stocks. Chapter 14 discusses models for the valuation of corporate stock; this is followed by a discussion of the firm's dividend policy (Chapter 15). The next three chapters deal with techniques used to analyze and select stocks for investments—the fundamental approach (Chapters 16 and 17) and the technical approach (Chapter 18).

Parts Five and Six discuss other assets that are possible alternatives to stocks and bonds. Part Five is devoted to options. Chapter 19 serves as a general introduction to options, and Chapters 20 and 21 cover warrants, calls, puts, and convertible bonds. Part Six explains a variety of specialized investments, some of which have recently become popular. Chapter 22 deals with investment companies, which provide an alternative to investing directly in stocks and bonds. Commodity futures, which are perhaps the riskiest of all the investments covered in this text, are then discussed (Chapter 23). The next two chapters in this part cover investing in physical assets. Chapter 24 is devoted to collectibles, such as art, and to gold, and Chapter 25 discusses investments in real estate. Chapter 26 broadens the investor's horizon by introducing international investments.

The text concludes with a discussion of financial planning and portfolio construction. This conclusion is a capstone chapter that stresses the need for financial planning, the establishment of financial goals, the enumeration of the investor's resources, and analysis of an asset's risks and expected returns.

Terms to Remember

Portfolio	Speculation
Investment	Marketability
Primary and secondary markets	Liquidity
Value	Systematic risk
Valuation	Unsystematic risk
Return	Business risk
Income	Financial risk
Capital gains	Market risk
Rate of return	Interest rate risk
Risk	Purchasing power risk

Questions

1. What is the distinction between liquidity and marketability?

2. What is risk and why may it be positive as well as negative?

3. What are the sources of risk that every investor must face?

4. A significant part of this text is devoted to valuation. What causes an asset to have value today?

5. What is the relationship between risk and expected return?

6. What is the implication of an efficient security market for the return an investor will earn over a period of time?

Annotated Bibliography and Readings

The subsequent chapters have lists of annotated readings. The criteria for selection included accessibility and readability. The lists are not exhaustive and do not include many references to academic journals; such readings may be found in more advanced texts. The suggested readings in this text are more pragmatic and develop the basic material covered in each chapter.

2

The Financing
of Business

LEARNING OBJECTIVES

After completing this chapter you should be able to

1. Explain the roles of the investment banker and the financial intermediary.
2. Illustrate the flow of funds from savers to firms.
3. Identify the components necessary for the sale of securities to the general public.
4. Differentiate an underwriting from a best efforts sale of securities.
5. Contrast the various financial instruments offered by commercial banks and other depository institutions.
6. Distinguish money market mutual funds from commercial banks and savings banks.
7. List several money market instruments.
8. Identify trends in the banking system and their primary cause.

There are many diverse types of businesses in many industries, but they all have at least two things in common: Somebody had to provide the funds to start them, and someone must supply the funds to sustain them. From the modest corner store to the large corporate giant, each must have a source of capital. This capital comes from owners who have equity in the firm and from creditors who have lent funds to the firm.

It is through the financing of business that securities come into existence. Firms issue securities, such as stocks or bonds, which are bought by the general public and by financial institutions such as pension funds or mutual funds. Once in existence, many of these securities may be traded in the secondary markets, such as the New York Stock Exchange. These secondary markets make securities more attractive to individuals, because investors know there is a place to sell the securities should the need arise.

This chapter is concerned with the financing of business needs, the role of financial intermediaries, and the advantages offered to individuals by short-term investments in various

financial intermediaries. It begins with a general discussion of transferring funds from savers to business. This transfer occurs either directly, when firms issue new securities, or indirectly through financial intermediaries. The second section describes the process of issuing new securities and the role of the investment banker. The last sections of the chapter are devoted to the role of financial intermediaries. Increased competition and the deregulation of banking has led to a blurring of distinctions among the various intermediaries; however, all offer individuals modest yields and safe short-term investments. The chapter concludes with a discussion of money market mutual funds that directly compete with the traditional financial intermediaries (e.g., commercial banks).

THE TRANSFER OF FUNDS TO BUSINESS

There are basically two methods for transferring funds to business. One is the direct investment of funds into businesses by the general public. This occurs when firms issue new securities that are purchased by investors or when individuals invest in partnerships or sole proprietorships. The second method is the indirect transfer through a **financial intermediary**, which transfers funds to firms and other borrowers from individuals such as savers or from firms that currently are not using the funds. The financial intermediary stands between the ultimate supplier and the ultimate user of the funds and facilitates the flow of money and credit between the suppliers and the users.

When a corporation issues a new security such as a bond and sells it to the general public, the following transaction occurs:

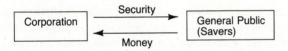

The saver purchases the security with money, thereby trading one asset for another. The firm acquires the funds by issuing the security; thus there is a direct transfer of money from the saver to the firm.

The indirect transfer is a little more complicated because an intermediary operates between the saver and the firm. The intermediary acquires funds from savers by issuing a claim on itself, such as a savings account at a commercial bank. The intermediary then lends the funds or buys new securities issued by an entity that is in need of money.

The flow of funds to the financial intermediary is illustrated by the following chart:

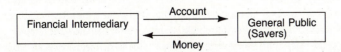

The saver trades one asset (the money) for another (the claim on the financial intermediary), and the financial intermediary acquires the funds by issuing a claim on itself.

The financial intermediary then lends the funds to an entity such as a firm, government, or household in need of the funds. That is, the financial intermediary buys a security such as a bond or makes a new loan, at which time the following transaction occurs:

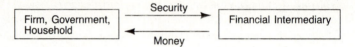

The financial intermediary gives up one asset, the money, to acquire another asset, the claim on the borrower. The borrower acquires the funds by promising to return them in the future and to pay interest while the loan is outstanding.

The preceding charts may be combined to illustrate the process of transferring funds from the ultimate lender (the saver) to the ultimate borrower.

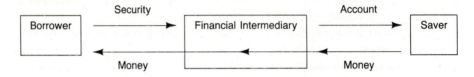

The saver's funds are transferred to the borrower through the financial intermediary. Through this process the borrower is able to acquire the funds because the financial intermediary was able to issue a *claim on itself* (i.e., the account) that the saver would accept.

Private placements

The direct sale of an entire issue of bonds or stock to a financial institution, such as a pension fund or a life insurance company, is called a **private placement.** The primary advantages of a private placement to the firm are the elimination of the cost of selling securities to the general public and the ready availability of large amounts of cash. In addition, the firm does not have to meet the disclosure requirements that are necessary to sell securities to the general public. This disclosure of information is for the protection of the investing public; it is presumed that the financial institution can protect itself by requiring information as a precondition for granting a loan.[1] The disclosure requirements are both a cost to the firm when securities are issued to the public and a possible source of information to its competitors that the firm may wish to avoid divulging. An additional advantage to both the firm and the financial institution is that the terms of securities may be tailored to meet both parties' needs.

The advantages of private placement are similar for the financial institution and for the firm that is obtaining the funds. A substantial amount of money may be invested at one time, and the maturity date can be set to meet the lender's needs. In addition, brokerage fees associated with purchasing securities on an organized exchange are avoided. The financial intermediary can gain more control over the firm that receives the funds by building restrictive covenants into the agreement. These covenants may restrict the firm from issuing additional securities without the prior

---

[1] Private lenders frequently negotiate for and receive a seat on the borrowing firm's board of directors.

permission of the lender and may limit the firm's dividends, its merger activity, and the types of investments that it may make. All of these restrictive covenants are designed to protect the lender from risk of loss and are part of any private sale of securities from a firm to a financial institution. Since each sale is separately negotiated, the individual terms vary with the bargaining powers of the parties and the economic conditions at the time of the agreement.

THE ISSUING AND SELLING OF NEW SECURITIES

Firms, in addition to acquiring funds through private placements, may issue new securities and sell them to the general public, usually through **investment bankers**. Firms employ this option when internally generated funds are insufficient to finance the desired level of investment spending and when the firm believes it to be advantageous to obtain outside funding from the general public instead of from a financial intermediary. Such outside funding may increase public interest in the firm and its securities and may also bypass some of the restrictive covenants that are required by financial institutions.

The following section deals with the sale of new securities to the general public through an investment banker.[2] It covers the role played by the investment banker, the mechanics of selling new securities, and the potential volatility of the new issue market.

The Role of Investment Bankers

A firm can market securities directly to the public in several ways: by contacting its current stockholders and creditors and asking them to purchase the new securities, by advertising the securities, or even by peddling them from door to door.[3] Although this last scenario is exaggerated, it illustrates that there is a cost to selling new securities, which may be considerable if the firm itself undertakes the task. For this reason, firms employ help in marketing new securities; they use the services of investment bankers, which sell new securities to the general public. In effect, an investment banker serves as a middleman to channel money from investors to the firm that needs the capital.

The role of middlemen

Investment banking is an important financial practice, but confusion exists concerning it, part of which may be attributable to the misnomer *investment banker*. An investment banker is rarely a banker and does not generally invest. Instead, the investment banker is usually a brokerage firm, like Merrill Lynch Pierce Fenner and Smith or First Boston Corporation. Although these brokerage firms may own securities, they do not necessarily buy and hold the newly issued securities on their own account for investment purposes.

Investment bankers perform a middleman function that brings together individuals who have money to invest and firms that need financing.[4] Since brokerage firms

---

[2] While the discussion is limited to the sale of stock, the mechanics of selling new stock also apply to new bonds.

[3] As is explained later, the formal offer to sell the securities must be made by a prospectus, and the securities must be registered with the SEC.

[4] Investment bankers are not financial intermediaries because they do not create claims on themselves.

have many customers, they are able to sell new securities without the costly search that the individual firm may have to make to sell its own securities. Thus, although the firm in need of financing must pay for the services, it is able to raise external capital at less expense through the investment banker than it could by selling the securities itself.

The Mechanics of Underwriting

An underwriting

If a firm needs funds from an external source, it can approach an investment banker to discuss an underwriting. The term **underwriting** refers to the process of selling new securities. In an underwriting the firm that is selling the securities, and not the firm that is issuing the shares, bears the risk associated with the sale. When an investment banker agrees to underwrite a sale of securities, it is agreeing to supply the firm with a specified amount of money. The investment banker buys the securities with the intention to resell them. If it fails to sell the securities, the investment banker must still pay the agreed-upon sum to the firm at the time of the offering (i.e., the sale) of the securities. Failure to sell the securities imposes significant losses on the underwriter, who must remit funds for securities that have not been sold.

The participants

The firm in need of financing and the investment banker discuss the amount of funds needed, the type of security to be issued, the price and any special features of the security, and the cost to the firm of issuing the securities. All of these factors are negotiated by the firm seeking capital and the investment banker. If mutually acceptable terms are reached, the investment banker will be the middleman through which the securities are sold by the firm to the general public.

The originating house

Because an underwriting starts with a particular brokerage firm, which manages the underwriting, that firm is called the **originating house**. The originating house need not be a single firm if the negotiation involves several investment bankers. In this case, several firms can join together to manage the underwriting and the sale of securities to the general public.

The syndicate

The originating house does not usually try to sell all of the securities by itself but forms a **syndicate** to market them. The syndicate is a group of brokerage houses that join together to underwrite a specific sale of securities. The firm that manages the sale is frequently referred to as the "lead underwriter." It is the lead underwriter that allocates the specific number of securities each individual member of the syndicate is responsible for selling.

The use of a syndicate has several advantages. First, the syndicate may have access to more potential buyers for the securities. Second, by using a syndicate the number of securities that each brokerage firm must sell is reduced. The increase in the number of potential customers and the decrease in the amount that each broker must sell increases the probability that the entire issue of securities will be sold. Thus, syndication makes possible both the sale of a large offering of securities and a reduction in the risk borne by each member of the selling group.

In some cases the firm seeking funds may not choose to negotiate the terms of the securities with an underwriter. Instead the firm designs the issue and auctions the securities to the investment banker making the highest bid. In preparation for bidding, the investment banker will form a syndicate as well as determine the price it is

willing to pay. The underwriter, and its syndicate that wins the auction and purchases the securities, marks up the price of the securities and sells them to the general public. Obviously, if the investment banker bids too high, it will be unable to sell the securities for a profit. Then the underwriter may sustain a loss when it lowers the securities' price in order to sell them.

Types of Agreements

The agreement between the investment bankers and the firm may be one of two types. The investment bankers may agree to purchase (i.e., to underwrite) the entire issue of securities and to sell them to the general public. This guarantees a specified amount of money to the firm issuing the securities. The alternative is a **best efforts agreement** in which the investment bankers make the best effort to sell the securities but do not guarantee that a specified amount of money will be raised. The former agreement places the risk of selling the securities on the investment bankers, and most sales of new securities are of this type.[5] The underwriters purchase all of the securities, pay the expenses, and bear the risk of selling the securities, with the anticipation of recouping the expenses through the sale. Since they have agreed to purchase the entire issue, the underwriters must pay the firm for all of the securities even if the syndicate is unable to sell them.

The guarantee of sale or best efforts agreements

It is for this reason that the pricing of securities is crucial. If the initial offer price is too high, the syndicate will be unable to sell the securities. When this occurs, the investment bankers have two choices: (1) to maintain the offer price and hold the securities in inventory until they are sold or (2) to let the market find a lower price level that will induce investors to purchase the securities. Neither choice benefits the investment bankers. If the underwriters purchase the securities and hold them in inventory, they either must tie up their own funds, which could be earning a return elsewhere, or must borrow funds to pay for the securities. Like any other firm, the investment bankers must pay interest on these borrowed funds. Thus, the decision to support the offer price of the securities requires the investment bankers to invest their own capital or (and this case is the more likely) requires that they borrow substantial amounts of capital. In either case, the profit margins on the underwriting are substantially decreased, and the investment bankers may even experience a loss on the underwriting.

The importance of the price of a new issue

Instead of supporting the price, the underwriters may choose to let the price of the securities fall. The inventory of unsold securities can then be sold, and the underwriters will not tie up capital or have to borrow money from their sources of credit. If the underwriters make this choice, they take losses when the securities are sold at less than cost. But they also cause the customers who bought the securities at the initial offer price to have a higher cost basis. The underwriters certainly do not want to inflict losses on these customers, because if they experience losses continually, the underwriters' market for future security issues will vanish. Therefore, the investment bankers do not try to overprice a new issue of securities, for overpricing will ultimately result in their suffering losses.

---

[5] Best efforts sales are generally limited to small issues of securities being sold by less well-known firms.

There is also an incentive to avoid underpricing new securities. If the issue is underpriced, all of the securities will be readily sold and their price will rise because demand will have exceeded supply. The buyers of the securities will be satisfied, for the price of the securities will have increased as a result of the underpricing. The initial purchasers of the securities reap windfall profits, but these gains are really at the expense of the company whose securities were underpriced. If the underwriters had assigned a higher price to the securities, the company would have raised more capital. Underwriting is a very competitive business, and each security issue is negotiated individually; hence, if one investment banker consistently underprices securities, firms will employ competitors to underwrite their securities.

Marketing Securities

The red herring

Once the terms of the sale have been agreed upon, the managing house may issue a **preliminary prospectus.** This is often referred to as a **red herring** because of the red lettering on the title page. This lettering informs the prospective buyer that the securities are being registered with the **Securities and Exchange Commission (SEC)** and may subsequently be offered for sale. **Registration** refers to the disclosure of information concerning the firm, the securities being offered for sale, and the use of the proceeds from the sale.[6]

The cost of printing the red herring is borne by the underwriters, who recoup this cost through the underwriting fees. This preliminary prospectus describes the company and the securities to be issued; it includes the firm's income statement and balance sheets, its current activities (such as a pending merger or labor negotiation), the regulatory bodies to which it is subject, and the nature of its competition. The preliminary prospectus is thus a detailed document concerning the company and is, unfortunately, usually tedious reading.

The preliminary prospectus does not include the price of the securities. That will be determined on the day that the securities are issued. If security prices decline or rise, the price of the new securities may be adjusted for the change in market conditions. In fact, if prices decline sufficiently, the firm has the option of postponing or even canceling the underwriting.

The final prospectus

After the shares have been approved for issue by the SEC, a final prospectus is published. The SEC does not approve the issue as to its investment worth but rather sees that all information has been provided and the prospectus is complete in format and content. Except for changes that are required by the SEC, it is virtually identical to the preliminary prospectus. The red lettering is removed, and information regarding the price of the security, the underwriting discount, and the proceeds to the company, along with any more recent financial data, is added. Exhibit 2.1 illustrates the title pages for the final prospectus for an issue of 9,359,416 shares of James River Corporation. The names of the managing underwriters are in large print at the bottom of the page. These managing underwriters formed the syndicate that sold the shares to the general public. In this example, more than 40 firms participated in the selling group.

---

[6]While unregistered corporate securities may not be sold to the general public, the debt of governments (e.g., state and municipal bonds) is *not* registered with the SEC and may be sold to the general public.

POINTS OF INTEREST
Tapping Your Customers

While firms generally acquire funds from the general public through investment bankers, a selected few also raise funds from their customers. Schwegmann Giant Supermarkets in New Orleans sells its bonds as well as groceries. These bonds have been very popular with its customers because Schwegmann will raise the interest rate it pays on outstanding bonds in response to general increases in interest rates. In addition, Schwegmann will redeem the bonds at par at the option of the holder. The bonds have been so popular that when a holder does redeem them, Schwegmann is able to sell more bonds to other customers.

Virginia Electric and Power permits its customers to subscribe to its common stock. Customers may pledge annually a specified amount that is paid in monthly installments. After the year has elapsed, the accumulated funds are applied to buy common stock at the average of the high and low sale prices on the twentieth day of each month during the twelve-month period. Like Schwegmann Giant Supermarkets, Virginia Electric and Power has found its customers to be a good source of funds. In the 1986–1987 plan, 34,000 customers elected to participate and subscribed for over $22 million of the common stock.

Underwriting fees

The cost of the underwriting, which is the difference between the price of the securities to the public and the proceeds to the firm, is also given in the prospectus shown in Exhibit 2.1. In this example, the cost is $.90 per share, which is 2.7 percent of the proceeds received by the firm for each share. The total cost is $8,423,474.40 for the sale of these shares. Underwriting fees tend to vary with the dollar value of the securities being underwritten and the type of securities being sold. Since some of the expenses are fixed (e.g., preparation of the prospectus), the unit cost for a large underwriting is smaller. Also, since it may be more difficult to sell speculative bonds than high-quality bonds, underwriting fees for speculative issues tend to be higher.

Indirect compensation

In addition to the fee, the underwriter may receive indirect compensation, which may be in the form of the right (or option) to buy additional securities or to have a membership on the firm's board of directors. Such indirect compensation may be as important as the monetary fee because it unites the underwriter and the firm. After the initial sale, the underwriter often becomes a market maker for the securities, which is particularly important to the investing public.[7] Without a secondary market in which to sell the security, investors would be less interested in buying the securities initially. By maintaining a market in the security, the brokerage firm eases the task of selling the securities originally.

Volatility of the New Issue Market

The new issue market (especially for common stock) is extremely volatile. There have been periods when the investing public seemed willing to purchase virtually any secu-

---

[7] For a detailed discussion of making a market, see "Market Makers" in Chapter 3.

Exhibit 2.1
Prospectus for an Issue of Shares of James River Corporation

9,359,416 Shares

JAMES RIVER CORPORATION
OF VIRGINIA

Common Stock, $.10 Par Value

All of the shares offered hereby will be offered for the accounts of the selling stockholders named herein under "Selling Stockholders". James River will not receive any of the proceeds of the offering.

The Common Stock is listed on the New York Stock Exchange. The last reported sale price of the Common Stock on such exchange on August 7, 1985 was $33 per share.

THESE SECURITIES HAVE NOT BEEN APPROVED OR DISAPPROVED BY THE SECURITIES AND EXCHANGE COMMISSION NOR HAS THE COMMISSION PASSED UPON THE ACCURACY OR ADEQUACY OF THIS PROSPECTUS. ANY REPRESENTATION TO THE CONTRARY IS A CRIMINAL OFFENSE.

	Price to Public	Underwriting Discount	Proceeds to Selling Stockholders(1)
Per Share...........................	$33.00	$.90	$32.10
Total...............................	$308,860,728	$8,423,474.40	$300,437,253.60

(1) James River estimates its expenses in connection with this offering to be $65,544. American Can Company, one of the Selling Stockholders, will bear certain expenses in connection with this offering estimated to be $177,956.

The above shares of Common Stock are offered by the several Underwriters when, as and if issued and accepted by the Underwriters and subject to their right to reject orders in whole or in part, and certain other conditions. It is expected that delivery of the shares will be made on or about August 15, 1985.

Kidder, Peabody & Co.
Incorporated

Morgan Stanley & Co.
Incorporated

Scott & Stringfellow, Inc.

Wheat, First Securities, Inc.

The date of this Prospectus is August 8, 1985

Source: Reprinted with permission of Scott & Stringfellow, Inc.

rity that was being sold on the market. There have also been periods during which new companies were simply unable to raise money, and large, well-known companies did so only under onerous terms.

"Hot" new issues

The new issue market is not only volatile regarding the number of securities that are offered but also regarding the price changes of new issues. When the new issue market is "hot," it is not unusual for the prices to rise dramatically. In many cases, however, prices subsequently decline even more remarkably. The dramatic price behavior of Four Seasons Nursing Homes is illustrated in Figure 2.1, which shows the annual price range of the stock and the firm's earnings per share. The firm went public on May 10, 1968. The price rose dramatically from the initial price of $11 to $102.

Figure 2.1
Annual Price Range and Earnings per Share of Stock of Four Seasons Nursing Homes (Anta Corporation)

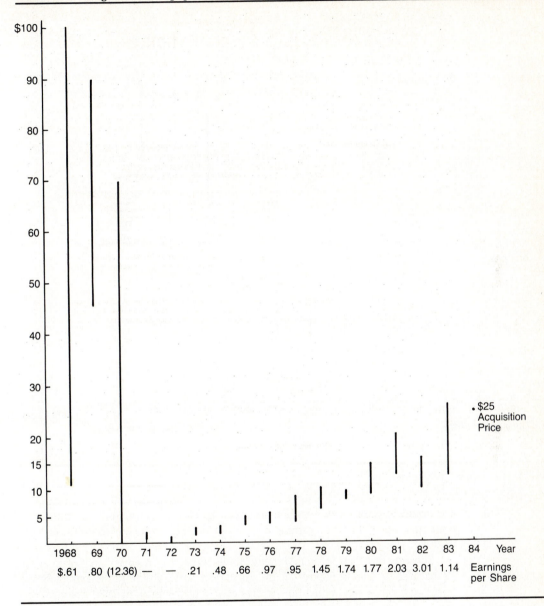

	1968	69	70	71	72	73	74	75	76	77	78	79	80	81	82	83	84	Year
	$.61	.80	(12.36)	—	—	.21	.48	.66	.97	.95	1.45	1.74	1.77	2.03	3.01	1.14		Earnings per Share

Source: Annual reports and Standard and Poor's *Stock Guide,* various issues.

Only two years later the firm was bankrupt, and the price of the stock declined to $0.16 (i.e., ³⁄₁₆ in the fractional prices that are used in the security markets).

A price of $102 for a share of Four Seasons Nursing Homes was indeed excessive. The company had 3.4 million shares outstanding, and, at a price of $102, the firm was worth $346.8 million ($102 × 3.4 million) according to the market. Since the firm

Figure 2.2
Annual Price Range and Earnings per Share of James River Corporation (Prices Adjusted for Stock Splits)

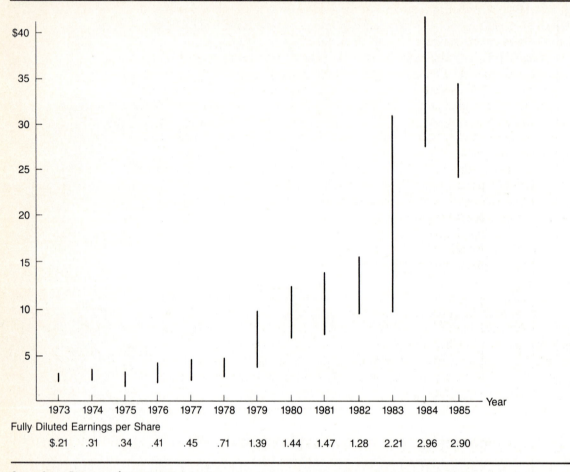

Fully Diluted Earnings per Share

	1973	1974	1975	1976	1977	1978	1979	1980	1981	1982	1983	1984	1985
	$.21	.31	.34	.41	.45	.71	1.39	1.44	1.47	1.28	2.21	2.96	2.90

Source: James River annual reports, various issues.

had revenues of only $19.3 million and earnings of less than $2 million, it made no sense in terms of the firm's earning capacity to value the company in excess of $300 million.

Subsequently Four Seasons Nursing Homes was reorganized as Anta Corporation. As may also be seen in Figure 2.1, the price of stock did rise from the extremely low prices at which it was valued during the years of bankruptcy. In 1984, the firm was acquired by Manor Care for $25 a share. While this acquisition price was a small fraction of the stock's price during the late 1960s, it is considerably higher than the valuation placed on the company during the period of bankruptcy.

Not all new issues perform like that of Four Seasons Nursing Homes. Despite the fact that some firms do not fulfill their development potential and fail, others succeed and grow steadily. For example, James River Corporation went public on March 16, 1973, and has done quite well. This performance is illustrated in Figure 2.2, which

plots the annual range of the stock's price and the firm's earnings per share. As may be seen from the figure, there has been a steady increase in the firm's earnings and in the price of the stock. Although the stock has not reached the heights achieved by that of Four Seasons Nursing Homes (and many other "high fliers"), it is an expanding firm that continues to offer growth potential to investors.

During the 1980s, price behavior like that seen for Four Seasons Nursing Homes occurred once again. In 1980, Genentech, a small genetic engineering research firm, went public and sold its stock for $35 a share. Initial trading in the over-the-counter market, however, started at $80, and the price quickly rose to $89 a share, for an increase of 154 percent in one day. In 1986, Home Shopping Network, Inc. went public at $18 and rose to $42⅝ during the first day. In less than three months, the stock sold above $100, for a 450 percent increase. However, such rapid price increases are rarely sustained. During 1981, the price of Genentech declined, and the stock traded for as low as $26 per share. Obviously those speculators who initially drove the price up above $80 a share and continued to hold the stock suffered significant losses when the price of the stock subsequently fell.

The potential for large gains is, of course, the lure that attracts speculative investors. All firms were small at one time, and each one had to go public to have a market for its shares. Someone bought the shares of IBM, Xerox, and Johnson & Johnson when these firms went public. The ability to spot the companies that promise the greatest growth for the future is rare. However, the new issue market has offered and continues to offer the opportunity to invest in emerging firms, some of which may achieve substantial returns for those investors or speculators who are willing to accept the risk. It is the possibility of such large rewards that makes the new issue market so exciting. However, if the past is an indicator of the future, many firms that go public will fail and will inflict significant losses on those investors who have accepted this risk by purchasing securities issued by the small, emerging firms.

THE ROLE OF FINANCIAL INTERMEDIARIES

While the securities of publicly held firms had to be sold to the public initially, these same firms acquire a substantial proportion of their financing from financial intermediaries. This is particularly true of short-term funds that are borrowed from commercial banks or are obtained by issuing short-term debt obligations that are purchased by a variety of financial intermediaries. Of course, for the intermediaries to make these loans, they too must have funds. These funds are acquired from savers and other economic units who do not currently need them and who thus invest the money in obligations issued by the financial intermediary. In effect, the savers are ultimately supplying the funds to the firms (or to any economic unit) in need of the funds. However, this transfer of money occurs indirectly through the financial intermediary instead of directly.

In advanced economies, a variety of financial intermediaries have developed to facilitate the indirect transfer of savers' funds to borrowers. These intermediaries include commercial banks, savings and loan associations, mutual savings banks, credit unions, life insurance companies, pension plans, and money market mutual funds.

Variety of financial intermediaries

Whenever these firms borrow from one group and lend to another, they are acting as financial intermediaries. However, it should be noted that if they purchase existing financial assets, such as stock traded on the New York Stock Exchange or existing mortgages, they are not acting as financial intermediaries. Instead they are investing in assets traded in secondary markets, in which case funds flow from buyer to seller and not to the economic unit that initially issued the security.[8]

Historically, a clear differentiation existed among the various financial intermediaries. For example, the differences between commercial banks and savings and loan associations (S & Ls) encompassed both the types of assets they acquired and the types of liabilities (accounts) they offered. Savings and loan associations were depository organizations that issued savings accounts and used the savers' funds to originate home mortgage loans. Such S & Ls were clearly differentiated from commercial banks, which issued a variety of accounts, especially checking accounts, and made various loans including personal loans (such as car loans) and short-term financing for businesses and governments.

Distinctions among financial intermediaries is blurred

Today it is probably safe to assert that many savers and potential borrowers are no longer aware of differences among financial intermediaries. Commercial banks, savings and loan associations, mutual savings banks, and credit unions offer similar services (e.g., checking accounts and savings accounts) and pay virtually the same rates of interest on deposits. In addition, the portfolio of assets acquired by each depository institution is more similar than in the past. For example, previously S & Ls made primarily mortgage loans, but now their portfolios have been broadened to include a more varied mix of assets.

Impact of deregulation

This blurring of the distinctions among the various financial intermediaries is the result of changes in the regulatory environment. Under the Depository Institutions Deregulation and Monetary Control Act of 1980, all depository institutions became subject to the regulation of the Federal Reserve. These regulations extended to the types of accounts these institutions may offer and the amount they must hold in reserve against deposits. In return for this change in the regulatory environment, the depository institutions were permitted to offer more accounts to depositors, such as checking accounts, which previously could be offered only by commercial banks. The intermediaries were also permitted to broaden the services offered depositors, such as brokerage services that link the accounts in the bank to brokerage accounts. Deregulation also led to the end of controls on maximum interest rates. Now the depository institutions may pay whatever rate of interest on deposits they deem necessary to compete with other financial intermediaries, such as the money market mutual funds.[9]

Advantages Offered by Financial Intermediaries

Investors will not deposit funds with a financial intermediary unless some benefit is offered. The advantages provided by the intermediaries include convenience, interest income, and safety of principal. Various accounts offer several features that make

---

[8] Secondary markets such as the New York Stock Exchange are discussed in the next chapter.

[9] Money market mutual funds are discussed later in this chapter.

Type of Deposit	Minimum Amount Required	Term	Annual Rate of Interest
Money market account	$1,000	None	7.15%
Savings account	250	None	5.25
Certificate of deposit	500	6 months	7.86
Certificate of deposit	500	1 year	8.33
Certificate of deposit	500	1½ years	8.37
Certificate of deposit	500	2 years	8.79
Certificate of deposit	500	2½ years	8.83
Certificate of deposit	500	3 years	9.11
Certificate of deposit	500	4 years	9.20
Certificate of deposit	500	5 years	9.29

Exhibit 2.2
Savings and Time Deposits Offered by a Savings and Loan Association

them convenient. Checking accounts and **NOW accounts** (NOW is an acronym that stands for "negotiable order of withdrawal" and is a checking account that pays interest) are a convenient means by which to make payments. Savings and checking accounts accommodate small deposits and small withdrawals. Other assets, such as stocks and bonds, may not be divisible into such small units or the commission costs associated with small units may make them impractical.

Time deposits

Interest is paid on savings accounts, NOW accounts, and time deposits that are called **certificates of deposit** or **CDs**. Funds deposited in savings accounts and NOW accounts may be withdrawn at will, making them among the most liquid assets available to investors. Certificates of deposit are time deposits that have a specified maturity date but that may be redeemed prior to maturity. Such early redemptions result in a penalty, such as the loss of interest for a quarter. The yields offered by these accounts depend on the term of the instrument. Exhibit 2.2 gives the term and yields provided by the savings accounts and certificates of deposit offered by a savings and loan association in early 1986. Notice that as the term increases, the interest rate paid on the certificate also increases.

Large denomination certificates

If the investor has $100,000 or more to invest, depository institutions may sell **negotiable certificates of deposit** or **jumbo CDs** directly to the investor in which case the yield and term of these certificates is agreed upon by the investor and the depository institution. In other cases the depository institutions establish the terms and yields they are willing to pay and offer the CDs for sale. Maturities are generally one to three months, and the yields are comparable to those earned on other money market instruments, such as commercial paper. While the CDs may not be redeemed prior to maturity, they are negotiable; that is, the holder may sell them because a secondary market in jumbo CDs exists.

The large amount required to purchase a jumbo CD (i.e., the $100,000 minimum investment, with $1 million being the usual unit of trading) precludes most investors. However, as is explained later, many investors do indirectly invest in negotiable certificates of deposit when they acquire shares in money market mutual funds, since these funds invest in negotiable certificates of deposit.

POINTS OF INTEREST
Eurodollar Certificates of Deposit

In addition to the traditional CDs discussed in the text, there are Eurodollar CDs. Eurodollar CDs are time deposits with fixed rates and specified maturity dates that are generally issued in units of $1 million by branches of major American banks. These CDs are sold in Europe (primarily in London) and pay yields that are usually higher than those available on domestic CDs. While the majority of investors who acquire Eurodollar CDs are foreign, some American portfolio managers acquire them when their yields rise sufficiently above the yields offered by domestic negotiable CDs.

Safety of bank deposits

Perhaps one of the most appealing features of an account with a depository institution is its safety. While there is the possibility of loss of purchasing power through the inflation rate exceeding the rate earned on the account, there is no risk of loss from default since the majority of these accounts are insured by the federal government. If an individual places $1,000 in a federally insured savings account, the $1,000 is safe. If the investor had invested $1,000 in a corporate bond, the market value of the bond could decline or the firm could default on the interest payment or principal repayment.

Deposit insurance

Federal government deposit insurance was one of the positive results of the Great Depression in the 1930s. The large losses sustained by commercial banks' depositors led to the establishment of the **Federal Deposit Insurance Corporation (FDIC)**. As of this writing, FDIC insures depositors with accounts in commercial banks and mutual savings banks up to $100,000. If a commercial bank were to fail, FDIC would reimburse each depositor up to the $100,000 limit. As most individuals do not have more than $100,000 on deposit, these investors know that their principal is completely safe. Similar insurance, which covers deposits in savings and loan associations, is administered by the Federal Savings and Loan Insurance Corporation (FSLIC). However, the investor should note that the insurance is *not* automatic but must be purchased from FDIC by the bank. A few banks have chosen not to purchase the insurance, and some S & Ls are insured by state agencies. Unfortunately, state insurance may not be adequate to cover depositors' losses. Thus, if safety of principal is a major concern, it is best for the funds to be deposited only in an account insured by the federal government.

MONEY MARKET MUTUAL FUNDS

One of the most important innovations in the realm of financial intermediaries has been the development and growth of **money market mutual funds**. While the discussion of mutual funds will be deferred to Chapter 22, money market mutual funds

differ from regular mutual funds. The money market funds directly compete with commercial banks and other depository institutions for the deposits of savers, while regular mutual funds offer investors an alternate means to own stocks and bonds. It was probably the development and rapid growth in the assets of money market mutual funds that forced banks to support deregulation.

Until the deregulation of the banking system, money market mutual funds offered investors an asset that was unique. Under regulation, the maximum rate of interest that banks could pay was constrained. Thus, when the rates paid by short-term securities (i.e., **money market instruments**) rose, the banks could not raise the interest rate they paid to be competitive with other money market yields. Investors sought means to acquire these short-term securities, which included treasury bills, negotiable certificates of deposit, commercial paper, and repurchase agreements. *Short-term securities*

The money market mutual funds were not subject to the same regulations as banks and thus could offer the higher yields. The money funds thus gave individuals the opportunity to invest indirectly in short-term securities and earn the higher yields available to the holders of these instruments. As a result, deposits flowed out of the financial intermediaries into the money funds.

Of course, individual investors may purchase money market instruments directly instead of acquiring the shares of the money funds who in turn acquire the securities. However, the large denominations (e.g., $100,000 minimum for negotiable CDs) exclude most investors. By pooling the resources of many savers, these funds are able to offer high money market yields to investors who otherwise would be limited in their choices. Those investors with $10,000 could acquire a treasury bill or purchase a non-negotiable certificate of deposit offered by a commercial bank. However, the money market mutual fund permits investors to broaden their portfolios of short-term securities and simultaneously to reduce risk as the portfolios of the funds are diversified. (The creation in 1983 of money market accounts with banks further expanded investors' choices.)

Since the portfolios are entirely invested in short-term obligations, the shares of money market funds are very liquid. The shares may be converted to cash with little risk of loss. This lack of risk emanates from the very nature of money market instruments. **U.S. Treasury bills** are short-term debt instruments issued by the federal government, and there is no question that the federal government has the capacity to retire the principal and pay the interest on its debt obligations. In addition, since the term of treasury bills is short, there is only a modest amount of interest rate risk. If interest rates were to rise and thus the prices of debt instruments were to fall, the quick maturity of T-bills means that any price decrease would be small and for a brief duration, because as the bills approach maturity, their value approaches the face amount (i.e., the principal). *Liquidity of money market shares*

Money market instruments

Treasury bills

As was discussed earlier in this chapter, negotiable certificates of deposit are issued by large commercial banks. While there is some risk of default, the possibility of several large banks failing seems remote. In general, the term of negotiable certificates of deposit is relatively short (one to three months), meaning that there is little interest rate risk associated with these CDs. Even if interest rates were to rise, the short term to maturity implies that the investor will soon recover the face amount of the debt. *Negotiable CDs*

Commercial paper—unsecured promissory notes

Commercial paper is an unsecured promissory note issued by a corporation as an alternative to borrowing funds from commercial banks. Since the paper is unsecured, only firms with excellent credit ratings are able to sell it; hence, the risk of default is small, and the repayment of principal is virtually assured. Once again the term is short, so there is little risk from an investment in commercial paper.

Federal agency debt

In addition to T-bills, negotiable CDs, and commercial paper, money market funds may acquire other short-term debt instruments, such as those issued by agencies of the federal government. These securities are virtually as safe as treasury bills, but since they are obligations of a federal agency and not the federal government, their yields are slightly higher than the yields on T-bills.

Repurchase agreements

Money market mutual funds also participate in **repurchase agreements**. In these agreements, which are often called "repos," the seller of a security agrees to buy back (i.e., repurchase) the security at a set price at a specified date. This repurchase price is higher than the initial sale price. The difference between the sale price and the repurchase price is the source of return to the holder of the security. Money market funds often participate in the market for repurchase agreements since they permit the money market funds to invest for short periods of time. The money market funds buy the securities knowing exactly when and for how much they can sell the securities in the future. Thus repurchase agreements offer the money market funds an attractive combination of return and liquidity.

While there are similarities among the portfolios of money market mutual funds, there can be many differences. For example, First Variable Rate Fund invests only in U.S. government securities or securities that are collateralized by obligations of the federal government. Other funds invest in a wider spectrum of short-term debt obligations and thus have a larger proportion of their portfolios in negotiable CDs and commercial paper. For example, Merrill Lynch's Retirement Reserves Money Fund had only 33.2 percent of its assets in treasury obligations, 4.3 percent in negotiable CDs, and 54.4 percent in commercial paper.[10]

Ease of withdrawal

Funds invested in a money market fund may be readily withdrawn by the investor. The individual who redeems the shares receives the amount invested plus any dividends that have been credited to the account.[11] Unless all investors sought to redeem their shares at the same time and thus forced the fund to liquidate its portfolio rapidly and perhaps at a loss, there is little risk that the investor would not receive the

Safety of principal

full value of the shares. It is this safety of principal plus the money market yields that were not available through other means (such as a savings account with a commercial bank) that made these funds so attractive to investors.[12]

The yields earned on investments in money market funds closely mirror the yields on short-term securities. This is illustrated in Figure 2.3, which plots the yields on three-month treasury bills and the yield on an investment in First Variable Rate Fund, which invests solely in government or government-backed securities. The yield

---

[10] The remaining 8.1 percent was a variety of short-term assets (as of December 31, 1985).

[11] Dividends are credited daily to the investor's account.

[12] In January 1983, commercial banks and other depository institutions were permitted to offer accounts that pay money market rates. These new accounts compete directly with the money market mutual fund shares for the funds of savers.

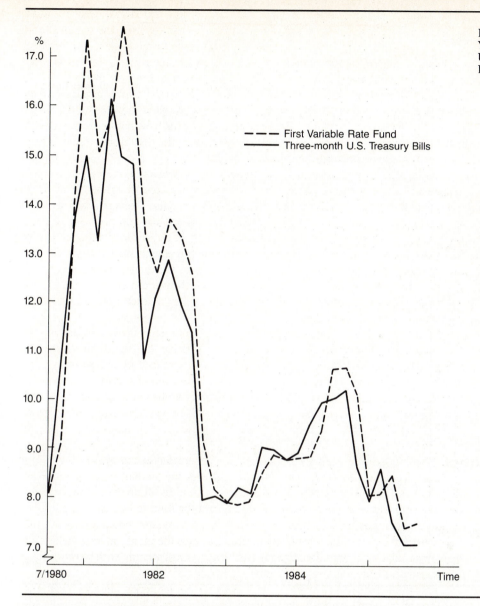

Figure 2.3
Yields on Three-month U.S. Treasury Bills and First Variable Rate Fund

First Variable Rate Fund
Three-month U.S. Treasury Bills

on the money market mutual fund closely parallels the yield on the T-bills. This relationship must occur because when the short-term debt held by the fund matures, the proceeds can be reinvested only at the going rate of interest. Hence changes in short-term interest rates are quickly felt by the individual money market mutual fund.

In addition to offering safety and money market yields, many money market mutual funds offer a service that is similar to a checking account. The investor is permitted to write drafts against his or her shares. The drafts are technically not checks, but

Checking privileges

Figure 2.4
**Money Market Mutual
Funds, Total Assets
(1976–1985)**

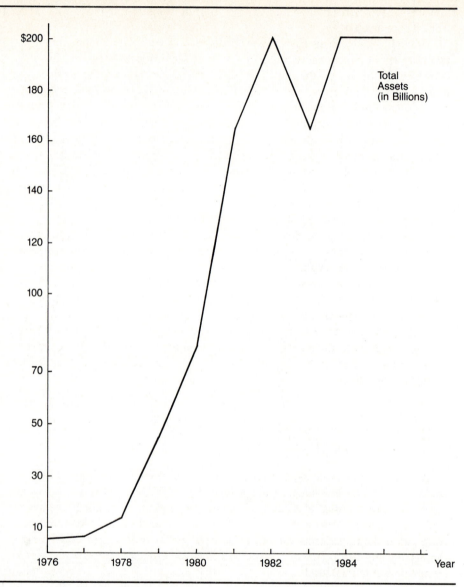

they do permit the transfer of funds from the money market mutual fund to whom-
ever the draft is payable. While there is a limit as to the minimum amount of the draft
(e.g., $250), these instruments are an excellent means for increased money manage-
ment. The investor can accumulate shares in the funds and, when disbursements become necessary, pay by the draft drawn on the fund. The funds invested in the money
market fund continue to earn interest until the draft clears, at which time shares are
redeemed to cover the amount of the draft. The existence of this service permits the
investor to earn interest while waiting for the disbursement of funds. Money that may

previously have been sitting in a noninterest-bearing checking account is now put to work for the investor.

Many brokerage firms have arrangements with money market funds that facilitate transfers of money between the two. Once a security is sold and the funds received by the broker on the settlement date, the broker transfers the funds to the money market fund. Later, when the investor buys a new security and must make payment, the funds are transferred back to the broker from the money market fund. All these transactions can occur without processing checks, as the money is transferred electronically from one account to another. This service permits the investor to earn interest on funds between investments even if the amount of time is only a few days. The amount of interest that the investor can earn by such transfers can be substantial. For example, at 8 percent, an investor earns about $22 per day on an investment of $100,000. Thus the transfer of $100,000 to a money market mutual fund for just a week will earn over $153.42 (i.e., $100,000 × 7/365 × 0.08).

Electronic transfers

Given the advantages offered by money market mutual funds, their initial popularity was not surprising. However, the growth in the assets of the money funds was nothing short of phenomenal. This is documented in Figure 2.4, which shows the huge increase in funds invested in money market mutual funds as the value of their assets rose from $3.6 billion in 1976 to more than $200 billion in just six years. Figure 2.4 also shows the decrease in the rate of growth that occurred with the beginning of the deregulation of the banking system. Once the various types of banks were better able to compete with the money funds, in addition to the general decline in interest rates, the rate of growth in the funds' assets stopped as dramatically as it had risen during 1978 to 1983.

Growth in money funds' assets

TRENDS IN COMPETITION AMONG FINANCIAL INTERMEDIARIES

A commercial bank or any other financial intermediary can only lend what has been lent to it. Unless the individual bank is able to induce individuals, firms, and governments to make deposits, that bank will be unable to grant loans and make investments. That general statement, of course, holds for all other financial intermediaries. None can make investments without a source of funds, whether these funds come through issuing certificates of deposit or selling life insurance or selling shares in money market mutual funds.

As this implies, financial intermediaries compete among each other for funds. This competition occurs through yields and services offered. With the deregulation of the interest rates that commercial banks and savings banks may pay, virtually all depository institutions offer competitive and comparable yields for comparable accounts. If a particular bank did not offer competitive yields, funds would be removed from that institution and deposited with a competitor.

Competition through yields and services

Historically, investors could differentiate one financial intermediary from another by the services it offered. Savers bought life insurance from insurance companies. The life insurance companies then used the funds to make investments. Banks offered checking accounts and other banking services to depositors, and stockbrokers bought

Financial intermediaries no longer specialize

and sold stocks and bonds for their customers. Those days of specialization are over. Bankers, stockbrokers, and insurance salespeople offer a wide spectrum of financial services and products. Commercial banks not only offer savers the traditional services of savings and checking accounts but other financial products such as discount brokerage (to compete with stockbrokers), money market accounts (to compete with money market mutual funds), and pension plans (to compete with insurance companies). Such a wide variety of products is also offered by the other savings banks (e.g., savings and loan associations and mutual savings banks).

Brokerage firms have also encroached on the domain of the banks through the creation of cash management accounts. For example, Merrill Lynch's pioneering Cash Management Account, which is known by a registered trademark—CMA—combines the traditional brokerage custodial services with checking privileges, a credit card (VISA), and money market yields on funds in the account. Other brokerage firms either have instituted similar accounts or have correspondent relationships with money market mutual funds that offer checking privileges, credit cards, and rates comparable to other money market yields.

Emergence of financial supermarkets

Today a type of financial supermarket that encompasses a variety of financial services is evolving. Several large brokerage firms have merged with other financial service firms. Prudential, the insurance company, acquired Bache Halsey Stuart Shields; American Express bought Shearson Loeb Rhodes; and Dean Witter was merged into Sears, which also owns Allstate Insurance.

In addition to consolidations amd mergers, the reduction in regulation and the lifting of interest rate ceilings has caused a blurring of the distinctions among the various types of financial intermediaries. Of course, some distinctions will remain. Commercial banks should continue to be the primary depository for checking accounts as well as a major source of short-term financing for corporations. Savings and loan associations will remain a major source of mortgage loans. Insurance companies will still provide their primary products—life, health, and casualty insurance. However, unless there is movement back toward regulation of the financial system, financial intermediaries will continue to encroach on their competitors' domains as each offers investors increasingly similar financial services and products.

SUMMARY

All firms must have a source of funds with which to acquire assets and retire outstanding liabilities as they come due. Besides retaining earnings, the firm may obtain these funds from savers who are not currently using all of their income to buy goods and services. The transfer of these savings may occur directly when firms issue new securities or indirectly through a financial intermediary.

When a firm issues new stocks or bonds, it usually employs the services of an investment banker to facilitate the sale of the securities by acting as a middleman between the firm and the savers. In many cases investment bankers underwrite the issue of new securities, which means that they guarantee a specified amount of money to the issuing firm and then sell the securities to the public. Since the underwriters are obligated to remit the specified amount for the securities, they bear the risk of the sale.

Firms may also obtain funds by borrowing from financial intermediaries, who raise funds by creating liabilities on themselves (e.g., a savings account), then lend the funds to the ultimate users. Prior to the deregulation of the banking system, the various types of financial intermediaries were clearly distinguished from one another. However, now that regulation is centralized with the Federal Reserve and depository institutions may offer whatever interest rates they deem necessary to raise funds, the differences among the intermediaries is disappearing, as they tend to offer comparable yields and services.

One of the newest and most important financial intermediaries is the money market mutual fund, which offers savers an important alternative to the traditional depository institution. These funds offer services similar to banks (e.g., checking privileges) and pay yields that are comparable to those available on money market instruments such as negotiable certificates of deposit, commercial paper, treasury bills, and repurchase agreements. Since the minimum denominations of these money market instruments are sufficiently large that most individuals are excluded from participating in the market for them, the money market mutual funds offer savers a means to indirectly acquire these money market securities.

Terms to Remember

Financial intermediary
Private placement
Investment bankers
Underwriting
Originating house
Syndicate
Best efforts agreement
Preliminary prospectus (red herring)
Securities and Exchange Commission (SEC)
Registration

NOW account
Certificate of deposit (CD)
Negotiable certificate of deposit (jumbo CD)
Federal Deposit Insurance Corporation (FDIC)
Money market mutual fund
Money market instruments
U.S. Treasury bills
Commercial paper
Repurchase agreements

Questions

1. In an underwriting, what role does each of the following play? (a) the investment banker, (b) the syndicate, (c) the red herring, (d) the SEC, and (e) the saver.

2. Why is it important that in an underwriting the investment banker does not overvalue (that is, overprice) the securities? If the securities are overpriced, who suffers the loss?

3. What differentiates an underwriting from a best efforts agreement? Who bears the risk in each of these agreements?

4. Why do investors buy new issues of securities? Besides the risk associated with fluctuations in the market as a whole and the loss of purchasing power through inflation, what is the source of risk associated with new issues?

5. What is a financial intermediary? What role does it play? What differentiates a financial intermediary from an investment banker?

6. What features differentiate savings accounts, certificates of deposit, and negotiable certificates of deposit?

7. Identify the trends that are directly related to the deregulation of the banking system.

8. If a saver had $12,540 to invest for a short period of time, what alternatives would be available?

9. What assets do money market mutual funds acquire? Could an individual saver acquire these assets?

10. Explain the initial rapid growth and subsequent decline in the rate of growth of money market mutual funds.

Suggested Readings

There are many excellent textbooks on money, banking, and other financial institutions. In general these texts discuss banking and financial intermediation in a macroeconomic context and include the impact of monetary and fiscal policy on the banking system and on the level of income and employment. See, for instance:

Ritter, Lawrence S., and William L. Silber. *Principles of Money Banking and Financial Markets.* 4th ed. New York: Basic Books, 1983.

Kaufman, George G. *Money, The Financial System and the Economy.* 3rd ed. Boston: Houghton Mifflin, 1981.

Kidwell, David S., and Richard L. Peterson. *Financial Institutions, Markets, and Money.* 3rd ed. Hinsdale, Ill.: The Dryden Press, 1987.

Meyer, Paul A. *Monetary Economics and Financial Markets.* Homewood, Ill.: Richard D. Irwin, 1982.

Other readings concerning financial intermediaries, investment banking, and the flow of resources from savers to business include:

Dougall, Herbert E., and Jack E. Gaumnitz. *Capital Markets and Institutions.* 5th ed. Englewood Cliffs, N.J.: Prentice-Hall, 1986.
This concise text covers various financial intermediaries, their sources of funds, and portfolios.

Hayes, Samuel L., III. "The Transformation of Investment Banking." *Harvard Business Review* (January–February 1979): 153–170.
This article details changes in investment banking that occurred during the 1970s in response to negotiated commissions, inflation, and the general decline in security prices.

Light, J. O., and William L. White. *The Financial System.* Homewood, Ill.: Richard D. Irwin, 1979.
This text discusses trends in savings and the demand for funds by corporations, governments, and households. It also describes the principal financial markets.

Sullivan, Brian. "An Introduction to 'Going Public.'" *The Journal of Accountancy* (November 1965): 48–53.
This article gives a general description of the process required for a public issue of securities.

Welch, Jonathan B. "Explaining Disintermediation at Mutual Savings Banks." *Financial Analysts Journal* (May–June 1980): 71–76.
This empirical study shows that increased differentials between rates of interest on U.S. Treasury bills and interest earned on savings accounts causes funds to flow out of savings banks.

For discussions of the evolving financial service industry, see:

Gart, Alan. *The Insider's Guide to the Financial Services Revolution.* New York: McGraw-Hill, 1984.

Perez, Robert C. *Marketing Financial Services.* New York: Praeger Publishers, 1983.

Havilesky, Thomas M., and Robert Schweitzer, eds. *Contemporary Developments in Financial Institutions and Markets.* Arlington Heights, Ill.: Harlan Davidson, 1983.

3

Security Markets

LEARNING OBJECTIVES

After completing this chapter you should be able to

1. Explain the role of market makers.
2. Distinguish between security exchanges and over-the-counter markets.
3. Illustrate how security transactions are reported in the financial press.
4. List the services provided by brokers.
5. Differentiate between the types of security orders.
6. Identify the costs of investing in securities.
7. Contrast cash and margin accounts.
8. State the purpose of the SEC and SIPC.

On January 9, 1986, over 2,000,000 shares of IBM traded on the New York Stock Exchange. In all over 176,000,000 shares of stock traded that day on the New York Stock Exchange. Not one penny of the proceeds of those sales went to the firms whose stocks were exchanged. Instead all of these transactions were among investors. Obviously, many individuals were altering their portfolios either through buying or selling these existing securities.

This buying and selling of securities has a certain mystique or fascination for both the novice and the seasoned investor. Investors may be drawn to securities by the jargon used in the stock market or the excitement generated by trading securities. Perhaps the investor's fascination is the result of the fact that many dollars can be earned or lost through investments in stocks and bonds. For whatever reason, investors who are drawn to Wall Street must understand both how security markets work and the mechanics of buying and selling securities.

It is the purpose of this chapter to explain the machinations of the market and the mechanics of buying and selling securities. The first section discusses security dealers and the role of security exchanges. The bulk of the chapter describes how the individual buys

securities. The role of the broker, the types of orders and accounts, the delivery of the se-curities, and the brokerage cost of buying and selling are explained. The chapter ends with a brief discussion of the regulation of the securities industry and the Securities Investor Protec-tion Corporation (SIPC), which insures investors against losses incurred from the failure of a brokerage firm.

MARKET MAKERS

Securities are bought and sold every day by investors who never meet each other. The market impersonally transfers securities from individuals who are selling to those who are buying. This transfer may occur on an **organized exchange,** such as the New York Stock Exchange, or on an unorganized, informal market that is called the **over-the-counter (OTC) market.** In either case there exist professional security dealers who make markets in securities and facilitate their transfer from sellers to buyers. Market makers for securities that are listed on the New York and American stock exchanges are called **specialists.** Market makers for over-the-counter securities are called **deal-ers.** These market makers offer to buy the securities from any seller and to sell the securities to any purchaser.[1]

How securities are traded

Transactions are made in either round lots or odd lots. A **round lot** is the basic unit for trading. For stock, it is usually 100 shares. Smaller transactions (for example, 37 shares), are called **odd lots.** The round lot does not have to be 100 shares for all stocks. For example, for very cheap stocks (sometimes called cats and dogs), a round lot may be 500 or 1,000 shares. For bonds, a round lot may be five $1,000 bonds (i.e., $5,000) or bonds totaling $10,000 or even $100,000 in face value. Odd lots are less profitable for brokerage firms and market makers because the paperwork and the time involved in executing a trade are the same for 10 shares or 100 shares, but the dollar volume of the trade is smaller for the odd lot. Thus, the price per share that the buyer is charged for an odd lot is usually higher than the price per share for a round lot. This additional fee may be hidden in a higher asking price for the security rather than being explicitly stated.[2]

Round lots and odd lots

Both specialists and dealers quote prices on a **bid and ask** basis; they buy at one price and sell at the other. For example, a market maker may be willing to purchase a specific stock for $20 per share and sell it for $21. The security is then quoted "20–21," which are the bid and ask prices. Selected quotes for over-the-counter stocks are illustrated in Exhibit 3.1. As can be seen in the exhibit, the market makers in Child World are willing to purchase (bid for) the stock at $12¼ and to sell (ask) the stock for $12½.

Bid and ask prices

The difference between the bid and the ask is the **spread** (i.e., the $0.25 differ-ence between $12¼ and $12½ for Child World). Although the value of the security is the bid price, the investor pays the asking price. The spread, like brokerage commis-

---

[1] As of January 1983, 64 firms operated as specialists on the New York Stock Exchange.

[2] There is no odd lot differential for a market order on the New York Stock Exchange. For a limit order, the odd lot fee is ⅛ of a point (i.e., $0.125 per share) for stock prices up to $50 and ¼ of a point for prices above $50. Thus if a stock cost $25, the price of an odd lot would be $25.125 to buy and $24.875 to sell through a limit order. (See "Types of Orders" later in this chapter for an explanation of market and limit orders.)

Exhibit 3.1
Selected Bid and Ask
Quotes for Over-the-
counter Stocks as of
January 2, 1986

| | Price | |
Company	Bid	Ask
Base Ten Class B	9	10½
Child World	12¼	12½
Waldbaum's	27	27½

Source: The Wall Street Journal, January 3, 1986.

sions, is part of the cost of investing. These two costs should not be confused. The spread is one source of compensation for maintaining a market in the security. The broker's commission is compensation for executing the investor's purchase or sale order.

The spread may be quite large (at least as a percentage of the bid price). In Exhibit 3.1, for example, the spread is 1½ points for the Base Ten Class B stock, which is 16.7 percent of the bid price. The spread for Child World is only ¼ point, which is 2.0 percent of the bid. The investor's effective cost of buying and selling a share of the Base Ten Class B stock is greater than that for buying and selling the stock of Child World even though the price of one share of Base Ten Class B is less than the cost of one share of Child World.

The size of the differential between the bid and the ask is affected by various factors. If there are several market makers in a particular security, the spread tends to be smaller because of competition. The difference is also affected by the volume of transactions in the security and the number of shares that the firm has outstanding. If the volume of transactions or the number of outstanding securities is large, then the spread between the bid and the ask is small. AT&T's stock may be used as an example. If the stock is quoted 24–24⅛, the spread is only ⅛ of a point (i.e., 0.5 percent of the bid). The spread is small because as of December 31, 1985, AT&T has 1,069.3 million shares outstanding and thousands of shares are traded daily. When the number of outstanding securities is small (i.e., it is a **thin issue**), the spread is usually larger. In the case of Base Ten in Exhibit 3.1, the firm has 3.5 million Class B shares outstanding and only a few hundred may be traded on a given day.

Sources of profit for security dealers

The spread is one source of profit for dealers as they turn over the securities in their portfolios. The market makers also earn income when they receive dividends and interest from the securities they own. Another source of profit is an increase in security prices, for the value of the dealers' portfolios rise. These profits are a necessary element of security markets because they induce the market makers to serve the crucial functions of buying and selling securities and of bearing the risk of loss from unforeseen price declines. These market makers guarantee to buy and sell at the prices they announce. Thus, an investor knows what the securities are worth at any given time and is assured that there is a place to sell current security holdings or to purchase additional securities. For this service, the market makers must be compensated, and this compensation is generated through the spread between the bid and ask prices, dividends and interest earned, and profits on the inventory of securities should their prices rise. (Of course, the market makers must bear any losses on securities that they hold when prices fall.)

Although the bid and ask prices are quoted by market makers, the security prices are set by the demand from all buyers and the supply from all sellers of securities. Market makers try to quote an **equilibrium price** that equates the supply with the demand. If market makers bid too low a price, too few shares will be offered to satisfy the demand. If they ask too high a price, too few shares will be purchased, which will result in a glut, or excess shares, in their portfolios.

The determination of security prices

Could market makers set a security's equilibrium price? For large companies the answer is probably no. If the market makers tried to establish a price above the equilibrium price that is set by supply and demand, they would have to absorb all of the excess supply of securities that would be offered at the artificially higher price. Conversely, if the market makers attempted to establish a price below the equilibrium price, they would have to sell a sufficient number of securities to meet the excess demand that would exist at the artificially lower price. The buying of securities requires the delivery of the securities sold. Market makers do not have an infinite well of money with which to purchase the securities nor an unlimited supply of securities to deliver. They may increase or decrease their inventory, but they cannot support the price indefinitely by buying securities, nor can they prevent a price increase by selling them.

Although market makers cannot set the market price, they perform an extremely important role: They maintain an orderly market in securities so that buyers and sellers will have an established market in which to trade securities. To establish this orderly market, the market makers offer to buy and sell at the quoted bid and ask prices but guarantee only one round lot transaction at these prices. If a market maker sets too low a price for a certain stock, a large quantity will be demanded by investors. The market maker is required to sell only one round lot at this price and then may increase the bid and ask prices. The increase in the price of the stock will (1) induce some holders of the stock to sell their shares and (2) induce some investors who wanted to purchase the stock to drop out of the market.

Market makers maintain an orderly market

If the market maker sets too high a price for the stock, a large quantity of shares will be offered for sale, but these shares will remain unsold. If the market maker is unable to or does not want to absorb all of these shares, the security dealer may purchase a round lot and then lower the bid and ask prices. The decline in the price of the stock will (1) induce some potential sellers to hold their stock and (2) induce some investors to enter the market by purchasing the shares, thereby reducing any of the market maker's surplus inventory.

SECURITY EXCHANGES

When a company first sells its securities to the public, the securities are traded in the over-the-counter market. However, the firm may subsequently desire to have its securities **listed** on one of the major organized exchanges—the **New York Stock Exchange** (**NYSE**, or "**the big board**") or the **American Stock Exchange** (**AMEX**, or "**the curb**"). (Although the inclusion of the word *stock* in the names implies a market that deals solely in stock, some bond issues and options are also traded on these exchanges.) The listing of a firm's securities on a major exchange has an element of prestige, for it indicates that the company has grown above local importance and has at-

Listed securities

Exhibit 3.2
Listing Requirements

Requirements	New York Stock Exchange	American Stock Exchange
Number of shares held by the general public	1,100,000	400,000
Number of stockholders owning 100 or more shares	2,000	1,200, of which 500 must own 100 to 500 shares
Pretax income for latest fiscal year	$2,500,000	$750,000
Pretax income for preceding two years	$2,000,000	
Minimum aggregate value of shares publicly held	$18,000,000	$300,000
Tangible assets	$16,000,000	$4,000,000

Regional exchanges

The NYSE and the AMEX

The listing requirements

tained a specified level of size and profitability.[3] Listing may also facilitate selling securities in the future, for investors may be more willing to purchase the securities of companies whose stocks or bonds are publicly traded on an exchange.

In addition to these national exchanges, there are several regional stock exchanges, including the Philadelphia Exchange, the Midwest Exchange, and the Pacific Exchange. These regional exchanges list companies of particular interest to their geographic areas. For example, Alaska Gold is primarily a regional company and is listed on the Pacific Exchange. Other firms in the region, like Georgia Pacific, are listed on several exchanges. This company has a national market for its stock but is also of particular interest to investors living on the West Coast, since it has large timber holdings there. Its securities are actively traded on both the New York and the Pacific stock exchanges.

The NYSE is the largest exchange and lists the securities of companies of national interest. The AMEX is smaller than the NYSE but, unlike the regional exchanges, lists smaller firms with national followings. Many of the firms listed on the NYSE were originally listed on the AMEX. After achieving larger earnings and size, these firms transferred their listing from the AMEX to the NYSE.

The listing requirements for both exchanges are presented in Exhibit 3.2. As may be seen in the exhibit, the criteria that must be fulfilled in order to be listed are essentially the same for both exchanges, but the required sums are larger for the NYSE. In addition to the conditions stated in Exhibit 3.2, listing requires the firm to conform to certain procedures, including publishing quarterly reports, soliciting proxies, and publicly announcing any developments that may affect the value of the securities.

Once the securities are accepted for trading on an exchange, the firm must continue to meet the listing requirements. The exchange may delist the securities if the firm is unable to continue to meet the criteria for listing. Such delistings do occur, but over a period of years the number of listed securities has increased. Whereas 1,253 stocks were traded on the NYSE in 1965, the number had grown to 2,319 issues of 1,543 companies in 1984.[4]

---

[3] Many corporations (e.g., Bob Evans, MCI Communications, and NIKE, Inc.) choose *not* to be listed.

[4] New York Stock Exchange, *1985 Fact Book*, 37.

Daily transactions on the listed exchanges are reported by the financial press (e.g., *The Wall Street Journal*). Weekly summaries are also reported in several publications (e.g., *The New York Times* and *Barron's*). Although there is variation in this reporting, the typical entry appears as follows:

The reporting of listed stock transactions

52 weeks High	Low	Stock (Company)	Dividend	Yield (%)	P/E	Sales in 100s	High	Low	Close	Net Change
158½	117⅜	IBM	4.40	2.8	16	9241	158¾	155	155½	−2¾

"High" and "low" at the far left indicate the high and low prices (158½ and 117⅜, respectively, for IBM) of the security during the preceding fifty-two weeks. Then the name of the company is given, usually in an abbreviated form, followed by the amount of the dividend ($4.40), which is generally the annual rate that the firm is paying. If the amount is not the annual rate, a symbol is placed after the dividend that refers the reader to a key explaining the particular exceptions. After the dividend the current yield is given, which is the amount of the dividend divided by the price of the stock (2.8 percent for IBM). This dividend yield is a measure of the flow of income that is produced by an investment in that particular stock. (Dividends are discussed in more detail in Chapter 15.) The **P/E ratio** (16 for IBM) is the ratio of the price of the stock to the earnings per share of the firm. The P/E ratio may be interpreted as a measure of what the market is willing to pay for the stock.

The last five entries of the typical listing pertain to the trading in that particular security on the preceding trading day. The first is the volume of transactions, which, for stocks, is expressed in hundreds of shares (i.e., 461 means 46,100). (For bonds the volume is expressed in terms of the face value in denominations of $1,000 of the bonds traded; for example, 7 means that the face value of the bonds that changed hands was $7,000.) After volume of trading are the price statistics, which include the high, low, and closing prices. If the stock is traded for a new high for the preceding 12 months, a "u" is placed next to the value. If it is traded at a new low, a "d" is placed next to the price. The last entry is the change in price from the closing price of the previous day of trading.

Securities of companies with shares issued to the general public that are not traded on an exchange are traded over the counter. The prices of many of these securities are also reported daily in the financial sections of newspapers. In *The Wall Street Journal* these entries are subdivided into the NASDAQ over-the-counter national market, NASDAQ bid and asked quotations, and additional OTC quotes. **NASDAQ** is an acronym for National Association of Security Dealers Automated Quotation system, which is the impressive system of communication for over-the-counter price quotations. All major unlisted stocks are included in this system. A broker may thereby readily obtain the bid and ask prices for many stocks and bonds by simply entering the firm's code into the NASDAQ system.

The reporting of OTC stock transactions

The national OTC market—NASDAQ

The reporting of the NASDAQ national market issues is virtually the same as the reporting of listed securities. The information given includes the 52-week high and low prices, the firm's dividend, the volume of transactions, the high, low, and closing prices, and the net change from the previous day. Only the yield and the P/E ratio may be excluded.

POINTS OF INTEREST
The P/E Ratio

One term often used by investors is the P/E ratio, which is the ratio of a stock's price to the firm's per-share earnings. By expressing each firm's stock price relative to its earnings, this ratio facilitates the comparison of firms. The P/E ratio indicates the amount that the market is willing to pay for each dollar of earnings. A P/E of 12 means that the stock is selling for 12 times the firm's earnings and that the market believes that $1 of earnings is currently worth $12. There is also the implication that if earnings increase by $1, the price of the stock will rise by $12.

Firms in the same industry tend to have similar P/E ratios. This is illustrated in Exhibit 3.3, which gives the earnings, the price of the stock, and the P/E ratio for ten chemical companies. The average P/E ratio for the industry (i.e., 14.2) may be indicative of the appropriate P/E ratio for an individual firm's stock. If the company's ratio is higher than the industry's average, the stock may be overpriced. Conversely, if the P/E ratio is lower than the industry's average, it may indicate that the stock is undervalued.

Unfortunately, security analysis and selection are not that simple. If a firm has an excellent record of earnings growth and the security market anticipates that this growth will continue, the P/E ratio tends to be higher than the industry's average. This higher growth has value. These earnings may achieve a higher price, in which case the stock sells for a higher P/E ratio. If a firm is considered to be riskier than is typical of firms in its industry, the P/E ratio tends to be lower. The earnings of a firm involving greater risk are worth less. Thus, the stock's price and the P/E ratio are lower than industry's average.

While the P/E ratio is frequently used, it does not tell the investor much about the firm. Of course, it does permit easy comparison of firms, but it considers only the earnings and the price of the stock. It tells nothing of how the earnings were achieved or why the market may view one firm's earnings as inferior or superior to the earnings of another firm.

Exhibit 3.3
Per-share Earnings, Stock Price, and P/E Ratios for Selected Chemical Companies as of January 1, 1986

Company	Per-share Earnings for the Preceding Twelve Months	Price of the Stock	P/E Ratio
Allied-Signal, Inc.	$ 4.74	$ 46¾	9.9
Celanese	11.97	150¼	12.6
Dow Chemical	2.45	41	16.7
DuPont	3.79	67⅞	17.9
Ethyl	1.76	27¼	15.5
Grow Group	.67	10¾	16.0
Monsanto	3.69	47¾	13.0
Pennwalt	3.25	42¾	13.2
Rohm and Haas	5.96	76⅝	12.9
Union Carbide	4.84	70⅞	14.6

Average P/E: 14.2

Source: Standard and Poor's *Stock Guide,* January 1986.

In addition to the NASDAQ national market issues, *The Wall Street Journal* and other papers that give thorough coverage of security prices report the NASDAQ over-the-counter bid and ask price quotations. These are generally limited to the company, the dividend (if any), the volume of transactions, the closing bid and ask prices, and the net change in the bid price from the previous day. A typical NASDAQ over-the-counter entry would read as follows:

Stock and Dividend	Sales 100s	Bid	Asked	Net Change
Santa Monica Bank .60	1	29½	33	. . .

This tells the investor that the bank pays an annual dividend of $0.60, that 100 shares traded, and that there was no net change (. . .) from the previous trading day's bid price.

Some papers also report additional OTC quotes. These are generally limited to the bid and ask prices, and, in many cases, these quotations are limited to small firms traded in the geographical area served by the paper.

With the development of NASDAQ, the distinction between the various exchanges and the over-the-counter market is being erased. Since New York Stock Exchange securities trade on other exchanges, the actual reporting of New York Stock Exchange listings includes all the trades and is reported as the NYSE-Composite transactions. The bulk of the transactions in listed securities, however, still occurs on the NYSE.

Composite transactions

In addition to listed securities and stocks traded over-the-counter through security dealers, there are also large block transactions executed through the exchange by brokers and not through specialists. This over-the-counter trading in listed securities is often referred to as the **"third market."** Large institutional investors such as pension plans, mutual funds, or insurance companies may seek to purchase or sell large amounts of stocks in listed securities, such as the stock of IBM, which usually trades on the NYSE. Such large transactions (i.e., 10,000 shares or more) are called "blocks" of stocks, and the brokers who organize and execute the trades are referred to as "block positioners."

Block trades—10,000 or more shares

The third market

In the third market the financial institution works through a large brokerage firm that serves to complete the transaction. If the financial institution desires to buy a large position, the brokerage firm seeks potential sellers. If the institution desires to sell a large position, the brokerage firm seeks potential buyers. After the brokerage firm finds the required sellers (or buyers), the block of securities is traded off the floor of the exchange.

In the "fourth market," the financial institutions do not use a brokerage firm but trade securities through a computerized system called "Instinet," which provides bid and ask price quotations and executes orders. This system is limited to those financial institutions that subscribe to the service. Transactions through Instinet are reported in the financial press through the composite transactions just as trades on the various exchanges are reported.

The fourth market

Block trades, the third market, and the fourth market offer financial institutions two advantages: lower commissions and quicker executions. Competition among brokerage firms for this business has reduced the commissions charged the financial institutions. In addition, the effort and time required to put together a block to purchase

or to find buyers for a sale is significantly reduced through the development of block trading and over-the-counter trading of listed securities. The effect of this trading and the change in the regulatory environment for financial institutions is leading to a national market system for the execution of security orders, since these orders need not go through an exchange in a particular geographical area.[5]

THE MECHANICS OF INVESTING IN SECURITIES

Individual investors usually purchase securities through **brokers,** who buy and sell securities for their customers' accounts. Whereas some securities may be purchased directly from firms, the majority of purchases are made through brokerage firms, such as Merrill Lynch Pierce Fenner and Smith or E. F. Hutton. The firms have salespersons who service the individual's account. These brokers are the investor's agents, who execute the investor's buy and sell orders. In order to be permitted to buy and sell, these salespersons must pass a proficiency examination that is administered by the National Association of Security Dealers. Once the individual has passed the test, he or she is referred to as a **registered representative** and can buy or sell securities for customers.

Brokers are not experts

Although registered representatives must pass this proficiency examination, the investor should not assume that the broker is an expert. There are many aspects of investing, and even an individual who spends a considerable portion of the working day servicing accounts cannot be an expert on all of the aspects of investing. Thus, many recommendations are based on research that is done by analysts employed by the brokerage firm rather than by individual salespersons.

Compensation through commissions

The investor should also realize that brokers make their living through transactions (i.e., buying and selling for their customers' accounts). There are essentially two types of working relationships between the brokerage firm and the salesperson. In one case the firm pays a basic salary, but the salesperson must bring in a specified amount in commissions, which go to the firm. After the minimum amount of sales has been met, the registered representative's salary is increased in proportion to the amount of additional commissions generated. In the second type of relationship, the salesperson's income is entirely related to the commissions generated. In either case the investor should realize that the broker's livelihood depends on the sale of securities. Thus, the broker's advice on investing may be colored by the desire to secure commissions. However, the investor is ultimately responsible for the investment decisions. Although advice may be requested from the broker, and it is sometimes offered even though unsolicited, the investor must weigh the impact of a specific investment decision in terms of fulfilling his or her personal goals.

Selecting a brokerage firm

Selecting a brokerage firm can be a difficult task. Various firms offer different services; for example, some may specialize in bonds and others may deal solely in the securities of corporations located in a particular geographic region. The best source of information on stocks of local interest (e.g., local commercial banks) is often the small regional brokerage firm. Other brokerage firms offer a variety of services, including

---

[5]For a detailed discussion of the development of a national market system, see Morris Mendelson and Junius W. Peake, "The ABCs of Trading on a National Market System," *Financial Analysts Journal* (September–October 1979): 31–42.

estate planning and life insurance, as well as the trading of stocks and bonds. Still other firms offer virtually no services other than executing orders at discount (i.e., lower commissions). Each investor therefore needs to identify his or her personal investment goals and decide on the strategies to attain those goals in order to select the firm that is best suited to that individual's needs.

Choosing a registered representative is perhaps a more difficult task than selecting a brokerage firm. This individual will need to know specific information, including the investor's income, other assets and outstanding debt, and financial goals, in order to give the best service to the account. Since people are reluctant to discuss some of this information, trust and confidence in the registered representative are probably the most important considerations in selecting a broker. Good rapport between the broker and the investor is particularly important if the relationship is going to be mutually successful.

Selecting a broker

The Long Position

Essentially, an investor has only two courses of action, which involve opposite positions. They are frequently referred to as the bull and bear positions and are symbolized by a statue, which is located outside the NYSE, of a bull and a bear locked in mortal combat.[6]

If an investor expects a security's price to rise, the security may be purchased. The investor takes a **"long position"** in the security in anticipation of the price increase. The investor is **"bullish"** because he or she believes that the price will rise. The long position earns profits for the investor if the price rises after the security has been purchased. For example, if an investor buys 100 shares of AB&C for $55 (i.e., $5,500 plus brokerage fees) and the price rises to $60, the profit on the long position is $5 per share (i.e., $500 on 100 shares before commissions).

The bullish position

Opposite the bullish position is the **"bearish"** position, in which the investor anticipates that the security's price will fall. The investor may sell the security and hold cash or place the funds in interest-bearing short-term securities, such as treasury bills or a savings account. Some investors who are particularly bearish or who are willing to speculate on the decline in prices may even "sell short," which is a sale for future delivery. Since few investors do sell short, a detailed discussion of it is deferred until Chapter 19, which is concerned with some of the more speculative investment alternatives.

The bearish position

Types of Orders

After an investor decides to purchase a security, a buy order is placed with the broker. The investor may ask the broker to buy the security at the best price currently available, which is the asking price set by the market maker. Such a request is a **market order.** The investor is not assured of receiving the security at the currently quoted price, since that price may change by the time the order is executed. However, the order is generally executed at or very near the asking price.

The market order

---

[6] The derivations of "bull" and "bear" are lost in time. "Bearish" may originate from trading in pelts when bearskins were sold before the bears were caught. Bullbaiting and bearbaiting were also sports in the eighteenth century. See Steele Commager, "Watch Your Language," *Forbes* (October 27, 1980): 113–116.

Purchase orders with specified prices

The investor may specify a price below the current asking price and wait until the price declines to the specified level. Such an order may be placed for one day (i.e., a **day order**), or the order may remain in effect indefinitely (i.e., a **good-till-canceled order**). Such an order remains on the books of the broker until it is either executed or canceled. If the price of the security does not decline to the specified level, the purchase is never made. Such an order may then become a nuisance for the broker, who must periodically inform the customer that the order is still in effect.

The stop loss order

After purchasing the security an investor may place a **limit order** to sell, which may be at a higher or lower price.[7] An investor who desires to limit potential losses may place a **stop loss order**, which specifies the price below the cost of the security at which the broker is authorized to sell. For example, if an investor buys a stock for $50 a share, a stop loss order at $45 limits the loss to $5 a share, plus the commission fees for the purchase and the sale. If the price of the stock should fall to $45, the stop loss order becomes a market order, and the stock is sold.[8] Such a sale protects the investor from riding the price of the stock down to $40 or lower. Of course, if the stock rebounds from $45 to $50, the investor has sold out at the bottom price.

The investor may also place a sell order above the purchase price. For example, the investor who purchases a stock at $50 may place a sell order at $60. Should the price of the stock reach $60, the order becomes a market order, and the stock is sold. Such an order puts a limit on the potential profit, for if the stock's price continues to rise, the investor who has already sold the stock does not continue to gain. However, the investor has protected the profit that resulted as the price increased from $50 to $60. In many cases the investor watches the stock's price rise, decides not to sell, and then watches the price subsequently decline. Sell orders are designed to reduce the possibility of this occurring.

The use of sell orders may be good strategy

The placing of sell orders can be an important part of an investor's strategy. For example, in the previous case the investor who purchased a stock at $50 may place sell orders at $45 and $60. If the price of the stock subsequently rises, this investor may change these sell orders. For example, if the price rises to $56 per share, the investor may change the sell orders to $52 and $64. This will preserve the capital invested, for the price of the stock cannot fall below $52 without triggering the sell order, but the price can now rise above $60, which was the previous upper limit for the sell order. By continuously raising the prices for the sell orders as the stock's price rises, the investor can continue to profit from any price increase and at the same time protect the funds invested in the security against price declines.

The confirmation statement

Once the purchase has been made, the broker sends the investor a **confirmation statement,** an example of which is shown in Exhibit 3.4. This confirmation statement gives the number of shares and name of the security purchased (100 shares of Clevepak Corporation), the unit price ($12⅛), and the total amount that is due ($1,244.26). The amount that is due includes both the price of the securities and the transaction fees. The major transaction fee is the brokerage firm's commission, but there may also be state transfer fees and other miscellaneous fees. The investor has five business days

---

[7] For a description of the 21 possible orders recognized by NYSE Rule 13, see Morris Mendelson and Junius W. Peake, "The ABCs of Trading on a National Market System," *Financial Analysts Journal* (September–October 1979): 39–40.

[8] Since the order is now a market order, there is no guarantee the investor will get $45. If there is an influx of sell orders, the sale may occur at less than $45.

Exhibit 3.4
Confirmation Statement for the Purchase of 100 Shares of Clevepak Corporation

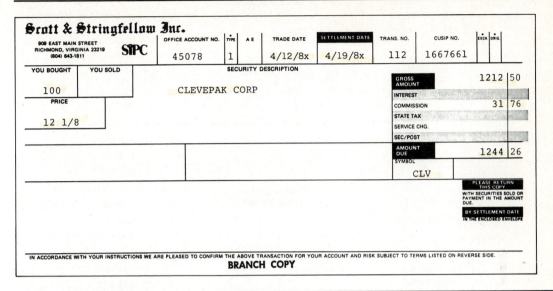

Source: Reprinted with permission from Scott & Stringfellow, Inc.

after the date of purchase (April 12, 198x) to pay the amount that is due; the date by which payment must be made (April 19, 198x) is called the **settlement date**.

Types of Accounts

The investor must pay for the securities as they are purchased. This can be done either with cash or with a combination of cash and borrowed funds. The latter is called buying on **margin**. The investor then has either a cash account or a margin account. A cash account is what the name implies: The investor pays the entire cost of the securities (i.e., $1,244.26 in Exhibit 3.4) in cash.

A cash account

When an investor uses margin, that is, purchases the security partially with cash and partially with credit supplied by the brokers, he or she makes an initial payment that is similar to a down payment on a house and borrows the remaining funds necessary to make the purchase. To open a margin account, the investor signs an agreement with the broker that gives use of the securities and some control over the account to the broker. The securities serve as collateral for the loan. Should the amount of collateral on the account fall below a specified level, the broker can require that the investor put more assets in the account. This is called a "margin call," and it may be satisfied by cash or additional securities. If the investor fails to meet a margin call, the broker will sell some securities in the account to raise the cash needed to protect the loan.

A margin account

The margin requirement is the minimum percentage of the total price that the investor must pay and is set by the Federal Reserve Board. Individual brokers, however, may require more margin. The minimum payment required of the investor is the

The margin requirement

Exhibit 3.5
Potential Return Earned on Cash and Margin Purchases

	Cash Purchase, No Margin	Margin Purchase
Purchase price	$1,244.26	$1,244.26 cash—$746.56 debt—$497.70
Sale price	$1,500.00	$1,500.00
Profit on sale	$ 255.74	$ 255.74
Percent earned	$\frac{\$\ 255.74}{\$1,244.26} \times 100\% = 20.6\%$	$\frac{\$\ 255.74}{\$746.56} \times 100\% = 34.3\%$

Exhibit 3.6
Potential Loss from Cash and Margin Purchases

	Cash Purchase, No Margin	Margin Purchase
Purchase price	$1,244.26	$1,244.26 cash—$746.56 debt—$497.70
Sale price	$1,000.00	$1,000.00
Loss on sale	$ 244.26	$ 244.26
Percent lost	$\frac{\$\ 244.26}{\$1,244.26} \times 100\% = 19.6\%$	$\frac{\$\ 244.26}{\$\ 746.56} \times 100\% = 32.7\%$

value of the securities times the margin requirement. Thus, if the margin requirement is 60 percent and the price plus the commission on 100 shares of Clevepak Corporation is $1,244.26, the investor must supply $746.56 in cash and borrow $497.70 from the broker, who in turn borrows the funds from a commercial bank. The investor pays interest to the broker on $497.70. The interest rate will depend on the rate that the broker must pay to the lending institution. The investor, of course, may avoid the interest charges by paying the entire $1,244.26 and not using borrowed funds.

The use of margin may increase the rate of return

Investors use margin to increase the potential return on the investment. When they expect the price of the security to rise, some investors pay for part of their purchases with borrowed funds. How the use of borrowed funds increases the potential return is illustrated in Exhibit 3.5. If the price of shares of Clevepak Corporation rises from 12⅛ to 15, the profit is $255.74 (excluding commissions on the sale). If the investor pays the entire $1,244.26, the percentage return is 20.6 percent. However, if the investor uses margin and pays for the stock with $746.56 in equity and $497.70 in borrowed funds, the investor's percentage return is increased (before the interest expense)[9] to 34.3 percent. In this case, the use of margin is favorable because it increases the investor's return on the invested funds.[10]

The use of margin may increase the percentage lost

Of course, if the price of the stock falls, the reverse occurs—that is, the percentage loss is greater, as is illustrated in Exhibit 3.6. If the price falls to $10, the investor loses $244.26 before commissions on the sale. The percentage loss is 19.6 percent.

---

[9] For ease and clarity, dividends received and interest paid are omitted. For a complete illustration, see Problem 3 at the end of this chapter.

[10] How a firm may increase its per-share earnings through the use of borrowed funds is explained in Chapter 14.

However, if the investor uses margin, the percentage loss is increased to 32.7 percent. Since the investor has borrowed money and thus reduced the amount of funds that he or she has committed to the investment, the percentage loss is greater. The use of margin magnifies not only the potential gain but also the potential loss. Because the potential loss is increased, buying securities on credit increases the element of risk that must be borne by the investor.

Delivery of Securities

Once the shares have been purchased and paid for, the investor must decide whether to leave the securities with the broker or to take delivery. (In the case of a margin account, the investor *must* leave the securities with the broker.) If the shares are left with the broker, they will be registered in the broker's name (i.e., in the **street name**). The broker then becomes custodian of the securities, is responsible for them, and sends a monthly statement of the securities that are being held in the street name to the investor. The monthly statement also includes any transactions that have taken place during the month and any dividends and interest that have been received. The investor may either leave the dividends and interest payments to accumulate with the broker or receive payment from the broker.

Securities may be left with the broker

An example of a monthly statement is shown in Exhibit 3.7. The statement is divided into two parts. The top half enumerates all of the transactions during the month. According to this monthly statement, the investor made no purchases, deposited 158 shares of Martha Manning in the account on March 16, sold those shares on March 22 for 2⅝, and received dividend payments from six firms. The investor also withdrew $633.80 from the account. The bottom half of the statement enumerates the investor's security position at the end of the month. In this exhibit the broker is holding ten stocks in nine companies for the customer.

The monthly statement

This monthly statement gives additional information that may be useful to the investor. Besides enumerating the securities held, it gives their prices as of a certain date. This may help in planning one's portfolio. The total dividends collected to date during the year are also given ($672). Since the total for the year must be reported to the Internal Revenue Service, the yearly total to date may aid in tax planning.

The main advantage of leaving the securities with the broker is convenience. The investor does not have to worry about storing the securities and can readily sell them, since they are in the broker's possession. The accrued interest and dividends may be viewed as a kind of forced savings program, for they may be immediately reinvested before the investor has an opportunity to spend the money elsewhere. The monthly statements are a readily accessible source of information for tax purposes.

Advantages of leaving securities with the broker

There are, however, several important disadvantages in leaving the securities in the broker's name. If the brokerage firm fails or becomes insolvent, the investor may encounter difficulty in transferring the securities into his or her name and even greater difficulty in collecting any accrued dividends and interest.[11] In addition, since the securities are registered in the brokerage firm's name, interim financial statements, annual reports, and other announcements that are sent by the firm to its stockholders are

Disadvantages of leaving securities with a broker

---

[11] The Securities Investor Protection Corporation (SIPC) has reduced the investor's risk of loss from the failure of a brokerage firm. SIPC is discussed later in this chapter.

Exhibit 3.7
**Brokerage Monthly
Statement**

**Statement of
Security Account**

ACCOUNT # 876 55352	A/E # 4265	PAGE # 1
SS OR ID # 000-00-0000	PERIOD ENDING 03 31 19XX	
ACCOUNT EXECUTIVE NAME POOLED ACCOUNT		

DATE	BOT/RECD	SOLD/DELD	DESCRIPTION	PRICE	AMOUNT
			US FDS BALANCE FEB 24		$77.75CR
02 27			100 AMER FILTRONA CORP	* DIV	$18.00CR
03 15			325 CONTL GRP $2CVPF SRA	* DIV	$162.50CR
03 15			150 CONTINENTL GROUP INC	* DIV	$82.50CR
03 16	158		MANNING MARTHA CO	RCD	
03 17			100 MAGIC CHEF INC	* DIV	$12.50CR
03 20			905 VIRGINIA ELECT POWER	* DIV	$280.55CR
03 22			CHECK F		$383.52
03 22		158	MANNING MARTHA CO	2 5/8	$383.52CR
03 27			CHECK F 03/23		$633.80
03 27			100 LENOX INC	* DIV	$28.00CR
			US FDS CLOSING BALANCE		$28.00CR

LONG	SHORT	POSITION IN YOUR ACCOUNT	PX AS OF 03 30
100		AMER FILTRONA CORP	9.625
100		ATLANTA NATL R&T SBI	N/A
325		CONTL GRP $2CVPF SRA	24.750
150		**CONTINENTL GROUP INC	29.750
100		**GENERAL MEDICAL CORP	12.000
100		**LENOX INC	25.500
100		**MAGIC CHEF INC	8.625
100		NEW JERSEY NATL CORP	23.250
71		**S C M CORP	15.875
905		**VIRGINIA ELECT POWER	14.125

---------YEAR TO DATE DIVIDEND, INTEREST AND/OR CHARGE INFORMATION---------

TOTAL DIV REPORTABLE TO IRS: $672

FOR AN EXPLANATION OF SYMBOLS, PLEASE SEE REVERSE SIDE
PLEASE ADVISE YOUR ACCOUNT EXECUTIVE IMMEDIATELY OF ANY DISCREPANCIES ON YOUR STATEMENT.
WHEN MAKING INQUIRIES, PLEASE MENTION YOUR ACCOUNT NUMBER AND ADDRESS ALL CORRESPONDENCE TO THE OFFICE SERVICING YOUR ACCOUNT.
WE URGE YOU TO PRESERVE THIS STATEMENT FOR USE IN PREPARING INCOME TAX RETURNS.

mailed to the brokerage firm and not to the investor. The brokerage firm should forward this material to the investor but may not, or the material may arrive late. To circumvent this problem, an investor may write to the firm and ask to be placed on its mailing list. The firm may choose not to do so, for it sends the material to the brokerage firm and may view the additional mailing as an unnecessary expense.

Whether the investor ultimately decides to leave the securities with the broker or to take delivery depends on the individual. However, if the investor frequently buys and sells securities (i.e., is a **trader**), the securities ought to be left with the broker to facilitate the transactions. If the investor is satisfied with the services of the broker and

is convinced that the firm is financially secure, leaving the securities registered in the street name may be justified for reasons of convenience.

If the investor chooses to take delivery of the securities, that individual receives *The storage of securities* the stock certificates or bonds. Since the certificates may become negotiable, the investor may suffer a loss if they are stolen. Therefore, care should be taken to store them in a safe place (e.g., a lockbox or safe-deposit box in a bank). If the certificates are lost or destroyed, they can be replaced, but only at considerable expense in terms of money and time.

The Cost of Investing

Investing, like everything else, is not free. The individual must pay certain costs, the *Commissions* most obvious of which is **commission** fees. There may also be transfer fees, and some states tax the transfer of securities. These last expenses tend to be small, but they do add up as the dollar value or the number of trades increases.

Commission costs are not insignificant, and for small investors they may constitute a substantial portion of the total amount spent on the investment. Commission rates are supposed to be set by supply and demand, but in reality only large investors (e.g., financial institutions such as insurance companies or mutual funds) are able to negotiate commissions with brokerage firms. These institutions do such a large dollar volume that they are able to negotiate lower rates. For these institutions, the commission rates (as a percentage of the dollar amount of the transaction) may be quite small.

Individuals, however, do not have this influence and generally have to accept the rate that is offered by the brokerage firm. Although the fee schedule may not be made public by the brokerage firm, the registered representative will generally tell the investor what the fee will be before executing the transaction.

In general, commission rates are quoted in terms of round lots of 100 shares. Most firms also set a minimum commission fee (e.g., $30) that may cover all transactions involving $1,000 or less. Then, as the value of the 100 shares increases to greater than $1,000, the fee also increases. However, this commission fee as a percentage of the dollar value of the transaction will usually fall.

There are some brokerage firms that offer lower commission rates. However, *Discount brokers* these firms may not offer some of the services that are provided by the nondiscount houses. Research facilities and advisory services cost money and therefore may not be available through **discount brokers**. If the individual does not need these services, the discount brokers may be a means to reduce the cost of investing by decreasing the commission fees.[12]

The commissions for a purchase (or sale) of 100 shares and 300 shares charged by a discount and a full service broker are presented in Exhibit 3.8. The fees of both brokers rise as the amount invested rises. For example, the commissions on a purchase of 100 shares at $20 ($2,000) is $30.90 at the discount broker, but the commission rises to $36.95 when the price of the stock rises to $30 ($3,000). The exhibit shows that the commissions as a percent of the amount invested decline as the cost of

---

[12] Full service brokers may offer discounts, but the investor must ask for them. Receiving the requested discount will depend on such factors as the volume of trades generated by the investor.

Exhibit 3.8
Commissions Charged
by Discount and Full
Service Brokers

Price of Stock	Discount Broker Commission	Commission as a Percent of Cost of Stock	Full Service Broker Commission	Commission as a Percent of Cost of Stock
	(100 shares)		(100 shares)	
$10	$30.00	3.00%	$29.28	2.98%
20	30.90	1.54	46.95	2.34
30	36.95	1.23	60.54	2.02
40	41.90	1.05	71.66	1.79
50	45.37	0.91	80.31	1.61
75	45.37	0.60	87.19	1.16
100	45.37	0.45	87.19	0.87
	(300 shares)		(300 shares)	
$10	$36.85	1.23%	$79.44	2.64%
20	58.38	0.97	126.09	2.10
30	75.14	0.83	162.09	1.80
40	97.91	0.77	198.53	1.65
50	108.68	0.72	234.74	1.56
75	121.10	0.54	261.57	1.16
100	125.00	0.42	261.57	0.87

Source: Two anonymous brokerage firms.

the investment rises. The commissions on 100 shares at $30 is only 1.23 percent of the purchase price, whereas the commission would be 1.54 percent on a purchase of 100 shares at $20.

The exhibit also illustrates the potential savings from using a discount broker. The difference on a purchase of 300 shares at $100 (an investment of $30,000) is $136.57. However, the difference in commission costs for small purchases is modest ($60.54 versus $36.95 for the purchase of 100 shares at $30). Investors with modest sums may find the services offered by the full service brokers to be worth the additional costs in commissions.

Implicit costs
Whereas commissions and other fees are explicit costs, there is also an important implicit cost of investing. This cost is the spread between the bid and the ask price of the security. As was explained earlier in this chapter, the investor pays the ask price but receives only the bid price when the securities are sold. This spread should be viewed as a cost of investing. Thus, if an investor wants to buy 100 shares of a stock quoted 20–21, he or she will have to pay $2,100 plus commissions to buy stock that is currently worth (if it were to be sold) only $2,000. If the commission rate is 2.5 percent on purchases and sales, the cost of a round trip in the security (i.e., a purchase and a subsequent sale) is substantial, as is illustrated in Exhibit 3.9. First, the investor pays 2.5 percent of $2,100 to buy the stock, for a total cost of $2,152.50 ($2,100 + $52.50). If the stock is then sold, the investor will receive $1,950 ($2,000 − [0.025 × $2,000] = $1,950). Although the investor paid $2,152.50, only $1,950 will be received in the event that the stock must be liquidated at the bid price.

The cost of this purchase and the subsequent sale exceeded $200. This loss through the spread is regarded as a capital loss for income tax purposes. It is not considered to

Purchase Price	Commission	Total Cost	Exhibit 3.9
$2,100.00	$52.50	$2,152.50	**Effect of the Spread on the Cost of Investing**
Sale Price	Commission	Total Received	
$2,000.00	$50.00	$1,950.00	

Net Loss
Total Cost Minus Total Received = Net Loss
$2,152.50 − $1,950.00 = $202.50

be part of the actual cost of investing. However, the individual investor should view this spread as an implicit cost of investing and should consider its impact on the total cost. As the previous example illustrates, the investor loses the difference in value between the bid and ask prices (the spread) upon purchasing the security. Thus, the bid price of the security must rise sufficiently to cover both the commission fees and the spread before the investor realizes any capital appreciation.

REGULATION

Like many industries, the securities industry is subject to a substantial degree of regulation from both the federal and state governments. Since the majority of securities are traded across state lines, most regulation is at the federal level.

The purpose of these laws is to protect the investor by ensuring honest and fair practices. The laws require that the investor be provided with information upon which to base decisions. Hence, these acts are frequently referred to as the **full disclosure laws,** because publicly owned companies must inform the public of certain facts relating to the firm. The regulations also attempt to prevent fraud and the manipulation of stock prices. However, they do not try to protect investors from their own folly and greed. The purpose of legislation governing the securities industry is not to ensure that investors will profit from their investments; instead the laws try to provide fair market practices while allowing investors to make their own mistakes. *The purpose*

Although current federal regulation developed during the 1930s as a direct result of the debacle in the security markets during the early part of that decade, state regulation started in 1911 with the pioneering legislation of the state of Kansas. These state laws are frequently called blue sky laws because fraudulent securities were referred to as pieces of blue sky. Although there are differences among the state laws, they generally require that (1) security firms and brokers be licensed, (2) financial information concerning issues of new securities be filed with state regulatory bodies, (3) new securities meet specific standards before they may be sold, and (4) regulatory bodies be established to enforce the laws. *Laws passed in the 1930s*

The Federal Security Laws

The first modern federal legislation governing the securities industry was the Security Act of 1933. This act is primarily concerned with the issuing of new securities. It requires that new securities be "registered" with the Security and Exchange Commission *Security Act of 1933*

(SEC). Registration consists of supplying the SEC with information concerning the firm, the nature of its business and competition, and its financial position. This information is then summarized in the prospectus (refer to Exhibit 2.1), which makes the formal offer to sell the securities to the public.

The impact on the sale of new securities

Once the SEC has determined that all material facts that may affect the value of the firm have been disclosed, the securities are released for sale. When the securities are sold, the buyer must be given a copy of the prospectus. If the investor incurs a loss on an investment in a new issue of securities, a suit may be filed to recover the loss if the prospectus or the registration statement that was filed with the SEC contained false or misleading information. Liability for this loss may rest on the firm, its executives and directors, the brokerage firm selling the securities, and any experts (e.g., accountants, appraisers) who were employed in preparing the documents. Owing to this legal accountability, those involved exercise caution and diligence in the preparation of the prospectus and the registration statement.

Security Exchange Act of 1934

Although the Security Act of 1933 applies only to new issues, the Security Exchange Act of 1934 (and subsequent amendments) extends the regulation to existing securities. This act forbids market manipulation, deception and misrepresentation of facts, and fraudulent practices. The SEC was also created by this act to enforce the laws pertaining to the securities industry.

Under the Security Exchange Act of 1934, publicly held companies are required to keep current the information on file with the SEC. This is achieved by having the firm file an annual report (called the 10-K report) with the SEC. The 10-K report contains a substantial amount of factual information concerning the firm, and this information is usually sent in summary form to the stockholders in the company's annual report. (Companies must upon request and without charge send a copy of the 10-K report to stockholders.)

Flow of information to the public

Firms are also required to release any information during the year that may materially affect the value of their securities. Information concerning new discoveries, lawsuits, or merger discussions must be disseminated to the general public. The SEC has the power to suspend trading in a company's securities for up to ten days if, in its opinion, the public interest and the protection of investors necessitate such a ban on trading. If a firm fails to keep investors informed, the SEC can suspend trading pending the release of the required information. Such a suspension is a drastic act and is seldom used, for most companies frequently issue news releases that inform the investing public of significant changes affecting the firm. Sometimes the company itself asks to have trading in its securities halted until a news release can be prepared and disseminated.

Inside information

The disclosure laws do not require that the company tell everything about its operations. All firms have trade secrets that they do not want known by their competitors. The purpose of the full disclosure laws is not to restrict the corporation but (1) to inform the investors so that they can make intelligent decisions and (2) to prevent a firm's employees from using privileged information for personal gain.

It should be obvious that employees ranging from president of the company to those of lesser positions may have access to information before it reaches the general public. Such information (called inside information) may significantly enhance the employees' ability to make profits by buying or selling the company's securities before the announcement is made. Such profiteering from inside information is illegal. Offi-

POINTS OF INTEREST
Illegal Use of Inside Information

The use of inside (privileged) information for personal gain is illegal. Management cannot buy a stock, make an announcement that causes the value of the stock to rise, and then sell the stock for a profit. If insiders do this, the corporation or its stockholders may sue, and if the defendants are found guilty, any profits must be returned to the corporation.

The law does not forbid insiders from buying and subsequently selling the stock. However, the Securities Exchange Act of 1934 requires that each officer, director, and major stockholder (i.e., any individual who owns more than 10 percent of the stock) of a publicly held corporation must file a report with the SEC disclosing the amount of stock held. These individuals must also file a monthly report if there are any changes in the holdings. This information is subsequently published by the SEC. If these insiders make a profit on a transaction that is completed (i.e., the stock is bought and sold) within six months, it is assumed the profit is the result of illegally using confidential corporate information.

Individuals who may be considered insiders are not limited to the corporation's officers and directors. An insider is any individual with "material information" not yet disclosed to the public. Material information implies information that could reasonably be expected to affect the value of the firm's securities. The individual need not necessarily be employed by the firm but could have access to inside information through business relationships, family ties, or being informed (tipped off) by insiders. Use of such privileged information even by nonemployees is also illegal. In one of the most famous cases concerning the illegal use of inside information, several officers and directors of Texas Gulf Sulfur became aware of new mineral discoveries. Not only were their purchases ruled illegal, but purchases made by individuals they had informed were also ruled illegal. Thus, an insider who may not directly profit through the use of inside information cannot pass that information to another party who profits from using that knowledge.

cers and directors of the company must report their holdings and any changes in their holdings of the firm's securities to the SEC. Thus, it is possible for the SEC to determine if transactions have been made prior to any public announcement that affected the value of the securities. If insiders do profit illegally from the use of such information, they may be prosecuted under criminal law and their gains may have to be surrendered to the firm.

Other Regulations

Although the Security Act of 1933 and the Security Exchange Act of 1934 are the backbone of such regulations, subsequent laws have been passed. These include the Public Holding Company Act of 1935, which reorganized the utility industry by requiring better methods of financial accounting and more thorough reporting and by constraining the use of debt financing. The Investment Company Act of 1940 extended the regulations to include mutual funds and other investment companies. The most recent act of importance is the Securities Investors Protection Act of 1970, which

is designed to protect investors from brokerage firm bankruptcies and is explained below.

Registration of advisors

In addition to the laws affecting the issuing of securities and their subsequent trading, there are also laws requiring disclosure by investment advisors. Investment advisory services and individuals who "engage for compensation in the business of advising others about securities shall register" with the SEC.[13] Investment advisors must disclose their backgrounds, business affiliations, and the compensation charged for their services. Failure to register with the SEC can lead to an injunction against supplying the service or to prosecution for violating the security laws.

Besides the state and federal securities laws, the industry itself regulates its members. The stock exchanges and the trade association, the National Association of Security Dealers, have established codes of behavior for their members. These include the relationships between brokers and customers, the auditing of members' accounts, and proficiency tests for brokers. While such rules may not have the force of law, they can have a significant impact on the quality and credibility of the industry and its representatives.

SIPC

FDIC insures commercial bank depositors

Most investors are aware that accounts in virtually all commercial banks are insured by the Federal Deposit Insurance Corporation (FDIC). Should an insured commercial bank fail, the FDIC reimburses the depositor for any losses up to $100,000.[14] If a depositor has more than $100,000 on account at the time of the commercial bank's failure, the depositor becomes a general creditor for the additional funds.

This insurance has greatly increased the stability of the commercial banking system. Small depositors know that their funds are safe and therefore do not panic if a commercial bank fails (as one occasionally does). This stability simply did not exist prior to the formation of the FDIC. When panicky depositors tried to make withdrawals, some commercial banks could not meet the sudden requests for cash. Many had to close, which only increased the panic that caused the initial withdrawals. Since the advent of the FDIC, however, such panic withdrawals should not occur because the FDIC reimburses depositors (up to the limit) for any losses they sustain.

SIPC insures accounts with brokers

Like commercial banks, brokerage firms are also insured by an agency that was created by the federal government—the **Securities Investor Protection Corporation (SIPC)**. The SIPC is managed by a seven-member board of directors. Five members are appointed by the president of the United States, and their appointments must be confirmed by the Senate. Two of the five represent the general public, and three represent the securities industry. The remaining two members are selected by the secretary of the treasury and the Federal Reserve board of governors.

The SIPC performs a role similar to that of the FDIC. Its objective is to preserve public confidence in the securities markets and industry. Although the SIPC does not

---

[13] Securities and Exchange Commission, *The Work of the Securities and Exchange Commission* (Washington, D.C.: Government Printing Office, 1978), 17.

[14] As of January 1987.

protect investors from losses resulting from fluctuations in security prices, it does insure investors against losses arising from the failure of a brokerage firm. The insurance provided by the SIPC protects a customer's cash and securities up to $500,000.[15] If a brokerage firm fails, the SIPC reimburses the firm's customers up to this specified limit. If a customer's claims exceed the $500,000 limit, that customer becomes a general creditor for the remainder of the funds.

The cost of this insurance is paid for by the brokerage firms that are members of the SIPC. All brokers and dealers that are registered with the Securities and Exchange Commission (SEC) and all members of national security exchanges must be members of the SIPC. Most security dealers are thus covered by the SIPC insurance. Some firms have even chosen to supplement this coverage by purchasing additional insurance from private insurance firms.

SUMMARY

This chapter has covered security markets and the mechanics of buying securities. Securities are traded on organized exchanges, such as the NYSE, or in the informal over-the-counter markets. Securities are primarily bought through brokers, who buy and sell for their customers' accounts. The brokers obtain the securities from dealers, who make markets in them. These dealers offer to buy and sell at specified prices (quotes), which are called the bid and the ask. Brokers and investors obtain these prices through a sophisticated electronic system that transmits the quotes from the various dealers.

After securities are purchased, the investor must pay for them with either cash or a combination of cash and borrowed funds. When the investor uses borrowed funds, that individual is buying on margin. Buying on margin increases both the potential return and the potential risk of loss for the investor.

Investors may take delivery of their securities or leave them with the broker. Leaving securities registered in the street name offers the advantage of convenience because the broker becomes the custodian of the certificates. Since the advent of the SIPC and its insurance protection, there is little risk of loss to the investor from leaving securities with the broker.

The federal laws governing the securities industry are enforced by the Securities and Exchange Commission (SEC). The purpose of these laws is to ensure that individual investors have access to information upon which to base investment decisions. Publicly owned firms must supply investors with financial statements and make timely disclosure of information that may affect the value of the firms' securities.

Investors' accounts with brokerage firms are insured by the Securities Investor Protection Corporation (SIPC). This insurance covers up to $500,000 worth of securities held by the broker for the investor. The intent of SIPC is to increase public confidence in the securities industry by reducing the risk of loss to investors from failure by brokerage firms.

---

[15] Only $100,000 of the $500,000 insurance applies to cash balances on an account.

Terms to Remember

Organized exchange

Over-the-counter (OTC) market

Specialist

Dealer

Round lot

Odd lot

Bid and ask

Spread

Thin issue

Equilibrium price

Listed security

New York Stock Exchange (NYSE or "big board")

American Stock Exchange (AMEX)

P/E ratio

NASDAQ

Third market

Brokers

Registered representative

Long position

Bullish

Bearish

Market order

Day order

Good-till-canceled order

Limit order

Stop loss order

Confirmation statement

Settlement date

Margin

Street name

Trader

Commissions

Discount broker

Full disclosure laws

Securities Investor Protection Corporation (SIPC)

Questions

1. What is the role of market makers, and how do they earn profits?

2. What is the difference between listed securities and securities traded in over-the-counter markets?

3. How is the market price of a security determined?

4. What is the difference between a market order, a good-till-canceled order, and a stop loss order?

5. In addition to commission fees, are there any costs of investing?

6. What are the advantages of leaving securities registered in the street name?

7. Why is it riskier to buy stocks on margin?

8. How is the SIPC similar to the FDIC?

9. Why are laws governing the securities industry frequently called "full disclosure laws"?

10. What are the roles of the SIPC and the SEC?

Problems

1. A stock sells for $10 per share. You purchase one hundred shares ($1,000), and after a year the price rises to $17½ per share. What will be the percentage return on your investment if you bought the stock on margin and the margin requirement was (a) 25 percent, (b) 50 percent, or (c) 75 percent? (Ignore commissions, dividends, and interest expense.)

2. Repeat Problem 1 to determine the percentage return on your investment but in this case suppose the price of the stock falls from $10 to $7½ per share. What generalization can be inferred from your answers to Problems 1 and 2?

3. Investor A makes a cash purchase of 100 shares of AB&C common stock for $55 a share. Investor B also buys 100 shares of AB&C but uses margin. Each holds the stock for one year, during which dividends of $5.00 a share are distributed. Commissions are 2 percent of the value of a purchase or sale; the margin requirement is 60 percent, and the interest rate is 10 percent annually on borrowed funds. What is the percentage earned by each investor if he or she sells the stock after one year for (a) $40, (b) $55, (c) $60, or (d) $70? If the margin requirement had been 40 percent, what would have been the annual percentage returns? What conclusion do these percentage returns imply?

Suggested Readings

For histories of the New York and American Stock Exchanges, see:

Sobel, Robert. *The Big Board: A History of the New York Stock Market.* New York: The Free Press, 1965.

Sobel, Robert. *The Curbstone Brokers: The Origins of the American Stock Exchange.* New York: Macmillan, 1970.

The impact of financial institutions and the concentration of financial resources has led to a considerable literature on competition in the financial community. For a sample of this literature, consult:

Bostian, David B., Jr. "The De-Institutionalization of the Stock Market in American Society." *Financial Analysts Journal* (November–December 1973): 30–37.

Murray, Roger F. "Institutionalization of the Stock Market to be Feared or Favored?" *Financial Analysts Journal* (March–April 1974): 18–22.

Peake, J. W. "The National Market System." *Financial Analysts Journal* (July–August 1978): 25–34.

For a discussion of the nature, origin, and workings of the SEC, see:

Skousen, K. Fred. *An Introduction to the SEC.* 3rd ed. Cincinnati: South-Western Publishing, 1983.

For a reference book on the NASDAQ market system that provides information on trading procedures, acquire:

National Association of Securities Dealers. *The NASDAQ Handbook.* Chicago: Probus Publishing, 1986.

4 Sources of Information

LEARNING OBJECTIVES

After completing this chapter you should be able to

1. Name four categories of financial information that are generally available to investors.

2. List several publications concerning investments that are available in many libraries.

3. Distinguish between the contents of an annual report, a brokerage firm's research report, and an investment advisory report.

4. Define inside information.

5. Identify several government publications concerning economic conditions.

Investing requires knowledge. Savers who want to buy securities have a vast supply of information available to them. Their problems lie not in obtaining information but in determining which information is useful and then interpreting it. This chapter will describe and illustrate the variety of sources that are available to investors who are interested in purchasing stocks and bonds. Other types of investments, such as art, require specialized knowledge and specialized sources of information, which are not discussed in this chapter.

The major sources of information available to potential investors include corporate publications, brokerage firms' research reports, and investment advisory services. Some of this information, such as a firm's annual report, may be obtained at very little cost. Other information, such as the Value Line Investment Survey, can be purchased only at considerable expense. The costly sources of information, however, may be available in the public library or in a local college library.

CORPORATE SOURCES OF INFORMATION

Publicly held firms must inform stockholders

Publicly held firms are required by both federal and state laws, including the full disclosure laws, to publish annual and quarterly reports, which are sent to stockholders. Furthermore, the SEC requires publicly held firms to publish news bulletins giving any pertinent changes in the firm's financial position and any other information that may alter the value of its securities.

Although this information is sent free of charge to all stockholders in whose name the securities are registered, other investors and potential investors may request that the firm place their names on its mailing list. Firms are not required to do this, but many will honor such requests.

The Annual Report

Perhaps the most important publication of the firm is its **annual report.** This covers a wide variety of topics, as may be seen in the table of contents of a CBS annual report (Exhibit 4.1).

Annual reports play a public relations role

Although the annual report includes a substantial amount of factual and financial information, it should be viewed as a public relations document. It is frequently printed on expensive paper and filled with colorful pictures of products and of smiling employees. One notable exception was the Coca-Cola Company, whose annual reports during the late 1970s were brief and designed to convey the impression of financial conservatism. In some years its annual report has even been printed on recycled paper to demonstrate the company's concern for the environment. However, in the 1980s, the company has published the colorful, public-relations type of annual report favored by most firms.

Firms use the annual report to explain, at least superficially, their achievements of the past year. These discussions are in general terms, but the firm's careful selection of

Exhibit 4.1
Table of Contents from an Annual Report of CBS

Annual Report to the Shareholders of CBS Inc.

Letter to Shareholders/3
Organization Chart/7
Operating Group Discussions/9
CBS/Broadcast Group/9
CBS/Records Group/17
CBS/Columbia Group/23
CBS/Publishing Group/29
CBS Technology Center/35
Financial Section/36
Report of Independent Certified Public Accountants/36
Consolidated Financial Statements/37
Notes to Financial Statements/42
Segments of Business and Supplementary Information/46
Five-Year Summary of Operations/50
Directors and Officers/52

Source: Reprinted with permission of CBS, Inc.

POINTS OF INTEREST
Reading an Annual Report

While there is no correct way to read an annual report, the fact that the report includes both factual financial information and public relations material suggests that the prudent investor should read the annual report with caution. The tone of most annual reports, especially the message from management or the descriptions of the firm's products, markets, and potential for success and growth, is upbeat and positive. Even a year in which the firm experienced serious problems such as declining sales and earnings, labor unrest, or internal strife may be described with optimistic rhetoric.

With this in mind, the investor approaching an annual report should probably stress reading the numbers and how they were computed (i.e., the financial statements and the footnotes). Immediately after the financial statements, the firm must state the general accounting principles used in the construction of the financial statements. These principles, along with the subsequent footnotes, may offer a better clue to the firm's true financial condition than the blurbs describing sales, earnings, and dividends. Legal problems, nonrecurring sources of income, unfunded pension liabilities, lease obligations not on the balance sheet, current and deferred tax obligations, and the calculation of fully diluted earnings will be discussed (if applicable) in the various footnotes. Since any of these factors could affect the future value of the firm's securities, the prudent investor should take the time and effort to be aware of them.

words may allow the investor to read between the lines. Generally, the more substantive material is presented in the financial statements, particularly in the explanatory footnotes.

The typical annual report begins with a letter from the president of the company to the stockholders. The chairman of the board of directors also frequently signs this letter. The letter reviews the highlights of the year and points out certain noteworthy events, such as a dividend increase or a merger. It may also forecast events in the immediate future, such as next year's sales growth and earnings.

After the letter to the stockholders, the annual report may describe the various components of the business. For example, it may illustrate with words and pictures the various products that the firm makes, the type of research and development in which the company is engaged, the particular application of the firm's goods and services in different industries, and the outlook for the firm's products in the various industries in which it operates.

Annual report includes financial statements

After the descriptive material, there follows a set of financial statements. These statements include the balance sheet as of the end of the firm's fiscal year, its income statement for the fiscal year, and the statement of changes in financial position. (These statements are discussed and illustrated in Chapter 7.) A summary of financial information for the past several years may also be given. This summary permits the investor to view the firm's growth in sales, earnings, and dividends as well as the book value of the stock. Some of this information is frequently illustrated by graphs. Since the financial data have been audited, the investors may assume that the information is accurate and that the appropriate accounting principles have been applied consistently. Without this audit, year-by-year comparisons may be meaningless.

POINTS OF INTEREST
The President's Letter

Every annual report includes a letter from the president or chairman of the board. Generally these are carefully worded documents that summarize the firm's achievements during the fiscal year. In addition, a discussion of the firm's prospects for the future may also be included. Does this forecast have useful information for investors? Does it "signal" how the firm's stock will perform in the near future?

These questions were addressed in a recent study that analyzed letters by corporate presidents or chairmen of the board of firms whose stocks subsequently performed very well or very poorly.* The letters of firms whose stocks subsequently did well tended to forecast gains and indicated confidence in the firm's potential. The letters of firms whose stock did poorly discussed the potential for losses and generally made references to forthcoming problems. Few of these letters forecasted gains in earnings or dividends.

The results of this research clearly suggest that the president's letter to stockholders offers more than public relations material. Instead, the investor may associate discussions of imminent losses, lack of confidence, or poor growth potential with poor future performance by the stock.

*See Dennis McConnell, John Haslem, and Virginia Gibson, "The President's Letter to Stockholders," *Financial Analysts Journal* (September–October 1986): 66–70.

Quarterly Reports and News Bulletins

During the year, the firm publishes **quarterly reports** that summarize its performance during the preceding three months. They usually include a brief account of pertinent events as well as various financial statements. Although these statements are rarely as complete as the financial statements in the annual report, they do permit the investor to see the changes in the firm's earnings and sales for the quarter and often for the last 12 months. Such quarterly statements are usually not audited and may subsequently be restated.

Additional information made public

In addition to the annual report and quarterly reports, a firm typically issues news bulletins to the financial press concerning any major event that may alter the value of its shares. These reports include announcements of new products, merger activity, dividend payments, and new financing that the firm is in the process of obtaining. This information is readily accessible because the financial press efficiently disseminates it to the general public. In many cases the firm also sends copies of the news bulletins to its stockholders.

Firms must file several documents with the Securities and Exchange Commission (SEC). These reports are available to investors. The first document is the **10–K report,** which gives a much more detailed statement of the firm's fundamental financial position than is provided to stockholders in the annual report. The 10–K report also gives sales information by product line and a more detailed breakdown of expenses. Although the 10–K report is not automatically sent to stockholders, a company must supply stockholders with this document upon written request.

The 10–K report

The second document is the **10–Q report,** which the firm issues quarterly. This document must be sent to the SEC and is also available to stockholders. Like the

The 10–Q report

The 8–K report

10–K, it is a detailed report of the firm's financial state. The quarterly report that the company sends to its stockholders is basically a summary of the 10–Q report.

A third document is the **8–K report,** which a firm must file with the SEC within 15 days after an event occurs that may materially affect the value of its securities. This document often details material previously announced through a press release.[1]

Prospectus

The firm also must file a prospectus when it sells securities to the general public. While the firm prepares a 10–K report annually, a prospectus is required only when the securities are initially sold to the general public. In some cases a preliminary prospectus (called a "red herring") also may be prepared. The final prospectus is published when the securities are sold, and the buyers receive a copy of the final prospectus along with their confirmation statements. (See Exhibit 2.1 for the cover page of a prospectus for an issue of James River Corporation common stock that was sold to the general public.)

Inside Information

In addition to the sources that have been previously discussed, there is the possibility of an investor's obtaining **inside information.** Inside information is not available to the general public, and it may be of great value in guiding investments in a particular firm. For example, news of a dividend cut or increment may affect a stock's price. Such knowledge before it is made public should increase the individual's ability to make profitable investment decisions. However, the use of such information for personal gain by employees of the firm, by brokers or investment managers, or by anyone else is illegal.

This does not mean that employees cannot own securities issued by their firm; however, the SEC requires holdings by management to be made public and changes in these holdings to be disclosed. These changes are periodically reported in the financial press, and one publication, *The Insiders' Chronicle,* is devoted solely to reporting transactions by insiders.

Insider activity as an indicator

The reasons for insiders buying or selling their shares are varied. For example, an individual may be using the proceeds of a sale to retire personal debt, or an executive may be exercising an option to buy the stock. Such transactions are legal and are done for reasonable, legitimate financial purposes. However, some financial analysts and investors believe that inside transactions offer a clue to management's perception of the future price performance of the stock.[2] If many insiders sell their shares, this may be interpreted as a bearish sign, indicating that the market price of the stock will decline in the future. Conversely, a large number of purchases by insiders implies that management expects the price of the stock to rise. Such purchases by insiders are interpreted as being bullish. The reason for these interpretations is obvious: If managers believe that the firm's earnings are growing, they will buy the stock. Insiders' purchases and sales may mirror management's view of the company's potential. This information may then be used by outside investors as a key to the direction of future stock prices.[3]

---

[1] For a complete list of forms and reports required by the SEC, see K. Fred Skousen, *An Introduction to the SEC,* 2d ed. (Cincinnati: South-Western Publishing, 1980), 58–60.

[2] See, for instance, Martin E. Zweig, "Canny Insiders," *Barron's* (June 21, 1976): 5.

[3] For a discussion of the use of inside information in selecting securities, see Chapter 18.

		Exhibit 4.2
How to Read a Financial Report	Merrill Lynch	**Selected Bibliography of**
How Over-the-Counter Securities Are Traded	Merrill Lynch	**Publications Available**
Investing for Tax-Free Income	Merrill Lynch	**from Brokerage Firms**
How to Buy and Sell Commodities	Merrill Lynch	**and Commercial Banks**
What Is Margin?	Merrill Lynch	
Guide to Writing Options	Merrill Lynch	
A Profile of Investment Banking	Securities Industry Association	
The U.S. Government Securities Market	Harris Bank	
Handbook of Securities of the United States Government and Federal Agencies	First Boston Corporation	
Money Market Investments and Investment Vocabulary	Bank of America	

BROKERAGE FIRMS' RESEARCH REPORTS

One service that some brokers offer to their customers is research on specific securities. Many brokerage firms have research staffs who analyze firms and their securities; the purpose of such research is to identify undervalued securities that have the potential for price appreciation. In some cases these findings are published by the brokerage firm and are readily available to its customers.[4] The cost of such research is included in the commission fee.

Brokerage firms' recommendations take the form of "buy," "sell," or "hold."[5] The word **buy** means that the investor should purchase the security or add to existing holdings. **Sell** indicates the opposite, and existing shares should be sold. **Hold** signifies that the investor should not purchase the security but should not sell shares that are already owned. A hold recommendation should not be considered to be neutral, because the investor still holds securities even though no additional shares are purchased.

In most cases, brokerage firms' research reports tend to recommend purchasing the security. Rarely do such reports recommend the outright sale of shares. For this reason, the individual investor should probably use such reports in conjunction with other information. It should be remembered that brokerage firms and their salespeople profit from commissions; hence, there is a natural bias to encourage purchasing securities as opposed to placing money in a savings account or money market mutual fund.

Some brokerage firms and commercial banks publish material that is purely informational and is available to the public without charge. The brokerage firm of Merrill Lynch Pierce Fenner and Smith Inc. is by far the largest supplier of this complimentary literature. These publications not only describe various securities and how they are acquired but also explain how they may be used as part of one's investment strategy. The investor may find some of this information extremely useful, especially in estate and portfolio planning. A selected bibliography of this material, along with a list of the firms that publish it, is given in Exhibit 4.2.

Brokerage firms' recommendations

Publications of brokerage firms

---

[4]One particularly useful source of information is the *Wall Street Transcript*, which compiles and publishes brokerage firm reports. This is a very detailed publication and it is relatively costly: $25 an issue or $990 annually. It may be obtained by writing the Wall Street Transcript, 120 Wall Street, New York, NY 10005.

[5]Some brokerage firms refine their buy and sell recommendations. For example, Merrill Lynch has five classes: buy, ok to buy, neutral, ok to sell, and sell.

Exhibit 4.3
Dividends Reported and
Earnings Announcement

* * *

Dividends Reported July 9

Company	Period	Amt.	Payable date	Record date
REGULAR				
ANR Pipeline $2.12pf	Q	.53	9– 1–86	8–21
ANR Pipeline $2.675pf	Q	.66⅞	9– 1–86	8–21
Bank of New York Co	Q	.57	8– 1–86	7–18
CBS Inc	Q	.75	9–12–86	8–27
CBS Inc $1pref	Q	.25	9–30–86	8–27
CSX Corp pfA	Q	1.75	10–31–86	9–30
CSX Corp	Q	.29	9–15–86	8–22
Coastal Corp pfG	Q	.528⅛	8–15–86	7–31
Dayton Hudson Corp	Q	.21	9–10–86	8–20
Fleet Financl Group	Q	.36	10– 1–86	9–15
Fleet Financial adj pf	Q	.75	9– 1–86	8–15
Flexsteel Industries	Q	.12	9– 8–86	8–27
Hanover Insurance Co	Q	.14	8–15–86	7–25
Media General Inc	Q	.29	9–12–86	8–15
Michaels (J) Inc	Q	.09	9– 2–86	8– 4
National Data Corp	Q	.11	8–29–86	8– 7
Noranda Inc	Q	b.12½	9–15–86	8–15
Ohio Mattress Co	Q	.10	7–31–86	7–21
Tokheim Corp	Q	.12	8–29–86	8– 8
Walgreen Co	Q	.12½	9–12–86	8–21
Woolworth (FW) Co pfA	Q	.55	9– 1–86	8– 1

CBS INC. (N)

Quar June 30:	1986	1985
Revenues	$1,217,200,000	$1,189,600,000
Inco cnt op	106,900,000	91,600,000
Inco dis op	a12,000,000	d22,300,000
Income	118,900,000	69,300,000
Extrd chg	e11,700,000	....
Net income	107,200,000	69,300,000
Shr earns:		
Inco cnt op	4.41	3.08
Income	4.92	2.33
Net income	4.42	2.33
6 months:		
Revenues	2,418,100,000	2,290,600,000
Inco cnt op	123,200,000	118,100,000
Inco dis op	a12,000,000	d32,000,000
Income	135,200,000	86,100,000
Extrd chg	e11,700,000	....
Net income	123,500,000	86,100,000
Shr earns:		
Inco cnt op	4.97	3.97
Income	5.48	2.89
Net income	4.98	2.89

a-From gain on disposal of discontinued operations. d-Loss. e-Loss on repurchase of debt.

Source: The Wall Street Journal, July 10, 1986. Reprinted by permission of *The Wall Street Journal,* © Dow Jones & Company, Inc. 1986. All Rights Reserved.

PURCHASED SOURCES OF INFORMATION

The investor may buy a variety of publications and services rendering information that is potentially useful in making investment decisions. This section will describe several of these sources of information.

Newspapers and Magazines

The Wall Street Journal

The foremost financial newspaper is *The Wall Street Journal.* This daily newspaper publishes not only daily stock prices and quotes but also bond prices and transactions, option transactions and prices, quotes on treasury securities, and prices of commodities and foreign currencies. In addition to financial news, *The Wall Street Journal* includes news bulletins that are issued by firms and editorial comments on national economic policy. Editorials tend to stress those policies that affect the investment community (e.g., the fiscal policy of the federal government, the monetary policy of the Federal Reserve Board, and proposed changes in federal tax laws).

The Wall Street Journal also publishes earnings reports and announcements of dividends that have been declared. These reports and dividends for CBS are illustrated in Exhibit 4.3. The right-hand side of the exhibit presents the earnings for CBS for the period ending June 30, 1986. These earnings are presented for both the last quarter and six months. The left-hand side of Exhibit 4.3 illustrates the announcement of a cash dividend. The entry indicates the per-share amount of the dividend ($0.75) (if it is a quarterly dividend, this will be indicated by Q), the date of record (8-27), and the payment date (9-12). The date of record is the day on which the firm closes its books.

General Financial News:

Business Week
Forbes
Fortune
Financial World
Fact
Personal Investor
Sylvia Porter's Personal Finance

Academic and Professional:

Financial Management
Journal of Finance
Harvard Business Review
Journal of Portfolio Management
Financial Analysts Journal

Specialized:

Oil and Gas Journal
Realty Trust Review
Public Utilities Fortnightly

Exhibit 4.4
Selected Magazines of
Potential Value to the
Investment Community

All stockholders owning shares at that time receive the dividend. The date of payment is the day on which the investor is to receive the dividend.

In addition to *The Wall Street Journal*, there are several newspapers of interest to the investment community. These include *Barron's, Media General Financial Weekly, The Journal of Commerce, Over-the-Counter Weekly Review,* and *The Wall Street Transcript.* Particularly noteworthy is *Barron's,* which, along with *The Wall Street Journal,* is published by Dow Jones. *Barron's* is a weekly newspaper that reports weekly security transactions and that includes various feature articles of interest to the financial community as well as investment advisory reports. One particularly important piece of information is *Barron's* confidence index, which will be described in Chapter 18.

Other financial newspapers

A variety of magazines also report financial news. These range from *Money,* which is a popular press magazine related primarily to personal finance and financial planning, to more sophisticated publications. A selected list of these publications is given in Exhibit 4.4. The list is divided into three categories to designate the nature of the publications. General investors should be particularly interested in *Forbes, Business Week,* and *Fortune,* all of which publish analytical articles concerning the general financial community and specific companies.

Financial magazines

These publications also cover specific topics on investment decisions and security selection. For example, *Forbes* periodically devotes specific issues to the reporting of financial information that facilitates comparisons of firms. There is the *Annual Report on American Industry* that ranks more than 1,000 firms with regard to sales and growth in earnings, stock price performance, and return on equity. The issue also classifies the firms by industry and reports such additional information as use of debt and profit margins for the individual firms and medians for the industry.

In addition to the *Annual Report on Industry, Forbes* also periodically presents other specialized information, such as an enumeration of the largest non-American

POINTS OF INTEREST
Standard and Poor's *Corporation Records* and Moody's *Manuals*

Two of the most important sources of factual information concerning firms and their securities are the *Corporation Records* published by Standard and Poor's and the various *Manuals* published by Moody's. S&P's *Corporation Records* contains descriptions of companies listed on the major exchanges and many over-the-counter stocks. (Firms that are included must pay a fee for the service, which for Standard & Poor's *Corporation Records* as of 1986 was $1,300 for the initial listing and $580 for subsequent years.) These corporate records are updated quarterly and include the most recent fiscal year's financial statements. For larger firms, S&P's *Corporation Records* includes descriptions of the firm's various securities, its earnings, dividends, and the annual range of security prices for the previous decade.

Moody's manuals compile information similar to S&P's *Corporation Records,* but Moody's publishes this material in specialized volumes. The titles include:

- *Moody's Industrial Manual*
- *Moody's Bank and Finance Manual*
- *Moody's Public Utility Manual*

- *Moody's Municipal & Government Manual*
- *Moody's Transportation Manual*
- *Moody's International Manual*
- *Moody's OTC Industrial Manual*

In addition to these annually published manuals, Moody's also publishes *News Reports,* which continually updates the material in the manuals.

Like S&P's *Corporation Records,* Moody's manuals require that the firm or government pay an annual fee for inclusion. Material in these manuals includes descriptions of the firm, its securities, and recent financial statements. The manuals are an excellent reference for descriptions of the important features of a firm's securities, especially its bonds.

S&P's *Corporation Records* and Moody's *Manuals* include essentially the same information. However, occasionally a firm is listed in one and not the other. This is particularly true for small firms whose securities are traded over the counter. Corporations whose securities are traded on the major exchanges generally choose to be included in both S&P's and Moody's.

firms and the annual performance of mutual funds. (*Barron's* also publishes quarterly the performance rating of over 800 mutual funds.) Perhaps one of the most awaited issues of *Forbes* is devoted to enumerating the 400 richest Americans. While that issue may not help the individual invest, it can illustrate the potential return for the successful management of investments and careers.

Academic and professional publications   The academically and professionally oriented journals are more specialized, and their contents tend to be more difficult for the inexperienced or untrained investor to understand. *Financial Management* and the *Journal of Finance* are primarily designed for individuals doing research in financial topics, such as capital budgeting, cost of funds, or valuation theory. The *Harvard Business Review* is not limited to topics in finance but covers the gamut of business operations. The *Journal of Portfolio Management* and the *Financial Analysts Journal* are a cross between academic and professional publications, as they include articles by both practitioners and academicians. The *Financial Analysts Journal,* which is a professional magazine published six times a year by the Financial Analysis Federation, is almost exclusively devoted to professional financial analysis.

The recent interest in financial planning has spawned publications devoted to the professional financial planner such as *Financial Planning,* published by the International Association of Financial Planners. Publications stressing financial planning have a more aggregate or macro emphasis that encompasses such topics as portfolio management, tax shelters, and retirement and estate planning. The publications also tend to be more descriptive and less theoretical than the other academic and professional journals.

The individual who is interested in a particular area of investment may also read specialized trade journals. For example, those who are considering investments in the oil and gas industry may find the *Oil and Gas Journal* a good source of information concerning discoveries of new oil fields and the amounts of reserves that have been determined to exist in these fields. Such trade publications will help the investor keep abreast of events in a particular industry.[6]

Specialized trade journals

Investment Advisory Services

For the investor who wants additional information or advice, a variety of sources may be purchased, some of which are illustrated in this chapter. These sources include the corporate records that are published by Standard & Poor and by Moody. In addition, Standard & Poor publishes each month a *Stock Guide* and a *Bond Guide.* Exhibit 4.5 reproduces a page from the *Stock Guide.* As may be seen in the exhibit, which highlights the stock of CBS, a considerable amount of information is given, including not only the price but also financial data such as dividends, earnings per share, and certain balance sheet items (current assets, current liabilities, long-term debt, and number of shares outstanding). Since this publication packs so much information into such a small space and is updated monthly, it is a widely used reference.

Standard & Poor's Stock Guide

In addition to the *Stock Guide, Bond Guide,* and *Corporation Records,* Standard & Poor publishes *The Outlook,* an investment advisory service that lists stocks appropriate for investors seeking income or growth. It also lists moderately speculative securities that may offer more potential for higher returns. Each issue describes several securities that the publisher believes are attractive investments. These lists and suggestions are continuously updated so that the subscriber may alter his or her portfolio as conditions and suggestions change. It should be noted that material is generally descriptive and does not report how the conclusions were determined.

The Outlook

One important investor advisory service is the *Value Line Investment Survey.* Each week this publication includes new information on selected industries and specific firms within these industries and updates previously published information. During a three-month period, *Value Line* evaluates most of the important firms that trade their securities on the major exchanges or in the over-the-counter markets. In addition to evaluating individual firms, this service analyzes the industry and makes a recommendation for the price performance of specific stocks relative to the price movements of the market for the immediate future. These recommendations consist of scores ranging from 5 (the lowest performance) to 1 (the highest performance). A score of 1 does not necessarily mean that the stock will earn a positive return;

Value Line Investment Survey

---

[6]A source of this material is the *Guide to Industry Publications for Security Analysts,* published by the New York Society for Securities Analysts.

Exhibit 4.5
Page from Standard & Poor's *Stock Guide*

46 Cat-Cen

Standard & Poor's Corporation

†S&P 500 ♦Options Index	Ticker Symbol	Name of Issue (Call Price of Pfd. Stocks) Market	Com. Rank. & Pfd. Rating	Par Val.	Inst.Hold Cos	Inst.Hold Shs. (000)	Principal Business	Price Range 1971-84 High	Low	1985 High	Low	1986 High	Low	Mar. Sales 100s	Last Sale Or Bid High	Low	Last	%Div. Yield	P-E Ratio
1	CEDC	Catalyst Energy Dev....OTC	NR	10¢	22	1930	Devel alternative energy sys	6⅛	6	15¼	9¾	15¼	15⅛	21743	15¼	11¼	15⅛		46
2	CAT	Caterpillar Tractor²¹....NY,B,C,M,P,Ph	B	No	421	57677	Earthmoving mchy: diesel eng	73¼	25⅜	43¼	29	55⅝	39¼	77936	55⅝	50	52⅝	1.0	26
3	CBTB	CBT Bancshares.........OTC	B	2½	10	332	Multi-bank hldg,Georgia	16½	3½	33	13¾	31	26	584	31	30	31	1.6	d
4	CBH	CBI Indus............NY,M	A	2½	91	9850	Steel plate structures,tanks	70⅜	5	34½	27⅛	27¾	19¼	7140	27¾	21¾	27¼	2.2	d
5	CBS	CBS Inc.............NY,B,C,M,P,Ph	A-	2½	254	14372	Broadcasting,records,publish	87¾	24¾	126½	70⅜	151⅞	110	31004	151½	131¾	147⅜	2.0	28
6	Pr	$1.00 cm Cv A Pref (43½)vtg....NY P	A	1			Home leisure time prod, toy	58½	17½	85¼	52½	95¾	85	8	95¾	94¾	100¾	1.0	
7	CCBF	CCB Financial..........OTC	A	5	4	1198	Bankhldg:No Carolina	24½	3½	34¼	24½	45	32¾	492	45	40¾	44¼	2.5	13
8	CCBL	C-COR Electrs.........OTC	B-	10¢	7	134	CATV equip-amplifiers	35¼	6	9½	4	5¾	4	694	5½	5¼	5⅝		d
9	CCX	CCX Inc.............NY,M,P	B	7	9	533	Wire & cable,alloy steels	11¼	2¾	8½	4	5¼	4¼	2037	5¼	4¼	4⅞		
10	Pr	5% cm Pfd (27).........NY	CCC	25			screening, rubber prdts	17¾	7½	12	9	12¾	10½	31	11¾	10½	10½	11.9	
11	CDI	CDI Corp............AS	B	10¢	8	697	Engr'g & technical services	11¾	1¢	25¼	9¾	32¾	24¾	722	32¾	30	33		15
12	CCP	Ceco Indus...........NY,M	B+	No	30	1703	Construction industry items	26	6⅛	29¼	20	34½	28½	2225	34½	29	33½	2.4	15
13	CCL	Celanese Canada.......To,Mo,Vc	B	No	10	921	Fibers,fabrics,chemicals	14½	2½	10⅞	6¼	16⅜	10½	2059	16⅜	14⅞	16⅛	2.9	13
14	CZ	Celanese Corp.........NY,B,C,M,P,Ph	B+	No	202	6531	Fibers, chemicals, plastics	82		151	46¼	57	45½	10362	203	55¾	54¾	2.4	14
15	CZ	4½% cm A Pfd(100)¹¹....NY	BBB	100	3	58	paints/industl coatings	65¼	30	46¼	37¾	57	45¼	137	55¾	54¾	54⅜	8.3	
16	CELP	Cellular Products.......OTC	NR	1	2	71	Protein substances:R&D,mfr	1⅞	1	4¼	1½	3½	2½	8752	3½	2½	3⅝		d
17	CNCR	CenCor Inc...........OTC	B+	1	7	167	Loans:day care:ed:temp help	19¾	½	17½	5¾	17¾	16	3648	17¾	16	16½	0.8	14
18	CRG	Cenergy Corp.........NY,Ph	A+	25¢	47	2852	Oil&gas prod:pipeline	15	7½	10¾	6¼	9¾	4¾	4705	9¾	4⅞	4⅞	4.6	11
19	CNT	Centel Corp..........NY,B,M	A+	50¢	236	12586	Telephone,elec,communic sys	40¾	13	47¼	36½	53½	45	5592	53½	49¾	52½		d
20	CEG	Centennial Group⁴⁴.....AS	NR		1	11	Real estate & development	9¾	3¾	9¾	4¾	10¼	7¾	566	10¼	9¼	9¾		d
21	CTBC	Centerre Bancorp......OTC	A-	10	58	2078	Multiple bank hldg:St Louis	29½	10½	35¼	26½	44½	34	6838	44	40¾	42¾	4.2	12
22	CTX	Centex Corp..........NY,M	B+	25¢	85	9582	R.E devel,constr,cement,o&g	33½	2¾	26½	20½	33½	24	14397	33½	29¼	31¾	0.8	12
23	CNTO	Centocor Inc..........OTC	NR		49	2615	Develops diagnostic test kits	25½	8	20¾	6¾	20	12½	2537	20	16½	17¾		
24	CBAN	Centrafarm Group NV...OTC	NR		24	2111	Markets pharmaceuticals			20½	9¾	51¾	38¾	1850	51¾	47	51¾	2.9	13
25	CBAN	Cent'l Bancorp'n Cin...OTC	A	5	35	1698	Multiple bank hldg:Cinn	24¾		40	24½	51¾	38¾						
26	CBSS	Cent'l Bancshrs South..OTC	A-	2	17	1358	Bank hldg: Alabama	15¾	3¹³⁄₁₆	24½	17¾	27¾	23¾	1966	24½	23¾	24¼	3.6	11
27	CSYS	Cent'l Banking Sys.....OTC	A	2½	6	89	Bank hldg: California	17½	1½	14½	12½	18½	14	1254	18½	16½	17¾	2.3	11
28	CBPI	Cent'l Fidelity Banks...OTC	A	5	20	2242	Bank holding, Virginia	19¾	3¾	31¾	19	32	24¾	2810	30¾	27¾	29¾	2.8	12
29	CNH	Central Hudson Gas&El..NY	A-	No	44	883	Utility:elec & gas, NY State	27½	11	31¼	23	35¼	28	9471	35¼	31¾	33¾	8.7	7
30	Pr	Dep1/4shr Adj Rt⁴⁴ A Pfd(**25.75)	A	100	5	333		27		20¼	27¾	23¾	27	24	493	26	25¼	25a	8.9	
31	CER	Central Ill E 4½% cm Pfd⁷¹...NY⁷¹	AA	100			Sub of CILCORP:elec/gas util	69	28½	46	40	50½	44¼	15	50½	47⅞	48⅛	9.3	
32	CIP	Central Ill Pub Sv.......NY,B,C,M,Ph	A	No	114	8421	Electric & natural gas utility	22⅝	8½	21½	17½	26½	23¾	20021	26½	22¼	23¾	6.9	13
33	CJER	Central Jersey Bancorp..OTC	A	2½		222	Gen'l comm'l bankg & a trust	21¾	6¾	35½	20	39¾	32¼	655	39¾	35¾	37⅜	3.8	12
34	CNL	Central La Elec........NY,B,M	A	4	68	3067	Electric sv in Louisiana	22¼	12¾	30½	21¼	38½	33¾	3137	38½	34	37⅜	7.7	11
35	Pr	$4.18 cm C Pfd⁷¹(**31.88)1/4 vtg	BBB+	25			Fueled:74% gas,20% coal	35	27½	37	32½	38¼	35¼	481	38¼	36¼	37¼	11.2	
36	CTP	Central Maine Power⁷¹...NY,B,M	NR	5	41	2041	Utility supplies electricity	21¼	7¾	14	9¾	17¾	15¼	13920	18	15½	17⅜	7.9	
37	CP	3.50% cm Pfd (101)....AS	B+	100			oil 50%,nuclear 31%,hyd 19%	53	20¾	31	23¾	34	29½	14	34	29½	34	10.3	
38	CPCO	Central Pacific........OTC	NR	No	3	223	Elec utility: Bakersfield,Cal	19½	4	8⅝	3¾	9¾	7¾	1075	9¾	8¼	8⅜		40
39	CRLC	Central Reserve Life....OTC	NR	1	3	83	Life,small group health ins	5¾	⅞	14¼	13¾	14¼	13¾	3396	13¾	14	13¾	1.5	11
40	CET	Central Securities......AS	NR	No	6	157	Closed-end investment co	16½	2½	14½	11¾	14¾	13¾	849	14	12¾	14	1.5	
41	Pr D	$2.00 cm Cv D Pref(27½)...AS	NR	No	20	723	Mfrs fire sprinkler sys	25¼	22½	27	23¼	29	25¾	16	29	26	27e	7.4	24
42	CNSP	Central Sprinkler.......OTC	NR	1¢			Integ elec utility hldg co	26½	10¾	28½	21¾	31½	26½	27526	31½	29¾	31¾	6.9	9
43	CSR	Central So. West......NY,B,C,M,P,Ph	A+	3½	349	42691	Electricity in Vt, N.H.	26½	10¾	28½	21¾	31½	26½	1811	25¾	23¼	25¼	7.6	7
44	CV	Central Vt Pub Serv....NY,M	A	6	19	796	Mfr computer printers	19¾	8½	22¼	16½	25¾	21¼	31645	63¼	1¾	5¾		
45	CEN	Centronics Data.......NY,B,M,Ph	C	1¢	25	1576	Hunt'g/fish'g eq:seafood prod	54¾	1½	9	2½	2½	1¾	9957	2½	1½	2a		d
46	CENT	Centuri Inc...........OTC	B		7	2902		13¾	¼	2	⅞	2½	1¾						

Uniform Footnote Explanations—See Page 1. Other: ¹AS:Cycle 2. ²CBOE:Cycle 2. ³CBOE:Cycle 3. ⁴NY. ⁵¹Vote Apr '9? on name chge to Caterpillar Inc. ¹¹⁵0.72,'81. ¹¹¹⁵0.82,'82. ²³⁵4.45,'85. ⁵³³3.31,'85. ⁵⁴³0.43,'91. ³²⁵0.82,'82. ⁵⁵³13.18,'85. ²⁴Co offer for all 4½% cm Pfd.⁵⁵5 to Mar 28. ⁴⁰40 Wk Mar'83. ⁴¹Stk distr of LaPatite Academy. ⁵⁴Co plan fiscal chge to Dec. ¹⁴Pfd in $M...

Common and Preferred Stocks

Cat-Cen 47

Splits ♦ Index	Cash Divs. Ea. Yr. Since	Dividends Latest Payment Per$	Date	Ex. Div.	Total $ So Far 1986	Ind. Rate	Paid 1985	Financial Position Mil-$ Cash& Equiv.	Curr. Assets	Curr. Liab.	Balance Sheet Date	Capitalization Lg Trm Debt Mil-$	Shs. 000 Pfd.	Com.	Earnings $ Per Shr. Years End	1981	1982	1983	1984	1985	Last 12 Mos.	Interim Earnings Period	$ Per Shr. 1984	1985	Index
1		None Since Public				Nil		4.66	20.3	26.6	12-31-85	16.1		*12248	Dc		Nil	0.06	0.33	0.33					1
2	1914	Q0.12½ 2-20-86	1-13		0.50	0.50	Nil	282	2982	1742	12-31-85	1177		96379	Dc	6.64	d2.04	6	5⁴.47	2.02	2.02			2
3	1930	Q0.12 4-1-86	3-11		0.24	0.48	0.403	57.2	367	265.	10-5-85	297		21641	Dc	0.71	0.66	0.80	1.10	1.35	1.35			3
4	1913	Q0.15 3-20-86	2-11		0.15	0.60	1.20	57.2	367		10-5-85			23449	Dc	4.73	5.06	2.36	2.18	d2.18				4
5	1931	Q0.75 3-12-86	2-20		0.75	3.00	3.00	120.	1836	1550	12-31-85	954.	1289	23449	Dc	6.56	4.83	6.31	6.96	5.26	5.26			5
6	1967	Q0.25 3-31-86	2-20		0.25	1.00	1.00	Conv into 0.6886 shrs common				26.4		4196	Dc	5.34	b4.73	6.86	b8.96	p2.98				6
7	1934	Q0.18 3-25-86	3-24		0.53	1.12	0.89	Book Value $17.85			12-31-85	0.65		3015	Dc	0.53	1.12	1.05	0.09	p⁹³3.42	3.42	6 Mo Dec	0.10	d1.44	7
8		None Since Public				Nil		5.54	17.7	2.74	12-31-85	0.28	119	3851	Je	0.53	d3.47	d1.49	¹0.18	0.01	d1.53	6 Mo Dec	⁵0.16	*d0.22	8
9		0.39 9-1-76	8-6			Nil		0.97	26.0	7.96	12-31-85		119	119	Je	0.70	b0.97	bd2.64	d0.89	¹0.39	0.01				9
10	1949	Q0.31¼ 3-1-86	2-10		0.31¼	1.25	1.25																		10
11		0.058 11-2-70	10-16			Nil		n/a	78.1	46.3	1-31-86	27.0		3980	Ap	0.58	d0.73	0.45	1.21	1.53	2.13	6 Mo Sep	d0.06	d0.07	11
12	1983	Q0.12 3-31-86	3-14		0.40	0.80	0.76	8.61	152.	82.5	6-30-85	15.5	495	13537	Dc	0.14	2.11	2.34	2.55	2.81	p2.61				12
13	1939	Q1.20 3-31-86	2-24		1.20	4.80	4.80	2.15	154.	65.0	6-30-85	58.8			Dc	9.01	d⁰0.05	0.79	0.87	1.70	13.70				13
14	1939	Q1.12½ 4-1-86	2-24		2.25	4.50	4.50	369.	1161	864.	12-31-85	434.	366	851	Dc	b2.93	b0.44	b2.91	b4.14						14
15	1951																								15
16		None Since Public				Nil		0.53	1.14	0.37	9-30-85	0.53		4952	Mr		d0.03	d0.09	d0.14	d0.15	d0.15	6 Mo Sep	d0.06	d0.07	16
17	1985	Q0.03 4-18-86	3-11		0.03	0.04	0.04	13.6	34.8	34.8	9-30-85	69.4	184	34172	Mr	1.30	0.48	0.92	0.65	P0.93	0.93	6 Mo Sep	0.16	0.16	17
18	1939	Q0.01 4-30-86	4-1		1.22	2.44	2.38	2.84	21.3	17.9	9-30-85	89.9	300	9739	Mr	1.33	4.84	4.12	4.50	P4.61	4.61	6 Mo Sep	Δ*d0.07	0.20	18
19		1.25 9-3-74	8-13			Nil		Equity per shr $8.12			9-30-85	2.80	185	27870	Dc		*ΔNil	b0.50	4.71	d⁴0.33					19
20											9-30-85	741.		1417	Dc										20
21	1919	Q0.30 4-30	4-30		1.80	1.80	1.80	Book Value $41.04			9-30-85	96.1		7704	Dc	4.61	b3.05	4.74	P3.53	3.53	3.53	9 Mo Dec	1.69	2.01	21
22	1973	Q0.06¼ 4-2-86	3-14		0.12½	0.25	0.25	Equity per shr $17.33			12-31-85	60.7		P17824	Mr	1.41	b1.84	2.55	2.99	E2.65	2.52				22
23		None Since Public				Nil		49.5	56.9	3.39	12-31-85	1.19		⁵³667	Dc	d0.48	d0.51	d0.12	d0.45	P0.46					23
24								6.41	15.5	4.17	12-31-85	27.1		8283	Dc	2.13	3.34	4.28	P4.04	4.06					24
25	1937	Q0.37½ 4-7-86	3-21		0.75	1.50	1.349																		25
26	1940	Q0.22 4-1-86	3-10		0.41	0.88	0.73½	Book Value $14.89			9-30-85	6.40		13704	Dc	⁶0.54	⁴⁴1.59	A1.81	⁴⁷1.85	P2.21	2.21				26
27	1940	Q0.10 4-15-86	3-25		0.18	0.40	0.31⅝	Book Value $15.07			12-31-85	29.2		3908	Dc	A1.85	B1.34	1.83	1.86	1.80	1.80				27
28	1969	Q0.21 4-15-86	3-20		0.42	0.84	0.73	Book Value $7.76			6-30-85	34.	368	14140	Dc	A1.86	2.41	P2.45	2.45	2.45					28
29	1980	Q0.90 4-1-86	3-14		1.48	2.90	2.90	16.0	156.	57.3	12-31-85	342.		12075	Dc	3.72	3.91	3.94	4.43	4.67	4.67	SF 32,000 fr Mar'93,$25			29
30	1983	0.56			1.171	4	2.272											3.72	3.91	3.94	4.43					30
31	1936	Q1.12½ 4-1-86	3-3		2.25	4.50	4.50	12.7	123.	51.5	9-30-85	309.	¹646	13564	Dc	b1.99	b2.27	b2.31		1.92	1.83	12 Mo Feb△	2.02	1.83	31
32	1947	Q0.41 3-10-86	2-11		0.82	1.64	1.63	120.	316.	126.	12-31-85	*523.	1115	34172	Dc	2.33	2.03	2.38	2.46	3.15	3.15				32
33	1925	Q0.35 4-1-86	3-14		0.70	1.40	1.17½	Book Value $19.85			9-30-85	²297	1278	11110	Dc	2.02	2.39	2.85	3.62	3.65	3.65				33
34	1982	Q0.52 4-1-86	3-1-86		1.04½	1.18	4.18	Red restr (15.20%)to			8-31-87		800		Dc	b1.77	b2.42	b2.62	3.62	3.65					34
35	1943	Q0.35 4-30-86	4-4		0.70	1.40	1.40	80.7	173.	127.	9-30-85	484.	1180	22494	Dc	1.81	2.04	2.51	1.99	P0.08	0.08				35
36	1946	Q0.87½ 4-1-86	3-24		1.75	3.50	3.50	Book Value $9.22			12-31-84	p7.60		*3697	Dc	1.68	1.81	1.80	2.11	P0.21	0.21				36
37		0.04 10-30-84	12-23			Nil		Book Value $3.82			9-30-85			3603	Dc	d0.17	d0.15	d0.44	0.89	PA1.17	1.17				37
38	1980	A0.20 4-29-86	4-9		0.20	0.20	0.12	Net Asset Val $15.25			12-31-86			3609	Dc	b1.50	b14.02	b17.25	b13.57	b15.38					38
39	1955	Q0.35 3-21-86	2-10		1.50	b0.20	¹1.57																		39
40	1984	Q0.50 5-1-86	4-7		1.00	2.00	2.00	Cv into 1.94 shrs com				223			Dc					1.11	1.18	3 Mo Jan△	0.23	0.30	40
41		None Since Public				Nil		11.1	27.0	7.48	10-31-85	19.3		1864	Dc	2.54	2.82	3.02	3.63	3.61	3.61				41
42	1947	Q0.53½ 2-28-86	1-31		0.53½	2.14	2.02	148.	649.	365.	10-31-85	131.	442	6420	Dc	2.81	2.82	2.94	3.19	P3.39	3.39				42
43	1944	Q0.47½ 3-15-86	1-27		0.47½	1.90	1.90	8.93	35.8	34.0	9-30-85	48.5		11975	Dc	2.54	2.89	3.26	3.40	P3.65	3.65	9 Mo Sep	*D0.06	*0.06	43
44								48.8	132.	61.0	9-30-85	7.25		16281	Dc	d0.46	¹²0.20								44
45		None Paid				Nil		1.39	61.3	52.2	9-30-85				Dc										45
46																									46

◆ Stock Splits & Divs By Line Reference Index ¹2-for-1,'84:3-for-2,'85. ¹²2-for-1,'84. ¹⁰3%,'81. ¹¹2-for-1,'84:3-for-2,'85...

Source: Reprinted with permission from the Standard & Poor's *Stock Guide*.

rather, it indicates that *Value Line* believes the stock should outperform the market, which in declining markets may mean that the investor will still suffer losses but that the losses will be smaller.

A page from the *Value Line Investment Survey* is given in Exhibit 4.6. As may be seen from this exhibit, *Value Line* reports a considerable amount of information. Most of these data are factual, but there are some projections. In this example *Value Line* suggests that the stock of CBS will perform in tandem with the market (i.e., the time-liness rating is 3) in the near term. However, the discussion suggests that the stock sells for less than its value and that the company may still be considered a takeover candidate.

Value Line asserts that the securities it recommends have outperformed the market.[7] It also maintains that the stocks ranked 1 and 2 by its analysis consistently achieve higher returns than those ranked 4 and 5. There is some outside empirical support for *Value Line*'s claims, for one study found that stocks ranked 1 by *Value Line* consistently outperformed (even after adjusting for risk) a strategy of randomly selected stocks.[8]

Performance of recommendations

For individual investors, *Value Line*'s performance is somewhat misleading because to achieve the same results, they would have to duplicate the recommendations. *Value Line* assigns a ranking of 1 to 100 stocks. Thus, if only $1,000 is invested in each, a total outlay of $100,000 would be required. Even if the investor could make the purchases as soon as the recommendations were made (which may be impossible), the large commission costs on so many small purchases would reduce the return. Generally investors must select among the recommendations, so the results could be very different from the return earned by all of *Value Line*'s recommendations, since some of the individual selections will outperform the market but others will not.[9]

Specialized Investment Advisory Services

In addition to the information published by publicly held firms, by Standard & Poor and Moody, and by advisory services such as *Value Line,* there is a host of specialized investment advice that the investor may purchase. A casual survey of the advertisements in *The Wall Street Journal* or *Barron's* proves this. A representative list of this material is given in Exhibit 4.7. Since these publishers and authors earn their living by selling these services and not by investing, the purchaser should be somewhat cautious when acting on any specific recommendations. Previous recommendations that proved successful do not guarantee future success.[10] Furthermore, if the service makes several recommendations, some, according to the laws of probability, should be correct. The service's true performance may be reflected in the number of successes

Other advisory services

---

[7] See, for instance, "The Value Line Ranking System," *The Value Line Investment Survey Selection & Opinion* (January 18, 1985): 960.

[8] Fisher Black, "Yes, Virginia, There Is Hope: Tests of the Value Line Ranking System," paper presented at the Center for Research in Security Prices, Graduate School of Business, University of Chicago, May 1971.

[9] *Value Line* also manages several mutual funds that permit the investor to obtain a diversified portfolio based on its analysts' recommendations.

[10] The SEC and state regulatory agencies forbid advisory services from providing single illustrations or examples of previously successful recommendations. All recommendations ever made must be presented.

Exhibit 4.6
Page from the *Value Line*
Investment Survey

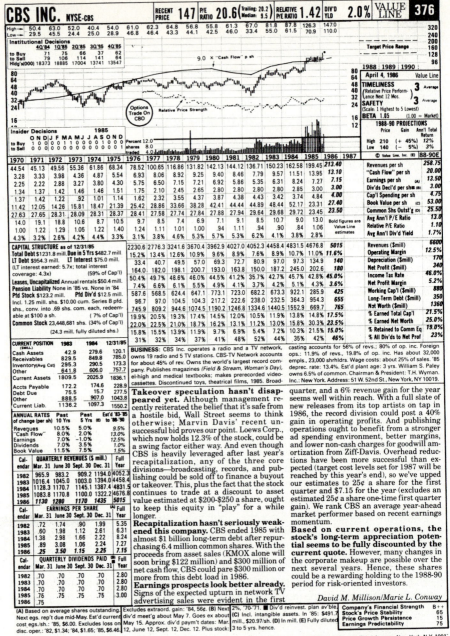

Exhibit 4.7
Selected Investment
Advisory Services

Commodity Timing
c/o Conceptual Management
850 Munras #2
Monterey, CA 93940

Dow Theory Forecasts
7412 Calumet Ave
Hammond, IN 46324

R.H.M. Survey of Warrants, Options, and Low-Priced Stocks
R.H.M. Associates
417 Northern Boulevard
Great Neck, NY 11021

Trendline Daily Action Stock Charts
Standard & Poor's
25 Broadway
New York, NY 10004

Value Line OTC Special Situations Service
c/o Arnold Bernhard & Co., Inc.
711 Third Avenue
New York, NY 10017

The Zweig Forecast
Zweig Services
747 Third Avenue
New York, NY 10017

relative to the number of recommendations or in the returns earned on all of the recommendations relative to a measure of the market, such as the Dow Jones industrial
average.

OTHER SOURCES OF INFORMATION

The U.S. federal government publishes a considerable amount of material that may be *Government publications*
useful to investors. These publications include the *Survey of Current Business,* which
presents business statistics, and the *Business Conditions Digest,* which provides information on business indicators. The *Economic Report of the President* and the *Annual
Report of the Council of Economic Advisors* are published annually; they cover business
conditions and provide economic forecasts. For statistics on interest rates, the money
supply, national income, and unemployment rates, the investor may consult the *Federal Reserve Bulletin,* which is published monthly by the board of governors of the
Federal Reserve.

Miscellaneous sources of investment advice also are available. An investor may *Professional investment
engage the services of a professional investment counselor. In addition, many banks counselors and trust
offer investment services through **trust departments.** Investment counseling and departments*
trusts are costly, particularly for small investors. Exhibit 4.8 illustrates the fees charged
by the trust department of a commercial bank. The first column gives the market
value of the portfolio, and the second column presents the trust department's fees. The
last column expresses the fees as a percentage of the value of the portfolio. As is obvious from the exhibit, the percentage costs decline as the value of the portfolio
increases.

Exhibit 4.8
Sample Fee Schedule for
Portfolio Management

UNITED JERSEY BANK
INVESTMENT MANAGEMENT DIVISION

INVESTMENT MANAGEMENT FEES

First $150,000 of principal .... $1,100 base fee
Next $350,000 .... .50%
Next $500,000 .... .40%
Next $2,000,000 .... .30%
Next $2,000,000 .... .20%
Next $5,000,000 .... .15%
Balance .... .10%

Fees on representative accounts:

Account Size:	Fee ($):	Fee as Percentage of Size of Account:
$ 150,000	$ 1,100	.73%
250,000	1,600	.64%
500,000	2,850	.57%
1,000,000	4,850	.49%
2,000,000	7,850	.39%
3,000,000	10,850	.36%
4,000,000	12,850	.32%
5,000,000	14,850	.30%
10,000,000	22,350	.22%
20,000,000	32,350	.16%

Source: Courtesy of United Jersey Bank—Investment Management Division.

Investment clubs

The investor may also join an **investment club.** Such clubs pool the members' funds and invest them in securities. Most clubs invest only moderate sums. For example, members may pay $10 per month in dues, which are then invested in the club's name. Although such sums of money are trivial, the potential knowledge and experience that can be gained through membership in such clubs is not. Since members must agree on the club's investment goals, strategies, and choice of investments, the individual may learn a considerable amount concerning investments as the club formulates and executes policy. These clubs may have an additional advantage in that they may be able to obtain professional help at a fraction of the cost. For example, a salesperson from a brokerage firm may be willing to talk with members of the club and execute orders for them. The broker may do this for the potential commissions not only from the club but also from individual members of the club who may become clients. Unfortunately, the club may be dominated by one or a few outspoken individuals, and the club's goals may not coincide with the individual's goals or financial needs. Because of these factors, the individual should not rely solely on investment clubs to make personal investment decisions.[11]

[11] For a description of the procedures for establishing an investment club consult the *Investors Manual* published by the National Association of Investment Clubs, 1515 E. 11 Mile Road, Royal Oak, MI 48067.

POINTS OF INTEREST

A Review of the *Encyclopedia of Investments*

The *Encyclopedia of Investments* is designed to fill a gap in the general literature on investments. It is a standardized compilation of articles on over 50 possible investments. Each piece is individually written by an expert in that particular field. The length and form of each article are uniform (about 15 to 20 pages), and each piece includes a glossary and a bibliography. The entries examine such practical considerations as how to buy and sell the asset, the primary factors that determine the asset's value, for whom the asset is suitable, the tax implications, and where professional advice may be obtained.

While the *Encyclopedia of Investments* covers traditional investments such as stocks, bonds, and mutual funds, its strength lies in the coverage given to the less traditional investments. These include financial futures, folk art, gemstones, mortgage-backed securities, motion pictures, paintings, period furniture, and stamps. Approximately one half of the book is devoted to these nontraditional investments. Since there is a dearth of conveniently compiled material on such investment alternatives, this encyclopedia may become a standard reference book for any library supporting programs in investments.

Source: This material appeared in slightly different form in *Choice,* February 1983, a publication of the Association of College and Research Libraries.

Last, the individual investor should not exclude the possibility of taking courses in investments. Many adult education programs offer special courses in areas of investing such as portfolio planning and management. These classes usually have nominal tuition fees and may offer the individual investor an excellent source of information.

Adult education courses

There is no shortage of readily available information. The problem for the investor is separating "the wheat from the chaff" and processing it into a useful form from which to draw conclusions. Even if the investor relies solely on the advice of others, such as brokers or investment services, that individual must still select from the alternatives that are suggested. For example, each week the *Value Line Investment Survey* recommends 100 stocks that should, in its opinion, outperform the market. No investor is going to buy all of them. If an investor follows the advice of the publication and purchases several of its recommended stocks, he or she must still choose from the various recommended investment alternatives. Hence, the final investment decision rests with the individual investor, who earns the returns and bears the risk.

No shortage of information

Data Bases

With the spread of personal computers, computer programs, and peripheral equipment, there have developed data bases such as *The Source* and the *Dow Jones News/Retrieval Service. The Source* and *CompuServe* are general information services, while the *Dow Jones News/Retrieval Service* specializes in on-line financial information. Other on-line financial information services include *Telescan, FCI-Invest/Net, Nite-Line,* and *Warner Computer Systems.* Subscribers pay a connection fee and usage rates. Such services provide current price quotations, historical price information, financial news items, and filings with the SEC such as annual reports and quarterly filings.

On-line trading

The next step after the development of data bases may be the institution of on-line trading. For example, *The Source* information network offers on-line trading through Spear Securities. Such services are not widely used by the general investing public, but the concept is being nurtured by discount brokerage firms. As may be expected, full commission brokerage firms are not inclined to encourage this development, since on-line investing can circumvent the broker. As an exception, two firms that seem to be moving toward on-line investing are E. F. Hutton and Dean Witter. Both offer on-line financial information that includes daily account statements, delayed stock quotes, and access to financial data bases, but as of 1986 neither offered on-line investing.[12]

SUMMARY

This chapter has described some of the extensive literature that is available to investors. These publications range from the annual and quarterly reports of publicly held firms to specialized investment advisory services. Some of this information is readily available and may be obtained with little effort and at little cost. Other sources require that the investor pay a substantial sum for the material. Many brokerage firms carry some of the publications that have been described, and the investor may often find them at a local library.

Although none of the publications can consistently predict the future (and the investor should be skeptical of any publication claiming that the subscriber can make a fortune), investors do need to be well informed. Reading financial literature from diverse sources is an excellent means of keeping abreast of events in the financial markets. The investor should be aware of the many sources of potentially useful financial information. In addition to the material cited in this chapter, each chapter in this text ends with a list of readings on the material covered in the chapter.

Investment services, which are available from a professional counselor or a bank, are another source of financial information. Although such services may be costly for the small investor, the effective cost of professional counseling decreases as the value of the portfolio increases.

There is no shortage of information on financial markets and investing. Instead, the problems for the investor are processing this information and putting it into a usable form for making financial decisions. Ultimately it is the individual who reaps the returns earned by the investment and bears the risk of loss.

Terms to Remember

Annual report
Quarterly report
10–K report
10–Q report
8–K report

Inside information
Buy, sell, or hold
Trust department
Investment club

[12] Pavan Sahgal, "Why Full-service Brokerage Firms Are Losing the Race to Win Customers," *Wall Street Computer Review* (July 1986), 28–37.

Questions

1. Describe the contents of an annual report.

2. What is a 10–K report? What is a prospectus?

3. Name several sources of information on investments that are available to individuals. In general, is there a shortage of available information?

4. Why may investment advisory research reports be self-serving?

5. The act of finding information is one of the best means to learn about the literature that is available to the investor. The student should try to locate the following and skim through each to become familiar with its contents. (a) *The Wall Street Journal* and *Barron's*; (b) *Value Line Investment Survey, The Outlook,* or some other advisory service publication; (c) *Forbes, Fortune,* or *Business Week*; and (d) *Moody's Industrial Manual* or *Standard & Poor's Corporation Records.*

Suggested Readings

In addition to the material presented in this chapter, the reader may consult the following general source material.

Consolidated Capital Communications Group, Inc. *The Financial Desk Book.* Emeryville, Calif.: Consolidated Capital Communications Group, 1985.

Moffat, Donald W., ed. *Concise Desk Book of Business Finance.* Englewood Cliffs, N.J.: Prentice-Hall, 1975.

New York Stock Exchange Fact Book, published annually.

Rachlin, Harvey, ed. *The Money Encyclopedia.* New York: Harper & Row, 1984.

Stock Market Encyclopedia. New York: Standard & Poor's Corp., published annually.

Sussman, D. H. "Information Sources: An Overview," in *Financial Analysts' Handbook,* edited by S. N. Levine. Homewood, Ill.: Dow Jones-Irwin, 1975.

Zarb, Frank G., and Gabriel T. Kerekes, eds. *The Stock Market Handbook.* Homewood, Ill.: Dow Jones-Irwin, 1975.

Zweig, Martin E. *Understanding Technical Forecasting: How to Use Barron's Market Laboratory Pages.* Princeton, N.J.: Dow Jones, 1980.

For descriptions of data base systems and investment software, see:

Hansen, Carol. *The Microcomputer User's Guide to Information On-line.* Hasbrouck Heights, N.J.: Hayden Book Co., 1985.

Meyers, Thomas A. *Dow Jones-Irwin Guide to On-line Investing: Sources, Services and Strategies.* Homewood, Ill.: Dow Jones-Irwin, 1985.

Schwaback, Robert. *Dow Jones-Irwin Guide to Investment Software.* Homewood, Ill.: Dow Jones-Irwin, 1985.

5

The Tax Environment

LEARNING OBJECTIVES

After completing this chapter you should be able to

1. Identify the taxes that affect investment decision making.
2. Define progressive, proportionate, and regressive taxes.
3. Distinguish between ordinary income and capital gains.
4. Illustrate how capital losses are used to offset ordinary income.
5. Explain how pension plans, IRAs, and Keogh accounts are tax shelters.
6. Differentiate between estate and inheritance taxes.
7. Explain the impact of accelerated depreciation on taxes owed.

*T*here are many laws that affect investments, but two general classes predominate: taxation and the regulation of security markets. Taxation influences investment decisions because it alters the potential return on an asset. Regulation affects investing by altering the environment in which the decisions are made.

Taxation is imposed by all levels of government. Investment income, profits from realized capital appreciation, and even the assets themselves may be subject to taxation. For this reason, considerable time and effort are devoted to reducing taxes and sheltering income from taxation.

This chapter briefly covers the main sources of taxation and offers several illustrations of tax shelters. Tax laws change virtually every year. This is unfortunate in that some of the specific information (e.g., tax rates) contained in this chapter may become outdated. However, the basic tax principles tend to remain the same, even though specific laws may have changed.

TAX BASES

Since one of the main purposes of taxes is to raise revenues, a tax base must be large in order to produce any sizable amount of revenue. In general, there are three bases that can be taxed: one's income, one's wealth, and one's consumption (i.e., spending). In the United States all three are used as tax bases at various levels of government. The federal government and many states tax income. Several states and virtually all local governments tax wealth (e.g., property taxes). The federal government also may tax an individual's wealth when that person dies (i.e., estate taxes). Many state governments tax spending (i.e., sales taxes), and the federal government taxes specific spending when it levies import duties, taxes telephone usage, and levies excise taxes on gasoline.

All three major sources of taxation may affect investment decisions. The tax that has the most impact on investments is the federal income tax, which is levied on investment income (i.e., interest and dividends) and on capital gains. Hence, the material on taxes appearing throughout this text emphasizes the federal income tax. However, taxes on wealth, such as the federal estate tax or property taxes on real estate, can be very important considerations for individual investors in specific circumstances. The least important general tax from an investment viewpoint is the sales tax (i.e., taxes on consumption). The purchase of securities or the acquisition of a savings account or shares in a mutual fund are not subject to sales tax. There are, however, a few investments, such as the purchase of gold or collectibles such as antiques, that are subject to sales tax in some localities. These taxes, of course, reduce the potential return from the investments and may reduce their attractiveness in comparison to financial assets that are exempt from sales taxes.

INCOME TAXATION

Personal and corporate income is subject to taxation. These taxes are levied both by the federal government and by many state governments. Some states also permit the taxation of income by their municipalities. For example, the income of New York City residents is subject to federal, state, and city taxes.

In general, income taxes apply to all sources of income. Thus, dividend and interest income is subject to this taxation. However, the tax is not applied evenly to the returns from all investments. For example, dividend income is taxed by the federal government, while interest on municipal bonds is not.

Tax rates are not evenly applied

Income taxes levied by the federal government and by many state governments are progressive. A tax is **progressive** if the tax *rate* increases as the tax base (e.g., income) rises. If the tax rate declines as the base increases, the tax is **regressive**. If the tax rate remains constant, the tax is **proportionate**.

Progressivity

Many individuals believe that taxes should be progressive, so that individuals with higher incomes or more wealth bear a larger proportion of the cost of government. It is on this basis that many regressive taxes are criticized. Regressive taxes place a greater share of the cost of government on those individuals with the least ability to afford the burden. This argument for progressive taxes, however, is based on

A normative question

Exhibit 5.1
State of Virginia's
Income Tax Rates
as of 1986

Taxable Income	Tax Rate
$0–$3,000	2.00%
$3,001–$5,000	3.00
$5,001–$12,000	5.00
Over $12,000	5.75

ethical or normative beliefs: It is a moral judgment that some people should pay a proportionately higher amount of tax.

A progressive tax is illustrated in Exhibit 5.1, which presents the Virginia state income tax. The left-hand column gives levels of income, and the right-hand column presents the tax rate on that income. This right-hand column is the tax rate on additional income and is frequently referred to as the individual's **marginal tax rate** or tax bracket. As may be seen in this column, the marginal tax rate increases as income increases, which indicates that the Virginia state income tax is progressive.

It is the marginal tax rate that influences an individual's investment decision making. Since investment income or profits on security transactions alter the individual's marginal income, they also affect the amount the individual nets after tax from the investment. This can play an important role in the selection of assets to include in the portfolio. Individuals in the highest tax brackets may prefer investments that offer some form of tax shelter, such as municipal bonds, whose interest is exempt from federal income taxation.

1986 tax reform reduced tax rates and number of brackets

Tax reform became a major political issue during the mid-1980s. Some of the proposed reforms centered around the progressivity of the federal income tax structure. It was argued that the progressive federal income tax and high marginal tax rates led to emphasis on ways to avoid taxes. Several proposals were made for a flat tax with only one tax rate (i.e., a proportionate tax). Other proposals suggested fewer tax brackets than the 14 that were in effect. In the federal tax reform act enacted during 1986 two income tax brackets emerged.

Starting in 1988, married couples filing a joint return pay 15 percent on the first $29,750 of taxable income. Income above $29,750 is taxed at 28 percent. For single taxpayers, up to $17,850 in income is taxed at 15 percent, and additional income is taxed at 28 percent. For couples with income exceeding $71,900 ($43,750 for single taxpayers), there is a 5 percent surcharge to phase out the benefit of the 15 percent tax bracket. For taxpayers who must pay the surcharge, the marginal tax rate is 33 percent.[1]

After tax reform the federal income tax may still be viewed as progressive, since as income rises, the marginal tax rate also increases (i.e., from 15 to 28 percent). However, for individuals subject to the surcharge, the tax is regressive. For these individu-

---

[1]After the benefit of the 15 percent tax bracket has been phased out, there is an additional 5 percent surcharge to phase out the benefits of personal exemptions. For taxpayers with sufficient income to have both the 15 percent bracket and personal exemptions phased out, the tax on *all* income will be 28 percent.

als the marginal tax bracket is 33 percent, and that rate falls back to 28 percent once their income has risen sufficiently so that they are no longer subject to the surcharge.

TAX SHELTERS AND STRATEGIES

Tax shelters avoid, reduce, or defer taxes

Even though tax reform reduced marginal tax rates, individuals are still concerned with sheltering income from taxation. A **tax shelter**, as the name implies, is anything that avoids, reduces, or defers taxes; it is a shelter or protection against taxes. An investor does not have to be wealthy to enjoy these benefits, and many investors of modest means use tax shelters. Unfortunately the term "tax shelter" may evoke a variety of emotions and misunderstandings. In the minds of some people, "tax shelter" means all those taxes that other people (especially the "rich") are not paying. For some investors, the possibility of sheltering income from taxation may be sufficient to make irrational (and costly) investments. Still others may not realize the tax shelters that they themselves enjoy.

An example of a tax shelter that avoids taxation is the municipal bond. These bonds are generally referred to as **tax-exempt bonds,** since the interest earned on state and municipal debt is exempt from federal income taxation. (Correspondingly, interest on federal debt is exempt from state and local government taxation). The interest is also exempt from state and local income taxes if the owner is a resident of the state of issue. Thus, for a resident of New York City, the interest on a New York state bond is exempt from federal income taxes, New York state income taxes, and New York City income taxes. This can be a significant tax shelter as one's income and marginal tax bracket rises. An individual living in New York City who has a combined federal, state, and local marginal tax rate near 40 percent will find that the after-tax yields on a 6.5 percent New York state bond are equivalent to a yield of 10.8 percent on a corporate bond.[2]

An example of a tax shelter that reduces taxes is the deductibility of interest on mortgages and property taxes. A home is, of course, an investment, and the deductibility of these expenses associated with home ownership reduces the individual's federal income taxes. In addition to being a major tax shelter, this makes home ownership less expensive and more attractive.

An example of a tax shelter that defers taxes is the tax-deferred retirement account. While the individual does not avoid paying the tax, the payment is postponed until some time in the future. In effect, the individual has the free use of the funds until the tax must be paid, which in this case will be during retirement. For a 30-year-old worker, this will be in the distant future.

Capital Gains and Losses

Many investments are purchased and subsequently sold. If the sale results in a profit, that profit is considered a **capital gain**; if the sale results in a loss, that is a **capital loss.** Under tax reform, capital gains are taxed at the individual's marginal tax rate

---

[2]How the equivalence of taxable and nontaxable yields is calculated is explained in Chapter 12.

POINTS OF INTEREST
The Wash Sale

An investor cannot sell a security for a loss, promptly buy it back, and take a tax loss. Such a transaction is called a *wash sale,* and while a wash sale is not illegal, the investor must wait 31 days before the security may be repurchased in order to take the tax loss. If the investor does not want to wait for the required time period, he or she can purchase additional securities, hold both positions for 31 days, and then sell the original shares. For example, suppose an investor owns 100 shares of AT&T and currently has an unrealized (i.e., paper) loss. The investor believes the firm will do well and thus wants to maintain a position in the stock. This individual could buy an additional 100 shares for a total of 200 shares. After 31 days the original shares could be sold in order to realize the tax loss. Of course, such a strategy increases the investor's risk exposure, since the value of all 200 shares could decline.

(i.e., either 15 or 28 percent). Thus, if an investor buys a stock for $10,000 and sells it for $13,000, the $3,000 capital gain is taxed as any other source of income. The taxpayer, however, may use capital losses to offset capital gains. If this investor bought a second stock for $15,000 and sold it for $12,000, the $3,000 loss would offset the $3,000 capital gain. If the investor has a net capital gain (i.e., a capital gain after deducting any capital losses), that gain is taxed as any other source of income.

Net capital loss is used to offset other income

If the investor has a net capital loss, it is used to offset income from other sources, such as dividends or interest. However, only $3,000 in capital losses may be used in a given year to offset income from other sources. If the individual has a larger loss (e.g., $5,000), only $3,000 may be used in the current year. The remainder is carried forward to offset capital gains or income received in future years. This $3,000 limitation suggests that many investors may seek to take profits if they already have realized losses rather than carry forward the losses.

Unrealized profits are not taxed

While capital gains are taxed at the same rate as ordinary income, they are still illustrative of a tax shelter. The taxes on capital gains may be deferred indefinitely, since investment profits are taxed only after they have been realized. Many profits on security positions are only **paper profits**, for some investors do not sell the securities and realize the gains. The tax laws encourage such retention of securities by taxing the gains only when they are realized.

If the holder gives the securities to someone as a gift (for example, if a grandparent gives securities whose value has risen to a grandchild), the cost basis is transferred to the recipient, and the capital gains taxes continue to be deferred. If the recipient sells the securities and realizes the gain, then capital gains taxes will have to be paid by the owner of the securities (i.e., the recipient of the gift).

Transfer at death avoids capital gains taxation

Capital gains taxes can be avoided entirely if the individual holds the securities until he or she dies. The value of securities are taxed as part of the deceased's estate. The securities are then transferred through the deceased's will to other individuals,

such as children or grandchildren, and the cost basis becomes the security's value as of the date of death. For example, suppose an individual owns shares of IBM that were purchased in the 1950s. The current value of the shares is probably many times their costs. If the investor were to sell these shares, he or she would incur a large capital gain. However, if the shares are held until the investor dies, their new cost basis becomes the current value of the shares, and the capital gains tax on the appreciation is avoided.

Tax-deferred Pension Plans

One tax shelter that may also ease the burden of retirement is the pension plan. Many firms contribute to these plans for their employees. The funds are invested in income-earning assets, such as stocks and bonds. In some cases the individual employee is required to make payments in addition to the employer's contributions. The amount of the employer's contribution is usually related to the employee's earnings. These contributions are not included in taxable income, so the worker does not have to pay taxes on the employer's payments to the pension plan. Instead, the funds are taxed when the worker retires and starts to use the money that has accumulated through the plan.

IRAs. One criticism of these pension plans was that they were not available to all workers. However, Congress passed legislation that enables all employees as well as the self-employed to set up their own pension plans; thus, the tax shelter that was previously provided only through employer-sponsored pension plans is now available to all. An employee who is not covered by a pension plan may set up an **individual retirement account (IRA).** In 1981 Congress passed additional legislation that extended IRAs to all employees, even if they were already participating in an employer-sponsored pension plan.

Under an IRA, an individual worker may open an account with a financial institution, such as a commercial bank, savings and loan association (S&L), insurance company, brokerage firm, or mutual fund and may deposit up to $2,000 per year. The funds must be earned, which means that any employee who earns $2,000 or more may place as much as $2,000 in an IRA account.[3] However, if the individual's source of income is dividends or interest, these funds cannot be placed in an IRA.

The amount invested in the IRA is deducted from the individual's taxable income. Income earned by the funds in the account is also not taxed. All taxes are deferred until the funds are withdrawn from the IRA, and then they are taxed as ordinary income. If the individual prematurely withdraws the funds (before age 59½), the money is taxed as ordinary income and a penalty tax is added.

IRA accounts soon became one of the most popular tax shelters, but in 1986 Congress placed important restrictions on the deductibility of the IRA contribution. For workers *covered by a pension plan,* full deductibility is applicable only for couples filing a joint return with adjusted gross income of *less than $40,000.* (For single workers covered by a pension plan the limit is $25,000.) Note that adjusted gross income is

Limitations on IRA deductions

---

[3] The ability of part-time workers to establish IRAs creates interesting possibilities for tax savings for spouses that work part-time while the other spouse maintains a full-time job.

POINTS OF INTEREST
When to Start an IRA

While an individual worker's ability to start an IRA is constrained by the availability of funds, the earlier the account is started, the better. Since many young workers often have other priorities for which they are saving (e.g., down payment on a house) and are not contemplating retirement, they may not open an IRA. This is unfortunate, since the final amount in the account is greatly enhanced if the deposits are made at an early age.

This difference in the terminal value is illustrated by the following examples. An individual deposits $1,000 in an IRA starting at age 25 and continues the contribution for 40 years (i.e., until age 65). If the funds earn 8 percent annually, the account grows to $259,050. If the same individual started the account at age 45 and contributed $2,000 annually until age 65, the account would have $91,524. (How these amounts may be calculated is explained in the next chapter.) Even though total contributions in both cases are $40,000, the final amounts are considerably different. When the funds are deposited earlier, they earn more interest, which produces the larger terminal value. Thus it is to the individual's benefit to start IRA contributions as soon as possible, even if the amount of the contributions is modest.

Income in IRA is still tax-deferred

used and not earned income. If an individual earns a modest salary but has significant amounts of interest or dividend income, this additional income counts when determining the deductibility of IRA contributions. Once the cutoff level of income is reached, the deductibility of the contribution is reduced, so that it is completely phased out once the couple reaches adjusted gross income of $50,000 ($35,000 for individuals).

It is important to realize that the complete loss of deductibility of the IRA contribution applies only to workers filing a joint return who earn more than $50,000 ($25,000 filing a single return). For the majority of workers, the deductibility of the IRA contribution still applies. And the deductibility still applies to any individual, no matter what the level of income, if that individual is not covered by an employer-sponsored pension plan.

Even if the individual loses the deductibility of the IRA contributions, there is still reason to establish an IRA because the income earned by the funds invested in the account is tax-deferred. If a worker places $2,000 in the account for 20 years, it would earn a substantial return and that return would not have been taxed. For example, if $2,000 were placed in an IRA each year for 20 years and it earns 8 percent annually, the amount in the account would grow to $91,524.[4] Only $40,000 of the total represents the annual contributions. The remaining $51,524 is earnings that have not been taxed but will be taxed when the funds are withdrawn from the account. Thus while the change in the tax laws did reduce the attractiveness of the IRA for workers with

---

[4]How this amount is determined is shown in Chapter 6, which explains how the value of a future sum is calculated.

POINTS OF INTEREST
Whose Name for an IRA

Consider a married man whose wife is not employed. He earns $35,000 a year and knows that he can contribute up to $2,000 in an IRA for himself and $250 in a spousal IRA. Is such a distribution of IRA funds optimal? Many financial planners may suggest the opposite division of the $2,250: place $2,000 in the wife's name and only $250 in the husband's name. Under the law an individual may place any amount up to $2,000 in one account, so the man could put $2,000 in his wife's name and $250 in his, or he could place $1,125 in either name. However, he cannot annually place more than $2,000 in an individual account, nor can he open a joint account. IRAs are *individual* retirement accounts.

What is the advantage of putting the larger amount in the wife's name? The answer really depends on the age of the wife. Women are frequently younger than their husbands. Withdrawals from IRA accounts do not have to start until the individual reaches 70½. If the wife is younger than the husband and the funds are in the wife's name, the potential tax shelter is greater, as the funds may remain tax-deferred for a longer period of time. In addition, the husband is better providing for his wife's old age, when the probability is greater that she will be a widow. Of course, once the funds are in the spouse's name, the spouse is the owner and controls the account.

---

substantial total income, it did not completely erase the tax shelter generated by IRA accounts.

Keogh Accounts. Self-employed persons may establish a pension plan called a **Keogh account** or **HR-10 plan.** The account is named after the congressman who sponsored the enabling legislation. A Keogh is similar to an IRA or a company-sponsored pension plan. The individual places funds in the account and deducts the amount from taxable income. The maximum annual contribution is the lesser of 25 percent of income or $30,000. The funds placed in the account earn a return that (like the initial contributions) will not be taxed until the funds are withdrawn. As in the case of the IRA, there is a penalty for premature withdrawals before age 59½, and withdrawals must start after reaching the age of 70½.

Keogh accounts— pension plans for the self-employed

The determination of the amount an individual may contribute to a Keogh account is somewhat confusing. The individual may contribute up to 25 percent of net earned income, but the calculation of net earned income subtracts the pension contribution as a business expense. The effect is that the individual can contribute 20 percent of income before the contribution. Consider a self-employed individual who earns $100,000 before the pension contribution. If that individual contributes $20,000 (i.e., 20 percent of $100,000), he or she has contributed 25 percent of income after deducting the pension contribution:

Net income after contribution:
$100,000 − $20,000 = $80,000.
Contribution as percent of net earned income: $20,000/$80,000 = 25%.

It is probably easier to determine one's maximum possible contribution by taking 20 percent of income before the contribution then by determining 25 percent of net earned income.[5]

A self-employed person may also open an IRA in addition to a Keogh account. For example, a doctor who earns $100,000 may place $20,000 in a Keogh account. That individual may also place $2,000 in an IRA, but the contribution may not be deducted from taxable income, since the doctor's income exceeds the IRA limits previously discussed. However, even though the contribution is not deductible, the income earned by the account is tax-deferred.

Keogh accounts apply to the employees of the self-employed

If a self-employed person does open a Keogh plan, it must also apply to other people employed by this individual. There are some exceptions, such as new and young employees; however, if a self-employed individual establishes a Keogh account for him- or herself, other regular employees cannot be excluded. By establishing the account, the self-employed individual takes on fiduciary responsibilities for the management of Keogh accounts for his or her employees. This individual can avoid these responsibilities by establishing a Simplified Employee Pension (SEP) plan. SEPs are a type of pension plan that was designed by Congress to encourage small employers to establish pension plans for their employees but that avoid the complexities of the pension laws.

401(k) Plans. Many employers also offer **supplementary retirement accounts (SRAs),** which are often referred to as **401(k) plans.** These programs permit individuals to contribute a portion of their earned income, up to a specified limit, to a savings plan. The contribution is deducted from the individual's earnings before determining taxable income; thus, a 401(k) plan is similar in its effect on the employee's federal income taxes to IRAs and Keogh accounts.[6] The company may or may not match the individual's contribution. If the firm matches the individual's contribution, the total amount accumulated is perceptibly increased. For example, the firm may contribute $1 for every $1 the employee contributes on the first 2 percent of earnings and $1 for each additional $2 of earnings up to some specified limit. The funds may be invested in one of several plans offered by the company. These often include a stock fund, a bond fund, and a money market fund. The individual has the choice as to the distribution of the contributions among the plans and may be allowed to shift the funds at periodic intervals.

Savings from Tax-deferred Pension Plans

An example of the savings that are possible with these tax shelters is presented in Exhibit 5.2. For illustrative purposes, it is assumed that the individual earns $40,000.

---

[5] The formula for determining the maximum contribution is

$$\frac{\text{Income} \times 0.25}{1 + 0.25}.$$

If the individual's income is $100,000, the maximum contribution is

$$\frac{\$100,000 \times 0.25}{1 + 0.25} = \frac{\$100,000 \times 0.25}{1.25} = \$20,000.$$

[6] Non-profit organizations such as hospitals, religious organizations, foundations, and public and private schools may offer similar savings plans referred to as 403(b) plans.

Variables	Case A	Case B
Present		
Taxable income	$40,000.00	$40,000.00
Contribution	0	2,000.00
Net taxable income	40,000.00	38,000.00
Taxes	11,200.00	10,640.00
Disposable income	28,800.00	27,360.00
Contribution to savings	2,000.00	0
Net disposable income	26,800.00	27,360.00
Tax savings	0	560.00
Year 1		
Amount invested	$ 2,000.00	$ 2,000.00
Interest earned	200.00	200.00
Taxes on interest	56.00	0
Net interest earned	144.00	200.00
Year 2		
Amount in account	$ 2,144.00	$ 2,200.00
Interest earned	214.40	220.00
Taxes on interest	60.03	0
Net interest earned	154.37	220.00
Year 3		
Amount in account	$ 2,298.37	$ 2,420.00
	.	.
	.	.
	.	.
Year 20		
Amount in account	$ 8,033.89	$13,455.00
Tax savings	0	5,421.00

Exhibit 5.2
**Potential Savings
with a Tax-Sheltered
Retirement Account**

The individual's personal income tax rate is assumed to be 28 percent, so for each dollar of additional income, the individual must pay $0.28 in taxes. The example illustrates two cases. In the first, the individual pays the income tax and then saves $2,000, which is placed in a taxable investment (e.g., a certificate of deposit) that pays 10 percent annually. The interest income earned by the account is, of course, taxable. In the second case the individual places $2,000 in a tax-sheltered retirement account, which also pays 10 percent annually. However, the tax on this interest is deferred until the individual retires and withdraws the money.

In case A the saver starts with the $40,000 and pays the income tax ($11,200), which leaves a disposable income of $28,800. Of this, $2,000 is invested, leaving $26,800. In case B the saver initially contributes $2,000 to an IRA, which reduces taxable income by $2,000 to $38,000. Taxes of $10,640 are then paid, which leaves a spendable income of $27,360. By placing $2,000 in the IRA account and reducing taxable income, the saver reduces taxes by $560.

The initial tax saving, however, is only the first part of the potential savings. The $2,000 in case A now earns $200 in interest, but $56 of that is lost in taxes. Hence,

POINTS OF INTEREST
The Use of Personal Computers to Complete Your 1040

For many investors, record keeping, tax planning, and the completion of tax forms required for filing with the IRS can be complicated, time consuming, and expensive. However, by using a personal computer and a tax preparation package, the investor may significantly reduce the amount of work necessary for the completion of the required tax forms. There are many tax packages to choose among. The following is a list of factors the investor should consider when acquiring such a program.

1. The investor needs to identify the use of the program. There are many tax packages available, offering a wide range of features. Modest tax packages will complete the most frequently used tax schedules (e.g., form 1040 and schedules A, B, C, D, E, and G). If, however, the investor needs to complete other schedules, a more elaborate (and more expensive) program may be necessary.

2. The investor must be certain the program is compatible with the computer to be used, as many programs can be used only on a specific computer. The investor may want to examine the tax packages before buying the personal computer.

3. Since tax laws change frequently, the investor should consider the adaptability of the program to changes in the tax laws. Otherwise he or she may have to purchase new programs to handle alterations in the tax laws.

4. Computer programs designed to complete tax papers are "cookbooks." They can only do what the investor tells them to perform. Their primary advantages are the reduction in mathematical errors and the simplification of both tax planning and the completion of the tax forms. For example, the investor may enter into the program charitable deductions, interest expenses, or business deductions throughout the year. Such running entries will simplify year-end tax planning. However, the investor must still know what to enter. The tax preparation package is not a substitute for knowledge of the tax laws.

the saver nets only $144 in interest. The 10 percent interest rate generates a return after taxes of only 7.2 percent. The $2,000 in the IRA earns $200 but none of that interest is currently subject to tax.

After the first year (i.e., the beginning of the second year), there is $2,144 in the account in case A, but in case B, in which the saver placed funds in the retirement account, the amount in the account is $2,200.[7] The amounts in the accounts in case A and in case B grow to $2,298.37 and $2,420, respectively, at the beginning of the third year. After 20 years the initial $2,000 placed in the account in case A will have grown to $8,033.89 after taxes have been paid, but the proceeds in the tax-deferred account will have grown to $13,455. The tax savings over 20 years will amount to $5,421.[8]

This example assumes that the saver makes only one payment of $2,000. However, savings plans usually imply that the investor periodically places funds in the

---

[7] This example assumes that the tax on interest in case A is deducted from the interest and is not paid from other disposable income.

[8] How these figures are determined is explained in the next chapter. See in particular Problems 3 and 9 at the end of that chapter.

account. If the investor were to place at the beginning of each year $2,000 in the taxable investment or the tax-sheltered retirement account every year for 20 years, the tax savings would be even greater. In that case the tax-sheltered account would have $126,005 but the taxable alternative would have $89,838 after taxes. The difference then would be $36,167. This difference is the result of the tax savings on the interest alone and does not include the $560 tax savings generated each year by depositing the $2,000 in the account. In 20 years, $11,200 ($560 each year × 20) would be saved in taxes, for a total tax savings of more than $47,300.

These tax savings would be even greater if the investor were to place a larger sum each year in the retirement plan account (as is possible under the Keogh plan). For the self-employed professional with a substantial amount of taxable income, such as a lawyer or a doctor, these retirement plans offer one of the best means available to shelter income from current taxation. However, the individual will still have to pay tax on this income when the funds are withdrawn from the plan, while the tax has already been paid on the funds in the taxable alternative.

Potential savings increase with the amount and the marginal tax rate

Tax-deferred Annuities

In addition to tax-deferred pension plans, an individual may acquire a **tax-deferred annuity,** which is a contract for a series of payments in the future whose earnings are not subject to current income taxation. Tax-deferred annuities are sold by life insurance companies, and they work like life insurance in reverse. Instead of periodically paying for the insurance, the insurance company makes regular payments to the individual who owns the annuity.[9] A tax-deferred annuity has two components: a period in which funds accumulate and a period in which payments are made by the insurance company to the owner of the annuity.

The investor buys the annuity by making a payment to the insurance company (e.g., a lump-sum distribution from a pension plan may be used to buy an annuity). The insurance company then invests the funds and contractually agrees to a repayment schedule, which can start immediately or at some other time specified in the contract. While the funds are left with the insurance company, they earn a return for the annuity's owner. The individual's personal income tax obligation on these funds is deferred until the earnings are actually paid out by the insurance company. In addition, the proceeds that are initially withdrawn from the annuity are considered to be funds that were invested and are not subject to income tax. In effect, the individual may withdraw the capital invested in the annuity without incurring any tax liability, and the tax deferral continues until after the individual has recouped all the money used to purchase the annuity contract.

Tax is deferred until earnings are withdrawn

Since the tax on the earnings is deferred, it is possible that the amount of tax actually paid will be less than would have been the case if the earnings were taxed as accumulated. Many individuals use these annuities to accumulate funds for retirement. If after reaching retirement their income has fallen, their tax bracket may be reduced. In this case the withdrawals from the annuity will be taxed at a lower rate. Of course, it is possible that if the individual has saved sufficiently through pension

[9] For descriptions of various types of annuities, see Robert S. Rubinstein, "Life Insurance Investments—Annuities," in *The Encyclopedia of Investments,* eds. M. E. Blume and J. P. Friedman (Boston: Warrent, Gorham & Lamont, 1982), 355–382.

plans, IRA accounts, Keogh accounts, and personal savings, the tax bracket could be higher instead of lower when funds are withdrawn from any of the tax-sheltered accounts (including the tax-deferred annuity). But even if a higher tax rate were to occur in the future, the individual still has had the advantage of tax-free accumulation during the period when the tax obligation was deferred.

TAXATION OF WEALTH

There are also taxes on wealth in the form of estate, gift, and property taxes. Two types of taxes are exacted when a person dies: estate taxes and inheritance taxes. Estate taxes are imposed on the corpus or body of the deceased's estate. That includes the value of investments such as stocks and bonds as well as the value of personal effects such as automobiles and other personal property. The inheritance tax is levied on the share of an estate received by another individual. Like the estate tax, it is imposed on the value of personal effects as well as on financial assets.

Estate taxes   **Estate taxes** are primarily the domain of the federal government, while both estate and inheritance taxes are levied by state governments. Like the personal income tax, estate and inheritance taxes are usually progressive. Selected rates from the federal estate tax are given in Exhibit 5.3.[10] As may be seen from this exhibit, the tax rates increase with the value of the estate.

Estate tax laws are extremely complex, and an investor who is planning the distribution of his or her estate should consult a lawyer or financial planner. However, the basic components of these taxes are as follows. First, a married individual may leave the entire estate to his or her spouse without the spouse's paying any tax. Thus, a married individual with a net worth of $1,000,000 may leave the entire estate to a spouse and avoid estate taxes. This is really only a deferment of the tax liability, because this wealth is added to the wealth of the surviving spouse and is thus subject to estate tax when the spouse dies. Unless there are perceptible differences in the net worth of the individuals, leaving the maximum amount possible to a spouse may only defer some of the tax.

Second, the estate receives a **tax credit**, which reduces the amount of taxes due. As of 1987, the maximum credit will be $192,800. The effect of this credit is to exempt all estates valued at less than $600,000 from federal estate taxation. As a result of this tax credit and the ability to leave tax-free funds to one's spouse, modest estates will avoid federal taxation. For example, in 1987 a husband with an estate whose taxable value is $400,000 can leave $250,000 to his wife without her paying federal estate taxes. This reduces the taxable value of the estate to $150,000. Tax on $150,000 would be $38,800, which is reduced to nothing by the tax credit. However, larger estates may be taxed heavily after the tax credit is applied, since the rates rise rapidly for sums over the sheltered amount.

Inheritance taxes   **Inheritance taxes** are levied by state governments on the distribution of the estates of individuals living in the state. Even though the recipient of the inheritance

---

[10] These rates also apply to gifts.

| | Tax | | |
Taxable Value of the Estate	On the Base*	Plus Percentage†	On Excess Over
$ 0–10,000	$ 0	18%	$ 0
10,000–20,000	1,800	20	10,000
20,000–40,000	3,800	22	20,000
.	.	.	.
.	.	.	.
.	.	.	.
100,000–150,000	23,800	30	100,000
150,000–250,000	38,800	32	150,000
250,000–500,000	70,800	34	250,000
.	.	.	.
.	.	.	.
.	.	.	.
1,000,000–1,250,000	345,800	41	1,000,000
1,250,000–1,500,000	448,800	43	1,250,000
.	.	.	.
.	.	.	.
.	.	.	.

Exhibit 5.3
Selected Federal Estate
Tax Rates in Effect as of
January, 1987

* The base is the tax paid on the amount shown in the left-hand column under the heading "Taxable Value of the Estate."

† The percentage applies to any amount in excess of that shown in the left-hand column and up to the amount shown in the right-hand column under the heading "Taxable Value of the Estate."

may live in another state, that individual's inheritance is subject to tax by the state in which the deceased resided.

As with state income taxes, there are substantial differences in state inheritance taxes. There are also differences in the tax rates for recipients of an inheritance, depending on their relation to the deceased. The deceased's immediate family pays lower rates. Maximum rates apply to nonrelatives who receive a share of the estate.

Variations in tax rates

In addition to estate and inheritance taxes, the investor must also be concerned with **property taxes.** These are primarily levied by counties, municipalities, and townships. Since there are thousands of such local governments, there is great diversity in property taxes.

Property taxes

Personal property taxes may be levied on tangible or intangible personal property. Tangible property is physical property, such as a house or an automobile. Intangible personal property includes nonphysical assets and financial assets, such as stocks and bonds. Many localities tax only tangible property, with particular emphasis on real estate. However, some states, including Florida and Pennsylvania, permit the taxation of intangible personal property. In such states the individual's portfolio of stocks and bonds may be subject to property taxation. Since there is considerable variation in this type of taxation, the investor would be wise to learn the specific tax laws that apply in his or her own state.

CORPORATE TAXATION

Like individuals, firms are subject to taxation by the various levels of government. Income, capital gains, and property may all be subject to taxation. Although any of these taxes may affect the individual firm, this brief discussion is limited to the federal corporate income tax.

As with the individual federal income taxes, the tax reform law enacted in 1986 reduced both the number of brackets and the corporate income tax rates. As of January 1988, the federal corporate income tax structure becomes:

The tax schedule

Corporate Income	Tax Rate
$0—$50,000	15%
$50,001—$75,000	25
over $75,000	34

Under this tax structure, the maximum rate applies to virtually all corporations of any significant size. Certainly for publicly held firms, the investor might as well view the amount of taxes owed as being about one-third of the firm's taxable income.[11] Although it is extremely difficult to isolate who ultimately bears the cost of the corporate income tax, it is at least partially borne by investors, since the tax reduces either cash dividends and/or the firm's capacity to reinvest its earnings and grow.

Depreciation—allocating the cost of an asset over time

Like individual investors, corporate managements seek to reduce or at least to defer tax payments by taking advantage of certain deductions and making selected investments. For example, the cost of long-term assets, such as plant and equipment, is allocated (i.e., deducted from income) over a period of time; that is, the asset is depreciated. Under **straightline depreciation**, the amount of the deduction is the same each year, but under **accelerated depreciation** this expense is increased during the early years of the asset's life. The effect of accelerated depreciation is to increase expenses in the early years of the asset's life, which decreases current income and current taxes. The tax is deferred until after the period of accelerated depreciation has elapsed.

Tax credit is repealed

Prior to tax reform, another means to alter the amount of taxes owed was the **investment tax credit**, which, as the name implies, is a credit to be applied against taxes for making certain investments. In an effort to stimulate spending on plant and equipment, the federal government permitted corporations to reduce their taxes if they made certain investments in plant and equipment. By channeling a firm's funds into these investments, management was able to reduce the amount of income tax that the firm had to pay.

The removal of the investment tax credit has a major implication for investors. Firms in industries that require a substantial investment in plant and equipment have lost a major tax advantage that was not available to firms whose operations do not require such investments. This suggests that the future profitability of firms requiring a large investment in plant and equipment may be reduced, while firms that provide

---

[11] For companies earning more than $100,000 the benefits of the 15 and 25 percent tax brackets are phased out, so that all income is taxed at the 34 percent tax rate.

services, such as retail operations, may experience increased profitability. The invest-ment tax credit offered service firms few tax benefits, but the lower tax rates associ-ated with tax reform should increase their future net income.

Another way corporate financial managers can reduce income taxes is through investments in the stock of other corporations. Only 20 percent of any dividends re-ceived are subject to corporate income tax, and the remaining 80 percent are excluded from federal income taxation. If the stock's value rises and is subsequently sold for a profit, this profit is a capital gain and is taxed, as any other source of income. How-ever, as with individuals, corporate capital gains taxes are paid only after the profits are realized. Management may defer this tax indefinitely by not realizing the gains. Thus, the exclusion of 80 percent of dividend income and the tax deferral of capital gains help explain why some firms own stock in other firms instead of operating as-sets such as plant and equipment.[12]

Corporate dividend exclusion

Accelerated depreciation and investments in other corporations' stocks are two means available to corporate management to reduce the firm's income taxes. The po-tential impact of taxes influences management's decision making (just as it affects an individual investor's choice of assets). From the viewpoint of the individual investor, corporate income tax laws make analyzing and comparing companies more difficult. However, if a firm pays less than one-third of its earnings in taxes, that may be a clue to the investor to examine the firm more closely. Although management may be able to reduce taxes temporarily, this may also imply that current earnings are overstated and that taxes may be higher in the future.

SUMMARY

Tax laws have a significant impact on the environment of investing. These laws are issued by all levels of government, but the most important laws affecting investment decisions have been passed by the federal government.

The federal government taxes income from investments, capital gains, and the individual's estate. Tax rates are progressive, which means that as the tax base in-creases, the tax rate increases. This taxation—especially the progressivity of tax rates—induces individuals to find ways to reduce their tax liabilities. Investments that re-duce, defer, or avoid taxes are called tax shelters. Important tax shelters include tax-exempt bonds and pension plans. The interest on tax-exempt bonds completely avoids federal income taxes, while pension plans (including IRAs, Keogh accounts, and 401(k) plans) defer taxes until the funds are withdrawn from the plans.

Capital gains occur when an investor buys an asset such as stock and subse-quently sells it for a profit. A capital loss occurs when the asset is sold for a loss. If the investor has capital losses that exceed capital gains, the losses may be used to offset up to $3,000 annually in income from other sources.

Estate taxes are levied on the value of a decedent's estate, and some states also levy taxes on an individual's share of an estate (i.e., the inheritance). State and local governments also tax an individual's property, which may include the investor's finan-cial assets.

---

[12] For additional discussion of the corporate dividend exclusion, see Chapter 11 on preferred stock.

Corporations also pay federal and state income taxes. The tax reform law enacted in 1986 reduced both corporate income tax rates and the ability of corporations to avoid paying income taxes. However, accelerated depreciation and the 80 percent exclusion of dividends earned on investments in the stock of other companies permit corporations to reduce or defer the current amount of taxes they must pay.

Terms to Remember

Progressive tax

Regressive tax

Proportionate tax

Marginal tax rate

Tax shelter

Tax-exempt bond

Capital gain

Capital loss

Paper profits

Individual retirement account (IRA)

Keogh account or HR-10 plan

Supplementary retirement account (SRA) or 401(k) plan

Tax-deferred annuity

Estate tax

Tax credit

Inheritance tax

Property tax

Straightline depreciation

Accelerated depreciation

Investment tax credit

Questions

1. What is a progressive tax? Why is the federal estate tax illustrative of a progressive tax?

2. Does a tax shelter necessarily imply that the investor avoids paying taxes?

3. What is a capital gain? When are capital gains taxes levied? May capital losses be used to offset capital gains and income from other sources?

4. Which of the following illustrate a tax shelter?
    a. dividend income
    b. interest earned on a savings account
    c. a stock purchased for $10 that is currently worth $25
    d. interest earned on a municipal bond

5. What are Keogh, 401(k), and IRA plans? What are their primary advantages to investors?

6. What is the difference between an estate tax and an inheritance tax?

7. What is depreciation? How does it reduce a firm's taxes? Should a firm use accelerated depreciation instead of straightline depreciation?

8. How can a corporation shelter income by purchasing stock in another company?

Problems

1. A corporation owns 10,000 shares of MNO Corp. The stock pays a dividend of $2.35 a share. If the corporation that owns the stock is in the 34 percent federal income tax bracket, how much tax does it owe on the dividend income?

2. **a.** An individual in the 28 percent federal income tax bracket sold the following securities during the year:

	Cost Basis of Stock	Proceeds of Sale
ABC	$24,500	$28,600
DEF	35,400	31,000
GHI	31,000	36,000

What are the taxes owed on the capital gains?

b. An individual in the 28 percent federal income tax bracket sold the following securities during the year:

	Cost Basis of Stock	Proceeds of Sale
ABC	$34,600	$28,600
DEF	29,400	31,000
GHI	21,500	19,000

What are the taxes owed as a result of these sales?

3. A corporation in the 34 percent federal income tax bracket collects the following investment income:

Dividends on preferred stock owned	$12,000
Interest on municipal bonds	10,000
Interest on corporate bonds	7,000
Dividends on common stock owned	8,500
Interest on federal government bonds	5,000

How much federal income tax does this firm owe on its investment income?

Suggested Readings

It is both difficult and time consuming to stay current on the tax laws, which partially explains why tax services such as H and R Block can be profitable. The individual should realize that recent tax reforms initiated in 1986 have rendered outdated much of the material previously published on federal income taxes.

Investors who do not use accountants to prepare their tax papers often do use the services of tax consultants. For the current federal tax laws, the investor may consult:

Federal Tax Course. Englewood Cliffs, N.J.: Prentice-Hall.

This book is published annually and is perhaps the most convenient means to keep current on the federal tax laws.

Lasser Institute. *J. K. Lasser's Your Income Tax.* New York: Simon & Schuster.

This annual publication is designed to help an individual file federal income tax forms; thus, it has current information on many of the tax laws pertaining to investments. It is also considerably easier to read than the Federal Tax Course; the latter, however, is both more comprehensive and more thorough.

A SHORT CASE STUDY FOR CHAPTERS 1–5
The Demise of a Savings Account

After completing a degree in education administration, Victor Patarcity accepted a position with the New Jersey Department of Education. He has worked there for seven years and has experienced annual salary increments and steady promotions. His benefit package includes full medical and dental insurance, pension plan, and life insurance equal to twice his annual salary. A year after graduating from college he married his childhood sweetheart, Doris Ulric, who works as an administrative assistant for the state. Victor and Doris are relatively frugal people and have accumulated $70,000, which is held in a National Bank of New Jersey savings account and which earns a modest 5 percent annually. They also own a three bedroom home with an 11 percent mortgage that has 20 years left before it is entirely paid off.

While Doris Patarcity has worked steadily, she is now pregnant with their first child. The Patarcitys are uncertain what changes this addition to the family will make to their economic situation. They doubt that Doris will be able to continue to work for a period of time, and Victor doubts that he will be able to add to their current savings account. He also thinks that this savings account may not be the best vehicle for their savings.

Patarcity decided that one possible course of action was to explore the various accounts and savings programs offered by the bank. National Bank of New Jersey is a moderate-sized regional bank that offers a variety of savings and checking accounts and a range of certificates of deposit. It also offers IRA and Keogh plans and has a working relationship with Strauss and Strauss Incorporated (S & S), a regional brokerage firm that will buy and sell securities for the bank's customers. Since the brokerage firm offers only minimal research services, it charges discount rates for transactions. However, it will hold securities in street name, and funds may be transferred directly from accounts with the bank to S & S and vice-versa. Individuals with IRA and Keogh accounts with National Bank of New Jersey may also buy and sell securities through S & S.

Patarcity asked a representative of the bank for suggestions and several alternatives to the savings account for the $70,000.

This representative made the following suggestions:

1. Open an IRA and place the maximum permitted by law in the certificate of deposit with the longest term and highest rate. The bank is offering for IRAs a CD that pays 7.75 percent and expires after 18 months. It may be automatically renewed at the then going rate.

2. Open a money market account with the bank. The account currently pays 6.7 percent, but this rate varies weekly with changes in short-term interest rates. The individual may write checks against the account and may deposit or withdraw funds at will. There are no fees unless the amount in the account is less than $2,500.

3. Consider making a modest gift to the child soon after birth and investing the funds in a high-yield certificate of deposit.

4. Complete the paperwork to open a brokerage account with S & S, even if any purchase decisions will be deferred.

5. Close the savings account.

To help make this investment decision, Patarcity asked the bank's representative the following questions:

1. How safe is each investment and is it insured against loss?

2. How liquid is each investment?

3. What are the tax implications of each suggestion?

QUESTIONS FOR DISCUSSION

a. If you were the bank's representative, how would you respond to each question?

b. What do you think Patarcity should do?

c. Why do you think the bank's representative suggested points 4 and 5?

II   The Tools of Investing

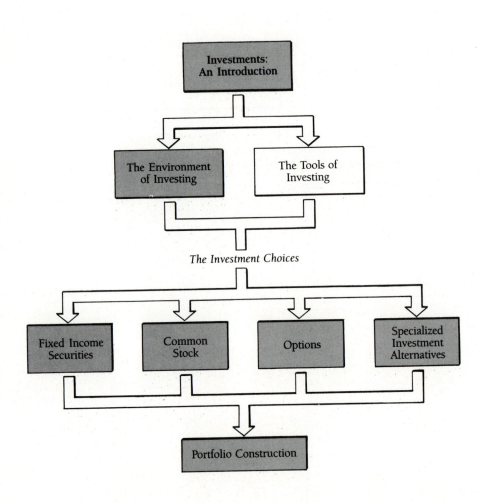

Once an understanding of the financial environment has been achieved, the investor needs several general tools with which to analyze specific assets. Like the material presented in Part One, the material presented in this section helps to lay the foundation for selecting securities and other assets.

Three tools are covered in Part Two. The first is a mathematical concept: the time value of money. A dollar received today and a dollar received tomorrow do not have the same value. Linking the future with the present is an extremely important concept for the valuation of assets, as investments are made in the present but the returns accrue in the future.

Financial statements are the next tool that is discussed in Part Two. A rudimentary ability to read financial statements is necessary to comprehend much of the analysis that is applied to firms in the evaluation of their securities.

The last chapter in Part Two discusses the sources of risk, how it may be measured, and the reduction of risk through diversification. Since virtually all investments involve risk, analysis of risk can play an important role in the selection of investments.

6

The Time Value of Money

LEARNING OBJECTIVES

After completing this chapter you should be able to

1. Explain why a dollar received tomorrow is not equal in value to a dollar received today.

2. Differentiate between compounding and discounting.

3. Distinguish between the present value of a dollar to be received in the future and the present value of an annuity.

4. Determine the future value of a dollar and the present value of a dollar to be received in the future.

5. Apply present value (i.e., discounting) to security analysis.

6. Solve problems concerning the time value of money.

If $2,000 is invested annually in an IRA, how much will be in the account in the year 2000? If your salary grows by 10 percent annually, how much will you be earning after 20 years? If you expect an investment in real estate to earn $10,000 a year for 15 years, how much is that investment worth to you today? These questions illustrate a major concept in finance—the time value of money. A dollar in the future is not equivalent in value to a dollar in the present: That is the time value of money.

The time value of money is one of the most crucial concepts in finance. An investment decision is made at a given time. For example, an investor buys stock or a firm decides to establish a pension plan today. The returns on these investment decisions will be received in the future. There has to be a means to compare the future results of these investments with their present cost. Such comparisons require an understanding of the time value of money, which is the subject of this chapter.

This chapter considers four concepts: (1) the future value of a dollar, (2) the present value of a dollar, (3) the future sum of an annuity, and (4) the present value of an annuity.

After each has been explained, several examples apply these concepts to investments. The chapter closes with a brief introduction to valuation, for the valuation of securities employs the time value of money.

THE FUTURE VALUE OF A DOLLAR

If $100 is deposited in a savings account that pays 5 percent annually, how much money will be in the account at the end of the year? The answer is easy to determine: $100 plus $5 interest, for a total of $105. This answer is derived by multiplying $100 by 5 percent, which gives the interest earned during the year, and then by adding this interest to the initial principal. That is,

Funds in a savings account grow

Initial principal + (Interest rate × Initial principal) = Principal after one year.

This simple calculation is expressed in algebraic form in Equation 6.1, in which P represents the principal and i is the rate of interest. This equation employs subscripts to represent time. The subscript 0 indicates the present, and 1 means the end of the first year. (The second year, third year, and so on to any number of years will be represented by 2, 3, . . . n, respectively.)

$$P_0 + iP_0 = P_1 \qquad\qquad (6.1)$$

If P_0 is the initial principal ($100) and i is the interest rate (5%), the principal after one year (P_1) will be

$$\$100 + 0.05(\$100) = \$105.$$

How much will be in the account after two years? This answer is obtained in the same manner by adding the interest earned during the second year to the principal at the beginning of the second year, that is, $105 plus 0.05 times $105 equals $110.25, which may be expressed in algebraic terms:

The interest left on deposit earns interest

$$P_1 + iP_1 = P_2. \qquad\qquad (6.2)$$

After two years the initial deposit of $100 will have grown to $110.25; the savings account will have earned $10.25 in interest. This total interest is composed of $10 representing interest on the initial principal and $0.25 representing interest that has accrued during the second year on the $5 in interest earned during the first year. This earning of interest on interest is called **compounding**. Money that is deposited in savings accounts is frequently referred to as being compounded, for interest is earned on both the principal and the previously earned interest.

The words *interest* and *compounded* are frequently used together. For example, banks may advertise that interest is compounded daily for savings accounts, or the cost of a loan may be expressed as 12 percent compounded annually. In the previous example, interest was earned only once during the year; thus it is an example of interest that is compounded annually. In many cases interest is not compounded annually but quarterly, semiannually, or even daily. The more frequently it is compounded (i.e., the more frequently the interest is added to the principal), the more rapidly the interest is put to work to earn even more interest.

How much will be in the account at the end of three years? This answer can be determined by the same general formula that was previously used. The amount in the account at the end of the second year ($110.25) is added to the interest that is earned during the third year (5% × $110.25); that is,

$$\$110.25 + \$5.5125 = \$115.76,$$

or the formula may be expressed algebraically as

(6.3) $$P_2 + iP_2 = P_3.$$

By continuing with this method, it is possible to determine the amount that will be in the account at the end of 20 or more years, but doing so is obviously a lot of work. Fortunately, there is a much easier way to ascertain how much will be in the account after any given number of years. This is by using an interest table called the future value of a dollar table.

A future value interest table

Appendix A consists of an interest table that gives the future value of a dollar. The interest rates at which a dollar is compounded periodically are read horizontally at the top of the table. The number of periods (e.g., years) is read vertically along the left-hand margin. To determine the amount to which $100 will grow in three years at 5 percent interest, find the interest factor (1.158) and multiply it by $100. That calculation yields $115.80, which is the answer that was derived previously by working out the equations (except for rounding). To ascertain the amount to which $100 will grow after 25 years at 5 percent interest compounded annually, multiply $100 by the interest factor, 3.386, to obtain the answer, $338.60. Thus, if $100 were placed in a savings account that paid 5 percent interest annually, there would be $338.60 in the account after 25 years.

A general formulation of the future value of a dollar

Interest tables for the future value of a dollar are based on a general formulation of the simple equations used previously. To determine the amount in the savings account at the end of Year 1, the following equation was used:

(6.1) $$P_0 + iP_0 = P_1,$$

which may be written as

$$P_0(1 + i) = P_1.$$

To calculate the amount after two years, the following equation was used:

(6.2) $$P_1 + iP_1 = P_2,$$

which may be written as

$$P_1(1 + i) = P_2.$$

Since P_1 equals $P_0(1 + i)$, the amount in the account at the end of Year 2 may be expressed as

$$P_0(1 + i)(1 + i) = P_2.$$

This equation uses the term $1 + i$ twice, for P_0 is being multiplied by $1 + i$ twice. Thus, it is possible to write Equation 6.2 as

$$P_0(1 + i)^2 = P_2.$$

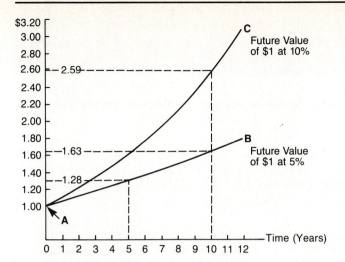

Figure 6.1
Future Value of One Dollar

The amount to which a dollar will grow may always be expressed in terms of the initial dollar (i.e., P_0). The general formula for finding the amount to which a dollar will grow in n number of years, if it is compounded annually, is

$$P_0(1 + i)^n = P_n. \qquad \textbf{(6.4)}$$

Thus, the general formula for finding the future value of a dollar for any number of years consists of (1) the initial dollar (P_0), (2) the interest factor $(1 + i)$, and (3) the number of years (n).

As may be seen in Appendix A, the value of a dollar grows with increases in the length of time and in the rate of interest. These relationships are illustrated in Figure 6.1. If $1 is compounded at 5 percent interest (*AB* in the figure), it will grow to $1.28 after five years and to $1.63 after ten years. However, if $1 is compounded at 10 percent interest (*AC* on the graph), it will grow to $2.59 in ten years. These cases illustrate the basic nature of compounding: The longer the funds continue to grow and the higher the interest rate, the higher will be the ultimate value.

The impact of time and the interest rate

It should also be noted that doubling the interest rate more than doubles the amount of interest that is earned over a number of years. In the example just given, the interest rate doubled from 5 percent to 10 percent; however, the amount of interest that will have accumulated in ten years rises from $0.63 at 5 percent to $1.59 at 10 percent. This is the result of the fact that compounding involves a geometric progression. The interest factor $(1 + i)$ has been raised to some power (n).

THE PRESENT VALUE OF A DOLLAR

In the preceding section, a dollar grew or compounded over time. In this section the reverse situation is considered. How much is a dollar that will be received in the future worth today? For example, how much will a payment of $1,000 20 years hence be

The opposite of compounding— discounting

worth today if the funds earn 10 percent annually? This question incorporates the time value of money, but instead of asking how much a dollar will be worth at some future date, it asks how much that future dollar is worth today. This is a question of **present value.** The process by which this question is answered is called **discounting.** Discounting determines the worth of funds that are to be received in the future in terms of their present value.

In the earlier section, the future value of a dollar was calculated by Equation 6.4.

(6.4)
$$P_0(1 + i)^n = P_n.$$

Discounting reverses this equation. The present value (P_0) is ascertained by dividing the future value (P_n) by the discount factor $(1 + i)^n$. This is expressed in Equation 6.5.

(6.5)
$$P_0 = \frac{P_n}{(1 + i)^n}.$$

The future amount is discounted by the appropriate interest factor to determine the present value. For example, if the interest rate is 10 percent, the present value of $100 to be received five years from today is

$$P_0 = \frac{\$100}{(1 + 0.1)^5}$$

$$= \frac{\$100}{1.611}$$

$$= \$62.07.$$

A present value table

Working with discount factors that are raised to a large power (n) is difficult, but as with the future value of a dollar, interest tables have been developed that ease the calculation of present values. Appendix B consists of a present value table. It gives the present value of a dollar for selected interest rates and time periods. The interest rates are read horizontally at the top, and time is read vertically along the left-hand side. To determine the present value of $1 that will be received in five years if the current interest rate is 10 percent, multiply $1 by the interest factor, which is found in the table under the vertical column for 10 percent and in the horizontal column for five years. The present value of $1 is

$$\$1 \times 0.621 = \$0.621.$$

Thus, $100 that will be received after five years is currently worth only $62.10 if the interest rate is 10 percent. This is the same answer that was determined with Equation 6.5 (except for rounding off).

The impact of time and the interest rate

As may be seen in Equation 6.5, the present value of a dollar depends on (1) the length of time before it will be received and (2) the interest rate. The further into the future the dollar will be received and the higher the interest rate, the lower the present value of the dollar. This is illustrated by Figure 6.2, which gives the relationship between the present value of a dollar and the length of time at various interest rates. Lines *AB* and *AC* give the present value of a dollar at 4 percent and 7 percent, respectively. As may be seen in this graph, a dollar to be received after 20 years is worth considerably less than a dollar to be received after five years when both are discounted

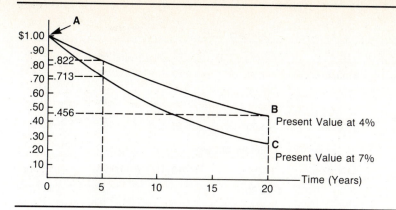

Figure 6.2
Present Value of One Dollar to be Received in the Future

at the same percentage rate. At 4 percent (line *AB*) the current value of $1 to be received after 20 years is only $0.456, whereas $1 to be received after five years is worth $0.822. Also, the higher the interest rate (i.e., discount factor), the lower the present value of a dollar. For example, the present value of $1 to be received after five years is $0.822 at 4 percent, but it is only $0.713 at 7 percent.

THE FUTURE SUM OF AN ANNUITY

How much will be in a savings account after three years if $100 is deposited annually and the account pays 5 percent interest? This is similar to the future value of a dollar except that the payment is not received as one lump sum but as a series. If the payments are equal, the series is called an **annuity**. The above question is then an illustration of the **future sum of an annuity**.

Flow of equal, annual payments

To determine how much will be in the account we must consider not only the interest rate earned but also whether deposits are made at the beginning of the year or the end of the year. If each payment is made at the beginning of the year, the series is called an **annuity due**. If the payments are made at the end of the year, the series is an **ordinary annuity**. What is the future sum of an annuity if $100 is deposited in an account for three years starting right now? What is the future sum of an annuity if $100 is placed in an account for three years starting at the end of the first year? The first question concerns an annuity due, while the second question illustrates an ordinary annuity.

Payment at the beginning or end of the year

The flow of payments for these two types of annuities is illustrated in Exhibit 6.1. In both cases the $100 is deposited for three years in a savings account that pays 5 percent interest. The top half of the figure shows the annuity due, while the bottom half illustrates the ordinary annuity. In both cases, three years elapse from the present to when the final amount is determined and three payments are made. The difference in the timing of the payment results in a difference in the interest earned. Since in an annuity due the payments are made at the beginning of each year, the annuity due

Exhibit 6.1
The Flow of Payments
for the Future Value of
an Annuity Due and an
Ordinary Annuity

Annuity Due

	1/1/x0	1/1/x1	1/1/x2	1/1/x3	Sum
	$100.00	5.00	5.25	5.51	115.76
		100.00	5.00	5.25	110.25
			100.00	5.00	105.00
Amount in the Account	$100.00	205.00	315.25	330.01	$330.01

Ordinary Annuity

	1/1/x0	1/1/x1	1/1/x2	1/1/x3	Sum
	—	$100.00	5.00	5.25	$110.24
			100.00	5.00	105.00
				100.00	100.00
Amount in the Account	—	100.00	205.00	315.25	$315.25

earns more interest ($30.01 versus $15.25) and thus has the higher terminal value ($330.01 versus $315.25). As will be illustrated later in the chapter, the greater the interest rate and the longer the time period, the greater will be this difference in terminal values.

Future sum of

The procedures for determining the future sum of an annuity due (FSAD) and the future sum of an ordinary annuity (FSOA) are stated formally in Equations 6.6 and 6.7, respectively. In each equation, I represents the equal, periodic payment, i represents the rate of interest, and n represents the number of years that elapse from the present until the end of the time period. For the annuity due, the equation is

1. an annuity due

(6.6)
$$FSAD = I(1 + i)^1 + I(1 + i)^2 + \cdots + I(1 + i)^n.$$

When this equation is applied to the previous example in which $i = 0.05$, $n = 3$, and the annual payment ($I = \$100$), the accumulated sum is

$$FSAD = \$100(1 + 0.05)^1 + 100(1 + 0.05)^2 + 100(1 + 0.05)^3$$

$$= \$105 + 110.25 + 115.76$$

$$= \$330.01.$$

2. an ordinary annuity

For the ordinary annuity the equation is

(6.7)
$$FSOA = I(1 + i)^0 + I(1 + i)^1 \cdots + I(1 + i)^{n-1}.$$

When this equation is applied to the above example, the accumulated sum is

$$FSOA = \$100(1 + 0.05)^0 + 100(1 + 0.05)^1 + 100(1 + 0.05)^{3-1}$$

$$= \$100 + 105 + 110.25$$

$$= \$315.25.$$

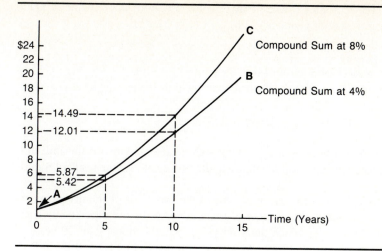

Figure 6.3
Future Sum of an Ordinary Annuity of One Dollar

Although it is possible to derive the sum of an annuity in this manner, it is very cumbersome. Fortunately, interest tables have been developed to facilitate these calculations. In Appendix C we find the interest table for the future sum of an ordinary annuity for selected time periods and selected interest rates. (Interest tables are usually presented only for ordinary annuities. How these tables may be used for annuities due is discussed below.) The number of periods is read vertically at the left, and the interest rates are read horizontally at the top. To ascertain the future sum of the ordinary annuity in the previous example, this table is used as follows. The FSOA at 5 percent interest for three years (three annual $100 payments with interest being earned for two years) is $100 times the interest factor found in Appendix C for three periods at 5 percent. This interest factor is 3.153; therefore, the future value of this ordinary annuity is $100 times 3.153, which equals $315.30. This is the same answer that was derived by determining the future value of each $100 deposit and totaling them. (The slight difference in the two answers is the result of rounding off.)

The value of an ordinary annuity of a dollar compounded annually depends on the number of payments (i.e., the number of periods over which deposits are made) and the interest rate. The longer the time period and the higher the interest rate, the greater will be the sum that will have accumulated in the future. This is illustrated by Figure 6.3. Lines *AB* and *AC* show the value of the $1 annuity at 4 and 8 percent, respectively. After five years the value of the annuity will grow to $5.87 at 8 percent but to only $5.42 at 4 percent. If these annuities are continued for another five years, they will be worth $14.49 and $12.01, respectively. Thus, both the rate at which the annuity compounds and the length of time affect the annuity's value.

Impact of interest and the number of payments

While the interest table in Appendix C is constructed for an ordinary annuity, it may be converted into a table for an annuity due by multiplying the interest factor given in the table by $(1 + i)$. For example, in the illustration of the $100 deposited annually in the savings account for three years, the interest factor for the ordinary

Adjusting interest table for an annuity due

annuity was 3.153. This interest factor may be converted for an annuity due at 5 percent for three years by multiplying 3.153 by 1 + 0.05. That is,

$$3.153(1 + 0.05) = 3.3107.$$

When this interest factor is applied to the example of $100 deposited in the bank at 5 percent for three years with the deposits starting immediately, the resulting terminal value is

$$\$100(3.3107) = \$331.07.$$

This is the same answer as derived by making each calculation individually and summing them. (Once again the small difference in the two answers is the result of rounding off.)

The difference between the terminal value of the two kinds of annuity payments can be quite substantial as the number of years increases or the interest rate rises. Consider an IRA account in which the saver places $2,000 annually for 20 years. If the deposits are made at the end of the year (an ordinary annuity) and the rate of interest is 7 percent, the terminal amount will be

$$\$2,000(40.995) = \$81,990.$$

However, if the deposits had been made at the beginning of each year (an annuity due), the terminal amount would be

$$\$2,000(40.995)(1 + 0.07) = \$87,729.30.$$

The difference is $5,739.30! Almost $6,000 in additional interest is earned if the deposits are made at the beginning, not at the end, of each year.

The difference between the ordinary annuity and the annuity due becomes even more dramatic if the interest rate rises. Suppose the above IRA offered 12 percent instead of 7 percent. If the deposits are made at the end of each year, the terminal value is

$$\$2,000(72.052) = \$144,104.$$

If the payments are at the beginning of the year, the terminal value will be

$$\$2,000(9.646)(1 + 0.12) = \$161,396.48.$$

The difference is now $17,292.48.

THE PRESENT VALUE OF AN ANNUITY

Discounting a flow of payments

In investment analysis, the investor is often not concerned with the future value but with the **present value of an annuity.** The investor who receives periodic payments often wishes to know the current (i.e., present) value. As with the future sum of an annuity, this value depends on whether the payments are made at the beginning of each period (an annuity due) or at the end of each period (an ordinary annuity).

If the annuity is an ordinary annuity, the present value of the future payments could be determined by obtaining the present value of each payment and summing

these values. This approach is illustrated by the following simple example. The recipient expects to receive $100 at the end of each year for three years and wants to know how much this series of annual payments is currently worth if 12 percent can be earned on alternative investments. One method to determine current worth is to calculate the present value of each of the $100 payments (find the appropriate interest factors in Appendix B and multiply them by $100) and to sum these individual present values, which in this case yields $240.20.

Payment	Year	Interest Factor	Present Value
$100	1	0.893	$ 89.30
100	2	0.797	79.70
100	3	0.712	71.20
			$240.20

This process is expressed in more general terms by Equation 6.8. The present value (PV) of the annual payments (I) is then found by discounting these payments at the appropriate interest factor (i).

$$PV = \frac{I}{(1 + i)^1} + \cdots + \frac{I}{(1 + i)^n},$$

$$PV = \sum_{t=1}^{n} \frac{I}{(1 + i)^t}.$$

(6.8)

When the values from the previous example are inserted into the equation, it reads

$$PV = \frac{\$100}{(1 + 0.12)} + \frac{\$100}{(1 + 0.12)^2} + \frac{\$100}{(1 + 0.12)^3}$$

$$= \frac{\$100}{1.120} + \frac{\$100}{1.254} + \frac{\$100}{1.405}$$

$$= \$240.20.$$

The present value of an annuity table

The calculation of the present value of an annuity can be a long and tedious process. To simplify this task, interest tables have been developed for the present value of an annuity. Appendix D is a table of this kind. Selected interest rates are read horizontally along the top, and the number of periods is read vertically at the left. To determine the present value of an annuity of $100 that is to be received for three years when interest rates are 12 percent, find the interest factor for three years at 12 percent (2.402) and then multiply $100 by this interest factor. The present value of this annuity is $240.20, which is the same value that was derived by obtaining each of the individual present values and summing them. The price that one would be willing to pay at the present time in exchange for three future annual payments of $100 when the rate of return on alternative investments is 12 percent is $240.20.

The impact of the interest rate and time

As with the present value of a dollar, the present value of an annuity is related to the interest rate and the length of time over which the annuity payments are made. The lower the interest rate and the longer the duration of the annuity, the greater the

Figure 6.4
**Present Value of an
Ordinary Annuity of
One Dollar**

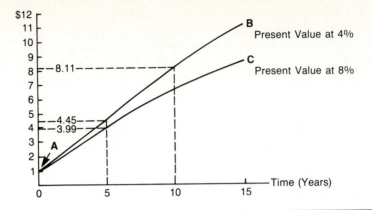

present value of the annuity. Figure 6.4 illustrates these relationships. As may be seen by comparing Lines *AB* and *AC*, the lower the interest rate, the higher the present dollar value. For example, if payments are to be made over five years, the present value of an annuity of $1 is $4.45 at 4 percent but only $3.99 at 8 percent. The longer the duration of the annuity, the higher the present value; hence, the present value of an annuity of $1 at 4 percent is $4.45 for five years, whereas it is $8.11 for ten years.

Many payments to be received in investments occur at the end of a time period and not at the beginning and thus are illustrative of ordinary annuities. For example, the annual interest payment made by a bond occurs after the bond is held for a while, and distributions from earnings (e.g., dividends from stock or disbursements from a real estate tax shelter) are made after, not at the beginning of, a period of time. There are, however, payments that may occur at the beginning of the time period, such as the annual distribution from a retirement plan; these would be illustrative of annuities due.

*Payment at the beginning
or end of the year*

The difference in the flow of payments and the determination of the present values of an ordinary annuity and an annuity due are illustrated in Exhibit 6.2. In each case the annuity is for $2,000 a year for three years and the interest rate is 10 percent. In the top half of the exhibit, the payments are made at the end of the year (an ordinary annuity), while in the bottom half of the exhibit, the payments are made at the beginning of the year (an annuity due). As may be seen by the totals, the present value of the annuity due is higher ($5,470 versus $4,972). This is because the payments are received sooner and, hence, are more valuable. As may also be seen in the illustration, since the first payment of the annuity due is made immediately, its present value is the actual amount received. Because the first payment of the ordinary annuity is made at the end of the first year, that amount is discounted, and, hence, its present value is less than the actual amount received.

*Adjusting present value
table for an annuity due*

The interest tables for the present value of an annuity presented in this text (and in other finance and investment texts) apply to ordinary annuities. These interest factors may be converted into annuity due factors by multiplying them by $(1 + i)$. Thus the interest factor for the present value of an ordinary annuity for $1 at 10 percent for

Exhibit 6.2
Flow of Payments and
Determination of the
Present Value of an
Ordinary Annuity and
an Annuity Due at 10
Percent for Three Years

Ordinary Annuity

1/1/x0	1/1/x1	1/1/x2	1/1/x3
$1,818 ◄── (0.909) 2,000			
1,652 ◄────────────── (0.826) 2,000			
1,505 ◄──────────────────────────── (0.751) 2,000			
$4,972			

Annuity Due

1/1/x0	1/1/x1	1/1/x2	1/1/x3
$2,000			
1,818 ◄── (0.909) 2,000			
1,652 ◄────────────── (0.826) 2,000			
$5,470			

three years (2.487) may be converted into the interest factor for an annuity due of $1 at 10 percent for five years as follows:

$$2.487(1 + i) = 2.487(1 + 0.1) = 2.736.$$

When this interest factor is used to determine the present value of an annuity due of $2,000 for three years at 10 percent, the present value is

$$\$2,000(2.736) = \$5,472.$$

The present value of an ordinary annuity of $2,000 at 10 percent for three years is

$$\$2,000(2.457) = \$4,974.$$

These are essentially the same answers given in Exhibit 6.2 with the small differences being the result of rounding.

APPLICATIONS OF COMPOUNDING AND DISCOUNTING

The previous sections have explained the various computations involving time value, and this section will illustrate them in a series of problems that the investor may encounter. These illustrations are similar to examples that are used throughout the text. If one understands these examples, comprehending the rest of the text material should be much easier, because the emphasis can then be placed on the analysis of the value of specific assets instead of on the mechanics of the valuation.

Answering the time value of money problems requires determining which of the four tables to use. The following decision tree may aid in this selection process. First, determine if the problem involves a lump sum payment or a set of equal payments (i.e., an annuity). Then determine if the problem concerns going from the present to the future (future value) or from the future to the present (present value).

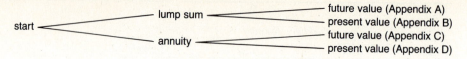

For example, if the current tuition cost of a four-year college education is $20,000, what will be the cost after ten years if prices rise annually by 6 percent? First, determine if the problem is concerned with an annuity or a lump sum. Since the question asks about total tuition costs, it is an illustration of a lump sum and not an annuity. Second, determine the time dimension. Since the problem is not concerned with the current cost of an education but with future costs, it is an example of future value and not present value. Thus, from the decision tree presented below, the appropriate table is determined to be the future value of a dollar table (Appendix A).

1. An investor buys a stock for $10 per share and expects to watch the value of the stock grow annually at 9 percent for ten years, at which time the individual plans to sell it. What is the anticipated sale price? This is an example of the future value of a dollar growing at 9 percent for ten years. The future value is

$$P_n = P_0(1 + i)^n,$$

$$P_{10} = \$10(1 + 0.09)^{10},$$

$$P_{10} = \$10(2.367) = \$23.67,$$

where 2.367 is the interest factor for the future sum of a dollar at 9 percent for ten years. The investor anticipates selling the stock for $23.67.

2. An investor sells a stock for $23.67 that was purchased ten years ago. A return of 9 percent was earned. What was the original cost of the investment? This is an example of the present value of a dollar discounted back at 9 percent for ten years. The initial value ten years ago, or the former price, was

$$P_{-n} = \frac{P_0}{(1 + i)^n},$$

$$P_{-10} = \frac{\$23.67}{(1 + 0.09)^{10}},$$

$$P_{-10} = \$23.67(0.4224) = \$10,$$

where 0.4224 is the interest factor for the present value of a dollar discounted at 9 percent for ten years. The investment cost $10 when it was purchased ten years ago.

The student should know that Questions 1 and 2 are two views of the same investment. In Question 1 the $10 investment grew to $23.67. In Question 2 the value at the time the stock was sold was brought back to the value of the initial investment. Another variation of this question would be as follows. If an investor bought stock for $10, held it for ten years, and then sold it for $23.67, what was the return on the

investment? In this case the values of the stock at the time it was bought and sold are known, but the rate of growth (the rate of return) is unknown. The answer can be found by using *either* the future value of a dollar table or the present value of a dollar table.

If the future value table is used, the question is at what rate (x) will $10 grow in ten years to equal $23.67. The answer is

$$P_0(1 + x)^n = P_n$$

$$\$10(1 + x)^{10} = \$23.67$$

$$(1 + x)^{10} = 2.367.$$

The interest factor is 2.367, which, according to the future value of a dollar table for ten years, makes the growth rate 9 percent. This interest factor is located under the vertical column for 9 percent and in the horizontal column for ten years.

If the present value table is used, the question asks what discount factor (x) at ten years will bring $23.67 back to $10. The answer is

$$P_0 = \frac{P_n}{(1 + x)^n}$$

$$\$10 = \frac{\$23.67}{(1 + x)^{10}}$$

$$0.4224 = \frac{1}{(1 + x)^{10}}.$$

The interest factor is 0.4224, which may be found in the present value of a dollar table for ten years in the 9 percent column (i.e., the growth rate is 9 percent). Thus, this problem may be solved by the proper application of either the future value or present value tables.

3. An employer offers to start a pension plan for a 45-year-old employee. The plan is to place $1,000 at the end of each year in a certificate of deposit that earns 12 percent annually. The employee wants to know how much will have accumulated by retirement at age 65.

This is an example of the future value of an ordinary annuity. The payment is $1,000 annually, and it will grow at 12 percent for 20 years. The fund will thus grow to

$$CS = I(1 + i)^0 + \cdots + I(1 + i)^{n-1}$$

$$= \$1,000(1 + 0.12)^0 + \cdots + \$1,000(1 + 0.12)^{19}$$

$$= \$1,000(72.052) = \$72,052,$$

where 72.052 is the interest factor for the future sum of an ordinary annuity of one dollar compounded annually at 12 percent for 20 years.

4. The same employer decides to place a lump sum in an investment that earns 12 percent and to draw on the funds to make the annual payments of $1,000. After 20 years all of the funds in the account will be depleted. How much must be deposited initially in the account?

This is an example of the present value of an ordinary annuity. The annuity is $1,000 per year at 12 percent for 20 years. Thus, the present value (i.e., the amount of the initial investment) is

$$PV = \sum_{t=1}^{n} \frac{I_1}{(1 + i)} + \cdots + \frac{I}{(1 + i)^n}$$

$$= \frac{\$1,000}{1 + 0.12} + \cdots + \frac{\$1,000}{(1 + 0.12)^{20}}$$

$$= \$1,000(7.469) = \$7,469,$$

where 7.469 is the interest factor for the present value of an ordinary annuity of one dollar at 12 percent for 20 years. Thus, the employer need invest only $7,469 in an account that earns 12 percent to meet the $1,000 annual pension payment for 20 years.

The student should notice the difference between the answers in the equations in Examples 3 and 4. In the equation in Example 3, a set of payments earns interest, and thus the future value is larger than just the sum of the 20 payments of $1,000. In the equation in Example 4, a future set of payments is valued in present terms. Since future payments are worth less today, the current value is less than the sum of the 20 payments of $1,000.

5. An investment pays $50 per year for ten years, after which $1,000 is returned to the investor. If the investor can earn 14 percent, how much should this investment cost? This question really contains two questions: What is the present value of an ordinary annuity of $50 at 14 percent for ten years, and what is the present value of $1,000 after ten years at 14 percent? The answer is

$$PV = \sum_{t=1}^{n} \frac{I_1}{(1 + i)^1} + \cdots + \frac{I_n}{(1 + i)^t} + \frac{P_n}{(1 + i)^t}$$

$$= \frac{\$50}{(1 + 0.14)} + \cdots + \frac{\$50}{(1 + 0.14)^{10}} + \frac{\$1,000}{(1 + 0.14)^{10}}$$

$$= \$50(5.216) + \$1,000(0.270) = \$530.80,$$

where 5.216 and 0.270 are the interest factors for the present value of an ordinary annuity of a dollar and the present value of a dollar, respectively, both at 14 percent for ten years.

This example illustrates that an investment may involve both a series of payments (the annuity component) and a lump sum payment. This particular investment is similar to a bond, the valuation of which is discussed in Chapter 10. Other examples of valuation and the computation of rates of return are given in Chapters 13 and 14, which consider investments in common stock.

6. A corporation's dividend has grown annually at the rate of 8 percent. If this rate is maintained and the current dividend is $5.40, what will the dividend be after ten years? This is a simple future value of a dollar problem. The dividend will grow to

$$P_n = P_0(1 + i)^n$$

$$= \$5.40(1 + 0.08)^{10}$$

$$= \$5.40(2.159) = \$11.66,$$

POINTS OF INTEREST
The Rule of 72

Do you want a short-cut method that answers the question, "How long will it take to double my money if I earn a specified percent?" The rule of 72 does just that! Divide 72 by the rate earned, and the answer is an approximation of how long it takes for the initial amount to double. For example, if the rate is 6 percent, funds double in $72/6 = 12$ years. At 10 percent, funds double in 7.2 years.

How accurate is this short cut? As may be seen from this table, the rule of 72 gives a rather accurate approximation of the time necessary to double one's funds at a specified rate of growth.

Rate (%)	Years for Funds to Double Using the Rule of 72	Actual Years for Funds to Double
5	14.4	14.3
7	10.3	10.2
10	7.2	7.3
12	6.0	6.1
16	4.5	4.7
20	3.6	3.8

where 2.159 is the interest factor for the future value of $1 at 8 percent for ten years. Although such a growth rate in future dividends may not be achieved, this problem illustrates how modest annual increments can result in a substantial increase in an investor's dividend income over a number of years.

The previous examples illustrate the use of interest tables. These problems could be done without such tables, but the amount of calculation would be substantial. The use of interest tables is obviously expeditious in solving any problems that are somewhat involved. Students with access to financial calculators may find these to be excellent substitutes for interest tables, since these models are programmed to include the tables. (The use of financial calculators is discussed later in this chapter.)

The importance of tables or electronic calculators

In addition to interest tables and electronic calculators, there is a simple method for determining how long it will take an amount to double. This method is the so-called "Rule of 72" presented in the "Points of Interest" section. While this technique is only an approximation, it permits you to determine easily how rapidly an amount is doubling.

NONANNUAL COMPOUNDING

The student should have noticed that in the previous examples compounding occurred only once a year. Since compounding can and often does occur more frequently, for example, **semiannually**, the equations that were presented earlier must be adjusted. This section extends the discussion of the compound value of a dollar to include compounding for time periods other than a year.

This discussion, however, is limited to the future value of a dollar. Similar adjustments must be made in the present value of a dollar or present value of an annuity when the funds are compounded more frequently than annually. These adjustments are not explained here but may be found in specialized texts concerning the time value of money.[1]

Modifications necessitated by nonannual compounding

Converting annual compounding to other time periods necessitates two adjustments in Equation 6.4. These adjustments are not particularly difficult. First, a year is divided into the same number of time periods that the funds are being compounded. For semiannual compounding a year consists of two time periods, whereas for quarterly compounding the year comprises four time periods.

After adjusting for the number of time periods, the individual adjusts the interest rate to find the rate per time period. This is done by dividing the stated interest rate by the number of time periods. If the interest rate is 8 percent compounded semiannually, then 8 percent is divided by 2, giving an interest rate of 4 percent earned in *each* time period. If the annual rate of interest is 8 percent compounded quarterly, the interest rate is 2 percent (8% ÷ 4) in each of the four time periods.

These adjustments may be expressed in more formal terms by modifying Equation 6.4 as follows:

(6.9)
$$P_0\left(1 + \frac{i}{c}\right)^{n \times c} = P_n.$$

The only new symbol is c, which represents the frequency of compounding. The interest rate (i) is divided by the frequency of compounding (c) to determine the interest rate in each period. The number of years (n) is multiplied by the frequency of compounding to determine the number of time periods.

The use of annual interest tables to solve nonannual compounding problems

The application of this equation may be illustrated in a simple example. An individual invests $100 in an asset that pays 8 percent compounded quarterly. What will the future value of this asset be after five years, that is, $100 will grow to what amount after five years if it is compounded quarterly at 8 percent? Algebraically, this is

$$P_5 = P_0 \left(1 + \frac{i}{c}\right)^{n \times c}$$

$$= \$100\left(1 + \frac{0.08}{4}\right)^{5 \times 4}$$

$$= \$100 \, (1 + 0.02)^{20}.$$

In this formulation the investor is earning 2 percent for 20 time periods. To solve this equation, the interest factor for the future value of a dollar at 2 percent for 20 years (1.486) is multiplied by $100. Thus, the future value is

$$P_5 = 100 \, (1.486) = \$148.60.$$

The difference between compounding annually and compounding more frequently can be seen by comparing this problem with a problem in which the values are identical except that the interest is compounded annually. The question is, then,

---

[1] See, for instance, Gary Clayton and Christopher Spivey, *The Time Value of Money* (Philadelphia: W. B. Saunders, 1978).

to what amount will \$100 grow after five years at 8 percent compounded annually? The answer is

$$P_5 = \$100 \, (1 + 0.08)^5$$

$$= \$100 \, (1.469)$$

$$= \$146.90.$$

This sum, \$146.90, is less than the amount that was earned when the funds were compounded quarterly, which suggests the general conclusion that the more frequently interest is compounded, the greater will be the future amount.

The discussion throughout this text is generally limited to annual compounding. There is, however, one important exception: the valuation of bonds. Bonds pay interest semiannually, and this affects their value. Therefore, semiannual compounding is incorporated in the bond valuation model that is presented in Chapter 10.

PRESENT VALUE AND SECURITY VALUATION

The valuation of assets is a major theme of this text. Investors must be able to analyze securities to determine their value. This valuation requires forecasting future gains and discounting them back to the present. The present value of an investment, then, is related to future benefits, in the form of either future income or capital appreciation. For example, stocks are purchased for their *future* dividends and potential capital gains but *not* for their previous dividends and price performance. Bonds are purchased for *future* income. Real estate is bought for the *future* use of the property and for the potential price appreciation. The concept of discounting future earnings back to the present applies to all investments: It is the future and not the past that matters. The past is relevant only to the extent that it may be used to predict the future.

Valuation is an application of present value

Some types of analysis (including the technical approach to selecting investments that is discussed in Chapter 18) use the past in the belief that it forecasts the future. Technical analysts employ such information as the past price movements of a stock to determine the most profitable times to buy and sell a security. However, most of the analytical methods that are discussed in this text use some form of discounting in the process of valuing the assets. Prices are the present value of anticipated future cash flows, such as dividends.

Subsequent chapters will discuss a variety of assets and the means for analyzing and valuing them. For debt, the current price is related to the series of interest payments and the repayment of the principal, both of which are discounted at the current market interest rate. The current price of a stock is related to the firm's future earnings and its investment opportunities. Cash flows are discounted back to the present at the appropriate discount factor. For these reasons it is important that the reader start in this introductory chapter to view current prices as the present value of future cash flows. The various features of the different investments, including stocks and bonds, will be discussed, and their prices will be analyzed in terms of present value. If the reader does not understand the material on the time value of money presented in this chapter, the analytical sections of subsequent chapters may be incomprehensible.

Future earnings are discounted to the present

Exhibit 6.3
**Face of a Financial
Calculator**

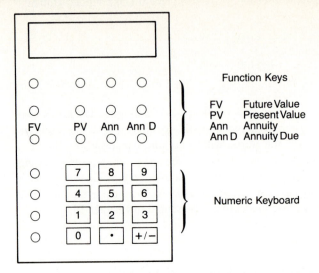

Function Keys

FV   Future Value
PV   Present Value
Ann   Annuity
Ann D   Annuity Due

Numeric Keyboard

FINANCIAL CALCULATORS

Once the student has mastered the concepts of future and present value and understands how the amounts are determined, the tedium associated with the actual calculations may be reduced through the use of electronic calculators programmed to solve financial problems. Such calculators permit the student to find future value and present value without using interest tables. Exhibit 6.3 displays the face of such a calculator, which has a numeric keyboard and several function keys that indicate such calculations as present and future value.

While financial calculators certainly ease the burden of the arithmetic, they can not set up the problems to be solved. The student still must determine if the problem concerns future value or present value and whether the problem deals with a lump sum or an annuity. Since failure to set up the problem correctly will only lead to incorrect results, it is imperative that the student be able to determine what is being asked and which of the various cases apply to the individual problem.

SUMMARY

Money has time value. A dollar to be received in the future is worth less than a dollar received today. People will forgo current consumption only if future growth in their funds is possible. Invested funds earn interest, and the interest in turn earns more interest—a process called compounding. The longer funds compound and the higher the rate at which they compound, the greater will be the final amount in the future.

Discounting, the opposite of compounding, determines the present value of funds to be received in the future. The present value of a future sum depends on how far

into the future the funds are to be received and on the discount rate. The further into future or the higher the discount factor, the lower will be the present value of the sum.

Compounding and discounting may apply to a single payment (lump sum) or to a series of payments. If the payments are equal, the series is called an annuity. When the payments start at the beginning of each time period, it is called an annuity due; when the payments are made at the end of each time period, the series is called an ordinary annuity.

Although an investment is made in the present, returns are earned in the future. These returns (e.g., the future flows of interest and dividends) must be discounted by the appropriate discount factor to determine the investment's present value. It is this process of discounting by which an investment's value is determined. As is developed throughout this text, valuation of assets is a crucial step in the selection of assets to acquire and hold in an investor's portfolio.

Terms to Remember

Compounding
Present value
Discounting
Annuity
Future sum of an annuity

Annuity due
Ordinary annuity
Present value of an annuity
Semiannual compounding

Questions

1. What is the difference between a lump sum payment and an annuity? Are all series of payments annuities?

2. What is the difference between compounding (the determination of future value) and discounting (the determination of present value)?

3. For a given interest rate, what happens to the numerical value of the interest factor as time increases for the
   a. future value of a dollar;
   b. future value of an annuity;
   c. present value of a dollar;
   d. present value of an annuity?

4. For a given time period, what happens to the numerical value of the interest factor as the interest rate increases for the
   a. future value of a dollar;
   b. future value of an annuity;
   c. present value of a dollar;
   d. present value of an annuity?

5. What does the phrase "discounting the future at a high rate" imply?

6. As is explained in subsequent chapters, increases in interest rates cause the value of assets to decline. Why would you expect this relationship?

Problems

1. An investor bought a stock ten years ago for $20 and sold it today for $35. What is the annual rate of return on the investment?

2. A saver places $1,000 in a certificate of deposit that matures after six years and that each year pays 7 percent interest, which is compounded annually until the certificate matures.

   a. How much interest will the saver earn if the interest is left to accumulate?

   b. How much interest will the saver earn if the interest is withdrawn each year?

3. At the end of each year a self-employed person deposits $1,500 in a Keogh retirement account that earns 12 percent annually.

   a. How much will be in the account when the individual retires at the age of 65 if the savings program starts when the person is age 45?

   b. How much additional money will be in the account if the saver defers retirement until age 70 and continues the annual contributions?

   c. How much additional money will be in the account if the saver discontinues the contributions but does not retire until the age of 70?

4. A saver wants $100,000 after ten years and believes that it is possible to earn an annual rate of 10 percent on invested funds.

   a. What amount must be invested each year to accumulate $100,000 if (1) the payments are made at the beginning of each year or (2) if they are made at the end of each year?

   b. How much must be invested annually if the expected yield is only 7 percent?

5. An investment offers $10,000 per year for 20 years. If an investor can earn 10 percent annually on other investments, what is the current value of this investment? If its current price is $120,000, should the investor buy it?

6. The price of an excellent quality Oriental rug rose from $1,500 to $3,650 in just six years. What is the annual rate of increase in the price?

7. Today graduating seniors may earn $18,000 each year. If the annual rate of inflation is 8 percent, what must these graduates earn after 20 years to maintain their current purchasing power? If the rate of inflation rises to 12 percent, will they be maintaining their standard of living if they earn $200,000 after 20 years?

8. A person who is retiring at the age of 65 and who has $200,000 wants to leave an estate of at least $30,000. How much can the individual draw annually on the $200,000 (starting at the end of the year) if the funds earn 10 percent and the person's life expectancy is 85 years?

9. A 40-year-old individual establishes an IRA account with a commercial bank. The account is expected to pay 12 percent annually, and deposits will be $2,000 annually at the beginning of each year. Initially the saver expects to start drawing on the account at age 60.

   a. How much will be in the account when the saver is age 60?

   b. If this investor found a riskier investment that offered 14 percent, how much in additional funds would be earned?

   c. The investor selects the 12 percent investment and retires at the age of 60. How much can be drawn from the account at the beginning of each year if life expectancy is 85 and the funds continue to earn 12 percent?

10. You are offered $900 five years from now or $150 at the end of each year for the next five years. If you can earn 6 percent on your funds, which offer will you accept? If you can earn 14 percent on your funds, which offer will you accept? Why are your answers different?

11. A racehorse may net $3,000,000 a year for three years. What is the maximum price you should pay for the horse if you require a 12 percent return on your funds?

12. The following questions illustrate nonannual compounding.

   a. $100 is placed in an account that pays 12 percent. How much will be in the account after one year if interest is compounded annually, semiannually, or monthly?

   b. $100 is to be received after one year. What is the present value of this amount if you can earn 12 percent compounded annually, semiannually, or monthly?

Suggested Readings

Cissell, Robert, Helen Cissell, and David Flaspohler. *Mathematics of Finance*. 6th ed. Boston: Houghton Mifflin, 1982.
This is a basic text that explains many of the variations on the four essential cases presented in this chapter.

Clayton, Gary, and Christopher B. Spivey. *The Time Value of Money*. Philadelphia: W. B. Saunders, 1978.
This is a primer illustrating many problems that can be solved by the basic time value of money tables.

Access to pocket calculators has greatly facilitated time value calculations. To increase your ability to use these calculators, consult:

Smith, Jon M. *Financial Analysis and Business Decisions on the Pocket Calculator*. New York: John Wiley, 1976.

For a reference book on time value of money calculations that includes loan amortization tables and mortgage balance tables, acquire:

Charles J. Woelfel. *The Desktop Guide to Money, Time, Interest and Yields*. Chicago: Probus Publishing, 1986.

7

Financial Statements

LEARNING OBJECTIVES

After completing this chapter you should be able to

1. Construct a list of current assets and current liabilities.
2. Distinguish between assets, liabilities, equity, book value, and net worth.
3. Differentiate the time periods covered by the income statement and the balance sheet.
4. Determine if receipts, income, profits, and cash are the same.
5. Define working capital.
6. Isolate the additional information that is learned from the statement of changes in financial position.
7. Identify several weaknesses in accounting data.

Many investors find financial statements unintelligible or dull or both. However, these statements can be a very important source of information concerning a firm's financial position. The firm's profits or losses, its assets and liabilities, and its sources of funds used to acquire its assets are all well documented in its financial statements.

While the investor need not understand all the subtleties concerning the construction of financial statements, a general knowledge of their content can be very helpful in the analysis of a firm and its securities. Much financial analysis employs the information reported on these statements. Hence, the investor should understand the content of financial statements in order to understand the analysis that employs accounting data.

This chapter covers the four basic financial statements: the balance sheet, the income statement, the statement of retained earnings, and the statement of changes in financial position. Unfortunately, it is not within the scope of this text to explain the subtleties and theories of accounting that are relevant to the construction of financial statements. This chapter does present the basic components of financial statements and gives a foundation for understanding them. The chapter is primarily descriptive and will concentrate on the com-

pone... ...tion of this information to investment decision maki... ...rs.

GEN... ...RINCIPLES

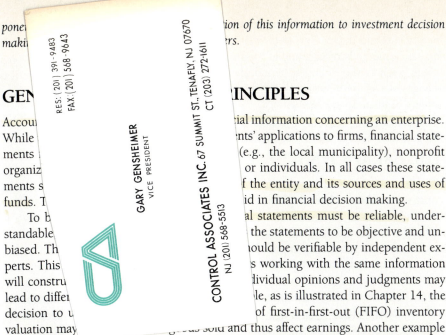

Accou... ...ial information concerning an enterprise. While ... ...nts' applications to firms, financial statements ... ...(e.g., the local municipality), nonprofit organiz... ...or individuals. In all cases these statements s... ...f the entity and its sources and uses of funds. T... ...id in financial decision making.

To b... ...al statements must be reliable, understandable ... ...the statements to be objective and unbiased. Th... ...ould be verifiable by independent experts. This... ...s working with the same information will constru... ...dividual opinions and judgments may lead to diffe... ...le, as is illustrated in Chapter 14, the decision to u... ...of first-in-first-out (FIFO) inventory valuation may ... ...oods sold and thus affect earnings. Another example that involves the accountant's judgment is the allowance for doubtful accounts receivable. Two accountants may establish differing amounts that will affect the firm's financial statements. However, it should not be concluded that two accountants will construct widely different statements; the amount of differentiation, if any, will probably be modest.

Financial statements should be
1. reliable

Accountants' second goal is that financial statements be understandable. The statement should be presented in an orderly manner and be readable by laypersons as well as professionals. Investors and other individuals who may use financial statements need not know all the principles used to construct them. However, a reasonably intelligent individual should be able to read a firm's financial statements and have some idea of the firm's profitability, its sources of funds, and those funds' uses.

2. understandable

Comparability requires that one set of financial statements can be compared with other sets of the same financial statements constructed over different accounting periods. The principles used to construct one year's statements should be used for subsequent years. If the principles being applied are changed, the previous years' statements should be restated. If the firm's operations change, the financial statements should also reflect these changes. If, for example, the firm discontinues part of its operations, its sales, expenses, and profits for previous years should be restated. If this adjustment is not made, the users of the financial statements will be unable to compare the firm's financial condition and performance over a period of time for its continuing operations.

3. comparable

To increase the objectivity of financial statements, a general framework for accounting and financial reports has been established by the Financial Accounting Standards Board (FASB). Accounting principles that are "generally accepted" also receive the support of the American Institute of Certified Public Accounts and the Securities and Exchange Commission. While these bodies establish the principles under which financial statements are constructed, it should not be concluded that the principles are static. Their conceptual framework changes over time with changes in the business

Generally accepted principles

environment and the needs of the statements' users. For example, increases in foreign investments and fluctuations in the value of foreign currencies have generated a need for better methods of accounting for these foreign investments. This problem plus others, such as the extended period of inflation during the 1970s, have resulted in changes in accounting principles as the profession seeks to improve the informational content of financial statements.

THE BALANCE SHEET

What have the owners invested in a firm? One method of answering this question is to construct a **balance sheet** that enumerates what a business owns (i.e., its **assets**) and what it owes (i.e., its **liabilities**) and to calculate the difference. This difference is called the **book value** or the **equity** that the stockholders have in the firm.

Assets

Exhibit 7.1 presents a simplified balance sheet for a hypothetical firm, EEM, Inc. For a publicly held firm, this balance sheet (and the other financial statements presented later in this chapter) would be published in the firm's annual report. This example combines the financial information for all the firm's subsidiaries and hence is called a **consolidated balance sheet**. The assets are divided into three groups: (1) **current assets**, which are expected to be used and converted into cash within a relatively short period of time, (2) **long-term assets**, which are those assets with a life span exceeding a year, and (3) **investments**. The liabilities and stockholders' equity are presented next, frequently on the right-hand side of the balance sheet across from the assets. While it is not necessary for a balance sheet to be arranged in this manner, many firms use this general form because it clearly enumerates the assets, liabilities, and equity of the firm.

While current assets are listed in order of liquidity (cash, accounts receivable, and then inventory), the following discussion considers these assets in reverse order. Inventory must be first sold, and then the firm obtains either an account receivable or cash.

Inventory

Firms must have goods or services or both to sell. These goods are the firm's **inventory**. Not all inventory is ready for sale. Some of the goods may be unfinished ("goods in process"), and there may also be inventories of raw materials. According to the EEM balance sheet, total inventory amounted to $315,000 in 19x1. The balance sheet does not subdivide the inventory into finished goods, work in process, and raw materials. The financial analyst should remember that only finished items are available for sale. Considerable time and cost may be involved in processing raw materials into finished goods. Therefore, much of a firm's inventory may not be salable and cannot be readily converted into cash.[1]

Accounts receivable

When goods or services are sold, the firm receives either cash or a promise of payment in the future. A credit sale generates an **account receivable**, which represents money that is due to the firm. EEM, Inc., had $510,000 in receivables; this is a net figure obtained by subtracting the doubtful accounts ($30,000) from the total amount of receivables. Since a firm does not always obtain payment from all of its

---

[1] Many balance sheets sent to stockholders present only aggregate numbers. Presumably management would have access to disaggregated figures and thus would know the amount of inventory that is finished goods and the amount that is raw materials.

	December 31		
	19x1	**19x0**	
Assets			Exhibit 7.1
Current assets			EEM, Inc.
Cash and cash equivalents	$ 200,000	$ 335,000	Consolidated Balance Sheet
Accounts receivable, less allowance for doubtful accounts (19x1, $30,000; 19x0, $20,000)	510,000	380,000	(for the time period ending December 31, 19x1 and 19x0)
Inventory	315,000	180,000	
Total current assets	$1,025,000	$ 895,000	
Investments	75,000	95,000	
Property, plant, and equipment			
Land	130,000	130,000	
Buildings	320,000	300,000	
Machinery and equipment	735,000	682,000	
	$1,185,000	$1,112,000	
Less accumulated depreciation	271,000	258,000	
Net property, plant, and equipment	$ 914,000	$ 854,000	
	$2,014,000	$1,844,000	
Liabilities			
Current liabilities			
Current maturities of long-term debt	$ 10,000	$ 10,000	
Accounts payable and accrued liabilities	342,000	318,000	
Notes payable to bank	38,000	17,000	
Taxes due	33,000	28,000	
Total current liabilities	$ 423,000	$ 373,000	
Long-term debt	100,000	110,000	
Total liabilities	$ 523,000	$ 483,000	
Shareholders' equity			
Common stock ($0.25 par value; 150,000 shares authorized; shares outstanding: 100,000 in 19x1; 90,000 in 19x0)	25,000	22,500	
Additional paid-in capital	75,000	72,500	
Retained earnings	1,391,000	1,266,000	
Total shareholders' equity	$1,491,000	$1,361,000	
	$2,014,000	$1,844,000	

accounts receivable, it is necessary to make an allowance for these "doubtful accounts." Thus, only the net realizable figure is included in the tabulation of the firm's assets.

A cash sale generates the asset " cash" for the firm. Since holding cash will earn nothing, some of it may be invested in short-term money instruments, such as U.S. Treasury bills. Cash and short-term money instruments may be combined under a classification called "cash and cash equivalents." For EEM, cash and marketable securities total $200,000. This money is available to meet the firm's immediate financial obligations.

Cash and cash equivalents

Cash and cash equivalents, accounts receivable, and inventory are the major short-term assets. In 19x1 EEM's total current assets amounted to $1,025,000. These short-term assets flow through the firm during its fiscal year and are used to meet its financial obligations that have to be paid during the year. The total value and the na-

Long-term assets

ture of these assets are very important in determining the firm's ability to meet its current obligations.

Long-term assets, which are used for many years, include the firm's property, plant, and equipment. The firm's employees utilize these long-term assets in conjunction with the current assets to create the products or services the company offers for sale. The type and quantity of long-term assets that a company uses vary with the industry. Some industries, such as utilities and transportation, require numerous plants and extensive equipment. Firms in these industries must have substantial investments in long-term assets to operate. Not all companies choose to own these assets; instead, they may rent them, which is called leasing. Regardless of whether the firm leases or owns these assets, it must have the use of the long-term assets to produce the company's output.

In 19x1 EEM, Inc. had $914,000 invested in long-term assets. The balance sheet indicates that the firm initially invested $1,055,000 in buildings and equipment. These assets had depreciated by $271,000 and were currently being carried on the books at $784,000 ($914,000 minus the value of the land). **Depreciation** is important because it is the process of allocating the cost of the plant and equipment over a period of time. Thus, the book value of long-term assets is reduced with time as the assets are used by the firm.

EEM owned land worth $130,000. Land does not depreciate with use, and hence the book value of the land is usually the purchase price unless the value of the land has been restated to indicate a price change. For example, the value of the land may rise as a result of inflation, in which case the accountants could increase the land's value on the books. However, because such revaluations rarely occur, many firms have **hidden assets** such as land whose market value is understated.

Other assets

The remaining entry on the asset side of the balance sheet is investments ($75,000 in 19x1 and $95,000 in 19x0). These include securities such as stock in other companies. Even though such stock can be sold and converted into cash, it may be considered separately from the firm's current assets. For example, if the securities were purchased with the intention of holding them for several years as an investment, they would be placed in a separate category on the balance sheet.[2]

The total assets owned by EEM, Inc. are the sum of the short-term assets ($1,025,000), the long-term assets ($914,000), and the investments ($75,000). These assets are financed by the claims of creditors and stockholders—the firm's liabilities and equity, which are presented on the other side of the balance sheet.

Short-term liabilities

The firm's liabilities are divided into two groups: **current liabilities,** which must be paid during the fiscal year, and **long-term liabilities,** which are due after the fiscal year. Current liabilities are primarily accounts payable and short-term loans. Just as the firm may sell goods on credit, it may also purchase goods and raw materials on credit. This trade credit is short term and is retired as goods are produced and sold. In the balance sheet for EEM, Inc., accounts payable ($342,000 in 19x1) also includes wages and salaries that have been earned but not paid out. (Many balance sheets have a separate entry called accrued liabilities to cover these current liabilities.) In addition to accounts payable, the firm has other short-term debt that must be paid during the

[2] Such investments can be substantial. For example, Teledyne reported in its *1985 Annual Report* that it owned 26 percent of Brockway, Inc., 54 percent of Curtiss-Wright Corp., 28 percent of Kidde, Inc., 26 percent of Litton Industries, and 21 percent of Reichold Chemical. The aggregate market value of these securities exceeded $1 billion.

fiscal year. This includes short-term notes for funds that the company has borrowed from commercial banks or other lending institutions ($38,000 in 19x1) and that portion of its long-term debt that must be retired this year ($10,000). The remaining current obligation is the taxes that must be paid during the year ($33,000).

Long-term debt obligations must be retired at some time after the current fiscal year. Such obligations, which may include outstanding bonds and mortgages on real property, represent part of the permanent financing of the firm because these funds are committed to financing the business for a long time. Short-term liabilities cannot be considered part of the firm's permanent financing because these liabilities must be paid within a relatively short time period. For EEM, Inc., the long-term liabilities consisted solely of long-term debt ($100,000 in 19x1). On other financial statements, a breakdown of the various debt issues (if the debt consists of more than one issue) may be given in a footnote that appears after the body of the financial statement.

Long-term liabilities

On most balance sheets, the stockholders' equity is listed after the liabilities. There are three essential entries: the stock outstanding, the additional paid-in capital, and the earnings that have been retained. The stock outstanding shows the various types of stock that have been issued and their quantities. EEM, Inc. had only one issue—common stock. Many firms, however, also have preferred stock.

Equity

When the term *book value* is used, it generally indicates the net worth of the common stock only. This book value of common stock is the sum of the common stock, the additional paid-in capital, and the **retained earnings**. Retained earnings, like common stock and paid-in capital, represent an investment in the firm by common stockholders. Since these stockholders would receive the earnings if they were distributed, retained earnings are part of the stockholders' contribution to the firm's financing. For EEM, Inc., the sum of the stock outstanding, additional paid-in capital, and retained earnings was $1,491,000 in 19x1. This sum is the book value of the firm and represents the common stockholders' investment in the firm.

Book value

The individual investor is primarily concerned with the value of a share of stock. To obtain the book value per share, the total equity available to the common stock is divided by the number of shares outstanding. For EEM, Inc., the per-share book value in 19x1 was $14.91 ($1,491,000/100,000). This amount is the accounting value of each of the 100,000 common shares held by the firm's many stockholders.

If EEM had ceased operations, sold its assets, and paid off its liabilities, the owners would have received their equity in the firm. If the assets and the liabilities were accurately measured by the dollar values on the balance sheet, then the book value is the amount the owners would have received in the liquidation. However, as is discussed subsequently, the book value may not be an accurate measure of the value of the firm.

Since a balance sheet presents both liabilities and equity, it gives an indication of the firm's financial position. The balance sheet for EEM, Inc. indicates that the firm owned assets valued at $2,014,000 and had liabilities of $523,000 and equity of $1,491,000. The sum of the liabilities and equity must equal the sum of all the assets, for it is the liabilities and equity that finance the assets. The assets could not be acquired if creditors and owners did not provide the funds. For EEM, Inc., the balance sheet indicates that liabilities finance 26 percent ($523,000/$2,014,000) and that equity finances 74 percent ($1,491,000/$2,014,000) of the total assets. Thus, the balance sheet indicates the proportion of the assets financed with debt and the proportion financed with equity.

Balance sheet is constructed at a given time

Two additional points need to be made about balance sheets. First, a balance sheet is constructed at the end of a fiscal period (e.g., a year) and indicates the value of the assets and liabilities, as well as the net worth, at that particular time. Since financial transactions occur continuously, the information contained in a balance sheet may become rapidly outdated. Second, the values assigned to the assets need not mirror their market value but may be overstated or understated. For example, the firm owns accounts receivable, and since not all of them will be paid, the value of the firm's accounts receivable may be overstated. As was explained earlier, while the firm does allow for these potential losses in an effort to make the balance sheet entries more accurate, they may be insufficient, and thus the value of the assets will be overstated. Conversely, the value of other assets may be understated. For example, the land on which the plant is built may have increased in value but may continue to be carried on the company's books at its cost.

Book value is not market value

For the book value of the firm to be a true indication of its worth, all assets on the balance sheet should be valued at their market prices; however, this practice is not necessarily followed. Accountants suggest that assets be valued conservatively (1) at the cost of the asset, or (2) at its market value, depending on which is less. Such conservatism is prudent but may result in assets having hidden or understated value if their appreciation is not recognized. Because of these accounting methods, the equity or net worth of a firm may not be a good measure of its value.

THE INCOME STATEMENT

The **income statement** tells investors how much accounting income the company has earned during a period of time (e.g., its fiscal year). It is a summary of revenues and expenses and hence indicates the firm's accounting profits or losses. It is not, however, a summary of cash receipts and disbursements.

The determination of profit or loss

Exhibit 7.2 is the 19x1 income statement for EEM, Inc. It gives earnings for both 19x1 and 19x0 to facilitate a year-to-year comparison. The statement starts with a summary of the firm's sources of revenues: sales of $10,375,000. Next follows a summary of the cost of goods sold ($9,234,000). The difference between the sales and the

---

Exhibit 7.2
Consolidated Income
Statement for EEM, Inc.
and Subsidiaries
(for the years ending
December 31, 19x1 and
19x0)

	19x1	19x0
Sales	$10,375,000	$9,872,000
Cost of goods sold	9,234,000	8,948,000
Gross profit	$ 1,141,000	$ 924,000
Selling and administrative expense	428,000	311,000
Operating profit	$ 713,000	$ 613,000
Other income	33,000	25,000
Income before interest and taxes	$ 746,000	$ 638,000
Interest expense	52,000	48,000
Taxes	310,000	275,000
Net income	$ 384,000	$ 315,000
Earnings per share	$3.84	$3.50

cost of goods sold is the gross profit ($1,141,000). Then the selling and administrative expenses are subtracted to determine the operating income ($713,000). If the firm has other sources of income (e.g., interest or dividends received), they are added to the operating income to determine the company's total income before interest and taxes. EEM, Inc. had $33,000 in other income, so this is added to the operating profit to give income before interest expense and taxes of $746,000. To determine net profits, interest expense ($52,000) and taxes ($310,000) must be subtracted from the $746,000, which in this case yields net income of $384,000.

Stockholders are generally not concerned with total earnings but with **earnings per share (EPS).** The bottom line of the income statement shows the earnings per share (EPS = $3.84), which is net income divided by the number of shares outstanding. This $3.84 is the amount of earnings available to each share of common stock.

Earnings per share

When the firm earns profits, management must decide what to do with these earnings. There are two choices: (1) to pay out some or all of these profits to stockholders in the form of cash dividends or (2) to retain the earnings. The retained earnings on the balance sheet are the sum of all the firm's profits that have accumulated but have not been paid out in dividends during the company's life. These retained earnings are used to finance the purchase of assets or to retire debt.

Earnings are retained or distributed

The income statement merely summarizes corporate revenues and expenses during the fiscal year and indicates whether the firm produced a net profit or loss. To learn how the earnings were employed and if there were changes in the firm's sources of financing during the fiscal year, it is necessary to consult the statement of retained earnings and the statement of changes in financial position.

THE STATEMENT OF RETAINED EARNINGS

The **statement of retained earnings** indicates the company's current earnings and adds this amount to its previously retained earnings. It then shows the division of these earnings between those distributed to stockholders and those retained to finance additional assets or to retire debt. The statement of retained earnings for EEM is illustrated in Exhibit 7.3.

The statement indicates that EEM, Inc. had previously retained $1,266,000 of its earnings. In 19x1, the corporation earned $384,000 and distributed cash dividends of $259,000. Thus, the firm retained $125,000 of its earnings and entered the 19x2 fiscal year with retained earnings of $1,391,000. This sum represents the accumulation of earnings over the life of EEM, Inc. These retained earnings are part of the

	19x1	19x0
Retained earnings at beginning of year	$1,266,000	$1,196,000
Net income	384,000	315,000
	$1,650,000	$1,511,000
Less cash dividends	259,000	245,000
Balance at end of the year	$1,391,000	$1,266,000

Exhibit 7.3
Consolidated Statement of Retained Earnings for EEM, Inc. and Subsidiaries (for the years ending December 31, 19x1 and 19x0)

stockholders' investment in the firm because they represent claims on the firm's assets. Therefore, this amount must also appear in the equity section of the corporation's 19x1 balance sheet. If the student reexamines Exhibit 7.1, the accumulated retained earnings of $1,391,000 are, in fact, given.

Retained earnings are not cash

There is a common misconception that if a company has retained earnings, it has cash and can pay cash dividends. Retained earnings are not cash. After the income has been earned and retained, it is used to purchase income-earning assets or to retire outstanding debt. Thus, the income is used to increase the firm's future profitability and is not held as cash.

THE STATEMENT OF CHANGES IN FINANCIAL POSITION

Link between the income statement and the balance sheet

The balance sheet shows the book value of a firm's assets and liabilities at a given time. The income statement summarizes the revenues and expenses and shows the profits or losses for the accounting period. The statement of retained earnings reveals whether the earnings were distributed or retained. None of these statements indicates how the income was used or what other sources of financing the firm acquired during the accounting period. The **statement of changes in financial position** is the link between the income statement and the balance sheet, because it identifies how funds were acquired and how they were used.

The importance of this statement is well recognized. Publicly held firms are required by the Securities and Exchange Commission to include it in their annual reports. The student should note that the statement is sometimes called by other names, such as the funds statement or the statement of sources and uses. However, the accounting profession recommends that it be called the statement of changes in financial position because it reveals the firm's sources of funds and their subsequent use in order to show changes in its financial position.

A company obtains funds from a variety of sources and puts them to use in a variety of ways. The term *funds* is not a synonym for *cash*. It is a broad term encompassing all of the sources available for financing a firm's assets. Some of these sources of funds are long-term, such as the sale of bonds and stocks, while others are short-term, such as accounts payable.[3] Correspondingly, some of the uses of these funds are long-term, including the purchase of plant and equipment, whereas others are short-term, including accounts receivable.[4] The statement of changes in financial position emphasizes the firm's current position (i.e., the management of short-term assets and liabilities).[5]

Working capital

This statement isolates changes in working capital. **Working capital** comprises the firm's current assets, and net working capital is the difference between the values of current assets and current liabilities. The bottom line of the statement indicates any

---

[3] An increase in an account payable is a source of funds because the company has the use of an asset, such as cash, until the account is paid.

[4] An increase in an account receivable is a use of funds because someone must provide the money to cover the account until the money is collected.

[5] Investors should analyze the appropriateness of the sources for particular uses. For example, short-term funds should not be used to acquire long-term assets.

Sources of Working Capital:	19x1
Income from operations	$ 384,000
Items not affecting working capital: depreciation	13,000
Working capital provided by operations	$ 397,000
Issuance of new stock	5,000
Issuance of long-term debt	0
Decrease in investments	20,000
Total sources	$ 422,000

Uses of Working Capital:	
Cash dividends	$ 259,000
Purchase of property, plant, and equipment	73,000
Decrease in long-term debt	10,000
Total uses	$ 342,000
Net change in working capital	$ 80,000

Changes in Working Capital:	
Increases (decreases) in current assets:	
Cash and cash equivalents	$(135,000)
Notes and accounts receivable	130,000
Inventory	135,000
	$ 130,000
(Increases) decreases in current liabilities:	
Current maturity of long-term debt	$ 0
Accounts payable and accrued liabilities	24,000
Notes payable	21,000
Taxes	5,000
	$ 50,000
Net increase (decrease) in working capital	$ 80,000

Exhibit 7.4
Consolidated Statement of Changes in Financial Position for EEM, Inc. (for the period ending December 31, 19x1)

change in the firm's working capital. Such changes can be very important in analyzing a firm's capacity to meet its financial obligations as they become due. An increase in the amount of net working capital shows that the firm has increased its current assets relative to its current liabilities: It has more current assets flowing through the firm relative to its current liabilities. This should increase its capacity to meet these obligations as they become due.

Sources of working capital

The statement of changes in financial position starts by listing all the sources of working capital. These are the firm's income and the funds generated by the sale of long-term assets, long-term borrowing, and the sale of new securities. Next listed are all of the uses of working capital, including the distribution of cash dividends, the purchase of long-term assets, the repayment of long-term debt, and the repurchase of outstanding stock. The difference between the amount obtained from these sources and the amount spent on the uses of these funds, then, is the change in working capital.

The statement of changes in financial position for EEM is shown in Exhibit 7.4. At the top of the statement the firm's sources of working capital are given. The working capital provided by operations is listed first. This is primarily income from operations and depreciation. Although it is obvious that income is a source of capital, deprecia-

tion is not so obvious. Depreciation is a noncash expense that allocates the cost of an asset over its useful life. Since it is a noncash expense, the firm has those funds in its possession and management can use them as it sees fit. To adjust for this depreciation expense, accountants add the depreciation charges to the income from operations to obtain the total working capital from operations. Operations provided $397,000 to working capital for EEM, Inc. in 19x1. This consisted of income ($384,000) and depreciation ($13,000).

The sources of working capital other than operations are listed next. For EEM these include $5,000 from issuance of new stock, $0 from new long-term debt, and $20,000 from the reduction in investments. The total of these nonoperating sources of working capital is $25,000, which yields $422,000 in new working capital from all sources.

Uses of working capital

Working capital was used by EEM primarily to pay cash dividends ($259,000) and to purchase property, plant, and equipment ($73,000). The summation of all of the uses of working capital is $342,000; thus there is a net change in working capital of $80,000 ($422,000 − $342,000).

The final section of the statement of changes in financial position presents changes in specific current assets and current liabilities. The current assets of EEM increased by $130,000. This sum is composed of increases in receivables of $130,000 and in inventory of $135,000, and a decrease in cash and cash equivalents of $135,000. Current liabilities rose by $50,000, which primarily reflects the increase in accounts payable and notes payable. Current assets increased by more than current liabilities, which again indicates that working capital rose (i.e., by $80,000). This is, of course, the same information that was presented earlier in the statement. This last set of entries shows specifically which current assets and current liabilities changed and, in this case, which current assets absorbed the increase in working capital.

By analyzing this statement of changes in financial position, it becomes clear that EEM, Inc. incurred fewer additional current liabilities than current assets. These current assets then had to be financed by some other source (e.g., long-term debt or equity). In this case the additions to current assets were financed by the increase in retained earnings.

THE ROLE OF THE AUDITOR

Accounts must be examined

Accounting statements of publicly held firms must be audited by an independent certified public accountant (CPA). These audits, which are official examinations of accounts, must be held annually. After conducting the audit, the CPA issues an **auditor's opinion** that attests to the reasonableness of the financial statements and their conformity with generally accepted accounting principles. This auditor's opinion must be included in the firm's annual report for publicly held firms.

The auditor's opinion

Exhibit 7.5 presents the auditor's opinion that was published in the 1985 CBS Annual Report. It is a brief document; the first paragraph covers the scope of the auditor's examination, and the second paragraph gives the opinion. On occasion, the evaluation may include a discussion of special factors that qualify the auditor's opinion concerning specific details of the financial statements.

Importance to the investor

Since audits are held by independent accountants, investors can have confidence in the financial statements. The accountants' objectivity enhances their credibility.

**Report of Independent
Certified Public Accountants**

Exhibit 7.5
An Auditor's Opinion

To the Shareholders of CBS Inc.:

We have examined the consolidated balance sheets of CBS Inc. and subsidiaries as of December 31, 1985, 1984 and 1983, and the related consolidated statements of income, retained earnings, additional paid-in capital and changes in financial position for the years then ended. Our examinations were made in accordance with generally accepted auditing standards and, accordingly, included such tests of the accounting records and such other auditing procedures as we considered necessary in the circumstances.

In our opinion, the financial statements referred to above present fairly the consolidated financial position of CBS Inc. and subsidiaries as of December 31, 1985, 1984 and 1983, and the results of their operations and the changes in their financial position for the years then ended, in conformity with generally accepted accounting principles applied on a consistent basis.

1251 Avenue of the Americas   COOPERS & LYBRAND
New York, New York 10020
February 12, 1986

Source: Reproduced with the permission of CBS Inc.

However, an auditor's opinion does not guarantee the accuracy of the statements. Responsibility for accuracy rests with the firm's management.

LIMITATIONS OF ACCOUNTING DATA

There are several weaknesses inherent in financial statements. While this does not mean that financial analysis employing accounting data should be discounted, the financial analyst needs to interpret financial statements in light of these weaknesses.

First, accounting data do not take into account nonmeasurable items, such as the quality of the research department or the marketing performance of the firm. Performance is measured solely in terms of money, and the implication of accounting data is that if the firm consistently leads its industry (or is at least above average), its management and divisions are qualitatively superior to those of its competitors. A strong relationship between performance and superior financial statements probably does exist. The strong financial statements of IBM mirror the quality of its management and its research and marketing staffs. However, many firms may be able to improve their financial position temporarily and achieve short-term superior performance that cannot be maintained.

Nonmeasurable items

Second, accounting data may not be sufficiently challenged by auditors. Although financial records are examined for reasonableness and conformity with accounting principles, the auditors may lack knowledge in specific areas pertinent to the firm's accounting statements. For example, the auditors may accept the estimates of the firm's engineers because the auditors lack the specialized knowledge necessary to challenge the estimates. This is not meant to suggest that the auditors are incompetent; they may, however, lack specific knowledge that is necessary to verify the authenticity of some of the data used by the corporation's accountants.

Auditors' insufficient knowledge

The problem of aggregate data

Third, financial statements that are available to the public give aggregate data. Although the company's management has access to itemized data, individual investors or security analysts may not receive sufficiently detailed information to guide investment decisions. For example, a company may not give its sales figures according to product lines. Aggregate sales data do not inform the public as to which of the company's products are its primary sources of revenue. The use of aggregate numbers in the firm's income statements and balance sheets may hide important information that the investor or security analyst could use in the study of the company.

Inaccurate valuation of assets

Fourth, accounting data may be biased. For example, the valuation of assets by the lower of either cost or market value may result in biased information if the dollar value of the assets has significantly risen (as may occur during periods of inflation). Such increases in value are hidden by the use of the historical cost, and thus the financial statements do not give a true indication of the value of the firm's assets. If the value of the assets has risen and this is not recognized by the accounting data, then the rate of return earned by the company on its assets is slanted upward. If the true value of the assets were used to determine the rate of return that the firm earns on its assets, the rate would be lower. In this case the use of historical cost instead of market value results in inaccurate measures of the company's performance.

Inflation

Fifth, within the last decade inflation has caused a problem in interpreting accounting data. Items that were purchased a number of years ago cannot currently be replaced for their original costs. As the firm's plant and equipment wear out, these assets will have to be replaced at higher prices. For the firm to maintain its current capacity, additional financing will be required to cover the higher costs. This decline in the purchasing power of money is not indicated by accounting data and poses one of the biggest problems that must be dealt with by accountants.[6]

Despite the problems that exist, financial analysis employing accounting data is a useful tool in evaluating a company's financial position. As long as the analyst is aware of the limitations of accounting data, financial statements may be interpreted in light of them.

SUMMARY

This chapter has briefly summarized the four major financial statements that are published in the annual reports of publicly held firms. The balance sheet enumerates what a firm owns (its assets), what it owes (its liabilities), and the stockholders' investment or equity. The income statement summarizes the firm's revenues and other income, its expenses, and its profit or loss for the accounting period. The statement of retained earnings indicates the distribution or retention of earnings. Finally, the statement of changes in financial position summarizes the sources of financing, their amounts, and how these funds were used. This statement emphasizes changes in the firm's net working capital, which is the difference between its current assets and its current liabilities.

---

[6]This is also one of industry's major problems. Firms must replace aging plant and equipment at a higher cost, which requires greater capital investments than some firms are able to afford.

Terms to Remember

Balance sheet	Hidden assets
Assets	Current liability
Liabilities	Long-term liability
Book value	Long-term debt
Equity (stockholders' equity)	Retained earnings
Consolidated balance sheet	Income statement
Current assets	Earnings per share (EPS)
Long-term assets	Statement of retained earnings
Investments	Statement of changes in financial
Inventory	position
Accounts receivable	Working capital
Depreciation	Auditor's opinion

Questions

1. Specify which of the following are assets and which are liabilities: (a) cash, (b) accrued interest, (c) equipment, (d) accounts payable, (e) goods in process, and (f) additional paid-in capital.

2. Why may the market value of an asset be different from its book value?

3. What time period is covered by a balance sheet and by an income statement?

4. Are a firm's profits equal to its cash? What may a corporation do with its profits?

5. Why do retained earnings represent an investment in the firm by the stockholders?

6. What is depreciation?

7. Which of the following represent a use of funds and which represent a source of funds?

    a. an increase in inventory
    b. an increase in accounts payable
    c. a decrease in accounts receivable
    d. a reduction in long-term debt
    e. an increase in equipment
    f. an increase in depreciation
    g. an increase in cash

8. What is working capital? What effect does each of the following have on net working capital?

    a. a new issue of stock
    b. an increase in accounts payable
    c. cash dividends paid by the firm
    d. a reduction in inventory
    e. a reduction in long-term debt

9. How does inflation affect the investor's interpretation of the accounting data used in financial statements?

10. From the investor's point of view, why is it important to have a firm's financial statements audited?

Problems

1. From the following information, construct a simple income statement and a balance sheet.

Sales	$1,000,000
Finished goods	200,000
Long-term debt	300,000
Raw materials	100,000
Cash	50,000
Cost of goods sold	600,000
Accounts receivable	250,000
Plant and equipment	400,000
Interest expense	80,000
Number of shares outstanding	100,000
Earnings before taxes	220,000
Taxes	100,000
Accounts payable	200,000
Other current liabilities	50,000
Other expenses	100,000
Equity	450,000

2. Given the following information, determine the per-share earnings of the common stock.

Earnings before interest and taxes	$100,000
Debt outstanding	$300,000
Income tax rate	30%
Interest rate on debt	12%
Preferred stock dividends	$20,000
Number of common shares outstanding	10,000

3. Given the following information, construct the firm's balance sheet.

Cash and cash equivalents	$300,000
Accumulated depreciation on plant and equipment	800,000
Plant and equipment	5,800,000
Accrued wages	400,000
Long-term debt	4,200,000
Inventory	6,400,000
Accounts receivable	4,100,000
Preferred stock	500,000
Retained earnings	7,700,000
Land	1,000,000
Accounts payable	2,100,000
Taxes due	100,000
Common stock	$10 par
Common shares outstanding	150,000
Current portion of long-term debt	$300,000

4. Fill in the blanks (—) with the correct entries.

Assets		Liabilities and Stockholders' Equity	
Current assets		Current liabilities	
Cash	$ 250,000	Accounts payable	$ 620,000
Accounts receivable (—less allowance for doubtful accounts of $20,000)	1,320,000	Notes payable to banks	130,000
		Accrued wages	—
		Taxes owed	100,000
Inventory	1,410,000	Total current liabilities	1,250,000
Total current assets	—	Long-term debt	—
Land	—	Stockholders' equity	
Plant and equipment ($2,800,000 less accumulated depreciation—)	2,110,000	Preferred stock	1,000,000
		Common stock ($1 par, 750,000 shares authorized, 700,000 outstanding)	—
Total assets	$5,390,000	Retained earnings	—
		Total common stockholders' equity	3,140,000
		Total liabilities and equity	—

5. Given the following information, construct a statement of changes in financial position for 19x1 and 19x2. What differences in sources of working capital for each year may be seen in these financial statements?

	19x2	19x1
Net income	$16,000,000	16,000,000
Increase in long-term debt	3,000,000	—
Sale of stock	—	3,000,000
Depreciation	4,000,000	4,000,000
Sale of preferred stock	—	10,000,000
Additions to plant and equipment	17,000,000	7,000,000
Dividends	6,000,000	5,000,000
Reduction in long-term debt	2,000,000	1,000,000
Increase (decrease) in cash	(4,000,000)	8,000,000
Increase (decrease) in accounts receivable	4,000,000	6,000,000
Increase (decrease) in inventory	(5,000,000)	10,000,000
(Decrease) increase in accounts payable	(2,000,000)	3,000,000
(Decrease) increase in notes payable	(2,000,000)	2,000,000
(Decrease) increase in taxes owed	1,000,000	(1,000,000)

Suggested Readings

The library of every financial analyst should include at least one good accounting text. Three possibilities are:

Keisco, Donald E., and Jerry J. Weygandt. *Intermediate Accounting*. 5th ed. New York: John Wiley, 1986.

Mosich, A. N., and E. A. Larsen. *Intermediate Accounting*. 6th ed. New York: McGraw-Hill, 1985.

Welsch, Glenn A., Charles T. Zlatkovich, and Walter T. Harrison, Jr. *Intermediate Accounting*. 7th ed. Homewood, Ill.: Richard D. Irwin, 1986.

The Kiesco-Weygandt text is quite comprehensive and well written. The Mosich-Larsen text is more concise. The text by Welsch et al is the most comprehensive of the three.

If the investor has little background in accounting, the following text (which has excellent pedagogical features) is recommended:

Meigs, Walter B., and Robert F. Meigs. *Financial Accounting*. 4th ed. New York: McGraw-Hill, 1983.

8 Risk and Efficient Markets

LEARNING OBJECTIVES

After completing this chapter you should be able to

1. Identify the general sources of risk.

2. Explain how diversification reduces risk.

3. Identify the relationship between securities that is necessary to achieve diversification.

4. Contrast the sources of return on an investment and differentiate between expected and realized returns.

5. Explain how standard deviations and beta coefficients measure risk.

6. Understand how beta coefficients can be used in portfolio construction.

7. Define what conditions are necessary to have efficient financial markets.

8. Explain the return an investor can anticipate according to the efficient market hypothesis.

In War As I Knew It, George Patton said, "Take calculated risks; that is quite different from being rash." Investors should realize that since the future is uncertain, they too must take calculated risks.

As a reward for bearing risk, an investor can anticipate a return. Until the 1950s, investors and financial analysts dealt with risk and return on an intuitive basis; there were no theoretical models to indicate the interrelationship between risk and return. However, with the pioneering work of several financial analysts, a theory of portfolio behavior and the measures of risk and return developed.

This chapter gives a brief introduction to the sources and analysis of risk and its use in modern portfolio construction. Risk may be measured by a standard deviation, which measures the dispersion around a central tendency such as an average return. Risk may also be measured by a beta coefficient, which is an index of the volatility of a security's return rela-

tive to the return on the market. Much of this chapter is devoted to these two measures of risk and the reduction of risk through diversification.

The chapter ends with a discussion of portfolio construction. An investor seeks to construct a portfolio that offers the highest return for a given level of risk or the least amount of risk for a given level of return. Such a portfolio, which is referred to as being efficient, is constructed in efficient and competitive financial markets. The major implication of the efficient market hypothesis is that an individual cannot expect to outperform the market consistently over a period of time.

SOURCES OF RISK

The word "risk" is used frequently in this text. As was explained in the first chapter, there are several sources of risk. These are frequently classified as systematic (or non-diversifiable) risk and unsystematic (or diversifiable) risk. **Systematic risk** refers to the risk associated with (1) fluctuating security prices in general, (2) fluctuating interest rates, and (3) the loss of purchasing power through inflation. **Unsystematic risk** refers to the risk associated with the individual firm itself, its operations, and its methods of financing.

Systematic and unsystematic risk

Asset returns tend to move together. If security prices rise in general, the price of a specific security tends to rise in sympathy with the market. Conversely, if the market were to decline, the value of an individual security would also tend to fall. Thus there is a systematic relationship between the price of a specific asset, such as a common stock, and the market as a whole. As long as the investor buys securities, that individual cannot avoid bearing this source of systematic risk.

Security prices move together

Asset values are also affected by changes in interest rates. As is explained in Chapter 10, rising interest rates depress the prices of fixed income securities, such as long-term bonds and preferred stock. Conversely, if interest rates fall, the value of these assets rises. There is a systematic negative relationship between the prices of fixed income securities and changes in interest rates. As long the investor acquires fixed income securities, that individual must bear the risk associated with fluctuations in interest rates.

Security prices move inversely to interest rates

The investor must also endure a third source of systematic risk: the loss of purchasing power through inflation.[1] It is obvious that rising prices of goods and services erode the purchasing power of both the investor's income and assets. Like fluctuating security prices or changes in interest rates, there is nothing the individual can do to stop inflation, so the goal should be to earn a return that exceeds the rate of inflation. If the investor cannot earn such a return, he or she may benefit more from spending the funds and consuming goods now.

Loss of purchasing power

Besides systematic risk, the investor also faces the unsystematic risk associated with each asset. Since the investor buys specific assets, such as the common stock of IBM or bonds issued by the township of Princeton, that individual must bear the risk associated with each specific investment.

For firms, the sources of unsystematic risk are the business and financial risks associated with the operation. Business risk refers to the nature of the firm's operations, and financial risk refers to how the firm finances its assets (i.e., whether the firm

Business and financial risks associated with the firm

---

[1]If systematic risk is defined as nondiversifiable risk, inflation may be considered part of systematic risk.

uses a substantial or modest amount of debt financing). For example, the business risk associated with TWA or Delta Airlines is affected by such factors as the cost of fuel, the legal and regulatory environment, the capacity of planes, and seasonal changes in demand. Financial risk for airlines depends on how the airline finances its planes and other assets—that is, whether the assets were acquired by issuing bonds, preferred stock, or common stock, by leasing, or by borrowing from other sources.

The investor may be unable to anticipate all the events that will affect a certain firm, such as a strike or natural disaster, but these events may affect the value of the firm's securities in positive or negative ways. In either case, the possibility of these events occurring increases the risk associated with investing in a specific asset.

Portfolio risk

The combination of systematic and unsystematic risk is defined as the total risk (or **portfolio risk**) that the investor bears. While the investor can do little to reduce systematic risk, he or she can affect unsystematic risk. Unsystematic risk may be significantly reduced through **diversification**, which occurs when the investor purchases the securities of firms in different industries. Buying the stock of five telephone companies is not considered diversification, because the events that affect one company tend to affect the others. A diversified portfolio may consist of stocks and bonds issued by a telephone company, an electric utility, an insurance firm, a commercial bank, an oil refinery, a retail business, and a manufacturing firm. This is a diversified mixture of industries and types of assets. The impact of particular events on the earnings and growth of one firm need not apply to all of the firms; therefore, the risk of loss in owning the portfolio is reduced.[2]

Diversification reduces unsystematic risk

How diversification reduces risk is illustrated in Figure 8.1, which shows the price performance of three stocks and their composite. Stock A's price initially falls, then rises, and starts to fall again. Stock B's price ultimately rises but tends to fluctuate. Stock C's price fluctuates the least of the three but ends with only a modest gain. Purchasing stock B and holding it would have produced a substantial profit while A would have generated a moderate loss.

The last quadrant illustrates what happens if the investor buys an equal dollar amount of each stock (i.e., buys a diversified portfolio).[3] First, the value of the portfolio as a whole may rise even though the value of an individual security may not. Second, and most importantly, the fluctuation in the value of the portfolio is less than the fluctuations in individual security prices. By diversifying the portfolio, the investor is able to reduce the risk of loss. Of course, the investor also gives up the possibility of a large gain (as was achieved by stock B).

In effect, a diversified portfolio reduces the element of unsystematic risk. The risk associated with each individual investment is reduced by accumulating a diversified portfolio of assets. Even if one company fails (or does extremely well), the impact on the portfolio as a whole is reduced through diversification. Distributing investments among different industries, however, does not eliminate systematic or market risk. The value of a group of securities will tend to follow the market values in general. The

---

[2] Since stock and bond prices may move together, even a diversified mixture of securities is not a completely diversified portfolio. Further diversification may be achieved by including such assets as real estate, gold, savings accounts, and collectibles in the portfolio. It is through such diversification of type of asset and industry that unsystematic risk is eliminated.

[3] Later in this chapter, the statistical condition that must be met to achieve diversification is discussed and illustrated using returns from investments in the common stocks of Mobil and Public Service Enterprise Group.

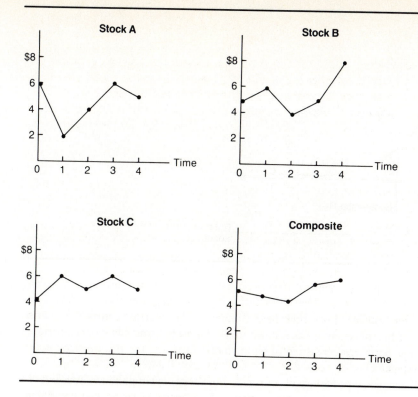

Figure 8.1
Prices of Three Stocks

price movements of securities will be mirrored by the diversified portfolio; hence the investor cannot eliminate this source of systematic risk.

How many securities are necessary to achieve a diversified portfolio that reduces and almost eliminates unsystematic risk? The answer may be "surprisingly few." Several studies have found that risk has been significantly reduced in portfolios consisting of from 10 to 15 securities.[4]

This reduction in unsystematic risk is illustrated in Figure 8.2. The vertical axis measures units of risk, and the horizontal axis gives the number of securities. Since market risk is independent of the number of securities in the portfolio, this element of risk is illustrated by a line, *AB,* that runs parallel to the horizontal axis. Regardless of the number of securities that an individual owns, the amount of market risk remains the same.

Portfolio risk (i.e., the sum of systematic and unsystematic risk), is indicated by line *CD*. The difference between line *AB* and line *CD* is the unsystematic risk associated with the specific securities in the portfolio. The amount of unsystematic risk de-

---

[4]For further discussion, see the following: John Evans and Stephen Archer, "Diversification and the Reduction of Dispersion: An Empirical Analysis," *Journal of Finance* (December 1968): 761–767; Bruce D. Fielitz, "Indirect Versus Direct Diversification," *Financial Management* (Winter 1974): 54–62; H. Latané and W. Young, "Tests of Portfolio Building Rules," *Journal of Finance* (September 1969): 595–612; and William Sharpe, "Risk, Market Sensitivity and Diversification," *Financial Analysts Journal* (January–February 1972): 74–79. However, George Frankfurter suggests that even well-diversified portfolios have a substantial amount of nonsystematic risk. See his "Efficient Portfolios and Non-Systematic Risk," *The Financial Review* (Fall 1981): 1–11.

Figure 8.2
Portfolio Risk
Consisting of Systematic
and Unsystematic Risk

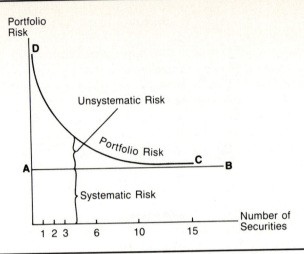

pends on the number of securities held. As this number increases, unsystematic risk diminishes; this reduction in risk is illustrated in Figure 8.2 where line *CD* approaches line *AB*. For portfolios consisting of ten or more securities, the risk involved is primarily systematic.

Such diversified portfolios, of course, do not consist of ten public utilities but of a cross section of American businesses. Investing $20,000 in ten stocks (i.e., $2,000 for each) may achieve a reasonably well-diversified portfolio. While such a portfolio may cost somewhat more in commissions than two $10,000 purchases, the small investor achieves a diversified mixture of securities, which should reduce the risk of loss associated with investment in a specific security. Unfortunately, the investor must still bear the systematic risk associated with investing and the risk of loss in purchasing power that results from inflation.

THE EXPECTED RETURN ON AN INVESTMENT

Portfolio theory is primarily concerned with systematic risk and expected return. Its purpose is to determine that combination of return and risk that will allow the individual investor to achieve the highest return for a given level of risk. To do this, a means for measuring return and risk must be devised. Such measurement is the focus of the next two sections of this chapter.

Sources of return: Income and price appreciation

The **expected return** is the anticipated flow of income and/or price appreciation. An investment may offer a return from either of two sources. The first source is the flow of income that may be generated by the investment. A savings account yields the holder a flow of interest income while the account is held. The second source of return is capital appreciation. If an investor buys stock and its price subsequently increases, the investor will receive a capital gain. All investments offer the investor either potential income and/or capital appreciation. Some investments, like the savings account,

offer only income, whereas other investments such as an investment in land, may offer only capital appreciation. In fact, some investments may require expenditures (e.g., property tax) on the part of the investor.

When the individual makes an investment, a return is anticipated. The yield that is achieved on the investment is not known until after the investment is sold and converted to cash. It is important to differentiate between *the expected return* and *the realized return*. The expected return is the incentive for accepting risk, and it must be compared with the investor's **required return,** which is the return necessary to induce that investor to bear the risk associated with a particular investment. The required return includes (1) what the investor may earn on alternative investments, such as the risk free return available on treasury bills, and (2) a premium for bearing risk that includes compensation for the expected inflation rate and for fluctuations in security prices. Since each individual's willingness to bear risk is different, the required rate of return differs from one investor to another.[5]

Return is anticipated

Required return encompasses alternate yields and a risk premium

Despite this difference, virtually all investors have the same attitude toward risk—they do not like to bear it. To induce them to bear additional risk, the expected return from the investment must be sufficient to compensate investors for assuming the risk inherent in the investment. Such a relationship between risk and expected return is consistent with investors' aversion to risk taking. A greater anticipated return is necessary to induce investors to bear an increased risk of loss; if the expected return is less than the required return, the investment will not be made.

Investors are averse to bearing risk

MEASURES OF RISK

Risk is concerned with the uncertainty that the realized return will not equal the expected return. Emphasis is placed on the extent to which the return may differ from the average return or on the volatility of the return. The former may be measured by a statistical concept called the standard deviation, while the latter may be measured by what has been termed a beta coefficient.

A measurement of risk is also frequently implied when individuals refer to the annual range in an asset's price. One may encounter statements such as "The stock is trading near its low for the year," or "245 stocks reached new highs while only 41 fell to new lows." Some individuals plan their investment strategy as if a stock trades within a price range. If the stock is near the low for the year, it may be a good time to purchase. Correspondingly, if it is trading near the high for the year, it may be a good time to sell. The range in the stock's price, then, can be used as a guide to strategy, because the price tends to gravitate to a mean between these two extremes. In other words, there is a "central tendency" for the price of the stock. The range in a stock's price than becomes a measure of risk. Stocks with wider ranges are "riskier" because their prices tend to deviate further from the average (mean) price.

High-low prices

One problem with using the range as a measure of risk is that two securities of different prices can have the same range. For example, a stock whose price ranges from $10 to $30 has the same range as a stock whose price varies from $50 to $70. The range is $20 in both cases, but an increase from $10 to $30 is a 200 percent

---

[5]The required rate of return is developed in depth in Chapter 14, which considers the valuation of common stock.

increment, whereas the increase from $50 to $70 is only a 40 percent increase. The price of the latter stock appears to be more stable; hence, less risk is associated with this security, even though both stocks involve equal risk according to the range.

Dispersion Around an Investment's Return

The problem that is inherent in using only two observations (e.g., a stock's high and low prices) to determine risk may be avoided by analyzing **dispersion** around an average value, such as an investment's return. This technique considers all possible outcomes. If there is not much difference among the possible returns (i.e., they are close together), then the dispersion will be small. If most of the returns are near the extremes and differ considerably from the average return, then the dispersion will be large. The larger this dispersion, the greater the risk associated with a particular stock.

Larger dispersion implies more risk

This concept is perhaps best illustrated by a simple example. An investment in either of two stocks yields an average return of 15 percent, but stocks could have the following returns:

Stock A	Stock B
13½%	11 %
14	11½
14¼	12
14½	12½
15	15
15½	17½
15¾	18
16	18½
16½	19

Although the average return is the same for both stocks, there is considerable difference in the possible returns. Stock A's returns are very close to the expected value, whereas stock B's returns are closer to the possible high and low values. The possible returns of stock A cluster around the average return. Since there is considerably less fluctuation in returns, it is the less risky of the two securities.

These differences in risk are illustrated in Figure 8.3, which plots the various returns on the horizontal axis and the frequency of their occurrence on the vertical axis. This is basically the same information that was previously given for stocks A and B, except that more observations would be necessary to construct such a graph.[6] Most of stock A's returns are close to the average return, so the frequency distribution is higher and narrower. The frequency distribution for stock B's return is lower and wider, which indicates a greater dispersion in that stock's returns.

Larger dispersion means more risk

The larger dispersion around the average return implies that the stock involves greater risk because the investor can be less certain of the stock's future return. The larger the dispersion, the greater is the chance of a large loss from the investment, and, correspondingly, the greater is the chance of a large gain. However, this potential for

---

[6]While there are only nine observations in the illustration, the figure is drawn as if there were a large number of observations.

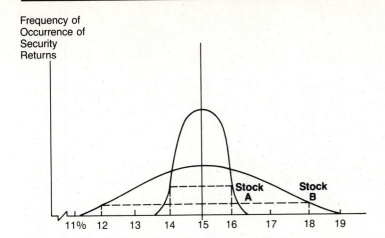

Frequency of
Occurrence of
Security
Returns

Stock A   Stock B

11% 12 13 14 15 16 17 18 19

Figure 8.3
**Distribution of the
Returns of Two Stocks**

increased gain is concomitant with bearing more risk. Stock A involves less risk; it has the smaller dispersion. But it also has less potential for a large gain. A reduction in risk also means a reduction in possible return on the investment.

This dispersion around the mean value (i.e., the average return) is measured by the standard deviation. Since the standard deviation measures the tendency for the various returns to cluster around the average return, it may be used as a measure of risk. The larger the dispersion, the greater the standard deviation and the larger the risk associated with the particular security.

The standard deviation is calculated as follows:

*How standard deviation
is computed*

1. For the range of possible returns, subtract the individual observations from the average return.

2. Square this difference.

3. Add these squared differences.

4. Divide this sum by the number of observations less 1.

5. Take the square root.

For stock A the standard deviation is determined as follows:

Expected Return	Individual Return	Difference	Difference Squared
15	13.50	1.5	2.2500
15	14	1	1.0000
15	14.25	0.75	0.5625
15	14.50	0.5	0.25
15	15	0	0
15	15.50	−0.5	0.25
15	15.75	−0.75	0.5625
15	16	−1	1.000
15	16.50	−1.5	2.2500
		The sum of the squared differences:	8.1250

Figure 8.4
**Distribution of the
Returns of Two Stocks**

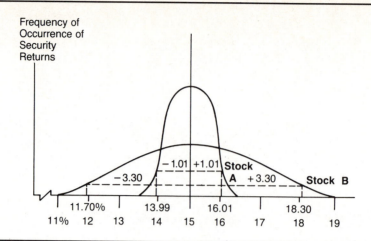

Frequency of
Occurrence of
Security
Returns

The sum of the squared differences divided by the number of observations less 1:

$$\frac{8.1250}{8} = 1.0156.$$

The square root: $\sqrt{1.0156} = \pm 1.01$

Thus, the standard deviation is ± 1.01

*Interpretations of the
standard deviation*

The investor must then interpret this result. Plus and minus one standard devia-tion has been shown to encompass approximately 68 percent of all observations (in this case, that is 68 percent of the returns). The standard deviation for stock A is $\pm$ 1.01, which means that approximately two thirds of the returns fall between 13.99 and 16.01 percent. These returns are simply the expected average return (15 percent) plus 1.01 and minus 1.01 percent (i.e., plus and minus the standard deviation).

For stock B the standard deviation is $\pm$ 3.30, which means that approximately 68 percent of the returns fall between 11.7 percent and 18.3 percent. Stock B's returns have a wider dispersion from the average return, and this fact is indicated by the greater standard deviation.

These differences in the standard deviations are illustrated in Figure 8.4, which reproduces Figure 8.3 but adds the standard deviations. The average return for both stocks is 15 percent, but the standard deviation is greater for stock B than for stock A (i.e., $\pm$ 3.30 for B versus $\pm$ 1.01 for A). By computing the standard deviation, the analyst quantifies risk. This will help in the selection of individual securities, since the investor will prefer those assets with the least risk for a given expected return.

While the above discussion was limited to the return on an individual security and the dispersion around that return, the concepts can be applied to an entire port-folio. A portfolio also has an average return and a dispersion around that expected return. The investor is concerned not only with the expected return and the risk asso-ciated with each investment, but also with the expected return and risk associated with the portfolio as a whole. This aggregate is, of course, the result of the individual investments and of each one's weight in the portfolio (i.e., the value of each asset, expressed in percentages, in proportion to the total value of the portfolio).

Consider two portfolios consisting of the following three stocks:

Stock	Expected Return
1	8.3%
2	10.6
3	12.3

If 25 percent of the total value of the portfolio is invested in stocks 1 and 2 and 50 percent is invested in stock 3, the expected return is more heavily weighted in favor of stock 3. The expected return is a weighted average of each return times its proportion in the portfolio.

Return is a weighted average

$$
\begin{array}{ccccc}
& & \text{Weight (percentage value} & & \\
\text{Expected return} & \times & \text{of stock in proportion to} & = & \text{Weighted average} \\
& & \text{total value of portfolio)} & &
\end{array}
$$

8.3%	×	0.25	=	2.075%
10.6	×	0.25	=	2.650
12.3	×	0.50	=	6.150.

The expected return is the sum of these weighted averages.

$$
\begin{array}{r}
2.075\% \\
2.650 \\
\underline{6.150} \\
10.875\%
\end{array}
$$

The previous example is generalized in Equation 8.1, which states that the return on a portfolio R_p is a weighted average of the returns of the individual assets $[(R_1) \ldots (R_n)]$, each weighted by its proportion in the portfolio $(w_1 \ldots w_n)$:

$$R_p = w_1(r_1) + w_2(r_2) + \ldots + w_n(R_n). \tag{8.1}$$

Thus, if a portfolio has 20 securities, each plays a role in the determination of the portfolio's return. The extent of that role depends on the weight that each asset has in the portfolio. Obviously those securities that compose the largest part of the individual's portfolio have the largest impact on the portfolio's return.[7]

Unfortunately, an aggregate measure of the portfolio's risk (i.e., the portfolio's standard deviation) is more difficult to construct than the weighted average. This is because security prices are not independent of each other. However, while security prices do move together, there can be considerable difference in these price movements. For example, prices of stocks of firms in homebuilding may be more sensitive to recession than stock prices of utilities, whose prices may decline only moderately. These relationships among the assets in the portfolio must be considered in the construction of a measure of risk associated with the entire portfolio. In more advanced texts, these inner relationships among stocks are called covariation. Covariation con-

Aggregate measure of portfolio risk

---

[7] The same general equation may be applied to expected returns, in which case the expected return on a portfolio, $E(R_p)$, is a weighted average of the expected returns of the individual assets $[(E(R_1) \ldots E(R_n)]$ each weighted by its proportion in the portfolio $(w_1 \ldots w_n)$:

$$E(R_p) = w_1 E(r_1) + w_2 E(r_2) + \ldots + w_n E(R_n).$$

Security prices are not
independent

siders not only the volatility of the individual asset but also its relationship with the other assets in the portfolio.

Since the determination of a portfolio's standard deviation becomes very complicated for a portfolio of many assets, the following illustrations will be limited to portfolios of only two assets. Three cases are illustrated. In the first case, the two assets' returns move exactly together; in the second, the two assets' returns move exactly opposite; and in the third, the returns are independent of each other. While these examples are simple, they do illustrate how a portfolio's standard deviation is determined and the effect of the relationships among the assets in the portfolio on the risk associated with the portfolio as a whole.

The standard deviation of the returns on a portfolio (S_d) with two assets is given in Equation 8.2:

(8.2)
$$S_d = \sqrt{w_a^2 S_a^2 + w_b^2 S_b^2 + 2w_a w_b \text{cov}_{ab}}$$

While this is formidable looking, it says that the standard deviation of the portfolio's return is the square root of the sum of (1) the squared standard deviation of the return of the first asset (S_a) times its squared weight in the portfolio (w_a) plus (2) the squared standard deviation of the return on the second asset (S_b) times its squared weight (w_b) in the portfolio plus (3) two times the weight of the first asset times the weight of the second asset times the covariance of the two assets.

The covariance of the returns on assets a and b (cov_{ab}) is

$$\text{cov}_{ab} = S_a \times S_b \times \text{(correlation coefficient of a and b)}.$$

Thus, to determine the covariation the analyst needs the standard deviations of each asset's return and the correlation coefficient between the returns on the two securities. The numerical values of correlation coefficients range from $+1.0$ for a perfect positive correlation to -1.0 for a perfect negative correlation.[8]

To illustrate the determination of the portfolio's standard deviation, consider the returns earned by securities A and B in the following three cases in which the portfolio is divided equally between the two securities. The three cases are also shown in Figure 8.5, which plots the returns on the assets and on the portfolio composed of equal amounts invested in each (i.e., 50 percent of the portfolio in each asset).

Impact on risk if returns
are exactly correlated

Case 1

1. *positive correlation*

Year		Return on Security A	Return on Security B	Return on Portfolio
1		10%	10%	10%
2		−12	−12	−12
3		−25	−25	−25
4		37	37	37
Average return		2.5%	2.5%	2.5%
Standard deviation of security returns		±.2716	±.2716	—

---

[8] How the correlation coefficient is determined may be found in an elementary text on statistics. See, for instance, George W. Summers, William S. Peters, and Charles P. Armstrong, *Basic Statistics in Business and Economics*, 4th ed. (Belmont, Calif.: Wadsworth, 1985), 307–308 and 534–537.

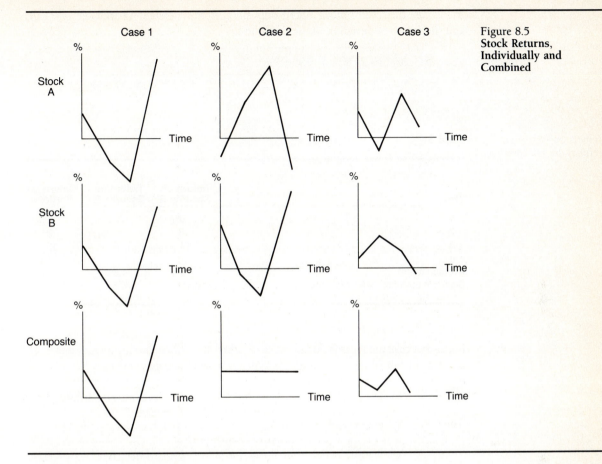

Case 1   Case 2   Case 3

Figure 8.5
**Stock Returns,
Individually and
Combined**

In this case the securities move exactly together (i.e., their correlation coefficient is 1.0). The standard deviation of the portfolio is computed as follows:

$$S_d = \sqrt{w_a^2 S_a^2 + w_b^2 S_b^2 + 2 w_a w_b \text{cov}_{ab}}$$

$$= \sqrt{.5^2(.2716)^2 + .5^2(.2716)^2 + 2(.5)(.5)(.2716)(.2716)(1)}$$

$$= \pm.2716.$$

Case 2   *2. negative correlation*

Year	Return on Security A	Return on Security B	Return on Portfolio
1	−15%	25%	10%
2	12	−2	10
3	25	−15	10
4	−37	47	10
Average return	−3.75%	−3.75%	10%
Standard deviation of security returns	±.277293	±.277293	—

In this case the returns move exactly opposite (i.e., the correlation coefficient is -1.0), and the standard deviation of the portfolio is

$$S_d = \sqrt{w_a^2 S_a^2 + w_b^2 S_b^2 + 2w_a w_b \text{cov}_{ab}}$$

$$= \sqrt{.5^2(.277293)^2 + .5^2(.277293)^2 + 2(.5)(.5)(.277293)(.277293)(-1)}$$

$$= 0.$$

Impact on risk when returns are not correlated

Case 3

Year	Return on Security A	Return on Security B	Return on Portfolio
1	10%	2%	6%
2	−8	12	2
3	14	6	10
4	4	−2	1
Average return	5%	4.5%	4.75%
Standard deviation of security returns	±.095917	±.0575	—

In this last case the returns do not move together. In the first and third years they both generated positive returns, but in the other two years one generated a loss while the other produced a positive return. In this illustration the correlation coefficient between the returns equals -0.524. Thus, the standard deviation of the portfolio is

$$S_d = \sqrt{w_a^2 S_a^2 + w_b^2 S_b^2 + 2w_a w_b \text{cov}_{ab}}$$

$$= \sqrt{.5^2(.095917)^2 + .5^2(.0575)^2 + 2(.5)(.5)(.095917)(.0575)(-.524)}$$

$$= ±.041.$$

Notice how, in the first case, the standard deviation of the portfolio is the same as the standard deviation of the two assets. Combining these assets in the portfolio has no impact on the risk associated with the portfolio. In Case 2, the portfolio's risk is reduced to zero (i.e., the portfolio's standard deviation is zero). This indicates that combining these assets whose returns fluctuate exactly in the opposite directions has the effect on the portfolio of completely erasing risk. The fluctuations associated with one asset are exactly offset by the fluctuations in the other asset.

In the third case, which is the most realistic of the three illustrations, the standard deviation of the portfolio is less than the standard deviations of the individual assets. The risk associated with the portfolio as a whole is less than the risk associated with either of the individual assets. Even though the assets' returns do fluctuate, the fluctuations partially offset each other, so that by combining these assets in the portfolio, the investor reduces his or her exposure to risk with almost no reduction in the return.

Diversification requires returns not be positively correlated

Diversification and the reduction in unsystematic risk require that assets' returns not be positively correlated. When there is a high positive correlation (as in Case 1), there is no risk reduction. When the returns are perfectly negatively correlated (as in Case 2), risk is erased. If one asset's return falls, the decline is exactly offset by the

increase in the return earned by the other asset. The effect is to achieve a risk-free return. In the third case, which is the most likely of the three illustrations, there is neither a perfect positive nor a perfect negative correlation. However, there is risk reduction, because the returns are negatively correlated. The lower the positive correlation and the greater the negative correlation among the returns, the greater will be the risk reduction achieved by combining the various assets in the portfolio.

While the above illustration is extended, it points out a major consideration in the selection of assets to be included in a portfolio. The individual asset's expected return and risk are important, but the asset's impact on the portfolio as a whole is also important. The asset's return and the variability of that return should be considered in a portfolio context. It is quite possible that the inclusion of a volatile asset will reduce the risk exposure of the portfolio as a whole if the return is negatively correlated with the returns offered by the other assets in the portfolio. Failure to consider the relationships among the assets in the portfolio could prove to be counterproductive if including the asset reduces the portfolio's potential return without reducing the variability of the portfolio's return (i.e., without reducing the element of risk).

Importance of the impact of the individual security on the portfolio

RISK REDUCTION THROUGH DIVERSIFICATION—AN ILLUSTRATION

The previous discussion has been in the abstract, but the concept of diversification through securities whose returns are not positively correlated may be illustrated by considering the returns earned on two specific stocks, Public Service Enterprise Group and Mobil Corporation. Public Service Enterprise Group is primarily an electric and gas utility whose stock price fell with higher interest rates and inflation. Mobil is a resource company whose stock price rose during inflation in response to higher oil prices but fell during the 1980s as oil prices weakened and inflation receded.

The annual returns (dividends plus price change) on investments in these two stocks are given in Figure 8.6 for the period 1971 through 1985. As may be seen in the graph, there were several periods when the returns on the two stocks moved in opposite directions. For example, during 1971 and 1978, an investment in Public Service Enterprise Group generated a loss while an investment in Mobil produced profits. However, the converse occurred during 1981 as the trend in Public Service Enterprise Group's stock price started to improve. From 1980 to 1985 the price of Public Service Enterprise Group doubled, but the price of Mobil's stock declined so that most of the return earned on Mobil's stock during the mid-1980s was its dividend.

Figure 8.7 presents a scatter diagram of the returns on these two stocks. The horizontal axis presents the average annual return on Public Service Enterprise Group, while the vertical axis presents the average annual return on Mobil Corporation. As may be seen in the graph, the individual points lie throughout the plane representing the returns. For example, point A represents a positive return on Mobil but a negative return on Public Service Enterprise Group, and point B represents a positive return on Public Service Enterprise Group but a negative return on Mobil.

Combining these securities in a portfolio reduces the individual's risk exposure, as is also shown in Figures 8.6 and 8.7. The line representing the composite return in Figure 8.6 runs between the lines representing the returns on the individual securities. Over the entire time period, the average annual returns on Mobil and Public

The portfolio's dispersion is less than the individual dispersions

Figure 8.6
Annual Returns

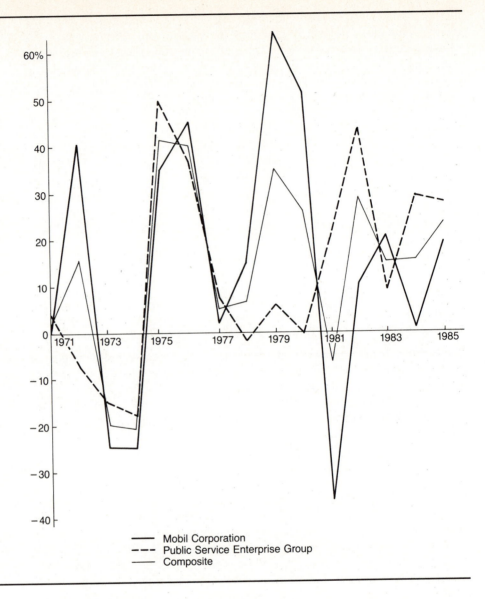

Mobil Corporation
Public Service Enterprise Group
Composite

Service Enterprise Group were 14.0 and 14.9 percent, respectively. The average annual return on the composite was 14.0 percent. The risk reduction (i.e., the reduction in the dispersion of the returns) can be seen by comparing the standard deviations of the returns. For the individual stocks the standard deviations were ±27.8 percent and ±21.5 percent, respectively, for Mobil and Public Service Enterprise Group. However, the standard deviation for the composite return was ±19.4, so the dispersion of the returns associated with the portfolio is less than the dispersion of the returns on either stock by itself.

Low correlation   In this illustration the correlation coefficient between the two returns is only 0.148. This lack of correlation is visible in Figure 8.7. If there were a high positive

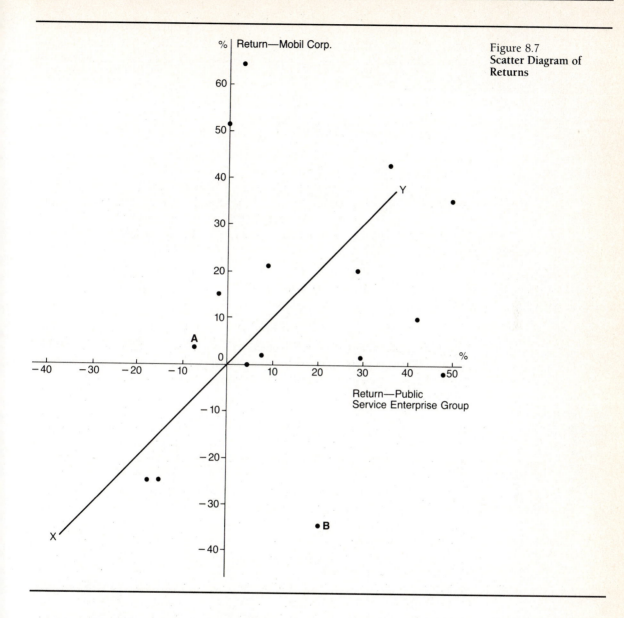

Figure 8.7
**Scatter Diagram of
Returns**

correlation between the two returns, the points would lie close to the line XY. Instead the points are scattered throughout the figure. Thus, there is little correlation between the two returns, which is why combining the two securities reduces the individual's risk exposure.

Diversification, then, is very desirable because it reduces the investor's risk exposure without necessarily reducing the portfolio's return. The problem facing investors is how to identify those assets whose returns are not positively correlated. Unfortunately, the returns on many assets, especially financial assets, are positively correlated. In addition, asset returns that are negatively correlated under one set of economic conditions may not be negatively correlated in a different economic en-

*Diverse assets may not
be correlated*

vironment. If, however, investors include a broad spectrum of assets (e.g., stocks, bonds, money market instruments, real estate, foreign securities, and physical assets) in their portfolios, a substantial amount of diversification and risk reduction should be achieved.

BETA COEFFICIENTS

Beta—an index of systematic risk

The standard deviation of a portfolio is an absolute number. Since absolute numbers are difficult to interpret, an alternative measure of risk is often employed. This measure, which is popularly referred to as a **beta coefficient**, is an index of risk that measures the volatility of the security's return relative to the market.[9] The reference point is an aggregate measure of the market such as the Standard & Poor's 500 stock index.

The beta coefficient for a specific security (β_i) is defined as follows:

$$\beta_i = \frac{\text{Standard deviation of the return on stock } i}{\text{Standard deviation of the return on the market}} \times \begin{array}{c} \text{Correlation coefficient of the} \\ \text{return on the stock and the} \\ \text{return on the market} \end{array}$$

Thus, beta depends on (1) the volatility of the individual stock's return, (2) the volatility of the market return (both measured by their respective standard deviations), and (3) the correlation between the return on the security and the return on the market. Beta coefficients are estimated by using linear regression analysis, which is illustrated in the appendix to this chapter.

Volatility of the asset's return relative to the volatility of the market

The more volatile a stock's return (i.e., the larger the standard deviation of the stock's return) relative to the variability of the market's return, the greater the risk associated with the individual stock. No longer is the investor interpreting an absolute number as a measure of risk. Since this beta coefficient is a relative number that measures the volatility of the stock's return relative to the return on the market as a whole, it is measuring the systematic risk associated with the particular stock. Systematic risk is, of course, the important risk facing the individual investor, since unsystematic risk is erased through the construction of a diversified portfolio.

A beta coefficient of 1 means that the stock's return moves exactly with an index of the market as a whole. A 10 percent return in the market could be expected to produce a 10 percent return on the specific stock. Correspondingly, a 10 percent decline in the market would result in a 10 percent decline in the return on the stock. A beta coefficient of less than 1 implies that the return on the stock would tend to fluctuate less than the market as a whole. A coefficient of 0.7 indicates that the stock's return would rise only 7 percent as a result of a 10 percent increase in the market but would fall by only 7 percent when the market declined by 10 percent. A coefficient of 1.2 means that the return on the stock could be expected to be 12 percent if the market return was 10 percent, but the return on the stock would decline by 12 percent when the market declined by 10 percent.

The greater the beta coefficient, the more the systematic risk associated with the individual stock. High beta coefficients may indicate exceptional profits during rising

---

[9] Beta coefficients offer an additional advantage in that they are available in financial publications such as the *Value Line Investment Survey*. Standard deviations of security returns are not generally available.

markets, but they also indicate greater losses during declining markets. Stocks with high beta coefficients are referred to as aggressive. The converse is true for stocks with low beta coefficients, which should underperform the market during periods of rising stock prices but outperform the market as a whole during periods of declining prices. Such stocks are referred to as defensive.

This relationship between the return on a specific security and the market index as a whole is illustrated in Figures 8.8 and 8.9. In each graph the horizontal axis represents the percentage return on the market index and the vertical axis represents the percentage return on the individual stock. The line *AB*, which represents the market, is the same in both graphs. It is a positive-sloped line that runs through the point of origin and is equidistant from both axes (i.e., it makes a 45° angle with each axis).

Figure 8.8 illustrates a stock with a beta coefficient greater than 1. Line *CD* represents a stock whose return rose and declined more than the market. In this case the beta coefficient is 1.2, so when the return on the market index is 10 percent, this stock's return is 12 percent.

Figure 8.9 illustrates a stock with a beta coefficient of less than 1. Line *EF* represents a stock whose return rose (and declined) more slowly than that of the market. In this case the beta coefficient is 0.8, so when the market's return is 10 percent, this stock's return is 8 percent.

Since a beta coefficient indicates the systematic risk associated with a particular stock, it can be used in security selection and portfolio construction. Some assets offer the investor modest returns for taking very little risk. Insured savings accounts and short-term obligations of the federal government are virtually risk-free. To induce investors to purchase risky securities such as common stock, the anticipated return must be sufficient to compensate the investor for the additional risk. Investors must anticipate sufficient returns for bearing systematic risk, and increases in systematic

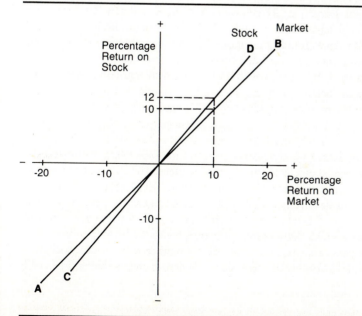

Figure 8.8
Stock with a Beta Coefficient of Greater than 1.0

Figure 8.9
**Stock with a Beta
Coefficient of Less than
1.0**

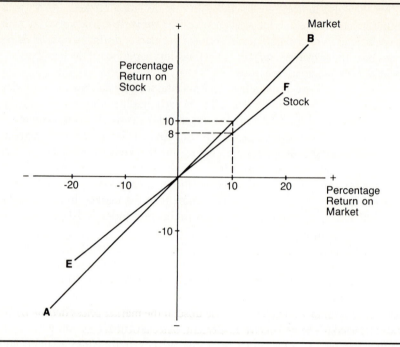

risk will require larger expected returns. (How beta coefficients are used in the valuation of a stock is explained in Chapter 14.)

Variations in beta coefficients

Beta coefficients do vary among firms. This is illustrated in Exhibit 8.1, which presents the beta coefficients for selected firms as computed by Value Line. As may be seen in the table, some firms (e.g., AT&T and Exxon) have relatively low beta coefficients, while the coefficients for other firms (e.g., Kmart and Boeing) are much higher. Investors who are willing to bear more risk may be attracted to these stocks with higher beta coefficients, because when stock market prices rise, these stocks tend to outperform the market. Investors who are less inclined to bear risk may prefer the stocks with low beta coefficients. Although these investors forgo some potential return during rising market prices, they should suffer milder losses during periods of declining stock prices.

Beta coefficients are available

Computing beta coefficients for a significant number of securities over a reasonably long period is an extremely time-consuming and tedious job.[10] Fortunately, the investor may obtain beta coefficients from several sources. The *Value Line Investment Survey* supplies beta coefficients for all securities covered by the service. The information may also be available through the investor's brokerage firm. Although not all brokers compute beta coefficients, the research departments of the larger brokerage firms determine beta coefficients, and these are available to the firms' customers.

Beta coefficients may be unreliable predictors

To be useful, beta coefficients must be reliable predictors of future stock price behavior. For example, a conservative investor who desires stocks that will be stable

---

[10] For an illustration of how beta coefficients are estimated, see the appendix to this chapter.

Company	Beta Coefficient 1978	Beta Coefficient 1986
AT&T	0.65	0.90
Exxon	0.90	0.80
Philip Morris, Inc.	0.90	0.95
Johnson & Johnson	0.95	0.95
IBM	0.95	1.05
GE	1.00	1.05
CBS, Inc.	1.00	1.05
E. I. DuPont	1.05	1.20
Kmart	1.05	1.15
McDonalds	1.05	1.10
Revlon, Inc.	1.10	0.85
Alcoa	1.15	1.15
Boeing	1.25	1.20

Exhibit 8.1
Selected Beta
Coefficients as
Computed by Value Line

will probably purchase stocks with low beta coefficients. An investor selecting a stock with a beta coefficient of 0.6 will certainly be upset if the market prices decline by 10 percent and this stock's price falls by 15 percent, since a beta coefficient of 0.6 indicates that the stock's expected return should decline by only 6 percent when the market declines by 10 percent.

Unfortunately, beta coefficients are constructed with historical price data. Although such data may be accumulated and tabulated for many years, it still does not mean that coefficients based on historical data will be accurate predictors of future returns earned on individual stocks. Beta coefficients can and do change over time. Empirical studies have shown that beta coefficients for individual securities may be very unstable (e.g., the decrease in Revlon's beta or increase in AT&T's beta in Exhibit 8.1).[11] Therefore, the investor should not rely solely on these coefficients for selecting a particular security. However, beta coefficients do give the investor some indication of the systematic risk associated with specific stocks and thus can play an important role in the selection of a security.

Unlike the beta coefficient for individual securities, the beta coefficient for a portfolio composed of several securities is fairly stable over time. Changes in the different beta coefficients tend to average out; while one stock's beta coefficient is increasing, the beta coefficient of another stock is declining. A portfolio's historical beta coefficients, then, can be used as a tool to forecast its future beta coefficient, and this projection should be more accurate than forecasts of an individual security's beta coefficient.

Since a portfolio's beta coefficient is stable, the investor can construct a portfolio that responds in a desired way to market changes. For example, in both 1978 and 1986 the average beta coefficient of the portfolio illustrated in Exhibit 8.1 is slightly greater than 1.[12] If an equal dollar account were invested in each security, the value of

Beta coefficients may help an investor construct a portfolio

---

[11] See Robert A. Levy, "Stationarity of Beta Coefficients," *Financial Analysts Journal* (November–December 1971): 55–62.

[12] The average for the 13 stocks in Exhibit 8.1 is 1.097 in 1978 and 1.031 in 1986.

the portfolio should follow the market values fairly closely, even though individual beta coefficients are greater or less than 1. This tendency of the portfolio to mirror the performance of the market should occur even though selected securities may achieve a return that is superior (or inferior) to that of the market as a whole. Hence, the beta coefficient for the portfolio may be a more useful tool than the beta coefficient for individual securities.

Beta coefficients may also be used in portfolio construction if the investor believes that the market prices will move in a particular direction. For example, if the individual anticipates an increase in prices, he or she may construct an aggressive portfolio consisting solely of securities with high beta coefficients. However, if the anticipated price increases do not occur and the market prices decline, such a strategy may result in a considerable loss.

PORTFOLIO CONSTRUCTION

Why systematic risk is important

Beta coefficients can play an integral part in the construction of an individual's portfolio. Since the investor constructs a diversified portfolio of assets (stocks, bonds, money market mutual funds) issued by firms in a variety of industries (utilities, banking, retailing) and by various governments (state, local, and federal), unsystematic risk is reduced and perhaps completely erased. Thus, the emphasis in portfolio construction has to be centered on systematic risk, which cannot be reduced through diversification. The question really becomes: How much systematic risk is the investor willing to bear, and what return that can be anticipated for bearing that risk?

Bearing more risk requires a higher expected return

To induce the investor to bear more systematic risk, the expected return must be higher. This relationship between risk and expected return is illustrated in Figure 8.10. The horizontal axis measures risk, and the vertical axis measures expected return. If the investor wishes to bear no risk, that individual buys a risk-free security and earns a return of R_F. This investor acquires short-term U.S. government securities (i.e., treasury bills) or perhaps shares in a money market mutual fund that invests

Figure 8.10
Trade-off between Risk and Expected Return

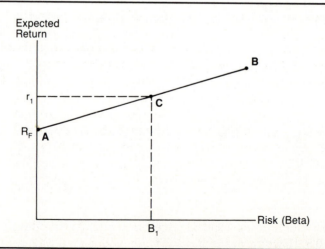

solely in T-bills or other short-term money market instruments guaranteed by the federal government. If, however, the investor wants a higher return, he or she must bear more risk and buy a security represented by point C, which offers an expected return of r_1 in association with B_1 of risk.

Since unsystematic risk is significantly reduced through diversification, the investor determines how much systematic risk he or she is willing to bear and constructs an optimal portfolio consistent with the willingness to endure such risk. The investor thus seeks that best combination of assets (i.e., the best portfolio) that achieves the highest expected return for the given level of risk.

Determining best combinations of assets

This process may be seen by considering the following universe of assets, its expected returns, and its index of risk (i.e., the beta coefficient):

Asset	Expected Return	Beta
Treasury bill	8.0%	0.0
Stock A	12.0	0.5
Stock B	13.5	1.0

The investor facing this universe of securities determines that he or she is willing to accept a portfolio with a beta of 0.8. Two possible portfolios that produce a beta of 0.8 are presented below. For example, a portfolio consisting of treasury bills and stock B can be constructed as follows:

Asset	Weight in Portfolio	Beta	Weighted Beta	Expected Return of Individual Asset	Weighted Expected Return
T-bill	20%	0.0	0.0	8.0%	1.6
Stock B	80%	1.0	0.8	13.5%	10.8
			$\Sigma = 0.8$		$\Sigma = 12.4\%$

In this case a portfolio of 20 percent of the investor's funds in the T-bills and 80 percent in stock B offers a 12.4 percent expected return and a beta of 0.8. Both the expected return and the beta of the portfolio are weighted averages that combine the expected return and the beta of the individual assets weighted by their proportions in the portfolio.

This portfolio, however, is not the only possible combination of these assets that yields a weighted beta of 0.8. Consider the following portfolio consisting of stocks A and B:

Asset	Weight in Portfolio	Beta	Weighted Beta	Expected Return of Individual Asset	Weighted Expected Return
Stock A	40%	0.5	0.20	12.0%	4.8
Stock B	60%	1.0	0.60	13.5%	8.1
			$\Sigma = 0.8$		$\Sigma = 12.9\%$

Investing 40 percent of the funds in stock A and 60 percent in stock B also provides a beta for the portfolio of 0.8. However, this combination also produces a higher ex-

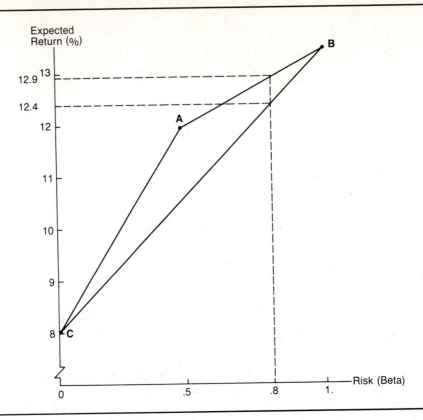

Figure 8.11
Risk and Expected
Return of Various
Portfolios Combining
Three Assets

pected return (12.9 percent versus 12.4 percent) than the previous portfolio of T-bills and stock B. Thus, the portfolio consisting of 40 percent stock A and 60 percent stock B is to be preferred as it offers a higher expected return for a given amount of risk.

In fact there are many possible combinations of T-bills, stock A, and stock B. These combination are illustrated in Figure 8.11. Point *C* represents the individual funds invested in T-bills. Points *A* and *B* represent all the funds invested in stock A and stock B, respectively. The line *CA*, then, represents all the possible combinations of risk and expected return for investments in the T-bills and stock A. Line *AB* represents all the combinations of risk and expected return for investments in stock A and stock B. Line *CB* represents all the combinations of risk and expected return for investments in the T-bills and stock B. As was illustrated above and now may be seen in the figure, some combinations offer inferior returns for a given amount of risk. The combination of 80 percent of the portfolio in stock B and 20 percent in T-bills offers a return of only 12.4 percent for a beta of 0.8. However, 40 percent in stock A and 60 percent in stock B produces an expected return of 12.9 percent for the same amount of risk. Obviously this latter portfolio will be preferred.

Efficient and inefficient portfolios
        All portfolios that offer a lower expected return for a given amount of risk are **inefficient portfolios.** Those portfolios that offer the highest expected return for a given amount of risk are **efficient portfolios.** Conversely, an efficient portfolio offers

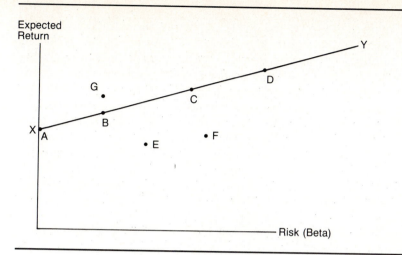

Figure 8.12
Efficient and Inefficient Portfolios

the least amount of risk for a given expected return. The investor's aim, then, is to select that efficient portfolio that is consistent with his or her willingness to bear risk.

Figure 8.11 was constructed using only three assets. In actuality the number of assets available to the individual investor is mind-boggling. However, the principle of modern portfolio construction is the same. The investor considers the expected return on each portfolio and its risk (which in turn depends on the risk and expected returns associated with the individual assets included in the portfolio). Then the individual portfolio is compared with all other portfolios, and those that offer the highest expected return for a given level of risk are considered to be efficient. This efficient set of portfolios is summarized by the line *XY* in Figure 8.12. Thus, portfolios *A, B, C,* and *D* are efficient because they lie on the line. Portfolios *E* and *F,* which lie below the line, are inefficient and would be discarded. Portfolio *G* would certainly be desirable since it lies above the line, but it does not exist. Since the line of all efficient portfolios is constructed by connecting all the points that represent the portfolios offering the highest expected return for a given amount of risk, portfolio *G,* which offers a higher return for a given level of risk, cannot exist. If it did exist, the line that represents all the efficient combinations of risk and expected return would connect *AGCD* and not *ABCD.*

While all the portfolios on line *XY* are efficient, the investor can select only one particular portfolio. A relatively conservative individual might select the portfolio represented by point *B.* Such an investor would be bearing only a modest amount of risk but then could expect only a modest return. An individual who is more willing to bear risk might select a portfolio such as *D,* which offers more expected return but requires more risk bearing. In either case the individual has selected an efficient portfolio, because no other portfolio offers a higher return for the given level of risk.

From a portfolio theory perspective, the biggest problems facing the investor are determining the acceptable level of risk and the risk/return trade-off for all possible assets. Even portfolio managers, who administer trust departments or mutual funds and have access to computers and statistical techniques that permit them to estimate the expected returns and risk for some combinations of assets, cannot estimate every possible combination. The individual investor may even find estimating the potential

returns and risks associated with a few securities to be too time-consuming, if not impossible. However, as is developed in the next section, such calculations need not be done by the individual investor. Instead the efficient market hypothesis suggests the current valuations (i.e., prices) of many assets reflect what the investment community as a whole believes the asset is worth. This valuation encompasses the risk and return associated with each asset. As long as the markets are efficient, the investor can combine the various assets available into a portfolio that meets his or her financial needs and goals. Over a period of time such a portfolio will in all likelihood generate a return that is consistent with the amount of risk borne by the investor. To understand this general conclusion, it is necessary to understand the efficient market hypothesis and its implications for the individual's strategy for portfolio construction.

THE EFFICIENT MARKET HYPOTHESIS

It is perhaps the conceit of some individuals to think that they can outperform the market. But the **efficient market hypothesis** suggests that they cannot. This hypothesis asserts that the security markets are so efficient that the current price of a stock properly values its future dividends and earnings, which are appropriately discounted back to the present. Today's price, then, is a true measure of the security's worth. For the individual investor, security analysis that is designed to determine if the stock is overpriced or underpriced is futile, because the stock is neither.

Undervaluation

This process by which security prices adjust may be illustrated by using the figures relating expected return and risk presented earlier in the chapter. Figure 8.13 reproduces this relationship between expected return and risk. Suppose stock C offered an expected return of r_2 for bearing B_2 of risk. What would the investor do? The obvious answer is rush to purchase the stock, because it offers an exceptional return for the given amount of risk. If several investors had a similar perception of this risk/return relationship, they also would seek to purchase the stock, which would certainly increase its price and reduce the expected return. This price increase and reduction in expected return stops when point C in Figure 8.13 moves back to line AB, which represents all the optimal combinations of risk and expected returns that are available. Thus, the security that was initially undervalued becomes fairly priced and no longer offers an exceptional return.

Overvaluation

The converse case (i.e., overvaluation) is illustrated by stock D in Figure 8.13, which offers an inferior expected return for the given amount of risk. In this case investors perceive the stock as being overvalued and will seek to sell it. This increased desire to sell will depress the stock's price and thus increase the expected return. The decline in the stock's price will cease only after the expected return has risen sufficiently to move point D in Figure 8.13 back to the line representing the optimal risk/return relationship. The efficient market hypothesis thus asserts that the price of any under- or overvalued stock is unstable and will change. The security's equilibrium price (when there is no incentive to change) is a true valuation of what the investment community believes the asset is worth.

The important implication of this theory of efficient markets is that the individual investor cannot consistently beat the market but will tend to earn a return that is consistent with the market and the amount of risk borne by the investor. The individual should realize that the probability of outperforming the market over any extended

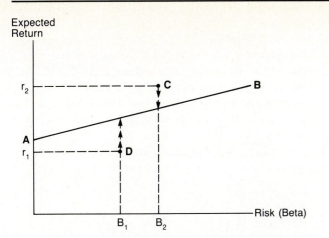

Figure 8.13
**Adjustments in
Expected Returns When
Securities are Under- or
Overvalued**

period is very small. That does not mean that an investor cannot outperform (or under-perform) the market during a short period of time. During a brief period, such as a year, some investors will earn returns that are different from the return earned by the market. However, there is very little chance that those investors will be able to achieve such results for a period of several years (i.e., to outperform the market consistently).

The Speed of Price Adjustments

The second facet of the efficient market hypothesis concerns the speed with which security prices adjust to new information. The hypothesis asserts that the market adjusts prices extremely rapidly as new information is disseminated. In the modern world of advanced communication, information is rapidly disbursed in the investment community. The market then adjusts security prices in accordance with the impact of the news on the firm's future earnings and dividends. By the time that the individual investor has learned the information, security prices probably will have already changed. Thus, the investor will not be able to profit from acting on the information.

Prices adjust rapidly

This adjustment process is illustrated in Figure 8.14, which plots the price of Guilford Mills stock during November 1982. Earlier in 1982 Guilford Mills announced that the company would be acquired for $23 a share. Thus, in early November the stock's price hovered at a modest discount from $23. Then, on November 16, the agreement to sell the company was terminated, and the price fell 3⅞ points from 21⅜ to 17½ in one day. Such price behavior is exactly what the efficient market hypothesis suggests: The market adjusts very rapidly to new information. By the time the announcement was reported in the financial press on November 17, it was too late for the individual investor to react, as the price change had already occurred.

If the market were not so efficient and prices did not adjust rapidly, some investors would be able to adjust their holdings and take advantage of differences in investors' knowledge. Consider the broken line in Figure 8.14. If some investors knew that the agreement had been terminated but others did not, the former could sell their holdings to those who were not informed. The price then may fall over a period of

Price adjustments in an inefficient market

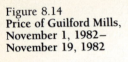

Figure 8.14
Price of Guilford Mills,
November 1, 1982–
November 19, 1982

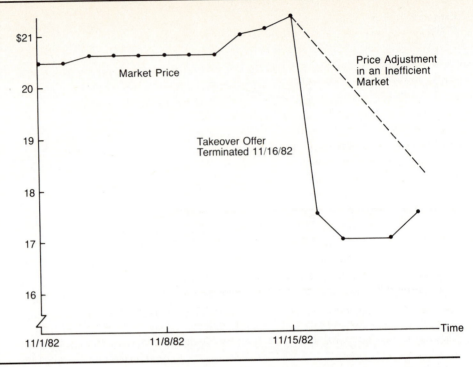

time as the knowledgeable sellers accepted progressively lower prices in order to unload their stock. Of course, if a sufficient number of investors had learned quickly of the termination, the price decline would be rapid as these investors adjusted their valuations of the stock in accordance with the new information. That is exactly what happened, because a sufficient number of investors were rapidly informed and the efficient market quickly adjusted the stock's price.

If an investor were able to anticipate the termination of the merger before it was announced, that individual could avoid the price decline. Obviously some investors did sell their shares just prior to the announcement, but it is also evident that some individuals bought those shares. Certainly one of the reasons for learning the material and performing the various types of analysis throughout this text is to increase one's ability to anticipate events before they occur. However, as the text unfolds, much evidence will be presented that supports the efficient market hypothesis and strongly suggests few investors will over a period of time outperform the market consistently.[13]

SUMMARY

Because the future is uncertain, all investment involves risk. The return the investor anticipates through income and/or capital appreciation may differ considerably from

---

[13] A summary of the empirical evidence in support of the efficient market hypothesis is presented in Chapter 27.

the realized return. This deviation of the realized return from the expected return is the risk associated with investing.

Risk emanates from several sources, which include fluctuations in market prices, fluctuations in interest rates, and loss of purchasing power through inflation. These sources of risk are often referred to as "systematic risk" because the returns on assets tend to move together (i.e., there is a systematic relationship between security returns and market returns). Systematic risk is also referred to as "nondiversifiable risk" because it is not reduced by the construction of a diversified portfolio.

Diversification does, however, reduce "unsystematic risk," which applies to the specific firm and encompasses the nature of the firm's operations and its financing. Since unsystematic risk applies only to the individual asset, there is no systematic relationship between the source of risk and the market as a whole. A portfolio composed of ten to fifteen unrelated assets—for example, stocks in companies in different industries or different types of assets such as common stock, bonds, mutual funds, and real estate—virtually eradicates the impact of unsystematic risk on the portfolio as a whole.

Risk may be measured by the standard deviation, which measures the dispersion around a central tendency, such as an asset's or portfolio's average return. If the realized returns differ considerably from the expected returns, the dispersion is larger (i.e., the standard deviation is larger) and the risk associated with the asset is increased.

An alternative measure of risk, the beta coefficient, measures the responsiveness of an asset's return relative to the return on the market as a whole. If the beta coefficient exceeds 1.0, the stock's return is more volatile than the return on the market, but if the beta is less than 1.0, the return on the stock is less volatile. Since the beta coefficient relates the return on the stock to the market's return, it is an index of the systematic risk associated with the stock.

Beta coefficients play an important role in portfolio construction. While individual beta coefficients may vary, the beta of a portfolio tends to be stable. Hence the portfolio's beta may be used by an investor to construct an efficient portfolio that offers the highest expected return for the amount of risk the individual is willing to bear.

Security selection and trading (i.e. the buying and selling of stocks and bonds) is executed in very competitive financial markets. This competition, as well as the rapid dissemination of information among investors and quick adjustment of asset values, results in efficient security markets. The efficient market hypothesis suggests that the individual investor cannot expect to outperform the market but instead should expect to earn a return consistent with the market return and the individual's risk exposure.

Terms to Remember

Systematic risk

Unsystematic risk

Portfolio risk

Diversification

Expected return

Required return

Dispersion

Beta coefficient

Efficient portfolio

Inefficient portfolio

Efficient market hypothesis

Questions

1. What is the difference between systematic risk and unsystematic risk?

2. What is a diversified portfolio? What type of risk is reduced through diversification? How many securities are necessary to achieve this reduction in risk? What characteristics must these securities possess?

3. What are the sources of return on an investment? What are the differences among the expected return, the required return, and the realized return?

4. Why is a stock's price range (i.e., its high and low prices) a poor measure of risk?

5. If the expected return of two stocks is the same but the standard deviation of the returns differs, which security is to be preferred?

6. If an investor desires diversification, should he or she seek investments that have a high positive correlation?

7. What is a beta coefficient? What do beta coefficients of 0.5, 1.0, and 1.5 mean?

8. How may beta coefficients be used by investors to aid in the construction of a portfolio?

9. What is the relationship between systematic risk (beta) and expected return?

10. What does it mean to say that security markets are efficient? If a stock is overvalued, what should happen to its price?

11. How rapidly will security prices adjust in an efficient market?

12. Why, according to the efficient market hypothesis, should investors not expect to outperform the market consistently?

Problems

1. You are considering three stocks with the following expected dividend yields and capital gains:

	Dividend Yield	Capital Gain
A	14%	0%
B	8	6
C	0	14

   a. What is the expected return on each stock?
   b. How may transactions costs affect your choice among the three securities?

2. A portfolio consists of assets with the following expected returns:

	Expected Return	Weight in Portfolio
Real estate	16%	20%
Low-quality bonds	15	10
AT&T stock	12	30
Savings account	5	40

   a. What is the expected return on the portfolio?
   b. What will be the expected return if the individual reduces the holdings of the AT&T stock to 15 percent and puts the funds into real estate investments?

3. An investor is considering constructing a portfolio. The individual can acquire a risk-free asset that pays 7 percent and can also acquire three securities with the following expected returns and betas:

	Expected Return	Beta
A	9%	0.6
B	11	1.3
C	14	1.5

a. What will be the portfolio's expected return and its beta if the investor constructs the following portfolios?
- Portfolios 1–4: all funds invested solely in each asset.
- Portfolio 5: one quarter of the funds invested in each alternative.
- Portfolio 6: one half of the funds in A and half in C.
- Portfolio 7: one third of the funds in each of the three stocks.

b. Draw a graph using the information in part (a) that relates the expected return and the risk (i.e., beta) associated with each portfolio.

c. According to the graph determined in part (b), are any of the portfolios efficient or inefficient? Is there any combination of the risk-free security and security C that is superior to portfolio 6?

Suggested Readings

Bluestein, Paul. "What's the Big Fuss About Modern Portfolio Theory?" *Forbes* (June 12, 1978): 41–51.

Wallace, Anise. "Is Beta Dead?" *Institutional Investor* (July 1980): 23–29.

These two articles describe in layman's terms modern portfolio theory and attempts to verify it.

Other articles that discuss beta include:

Levy, Robert A. "Stationarity of Beta Coefficients." *Financial Analysts Journal* (November–December 1971): 55–62.

Rosenberg, Barr, and James Guy. "Prediction of Beta from Investment Fundamentals." *Financial Analysts Journal* (May–June 1976): 60–73, and *Financial Analysts Journal* (July–August 1976): 62–71.

Sharpe, William. "Risk, Market Sensitivity, and Diversification." *Financial Analysts Journal* (January–February 1972): 74–79.

The Sharpe article discusses beta in general terms and explains how it is computed. The Levy article shows that betas for individual stocks may not be stable but that betas for a portfolio are stable and can be used as predictors. The Rosenberg and Guy article discusses the estimation of beta with historical data and explains why betas may change, thus reducing their usefulness as predictors for individual securities.

The following books include discussions of risk, security selection, and returns earned by investors.

Brealy, Richard A. *An Introduction to Risk and Return from Common Stocks.* 2d ed. Cambridge, MA.: The MIT Press, 1983.

Lorie, James H., et al. *The Stock Market: Theories and Evidence.* 2d ed. Homewood, Ill.: Richard D. Irwin, 1985.

Malkiel, Burton G. *A Random Walk Down Wall Street.* 2d ed. New York: W. W. Norton, 1981.

Appendix   The Estimation of Beta Coefficients

As was explained in the body of this chapter, investors must bear the systematic and unsystematic risks associated with an individual security. This appendix explains and illustrates how systematic risk may be estimated. The estimation technique uses linear regression analysis, and thus this appendix assumes that the student has had exposure to the use of regression to estimate equations.

Figure 8.15 presents the price of CBS stock and the Dow Jones Industrial average for a period of time. As would be expected, the price of CBS stock tends to follow the market as a whole. For example, when the market declined during 1977, the price of CBS stock also declined. A similar pattern occurred during 1980 when both the price of CBS stock and the Dow Jones Industrial average rose. However, in neither case is there an exact relationship between the two. For example, during 1977 the price of CBS stock declined from $60 to $46, for a 23.3 percent decline, but the Dow Jones Industrial average only fell from 950 to 850, for a 10.5 percent decline. During that period the decline in the value of the individual stock was greater than the decline in the market as a whole.

The tendency for the returns on an investment in a stock to follow the market is shown in Figure 8.16, which is a scatter diagram of monthly returns earned by CBS stock and the Dow Jones Industrial average. The horizontal axis measures the monthly return earned by the Dow Jones Industrial average, while the vertical axis gives the monthly returns earned on the stock. For example, point A represents a return on the Dow Jones Industrials of 7.0 percent and a return on CBS stock of 8.8 percent.

As may be seen from Figure 8.16, the returns on the stock and the returns on the market move in the same direction. The individual points rise from the third quadrant

Figure 8.15
The Price of CBS Stock and the Dow Jones Industrial Average

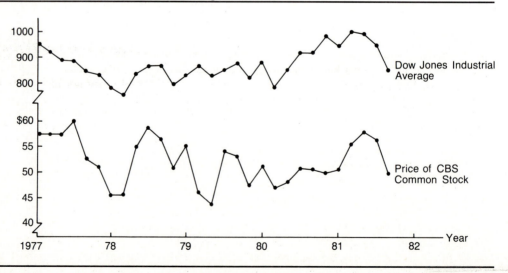

Figure 8.16
Returns on CBS Stock and the Dow Jones Industrial Average

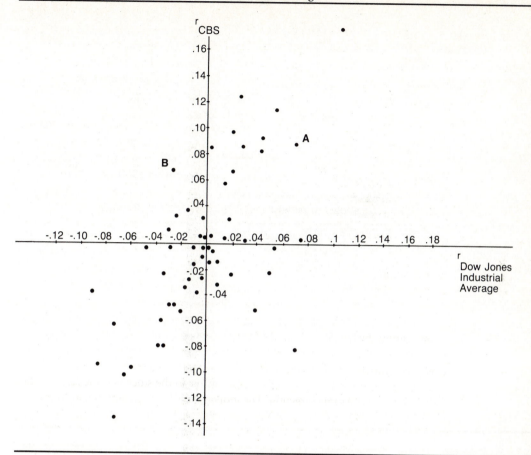

to the first quadrant, which indicates the positive relationship between the return on the market and the return on the individual stock. This relationship is the systematic risk associated with the market. Even though individual observations (e.g., point B, which represents a positive return on the stock when the market fell) may not be consistent with the general pattern, most of the individual observations seem to indicate the positive relationship between movements in the market and the individual stock's price.

Simple linear regression analysis may be used to estimate an equation that summarizes these observations relating returns on CBS stock to changes in the Dow Jones Industrial average. The analysis estimates the linear equation:

$$r_s = a + br_m.$$

The r_s is the return on the stock, while the r_m is the return on the market. The a is the Y intercept, and the b is the slope of the line. This slope is the beta coefficient, which measures the systematic risk associated with the stock.

Figure 8.17
Regression Line Relating Returns on CBS Stock and the Dow Jones Industrial Average

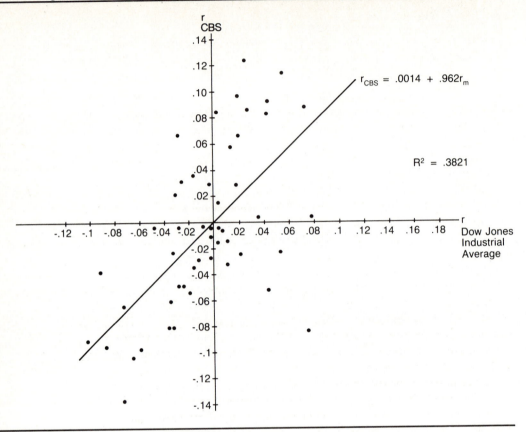

When linear regression analysis is applied to the data used to construct Figure 8.17, the following equation is estimated:

$$r_s = 0.0014 + 0.962\, r_m.$$

The Y intercept (0.0014) is virtually zero, and the slope of the line (i.e., the beta coefficient) is 0.962. This equation is line *AB* in Figure 8.17, which reproduces Figure 8.16 and adds the estimated regression equation. As may be seen in Figure 8.17, the line *AB* runs through the points. Some of the observations are above the line while others are below it. Some of the individual points are close to the line while others appear further away. The closer the points are to the line, the stronger is the relationship between the two variables. This closeness may be measured by the correlation coefficient. A perfect positive correlation would yield a correlation coefficient of 1. No relationship would yield a correlation coefficient of 0. In this illustration the correlation coefficient is 0.6181.

The estimated regression equation may be used to forecast the expected return on the stock. If the analyst expects that the market will rise by 20 percent (i.e., $r_m = 0.2$), the stock should yield a return of

$$r_s = 0.0014 + 0.962(0.2)$$

$$= 0.0014 + 0.1924$$

$$= 19.38\%.$$

As with any forecast, the expected result may not be realized because factors other than a change in the market may affect the stock's price (i.e., the factors associated with nonsystematic risk). The proportion of the return on an investment in CBS stock explained by the movement in the market is measured by the coefficient of determination. This coefficient is the square of the correlation coefficient and is commonly referred to as R^2. In this illustration the R^2 is 0.3821 (0.6181×0.6181), which indicates that about 38 percent of the variation in the return on CBS stock is explained by fluctuations in the market. Obviously some other variables must cause the remaining 62 percent of the variability in the return on CBS stock. These factors are the sources of the unsystematic risk associated with the investment.

Since there is considerable unsystematic risk in this illustration, the estimated beta coefficient may be a poor predictor. That, however, need not mean the coefficient is useless. As was explained in the body of this chapter, the portfolio's beta, which is an aggregate of the individual stocks' betas, may be a good predictor of the return the individual can expect from movements in the market. Factors that adversely affect the return earned on one security may be offset by factors that enhance the return earned on other securities in the portfolio.

Since unsystematic risk can be significantly reduced, the investor needs to determine how much systematic risk he or she is willing to bear. Such determination is subjective and is affected by considerations such as age, family responsibilities, and stability of employment. Once each security's beta coefficients are known, the investor can construct a diversified portfolio with an aggregate beta that is consistent with that individual's willingness to bear systematic risk.

III Investing in Fixed-Income Securities

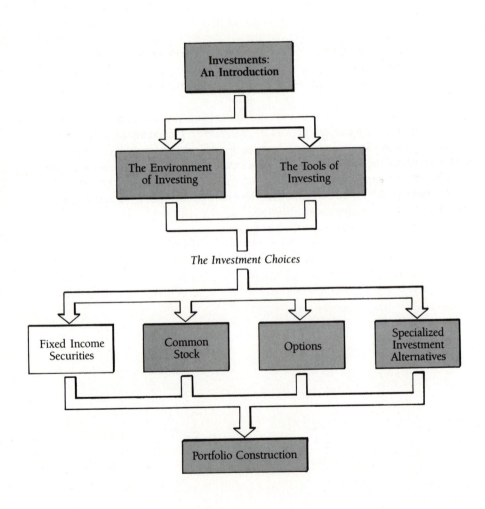

Investments:
An Introduction

The Environment
of Investing

The Tools of
Investing

The Investment Choices

Fixed Income
Securities

Common
Stock

Options

Specialized
Investment
Alternatives

Portfolio Construction

*P*art Three considers investments in securities that pay a fixed annual income. The annual interest or dividend payments are the same each year. Since such investments consist primarily of long-term bonds issued by corporations and governments, most of Part Three is devoted to these bonds.

These securities produce a constant flow of income and for many years were considered to be good investments for conservative individuals. However, the wide fluctuations in bond prices during the 1970s and early 1980s have increased the risk associated with investing in bonds. While bonds still offer a flow of interest income and safety associated with the legal obligation to repay the principal, many bonds can no longer be considered safe investments that are appropriate for conservative investors seeking income and the preservation of capital.

9

The Market for Debt

LEARNING OBJECTIVES

After completing this chapter you should be able to

1. Understand the features common to all bonds.
2. Explain the purpose of the indenture and the role of the trustee.
3. Differentiate between bearer bonds and registered bonds.
4. Ascertain the sources of risk to the bondholder.
5. Describe the procedure for buying a bond.
6. Differentiate among the types of corporate bonds.
7. Distinguish between the ways bonds are retired.

M*any corporations and governments have issued long-term debt to finance long-term investments, such as the expansion of plant and equipment or the construction of roads and schools. Internally generated funds (profits and depreciation for corporations and tax revenues for governments) may be insufficient to finance such investments on a pay-as-you-go basis. Long-term debt, which matures at a specified time longer than one year, permits firms and governments to acquire assets now and pay for them over a period of years. The debt is then retired for corporations by the cash flow that is generated by plant and equipment and for governments by the fees or tax revenues that are collected.*

This chapter is concerned with long-term debt and covers (1) the characteristics common to all of these debt instruments, (2) the risks associated with investing in debt, (3) the mechanics of purchasing debt instruments, and (4) the retirement of debt. Chapter 10 covers the valuation of debt. Like stock, debt may be purchased initially either by financial institutions in a private placement or by individuals through a public offering. Once the securities have been issued, secondary markets develop. These debt instruments may be bought and sold on the organized security exchanges or in the over-the-counter markets. These securities are generally very marketable, since there is an active secondary market in many corporate and government bonds.

GENERAL FEATURES OF DEBT INSTRUMENTS

Interest and Maturity

All **bonds** (i.e., long-term debt instruments) have similar characteristics. They represent the indebtedness (liability) of their issuers in return for a specified sum, which is called the **principal.** Virtually all debt has a **maturity date**, which is the particular date by which it must be paid off. When debt is issued, the length of time to maturity is set, and it may range from one day to 20 or 30 years or more. If the maturity date falls within a year of the date of issuance, the debt is referred to as short-term debt. Long-term debt matures more than a year after it has been issued. (Debt that matures in from one to ten years is sometimes referred to as intermediate debt.) The owners of debt instruments receive a flow of payments, which is called **interest,** in return for the use of their money. Interest should not be confused with other forms of income, such as the cash dividends that are paid by common and preferred stock. Dividends are distributions from earnings, whereas interest is an expense of borrowing.

Principal

Maturity

Interest

A bond is illustrated in Exhibit 9.1. This exhibit reproduces the face of a registered 8¾ percent debenture of AT&T. If this bond were not a sample, the principal amount would have been stated immediately following the words "the principal sum of." This bond matures on May 15, 2000. A bond is also individually numbered for identification, and the name of the owner is recorded on the certificate's face. The certificates may be endorsed on the back by the owner, and the title may be readily

Exhibit 9.1
Example of the Face of a Corporate Bond

Coupon rate
Maturity date

Trustee

changed from one owner to another by the transfer agent, which is usually the bank that countersigns the security and acts as the trustee for the bond issue.

When a debt instrument such as this bond is issued, the rate of interest to be paid by the borrower is established. This rate is frequently referred to as the bond's **coupon rate** (e.g., the 8¾ percent in Exhibit 9.1). The amount of interest is usually fixed over the lifetime of the bond. (There are exceptions; for example, see the section on variable interest rate bonds later in this chapter.) The return earned by the investor, however, need not be equal to the specified rate of interest because bond prices change. They may be purchased at a discount (a price below the face amount or principal) or at a premium (a price above the face amount of the bond). The return actually earned, then, depends on the interest received, the purchase price, and what the investor receives upon selling the bond or redeeming it.

Yields: Current and to maturity

The potential return offered by a bond is referred to as the yield. Yield is frequently expressed in two ways: the **current yield** and the **yield to maturity**. Current yield refers only to the annual flow of interest or income. The yield to maturity refers to the yield that the investor will earn if the debt instrument is held from the moment of purchase until it is redeemed at par (face value) by the issuer. The difference between the current yield and the yield to maturity is discussed at length in the section on the pricing of bonds in Chapter 10.

Structure of yields

There is a relationship between yield and the length of time to maturity for debt instruments of the same level of risk. Generally, the longer the time to maturity, the higher the rate of interest. This relationship is illustrated in Figure 9.1, which plots the yield on various United States government securities as of July 16, 1986. This figure, which is frequently referred to as a **yield curve**, shows that the bonds with the longest time to maturity have the highest interest rates. For example, bonds with one

**Figure 9.1
Positively Sloped Yield
Curve**

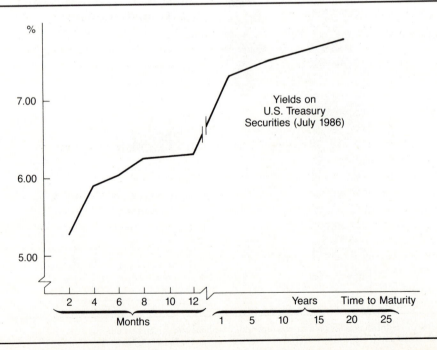

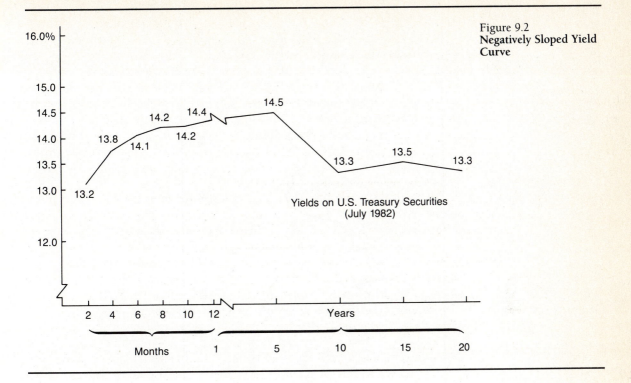

Figure 9.2
Negatively Sloped Yield Curve

Yields on U.S. Treasury Securities
(July 1982)

year to maturity yield 6.4 percent, whereas bonds that mature after ten years offer more than 7.5 percent.

One would expect such a relationship because the longer the time to maturity, the longer the investor will have his or her funds tied up. To induce investors to lend their money for lengthier periods, it is usually necessary to pay them more interest. Also, there is more risk involved in purchasing a bond with a longer period to maturity, since the fortunes of the issuer are more difficult to estimate for the longer term. This means that investors will ordinarily require additional compensation to bear the risk associated with long-term debt.

Although such a relationship between time and yield does usually exist, there have been periods when the opposite has occurred (i.e., when short-term interest rates exceeded long-term interest rates). This happened from 1978 to 1979, and again in 1981, when short-term interest rates were higher than long-term rates. The yields on treasury securities (securities issued by the Treasury Department) in July 1982 are illustrated in Figure 9.2. In this case the yield curve has a slight negative slope, which indicates that as the length of time to maturity increased, the interest rates declined. Thus, securities maturing in less than a year had a yield of greater than 14 percent, while the long-term debt that matured after ten years yielded less than 14 percent.

Such a yield curve can be explained by inflation, which exceeded 10 percent in 1981 to 1982. The board of governors of the Federal Reserve was pursuing a tight monetary policy in order to fight inflation. It sold short-term government securities (i.e., treasury bills) in an effort to reduce the capacity of commercial banks to lend. These sales depressed the prices of all fixed-income securities, which resulted in

Negative-sloped yield curves

Figure 9.3
Yield on Treasury Bills and Treasury Bonds (1972–January 1986)

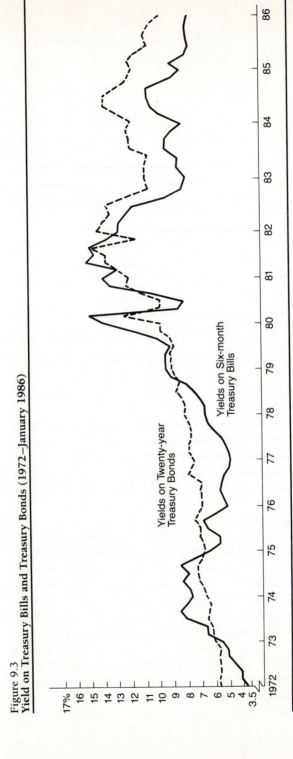

higher yields. (As is explained in detail in Chapter 10, yields on debt instruments rise as their prices fall.) The yields on short-term securities rose more than those on long-term securities, and this, coupled with other events in the money and capital markets, resulted in the negative-sloped yield curve. When the rate of inflation abated during the mid-1980s, the yield curve returned to the positive slope that it has maintained during most periods.

Figures 9.1 and 9.2 also illustrate that interest rates do change. (The student should remember that the interest rate is the current rate paid for the use of credit. This should not be confused with the coupon rate, which is fixed when the debt instrument is issued.) Although all interest rates fluctuate, short-term rates are more volatile than long-term interest rates. This is illustrated in Figure 9.3, which plots the yields on a six-month treasury bill and on a twenty-year treasury bond. As may be seen from the figure, the fluctuation in yields for the short-term bill is greater than that for the long-term bond. For example, the yield on a six-month treasury bill increased from 3.6 percent per year in January 1972 to over 8.5 percent in August 1973, while the yield on a twenty-year treasury bond rose from 5.6 to only 6.8 percent during the same period. This figure illustrates not only the greater fluctuation in short-term yields but also how quickly changes can occur. For example, the annual short-term rate rose from 10.1 percent to 15 percent in only *three* months in 1979 to 1980 in response to changes in the demand for the supply of short-term credit.[1]

Interest rates fluctuate

The Indenture

Each debt agreement has terms that the debtor must meet. These are stated in a legal document called the **indenture**.[2] These terms include the coupon rate, the date of maturity, and any other conditions required of the debtor. One of the more frequent of these requirements is the pledging of collateral, which is property that the borrower must offer to secure the loan. For example, the collateral for a mortgage loan is the building. Any other assets owned by the borrower, such as securities or inventory, may also be pledged to secure a loan. If the borrower defaults on the debt, the creditor may seize the collateral and sell it to recoup the principal. **Default** occurs when the borrower fails to meet not only the payment of interest but *any* of the terms of the indenture. The other conditions of the indenture are just as important as meeting the interest payments on time, and often they may be more difficult for the debtor to satisfy.

Terms are specified in the indenture

Examples of common loan restrictions include (1) limits on paying dividends, (2) limits on issuing additional debt, and (3) restrictions on merging or significantly changing the nature of the business without the prior consent of the creditors. In addition, loan agreements usually specify that if the firm defaults on any other outstanding debt issues, this debt issue is also in default, in which case the creditors may seek immediate repayment. Default on one issue, then, usually puts all outstanding debt in default.

These examples do not exhaust all the possible conditions of a given loan. Since each loan is separately negotiated, there is ample opportunity for differences among

---

[1] For additional discussions of the structure of yields, see the appendices to this chapter and Chapter 12.

[2] For publicly held corporate bond issues, the indenture is filed with the Securities and Exchange Commission.

loan agreements. During periods of scarce credit, the terms of a loan agreement will be stricter, whereas during periods of lower interest rates and more readily available money, the restrictions will tend to be more lenient. The important point, however, is that if any part of the loan agreement is violated, the creditor may declare that the debt is in default and may seek a court order to enforce the terms of the indenture.

The Role of the Trustee

A trustee is appointed for publicly held bonds

Many debt instruments are purchased by individual investors who may be unaware of all of the terms of the indenture. Even if individual investors are aware of the terms, they may be too geographically dispersed to take concerted action in case of default. To protect their interests, a **trustee** is appointed for each publicly held bond issue. It is the trustee's job to see that the terms of the indenture are upheld and to take remedial action if the company defaults on the terms of the loan. For performing these services, the trustee receives compensation from the issuer of the debt.

Trustees are usually commercial banks that serve both the debtor and the bondholders. They act as transfer agents for the bonds when ownership is changed through sales in the secondary markets. The signature of a trustee on the bond is a guarantee of the authenticity of the bond. These banks receive from the debtor the funds to pay the interest, and this money is then distributed to the individual bondholders. It is also the job of the trustee to inform the bondholders if the firm is no longer meeting the terms of the indenture. In case of default, the trustee may take the debtor to court to enforce the terms of the contract. If there is a subsequent reorganization or liquidation of the company, the trustee continues to act on behalf of the individual bondholders to protect their principal.

Forms of Debt

Registered and bearer bonds

Debt instruments are issued in one of two forms: (1) **registered bonds** or (2) **bearer bonds** to which coupons are attached (therefore, they are also called **coupon bonds**). Registered bonds are similar to stock certificates; the bonds are registered in the owner's name, and the interest payments are sent to the owner. When the bond is sold, it is registered in the name of the new owner by the transfer agent (i.e., the trustee). The AT&T bond in Exhibit 9.1 is an example of a registered bond. The names of both the owner (because this is a sample bond, the owner's name has been omitted) and the trustee (the Bank of New York) are stated on the front of such bonds.

Bearer bonds are entirely different. Ownership is evidenced by mere possession of the bond and is transferred simply by passing the debt instrument from the seller to the buyer; no new certificates are issued. Thus, securities in this form are extremely easy to transfer. However, if they are lost, they are like currency. Therefore, the possibility of theft is a real concern that requires the owner to be extremely cautious when handling these bonds.

Coupons and coupon clippers

Since the debtor does not know the names of the owners of bearer securities, coupons for interest payments are attached to the bond. The owner must detach the coupon and send it to the paying agent (the trustee) to collect the interest. In the past, most bonds were of this type. Investors who relied on fixed interest income for their livelihood were frequently called coupon clippers.

Today some bonds are available in both registered and coupon form. Under current law, all newly issued bonds have to be registered in the owner's name. However,

previously issued coupon bonds will still exist. An investor who prefers a certain type can consult a bond publication, such as *Standard & Poor's Bond Guide,* to determine which are coupon bonds and which are registered bonds. If the bond issue has both forms, the investor may specify the type desired when the bond is purchased from the broker.

An example of a bearer bond with coupons attached is shown in Exhibit 9.2. The bond has 50 coupons (only the first one is illustrated), and each represents a six-month interest payment. This particular bond is an income nonmortgage bond, which means that it is unsecured and among the riskiest of all debt instruments. The bond was never retired, and not one interest payment was ever made!

RISK

An important characteristic of all debt is risk: risk that the interest will not be paid, risk that the principal will not be repaid, risk that the price of the debt instrument may decline, and risk that inflation will continue, thereby reducing the purchasing power of the interest payments and of the principal when it is repaid. These risks vary significantly with different types of debt. For example, there is no risk of default on the interest payments and principal repayments of the debt of the federal government. The reason for this absolute safety is that the federal government has the power to tax and to create money. The government can always issue the money that is necessary to pay the interest and repay the principal.[3]

The safety of federal government debt

The procedure is more subtle than just printing new money. The federal government issues new debt and sells it to the Federal Reserve Board. With the proceeds of these sales, the federal government retires the old debt. The money supply increases because newly created money is used to pay for the debt. The effect of selling debt to the Federal Reserve Board and then using the proceeds to retire existing debt (or to finance a current deficit) is no different from printing and spending new money. The money supply expands in either case. Thus, the federal government can always pay its interest expense and retire its debt when it becomes due.

Even though the federal government can refund its debt and hence is free of the risk of default, the prices of the federal government's bonds can and do fluctuate. In addition, the purchasing power of the dollar may decline as a result of inflation, and, therefore, the purchasing power of funds invested in debt also may decline. Thus, investing in federal government securities is not entirely free of risk, since the investor may suffer losses from price fluctuations of the debt or from inflation.

Risk from price fluctuations and inflation

The debt of firms, individuals, and state and local governments involves even greater risk, for all of these debtors may default on their obligations. To aid buyers of debt instruments, several companies have developed **credit rating systems**. The most important of these services are Moody, Dun and Bradstreet, and Standard & Poor. Although these firms do not rate all debt instruments, they do rate the degree of risk of a significant number.

Exhibit 9.3 gives the risk classifications presented by Moody and Standard & Poor. The rating systems are quite similar, for each classification of debt involving little

Risk classifications and ratings

---

[3] The decline in the value of the dollar in foreign countries may reduce the attractiveness of federal obligations. Fluctuations in the value of the dollar, then, do impose significant risk for foreigners who invest in these securities.

Exhibit 9.2
A Coupon Bond

Coupon no. 1

risk (high-quality debt) receives a rating of triple A, while debt involving greater risk (poorer quality debt) receives progressively lower ratings.

Since the rating firms are analyzing similar data, their ratings of specific debt issues should be reasonably consistent. This consistency is illustrated by Exhibit 9.4, which gives the ratings for several different bond issues. In most cases, both Moody and Standard & Poor assigned comparable ratings to certain debt instruments. Even when the ratings are different (e.g., the Gulf and Western 7 percent bond that is due in 2003), the discrepancies are small.

Moody's Bond Ratings*

Aaa	Bonds of highest quality	B	Bonds that lack characteristics of a desirable investment
Aa	Bonds of high quality		
A	Bonds whose security of principal and interest is considered adequate but may be impaired in the future	Caa	Bonds in poor standing that may be defaulted
Baa	Bonds of medium grade that are neither highly protected nor poorly secured	Ca	Speculative bonds that are often in default
Ba	Bonds of speculative quality whose future cannot be considered well assured	C	Bonds with little probability of any investment value (lowest rating)

For ratings Aa through B, 1 indicates the high, 2 indicates the middle, and 3 indicates the low end of the rating class.

Standard & Poor's Bond Ratings†

AAA	Bonds of highest quality	BB	Bonds of lower medium grade with few desirable investment characteristics
AA	High-quality debt obligations		
A	Bonds that have a strong capacity to pay interest and principal but may be susceptible to adverse effects	B	Primarily speculative bonds with great uncertainties and major risk if exposed to adverse conditions
BBB	Bonds that have an adequate capacity to pay interest and principal but are more vulnerable to adverse economic conditions or changing circumstances	CCC	
		C	Income bonds on which no interest is being paid
		D	Bonds in default

Plus (+) and minus (−) are used to show relative strength and weakness within a rating category.

Exhibit 9.3
Bond Ratings

* *Source:* Adapted from *Moody's Bond Record,* January 1984.
† *Source:* Adapted from *Standard & Poor's Bond Guide,* January 1984.

Firm	Interest (Coupon %)	Year of Maturity	Moody's Rating	Standard & Poor's Rating
AT&T	7	2001	Aa3	AA
Consumers Power	7½	2001	Ba3	BB
Dow Chemical	8⁹⁄₁₀	2000	A2	A−
Gulf & Western	7	2003	A3	BBB
Mobil	7⅜	2001	Aa3	AA
World Airways	10	1993	Caa	CCC
Xerox	8⅝	1999	A2	AA−

Exhibit 9.4
Ratings for Selected Bonds as of January 1986

Sources: Moody's Bond Record, January 1986, and *Standard & Poor's Bond Guide,* January 1986.

These ratings play an important role in the marketing of debt obligations. Since the possibility of default may be substantial for poor-quality debt, some financial institutions and investors will not purchase debt with a low credit rating. Many financial institutions, especially commercial banks, are prohibited by law from purchasing bonds with a rating below Baa. Thus, if the rating of a bond issued by a firm or a municipality is low or declines from the original rating, the issuer may have difficulty selling its debt. Corporations and municipal governments try to maintain good credit ratings, since high ratings reduce the cost of borrowing and increase the marketability of the debt.

While the majority of corporate and municipal bonds are rated, there are exceptions. If a firm or municipality believes it will be able to market the securities without a rating, it may choose not to incur the costs necessary to have the securities rated. Unrated securities tend to be small issues and, since they lack the approval implied by a rating, probably should be viewed as possessing considerable risk.

Besides the risk of default, creditors are also subject to the risk of price fluctuations. Once debt has been issued, the market price of the debt will rise or fall depending on market conditions. If interest rates rise, the price of existing debt must fall so that its fixed interest payments relative to its price become competitive with the higher rates. In the event that interest rates decline, the opposite is true. The higher fixed interest payments of the bond make the debt more attractive than comparable newly issued bonds, and buyers will be willing to pay more for the debt issue. Why these fluctuations in the price of debt instruments occur is explained in more detail in Chapter 10, which discusses the valuation of debt instruments.

The importance of maturity

There is, however, one feature of debt that partially compensates for the risk of price fluctuations. The holder knows that the debt ultimately matures: The principal must be repaid. If the price of the bond decreases and the debt instrument sells for a discount (i.e., less than the face value), the value of the debt must appreciate as it approaches maturity, because on the day of maturity, the full amount of the principal must be repaid.

The loss of purchasing power through inflation

The final risk that all creditors must endure is inflation, which reduces the purchasing power of money. During periods of inflation the debtor repays the loan in money that purchases less. Creditors must receive a rate of interest that is at least equal to the rate of inflation to maintain their purchasing power. If lenders anticipate inflation, they will demand a higher rate of interest to help protect their purchasing power. For example, if the rate of inflation is 8 percent, the creditors may demand 10 percent, which nets them 2 percent in real terms (before income tax). Although inflation still causes the real value of the capital to decline, the higher interest rate partially offsets the effects of inflation.

The importance of anticipating the rate of inflation

If creditors do not anticipate inflation, the rate of interest may be insufficient to compensate for the loss in purchasing power. Inflation, then, hurts the creditors and helps the debtors, who are repaying the loans with money that purchases less.

The supposed inability of creditors to anticipate inflation has led to a belief that during inflation it is better to be a debtor. However, creditors invariably make an effort to protect their position by demanding higher interest rates. There is a transfer of purchasing power from creditors to debtors only if the creditors do not fully anticipate the inflation and do not demand sufficiently high interest rates. A transfer of purchasing power from debtors to creditors will occur in the opposite situation. If inflation is anticipated but does not occur, many debtors may pay artificially high interest

rates, which transfers purchasing power ~~~~~~~~~~~eir creditors.[4] Hence, the
transfer of purchasing power ~~~~~~~~~~~~ inaccurately anticipates
the future rate of infla~~~~~

THE MECHANIC~~~~~~~~~~~~~~DS

Bonds may be purchased in~~~~~~~~~~~~~~~~~~~~~vestor can buy them   *Bonds are purchased*
through a brokerage firm, a~~~~~~~~~~~~~~~~~~~~nent securities) can   *through brokers*
be purchased through comm~~~~~~~~~~~~~~~~~~~~~orders that may be
used to buy stock (e.g., the ma~~~~~~~~~~~~~~~pecified price) also
apply to the purchase of bonds.~~~~~~~~~~~~~~~hrough the use of
margin.

The bonds of many compani~~~~~~~~~~~~~~~~American stock   *Listed bonds*
exchanges. In addition, there is a ~~~~~~~~~~~n the over-the-
counter markets. Like listed stocks, ~~~~~~~~~by the financial
press. Exhibit 9.5 is an example of ~~~~~~~~~~reporting the
trading in the 8¾ AT&T bond that w~~~~~~~~~~~is a bit tricky
to read. The entry is for a $1,000 bond~~~~~~~~units greater
than $1,000). Bond prices are reported~~~~~~~~91¼ means
91¼% of $1,000, or $912.50. The bond ~~~~~~~~~~~percent and matures
in the year 2000, which is reported as 8¾~~~~~~~current yield is the annual interest
payment divided by the price ($87.50 ÷ $906.25 = 9.7%). The number of bonds
traded was 94, which means that, according to face value, $94,000 worth of these
bonds changed ownership. The remaining entries are the same as those of stock transactions. These include the high (91¼), low (90¼), and closing (90⅝) prices and the
net change (−¾) from the previous day.

After the debt has been purchased, the broker sends a **confirmation statement**.   *The confirmation*
Exhibit 9.6 presents the confirmation statements for the purchase and subsequent sale   *statement*
of $2,000 in face value worth of Tesoro Petroleum bonds. In addition to a description
of the securities, the confirmation statements include the price, the day of the transaction, the settlement day, the commission (note the increase in commission rates
from $10 to $20 between the time of purchase and the time of sale), any fees, and
accrued interest.

Bonds earn interest every day, but the firm distributes the interest payments only   *The handling of accrued*
twice a year. Thus, when a bond is purchased, the buyer owes the previous owner   *interest*
accrued interest for the days that the owner held the bond. In the case of the first
transaction, the purchase was made several months after the last interest payment, so
the accrued interest amounted to $43.46. This interest is added to the purchase price
that the buyer must pay. When the bond is sold, the seller receives the accrued interest. The second transaction occurred soon after the interest payment, and in this case
the accrued interest was only $13.13, which was added to the proceeds of the sale.

The profit or loss from the investment cannot be figured as the difference between
the proceeds of the sale and the amount that is due after the purchase (i.e., $1,548.13

---

[4]Debtors may seek to protect themselves from the anticipated inflation *not* occurring by having the bond be callable. The
call feature is discussed later in this chapter.

Exhibit 9.5
Illustration of an Entry for a $1,000 Bond Traded on the New York Stock Exchange

NEW YORK EXCHANGE BONDS

Thursday, January 2, 1986

Total Volume $30,860,000

SALES SINCE JANUARY 1

1986	1985	1984
$30,860,000	$28,795,000	$23,222,000

	Domestic Thu.	Domestic Tue.	All Issues Thu.	All Issues Tue.
Issues traded	899	895	901	897
Advances	365	411	366	412
Declines	318	291	318	291
Unchanged	216	193	217	194
New highs	112	122	112	123
New lows	3	6	3	6

CORPORATION BONDS
Volume, $30,810,000

Bonds	Cur Yld	Vol	High	Low	Close	Net Chg.
AMR 10¼06	12.	2	88	88	88	−1½
APL 10¾97	16.	25	68½	67	67	−1½
ARX 9⅜05	cv	5	126	126	126	−1
Advst 9s08	cv	21	101½	101	101	− ¼
AetnLf 8⅛07	9.6	1	84⅜	84⅜	84⅜	.....
ACan 6s97	8.5	3	70⅝	70⅝	70⅝	+ ⅝
AExC 7.8s92	8.4	5	93	93	93	+ ½
AExC 7.7s87	7.8	10	99⅛	99⅛	99⅛	− ⅜
AExC 10.1s90	9.9	10	101¾	101⅝	101⅝	−1⅛
AmGn 11s08	cv	19	190½	190¼	190¼	−4¾
AmMed 9½01	cv	430	103½	102¾	103	.....
AmMed 8¼08	cv	25	85	85	85	+ ½
AmMed 11¾99	12.	5	101	100¼	100¼	−2⅝
ATT 2⅝s86	2.7	20	98½	98	98	.....
ATT 2⅞s87	3.1	6	94	94	94	.....
ATT 3⅞s90	4.5	80	86½	86	86½	+ ¾
ATT 8¾00	9.7	94	91¼	90¼	90⅝	− ¾
ATT 7s01	9.0	57	77⅜	77	77⅜	+ ¼
ATT 7⅛s03	9.3	26	77	76¾	76¾	+ ⅜
ATT 8.80s05	9.8	125	90⅝	89¾	90	.....
ATT 8⅝s07	9.7	19	88⅝	88½	88½	− ⅜
ATT 10⅜90	10.	462	101⅞	101½	101⅞	.....
ATT 13¼91	13.	658	103⅛	103	103⅛	.....
Ames 8½09	cv	35	146½	145⅛	145⅛	− ⅞
Amoco 6s91	7.0	37	85½	85½	85½	−1⅛

Source: The Wall Street Journal, Jan. 3, 1986. Reprinted by permission of *The Wall Street Journal,* © Dow Jones & Company Inc., 1986. All Rights Reserved.

minus $1,610.96 in Exhibit 9.7). Instead, an adjustment must be made for the accrued interest. This procedure is illustrated in Exhibit 9.7. First, the accrued interest must be subtracted from the amount due to obtain the cost of the bond. Thus, $1,610.96 minus $43.46 is the cost ($1,567.50) of this purchase. Second, the accrued interest must also be subtracted from the proceeds of the sale. Thus, $1,548.13 minus $13.13 yields the revenues from the sale. To determine the profit or loss, the cost basis is subtracted from the sale value. In this particular instance, that is $1,535 (the sale value) minus $1,567.50 (the cost basis), which represents a loss of $32.50.

Bonds that trade flat

A few bonds do trade without accrued interest. These bonds are currently in default and are not paying interest. Such bonds are said to trade **flat**, and an *F* is placed next to them in the transactions reported by the financial press. These bonds are of little interest except to speculators. The risk in buying them is substantial, but some

190

Scott & Stringfellow

MEMBERS

NEW YORK, AMERICAN (ASSOC.) AND RICHMOND STOCK EXCHANGES

909 EAST MAIN STREET
RICHMOND, VIRGINIA 23219
(703) 643-1811

7 HOTEL STREET
WARRENTON, VIRGINIA 22186
(703) 347-2820

29 EAST BEVERLEY STREET
STAUNTON, VIRGINIA 24401
(703) 886-2396

8 SOUTH BRADDOCK STREET
WINCHESTER, VIRGINIA 22601
(703) 667-3311

WE CONFIRM THE FOLLOWING TRANSACTION SUBJECT TO CONDITIONS ON REVERSE SIDE.

PLEASE RETAIN THIS COPY FOR YOUR INCOME TAX RECORDS

YOU BOUGHT	YOU SOLD	SECURITY DESCRIPTION	PRICE
2000		TESORO PETROLEUM 5 1/4 2/1/89RGD	77 7/8

TRADE DATE AND NUMBER	SECURITY NUMBER	PRINCIPAL	COMMISSION	STATE TAX OR INTEREST	S.E.C. FEE	POSTAGE MISCELLANEOUS
072	936492	1,557.50	10.00	43.46		

ACCOUNT NUMBER | TYPE | V | BRANCH | REG REP | CODES A B C D
34295 1 1 01 03 2 1 2

SEE REVERSE SIDE FOR EXPLANATION OF CODES.

8

SETTLEMENT DATE　　NET AMOUNT DUE *　1,610.96

Scott & Stringfellow Inc.

909 EAST MAIN STREET　RICHMOND, VIRGINIA 23219

(804) 643-1811

MEMBERS

NEW YORK, AMERICAN (ASSOC.) AND RICHMOND STOCK EXCHANGES

OFFICES IN

BLUEFIELD, W. VIRGINIA 24701
(304) 325-3631

STAUNTON, VIRGINIA 24401
(703) 886-2396

CULPEPER, VIRGINIA 22701
(703) 825-0783

WARRENTON, VIRGINIA 22186
(703) 347-2820

WINCHESTER, VIRGINIA 22601
(703) 667-3311

WE CONFIRM THE FOLLOWING TRANSACTION SUBJECT TO CONDITIONS ON REVERSE SIDE.

PLEASE RETAIN THIS COPY FOR YOUR INCOME TAX RECORDS

YOU BOUGHT	YOU SOLD	SECURITY DESCRIPTION	PRICE
	2000	TESORO PETROLEUM 5 1/4 2/1/89RGD	77 3/4

TRADE DATE AND NUMBER	SECURITY NUMBER	PRINCIPAL	COMMISSION	STATE TAX OR INTEREST	S.E.C. FEE	POSTAGE MISCELLANEOUS
182	936492	1,555.00	20.00	13.13		

ACCOUNT NUMBER | TYPE | V | BRANCH | REG REP | CODES A B C D
46078 1 8 01 19 1 1 8

SEE REVERSE SIDE FOR EXPLANATION OF CODES.

8

223-54-4369

SETTLEMENT DATE　　NET AMOUNT DUE *　1,548.13

CUSIP 881609AA9

Exhibit 9.6
Confirmation
Statements from
Purchase and Sale

Source: Reprinted with permission from Scott & Stringfellow, Inc.

Cost basis of the bond:	
Purchase price plus commissions	$1,610.96
Less accrued interest	−43.46
	$1,567.50
Revenue from the sale:	
Proceeds of the sale less commissions	$1,548.13
Less accrued interest	−13.13
	$1,535.00
Profit (or loss) on the investment:	
Return from the sale of the bond	$1,535.00
Cost basis of the bond	−1,567.50
Profit (or loss) on the investment	$ (32.50)

Exhibit 9.7
Determination of Profit
or Loss on the Sale of
a Bond

do resume interest payments that can result in substantial returns. (See, for instance, the TWA bond illustrated in Exhibit 9.8, which is discussed later under income bonds.)

VARIETY OF CORPORATE BONDS

Corporations issue many types of bonds: mortgage bonds, equipment trust certificates, debenture bonds and subordinated debentures, income bonds, convertible bonds, variable interest rate bonds, and zero coupon bonds. These corporate debt instruments are either secured or unsecured. If a debt instrument is secured, the debtor pledges a specific asset as collateral. In case of default, the creditor may seize this collateral (through a court proceeding). Bonds that are not collateralized by specific assets are unsecured. If the debtor were to default, there would be no specific assets the creditors could seize to satisfy their claims on the borrower. Such unsecured debt instruments are supported by the general capacity of the firm to service its debt (i.e., pay the interest and repay the principal). Thus, the capacity of the borrower to generate operating income (i.e., earnings before interest and taxes) is crucial to the safety of unsecured debt obligations.

Mortgage Bonds

Mortgage bonds are secured by real estate

Mortgage bonds are issued to purchase specific fixed assets, which are then pledged to secure the debt. This type of bond is frequently issued by utility companies. The proceeds that are raised by selling the debt are used to build power plants, and these plants secure the debt. As the plants generate revenues, the firm earns the cash flow that is necessary to service (pay interest on) and retire the debt. If the firm defaults on the interest or principal repayment, the creditors may take title to the pledged property. They may then choose to hold the asset and earn income from it (to operate the fixed asset) or to sell it. These options should give investors cause for thought: How many creditors could operate a power plant? If the investors choose to sell it, who would buy it?

These two questions illustrate an important point concerning investing in corporate debt. Although property that is pledged to secure the debt may decrease the lender's risk of loss, the creditor is not interested in taking possession of and operating the property. Lenders earn income through interest payments and not through the operation of the fixed assets. Such creditors are rarely qualified to operate the assets should they take possession of them. If they are forced to seize and sell the assets, they may find few buyers and may have to sell at distress prices. Despite the fact that pledging assets to secure debt increases the safety of the principal, the lenders prefer the prompt payment of interest and principal.

Equipment Trust Certificates

Long-term debt is secured by equipment

Not all collateral has questionable resale potential. Unlike the mortgage bonds that are issued by utility companies, **equipment trust certificates** are secured by assets with substantial resale value. These certificates are issued to finance specific equipment, which is pledged as collateral. Equipment trust certificates are primarily issued by

railroads and airlines to finance rolling stock (railroad cars) and airplanes. As the equipment is used to generate cash flow, the certificates are retired. The collateral supporting these certificates is generally considered to be of excellent quality, for, unlike some fixed assets (e.g., the aforementioned utility plants), this equipment may be readily *moved* and sold to other railroads and airlines in the event that the firm defaults on the certificates.

Investors, however, should realize that while equipment may be more readily sold than power plants, these investors could still suffer losses. For example, in 1981 to 1982 the bankruptcies of Braniff Airlines and Freddie Laker's Skytrain dumped a large number of aircraft on the market. The market for used planes was already soft from a worldwide recession, so prices for used aircraft declined. This, of course, meant that even the secured creditors might not receive their principal from the proceeds of the sales of the planes.

Debentures

Debentures are unsecured promissory notes that are supported by the general creditworthiness of the firm. This type of debt involves more risk than bonds that are supported by collateral. In the case of default or bankruptcy, the unsecured debt is redeemed only after all secured debt has been paid off. Some debentures are subordinated, and these involve even more risk, for they are redeemed after the other general debt of the firm has been redeemed. Even unsecured debt has a superior position to the subordinated debenture. These bonds are among the riskiest debt instruments issued by firms and usually have higher interest rates or other attractive features, such as convertibility into the stock of the company, to compensate the lenders for assuming the increased risk.

Unsecured long-term debt

Financial institutions, such as commercial banks or insurance companies, prefer a firm to sell debentures to the general public. Since the debentures are general obligations of the company, they do not tie up its specific assets. Then, if the firm needs additional funds from a commercial bank, it can use specific assets as collateral, in which case the bank will be more willing to lend the funds. If the assets had been previously pledged, the firm would lack this flexibility in financing.

Although the use of debentures may not decrease the ability of the firm to issue additional debt, default on the debentures usually means that all senior debt is in default as well. A common indenture clause states that if any of the firm's debt is in default, all debt issues are also in default, and in this case the creditors may declare that all outstanding debt is due. For this reason, a firm should not overextend itself through excessive amounts of unsecured debt.

Income Bonds

Income bonds are the riskiest bonds issued by corporations. Interest is paid only if the firm earns it. If the company is unable to cover its other expenses, it is not legally obligated to pay the interest on these bonds. Owing to the great risk associated with them, income bonds are rarely issued by corporations, but a few have existed. Exhibit 9.8 briefly chronicles the history of one of the most interesting examples of an income bond: the TWA 6½ percent income bond that was due in 1978. The interest payments were sporadic. For several years (1971, 1975, and 1976) the bond did not pay inter-

Interest is paid only if earned

Exhibit 9.8
Interest Payments Made
by the TWA 6½ 78
Income Bond

Year	Payment
1970	$ 65.00
1971	0
1972	109.00
1973	86.00*
1974	65.00
1975	0
1976	0
1977	195.00*

*Arrearage cleared.

est, but in 1977 interest payments were resumed and the arrearage in payments was erased. This payment of interest had a very positive effect on the price of the bonds, which had reached a low of 46 in 1974 (i.e., a $1,000 bond could be purchased for $460). In 1977, the bond traded near par and was retired at par in 1978. Those speculators who were willing to buy the bond in 1974 for less than one half of its face value were well rewarded for taking the risk.

Although income bonds are rarely issued by firms, a similar type of security is often issued by state and municipal governments. These are revenue bonds, which are used to finance a particular capital improvement that is expected to generate revenues (e.g., a toll road or a municipal hospital). If the revenues are insufficient, the interest is not paid.

There is, however, one significant difference between income bonds and revenue bonds. Failure to pay interest does not result in default for an income bond, but it does mean that a revenue bond is in default. Most projects financed by revenue bonds have generated sufficient funds to service the debt, but there have been notable exceptions. For example, the Chesapeake Bay Bridge and Tunnel Authority bonds went into default during the 1970s. Toll revenues have risen sufficiently, however, that interest payments have been resumed. Perhaps the most famous default was the multibillion-dollar default by the Washington Public Power Supply System. As of 1986, the defaulted bonds sold for $.10 to $.15 per $1.00 face amount.

Convertible Bonds

Bonds that may be
exchanged for stocks

Convertible bonds are a hybrid type of security. Technically they are debt: The bonds pay interest, which is a fixed obligation of the firm, and have a maturity date. But these bonds have a special feature—the investor has the option to convert the bond into a specified number of shares of common stock. For example, the Xerox 6 percent of 1995 bond may be converted into 10.87 shares of Xerox common stock. The market price of convertible bonds depends on both the value of the stock and the interest that the bonds pay. If the price of the common stock rises, then the value of the bond must rise. The investor thus has the opportunity for capital gain should the price of the common stock rise. If, however, the price of the common stock does not appreciate, the investor still owns a debt obligation of the company and therefore has the security of an investment in a debt instrument.

Convertible bonds have been popular with both firms and investors. However, since they are a hybrid type of security, they are difficult to analyze. In addition, a convertible bond is, in part, an option (i.e., the option to convert the bond into stock). For these reasons, a detailed discussion is deferred until Chapter 21, which follows the material on options in Chapter 19.

Variable Interest Rate Bonds

Prior to the mid 1970s the interest rate that a bond paid was fixed at the date of issuance. With the advent of increased inflation in the 1970s, corporations started issuing **variable interest rate bonds.** Citicorp was the first major American firm to offer bonds with variable interest rates to the general public. Two features of the Citicorp bond were unique at the time it was issued: (1) a variable interest rate that was tied to the interest rate on treasury bills and (2) the right of the holder to redeem the bond at its face value.

Interest coupons are not fixed

The interest rate to be paid by the Citicorp bond was set at 1 percent above the average treasury bill rate during a specified period. This variability of the interest rate means that if short-term interest rates rise, the interest rate paid by the bond must increase. The bond's owner participates in any increase in short-term interest rates. Of course, if the short-term interest rates decline, the bond earns a lower rate of interest.

The second unique feature of the Citicorp bond was that two years after it was issued, the holder had the option to redeem the bond for its face value or principal. This option recurred every six months. If the owner needed the money more quickly, the bond could have been sold in the secondary market, for it was traded on the New York Stock Exchange. Therefore, the Citicorp bonds were very liquid debt instruments that offered the holder an opportunity to participate in higher short-term interest rates if they occurred.

The interest paid by this bond varied over time. When it was initially issued in 1974, it offered a current yield of 9.7 percent. However, short-term interest rates subsequently declined. By 1977, the current annual yield was only 6.6 percent, and many of the bondholders exercised their option to redeem the bonds. The decline in short-term interest rates resulted in a decline in investor fascination with variable interest rate bonds. However, with the return of high short-term interest rates in 1980 and 1981, these bonds were again attractive investments, and several firms subsequently issued them.

One of the advantages offered by variable interest rate bonds is that the coupon is not fixed. An important implication of the variable coupon is that the market price of the bond fluctuates less than the price of a fixed coupon bond. As is explained in the next chapter, the price of a fixed coupon bond fluctuates inversely with interest rates. Such price changes will not occur with a variable rate bond because the interest paid fluctuates with interest rates in general. Hence these bonds avoid one of the major sources of risk associated with investing in bonds—the risk associated with higher interest rates driving down the bond's market value.

Zero Coupon and Discount Bonds

In 1981 a new type of bond was sold to the general public. These bonds pay no interest and are sold at large discounts. The pathbreaking issue was the J.C. Penney **zero coupon bond** of 1989. This bond was initially sold for a discount ($330) but will pay

$1,000 at maturity in 1989. The investor's funds grow from $330 to $1,000 after eight years. The rate of growth (i.e., the yield on the bond) is 14.86 percent.[5]

After the initial success of this issue, several other firms including IBM Credit Corporation (the financing arm of IBM) and ITT Financial issued similar bonds. In each case the firm pays no interest. The bond sells for a large discount, and the investor's return accrues from the appreciation of the bond's value as it approaches maturity.

Since the return on an investment in a zero coupon bond depends solely on the firm's capacity to retire the debt, the quality of the firm is exceedingly important. Zero coupon bonds issued by firms such as Sears or IBM Credit Corporation are of excellent quality and should be retired at maturity. In these cases the investor will earn the expected return that accrues when the bond approaches maturity. If, however, the investor purchases low-quality zero coupon bonds, these bonds may never be redeemed. If the firm were to go bankrupt, the investor may receive nothing. Thus, it is possible for the individual who buys zero coupon bonds to lose the entire investment and never receive a single interest payment.

Interest taxed as accrued and not when received

There is, however, a tax feature that reduces the attractiveness of zero coupon bonds. The IRS taxes the accrued interest as if it were received. Thus the investor must pay federal income tax on the earned interest even though the investor receives the funds only when the bond matures. Thus zero coupon bonds are of little interest to investors except as part of pension plans. Zero coupon bonds may be included in an individual's Keogh account or IRA because the tax on the accrued interest in the account is deferred until the funds are withdrawn. So the primary reason for acquiring a zero coupon bond is to use it in conjunction with a tax-deferred pension plan.

Junk Bonds

Junk bonds are not a particular type of bond but a name given to debt of low quality. Junk bonds are usually debentures and may be subordinated to the firm's other debt obligations. The poor quality of this debt requires that junk bonds offer high yields, which may be three to four percentage points greater than the yield available on high-quality bonds (i.e., bonds rated double or triple A). Junk bonds are often issued to finance takeovers and mergers, and they may be bought by financial institutions and individuals who are accustomed to investing in poor-quality bonds and who are willing and able to accept the larger risk in order to earn the higher yields.

---

[5]The yield on a zero coupon bond is calculated using the time value formula:

$$P_0(1 + g)^n = P_n,$$

which is solved for g. In this example,

$$\$330(1 + g)^8 = \$1,000$$
$$(1 + g)^8 = \$1,000/\$330 = 3.030$$
$$g = \sqrt[8]{3.030} - 1$$
$$g = 0.1486 = 14.86\%.$$

The 14.86 percent was derived by the use of a calculator. If the student does not have access to a calculator, then the future value table is used and that derives an answer of approximately 15 percent.

RETIRING DEBT

Debt issues must ultimately be retired, and this retirement must occur on or before the maturity date of the debt. When the bond is issued, a method for periodic retirement is usually specified, for very few debt issues are retired in one lump payment at the maturity date. Instead, part of the issue is systematically retired each year. This systematic retirement may be achieved by issuing the bond in a series or by having a sinking fund.

Serial Bonds

In an issue of **serial bonds,** some bonds mature each year. This type of bond is usually issued by corporations to finance specific equipment, such as railroad cars, which is pledged as collateral. As the equipment depreciates, the cash flow that is generated by profits and depreciation expense is used to retire the bonds in a series as they mature.

Bonds that are issued in a series

The advertisement presented in Exhibit 9.9 for equipment trust certificates issued by Union Pacific Railroad Company is an example of a serial bond. This issue of equipment trust certificates is designed so that one-fifteenth of the bonds matures each year. Thus, the firm retires $2,337,000 of the certificates annually as each series within the issue matures. At the end of 2001, the entire issue of certificates will have been retired.

Few corporations, however, issue serial bonds. They are primarily issued by state and local governments to finance capital improvements, such as new school buildings, or by ad hoc government bodies, such as the Port Authority of New York, to finance new facilities or other capital improvements. The bonds are then retired over a period of years by tax receipts or by revenues generated by the investment (e.g., toll roads).

Serial bonds are primarily issued by governments

Sinking Funds

Sinking funds are generally employed to ease the retirement of long-term corporate debt. A **sinking fund** is a periodic payment to retire part of the debt issue. One type of sinking fund requires the firm to make payments to a trustee, who invests the money to earn interest. The periodic payments plus the accumulated interest retire the debt when it matures.

Types of sinking funds

Another type of sinking fund requires the firm to set aside a stated sum of money and to randomly select the bonds that are to be retired. The selected bonds are called and redeemed, and the holder surrenders the bond because it ceases to earn interest once it has been called. This type of sinking fund is illustrated in Exhibit 9.10 by an advertisement taken from *The Wall Street Journal*. The principal amount of $3,405,000 Industrial Development Authority of the County of Isle of Wight bonds is being retired through a sinking fund. The specific bonds being retired were selected by a lottery. Once they are chosen, these bonds are called. The owners must surrender the bonds to obtain their principal. If the bonds are not presented for redemption, they are still outstanding and are obligations of the company, but the debtor's obligation is limited to refunding the principal, since interest payments ceased at the call date.

Since each debt issue is different, there can be wide variations in sinking funds. A strong sinking fund retires a substantial proportion of the debt before the date of ma-

Strong and weak sinking funds

Exhibit 9.9
Example of a Serial
Bond Issue (Equipment
Trust Certificate)

This announcement is under no circumstances to be construed as an offer to sell or as a solicitation of an offer to buy any of these securities. The offering is made only by the Offering Circular Supplement and the Offering Circular to which it relates.

NEW ISSUE   July 17, 1985

$35,055,000

Union Pacific Railroad Company

Equipment Trust No. 1 of 1985

Serial Equipment Trust Certificates
(Non-callable)

Price 100%
(Plus accrued dividends, if any, from the date of original issuance.)

MATURITIES AND DIVIDEND RATES.

(To mature in 15 equal annual installments
of $2,337,000, commencing July 15, 1987.)

1987	6.500%	1992	7.500%	1997	7.800%
1988	7.000	1993	7.600	1998	7.800
1989	7.125	1994	7.700	1999	7.875
1990	7.300	1995	7.700	2000	7.875
1991	7.375	1996	7.750	2001	7.875

These Certificates are offered subject to prior sale, when, as and if issued and received by us, subject to approval of the Interstate Commerce Commission.

Merrill Lynch Capital Markets

Thomson McKinnon Securities Inc.

Source: Reprinted with permission of the Union Pacific Railroad Company.

turity. For example, if a bond issue is for $10 million and it matures in ten years, a strong sinking fund may require the firm to retire $1 million, or 10 percent, of the issue each year. Thus, at maturity only $1 million is still outstanding. With a weak sinking fund, a substantial proportion of the debt is retired at maturity. For example, a sinking fund for a debt issue of $10 million that matures in ten years may require

NOTICE OF REDEMPTION

Industrial Development Authority of
The County of Isle of Wight

Industrial Development Revenue Bonds
(Union Camp Corporation Project)

Dated August 1, 1968   Due August 1, 1990

$3,405,000 principal amount being redeemed ➤

NOTICE IS HEREBY GIVEN that pursuant to the terms of the Trust Indenture, dated as of August 1, 1968 between the Industrial Development Authority of the County of Isle of Wight (Union Camp Corporation Project) and Virginia National Bank (now Sovran Bank, N.A.), as Trustee, the following bonds of the Industrial Development Authority of the County of Isle of Wight Industrial Development Revenue Bonds (Union Camp Corporation), aggregating $3,405,000 in principal amount, dated August 1, 1968, bearing interest at the rate of 5½% per annum, and due August 1, 1990, are hereby called for redemption on August 1, 1986 from moneys in the Sinkng Fund for said bonds, at the principal amount thereof, together with interest accrued thereon to August 1, 1986:

The numbers of the coupon bonds in the denomination of $5,000 each
to be redeemed are as follows:

Specific bonds being retired ➤

2323	2731	3933	4315	4762	5707	6169	6573	7104	7765	8622	9110	9332	9557
2327	2769	3935	4324	4807	5724	6184	6597	7130	7827	8625	9114	9336	9562
2329	2815	3936	4326	4809	5736	6187	6602	7138	7830	8632	9118	9338	9568
2363	2826	3980	4330	4839	5741	6205	6603	7145	7842	8651	9120	9347	9640

The numbers of the registered bonds without coupons in the denomination of $5,000 each
are to be redeemed are as follows:

2354	2754	3073	3894	4371	4722	4993	5737	5890	6668	7483	7861	8730	9596
2433	2788	3084	3946	4372	4729	5036	5758	5904	6782	7487	7894	8773	9600
2464	2806	3085	3955	4414	4779	5041	5759	6049	6811	7514	7895	8775	9752
2472	2809	3771	3956	4474	4788	5042	5802	6054	6893	7547	7896	8859	9874

On said August 1, 1986, the coupon bonds and the registered bonds hereby called for redemption will become and be due and payable, the coupon bonds at the principal office of Sovran Bank, N.A. in Richmond, Virginia, or, at the option of the holder at the principal office of the Bank of New York, in the Borough of Manhattan, City and State of New York, Citizens and Southern Bank in Atlanta, Georgia, and Comerica, Inc., Detroit, Michigan, and the registered bonds without coupons at the principal office of the Trustee in Richmond, Virginia, at the redemption price above set forth, interest on said bonds shall

Interest will cease to accrue ➤

cease to accrue, the coupons subsequent to August 1, 1986 shall be void, said bonds shall cease to be entitled to any benefit or security under said Trust Indenture and the holders or registered owners of said bonds shall have no rights in respect thereof except to receive payment of the redemption price thereof.

The coupon bonds should be accompanied by all coupons appertaining thereto and maturing subsequent to August 1, 1986. Coupons maturing August 1, 1986 or prior thereto should be detached and presented for payment in the usual manner. Checks in payment of called registered bonds without coupons will be paid to the order of the registered owner. Accordingly, the registered bond need not be signed by the registered owner.

As of June 15, 1986, the following numbered bonds previously called for redemption
on August 1, 1985 have not been presented for payment:

2638	2979	4711	5507	7019	7618	7730	8599	8828	8921	9694
2860	4249	4715	6268	7076	7658	7897	8749	8836	8926	D4182
2888	4536	4725	6607	7495	7729	7951	8766	8890	9166	

The numbers of registered bonds called on August 1, 1985
and not yet presented for payment are:

2420	3939	4812	5877	5892	5893	5902	6898	7055

SOVRAN BANK, N.A.
Trustee

Dated: July 1, 1986

Exhibit 9.10
Example of a Sinking
Fund Retiring Debt

annual payments of $1 million commencing after five years. In this example, only $5 million is retired before maturity. The debtor must then make a lump sum payment to retire the remaining $5 million. Such a large final payment is called a **balloon payment**.

Several different types of sinking funds are illustrated in Exhibit 9.11, which presents the sinking fund requirements for selected debt issues. Some of these sinking funds are quite strong. For example, the Uniroyal bond requires that 6.67 percent of the issue be retired each year. In this example, the entire issue is retired through the sinking fund. Other sinking funds are quite weak, and there is no sinking fund for the General Telephone and Electronics' 4 90 bond (i.e., the 4 percent bond that matures in 1990).

	Bond	Sinking Fund
Exhibit 9.11 Selected Examples of Sinking Funds	General Telephone and Electronics 4 90	None
	General Telephone and Electronics 5 92	5% to be retired annually starting in 1978 (75% of issue retired prior to maturity)
	Uniroyal, Inc. 5½ 96	6⅜% to be retired annually starting in 1982 (100% of issue retired through the sinking fund)

The strength of a sinking fund affects the element of risk. A strong sinking fund requirement means that a substantial amount of the debt issue is retired during its lifetime, which makes the entire debt issue safer. The sinking fund feature of a debt issue, then, is an important factor in determining the amount of risk associated with investing in a particular debt instrument.

Repurchasing Debt

Debt may be repurchased

If bond prices decline and the debt is selling at a **discount,** the firm may try to retire the debt by purchasing it on the open market.[6] The purchases may be made from time to time, in which case the sellers of the bonds need not know that the company is purchasing and retiring the debt. The company may also announce its intentions and offer to purchase a specified amount of the debt at a certain price within a particular period. Bondholders may then tender their bonds at the offer price; however, they are not required to sell their bonds and may continue to hold the debt.[7] The firm must then continue to meet the terms of the debt's indenture.

If debt is bought at a discount, it increases income

The advantage of repurchasing debt that is selling at a discount is the savings to the firm. If a firm issued $10 million in face value of debt and the bonds are currently selling for $0.60 on the $1, the firm may reduce its debt by $1,000 with a cash outlay of only $600, resulting in a $400 savings for each $1,000 bond that is purchased. This savings is translated into income, because a reduction in debt at a discount is an extraordinary item that is treated in accounting as income.

On the surface, a firm's retiring debt at a discount may appear desirable. However, using money to repurchase debt is an investment decision, just like buying plant and equipment. If the company repurchases debt, it cannot use the funds for other purposes. Management must decide which is the better use of the money: purchasing other income-earning assets or retiring the debt. Unlike a sinking fund requirement (which management must meet), purchasing and retiring debt at a discount is a voluntary act. The lower price of the debt, the greater the potential benefit from the purchase, but management must still determine if it is the best use of the firm's scarce resource, cash. Many firms do not repurchase their debt, for the discount is not sufficient to justify such a use of funds. These corporations have better uses for their funds.

---

[6] Some indentures, however, forbid open market repurchases.

[7] If more bonds are tendered than the company offered to buy, the firm prorates the amount of money that it had allocated for the purchase among the number of bonds being offered.

Year	Percentage of Face Value	Amount Required to Retire $1,000 of Debt	Amount of Call Penalty
1987	103.15	$1,031.50	$31.50
1988	102.80	1,028.00	28.00
1989	102.45	1,024.50	24.50
1990	102.10	1,021.00	21.00
1991	101.75	1,017.50	17.50
1992	101.40	1,014.00	14.00
1993	101.05	1,010.50	10.50
1994	100.70	1,007.00	7.00
1995	100.35	1,003.50	3.50
2000	100.00	1,000.00	0.00

Exhibit 9.12
Schedule for the Call Penalty of the 8¾ Debenture of AT&T Maturing in 2000

Call Feature

Some bonds may have a **call feature** that allows for redemption prior to maturity. In most cases after the bond has been outstanding for a period of time (e.g. five years), the issuer has the right to call and retire the bond. The bond is called for redemption as of a specific date. After that date, interest ceases to accrue, which forces the creditor to relinquish the debt instrument.

Some bonds may be called prior to maturity

Such premature retiring of debt through a call feature tends to occur after a period of high interest rates. If a bond has been issued during such a period and interest rates subsequently decline, it may be advantageous for the company to issue new bonds at the lower interest rate. The proceeds can then be used to retire the older bonds with the higher coupon rates. Such **refunding** reduces the firm's interest expense.

Of course, premature retirement of debt hurts the bondholders who lose the higher yield bonds. To protect these creditors, a call feature usually has a **call penalty**, such as the payment of one year's interest. If the initial issue had a 9 percent interest rate, the company would have to pay $1,090 to retire $1,000 worth of debt. This call penalty usually declines over the lifetime of the debt. Exhibit 9.12 illustrates the call penalty associated with the AT&T 8¾ of 2000 (i.e., the bond in Exhibit 9.1). In 1990 the penalty is $21 per $1,000, but it declines to nothing at maturity. Such a call penalty does protect bondholders, and the debtor has the right to call the bond and to refinance debt if interest rates fall sufficiently to justify paying the call penalty.[8]

The call penalty is partial compensation for premature retirement

Several such refinancings occurred during 1977 and 1978, when interest rates fell below the levels of the mid-1970s. In particular, utility companies that had issued debt with higher interest rates issued new bonds with lower yields, called the old debt, and paid the call penalty. More recently, in 1986 Texas Instruments retired $200 million of its 12.7 percent bonds that were due in 2005. It paid $1,047 to retire $1,000 in face value of debt (i.e., the premium penalty was $47 per $1,000 bond). The refinancing, however, sufficiently reduced the company's interest expense to justify the refunding.

---

[8]How the call feature may affect the price of a bond is discussed in Chapter 10.

SUMMARY

This chapter discussed the general features of long-term debt. The terms of a debt issue include the coupon rate of interest and the maturity date. A trustee is appointed for each bond issue to protect the rights of the individual investors. The risks associated with investing in debt are attributable to price fluctuations and inflation as well as to the possibility of default on interest and principal repayment. To help investors, several firms have developed rating services that classify debt issues according to risk.

The mechanics of purchasing debt are very similar to those of buying stocks. However, while stocks are purchased through brokerage firms, some debt instruments (e.g., federal government securities) may be purchased through banks.

Debt may be retired in several ways. Some bonds are issued in a series, with a specified amount of debt maturing each year. Other debt issues have sinking funds that retire part of the bond issue prior to maturity. For some debt issues, the firm has the right to call the bonds prior to maturity. The debtor can also offer to buy the debt back from investors before it matures. Since creditors are as concerned with the return of their principal as they are with the payment of interest, the ability of the firm or government to retire its liabilities is one of the foremost factors in determining the risks associated with investing in debt.

Terms to Remember

Bonds	Accrued interest
Principal (face amount)	Flat
Maturity date	Mortgage bond
Interest	Equipment trust certificate
Coupon rate	Debenture
Current yield	Income bond
Yield to maturity	Convertible bond
Yield curve	Variable interest rate bond
Indenture	Zero coupon bond
Default	Serial bonds
Trustee	Sinking fund
Registered bond	Balloon payment
Bearer bond	Discount
Coupon bond	Call feature
Credit rating systems	Refunding
Confirmation statement	Call penalty

Questions

1. What is the difference between bearer bonds and registered bonds? Which type is safer and why?

2. What is the relationship between the yield earned on bonds and the length of time to maturity? Does this relationship always hold?

3. Even though bonds are debt obligations, investing in them involves risk. What are the sources of risk? What service is available to aid the buyers of debt instruments in selecting a particular bond?

4. How may bonds be purchased?

5. What is the difference between a serial issue of bonds and term bonds with a specific maturity date and a sinking fund?

6. A call penalty protects whom from what? Why may firms choose to retire debt early after a period of high interest rates?

7. What advantages and disadvantages do bonds offer to investors?

8. What secures mortgage bonds and equipment trust certificates?

9. Why are many debentures and income bonds considered to be risky investments?

Suggested Readings

For an easy-to-read discussion of the various types of bonds (e.g., the various issues of corporations, municipalities, and the federal government and its agencies), see:

Sherwood, Hugh. *How To Invest in Bonds.* Revised ed. New York: McGraw-Hill, 1983.

Bonds are sold to the general public through investment bankers or may be privately placed with a financial institution. For a discussion of these processes and the terms of the sales, consult:

Atamian, Elliot L. "Negotiating the Restrictive Covenants of Loan Agreements Associated With the Private Placement of Corporate Debt Securities." Reprinted in W. Serraino, S. Singhvi, and R. Soldofsky: *Frontiers of Financial Management,* 210–225. Cincinnati: South-Western Publishing, 1971.

Bloch, Ernest. "Pricing a Corporate Bond Issue: A Look Behind the Scenes." Reprinted in E. F. Brigham, *Readings in Managerial Finance,* 280–287. New York: Holt, Rinehart and Winston, 1971.

How bonds are rated is obviously important for determining the amount of interest the borrower must pay to obtain the funds. For a discussion of the objective and subjective techniques used by Standard & Poor to rate debt, see:

Sherwood, Hugh C. *How Corporate Debt Is Rated.* New York: John Wiley & Sons, 1976.

A more technical analysis of rate determination may be found in:

Pinches, George E., and Ken A. Mingo. "A Multivariate Analysis of Industrial Bond Ratings." *Journal of Finance* (March 1973): 1–18.

For a discussion of bond repurchases, see:

Johnson, Rodney, and Richard Klein. "Corporate Motives in Repurchases of Discounted Bonds." *Financial Management* (Autumn 1974): 44–49.

This article suggests that the temporary increase in earnings from retiring debt at a discount is a primary motive for such refundings.

The variety of zero coupon bonds is discussed in:

"Unzipping the Zeros." *Money,* April 1985, 103–110.

For terms of specific bonds, the investor may consult:

Standard & Poor's Corporation. *Bond Guide.* Published monthly.

This gives a calendar of new offerings, as well as descriptions of corporate bonds (i.e., coupon, maturity date, amount outstanding, prices, and yields). More detailed information concerning features such as sinking funds and call features may be found in Standard & Poor's Corporation Records.

Appendix   The Term Structure of Interest Rates

The relationship between the rate of interest and the length of time to maturity is often referred to as the "term structure of interest rates." During most periods of history, the longer the term to maturity, the higher the rate of interest (for example, see the yields offered by the savings and loan association in Exhibit 2.2 and the yields in Figure 9.1). One possible explanation for this relationship is that investors have a preference for liquidity. To induce these individuals to commit their funds for a longer term, the interest rate has to be higher to compensate them for the loss of liquidity.

This explanation is very plausible, but there have been periods when short-term interest rates have been higher than long-term rates. This has led to the development of an alternative explanation of the structure of yields based on investor expectations concerning future interest rates. This expectations theory suggests that the long-term rate is an average of the current short-term rate and the expected future short-term rate.

Consider an investor faced with the two following investment alternatives:

One-year bond	10%
Two-year bond	12%

If the investor purchases the two-year bond, the yield is locked in for two years. However, if the one-year bond is purchased, the investor will have to reinvest the proceeds when the bond matures. He or she will seek to earn the same return on either alternative: (1) the one-year bond in combination with a second one-year bond or (2) the two-year bond. Thus, the choice between the two alternatives depends on what the expected future rate on the one-year bond will be.

For the yields on the two alternatives to produce the same return over two years, the funds reinvested when the one-year bond matures must earn 14 percent during the second year. The average yield is 12 percent in both cases. The yield on the two-year bond equals the yield on the combination of the 10 percent and 14 percent one-year bonds.

However, suppose the investor anticipates that the one-year rate in the future will be 15 percent. If the current one-year bond is purchased, the individual can reinvest the funds when it matures and earn 15 percent for one year. The average return over the two years is 12.5 percent and beats the 12 percent annual yield on the two-year bond. Obviously, the two one-year securities will be preferred. However, if the investor anticipates that the future one-year rate will be 13 percent, the average yield over the two years is 11.5 percent annually, which is inferior to the 12 percent earned annually on the two-year bond.

While an individual may move between the one- and two-year bonds, this is not true in the aggregate. Investors as a whole cannot alter their portfolios by selling one security and purchasing another. Such attempts to alter portfolios change the securities' prices and yields. If all investors expected the future one-year rate to be 15 percent, they would seek to sell the two-year bond and purchase the one-year bond. The effect would be to drive up the yield on the two-year bond and drive down the yield on the one-year bond. One possible set of yields that could emerge is

| One-year bond | 10.0% |
| Two-year bond | 12.5% |

In this case the average yield on the two one-year bonds is 12.5 percent (10 percent for one year and 15 percent for the other year). The average yield on the two-year bond is 12.5 percent. Since the average yield on either investment alternative is the same (for a given risk class), an expectation of higher future interest rates requires a positively sloped yield curve. If investors anticipate that the one-year rate next year will be 14 percent and that two-year bonds are paying 12 percent, the one-year rate today *must be 10 percent*. At 10 percent the average yield on the two alternatives is 12 percent for both. If the current rate on the one-year bond is 10 percent, the term structure is positive. The one-year bond is paying 10 percent and the two-year bond is paying 12 percent, which is a positive relationship between yields and time to maturity.

If, however, investors expect the future one-year rate to be 11 percent while the two-year bond pays 12 percent annually, the current one-year rate must be 13 percent. Only if the current rate is 13 percent will a combination of it and the expected future one-year rate of 11 percent equal the average annual yield offered by the two-year bond. If the current one-year rate is 13 percent, then the current term structure of yields is negative. The one-year bond offers 13 percent and the two-year bond offers 12 percent, which is a negative relationship between yields and time to maturity. Thus, the expectation of lower rates in the future requires a negatively sloped yield curve in the present.

In addition to the liquidity preference and expectations theories of the term structure of yields, a third alternative explanation has been suggested. It is referred to as the "segmentation theory," and it suggests that yields depends on the demand for and supply of credit in various segments of the financial markets. For example, suppose funds were to flow from savings and loan associations to money market mutual funds. Since the S&Ls make mortgage loans but money market mutual funds make only short-term loans and no mortgage loans, there has been a change in the supply of credit in the two markets. The supply of mortgage money has decreased, and the rate charged on these loans should rise. Simultaneously, the supply of short-term credit has increased, which should tend to reduce short-term interest rates. The structure of yields thus depends on the supply and demand for credit from the various segments of the economy. A flow from one segment to another alters the supply of this credit, causing yields (i.e., the term structure of interest rates) to change. A flow of funds from financial institutions that grant short-term loans to those making long-term loans will then result in a negatively sloped yield curve.

There is no consensus as to which of the three theories is correct. Each has appealing elements, but there is insufficient empirical evidence to suggest that the structure of yields is solely explained by only one of the three theories. It is probably safe to assume that all three play some role in the determination of the term structure of interest rates.[9]

---

[9] See J. O. Light and William L. White, *The Financial System*, (Homewood, Ill.: Richard D. Irwin, 1979), especially Chapters 8 and 9. It should be noted that the illustration of the expectation theory in this appendix is limited to two years. However, it may be generalized into more time periods so that the current structure of yields reflects expected short-term rates in three, four, five, or more years in the future. See Light and White, 153–155.

10 The Valuation of Debt

LEARNING OBJECTIVES

After completing this chapter you should be able to

1. Determine the price of a bond.
2. Isolate the factors that affect a bond's price.
3. Explain the relationship between changes in interest rates and bond prices.
4. Differentiate among current yield, yield to maturity, and yield to call.
5. Illustrate how discounted bonds may be used to help finance an individual's retirement.

As was learned in the previous chapter, corporations sell a variety of debt instruments to the general public. There is a very active secondary market for these bonds. Since bonds trade daily, what establishes their prices? What yields do they offer investors? If interest rates in general change, what will happen to the prices of existing bonds? Which bonds' prices tend to be more volatile? These are some of the essential questions concerning investing in debt instruments that are addressed in this chapter.

Although there is a variety of debt instruments, each with its specific name and characteristics, for the purpose of this chapter the term **bond** will be used to include all types of debt instruments. The price of any bond (for a given risk class) is primarily related to (1) the interest paid by the bond, (2) the interest rate that investors may earn on competitive bonds, and (3) the maturity date of the bond. This chapter will explore the effect of each. Next follows a discussion of the various uses of the word yield, including the current yield, the yield to maturity, and yield to call. The chapter concludes with brief discussions of yields and risk, and duration.

PERPETUAL DEBT

A **perpetual bond** is a bond that never matures. The issuer never has to retire the
principal; it has only to meet the interest payments and the other terms of the indenture. Although such a bond may sound absurd, there are some in existence. For example, the British government issued perpetual bonds called consols to refinance the
debt that was issued to support the Napoleonic Wars. These bonds will never mature,
but they do pay interest, and there is an active secondary market in them.

*Some bonds
never mature*

How much can a perpetual bond be worth? The answer depends on the interest
paid by the bond and the return the investor can earn elsewhere. For example, a perpetual bond pays the following stream of interest income annually:

*Their value is related to
the amount of interest
that they pay*

Year 1	Year 2	. . .	Year 20	. . .	Year 100	. . .	Year 1000	. . .
$100	$100		$100		$100		$100	

How much are these interest payments worth? The question really is, what is the
present value of each one of these $100 payments? To answer the question, the inves-
tor must know the rate of interest that may be earned on alternative investments. If the
investor can earn 15 percent elsewhere, the present value (PV) of the perpetual stream
of $100 payments is

*Their value is related to
what the investor may
earn elsewhere*

$$PV = \frac{\$100}{(1 + 0.15)^1} + \frac{\$100}{(1 + 0.15)^2} + \cdots + \frac{\$100}{(1 + 0.15)^{20}}$$

$$+ \cdots + \frac{\$100}{(1 + 0.15)^{100}} + \cdots + \frac{\$100}{(1 + 0.15)^{1,000}}$$

$$= \$100(0.870) + \$100(0.756) + \cdots + \$100(0.037)$$

$$+ \cdots + \$100(0.000) + \cdots + \$100(0.000)$$

$$= \$87 + \$75.60 + \cdots + \$3.70 + \cdots + 0$$

$$= \$667.$$

As may be seen in this example, the $100 interest payments received in the near future
contribute most to the present value of the bond. Dollars received in the distant future
have little value today. The sum of all of these present values is $667, which means
that if alternative investments yield 15 percent, an investor would be willing to pay
$667 for a promise to receive $100 annually for the indefinite future.

The preceding may be stated in more formal terms. If I is the annual interest
payment and i is the rate of return that is being earned on comparable investments,
then the present value is

$$PV = \frac{I}{(1 + i)^1} + \frac{I}{(1 + i)^2} + \frac{I}{(1 + i)^3} + \cdots .$$

This is a geometric series, and its sum may be expressed as

$$PV = \frac{I}{i} .$$

(10.1)

Exhibit 10.1
Relationship Between
Interest Rates and
the Price of a
Perpetual Bond

Current Interest Rate (i)	Annual Interest Paid by the Bond (I)	Present Price of the Bond $\left(PV = \dfrac{I}{i} \right)$
4%	$100	$2,500
6	100	1,667
8	100	1,250
10	100	1,000
15	100	667
20	100	500

Their prices can fluctuate

Equation 10.1 gives the current value of an infinite stream of interest payments. If this equation is applied to the previous example in which the annual interest payment is $100 and alternative investments can earn 15 percent, then the present value of the bond is

$$PV = \frac{\$100}{0.15} = \$667.$$

If interest rates rise, bond prices fall

If market interest rates of alternative investments were to increase, say, to 20 percent, the value of this perpetual stream of interest payments would decline; if market interest rates were to fall to, say, 8 percent, the value of the bond would rise. These changes occur because the bond pays a **fixed flow of income**; that is, the dollar amount of interest paid by the bond is constant. Lower interest rates mean that more money is needed to purchase this fixed stream of interest payments, and with higher interest rates, less money is needed to buy this fixed flow of income.

If interest rates fall, bond prices rise

The inverse relationship between interest rates and bond prices is illustrated in Exhibit 10.1, which presents the value of the preceding perpetual bond at different interest rates. As may be seen from the exhibit, as current market interest rates rise, the present value of the bond declines. Thus, if the present value is $1,000 when interest rates are 10 percent, the value of this bond declines to $500 when interest rates rise to 20 percent.

A simple example may show why this inverse relationship between bond prices and interest rates exists. Suppose two investors offered to sell two different bond issues. The first is the perpetual bond that pays $100 per year in interest. The second is also a perpetual bond, but it pays $120 per year in interest. If the offer price in each case is $1,000, which bond would be preferred? Obviously, if they are equal in every way except in the amount of interest, a buyer would prefer the second bond that pays $120. What could the seller of the first bond do to make the bond more attractive to a buyer? The obvious answer is to lower the asking price so that the yield the buyer receives is identical for both bonds. Thus, if the seller were to ask only $833 for the bond that pays $100 annually, the buyer should be indifferent as to which he or she chooses. Both bonds would then offer a yield of 12 percent (i.e., $100 ÷ $833 for the first bond and $120 ÷ $1000 for the second bond).

BONDS WITH MATURITY DATES

The majority of bonds are not perpetual but have a finite life. They mature, and this fact must affect their valuation. A bond's price is related not only to the interest that it pays but also to its face amount (i.e., the principal). The current price of a bond equals the present value of the interest payments plus the present value of the principal to be received at maturity.

The date of maturity affects value

Annual Compounding[1]

The value of a bond is expressed algebraically in Equation 10.2 in terms of the present value formulas discussed in Chapter 6. A bond's value is

A bond valuation model

$$P_B = \frac{I_1}{(1 + i)^1} + \frac{I_2}{(1 + i)^2} + \cdots + \frac{I_n}{(1 + i)^n} + \frac{P}{(1 + i)^n},$$

(10.2)

where P_B indicates the current price of the bond; I, the annual interest payment (with the subscripts indicating the year); n, the number of years to maturity; P, the principal; and i, the current interest rate.

The calculation of a bond's price using Equation 10.2 may be illustrated by a simple example. A firm has a $1,000 bond outstanding that matures in three years with a 10 percent coupon rate ($100 annually). All that is needed to determine the price of the bond is the current interest rate, which is the rate being paid by newly issued, competitive bonds with the same length of time to maturity and the same degree of risk. If the competitive bonds yield 10 percent, the price of this bond will be par ($1,000), for

Applications of the model

$$P_B = \frac{\$100}{(1 + 0.10)^1} + \frac{\$100}{(1 + 0.10)^2} + \frac{\$100}{(1 + 0.10)^3} + \frac{\$1,000}{(1 + 0.10)^3}$$

$$= \$100(0.909) + 100(0.826) + 100(0.751) + 1,000(0.751)$$

$$= \$999.60 \approx \$1,000.$$

If competitive bonds are selling to yield 12 percent, this bond will be unattractive to investors. They will not be willing to pay $1,000 for a bond yielding 10 percent when they could buy competing bonds at the same price that yield 12 percent. For this bond to compete with the others, its price must decline sufficiently to yield 12 percent. In terms of Equation 10.2, the price must be

$$P_B = \frac{\$100}{(1 + 0.12)^1} + \frac{\$100}{(1 + 0.12)^2} + \frac{\$100}{(1 + 0.12)^3} + \frac{\$1,000}{(1 + 0.12)^3}$$

$$= \$100(0.893) + 100(0.797) + 100(0.712) + 1,000(0.712)$$

$$= \$952.20.$$

The price of the bond must decline to approximately $952; that is, it must sell for a **discount** (a price less than the stated principal) in order to be competitive with comparable bonds. At that price investors will earn $100 per year in interest and approxi-

---

[1]While bonds pay interest semiannually, this discussion uses annual compounding to facilitate the explanation.

mately $50 in capital gains over the three years, for a total annual return of 12 percent on their investment. The capital gain occurs because the bond is purchased for $952.20, but when it matures, the holder will receive $1,000.

If comparable debt were to yield 8 percent, the price of the bond in the previous example would have to rise. In this case the price of the bond would be

$$P_B = \frac{\$100}{(1 + 0.08)^1} + \frac{\$100}{(1 + 0.08)^2} + \frac{\$100}{(1 + 0.08)^3} + \frac{\$1,000}{(1 + 0.08)^3}$$

$$= \$100(0.926) + 100(0.857) + 100(0.794) + 1,000(0.794)$$

$$= \$1,051.70.$$

The bond, therefore, must sell at a **premium** (a price greater than the stated principal). Although it may seem implausible for the bond to sell at a premium, this must occur if the market interest rate falls below the coupon rate of interest stated on the bond.

Bond's value is the present value of 1. the annuity (the interest payments) and 2. the lump sum (the principal repayment)

These price calculations are lengthy, but the number of computations can be reduced when one realizes that the valuation of a bond has two components: a flow of interest payments and a final repayment of principal. Since interest payments are fixed and are paid every year, they may be treated as an annuity. The principal repayment may be treated as a simple lump-sum payment. If a $1,000 bond pays $100 per year in interest and matures after three years, its current value is the present value of the $100 annuity for three years and the present value of the $1,000 that will be received after three years. If the interest rate is 12 percent, the current value of the bond is

$$P_B = \$100(2.402) + \$1,000(0.712) = \$952.20,$$

where 2.402 is the interest factor for the present value of a $1 annuity at 12 percent for three years and 0.712 is the interest factor for the present value of $1 at 12 percent after three years. This is the same answer that was derived earlier (except for the rounding error), but the amount of arithmetic has been reduced.

The inverse relationship restated

These examples illustrate the same general conclusion that was reached earlier concerning bond prices and changes in market interest rates: They are inversely related. *When market interest rates rise, bond prices decline. When market interest rates fall, bond prices rise.* This relationship is illustrated in Figure 10.1, which plots the price of the aforementioned $1,000 bond at various interest rates. As may be seen from the figure, higher interest rates depress the bond's current value. Thus, the bond's price declines from $1,000 to $952.20 when interest rates rise from 10 to 12 percent, but the price rises to $1,051.70 when interest rates decline to 8 percent. (Factors that affect the amount of price change are covered later in this chapter.)

Correct anticipation of direction of change produces profits

The inverse relationship between the price of a bond and the interest rate suggests a means to make profits in the bond market. All that investors need to know is the direction of future changes in the interest rate. If investors anticipate that interest rates will decline, then they are expecting the price of previously issued bonds with a given number of years to maturity and of a certain risk to rise. This price increase must occur in order for previously issued bonds to have the same yield as currently issued bonds. The reverse is also true, for if investors anticipate that interest rates will rise, they are also anticipating that the price of currently available bonds will decline. This decline must occur for previously issued bonds to offer the same yield as currently

POINTS OF INTEREST
Bull Market for Bonds?

With interest rates reaching historic highs in 1982, the possibility of a historic bull market in bonds came into sharp focus. Long-term bonds with much lower coupons than the current rate were selling for substantial discounts. By purchasing these bonds, an investor locked in the current yields, and if interest rates did decline, the investor would also receive capital gains.

Consider the AT&T 8¾ 00 debenture shown in Exhibit 9.1. In early 1982, that bond offered a yield to maturity in excess of 14 percent when it sold for $640. If an investor bought it, this 14+ percent yield was assured if the bond was held to maturity. However, if interest rates were to decline to 12 percent within a year, the bond would sell for about $850. The investor thus would earn $87.50 interest and have a capital gain of $210 ($850 − 640) for a total profit of $297.50. On an investment of $640, this gives a total return of 46 percent in one year.

While few investors anticipated a scenario of declining interest rates, some analysts did suggest buying long-term bonds. (See, for instance, David Dreman, "Buy of a Lifetime," *Forbes,* June 7, 1982, 203.) Of course, such a strategy would require the investor to go against current popular sentiment, which is one reason the potential return is so large. Even in the bond market, the possibility of a large return requires that the investor bear risk. If interest rates were to continue to rise, the anticipated bull market in bonds would not materialize. Bond prices would decline further (if interest rates rose) and would inflict losses on those investors who purchased long-term debt in anticipation of declining interest rates.

After 1982, interest rates did fall and bond prices rose. By January 1986, the AT&T 8¾ 00 debentures were selling for $913.75 with a yield to maturity of 9.88 percent. Any investor who purchased the bond in 1982 and held it to 1986 not only collected the interest but also experienced a capital gain. The amount of this capital gain will continue to increase if interest rates decline further, but, of course, if the downward trend in interest rates were to be reversed, the bond's value would decline as interest rates rose.

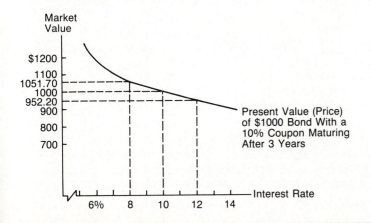

Figure 10.1
Relationship between Interest Rates and a Bond's Price

issued bonds. Therefore, if investors can anticipate the direction of change in interest rates, they can also anticipate the direction of change in the price of bonds.

Incorrect anticipation of direction of change produces losses

Investors, however, may anticipate incorrectly and thus suffer losses in the bond market. If they buy bonds and interest rates rise, then the market value of their bonds must decline, and the investors suffer capital losses. These individuals, however, have something in their favor: The bonds must ultimately be retired. Since the principal must be redeemed, an investment error in the bond market may be corrected when the bond's price rises as the bond approaches maturity. The capital losses will eventually be erased. The correction of the error, however, may take years, during which time the investors have lost the higher yields that were available on bonds issued after their initial investments.

Semiannual Compounding

Bonds pay interest semiannually

The valuation of a bond with a finite life presented in Equation 10.2 is a bit misleading, because bonds pay interest twice a year (i.e., semiannually), and the equation assumes that the interest payments are made only annually. However, Equation 10.2 may be readily modified to take into consideration semiannual (or even quarterly or weekly) compounding. This is done by adjusting the amount of each payment and the total number of these payments. To adjust the previous example, each interest payment will be $50 if payments are semiannual, and instead of three annual payments, the bond will make a total of six $50 semiannual payments. Hence, the flow of payments that will be made by this bond is

Bonds pay interest semiannually

Year 1		Year 2		Year 3		
$50	$50	$50	$50	$50	$50	$1,000

This flow of payments would then be discounted back to the present to determine the bond's current value. The question then becomes, what is the appropriate discount factor?

Modifying the valuation model for semiannual compounding

If comparable debt yields 12 percent, the appropriate discount factor is not 12 percent; it is 6 percent. Six percent interest paid twice a year yields 12 percent interest compounded semiannually. Thus, to determine the present value of this bond, the comparable interest rate is divided in half (just as the annual interest payment is divided in half). However, the number of interest payments to which this 6 percent is applied is doubled (just as the number of payments is doubled). Hence, the current value of this bond, which pays interest twice a year (is compounded semiannually), is

$$P_B = \frac{\$50}{(1 + 0.06)^1} + \frac{\$50}{(1 + 0.06)^2} + \frac{\$50}{(1 + 0.06)^3} + \frac{\$50}{(1 + 0.06)^4}$$

$$+ \frac{\$50}{(1 + 0.06)^5} + \frac{\$50}{(1 + 0.06)^6} + \frac{\$1,000}{(1 + 0.06)^6}$$

$$= \$50(0.943) + 50(0.889) + 50(0.840)$$
$$+ 50(0.792) + 50(0.747) + 50(0.705) + 1,000(0.705)$$

$$= \$47.15 + 44.45 + 42.00 + 39.60 + 37.35 + 35.25 + 705$$

$$= \$950.85.$$

With semiannual compounding, the current value of the bond is slightly lower (i.e., $950.85 versus $952.20). This is because the bond's price must decline more to compensate for the more frequent compounding. An investor would prefer a bond that pays $50 twice per year to one that pays $100 once per year, because the investor would have use of some of the funds more quickly. Thus, if interest rates rise, causing bond prices to fall, the decline will be greater if the interest on bonds is paid semi-annually than if it is paid annually.

Equation 10.2 may be altered to include semiannual compounding. This is done in Equation 10.3. Only one new symbol, c, is added, which represents the frequency of compounding (i.e., the number of times each year that interest payments are made).

$$P_B = \frac{\dfrac{I}{c}}{\left(1+\dfrac{i}{c}\right)^1} + \frac{\dfrac{I}{c}}{\left(1+\dfrac{i}{c}\right)^2} + \cdots + \frac{\dfrac{I}{c}}{\left(1+\dfrac{i}{c}\right)^{n \times c}} + \frac{P}{\left(1+\dfrac{i}{c}\right)^{n \times c}}. \qquad (10.3)$$

When Equation 10.3 is applied to the earlier example, the price of the bond is

$$P_B = \frac{\dfrac{\$100}{2}}{\left(1+\dfrac{0.12}{2}\right)^1} + \frac{\dfrac{\$100}{2}}{\left(1+\dfrac{0.12}{2}\right)^2} + \cdots + \frac{\dfrac{\$100}{2}}{\left(1+\dfrac{0.12}{2}\right)^{3 \times 2}} + \frac{\$1,000}{\left(1+\dfrac{0.12}{2}\right)^{3 \times 2}}$$

$$= \$50(0.943) + 50(0.890) + \cdots + 50(0.705) + 1,000(0.705)$$

$$= \$950.85,$$

which, of course, is the same answer derived in the immediately preceding example.

Performing such calculations can obviously be quite tedious and time-consuming. *Bond tables* However, the required effort will greatly be reduced if the individual has access to a bond table. A bond table has the following general presentation:

Bond Table for a Bond with an 8 Percent Coupon

Current Interest Rate	Years to Maturity			
	1	3	5	10
6.5%	$101.43	$104.03	$106.32	$110.09
7.0	100.95	102.66	104.16	107.11
7.5	100.47	101.32	102.05	103.47
8.0	100.00	100.00	100.00	100.00
8.5	99.53	98.70	98.00	96.68
9.0	99.06	97.42	96.04	93.50
9.5	98.60	96.16	94.14	90.45

The bond's coupon (i.e., 8 percent) is given in the title. The current rate of interest is read vertically at the left, and the number of years to maturity is read horizontally across the top. If an individual wanted to know the price of an 8 percent bond with a maturity of five years that was priced to yield 7.5 percent to maturity, that investor could consult the bond table and learn that the price would be $102.05 ($1,020.50 for a $1,000 bond).

Not every investor has access to a bond table, but the advent of the pocket calculator has put price calculations at the fingertips of virtually everyone. Sophisticated calculators (some of which are manufactured by Texas Instruments or Hewlett Packard) can be used to determine bond prices, and even the less sophisticated models can perform such computations. As was illustrated previously, all the investor needs to know to determine the bond's price are the interest factors for the present value of an annuity and of a dollar compounded semiannually. Such interest factors may be generated using the less sophisticated pocket calculators. Thus, the individual investor does not need a computer, present value tables, or a bond table to price bonds. Pocket calculators have reduced both the tedium of the calculations and the reliance on sophisticated equipment or mathematical tables.

FLUCTUATIONS IN BOND PRICES

As the preceding examples illustrate, a bond's price depends on the interest paid, the maturity date of the bond, and the yield currently earned on comparable securities. The illustrations also demonstrated that when interest rates rise, bond prices fall, and when interest rates fall, bond prices rise.

The amount of price fluctuation depends on (1) the amount of interest paid by the bond, (2) the length of time to maturity, and (3) risk. The smaller the amount of interest, the larger the relative price fluctuations will tend to be. The longer the term or time to maturity, the greater the price fluctuation will be. Riskier bonds will also experience greater fluctuations in their prices.

This section is concerned with the first two factors that affect price fluctuations, the amount of interest and the term to maturity. The impact of risk is covered in a subsequent section. The effect of the amount of interest and the length of time to maturity may be seen by the following illustrations. In the first case, consider two bonds with equal lives (e.g., ten years to maturity) but unequal coupons. Bond A pays $40 a year (a 4 percent coupon), and Bond B pays $140 annually (a 14 percent coupon). If interest rates are 10 percent, the bonds' prices are

$$P_A = \$40(6.145) + \$1,000(0.386) \approx \$632,$$

$$P_B = \$140(6.145) + \$1,000(0.386) \approx \$1,246.$$

If interest rates rise to 14 percent, the bonds' prices become

$$P_A = \$40(5.216) + \$1,000(0.270) = \$478.64,$$

$$P_B = \$140(5.216) + \$1,000(0.270) = \$1,000.$$

The price of Bond A falls by 25 percent from $632 to $478.64, while the price of Bond B falls 20 percent from $1,246 to $1,000. As may be seen in Figure 10.2, if interest rates continue to rise, the bonds' prices decline further. At 20 percent, the values of the bonds are $330 and $749, respectively. These prices represent declines of approximately 48 and 40 percent from the bonds' initial prices.

The length of time to maturity also affects the fluctuation in a bond's price. Consider the following two bonds. Each pays $100 interest annually (a 10 percent coupon). Bond A matures after ten years, and Bond B matures after one year. If interest rates are 10 percent, the price of each bond is

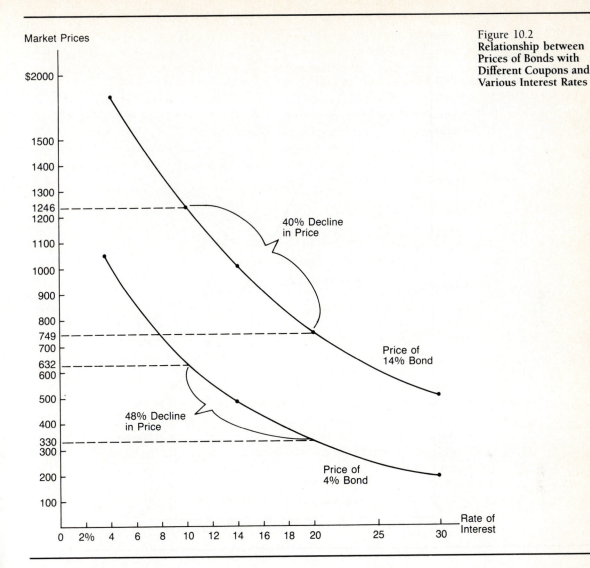

Market Prices

Figure 10.2
**Relationship between
Prices of Bonds with
Different Coupons and
Various Interest Rates**

40% Decline
in Price

Price of
14% Bond

48% Decline
in Price

Price of
4% Bond

Rate of
Interest

$$P_A = \$100(6.145) + \$1,000(0.386) = \$1,000,$$

$$P_B = \$100(0.909) + \$1,000(0.909) = \$1,000.$$

If interest rates rise to 12 percent, the price of each bond declines to

$$P_A = \$100(5.650) + \$1,000(0.322) = \$887.00,$$

$$P_B = \$100(0.893) + \$1,000(0.893) = \$982.30.$$

The price of Bond A falls approximately 12 percent from $1,000 to $887, but Bond B suffers only a modest price decline to $982.30.

Figure 10.3
**Relationship between
Bond Prices and Term
to Maturity**

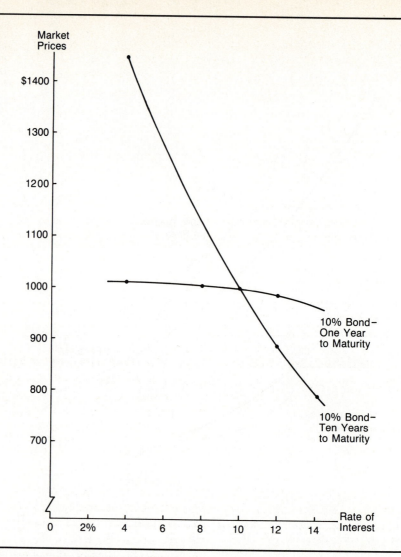

If interest rates fall, the price of the longer-term bond increases. This price increase (and the price decline caused by higher interest rates) is illustrated in Figure 10.3, which vividly shows the larger price fluctuations in the ten-year bond. Thus Figure 10.3 clearly illustrates that investors in long-term debt bear more risk from changes in bond prices caused by fluctuations in interest rates. For this reason investors who are concerned with the preservation of principal will stress short-term debt instruments. These offer both interest income and safety of principal. However, most investors do not actually buy short-term securities. Instead, they buy shares in money market mutual funds that in turn invest in short-term debt. Money market mutual funds thus offer investors liquidity that cannot be obtained through investments in long-term debt.

YIELDS

The word *yield* is frequently used with regard to investing in bonds. There are three important types of yields that the investor must be familiar with: the current yield, the yield to maturity, and the yield to call. This section will differentiate among these three yields.

The Current Yield

The **current yield** is the percentage that the investor earns annually. It is simply

$$\frac{\text{Annual interest payment}}{\text{Price of the bond}}.$$

(10.4)

The bond discussed previously in the section on discounted bonds has a coupon rate of 10 percent. Thus, when the price of the bond is $952, the current yield is

$$\frac{\$100}{\$952} = 10.5\%.$$

The current yield is important because it gives the investor an indication of the current return that will be earned on the investment. Investors who seek high current income prefer bonds that offer a high current yield.

However, the current yield can be very misleading, for it fails to consider any change in the price of the bond that may occur if the bond is held to maturity. Obviously, if a bond is bought at a discount, its value must rise as it approaches maturity. The opposite occurs if the bond is purchased for a premium, because its price will decline as maturity approaches. For this reason it is desirable to know the bond's yield to maturity.

The current yield does not consider price changes

The Yield to Maturity

The **yield to maturity** considers the current income generated by the bond as well as any change in its value when it is held to maturity. If the bond referred to earlier is purchased for $952 and is held to maturity, after three years the investor will receive a return of 12 percent. This is the yield to maturity, because this return considers not only the current interest return of 10.5 percent but also the price appreciation of the bond from $952 at the time of purchase to $1,000 at maturity. Since the yield to maturity considers both the flow of interest income and the price change, it is a more accurate measure of the return offered to investors by a particular bond issue.

The yield to maturity includes any price change

The yield to maturity may be determined by using Equation 10.2.[2] That equation reads

$$P_B = \frac{I_1}{(1 + i)^1} + \frac{I_2}{(1 + i)^2} + \cdots + \frac{I_n}{(1 + i)^n} + \frac{P}{(1 + i)^n}.$$

The i is the current rate of interest paid by newly issued bonds with the same term to maturity and the same degree of risk. If the investor buys a bond and holds it to matu-

---

[2] Equation 10.3 is more accurate, since bonds pay interest semiannually. However, Equation 10.2 is less formidable and still illustrates the point.

rity, the yield that is being paid by newly issued bonds (i) will also be the yield to maturity.

Determining the yield to maturity when the coupon rate of interest, the bond's price, and the maturity date are known is not easy, even with the use of an electronic calculator. For example, if the bond were selling for $952 and the investor wanted to know the yield to maturity, the calculation would be

$$\$952 = \frac{\$100}{(1 + i)^1} + \frac{\$100}{(1 + i)^2} + \frac{\$100}{(1 + i)^3} + \frac{\$1,000}{(1 + i)^3}.$$

Solving this equation can be a formidable task because there is no simple arithmetical computation to determine the value of i. Instead, the investor selects a value for i and plugs it into the equation. If this value equates the left-hand and right-hand sides of the equation, then that value of i is the yield to maturity.

If the value does not equate the two sides of the equation, another value must be selected. This process is repeated until a value for i is found that equates both sides of the equation. Obviously, that can be a long process. For example, suppose the investor selects 14 percent and substitutes it into the right-hand side of the equation. The result is

$$P_B = \frac{\$100}{(1 + 0.14)^1} + \frac{\$100}{(1 + 0.14)^2} + \frac{\$100}{(1 + 0.14)^3} + \frac{\$1,000}{(1 + 0.14)^3}$$

$$= \$100(2.321) + 1,000(0.675)$$

$$= \$232.10 + 675$$

$$= \$907.10.$$

$907.10 does not equal $952. That means the selected yield to maturity was too high, so the investor selects another, lower rate. If the investor had selected 12 percent, then

$$P_B = \$100(2.402) + \$1,000(0.712)$$

$$= \$240.20 + 712$$

$$= \$952.20,$$

and thus 12 percent is the yield to maturity (compounded annually).[3]

The above process to determine the yield to maturity is quite tedious. However, the yield to maturity can be approximated by Equation 10.5.

(10.5)
$$i = \frac{I + \dfrac{\$1,000 - P_B}{n}}{\dfrac{\$1,000 + P_B}{2}}.$$

The symbols are the same that were used in Equation 10.2. If the current price of a $1,000 bond with a 10 percent coupon ($I = \$100$) is $952 ($P_B = \$952$) and the bond matures in three years ($n = 3$), then the approximate yield to maturity is

---

[3] If the investor obtains a price greater than the correct price, the yield to maturity is too low, and the investor should select a higher rate.

$$i = \frac{\$100 + \dfrac{\$1,000 - 952}{3}}{\dfrac{\$1,000 + 952}{2}}$$

$$= \frac{100 + 48/3}{976}$$

$$= 11.88\%.$$

This answer, 11.88 percent, is approximately the 12 percent derived above by the more tedious, but technically correct, method.

A Comparison of the Current Yield and the Yield to Maturity

The current yield and the yield to maturity are equal only if the bond sells for its principal amount or par. If the bond sells at a discount, the yield to maturity exceeds the current yield. This may be illustrated by the bond in the previous example. When it sells at a discount (e.g., $952), the current yield is only 10.5 percent. However, the yield to maturity is 12 percent. Thus, the yield to maturity exceeds the current yield.

Effect on yield if bond sells for a premium or discount

If the bond sells at a premium, the current yield exceeds the yield to maturity. For example, if the bond sells for $1,052, the current yield is 9.5 percent ($100 ÷ $1,052) and the yield to maturity is 8 percent. The yield to maturity is less in this case because the loss that the investor must suffer when the price of the bond declines from $1,052 to $1,000 at maturity has been incorporated.

Exhibit 10.2 presents the current yield and the yields to maturity at different prices for a bond with an 8 percent coupon that matures in ten years. As may be seen in the table, the larger the discount (or the smaller the premium), the greater are both the current yield and the yield to maturity. For example, when the bond sells for $881.50, the yield to maturity is 9.9 percent, but it rises to 11.5 percent when the price declines to $795.10.

Discounted bonds offer conservative investors attractive opportunities for financial planning. For example, a person who is currently 55 years old may purchase dis-

Discounted bonds may be attractive investments

Price of Bond	Current Yield	Yield to Maturity
$1,109.00	7.2%	6.5%
1,049.10	7.6	7.3
1,000.00	8.0	8.0
966.80	8.3	8.5
910.50	8.8	9.4
881.50	9.1	9.9
831.30	9.6	10.8
795.10	10.1	11.5
687.28	11.6	14.0

Exhibit 10.2
Current Yields and Yields to Maturity for a Ten-year Bond with an 8 Percent Coupon

POINTS OF INTEREST
The Accuracy of the Approximate Formula

If the student does not have access to a financial function calculator, the approximation formula is a convenient means to estimate the yield to maturity. How accurate is the approximation? To help answer that question, consider two bonds that each have a 10 percent coupon ($100 per $1,000 face amount). Bond A matures in five years, while bond B matures in twenty years. The following table is constructed to show the correct and the approximate yield to maturity at various prices.

As may be seen in this illustration, the approximate yield to maturity is a reasonable estimate of the actual yield to maturity. Only when the bond sells for a large discount does the approximation significantly understate the true yield the bond offers over its lifetime.

Bond A

Price	Correct Yield to Maturity	Approximate Yield to Maturity
$1,100	7.56%	7.62%
1,000	10.00	10.00
900	12.76	12.63
800	15.94	15.55
500	29.86	26.67

Bond B

Price	Correct Yield to Maturity	Approximate Yield to Maturity
$1,100	8.90%	9.05%
1,000	10.00	10.00
900	11.26	11.05
800	12.78	12.22
500	20.42	16.67

Exhibit 10.3
Selected AT&T Bonds
Selling at a Discount
as of January 1, 1986

Coupon Rate	Maturity Year	Current Price (per $100 Face Value)	Yield to Maturity
4⅝	1994	$68½	10.50%
5⅝	1995	70	10.70
4⅜	1996	59¾	10.79
5½	1997	66½	10.77
4¾	1998	59	10.83
4⅜	1999	55	10.83

Source: Moody's Bond Record, January 1986.

counted bonds that mature after ten years to help finance retirement. This investor may purchase several bonds that mature 10, 11, 12 years, and so on, into the future. This portfolio will generate a continuous flow of funds during retirement as the bonds mature. Such a portfolio of AT&T bonds maturing during the 1990s is illustrated in Exhibit 10.3. The first column gives the coupon rate of interest, the second column gives the year of maturity, the third column presents the current discounted price for

$1,000 in face value worth of debt, and the last column gives the yield to maturity. By purchasing this portfolio for a total cost of $3,787.50, the investor will own $6,000 worth of bonds that mature between 1994 and 1999. Of course, by purchasing more discounted bonds that mature between 1994 and 1999, the investor will have an even greater flow of income during the particular time period to meet his or her financial goals (e.g., financing retirement or paying for children's college education).

The Yield to Call

Some bonds will never reach maturity but are retired before they become due. In some cases the issuer may call the bonds before maturity and redeem them. In other cases, the sinking fund will randomly call selected bonds from the issue and retire them. For these reasons the **yield to call** may be a more accurate estimate of the return actually earned on an investment in a bond that is held until redemption.

The yield to call is calculated in the same way as the yield to maturity except that (1) the expected call date is substituted for the maturity date and (2) the principal plus the call penalty (if any) is substituted for the principal. Note that the anticipated call date is used. Unlike the maturity date, which is known, the date of a call can only be anticipated.

A call feature will affect a bond's value

The following example illustrates how the yield to call is calculated. A bond that matures after ten years and pays 8 percent interest annually is currently selling for $935.00. The yield to maturity is 9 percent. However, if the investor believes that the company or government will call the bond after five years and will pay a penalty of $50 per $1,000 bond to retire the debt permanently, the yield to call (i_c) is approximately

The valuation model can be adjusted for a call feature

$$\$935 = \frac{\$80}{(1 + i_c)^1} + \cdots + \frac{\$80}{(1 + i_c)^5} + \frac{\$1,050}{(1 + i_c)^5}$$

$$i_c = 10.5\%.$$

(This answer, like the yield to maturity, may be derived by using the present value tables. To do so, select an interest rate, find the appropriate interest factors, and substitute them for i_c. This process is continued until a value for i_c is found that equates both sides of the equation. This lengthy process may be avoided by the use of computers or calculators that are programmed to determine yields to maturity.)

In this example, the yield to call is higher than the yield to maturity because (1) the investor receives the call penalty and (2) the principal is redeemed early and hence the discount is erased sooner. Thus, in the case of a discounted bond, the actual return the investor earns exceeds the yield to maturity if the bond is called and retired before maturity.

However, if this bond were selling for a premium (e.g., $1,146.80 with a yield to maturity of 6 percent) and the firm were to call the bond after five years, the yield to call would become

$$\$1,146.80 = \frac{\$80}{(1 + i_c)^1} + \cdots + \frac{\$80}{(1 + i_c)^5} + \frac{\$1,050}{(1 + i_c)^5}$$

$$i_c = 5.5\%.$$

This is less than the anticipated yield to maturity of 6 percent. The early redemption produces a lower return for the investor, because the premium is spread out over fewer years, reducing the yield on the investment.

Bonds selling for a premium may be called

Which case is more likely to occur? If a firm wanted to retire debt that was selling at a discount before maturity, it would probably be to its advantage to purchase the bonds instead of calling them. By doing so, the firm would avoid the call penalty and might even be able to buy the bonds for less than par. If the firm wanted to retire debt that was selling at a premium, it would probably be advantageous to call the bonds and pay the penalty. If the bonds were selling for more than the call penalty, this would obviously be the chosen course of action.

An investor should not expect a firm to call prematurely a bond issue that is selling at a discount. However, if interest rates fall and bond prices rise, the firm may refinance the debt. It will then issue new debt at the lower (current) interest rate and use the proceeds to retire the old and more costly debt. In this case the yield to the anticipated call is probably a better indication of the potential return offered by the bonds than is the yield to maturity.

The call penalty increases the bond's value

The preceding example also illustrates the importance of the call penalty. If an investor bought the bond in anticipation that it would yield 6 percent at maturity (i.e., pay $1,146.80) and the bond is redeemed after five years for $1,000, the return on the investment is only 4.6 percent. Although the $50 call penalty does not restore the return to 6 percent, the investor does receive a yield of 5.5 percent, which is considerably better than 4.6 percent.

RISK AND FLUCTUATIONS IN YIELDS

Investors will bear risk only if they anticipate a sufficient return to compensate for the risk, and a higher anticipated return is necessary to induce them to bear additional risk. This principle also applies to investors who purchase bonds. Bonds involving greater risk must offer higher yields to attract investors. Therefore, the lowest yields are paid by bonds with the highest credit ratings, and low credit ratings are associated with high yields.

This relationship is illustrated by Exhibit 10.4, which presents Moody's ratings and the anticipated yields to maturity for three bonds issued by industrial firms that will mature in the year 2000. As may be seen in the exhibit, the bonds with the highest credit ratings have the lowest anticipated yield to maturity. An AT&T bond with an Aa1 rating was selling to yield less than the Baa1-rated bond of Georgia Power Com-

Exhibit 10.4
Credit Ratings and
Yields to Maturity
for Selected Bonds
Maturing in the
Year 2000

Bond Issue	Moody's Bond Rating	Yield to Maturity
AT&T, 8¾ 00	Aa1	9.02%
Tenneco Corp., 9⅞ 00	A3	10.07
Georgia Power Co., 8⅝ 00	Baa1	11.15

Source: Moody's Bond Record, March 1986.

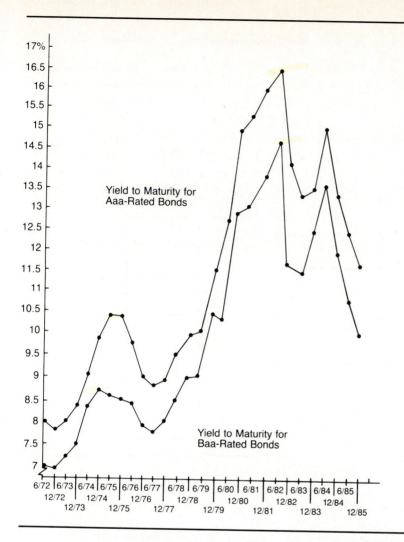

Figure 10.4
Fluctuations in Yield to Maturity for Moody's Aaa- and Baa-rated Industrial Bonds

pany. The difference, or "spread," in the yields is partially due to the difference in risk between the two bonds. While the AT&T bond is considered to be quite safe (as judged by its rating), the Georgia Power Company bond is viewed as involving considerably more risk.

Because interest rates change over time, the anticipated yields on all debts vary. However, the yields on debt involving greater risk tend to fluctuate more. This is illustrated in Figure 10.4, which plots the yields on Moody's Baa-rated bonds in the top line and the yields on its Aaa-rated bonds in the bottom line. In this particular period there was considerable change in the yields to maturity. During periods of higher interest rates, the poorer quality debt offered a higher yield and the spread between the yields was also greater. For example, during 1974, the yields to maturity on Aaa- and Baa-rated bonds rose to 8.6 and 10.4 percent, respectively, for a spread of 1.8 percent. During 1982, the yields rose even further to 14.8 and 16.9 percent, and the spread

Yields on riskier bonds fluctuate more

Figure 10.5   **Yearly Price Ranges of an AT&T and a Jersey Central Power and Light Bond**

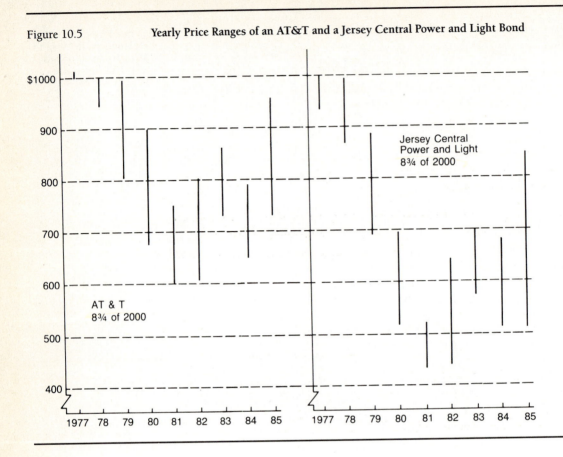

Price fluctuations of riskier bonds are larger

between the bonds also rose to 2.1 percent. When interest rates subsequently declined in the mid-1980s, the spread also declined.

As may be expected, all bond prices fall when interest rates rise, but the prices of bonds issued by financially weaker (riskier) firms tend to decline more. As the spread between yields rises, so too does the difference between bond prices. Such price fluctuations are illustrated in Figure 10.5, which plots the annual price range of two bonds with equal length of time to maturity and equal coupons but considerable difference in risk. The AT&T 8¾% bond that matures in 2000 was rated Aa1 (as of January 1986) while the Jersey Central Power and Light 8¾% bond that also matures in 2000 was rated Baa2. As would be expected, the price of the latter bond has experienced greater fluctuations. While the price of the AT&T bond declined from about $1,000 in 1977 to $600 in 1982, the JCP&L bond declined from $1,000 to $435 during the same period.

These differences in the fluctuations of bond prices and spreads are the market's way of adjusting for the relative risk of investing in debt instruments of different quality. During periods of high interest rates and relatively scarce credit, weaker firms find it more difficult to finance their assets. Issuing new debt either to finance new assets or to retire old debt is more costly. Lenders must allocate the scarce supply of available credit, meaning that the price of credit (i.e., the interest rate) must rise. In addition,

the possibility of default by the borrower is greater when interest rates are higher and the ability to borrow is reduced. The creditor must be compensated for assuming this increased risk of loss. Thus, despite the fact that all yields rise, the yields on the weakest debt instruments rise the most. These bonds, then, sell for the largest discounts and experience greater price volatility than high-quality bonds.

DURATION

Investors in bonds are exposed to the risks associated with (1) the loss of purchasing power through inflation, (2) the default on an obligation by a debtor, and (3) changes in interest rates. Individual investors cannot stop inflation but can seek to reduce its impact by earning a return that exceeds the inflation rate. They cannot stop a debtor from defaulting but can reduce the probability of default by selecting bonds with high credit ratings. Investors can further reduce the risk of loss through default by constructing a diversified portfolio composed of debt issued by different types of firms.

However, a diversified portfolio with a return exceeding the expected rate of inflation is still subject to the risk associated with fluctuations in interest rates. This source of risk can be reduced through the use of a concept referred to as **duration**. Duration is a means to compare the price sensitivity of bonds with different coupons and different maturity dates. This comparability is achieved by considering when all of the bond's payments are made.

Comparing price sensitivity of bonds

Duration is defined as the average time it takes the bondholder to receive the interest and the principal. It is a weighted average that encompasses the total amount of the bond's payments and their timing, then standardizes for the bond's price. To illustrate how duration is determined, consider a $1,000 bond with three years to maturity and a 9 percent coupon. The annual payments are as follows:

Year	Payment
1	$90
2	90
3	1,090

Currently the rate of interest on comparable bonds is 12 percent, so this bond's price is $928.18. The bond's duration is the sum of the present value of each payment weighted by the time period in which the payment is received, with the resulting quantity divided by the price of the bond. Thus, for this bond, the duration is determined as follows:

Number of payments		Amount of payment		Present value interest factor at 12%		
1	×	$90	×	0.893	=	80.37
2	×	90	×	0.797	=	143.46
3	×	1,090	×	0.712	=	2,319.24
						2,543.07

$$\text{Duration} = \frac{2,543.07}{928.18} = 2.74 \text{ periods.}$$

By making this calculation for bonds with different coupons and different maturities, the investor standardizes for price fluctuations. Bonds with the same duration will experience similar price fluctuations, while the prices of bonds with a longer duration will fluctuate more. For example, consider the following two bonds. Bond A has a 10 percent coupon, matures in twenty years, and currently sells for $1,000. Bond B has a 7 percent coupon and matures after ten years with a current price of $815.66.[4] If interest rates rise, the price of both bonds will fall, but which bond's price will fall more? Since the bonds differ with regard to maturity date and coupon, the investor does not know which bond's price will be more volatile.

Smaller duration means smaller price volatility

In general, the longer the term to maturity, the more volatile the bond's price. By that reasoning, bond A will be more volatile. However, lower coupons are also associated with greater price volatility, and by that reasoning bond B's price should be more volatile. Thus, the investor cannot tell on the basis of term and coupon which of these two bonds' prices will be more volatile. However, once their durations have been determined (9.36 and 7.22, respectively), the investor knows that the price of bond A will decline more in response to an increase in interest rates. For example, if interest rates rose to 12 percent, the prices of the two bonds become $850.61 and $717.49, respectively. Bond A's price declined by 15 percent while bond B's price fell by 12 percent, so bond A's price was more volatile.

Since bonds with larger durations are more volatile, investors reduce the risk associated with changes in interest rates by acquiring bonds with shorter durations. This, however, is not synonymous with buying bonds with shorter maturities.[5] If two bonds have the same term to maturity, the bond with the smaller coupon will have the longer duration, since most of the bond's total payment is repayment of principal. If two bonds have the same coupon, the one with the longer maturity will have the longer duration, as the payments are spread over a longer period of time. However, if one bond has a smaller coupon and a shorter term, its duration could be either greater or smaller than the duration of a bond with a higher coupon and longer term to maturity. Thus, it is possible to buy a bond with a longer term to maturity that has a shorter duration. In such a case, the longer term bond will experience smaller price fluctuations than the bond with the shorter maturity but longer duration.

Duration is primarily used by portfolio managers, such as managers of pension plans, who know when the funds will be needed. They seek to match the duration of their portfolios with the timing of the needs for their funds. Such matching reduces the interest-rate risk associated with their portfolios. An individual investor may have difficulty using duration because he or she may not know when the funds will be needed or whether the funds may be required for different purposes at various times in the future. In addition, each bond's duration is not reported in publications such as Standard & Poor's *Bond Guide*. An individual would have to perform the calculation, which is quite tedious. However, access to a financial spreadsheet such as *Lotus 1-2-3®* can facilitate the calculation and thereby permit an individual to compare the duration of many bonds being considered for inclusion in his or her portfolio.

---

[4] In this illustration it is assumed that the bonds sell for the same yield. Generally the long-term bond offers a higher yield. This assumption facilitates comparisons for a given change in interest rates but tends to overstate the duration of bond B.

[5] The only time when duration equals the term to maturity occurs when the bond makes no interest payments (i.e., it is a zero coupon bond). All the payments then occur at maturity.

SUMMARY

The price of a bond depends on the interest paid, the maturity date, and the return offered by comparable bonds. If interest rates rise, the price of existing bonds falls. The opposite is also true—if interest rates fall, the price of existing bonds rises.

The current yield considers only the flow of interest income relative to the price of the bond. The yield to maturity considers the flow of interest income as well as any price change that may occur if the bond is held to maturity. The yield to call is similar to the yield to maturity, but it substitutes the call date and the call price for the maturity date and the principal.

Discounted bonds may be attractive to investors seeking current income, some capital appreciation, and the return of the principal at a specified date. Since most bonds mature, the investor knows exactly when the principal is to be received.

All bond prices fluctuate in response to changes in interest rates, but the prices of bonds with longer maturities or poorer credit ratings tend to fluctuate more. These bonds may sell for larger discounts or higher premiums than bonds with shorter maturities or better credit ratings. Such bonds may be attractive investments for individuals who seek higher returns and who are willing to bear additional risk.

Investors may determine bonds' duration to ascertain which bonds' prices will fluctuate more. Duration is a weighted average of all of the bond's interest and principal payments standardized by the bond's price. Bonds with smaller durations tend to have smaller price fluctuations in response to changes in interest rates.

Summary of Bond Valuations

Perpetual Bond

$$PV = \frac{I}{i}. \tag{10.1}$$

Finite Maturity—Annual Compounding

$$P_B = \frac{I_1}{(1 + i)^1} + \frac{I_2}{(1 + i)^2} + \cdots + \frac{I_n}{(1 + i)^n} + \frac{P}{(1 + i)^n}. \tag{10.2}$$

Finite Maturity—Semiannual Compounding

$$P_B = \frac{\frac{I}{c}}{\left(1 + \frac{i}{c}\right)^1} + \frac{\frac{I}{c}}{\left(1 + \frac{i}{c}\right)^2} + \cdots + \frac{\frac{I}{c}}{\left(1 + \frac{i}{c}\right)^{n \times c}} + \frac{P}{\left(1 + \frac{i}{c}\right)^{n \times c}}. \tag{10.3}$$

Current Yield

$$\text{Current yield} = \frac{\text{Annual interest payment}}{\text{Price of the bond}}. \tag{10.4}$$

Approximate Yield to Maturity

$$i = \frac{I + \dfrac{\$1{,}000 - P_B}{n}}{\dfrac{\$1{,}000 + P_B}{2}}. \tag{10.5}$$

Terms to Remember

Perpetual bond   Current yield
Fixed flow of income   Yield to maturity
Discount   Yield to call
Premium   Duration

Questions

1. What causes bond prices to fluctuate?
2. Define the current yield and the yield to maturity. How are they different?
3. When is the yield to maturity greater than the current yield?
4. What advantages do discounted bonds offer to investors?
5. Why may a bond be called if it is selling at a premium?
6. Although all bond prices fluctuate, the price of which bonds tends to fluctuate more?
7. What is the yield to call? How does it differ from the yield to maturity?
8. What differentiates the term of a bond and its duration? If bond A has a 10 percent coupon while bond B has a 5 percent coupon and they both mature after 10 years, which bond has the shorter duration?

Problems

1. A $1,000 bond has the following features: a coupon rate of 14 percent, interest that is paid semiannually (i.e., $70 every six months), and a maturity date of ten years.
    a. What is the bond's price if comparable debt yields 14 percent?
    b. What is the bond's price if comparable debt yields 10 percent?
    c. What is the current yield if the bond sells for the prices determined in Questions a and b?
    d. Why are the prices different for Questions a and b?
2. A $1,000 bond has a coupon rate of 10 percent and matures after eight years. Interest rates are currently 7 percent.
    a. What will the price of this bond be if the interest is paid annually?
    b. What will the price be if investors expect that the bond will be called with no call penalty after two years?
    c. What will the price be if investors expect that the bond will be called after two years and there will be a call penalty of one year's interest?
    d. Why are your answers different for the Questions a, b, and c?
3. A company has two bonds outstanding. The first matures after five years and has a coupon rate of 12 percent. The second matures after ten years and has a coupon rate of 12 percent. Interest rates are currently 14 percent. What is the present price of each bond? Why are these prices different?
4. If a bond with a 9 percent coupon (paid annually) and a maturity date of ten years is selling for $939, what is the current yield and the yield to maturity? (Hint: Try 8 percent or 12 percent.)

5. A zero coupon bond sells for $519 and matures after five years. What is the yield to maturity? (Consult the previous chapter for the discussion of zero coupon bonds, if necessary.)

6. You are offered a $1,000 bond for $850. It pays $75 in interest annually and matures after 12 years. Currently interest rates are 10 percent. Is this bond a good buy?

7. Given the following information:

> XY Inc. 5% bond
> AB Inc. 14% bond
> Both bonds are for $1,000, mature in 20 years, and are rated AAA.

   a. What should be the current market price of each bond if the interest rate on triple A bonds is 10 percent?

   b. Which bond has a current yield that exceeds its yield to maturity?

   c. Which bond would you expect to be called if interest rates are 10 percent?

   d. If CD Inc. had a bond outstanding with a 5 percent coupon and a maturity date of 20 years but it was rated BBB, what would you expect its price to be relative to the XY Inc. bond?

8. Company X has the following bonds outstanding:

Bond A	Coupon	8%
	Maturity	10 years
Bond B	Coupon	Variable—changes annually
	Maturity	10 years

Initially, both bonds sold at $1,000 with yields to maturity of 8 percent.

   a. After two years, the interest rate on comparable debt is 10 percent. What should be the price of each bond?

   b. After two additional years (i.e., four years after issue date), the interest rate on comparable debt is 7 percent. What should be the price of each bond?

   c. What generalization may be drawn from the prices in Questions a and b?

Suggested Readings

Most of this chapter is devoted to changes in bond prices caused by interest rate fluctuations. Controlling the impact of these fluctuations (called "immunization") has become a major consideration of professional money managers. For discussion of techniques to reduce the sensitivity of a portfolio's value to changes in interest rates, see:

Kolb, Robert W. *Investments.* Glenview, Ill.: Scott, Foresman, 1985, 229–236.

Radcliffe, Robert C. *Investment Concepts, Analysis, and Strategy.* Glenview, Ill.: Scott, Foresman, 1982, 227–230.

Kaufman, George G., G. O. Bierwag, and Alden Toevs. *Innovations in Bond Portfolio Management.* Greenwich, Conn.: JAI Press, 1983.

For material on duration, see:

Edwards, Bob. "Bond Analysis: The Concept of Duration," *IIAA Journal* (March 1984): 33–37.

11

Preferred Stock

LEARNING OBJECTIVES

After completing this chapter you should be able to

1. Compare and contrast long-term bonds and preferred stock.
2. Explain why firms prefer debt issues to preferred stock as a source of funds.
3. Illustrate the pricing of preferred stock.
4. Isolate the sources of risk to investors in preferred stock.
5. Determine earnings per preferred share.
6. Explain why corporations may own preferred stock of other corporations.

An alternative to investing in long-term debt is preferred stock. Legally, preferred stock represents ownership in a corporation; it is not debt and appears on the balance sheet under equity. As the name implies, it is senior to common stock, as preferred stockholders are paid dividends before common stockholders. In case of liquidation, preferred stock is redeemed before the common stockholders receive any proceeds from the sale of the firm's assets. While there is no legal obligation on the part of the firm to pay a dividend to preferred stockholders, it is generally understood that if the firm has sufficient funds, it will pay the preferred dividends.

Preferred stock is similar to debt in that it pays a fixed dividend just as bonds pay a fixed amount of interest. Thus preferred stock is a hybrid type of security that combines some elements of debt and some of equity. While it is legally equity, the fact that it pays a fixed dividend means that investors should analyze preferred stock as if it were debt.

Since preferred stock is an alternative to investing in debt, it will be discussed in this section on fixed-income securities. This chapter initially considers the general features of preferred stock. Then the bond valuation model presented in the previous chapter is applied to the valuation of preferred stock. Next, preferred stock and long-term bonds are contrasted.

The chapter ends with a brief discussion of yields and special features offered by selected preferred stocks that differentiate them from the general class of preferred stock.

THE FEATURES OF PREFERRED STOCK

Preferred stock is an equity instrument that pays a fixed dividend. While most firms have only one issue of common stock, they may have several issues of preferred stock.[1] As may be seen in Exhibit 11.1, Virginia Electric and Power has 18 issues of preferred stock. In each case the dividend rate is fixed. Thus, for the series $8.84 preferred, the annual dividend is $8.84, which is distributed at the rate of $2.21 per share quarterly.

Fixed dividend

This fixed dividend is paid from the firm's earnings. If the firm does not have the earnings, it may not declare and pay the preferred stock dividends. If the firm should omit the preferred stock's dividend, the dividend is said to be *in arrears*. The firm does not have to remove this **arrearage.** In most cases, however, any omitted dividends have to be paid in the future before dividends may be paid to the holders of the common stock. Such cases in which the preferred stock's dividends accumulate are called **cumulative preferred.** Most preferred stock is cumulative, but there are examples of **noncumulative preferred stocks** whose dividends do not have to be made up if missed (e.g., the Uniroyal $8 preferred stock is noncumulative). For investors holding preferred stock in firms having financial difficulty, the difference between cumulative and noncumulative may be immaterial. Forcing the firm to pay dividends to erase the arrearage may further weaken it and hurt the owners of the preferred stock more than would forgoing the dividends. Once the firm has regained its profitability, erasing the arrearage may become important not only to holders of the stock but also to the company, as a demonstration of its improved financial condition.

Chrysler Corporation provides an example of a firm clearing the arrearage on its preferred stock. In December 1979, Chrysler suspended payments on its $2.75 preferred stock. The dividends accumulated for four years, by which time the arrearage had reached $11 per share. In December 1983, Chrysler paid sufficient dividends to the preferred stockholders to erase the arrearage, and less than a year later (October 31, 1984) it redeemed each share of the preferred stock.

Once the preferred stock is issued, the firm may never have to concern itself with its retirement: It is perpetual. This may be both an advantage and a disadvantage. Since the firm may never have to retire the preferred stock, it does not have to generate the money to retire it but may instead use its funds elsewhere (e.g., to purchase plant and equipment). However, should the firm ever want to change its capital structure and substitute debt financing for the preferred stock, it may have difficulty retiring the preferred stock. The firm may have to purchase the stock on the open market, and, to induce the holders to sell the preferred shares, the firm will probably have to bid up the preferred stock's price.

Preferred stock may be perpetual

---

[1] Some corporations have also issued a "preference" stock which is subordinated to preferred stock but has preference over common stock with regard to the payment of dividends. Such stock is another level of preferred stock, and in this text no distinction is made between the two.

Exhibit 11.1
The Preferred Stocks
of Virginia Electric
and Power

Preferred stock not subject to mandatory retirement	Annual Dividend per Share	Outstanding Shares
	$4.04	12,926
	4.20	14,797
	4.12	32,534
	4.80	73,206
	5.00	106,677
	7.72	350,000
	8.84	**350,000**
	7.45	400,000
	7.20	450,000
	7.72	500,000
	9.75	600,000

Preferred stock subject to mandatory retirement	Annual Dividend per Share	Outstanding Shares 12/31/81	12/31/85
	$9.125	192,000	160,000
	8.925	280,000	259,000
	8.60	**347,000**	**299,768**
	8.625	370,000	333,000
	8.20	600,000	510,000
	7.325	700,000	644,000
	8.40	800,000	768,000

Source: 1982 and 1985 Annual Reports.

Call features

    To maintain some control over the preferred stock, the firm may seek to add a call feature to the preferred issue. This feature gives the firm the option to call and redeem the issue. Such a call is illustrated in Exhibit 11.2, in which Delmarva Power & Light is redeeming an issue of preferred stock. While the actual terms of the call feature will vary with each preferred stock issue, the general features are similar. First, the call is at the option of the firm. Second, the call price is specified. Third, the firm may pay a call penalty (e.g., a year's dividends). Fourth, after the issue is called, future dividend payments will cease; this, of course, forces any recalcitrant holders to surrender their certificates.

    Some preferred stocks also have mandatory sinking funds requiring that the firm periodically retire some of the issue. For example, the $8.60 preferred stock in Exhibit 11.1 has a mandatory sinking fund that started in 1985. It requires Virginia Electric and Power to redeem annually 4 percent of the shares originally issued at $100 per share. Thus, by 2010 all the shares will have been retired. Such issues of preferred stock with mandatory sinking funds are very similar to bonds, which also are not perpetual and must be retired.[2]

---

[2] In 1979 a change in how property and casualty insurance companies account for investments in preferred stock shifted their preference for sinking fund preferred stock vis-a-vis perpetual preferred stock. Utilities, which are the primary issuers of preferred stock, responded to this change by starting to issue preferred stock with mandatory retirement features (sinking funds). See M. J. C. Roth, "New Look at Preferred Stock Financing," *Public Utilities Fortnightly* (March 27, 1980): 26–28.

Exhibit 11.2
**Redemption of an Issue
of Preferred Stock**
The issue

**NOTICE OF REDEMPTION
OF
ALL OUTSTANDING SHARES OF
12.56% PREFERRED STOCK
OF
DELMARVA POWER & LIGHT COMPANY**

The company

Notice is hereby given that Delmarva Power & Light Company (the "Company") has called for redemption and will redeem on December 31, 1985 (the "Redemption Date") all outstanding shares of its 12.56% Preferred Stock (the "12.56% Stock"), for the redemption price of $108.38 per share (the "Regular Redemption Price"). Dividends will be paid directly by the Company on December 31, 1985 to stockholders of record on December 10, 1985, and the redemption price will thus not include any dividends. The Company intends to deposit in trust with the Redemption Agent on or before December 31, 1985 moneys sufficient in amount to pay the aggregate Regular Redemption Price of the shares of 12.56% stock to be redeemed. Pursuant to the terms of the Certificate of Incorporation, all rights of the holds of shares of 12.56% stock to be redeemed, as stockholders of the Company, shall thereupon cease and terminate, excepting only the right to receive the Regular Redemption Price upon surrender of the certificates for the 12.56% Stock.

The call price

*The rights of stockholder
cease*

Payment of the Regular Redemption Price will be made on or after the Redemption Date upon surrender of the 12.56% Stock certificates, accompanied by a properly completed and executed Letter of Transmittal, to Manufacturers Hanover Trust Company (the "Redemption Agent") at either of the addresses listed below.

By Mail:

Manufacturers Hanover Trust Company
Reorganization Department
P.O. Box 3083, G.P.O. Station
New York, New York 10116

By Hand:

Manufacturers Hanover Trust Company
Securities Window
130 John Street, Street Level
New York, New York 10038

This redemption is being made pursuant to the Certificates of Incorporation under which the Company has elected to call 12.56% Stock for redemption

DELMARVA POWER & LIGHT COMPANY
Roger D. Campbell
Vice President, Treasurer & CFO

November 27, 1985

Source: Reprinted with permission of the Delmarva Power & Light Company.

THE VALUATION OF PREFERRED STOCK

The process of valuing (pricing) preferred stock is essentially the same as that used to price debt. The future payments are brought back to the present at the appropriate discount rate. If the preferred stock does not have a required sinking fund or call feature, it may be viewed as a perpetual debt instrument. The fixed dividend (D) will continue indefinitely. These dividends must be discounted by the yield being earned on newly issued preferred stock (k). This process for determining the present value of the preferred stock (P) is given in Equation 11.1:

$$P = \frac{D}{(1 + k)^1} + \frac{D}{(1 + k)^2} + \frac{D}{(1 + k)^3} + \cdots .$$

(11.1)

As in the case of the perpetual bond, this equation is reduced to

$$P = \frac{D}{k} .$$

(11.2)

Thus, if a preferred stock pays an annual dividend of $4 and the appropriate discount rate is 12 percent, the present value of the preferred stock is

$$P = \frac{\$4}{(1 + 0.12)^1} + \frac{\$4}{(1 + 0.12)^2} + \frac{\$4}{(1 + 0.12)^3} + \cdots$$

$$= \frac{\$4}{0.12} = \$33.33.$$

If an investor buys this preferred stock for $33.33, he or she can expect to earn 12 percent ($33.33 × 0.12 = $4) on the investment. Of course, the realized rate of return on the investment will not be known until the investor sells the stock and adjusts this 12 percent return for any capital gain or loss. However, at the current price, the preferred stock is selling for a 12 percent dividend yield.

The impact of finite life on valuation

    If the preferred stock has a finite life, this fact must be considered in determining its value. As with the valuation of long-term debt, the amount that is repaid when the preferred stock is retired must be discounted back to the present value. Thus, when preferred stock has a finite life, the valuation equation becomes

(11.3)
$$P = \frac{D}{(1 + k)^1} + \frac{D}{(1 + k)^2} + \cdots + \frac{D}{(1 + k)^n} + \frac{S}{(1 + k)^n},$$

where S represents the amount that is returned to the stockholder when the preferred stock is retired after n number of years. If the preferred stock in the previous example is retired after 20 years for $100 per share, its current value would be

$$P = \frac{\$4}{(1 + 0.12)^1} + \cdots + \frac{\$4}{(1 + 0.12)^{20}} + \frac{\$100}{(1 + 0.12)^{20}}$$

$$= \$4(7.470) + \$100(0.104)$$

$$= \$40.28,$$

where 7.470 is the interest factor for the present value of an annuity of $1 for 20 years at 12 percent and 0.104 is the present value of $1 to be received after 20 years when yields are 12 percent. Instead of selling the stock for $33.33, the nonperpetual preferred stock would sell for $40.28. The yield is still 12 percent, but the return in this case consists of a current dividend yield of 9.93 percent ($4 ÷ $40.28) and a capital gain as the price of the stock rises from $40.28 to $100 when it is retired 20 years hence.

PREFERRED STOCK AND BONDS CONTRASTED

Since preferred stock pays a fixed dividend, it is purchased primarily by investors seeking a fixed flow of income, and it is analyzed and valued like any other fixed-income security (i.e., long-term bonds). But preferred stock differs from long-term debt, as the subsequent discussion will demonstrate, and these differences are significant.

Preferred stock is riskier than debt

    First, preferred stock is riskier than debt. The terms of a bond are legal obligations of the firm. If the corporation fails to pay the interest or meet any of the terms of the indenture, the bondholders may take the firm to court to force payment of the interest or to seek liquidation of the firm in order to protect their principal. Preferred

stockholders do not have that power, for the firm is not legally obligated to pay the preferred stock dividends.

In addition, debt must be retired, while preferred stock is often perpetual. If the security is perpetual, the only means to recoup the amount invested is to sell the preferred stock in the secondary market. The investor cannot expect the firm to redeem the security. Market price fluctuations tend to be greater for preferred stock than for long-term bonds. Figure 10.2 (in Chapter 10) illustrated that price fluctuations for long-term bonds were greater than price fluctuations experienced by short-term debt. This principle holds when comparing long-term bonds and preferred stock. The price of a perpetual preferred stock will fluctuate more than the price of a long-term bond that has a finite life.

Importance of secondary markets

Price fluctuations

This generalization is illustrated in Figure 11.1, which presents the dividend yield, the yield to maturity, and the prices of a Philadelphia Electric bond and preferred stock. The stock is the $4.68 preferred, and the bond is the 4⅝ of 1987. As may be seen in the graph, there is an inverse relationship between the yields and the prices of both the preferred stock and the bond. However, since the bond has a finite life (i.e., it matures in 1987), its price is not as volatile as the preferred stock's price. Thus, when yields rose to over 14 percent in 1981, the bond's price declined from $740 in 1977 to about $600, but the stock's price declined from $50 to under $30 per share during the same time period.

Figure 11.1 also demonstrates that although the yield on the bond and stock move together, the differential between the two yields is relatively small. While the differential was 1.8 percent in 1981, there was virtually no difference in the yields in 1978 to 1979. This similarity in yields is surprising since from the investor's viewpoint the bond is less risky than the preferred stock. Presumably the riskier security should offer a higher return.

This small differential between the yields on bonds and preferred stock may be explained by the corporate income tax laws. Dividends paid by one corporation to another receive favorable tax treatment. Only 20 percent of the dividends are taxed as income of the corporation receiving them. Thus, for a firm such as an insurance company in the 34 percent corporate income tax bracket, this shelter is very important. If the company receives $100 in interest, it nets only $66 as $34 is taxed away. However, if this company were to receive $100 in preferred stock dividends, only $20 would be subject to federal income tax. Thus the firm pays only $6.80 ($20 × 0.34) in taxes and gets to keep the remaining $93.20 of the dividends.

Corporate dividend exclusion

For this reason, a corporation may choose to purchase preferred stocks instead of long-term bonds. This preference drives up the price of preferred stocks, which reduces their yields. Since individual investors do not enjoy the tax break, they may prefer bonds, which offer yields comparable to preferred stock but are less risky. To induce investors to purchase preferred stock, the firm often offers other features, such as the convertibility of the preferred stock into common stock.

A second important difference between debt and preferred stock (at least from the viewpoint of the firm) is that the interest on debt is a tax-deductible expense while the dividend on preferred stock is not. Preferred dividends are paid out of earnings. This difference in the tax treatment of interest expense and preferred stock dividends affects the earnings available to the firm's common stockholders. Using debt instead of preferred stock as a source of funds will result in higher earnings per common share.

Preferred dividends are not an expense

Figure 11.1
Prices and Yields on a Philadelphia Electric Bond and a Preferred Stock

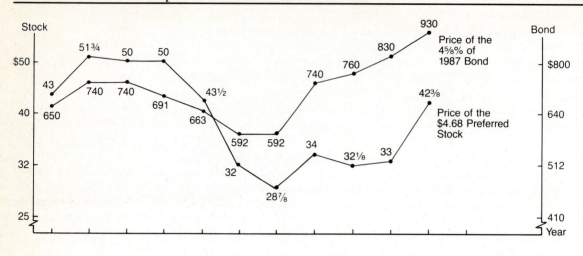

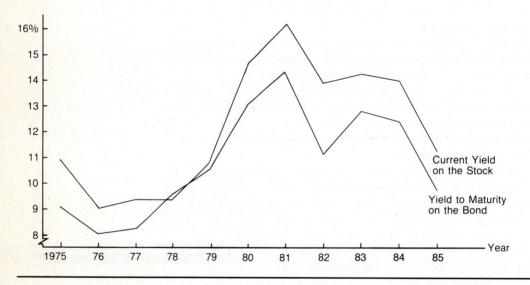

Consider a firm with operating income (earnings before interest and taxes) of $1,000,000. The firm has 100,000 common shares outstanding and is in the 40 percent corporate income tax bracket. If the firm issues $2,000,000 of debt with a 10 percent rate of interest, its earnings per common share are

Earnings before interest and taxes	$1,000,000
Interest	200,000
Earnings before taxes	800,000
Taxes	320,000
Net income	$480,000
Earnings per common share: $480,000/100,000 =	$4.80

If the firm had issued $2,000,000 in preferred stock that also paid 10 percent, the earnings per common share would be

Earnings before interest and taxes	$1,000,000
Interest	00
Earnings before taxes	1,000,000
Taxes	400,000
Earnings before preferred stock dividends	600,000
Preferred stock dividends	200,000
Earnings available to common stock	$400,000
Earnings per common share: $400,000/100,000 =	$4.00

The use of preferred stock has resulted in lower earnings per common share. This reduction in earnings is the result of the different tax treatment of interest, which is a tax-deductible expense, and preferred stock dividends, which are not deductible.

ANALYSIS OF PREFERRED STOCK

Since preferred stock is similar to debt, the tools used to analyze it are similar as well. Because preferred stock is an income-producing investment, the analysis is primarily concerned with the capacity of the firm to meet the dividend payments. Although dividends must ultimately be related to current earnings and the firm's future earning capacity, preferred dividends are paid from cash. Even if the firm is temporarily running a deficit (i.e., experiencing an accounting loss), it may still be able to pay dividends to the preferred stockholders if it has sufficient cash. In fact, cash dividends might be paid despite the deficit to indicate that the losses are expected to be temporary and that the firm is financially strong.

An analysis of the firm's financial statements (such as the ratios used to analyze common stock in Chapter 17) may reveal its liquidity position and profitability. The more liquid and profitable the firm, the safer the dividend payment should be. The investor may also analyze how well the firm covers its preferred dividend. This analysis is achieved by computing the **times-dividend-earned ratio**, which is

The ratio of dividends to earnings

$$\frac{\text{Earnings after taxes}}{\text{Dividends on preferred stock}}$$

The larger this ratio, the safer the preferred stock's dividend should be. Notice that the numerator consists of *total* earnings. Although the preferred stock dividends are subtracted from the total earnings to derive the earnings available to the common stockholders, all of the firm's earnings are available to pay the preferred stock dividend.

A variation on this ratio is **earnings per preferred share**. This ratio is

Earnings per preferred share

$$\frac{\text{Earnings after taxes}}{\text{Number of preferred shares outstanding}}$$

The larger the earnings per preferred share, the safer the dividend payment. However, neither of these ratios indicates whether the firm has sufficient cash to pay the dividends. They can only indicate the extent to which earnings cover the dividend requirements of the preferred stock.

How each ratio is computed can be illustrated by the following simple example. A firm has earnings of $6 million and is in the 40 percent tax bracket. It has 100,000 shares of preferred stock outstanding, and each share pays a dividend of $5. The times-dividend-earned ratio is

$$\frac{\$6,000,000 - \$2,400,000}{\$500,000} = 7.2,$$

and the earnings per preferred share are

$$\frac{\$6,000,000 - \$2,400,000}{100,000} = \$36.$$

Both ratios, in effect, show the same thing. In the first, the preferred dividend is covered by a multiple of 7.2:1. The second ratio shows an earnings per preferred share of $36, which is 7.2 times the $5 dividend paid for each share.

THE VARIETIES OF PREFERRED STOCK

Convertible preferred

While most of this chapter considers straight preferred stock that is either perpetual or subject to mandatory retirement, other features may be built into a preferred stock. The first and most important of these is convertibility. Some preferred stocks may be converted into common stock. For example, as of January 1986, Household International had three issues of convertible preferred stock that may be exchanged at the owner's option for a specified number of shares of common stock. Convertible preferred stock differs considerably from nonconvertible preferred and is discussed in more detail in Chapter 21, which covers convertible securities.

Adjustable rate preferred stock

The second possible variation is adjustable rate preferred stock, which does not pay a fixed dividend but a variable rate. For example, the Integrated Resources adjustable rate preferred stock pays a dividend that can range from a high of $7.50 to a low of $4.00 annually. As with variable interest rate bonds, adjustable rate preferred stock removes some of the potential for price fluctuations generated by changing interest rates. If interest rates rise, the rate paid by the preferred stock increases. However, if interest rates fall, the dividend is decreased. Thus, while the variable dividend reduces price fluctuations, it also reduces the attractiveness of the stock for an individual seeking a fixed flow of dividend income.

The third possible variation is the substitution of stock dividends for cash dividends. For example, the LTV AA convertible preferred stock does not pay a cash dividend but instead pays a 3 percent stock dividend.[3] Another possible variation is the participating preferred stock whose dividend is tied to the dividends paid to the firm's common stock. Such preferred stock would participate in the dividend growth experienced by the common stock. However, the number of preferred stocks that pay stock dividends or have participating dividends are very small. Such hybrid securities are difficult to evaluate, which probably explains why there are so few of these types of preferred stock.

---

[3] LTV suspended payment of the stock dividend in 1985 when it suspended cash dividend payments to its other issues of preferred stock.

DISADVANTAGES OF PREFERRED STOCK

While most preferred stock offers the investor the advantage of a fixed flow of income, this may be more than offset by several disadvantages. Like any fixed-income security, preferred stock offers no protection from inflation. If the inflation rate were to increase, the real purchasing power of the dividend would be diminished. In addition, increased inflation would probably lead to higher interest rates, which would drive down the market value of the preferred stock. Thus, higher rates of inflation doubly curse preferred stock, as the purchasing power of the dividend and the market value of the stock both will be diminished.[4]

No inflation protection

Preferred stock also tends to be less marketable than other securities. Marketability of a particular preferred stock depends on the size of the issue. However, most preferred stock is bought by insurance companies and pension plans. The market for the remaining shares may be quite thin, so there can be a substantial spread between the bid and ask prices. While this may not be a disadvantage if the investor intends to hold the security, it will reduce the attractiveness of the preferred stock in cases in which marketability is desired.

Less marketability

Several other disadvantages were alluded to earlier in the chapter. The first of these is the inferior position of preferred stock to debt obligations. The investor must realize that preferred stock is perceptibly riskier than bonds. For example, in May 1986, Zapata Corporation omitted dividends on its two issues of preferred stock but continued to make the interest payments on its debentures. One of these issues is noncumulative, so those dividend payments have been lost forever.

Subordinated to debt

A second disadvantage is that the yields offered by preferred stock are probably insufficient to justify the additional risk. The yields on preferred stock are not necessarily higher than those available on bonds because of the tax advantage preferred stock offers corporate investors and pension managers. As was explained before, only 20 percent of the preferred dividends are subject to corporate income tax, and none of the dividends paid to pension plans are subject to tax. (Any tax is paid by the recipient of the pension.) These tax advantages artificially drive up the price of preferred stock and drive down the yield. Unfortunately, individual investors are unable to take advantage of these tax breaks except as part of retirement plans. Thus, individual investors may earn inferior yields after adjusting for the risks associated with investing in a security inferior to the firm's bonds.

Inferior yields

SUMMARY

While preferred stock is legally equity, the fact that it pays a fixed dividend makes it similar to debt. Preferred stock's value fluctuates with changes in interest rates. When interest rates rise, the price of preferred stock falls; when interest rates decline, the price of preferred stock rises. Since its price behavior is the same as the price behavior of bonds, preferred stock is valued and analyzed as an alternative to long-term debt. The prime advantage to the firm issuing preferred stock is that it is less risky than debt because the terms of the preferred stock are not legal obligations. The major

---

[4]This disadvantage, of course, applies to all fixed-income, long-term securities.

disadvantage is that the dividends are not a tax-deductible expense. The main reason for purchasing a preferred stock is the flow of dividend income. However, since preferred stock is riskier than debt (from the viewpoint of the individual investor), it has not been a popular investment vehicle with individuals. The majority of preferred stock is purchased by corporations, especially insurance companies, and pension funds, which receive favorable tax treatment on the preferred stock dividends they receive.

Terms to Remember

Preferred stock	Noncumulative preferred stock
Arrearage	Times-dividend-earned ratio
Cumulative preferred stock	Earnings per preferred share

Questions

1. What are the features common to most preferred stock?

2. Must a firm pay preferred stock dividends? What does being in arrears mean? What advantage is offered investors by a cumulative preferred stock?

3. From the viewpoint of the corporation, preferred stock is less risky than debt. However, from the viewpoint of the investor the reverse is true: debt is less risky than preferred stock. Why are these statements concerning risk true?

4. What affects the price of a preferred stock? What will happen to the price of a preferred stock if interest rates rise?

5. What is the earnings per preferred share ratio? Why is it a measure of safety?

6. What types of investors may select preferred stock? What are the advantages and disadvantages associated with investments in preferred stock?

Problems

1. **a.** If a preferred stock pays an annual dividend of $6 and investors can earn 10 percent on alternative and comparable investments, what is the maximum price that should be paid for this stock?
   b. If the preferred stock in part a had a call feature and investors expected the stock to be called for $100 after ten years, what is the maximum price that investors should pay for the stock?
   c. If investors can earn 12 percent on comparable investments, what should be the price of the preferred stock in part a? What would be the price if comparable yields are 8 percent? What generalization do these answers imply?

2. What is the times-dividends-earned ratio given the following information?

30% corporate income tax rate
$10,000 EBIT (earnings before interest and taxes)
$2,000 interest owed
$2,000 preferred stock dividends

3. A firm with earnings before interest and taxes of $500,000 needs $1 million of additional funds. If it issues debt, the bonds will mature after 20 years and have a coupon of 10 percent. The firm could issue a preferred stock with a dividend rate of 10 percent. The firm has 100,000 shares of common stock outstanding and is in the 30 percent corporate income tax bracket. What are the earnings per common share under the two alternative financings?

4. What should be the prices of the following preferred stocks if comparable securities yield 8 percent, 10 percent, and 14 percent?

    a. MN, Inc. $4 preferred ($100 par).

    b. CH, Inc. $4 preferred ($100 par with the additional requirement that the firm must retire the preferred after 20 years).

Why should the prices of these securities be different?

Suggested Readings

Preferred stock is generally believed to be an inferior source of funds for industrial firms. Arguments *in favor* of the use of preferred stock may be found in:

Donaldson, Gordon. "In Defense of Preferred Stock." *Harvard Business Review* (July–August 1962): 123–136.

Elsaid, Hussein H. "The Function of Preferred Stock in the Corporate Financial Plan." *Financial Analysts Journal* (July–August 1969): 112–117.

Many preferred stocks now have provisions for mandatory retirement. For an explanation why, see:

Roth, M. J. C. "New Look At Preferred Stock Financing." *Public Utilities Fortnightly* (March 27, 1980): 26–28.

Information on specific preferred stocks may be found in:

Standard & Poor's Daily Dividend Record or *Moody's Dividend Record,* which report the amount of dividends, and their record and payment dates.

Standard & Poor's Stock Guide, which gives basic financial information on preferred stocks.

12 Government Securities

LEARNING OBJECTIVES

After completing this chapter you should be able to

1. Distinguish among the types of federal government debt.
2. Identify the sources of risk from investing in federal government securities.
3. Distinguish between the federal government's moral obligation and its full-faith and credit obligations to its agencies' debt.
4. Name the primary advantage of state and local government bonds.
5. Illustrate how to equalize yields on corporate bonds and state and local government bonds.
6. Differentiate revenue bonds from general obligation bonds.
7. Compare treasury bonds, T-bills, federal agency debt, municipal bonds, anticipation notes, and project notes.

During 1985 one of the big political issues in Washington was the size of the federal government's deficit. This deficit is the result of expenditures exceeding revenues. Whenever such a deficit occurs, the general public or various financial institutions must finance the deficit. In order to raise money to cover its expenditures, the federal government issues a variety of securities. This variety helps the government tap the different sources of funds that are available in the money and capital markets.

This chapter is concerned with government securities. The first section discusses the various types of debt issued by the federal government, which range from short-term treasury bills to long-term treasury bonds. The second section briefly considers the debt issued by the various agencies of the federal government, and the last section discusses the debt issued by state and local governments. Special emphasis is placed on the feature that distinguishes state and local government debt from other securities: The interest paid to bondholders is exempt from federal income taxation.

THE VARIETY OF FEDERAL GOVERNMENT DEBT

In 1985 the federal government made interest payments of $111.1 billion on its debt. This sum was substantial and amounted to about 13.0 percent of the total expenditures made by the federal government in that year. The debt was financed by a variety of investors, including individuals, corporations, and financial institutions. To induce this diverse group of investors to purchase its debt, the federal government issued different types of debt instruments that appealed to the various potential buyers.

For investors, the unique advantage offered by the federal government's debt is its safety. These debt instruments are the safest of all possible investments, for there is no question that the U.S. Treasury is able to pay the interest and repay the principal. The source of this safety is the federal government's constitutional right to tax and to print money. Because there is no legal limitation on the federal government's capacity to create money, there is no restriction on its ability to pay interest and retire (or at least refinance) its debt.

The safety of the principal and interest

The various types of federal government debt and the amount outstanding of each are illustrated in Exhibit 12.1. As may be seen in the exhibit, there has been an emphasis on the use of short- and intermediate-term financing by the Treasury. This emphasis is partially explained by interest costs. Interest rates on short-term debt are usually lower than those on long-term debt. Hence, the use of short-term financing reduces the Treasury's interest expense. Furthermore, Congress restricts the interest rate that the Treasury may pay on long-term debt, but it does not restrict the interest rate on short-term securities. Thus, during periods of high interest rates, the Treasury may not be permitted to sell long-term securities even if it desires to do so.

The emphasis is on the use of short-term debt

Nonmarketable Federal Government Debt

Perhaps the most widely held federal government debt is the **series E** and **series EE bonds.** The series E bond was designed to encourage saving by people of modest means, as it was sold in small denominations (e.g., $25, $100, $500, and up to $10,000). Although virtually every person should have been able to place modest amounts of savings in these bonds, an individual was allowed to purchase no more than $10,000 worth of series E bonds in a calendar year.

Series E and EE bonds

	Length of Time to Maturity	Value (in Billions of Dollars)	Percentage of Total Debt	
Treasury bills	Less than 1 year	$399.9	20.6%	Exhibit 12.1
Intermediate-term notes	One to 5 years	812.5	41.8	The Variety of Federal Government Debt as of April 1986
Long-term bonds	Over 5 years	211.1	10.8	
Savings bonds	Various maturities	78.1	4.0	
Other debt*	Various maturities	444.3	22.8	

Source: *Federal Reserve Bulletin,* May 1986.
*Debt held by U.S. government agencies and trust funds and state and local governments.

Series E bonds are purchased at a discount

Series E bonds paid no interest but were purchased at a discount (i.e., below their face value). For example, if a saver purchased a $25 series E bond for $18.75 and held it until maturity five years and five months later, he or she received $25 and earned 6 percent annually on the investment. If the bonds were cashed in prior to maturity, the holder received less than $25 and earned a yield of less than 6 percent. (The yield started at 4 percent and rose over the lifetime of the bond until it reached 6 percent at the bond's maturity. This ascending structure of yields is an incentive to hold the bonds until maturity).

Series E bonds were initially issued in 1941 to help finance World War II expenditures. At that time the bonds had a maturity of ten years and a yield of 2.9 percent. As interest rates have risen, the length of time to maturity has been reduced, which has had the effect of increasing the yield on the bonds.

The extension of maturity

Although series E bonds did mature, the Treasury initially did not require that the bonds be redeemed. Instead, the maturities were extended and interest continued to accrue. The rate earned on these older bonds has been increased, so the yield is comparable to that earned by the series EE bond that is currently being sold. The Treasury, however, will no longer extend the maturity of E bonds.[1] As they reach final maturity, the bonds will cease to earn interest, and holders will have to redeem or exchange them for other bonds.

Series EE bond

On January 2, 1980, the Treasury started to issue a new bond, series EE, to replace the series E bonds. Like the E bonds, the new bonds are issued at a discount. The smallest denomination is $50, which costs $25. In November 1982, the Treasury changed the method for computing interest on EE bonds from a fixed rate to a variable rate. The new rate will be 85 percent of the average rate on five-year Treasury securities. This rate will change every six months, but the bonds will guarantee a minimum annual yield of 6.0 percent. This last feature sets a floor on the yield while the variable rate permits the investor to participate in higher yields if interest rates rise in the future.

There are several major differences between series E and EE bonds and most other investments, such as savings accounts. The interest earned on series E and EE bonds is not subject to federal income taxation until the bonds are redeemed or reach final maturity. The interest earned on other investments, including savings accounts, is subject to federal income taxation during the year in which it is earned. Although the federal income tax on the E or EE series may be deferred until the bonds are redeemed, are disposed of, or mature (whichever comes first), the owner does have the option to have the interest taxed each year. Even though the funds are not received until the bond is redeemed, the owner may report the interest to the Internal Revenue Service on an accrual basis. However, most holders of series E bonds have preferred to defer the tax payment. Presumably owners of series EE bonds will follow the same strategy.

Tax deferment

The deferment of interest income until the bonds are redeemed can be advantageous in that the saver can cash in series E and EE bonds in those years when income from other sources is lower. For example, these bonds are potentially good investments to be redeemed during retirement or times of temporary unemployment. It

---

[1] An E bond issued in May 1946 will reach final maturity in May 1986 (i.e., 40 years after date of issue).

is likely that the individual's taxable income will be lower during these periods, and thus the taxes paid on the accrued interest earned by the bonds will be lower. By allowing investors to determine when the interest will be subject to taxation, series E and now series EE bonds offer the investor an opportunity to reduce the amount of taxes paid on the interest. Since they are sold in small units, these bonds offer a means that is available to virtually every investor to shelter income from taxes. Such tax sheltering of interest income is not available through other savings instruments, such as accounts in commercial banks or savings and loan associations.

No secondary market

Another important difference between series E and EE bonds and other bonds is that there is no secondary market in these bonds. If the owner wants immediate cash, the bonds cannot be sold. Instead, the investor redeems them at a commercial bank. Nor can the bonds be transferred as a gift, although they can be transferred through an estate. The Treasury also forbids the use of series E and EE bonds as collateral. Thus, while corporate debt may be used to secure a personal loan, these bonds cannot.

Series H and HH bonds

The investor may exchange series E for **series H bonds**, and as of 1980 they may exchange them for **HH bonds**. The HH series (like the EE bonds) is a new series that is designed to replace the series H bonds. Series H and HH bonds are different from E and EE bonds in several ways. They are sold at par in larger denominations, with $500 being the minimum investment. The bonds mature in ten years and pay 7½ percent interest if held to maturity. The interest is paid every year and does not accumulate as it does with the series E and EE bonds. Thus, interest is subject to federal income taxation each year, while taxation on series E and EE bonds may be deferred until the bonds are redeemed. Series HH bonds are more attractive to investors who need safe sources of current income, while series EE bonds are attractive to conservative investors who wish to build up capital but who do not need current income.

Marketable Securities

Short-term debt

Treasury Bills. Short-term federal government debt is in the form of **treasury bills**. These bills are sold in denominations of $10,000 to $1,000,000 and mature in 3 to 12 months. Like series EE bonds, they are sold at a discount; however, unlike series EE bonds, the discounted price is not set. Instead, the Treasury continually auctions off the bills, which go to the highest bidders. For example, if an investor bids $9,700 and obtains the bill, he or she will receive $10,000 when the bill matures, which is a yield of 3.1 percent ($300 ÷ $9,700). If it is a three-month bill, the annual rate of interest is 12.4 percent. If the bid price had been higher, the interest cost to the Treasury (and the yield to the buyer) would have been lower.

Treasury bills have a secondary market

Once treasury bills have been auctioned, they may be bought and sold in the secondary market. They are issued in bearer form, which makes them highly negotiable and easily marketed. There is an active secondary market in these bills, and they are quoted daily in the financial press and many city newspapers. These quotes and the quotes for other federal government securities are illustrated in Exhibit 12.2. For treasury bills the quotes are given in the following form:

Maturity	Bid Discount	Asked Discount	Yield
10-30	7.35	7.31	7.79

Exhibit 12.2
Yields or Price Quotes for Selected Government Bills, Notes, and Bonds and for Selected Government Agency Issues

Bills

U.S. Treas. Bills

Mat. date	Bid	Asked	Yield	Mat. date	Bid	Asked	Yield
	Discount				Discount		
-1986-				-1986-			
1-16	5.75	5.59	5.67	5- 8	7.25	7.21	7.48
1-23	7.00	6.96	7.07	5-15	7.26	7.22	7.50
1-30	6.93	6.31	6.42	5-22	7.25	7.23	7.54
2- 6	6.75	6.71	6.83	5-29	7.14	7.10	7.40
2-13	6.88	6.82	6.86	6- 5	7.28	7.24	7.56
2-20	7.09	7.05	7.20	6-12	7.29	7.25	7.59
2-27	7.09	7.07	7.23	6-19	7.15	7.11	7.45
3- 6	7.11	7.07	7.24	6-26	7.23	7.21	7.56
3-13	7.09	7.05	7.23	7- 3	7.30	7.28	7.56
3-20	7.18	7.14	7.34	7-10	7.32	7.28	7.67
3-27	7.17	7.15	7.36	8- 7	7.22	7.18	7.56
4- 3	7.19	7.15	7.37	9- 4	7.32	7.30	7.70
4-10	7.18	7.16	7.39	10- 2	7.33	7.31	7.74
4-17	7.20	7.18	7.42	10-30	7.35	7.31	7.79 ←
4-86	7.21	7.17	7.42	11-28	7.23	7.21	7.69
5 1	7.22	7.18	7.44	12-26	7.30	7.28	7.79

Notes and Bonds

Rate	Mat.	Date	Bid	Asked	Bid Chg.	Yld.
15 3/8s,	1988	Oct n	116.14	116.22	-.16	8.46
11 3/8s,	1988	Sep p	106.24	106.28	.17	8.49
8 5/8s,	1988	Nov p	100.10	100.14	-.17	8.45
8 3/4s,	1988	Nov n	100.18	100.26	-.17	8.42
11 3/4s,	1988	Nov n	107.27	107.31	-.20	8.53
10 5/8s,	1988	Dec p	105.7	105.11	-.18	8.55
14 5/8s,	1989	Jan n	115.20	115.24	-.18	8.57
11 3/8s,	1989	Feb n	107.6	107.10	-.21	8.63
11 1/4s,	1989	Mar p	107.1	107.9	-.22	8.61
14 3/8s,	1989	Apr n	115.23	115.31	-.22	8.64
9 1/4s,	1989	May n	102	102.8	-.23	8.46
11 3/4s,	1989	May n	108.20	108.24	.22	8.68
9 5/8s,	1989	Jun p	102.24	102.28	.21	8.65
14 1/2s,	1989	Jul n	115.7	115.11	-2.12	8.80
13 7/8s,	1989	Aug n	115.30	116.2		8.59
9 3/8s,	1989	Sep p	102	102.4	-.22	8.69
11 7/8s,	1989	Oct n	109.21	109.25	-.22	8.76
10 3/4s,	1989	Nov n	106.9	106.13	-.23	8.75
12 3/4s,	1989	Nov p	112.10	112.14	1.3	8.86
8 3/8s,	1989	Dec p	99.1	99.5	-.22	8.63
10 1/2s,	1990	Jan n	105.12	105.16	-.26	8.84
→ 3 1/2s,	1990	Feb	90.19	91.19	-.12	5.84 ←
11s,	1990	Feb p	107	107.4	-.25	8.88
10 1/2s,	1990	Apr n	105.18	105.22	-.24	8.87
8 1/4s,	1990	May	100.28	101.12	.19	7.87
11 3/8s,	1990	May p	108.17	108.21	-.25	8.93
10 3/4s,	1990	Jul n	106.18	106.22	.26	8.92

Rate	Mat.	Date	Bid	Asked	Bid Chg.	Yld.
10 3/4s,	2003	Feb	108.20	108.28	1.3	9.68
10 3/4s,	2003	May	108.20	108.28	1.3	9.68
11 1/8s,	2003	Aug	111.11	111.19	1.3	9.74
11 7/8s,	2003	Nov	117.19	117.27	1.4	9.75
12 3/8s,	2004	May	121.30	122.6	-1.6	9.75
13 3/4s,	2004	Aug	133.27	134.3	1.11	9.74
11 5/8s,	2004	Nov k	116.27	117.3	.31	9.65
8 1/4s,	2000-05	May	88.17	89.1	-1.4	9.50
12s,	2005	May k	120.5	120.13	-1.9	9.65
10 3/4s,	2005	Aug k	109.1	109.9	-1.6	9.68
7 5/8s,	2002-07	Feb	83.1	83.17	-.21	9.44
7 7/8s,	2002-07	Nov	85.10	85.26	-.31	9.42
8 3/8s,	2003-08	Aug	89.31	90.7	-1	9.43
8 3/4s,	2003-08	Nov	93.2	93.10	-1.3	9.47
9 1/8s,	2004-09	May	96.3	96.11	-1	9.52
10 3/8s,	2004-09	Nov	105.20	105.28	-1.7	9.69
11 3/4s,	2005-10	Feb	116.24	117	-1.7	9.77
10s,	2005-10	May	102.14	102.22	-1.7	9.69
12 3/4s,	2005-10	Nov	125.2	125.10	-1.17	9.83
13 7/8s,	2006-11	May	135.19	135.27	-1.15	9.78
14s,	2006-11	Nov	136.17	136.25	-1.20	9.82
10 3/8s,	2007-12	Nov	105.15	105.23	-1.7	9.74
12s,	2008-13	Aug	119.16	119.24	1.17	9.81
13 1/4s,	2009-14	May	131.29	132.5	1	9.74

Agency Issues

GOVERNMENT AGENCY ISSUES

Thursday, January 9, 1986

Mid-afternoon Over-the-Counter quotations usually based on large transactions, sometimes $1 million or more. Sources on request.

Decimals in bid-and-asked represent 32nds; 101.1 means 101 1/32. a-Plus 1/64. b-Yield to call date. d-Minus 1/64.

FNMA Issues

Rate	Mat	Bid	Asked	Yld
13.00	1-86	99.30	100.2	0.00
11.70	2-86	100.7	100.11	7.20
8.20	3-86	100.1	100.5	7.06
9.50	3-86	100.7	100.11	7.19
9.95	3-86	100.9	100.13	7.24
10.95	4-86	100.24	100.28	7.19
9.20	4-86	100.10	100.14	7.25
11.00	5-86	101	101.4	7.46
11.95	1-95	114.6	114.22	9.49
11.50	2-95	111.2	111.18	9.56
11.70	5-95	112.18	113.2	9.55
11.15	6-95	109.14	109.26	9.55
10.50	9-95	106.4	106.20	9.44

Federal Farm Credit

Rate	Mat	Bid	Asked	Yld
10.90	1-86	99.31	100.3	7.15
15.80	1-86	100.6	100.10	4.22
8.05	2-86	99.29	100.1	7.30
8.70	2-86	99.31	100.3	6.82
7.70	3-86	99.29	100.1	7.29
7.95	3-86	99.28	100.1	7.38
9.90	1-87	101.18	101.26	8.02
13.20	1-87	104.26	105.2	7.97
14.63	1-87	106.6	106.14	7.97
11.45	3-87	103.2	103.10	8.33
12.40	3-87	104.3	104.11	8.32
14.38	4-87	107.8	107.20	7.95
14.40	4-87	107.4	107.16	8.08
9.13	6-87	100.25	100.31	8.36
10.55	6-87	102.18	102.30	8.26
10.63	7-87	103	103.12	8.23
10.13	9-87	102.13	102.25	8.26
10.45	10-87	102.30	103.10	8.39
10.55	10-87	103.2	103.14	8.41
10.30	12-87	102.20	102.28	8.61
10.65	12-87	103.8	103.16	8.59
9.45	1-88	101.17	101.23	8.50
10.90	3-88	104.2	104.14	8.56
11.35	3-88	104.28	105.8	8.60
10.25	4-88	103.5	103.11	8.59
12.65	4-88	107.26	108.6	8.60
15.65	10-89	119.14	119.30	9.27
12.45	10-89	109.16	110	9.25
10.95	1-90	105.4	105.20	9.25
11.15	1-90	105.26	106.6	9.27
10.85	2-90	104.24	105.8	9.26
11.35	4-90	106.18	106.30	9.34
14.10	6-90	115.28	116.12	9.45
9.55	7-90	100.20	101.4	9.24
10.40	7-90	103.8	103.24	9.36
12.50	9-90	110.20	111.4	9.48
10.60	10-90	104.4	104.20	9.37
8.70	12-90	99.2	99.6	8.90
14.10	4-91	118.16	119.6	9.44
9.10	7-91	98.24	99.8	9.27
14.70	7-91	121.8	121.24	9.55
13.00	9-94	117.24	118.16	9.77
11.45	12-94	110.6	110.26	9.61
11.90	10-97	114.20	115.12	9.68

Student Loan Marketing

Rate	Mat	Bid	Asked	Yld
11.25	10-87	104.16	104.28	8.15
10.10	1-88	103.4	103.16	8.16
9.63	5-88	102.20	102.28	8.26
11.70	7-88	106.18	106.30	8.54
12.85	9-89	111.14	111.30	8.93
10.90	2-90	105.28	106.12	9.01
10.50	4-93	105	105.16	9.43

Fed. Home Loan Bank

Rate	Mat	Bid	Asked	Yld
9.20	1-86	99.31	100.3	6.92
12.75	1-86	100.4	100.8	7.03
13.85	1-86	100.5	100.9	7.41
9.55	2-86	100.5	100.9	7.03
15.30	2-86	100.25	100.29	7.55
10.20	3-86	100.12	100.16	7.54
15.75	3-86	101.16	101.20	7.48
9.15	4-86	100.11	100.15	7.37

World Bank Bonds

Rate	Mat	Bid	Asked	Yld
8.85	12-85	101.21	102.5	8.66
11.26	3-86	100.9	100.25	7.80
10.38	3-87	102.1	102.17	8.10
7.75	8-87	98.15	98.31	8.43
14.63	8-87	108.6	108.22	8.75
13.45	9-87	106.22	107.6	8.80
10.38	3-88	102.20	103.4	8.80
10.00	5-88	102.1	102.17	8.80
15.00	12-88	114.28	115.12	9.02
11.00	10-89	100.21	101.5	10.61
4.50	2-90	85.26	86.10	8.50
5.38	7-91	84.23	85.7	8.80

Federal Land Bank

Rate	Mat	Bid	Asked	Yld
7.60	4-87	99.6	99.18	7.95
7.25	7-87	98.6	98.18	8.27
7.85	1-88	98.24	99.4	8.33
8.20	1-90	96.24	97.8	9.03
7.95	4-91	94.20	95.4	9.13
7.95	10-96	89	89.24	9.49
7.35	1-97	84.24	85.16	9.50

Inter-Amer. Devel. Bk.

Rate	Mat	Bid	Asked	Yld
8.38	2-86	100.28	101.12	0.00
14.00	12-86	104.21	105.5	8.25
10.75	8-87	101.4	101.20	9.63
15.00	4-89	115.14	115.30	9.25
5.20	1-92	87.17	88.1	7.70
14.63	8-92	121.7	121.23	10.05

Asian Development Bank

Rate	Mat	Bid	Asked	Yld
8.63	8-86	101	101.16	6.11
	7-92	52.9	52.25	9.95
7.75	4-96	85.15	85.31	9.95
10.75	6-97	103.16	104	10.15
11.13	5-98	106.8	106.24	10.15

GNMA Issues

Rate	Mat	Bid	Asked	Yld
8.00		89.12	89.20	9.51
9.00		93.26	94.2	9.86
9.50		96.26	97.2	9.91
10.00		99.9	99.17	10.04
10.50		101.21	101.29	10.18

FIC Bank Debs.

Rate	Mat	Bid	Asked	Yld
7.95	4-86	99.26	100.2	7.50
6.95	1-87	98.28	99.8	7.75

Private Expt. Fndg. Corp.

Rate	Mat	Bid	Asked	Yld
14.125P	6-91	106	106 3/4	12.36
12.35Q	11-90	103 1/2	104 1/4	11.17
10.75R	11-89	103	103 1/2	9.62
11.25S	2-92	104	104 3/4	10.16
11.25T	10-95	105	105 3/4	10.30

Source: The Wall Street Journal, Jan. 10, 1986. Reprinted by permission of *The Wall Street Journal*,

These quotes indicate that for a treasury bill maturing on October 30, buyers were willing to bid a discounted price that produced a discount yield of 7.35 percent. Sellers, however, were willing to sell (offer) the bills at a smaller discount (higher price) that returned a discount yield of 7.31 percent. The annualized yield on the bill based on the asked price is 7.79 percent.

The reason for the difference between the discount yield and the annualized yield is that treasury bills are sold at a discount and are quoted in terms of the discount

yield. The discount yield is not the same as (nor is it comparable to) the annualized yield on the bill or the yield to maturity on a bond. It is calculated on the basis of the face amount of the bill and uses a 360-day year. The annualized yield on the bill depends on the price of the bill and uses a 365-day year.

The difference between the two calculations may be seen in the following example. Suppose a three-month $10,000 treasury bill sells for $9,800. The discount yield (y_d) is

$$y_d = \frac{\text{Par value} - \text{Price}}{\text{Par value}} \times \frac{360}{\text{Number of days to maturity}}$$

$$\frac{\$10,000 - \$9,800}{\$10,000} \times \frac{360}{90} = 8\%.$$

The annualized yield (y_a) is

$$y_a = \frac{\text{Par value} - \text{Price}}{\text{Price}} \times \frac{365}{\text{Number of days to maturity}}$$

$$\frac{\$10,000 - \$9,800}{\$9,800} \times \frac{365}{90} = 8.277\%.$$

Since the discount yield uses the face amount and a 360-day year, it understates the true yield the investor is earning.[2]

How they are purchased

Treasury bills may be purchased through brokerage firms, commercial banks, and any Federal Reserve Bank. These purchases may be new issues or bills that are being traded in the secondary market. Bills with one year to maturity are auctioned once a month. Shorter term bills are auctioned weekly. If the buyer purchases the bills directly through the Federal Reserve Bank, there are no commission fees. Brokers and commercial banks do charge commissions, but the fees are modest compared with those charged for other investment transactions, such as the purchase of stock.

Treasury bills are among the best short-term debt instruments available to investors who desire liquidity and safety.[3] The bills mature quickly, and there are many issues from which the investor may choose. Thus, the investor may purchase a bill that matures when the principal is needed. For example, an individual who has ready cash today but who must make a payment after three months may purchase a bill that matures at the appropriate time. In doing so, the investor puts the cash to work for three months.

Like all treasury debt, the bills are safe, for there is no question that the federal government has the capacity to refund or retire the bills. Although companies with excess cash or commercial banks with an unused lending capacity are the principal buyers of treasury bills, individual savers may also purchase them. However, the large

---

[2] The discount yield may be converted to the annualized yield by the following equation:

$$y_a = \frac{365 \times Y_d}{360 - (y_d \times \text{Days to maturity})}.$$

Thus, if the discount rate on a three-month treasury bill is 8 percent, true yield is

$$y_a = \frac{365 \times 0.08}{360 - (0.08 \times 90)} = 8.277\%.$$

[3] Treasury bills are issued in bearer form and thus are easily transferred if *stolen*. In that sense, they lack some element of safety.

minimum denomination of $10,000 virtually excludes most savers. Individual investors who desire such safe short-term investments may purchase shares in mutual funds that specialize in buying short-term securities, including treasury bills. For a discussion of these investments, see the section on money market funds in Chapter 2.

Intermediate- and long-term debt

Treasury Notes and Bonds. Intermediate-term federal government debt is in the form of **treasury notes.** These notes are issued in denominations of $1,000 to more than $100,000 and mature in one to ten years. **Treasury bonds,** the government's debt instrument for long-term debt, are issued in denominations of $1,000 to $1,000,000, and these bonds mature in more than five years from the date of issue. Notes and bonds are issued in both bearer and registered forms. These issues are the safest intermediate- and long-term investments available and are purchased by pension funds, financial institutions, or savers who are primarily concerned with moderate income and safety. Since these debt instruments are so safe, their yields are generally lower than that which may be obtained with high-quality corporate debt, such as AT&T bonds. For example, in early 1986, IBM bonds that were rated triple A yielded about 9.9 percent, while treasury bonds with approximately the same time to maturity yielded 9.3 percent. Although the difference is less than a percentage point, the market still placed a higher return on the IBM bonds.

How treasury bonds are purchased

Like treasury bills, new issues of treasury bonds may be purchased through commercial banks and brokerage firms. These firms will charge commissions, but the individual may avoid such fees by purchasing the securities from any of the Federal Reserve banks or their branches. Payment, however, must precede purchase, except when the individual pays cash. Unless the individual investor submits a competitive bid, the purchase price is the average price charged institutions that buy the bonds through competitive bidding. By accepting this noncompetitive bid, the individual assures matching the average yield earned by financial institutions, which try to buy the securities at the lowest price (highest yield) possible.

Active secondary market

Once the bonds are purchased, they may be readily resold, as there is an active secondary market in U.S. Treasury bonds. Like corporate stocks and bonds, treasury bonds are quoted in the financial press under the general heading "Treasury Issues." How these bonds are reported was illustrated in Exhibit 12.2, which presented quotes for selected treasury notes and bonds. These price quotes are different than the bid and ask prices for stocks because treasury securities are quoted in 32nds. Thus the $3\frac{1}{2}$ percent bond due in 1990, which was quoted 90.19–91.19, had a bid price of $90^{19}/_{32}$ and an asking price of $91^{19}/_{32}$ (i.e., $9,059.38 and $9,159.38 per $10,000 face amount).

Treasury bonds are among the safest investments available to investors. However, while there is no question that the federal government can pay the interest and refund its debt, there are ways in which the holder of treasury notes and bonds can suffer losses. These debt instruments pay a fixed amount of interest, which is determined when the notes and bonds are issued. If interest rates subsequently rise, existing issues will not be as attractive, and their market prices will decline. If an investor must sell the debt instrument before it matures, the price will be lower than the principal amount and the investor will suffer a capital loss.

Interest rate risk

Yields have varied

Interest rates paid by treasury debt have varied over time. The extent of this variation was illustrated by Figure 9.3 in Chapter 9, which showed the yields on treasury bills and treasury bonds from 1972 to 1986. Yields also can fluctuate rapidly. For

example, yields on three-month treasury bills changed from a high of 15 percent in March 1980 to 8.7 percent only two months later. These fluctuations in yields are due to variations in the supply of and demand for credit in the money and bond markets. As the demand and supply vary, so will the market prices and the yields on all debt instruments, including the debt of the federal government. When demand for bonds becomes strong and exceeds supply at the old prices, bond prices will rise and yields will decline. The reverse occurs when supply exceeds demand: bond prices decline and yields rise.

An investor may also lose through investments in treasury debt when the rate of inflation exceeds the interest rate earned on the bonds. For example, during 1974 the yields on government bonds rose to 7.3 percent, but the rate of inflation for consumer goods exceeded 10 percent. The investor then suffered a loss in purchasing power, for interest payments were insufficient to compensate for the inflation.

Purchasing power risk

These two factors, fluctuating yields and inflation, illustrate that investing in federal government debt, like all types of investing, subjects the investor to interest rate risk and purchasing power risk. Therefore, although federal government debt is among the safest of all investments with regard to the certainty of payment of interest and principal, some element of risk still exists.

Zero Coupon Treasury Securities

With the advent of Individual Retirement Accounts (IRAs), corporations started issuing zero coupon bonds. Because the Treasury did not issue such bonds at that time, selected brokerage firms created their own zero coupon treasury securities. For example, in 1982 Merrill Lynch created the Treasury Investment Growth Receipt (TIGR, generally referred to as "tigers"). Merrill Lynch bought a block of treasury bonds, removed all the coupons, and offered investors either the interest to be received in a specific year or the principal at the bonds' maturity. Since payment was limited to the single payment at the specified time in the future, these "tigers" were sold at a discount. In effect, they were zero coupon bonds backed by treasury securities originally purchased by Merrill Lynch and held by a trustee.

Other brokerage firms created similar securities by removing coupons from existing treasury bonds. Some of these zero coupon treasury securities were given clever acronyms, such as Salomon Brothers' CATS (Certificates of Accrual on Treasury Securities). In other cases they were just called Treasury Receipts (T.R.s). In each case, however, the brokerage firm owns the underlying treasury securities. The actual security purchased by the investor is an obligation of the brokerage firm and not of the federal government.

In 1985, the Treasury introduced its own zero coupon bonds called STRIPS for Separate Trading of Registered Interest and Principal Securities. Investors who purchase such STRIPS acquire a direct obligation of the federal government. Since these securities are direct obligations, they tend to have slightly lower yields than Tigers, CATS, and the other zero coupon securities created by brokerage firms.

In any case, the primary appeal of these securities is their use in retirement accounts. The interest earned on a zero coupon bond is taxed as it accrues, even though the holder does not receive annual cash interest payments. Thus, there is little reason to acquire these securities in accounts that are not tax sheltered. They are, however, excellent vehicles for retirement accounts, since all the funds (i.e., principal and ac-

POINTS OF INTEREST

Fluctuations in the Market Prices of Zero Coupon Bonds

As was discussed in Chapter 10, changing interest rates generate fluctuations in bond prices. The longer the term to maturity, the greater the price fluctuation (see Figure 10.3). For bonds of a given risk class and given term (e.g., ten years or twenty years to maturity), zero coupon bonds are the most volatile. For example, if interest rates currently were 10 percent, a ten-year zero coupon bond would sell for $385.50 while a ten-year 10 percent coupon bond would sell for $1,000.* If interest rates rose to 14 percent, the price of the zero coupon bond would fall to $269.70, for a decline of approximately 30 percent. The price of the 10 percent coupon bond would fall to $791.31, for a decline of approximately 21 per-

cent. If the terms of these bonds had been 20 years, their respective prices at 10 percent would be $148.60 and $1,000 but would fall to $72.80 and $735.11 at 14 percent. Such declines are approximately 51 and 26 percent.

The reason for a zero coupon bond's increased price volatility is that the entire return falls on the single payment at maturity. Since the current price of any bond is the present value of the interest and principal payments, the price of a zero coupon bond is the present value of the face amount received at the end of the term. There are no interest payments in the early years of the bond's life that reduce the responsiveness of the bond's price to changes in interest rates.

*The calculations assume annual compounding.

crued interest) are paid in one lump sum at maturity. Because any tax on a retirement account is paid when the funds are withdrawn, the tax disadvantage of zero coupon bonds is circumvented. The investor can purchase issues that mature at a desired date to meet retirement needs. For example, a 40-year-old investor could purchase zero coupon government securities that mature when he or she is age 65, 66, and so on. Such a strategy would assure that the funds were received after retirement, at which time they would replace the individual's earned income that ceases at retirement.

FEDERAL AGENCIES' DEBT

In addition to the debt issued by the federal government, certain agencies of the federal government and federally sponsored corporations issue debt. These debt instruments encompass the entire spectrum of maturities, ranging from short-term securities to long-term bonds. Like many U.S. Treasury debt issues, there is an active secondary market in some of the debt issues of these agencies, and price quotations for many of the bonds are given daily in the financial press (i.e., see Exhibit 12.2).

Several federal agencies have come into existence to fulfill specific financial needs. For example, the Banks for Cooperatives were organized under the Farm Credit Act. These banks provide farm business services and make loans to farm cooperatives to help purchase supplies. The Federal Home Loan Mortgage Corporation was established to strengthen the secondary market in residential mortgages insured by the Federal Housing Administration. This federal corporation buys and sells home mortgages to give them marketability and thus increase their attractiveness to private

investors. The Student Loan Marketing Association was created to provide liquidity to the insured student loans made under the Guaranteed Student Loan Program by commercial banks, savings and loan associations, and schools that participate in the program. This liquidity should expand the funds available to students from private sources.

Federal agency bonds are not issued by the federal government and are not the debt of the federal government. Hence, they tend to offer higher yields than those available on U.S. Treasury debt. However, the bonds are extremely safe because they have government backing. In some cases this is only **moral backing,** which means that in case of default the federal government does not have to support the debt (i.e., to pay the interest and meet the terms of the indenture). Some of the debt issues, however, are secured by the U.S. Treasury. Should these issues go into default, the federal government is legally bound to assume the obligations of the debt's indenture.

Agency bonds have higher yields than treasury debt

The matter of whether the bonds have the legal or the moral backing of the federal government is probably academic. All of these debt issues are excellent credit risks, because it is doubtful that the federal government would let the debt of one of its agencies go into default. Since these bonds offer slightly higher yields than those available on U.S. Treasury debt, the bonds of federal agencies have become very attractive investments for conservative investors seeking higher yields. This applies not only to individual investors who wish to protect their capital but also to financial institutions, such as commercial banks, insurance companies, or credit unions, which must be particularly concerned with the safety of the principal in making investment decisions.

These bonds are excellent credit risks

Federal agency debt can be purchased by individuals, but few individual investors do own these bonds, except indirectly through pension plans, mutual funds, and other institutions that own the debt. Many individual investors are probably not even aware of the existence of this debt and the potential advantages it offers. Any investor who wants to construct a portfolio with an emphasis on income and the relative safety of the principal should consider these debt instruments.

Ginnie Mae Securities

One of the most important and popular debt securities issued by a government agency and supported by the federal government is the **Ginnie Mae,** a debt security issued by the Government National Mortgage Association (GNMA or Ginnie Mae), a division of the Department of Housing and Urban Development (HUD). The funds raised through the sale of Ginnie Mae securities are used to acquire a pool of FHA/VA guaranteed mortgages. (FHA and VA are the Federal Housing Authority and Veteran's Administration, respectively.) The mortgages are originated by private lenders, such as savings and loan associations, and packaged into securities that are sold to the general public and guaranteed by GNMA. The minimum size of each issue is $1 million, and the minimum size of the individual Ginnie Mae securities sold to the public is $25,000.[4]

Ginnie Mae securities serve as a conduit through which interest and principal repayments are made. An investor who buys a Ginnie Mae acquires part of the pool. As interest payments and principal repayments are made to the pool, the funds are channeled to the Ginnie Mae's owners. The investor receives a monthly payment that is his or her share of the principal and interest payment received by the pool. Since

Conduit for interest and principal payments

---

[4]Individuals with more modest sums to invest may acquire shares in a mutual fund that invests solely in Ginnie Maes.

such payments may vary from month to month, the amount received by the investor also varies monthly. Thus the Ginnie Mae is one example of a long-term debt security whose periodic payments are not fixed.

Popular for retirement plans

Ginnie Mae securities have become particularly popular with individuals financing retirement or accumulating funds in retirement accounts. The reason for their popularity is safety, since the federal government insures the payment of principal and interest. Thus, if a mortgage payer were to default, the federal government would make the required payments. This guarantee virtually assures the timely payment of interest and principal to the holder of the Ginnie Mae.

Enhanced yields

In addition to safety, Ginnie Maes offer yields that exceed what may be obtained through the purchase of federal government securities. Since the yields are ultimately related to the mortgages acquired by the pool, they depend on mortgage rates rather than on the yields of federal government bills and bonds. This yield differential can be as great as 2 percent (sometimes referred to as 200 basis points, with one basis point equaling 0.01 percent) over the return offered by long-term federal government bonds.

Ginnie Mae securities are exceptionally desirable to investors seeking a monthly flow of payments since interest and principal repayments are distributed monthly. The mortgage repayment schedules define the minimum amount of the anticipated payments. However, if the homeowners speed up payments or pay off their loans before the full term of the mortgage, the additional funds are passed on to the holder of the Ginnie Mae securities.

Risks:
1. loss of purchasing power

While these securities are supported by the full faith and credit of the federal government, there are risks associated with Ginnie Maes. One is the loss of purchasing power through inflation. Of course, investors will not purchase Ginnie Maes if the anticipated yield is less than the anticipated rate of inflation.

2. fluctuations in interest rates

Even if the anticipated return is sufficient to justify the purchase, investors could still lose if interest rates rise. All the mortgages in a particular pool have the same interest rate, and since Ginnie Maes are fixed-income debt securities, their prices fluctuate with interest rates. Higher interest rates will drive down their prices. Thus, if an investor were to seek to sell the security in the secondary market (and there is an active secondary market in Ginnie Maes), he or she could sustain a capital loss resulting from the rise in interest rates. Of course, the investor could experience a capital gain if interest rates were to decline, thus causing the security's value to rise.

Timing of payments is not certain

The valuation of Ginnie Mae securities is essentially the same as for other debt instruments described in Chapter 10. The interest payments and principal repayments are discounted back to the present at the current rate of interest. There is, however, one important difference. Individuals owning their homes can (and do) repay their mortgage loans prematurely. This is particularly true when the individuals move and sell their homes (unless the new owners are allowed to assume the old mortgage). Thus, the timing and amount of principal repayments that the holder of the Ginnie Mae will receive is not certain. If a large number of homeowners rapidly pay off their mortgage loans, these payments will quickly retire the Ginnie Mae securities.

Average life: 12 years

This uncertainty of future payments can lead to differences in the estimated yields. Consider a Ginnie Mae that has an expected life of 12 years[5] and that is currently selling for a discount (which could result if interest rates rose after this Ginnie

---

[5]While the maturity of a Ginnie Mae may be 25 to 30 years, the average life (according to the Government National Mortgage Association) is 12 years.

Mae pool had been assembled and sold). In such a case the price of the Ginnie Mae would decline so that the anticipated yield is comparable with securities currently being issued. For the Ginnie Mae selling at a discount, the yield would depend on the flow of interest payments and how rapidly the mortgage loans are paid off.

If the mortgages are paid off more rapidly than expected (i.e., if the life of the pool is less than the expected 12 years), the realized return will be higher. However, if the mortgages are retired more slowly, the realized return will be less than the expected return. Thus it is possible that the actual yield may differ from the yield assumed when the security was purchased. This makes it possible for two security dealers to assert different yields for the same Ginnie Mae sold at the same price. If one dealer assumes that the mortgage loans will be retired more quickly, a higher yield is anticipated. However, another security dealer may make a more conservative assumption as to the rate at which the mortgages will be retired.

The speed with which the mortgages are paid off depends in part on the interest rates being paid on mortgage loans. If the Ginnie Mae mortgage loans have relatively high rates, homeowners will seek to refinance these loans when rates decline, so the original mortgages are retired rapidly. The opposite holds when the rates on the Ginnie Maes' mortgage loans are lower than current interest rates. In this case there is less incentive for early retirement, which will tend to extend the life of the mortgage pool. Thus, a Ginnie Mae that sells for a discount because the mortgage loans have lower interest rates will tend to have a longer life than a Ginnie Mae selling at a premium because its mortgage loans have a higher rate of interest.

Factors affecting the speed of principal repayments

The investor who purchases a Ginnie Mae security should be aware that the payment received represents both earned interest income and return of invested funds. If the investor spends all the payment, that individual is depleting his or her principal. Thus the investor should be fully aware that the individual payments received are composed of both interest and principal repayment and that the latter should be spent only if there is reason for the investor to consume the principal.

Other Mortgage-backed Securities

While Ginnie Maes were the first mortgage-backed securities, other issues have been created by the Federal Home Loan Mortgage Corporation (FHLMC or "Freddie Mac"), the Federal National Mortgage Association (FNMA or "Fannie Mae"), and other lending institutions. The FHLMC Participation Certificate (PC) is similar to the Ginnie Mae; they are both conduits through which interest and principal payments pass from the homeowner to the certificate holder. There is, however, one important difference—Freddie Mac PCs' payments are not guaranteed by the federal government. The absence of this guarantee means that even though the individual mortgages are insured by private mortgage insurance companies, Freddie Mac PCs offer a higher yield than is available through Ginnie Maes.

Freddie Mac and Fannie Mae

Mortgage-backed securities are also issued by the FNMA. Fannie Mae sells both general obligation debentures and mortgage-backed securities. The funds are used to finance mortgages, and, like the Freddie Mac PC, the securities issued by Fannie Mae are secured by mortgage loans. Since the Federal National Mortgage Corporation is a private corporation (its stock trades on the New York Stock Exchange), its debt obligations are not guaranteed by the federal government; thus, these bonds offer higher yields than Ginnie Maes.

STATE AND LOCAL GOVERNMENT DEBT

State and local governments also issue debt to finance capital expenditures, such as schools or roads. The government then retires the debt as the facilities are used. The funds used to retire the debt may be raised through taxes (e.g., property taxes) or through revenues generated by the facilities themselves.

Variations in the quality

Unlike the federal government, state and local governments do not have the power to create money. These governments must raise the funds necessary to pay the interest and retire the debt, but the ability to do so varies with the financial status of each government. Municipalities with wealthy residents or valuable property within their boundaries are able to issue debt more readily and at lower interest rates because the debt is safer. The tax base in these communities is larger and can support the debt.

The Tax Exemption

Interest is exempt from federal taxation

The primary factor that differentiates state and local government debt from other forms of debt is the tax advantage that it offers to investors. The interest earned on state and municipal government debt is exempt from federal income taxation. Hence, these bonds are frequently referred to as **tax-exempt bonds** or **municipal bonds.** Although state and local governments may tax the interest, the federal government may not. The rationale for this tax exemption is legal and not financial. The Supreme Court ruled that the federal government does not have the power to tax the interest paid by the debt of state and municipal governments. Since the interest paid by all other debt, including corporate bonds, is subject to federal income taxation, this exemption is advantageous to state and local governments, for they are able to issue debt with substantially lower interest rates.

The after-tax return is competitive

Investors are willing to accept a lower return on state and local government debt because the after-tax return is equivalent to higher yields on corporate debt. For example, if an investor is in the 30 percent income tax bracket, the return after taxes is the same for a corporate bond that pays 10 percent as for a state or municipal government bond that pays 7 percent: The after-tax return is 7 percent in either case.

The importance of the individual's tax bracket

The willingness of investors to purchase state and local government debt instead of corporate and U.S. Treasury debt is related to their income tax bracket. If an investor's federal income tax rate is 30 percent, a 7.5 percent nontaxable municipal bond gives the investor the same yield after taxes as a 10.71 percent corporate bond the interest of which is subject to federal income taxation. The individual investor may determine the equivalent yields on tax-exempt bonds and nonexempt bonds by using the following equation:

(12.1)
$$i_c(1 - t) = i_m,$$

where i_c is the interest rate paid on corporate debt, i_m is the interest rate paid on municipal debt, and t is the individual's tax bracket (i.e., the marginal tax rate). This equation is used as follows. If an investor's tax bracket is 30 percent and tax-exempt bonds offer 7.5 percent, then the equivalent corporate yield is

$$i_c(1 - 0.3) = 0.075$$

$$i_c = \frac{0.075}{0.07} = 10.71\%.$$

Exempting the interest on these bonds from federal income taxation has been *A tax shelter*
frequently criticized because it is an apparent means for the rich to avoid federal income taxation. The exemption does, however, reduce the interest cost for the state
and municipal governments that issue debt, which in effect is a subsidy to those governments. From an economic point of view, the important question is whether the
exemption is the best means to aid or subsidize state and local governments. Other
means, such as federal revenue sharing, could be used for this purpose.

The interest exemption is primarily a political question. Changes in the legal
structure may alter the tax exemption in the future. Until that time, however, the interest on state and municipal debt remains exempt from federal income taxation, with
the effects being that (1) state and local governments can issue debt with interest rates
that are lower than individuals and corporations must pay, and (2) these bonds offer
the wealthier members of our society a means to obtain tax-sheltered income.

While state and local government interest is tax-exempt at the federal level, it may
be taxed at the state level. States do exempt the interest paid by their own local governments but tax the interest paid by other states and their local governments. Thus
while interest earned on New York City obligations is not taxed in New York, it is
taxed in New Jersey.

It should also be noted that state and local governments cannot tax the interest *State and local*
paid by the federal government. While interest earned on Series EE and HH bonds, *governments cannot tax*
treasury bills, notes, and bonds is taxed by the federal government, this interest can- *interest paid on federal*
not be taxed by state and local governments. In states with modest or no income *securities*
taxes, this exemption is meaningless. However, in states with high income taxes such
as Massachusetts or New York, this tax exemption may be a major reason for acquiring
U.S. Treasury securities. For example, the yield on a treasury bill on an after-tax basis
may exceed the yield on a federally insured certificate of deposit or the yield offered by
a money market mutual fund. In such cases the tax laws will certainly encourage the
investor to acquire the federal security, because that investor has both a higher after-
tax yield and less risk (i.e., the support of the full faith and credit of the federal
government).

Yields and Prices of State and Local Government Bonds

Like yields on other securities, yields on tax-exempt bonds have varied over time. *Fluctuations and*
Figure 12.1 shows the average yields on Moody's Aaa- and Baa-rated bonds over sev- *differences in yields*
eral years. During this period there was considerable fluctuation in the interest rates
paid by tax-exempt bonds. For example, in 1978 the yields to maturity were 5.5 percent for the Aaa-rated bonds, but these yields rose to 12 percent in 1982. There was a
comparable fluctuation in the yields of the Baa-rated bonds, which rose from 6.2 percent to 13.3 percent during the same period. A yield of 12 percent is comparable to a
yield of 17.1 percent on a corporate bond for an individual in the 30 percent income
tax bracket.

In addition to showing the fluctuations in yields, the figure shows the difference
in yields. As would be expected, the yields on Baa-rated bonds exceed those on the
Aaa-rated bonds, but the spread in the yields between the Aaa- and Baa-rated bonds
varies. During the periods of higher interest rates, the spread widens. For example, the
spread rose to over 1.5 percent during 1982. However, when interest rates declined,

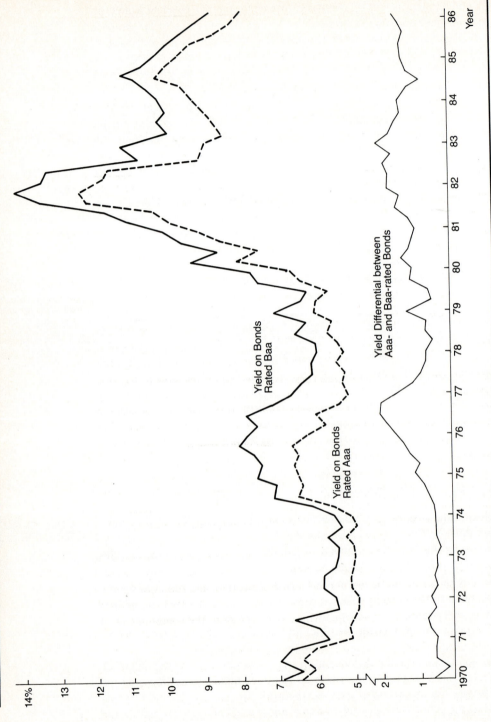

Figure 12.1
Average Yields and the Spread Between Aaa- and Baa-rated Municipal Bonds from 1970 to 1986

Yield on Bonds Rated Baa

Yield on Bonds Rated Aaa

Yield Differential between Aaa- and Baa-rated Bonds

Year

Source: Moody's Bond Record, various issues.

Figure 12.2
Yields on Twenty-year Federal Government Bonds and Aaa-rated Municipal Bonds

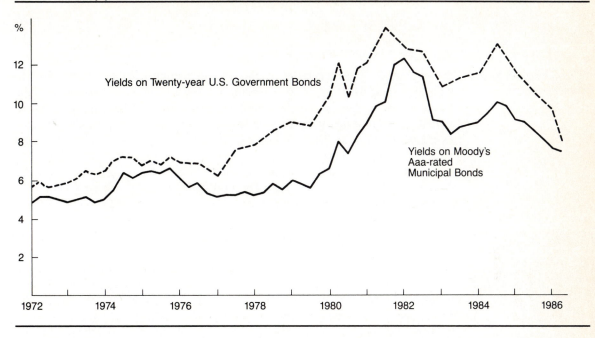

the spread between the yields on the Aaa- and Baa-rated bonds declined to less than 1.0 percent in 1984.

Figure 12.2 presents similar information except it plots the yields on 20-year U.S. government bonds and Moody's Aaa-rated municipal bonds. A similar pattern emerges. When interest rates in general rose, the yields on both bonds rose (e.g., 1980–1982), and when interest rates fell, the yields on both federal government and municipal bonds fell (e.g., 1983–1985). The yields on the federal government securities exceeded the yields on the municipal bonds throughout the time period. However, the differential between the yields started to diminish during 1986, as tax reform and lower federal income tax rates reduced the attractiveness of municipal securities vis-a-vis the bonds of the federal government.

This change in the relative attractiveness of one bond to another points out that the yields (and prices) of municipal bonds, like the prices and yields on corporate and federal government debt, ultimately depend on the demand for and supply of the various types of bonds. When many state and local governments seek credit and desire to issue bonds, the yields on tax exempts will rise. In addition, the conditions in the financial markets will affect yields. As Figures 12.1 and 12.2 illustrate, when interest rates rise in general, the yields on tax-exempt bonds will also rise.

Of course, an increase in yields means that the prices of existing municipal bonds must fall. The equations used to determine the value of a bond that were presented in Chapter 10 also apply to the valuation of municipal and state bonds. The yields on these bonds are inversely related to their prices. When a state or municipality government bond's price rises, its yield declines. When the bond's price falls, the yield rises.

Municipal bond pricing

Like corporate debt, these bonds can sell at a discount or for a premium, depending on the direction of change in interest rates. Hence investors in tax-exempt bonds bear the risk associated with fluctuations in interest rates.

Types of Tax-Exempt Securities

General obligation and revenue bonds

State and local governments issue a variety of debt instruments; these can be classified either according to the means by which the security is supported or according to the length of time to maturity (i.e., short- or long-term). State and municipal debt is supported by either the taxing power of the issuing government or the revenues generated by the facilities that are financed by the debt. If the bonds are secured by the taxing power, the debt is a **general obligation** of the government.

Bonds supported by the revenue generated by the project being financed with the debt are called **revenue bonds.** These are issued to finance particular capital improvements, such as a toll road that generates its own money. As these revenues are collected, they are used to pay the interest and retire the principal.

General obligation bonds are commonly thought to be safer than revenue bonds, since the government is required to use its taxing authority to pay the interest and repay the principal.[6] Revenue bonds are supported only by funds generated by the project financed by the sale of the bonds. If the project does not generate sufficient revenues, the interest cannot be paid, and the bonds go into default. For example, the Chesapeake Bay Bridge and Tunnel did not produce sufficient toll revenues, so its publicly held bonds went into default. The default, of course, caused the price of the bonds to fall. Since the bondholders could not foreclose on the bridge, their only course of action was to wait for a resumption of interest payments. After several years elapsed, toll revenues rose sufficiently so that interest payments to the bondholders were resumed.

Registered bonds in units of $5,000

Tax-exempt bonds are issued in both registered and coupon form. The minimum denomination is $5,000 in face value. There is an active secondary market in this debt; however, the bonds are traded only in the over-the-counter market, and only a handful are quoted in the financial press. Small denominations (e.g., $5,000) tend to lack marketability, but that does not mean that an investor trying to sell one $5,000 bond issued by a small municipality cannot sell it. It does imply, however, that the market is extremely thin and that the spread between the bid and ask prices may be substantial.

Serial bonds

Although most corporate bonds are issued with a particular term to maturity and a sinking fund requirement, many tax-exempt bonds are issued in a series. With a serial issue, a specific amount of the debt falls due each year. Such an issue is illustrated in Exhibit 12.3, which reproduces a tombstone advertisement for bonds sold by the Alabama Municipal Electric Authority. (These advertisements are placed by the underwriting syndicate to describe a public offering. They are frequently referred to as "tombstones" because they resemble an epitaph on a tombstone.) About half of this $140 million issue is in serial bonds. A portion of the issue matures each year. For

---

[6]General obligation bonds may have to be approved by popular referendum. Such referendums can be costly, and public approval of the bonds may be difficult to obtain. These characteristics associated with issuing the debt reduce the risk of investing in general obligation bonds.

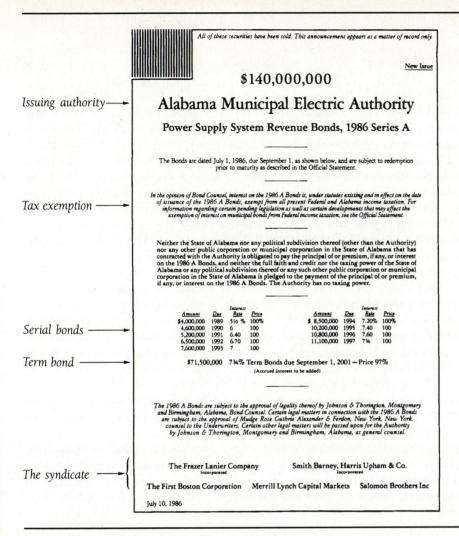

Issuing authority→

Tax exemption →

Serial bonds →

Term bond →

The syndicate →

All of these securities have been sold. This announcement appears as a matter of record only.

New Issue

$140,000,000

Alabama Municipal Electric Authority

Power Supply System Revenue Bonds, 1986 Series A

The Bonds are dated July 1, 1986, due September 1, as shown below, and are subject to redemption prior to maturity as described in the Official Statement.

In the opinion of Bond Counsel, interest on the 1986 A Bonds is, under statutes existing and in effect on the date of issuance of the 1986 A Bonds, exempt from all present Federal and Alabama income taxation. For information regarding certain pending legislation as well as certain developments that may affect the exemption of interest on municipal bonds from Federal income taxation, see the Official Statement.

Neither the State of Alabama nor any political subdivision thereof (other than the Authority) nor any other public corporation or municipal corporation in the State of Alabama that has contracted with the Authority is obligated to pay the principal of or premium, if any, or interest on the 1986 A Bonds, and neither the full faith and credit nor the taxing power of the State of Alabama or any political subdivision thereof or any such other public corporation or municipal corporation in the State of Alabama is pledged to the payment of the principal of or premium, if any, or interest on the 1986 A Bonds. The Authority has no taxing power.

Amount	Due	Interest Rate	Price		Amount	Due	Interest Rate	Price
$4,000,000	1989	5½ %	100%		$ 8,500,000	1994	7.20%	100%
4,600,000	1990	6	100		10,200,000	1995	7.40	100
5,200,000	1991	6.40	100		10,800,000	1996	7.60	100
6,500,000	1992	6.70	100		11,100,000	1997	7¾	100
7,600,000	1993	7	100					

$71,500,000   7¾% Term Bonds due September 1, 2001 — Price 97%

(Accrued interest to be added)

The 1986 A Bonds are subject to the approval of legality thereof by Johnson & Thorington, Montgomery and Birmingham, Alabama, Bond Counsel. Certain legal matters in connection with the 1986 A Bonds are subject to the approval of Mudge Rose Guthrie Alexander & Ferdon, New York, New York, counsel to the Underwriters. Certain other legal matters will be passed upon for the Authority by Johnson & Thorington, Montgomery and Birmingham, Alabama, as general counsel.

The Frazer Lanier Company
Incorporated

Smith Barney, Harris Upham & Co.
Incorporated

The First Boston Corporation   Merrill Lynch Capital Markets   Salomon Brothers Inc

July 10, 1986

Exhibit 12.3
Tombstone for an Issue of Serial and Term Bonds

Source: Reprinted with permission of the Alabama Municipal Electric Authority.

example, $4,000,000 worth of the bonds matures on September 1, 1989, and another $4,600,000 matures on September 1, 1990. Serial bonds offer advantages to both the issuer and the buyer. In contrast to corporate debt, in which a random selection of the bonds is retired each year through the sinking fund, the buyer knows when each bond will mature. The investor can then purchase bonds that mature at the desired time, which helps in portfolio planning. Because a portion of the issue is retired periodically with serial bonds, the issuing government does not have to make a large, lump-sum payment. Since these bonds are scheduled to be retired, there is no call penalty. If the government wants to retire additional debt, it can call some of the remaining bonds. For example, if the Alabama Municipal Electric Authority wanted to retire some of these bonds prematurely, it would call the term bonds that are due in 2001. (Most issues like the bonds shown in Exhibit 12.3 require that any debt retired before matu-

rity be called in reverse order. Thus, the term bonds with the longest time to maturity are called and redeemed first.)

Anticipation notes

Although most of the debt sold to the general public by state and local governments is long-term, there are two notable exceptions: tax or revenue anticipation notes and project notes. Tax or revenue **anticipation notes** are what their name implies. The issuing government anticipates certain receipts in the future and issues a debt instrument against these receipts. When the taxes or other revenues are received, the notes are retired. The maturity date is set to coincide with the timing of the anticipated receipts so that the notes may be easily retired.

Project notes

Project notes are short-term debt issued to finance urban renewal. States have formed local public agencies to plan and carry out urban renewal projects. Before low-rent housing can be built or slum neighborhoods can be redeveloped, the agencies need short-term financing for land acquisition, site improvement, construction, and working capital. After the projects are completed, the agencies issue long-term bonds that provide the projects with more permanent financing. However, during the initial stages of development, the agencies need a major source of short-term financing, and this has led to the development of project notes.

Issued through HUD

Each agency does not market its own project notes. Instead, the U.S. Department of Housing and Urban Development (HUD) combines the various issues into one large issue of notes. In effect, HUD is the conduit through which the various notes are initially sold to the public. The notes are auctioned twice a month and are issued in bearer form, with denominations ranging from $1,000 to $100,000. Interest is payable at maturity, which ranges from 3 to 12 months.

Although project notes are sold through HUD, they are the obligations of the issuing state and local housing and urban renewal agencies. Since the notes represent the obligations of state and local agencies, the interest they pay is exempt from federal income taxation and may also be exempt from income taxes in the state of issue.

Backed by full faith and credit of the federal government

In addition to the tax exemption, project notes are guaranteed by HUD. Thus, they are backed by the full faith and credit of the U.S. government. Since the notes are fully secured by the federal government, they are as safe as treasury bills. Project notes and treasury bills, then, have strong similarities, and one may be preferred to the other on the basis of any difference in yields.

Tax-exempt Securities and Risk

Interest rate risk

While the sources of risk associated with investing in tax-exempt bonds were alluded to in the above discussion, it is desirable to summarize them. First, there is the market risk associated with changes in interest rates. Higher interest rates will drive down the prices of existing bonds. This source of risk, of course, applies to all bonds and is not unique to the bonds of state and municipal governments. The investor may reduce this source of risk by purchasing bonds of shorter maturity, because the prices of bonds with longer terms to maturity fluctuate more. If the investor is concerned with price fluctuations and the preservation of capital, then shorter term tax-exempt bonds should be preferred to long-term bonds. The investor, however, should realize that shorter term bonds generally pay less interest.

Municipal debt is not registered with the SEC

The second source of risk is the possibility that the government might default on the interest and principal repayment. Unfortunately, finding information on particular

bond issues can be fairly difficult for the individual investor. Municipal bonds are not registered with the Securities and Exchange Commission (SEC) prior to their sale to the general public, and many state and local governments do not publish annual reports and send them to bondholders. Instead, investors may consult the latest issues of Moody's *Municipal and Government Manual* or *Standard & Poor's Bond Guide*. Fortunately for investors, both of these firms rate a considerable number of the tax-exempt bonds that are sold to the general public. These ratings are based on a substantial amount of data, for the rating services require the municipal and state governments to provide them with financial and economic information. Since failure of the bond issue to receive a favorable rating will dissuade many potential buyers, the state and local governments supply the rating services with the required information.

The importance of rating services

The investor can take several steps that will reduce the risk associated with default. The first is to purchase a diversified portfolio of tax-exempt bonds, which spreads the risk associated with any particular government. Second, the investor may limit purchases to debt with high credit ratings.[7] If the investor purchases only bonds with AAA or AA credit ratings, there is little risk (perhaps no real risk) of loss from default.

A third means by which the investor may limit the risk of default is to limit purchases to bonds that are insured. Several insurance companies guarantee the payment of interest and principal of the municipal bonds they insure. Insured bonds almost inevitably have high credit ratings. For example, the Virginia Port Authority Facility revenue bonds are insured by AMBAC and have an AAA rating by Standard & Poor's. AMBAC is the American Municipal Bond Assurance Corporation, which is owned by several financial institutions including Citicorp and Xerox Financial Services. Other municipal bond insurers include MBIA (Municipal Bond Insurance Association), which is composed of a consortium of leading insurance companies, FGIC (Financial Guaranty Insurance Co.), which is owned by several large financial institutions including General Electric Credit and Merrill Lynch, and Industrial Indemnity, a division of Xerox's Crum & Foster insurance subsidiary.

Insured bonds

The investor who acquires insured bonds should realize that lower yields accompany lower risk. As a result of the insurance guarantees, the yield on the bonds will be lower than the yield available on non-insured bonds. The reduction in risk and yields is also affected by the quality of the company offering the insurance. If the insurance company has a lower credit rating than other insurers, the quality of the insurance may be lower, raising the possibility of default by the insurance company should the municipality default. While such a default has not occurred, its possibility should be considered.

In addition to the risks associated with fluctuations in security prices and the possibility of default, the investor should be aware that tax-exempt bonds may lack marketability and liquidity. Bonds issued by small governments may be resold, but the secondary markets are thin (i.e., small). Common sense should tell the investor that bonds issued by the Industrial Development Authority of Medium-Town, USA, are not very liquid. If the investor must sell the bonds before maturity, he or she may suffer a loss as the price of the bonds is marked down to induce someone to purchase

---

[7] Some tax-exempt bonds are secured by lines of credit with commercial banks. If the government defaults, the banks pay the interest and principal.

them. Many investors may not be aware of this lack of liquidity until they seek to sell the bonds and receive bids that are below the anticipated price. This is particularly true during periods of high interest rates, such as in 1981, when the market for existing municipal bonds dries up and prices are significantly marked down.

The existence of these risks does not imply that an investor should avoid tax-exempt bonds. The return offered by these bonds is probably consistent with the amount of risk the investor must bear. If a particular bond were to offer an exceptionally high return, it would be readily purchased and its price driven up so that the return was in line with comparable risky securities. Tax-exempt bonds should be examined by investors with moderate-to-high incomes who are seeking tax-free income and who do not need liquidity. Like any investment, tax-exempt bonds may fit into an individual investor's portfolio and offer a return (after tax) that is in line with the risk the investor must endure.

SUMMARY

When the federal government spends more than it receives in tax revenues, this deficit must be financed. In order to tap funds from many sources, the federal government issues a variety of debt instruments. These include series EE and HH bonds, which are sold in small denominations, and treasury bills and bonds, which are sold in large denominations.

Federal government debt is the safest of all possible investments, as there is no possibility of default. However, the investor still bears the risk of loss through fluctuations in the price of the marketable debt and through inflation. If the rate of inflation exceeds the yield on the debt instruments, the investor then experiences a loss of purchasing power.

In addition to the debt issued by the federal government itself, bonds are issued by its agencies. These bonds tend to offer slightly higher yields, but they are virtually as safe as the direct debt of the federal government. In some cases the agency's debt is even secured by the full faith and credit of the U.S. Treasury.

Among the most popular securities issued by a federal government agency are the mortgage pass-through bonds issued by the Government National Mortgage Association or "Ginnie Mae." These bonds serve as a conduit through which interest and principal repayments are made from homeowners to the bondholders. Payments are made monthly, so Ginnie Mae bonds are popular with individuals seeking a flow of cash receipts. While these bonds do expose investors to some risk of loss from fluctuating interest rates or from inflation, the interest payments and principal repayments are guaranteed by an agency of the federal government. Thus Ginnie Mae bonds are considered to be among the safest of all long-term debt instruments.

State and local governments issue long-term debt instruments to finance capital improvements such as schools and roads. The debt is retired over a period of time by tax receipts or revenues. While some of these bonds are supported by the taxing authority of the issuing government, many are supported only by the revenues generated by the facilities financed through the bond issues.

State and municipal debt differs from other investments because the interest is exempt from federal income taxation. These bonds pay lower rates of interest than

taxable securities (e.g., corporate bonds), but their after-tax yields may be equal to or even greater than the yields on taxable bonds. The nontaxable bonds are particularly attractive to investors in high income tax brackets, because they provide a means to shelter some income from taxation.

Tax-exempt bonds can be risky investments, since the capacity of state and local governments to service the debt varies. Moody's and Standard & Poor's rating services analyze this debt based on the government's ability to pay the interest and retire the principal. Such ratings indicate the risk associated with investing in a particular debt issue. In addition, investors must bear the risks associated with fluctuations in security prices and the lack of liquidity associated with tax-exempt bonds.

Terms to Remember

Series E and EE bonds	Ginnie Mae
Series H and HH bonds	Tax-exempt bond
Treasury bills	Municipal bond
Treasury notes	General obligation bond
Treasury bonds	Revenue bond
Federal agency bonds	Anticipation note
Moral backing	Project note

Questions

1. Why is the debt of the federal government considered to be the safest of all possible investments?

2. What distinguishes series EE bonds from treasury bills?

3. When interest rates rise, what happens to the price of federal government bonds? What happens to the price of state and local government bonds?

4. What is the difference between the following:
   a. a bond secured by a moral obligation and a bond secured by full faith and credit?
   b. a revenue bond and a general obligation bond?
   Are there any similarities between a bond secured by a moral obligation and a revenue bond?

5. What are the sources of risk investing in
   a. federal government debt?
   b. municipal debt?

6. What is the difference between a term bond issue and a serial bond issue? Why are many capital improvements made by state and local governments financed through serial bonds?

7. If an investor or corporation wants to invest in a short-term government security, what alternatives are available? How safe are these securities, and do they offer any tax advantages?

8. What is a mortgage pass-through bond? What risks are associated with investing in Ginnie Mae bonds? What is the composition of the payment received from a mortgage pass-through bond?

9. If interest rates increase, what should happen to
    a. the price of a Ginnie Mae bond and the price of a municipal bond?
    b. the payments received from a Ginnie Mae bond and the payments received from a municipal bond?

Contrast your answers to parts a and b.

10. What government securities may be appropriate for the following investors?
    a. a retired couple seeking income
    b. an individual in the highest tax bracket seeking a liquid investment
    c. an individual seeking a government bond for inclusion in an individual retirement account (IRA)
    d. a child with no income and a modest amount to invest
    e. a corporation with $100,000,000 to invest for less than three months
    f. a church seeking to invest a modest endowment fund.

Problems

1. If a six-month treasury bill is purchased for $0.9675 on a dollar (i.e., $96,750 for a $100,000 bill), what is the approximate annual rate of interest? What will be the yield if the discount price falls to $0.94 on a dollar (i.e., $94,000 for a $100,000 bill)?

2. An investor is in the 28 percent income tax bracket and can earn 8.3 percent on a nontaxable bond. What is the comparable yield on a taxable bond? If this same investor can earn 13.2 percent on a taxable bond, what must be the yield on a nontaxable bond so that the after-tax yields are equal?

3. An investor in the 30 percent tax bracket may purchase an AT&T bond that is rated double A and is traded on the New York Stock Exchange (the bond division). This bond yields 12 percent. The investor may also buy a double A-rated municipal bond with an 8.4 percent yield. Why may the AT&T bond be preferred? (Assume that the terms of the bonds are the same.)

4. What is the price of the following zero coupon bonds if interest rates are (a) 5%, (b) 10%, and (c) 15%?
   • Bond A: zero coupon; maturity 10 years
   • Bond B: zero coupon; maturity 20 years
   • Bond C: zero coupon; maturity 30 years

What generalization can be made concerning the term of a zero coupon bond and its price to changes in the level of interest rates?

Suggested Readings

Detailed descriptions of the various securities issued by governments may be found in

Barnes, Leo, and Stephen Feldman. *Handbook of Wealth Management.* Chapters 26–28. New York: McGraw-Hill, 1977.

First Boston Corporation. *Handbook of Securities of the United States Government and Federal Agencies.* Boston. Published biennially.

Hawk, William A. *The U.S. Government Securities Market.* Chicago: Harris Trust and Savings Bank, 1976.

Stigum, Marcia. *The Money Market—Myth, Reality, and Practice.* Chapters 7, 13, and 20. Homewood, Ill.: Dow Jones-Irwin, 1978.

The process by which all bonds are rated is covered in

Sherwood, Hugh C. *How Corporate and Municipal Debt Is Rated.* New York: John Wiley & Sons, 1976.

For information on particular issues or the debt of particular states and municipalities, consult:

Moody's Investors Service. *Moody's Bond Record* or *Moody's Bond Survey.*
(These publications are updated continuously and present a wealth of information on particular debt issues.)

Standard & Poor's Corporation. *Bond Guide.* Published monthly.
(While primarily limited to corporate debt, these bond guides are a convenient source of S & P's ratings of municipal debt.)

For a book of readings on treasury securities that includes returns, yield curves, cash management strategies, and options, consult:

Frank J. Fabozzi, ed. *The Handbook of Treasury Securities.* Chicago: Probus Publishing, 1986.

For a discussion of recent developments in and uses of mortgage-backed securities, see:

Frank J. Fabozzi. *Mortgage-Backed Securities.* Chicago: Probus Publishing, 1986.

Blume, Marshall E., and Jack P. Friedman, eds. *The Encyclopedia of Investments.* Boston: Warren, Gorham & Lamont, 1982.
This book devotes chapters to mortgage-backed securities, municipal securities, Treasury bonds and agency securities, and treasury bills.

Riding the Yield Curve

Appendix

The positively sloped yield curve suggests a means by which an investor may magnify the return on a short-term investment. Consider an individual with $10,000 to invest in treasury bills. Four investment possibilities are

Term	Price	Annual Yield
3 months	$9,800	8.2%
6 months	9,500	10.5
9 months	9,000	13.2
12 months	8,800	13.6

Notice that in this example the yield curve in Figure 12.3 is positively sloped because as the term of the bill increases, the yields become higher (e.g., 8.2 percent for the three-month bill and 13.6 percent for the twelve-month bill).

The investor may purchase any of the four T-bills. For example, if the individual wants to invest the funds for one year, he or she can buy the twelve-month bill or buy

Figure 12.3
Riding the Yield Curve

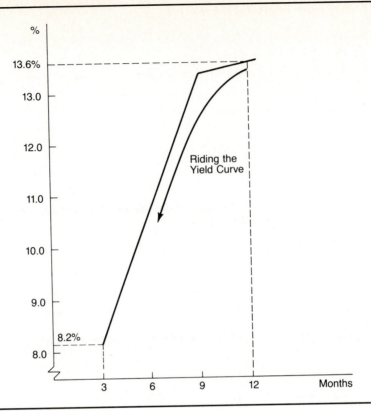

the three-month bill and reinvest the funds for an additional nine months when the three-month bill matures. Even if the individual wants the investment for only six months, any of the T-bills may be purchased, because the three-month bill can be rolled over into another bill and the nine-month or twelve-month bills can be sold after six months. Since there are active secondary markets in T-bills, the investor could buy the twelve-month bill, hold it for six months, and then sell it.

Whether the individual wants to invest for three months, six months, or a year, it may be possible to increase the yield by purchasing the twelve-month bill and selling it after a period of time. This strategy is referred to as "riding the yield curve." To see how the yield may be increased, consider the investor who buys the twelve-month bill with the intention of selling it after six months. What will be the price of the bill when it is sold? There are three general possibilities: (1) the structure of yields will remain the same, (2) yields will rise, and (3) yields will fall.

If after six months the structure of yields has not changed, the twelve-month bill becomes a six-month bill with a price of $9,500 and an annual yield of 10.5 percent. (Remember: T-bills are sold at a discount that declines as the bill approaches maturity.) The bill has moved up two steps in the table of prices and yields given above and has moved down the yield curve in Figure 12.3. That means the investor may sell the bill for a profit of $700 ($9,500 − $8,800), for a six-month return of 7.95 percent

(15.9 percent annually). This profit and yield is greater than the $500 earned (10.5 percent) by purchasing the six-month bill.

If interest rates have risen, the prices of the bills will not rise as much. For example, suppose after six months the structure of yields is

Term	Price	Annual Yield
3 months	$9,750	10.2%
6 months	9,410	12.5
9 months	9,000	14.8
12 months	8,700	14.9

The original twelve-month bill can now be sold for $9,410, which generates an annual return of 13.8 percent. The investor did not fare as well in this case (13.8 percent versus 15.9 percent) because the bill's price did not rise as much. However, unless interest rates rise precipitously and rapidly, as did occur during 1979 and 1980 (see Figure 9.3), the investor will earn a return that exceeds the yield available through purchasing the six-month bill and holding it to maturity.

If interest rates have fallen, the strategy of buying the twelve-month bill produces an even higher return. Suppose after six months the structure of yields is

Term	Price	Annual Yield
3 months	$9,850	6.1%
6 months	9,600	8.3
9 months	9,400	8.5
12 months	9,820	8.7

Since interest rates have fallen, the price of the twelve-month bill has risen even more than it would have had there been no change in the yield structure. In this case the investor may now sell the bill for $9,600, generating a profit of $800 and an annual return of 18.2 percent. This is obviously the best scenario since the investor benefits from both riding the yield curve and the declining interest rates.

The opportunity to increase returns by riding the yield curve suggests that a positively sloped yield curve may be unstable. If many investors try to ride the yield curve, they will seek to sell the shorter term bills in order to purchase the longer term bills. This will depress the price of the shorter term bills and increase their yields while simultaneously increasing the price of the longer term bills and decreasing their yields. These forces will tend to flatten the yield curve. The actual shape of the yield curve at a point in time will depend on the interplay of many factors, including those explained in Chapter 9 (i.e., individuals' preference for liquidity and expectations of future interest rates), in addition to the impact of individuals seeking higher returns by riding the yield curve.

A SHORT CASE STUDY FOR CHAPTERS 9–12
Bonds, Bonds, and More Bonds

Frank Duesing is a relatively conservative individual who has just inherited $100,000. He has no immediate needs for the funds but would like to supplement his current income. Thus, Duesing is considering investing these funds in debt instruments, since the interest and repayment of principal are legal obligations of the issuer. While Duesing realizes that the borrower could default on the payments, he thinks this is unlikely, especially if he decides to limit his choices to triple- or double-A rated bonds. Duesing does realize that he could earn more interest by purchasing lower rated bonds but is not certain if he is capable of bearing the risk.

Besides risk and expected return, Duesing decides that tax considerations must also play a role in this investment decision. He is currently in the 30 percent federal income tax bracket, and he pays state income tax of 5 percent. He believes that his job is relatively secure and that his salary will increase over time but does not expect it to rise sufficiently so that his income tax brackets will be significantly increased.

Duesing quickly learned that there are many bonds to choose among. For example, the PHONE Company has three triple-A bonds outstanding. Their annual interest payments (or coupon rate), term to maturity, and price are

Bond	Interest per $1,000 Bond	Coupon	Term	Price
A	$ 50	5%	1 year	$ 970
B	100	10	5 years	1,000
C	100	10	10 years	1,000

Currently the interest rate of long-term debt is approximately 10 percent, but Duesing expects that this rate will fall, as inflation is declining. In addition, the level of unemployment is increasing, so Duesing anticipates that the Federal Reserve will take actions to stimulate the economy through reductions in the rate of interest. Duesing believes that interest rates could fall to 8 percent within a year. Of course, he also realizes that this decline may not occur or even if it did, that interest rates could rise again after the initial decline. Duesing decided to analyze the three PHONE Company bonds to determine which may be the better investment under various assumptions concerning future interest rate behavior. To do this he sought to answer the following questions:

1. **a.** What would be the expected price of each bond one year from now if interest rates were 8 percent?

   b. What would be the expected price two years from now if interest rates initially fall but subsequently rise to 12 percent at the end of the second year?

2. If interest rates were expected to fall and not rise back to 12 percent, which alternative is best?

3. If interest rates were expected to decline initially and then rise, which alternative should be selected?

4. If bond A were selected, what would happen after a year elapses? What decision must then be made?

After answering these questions, Duesing realized the importance of expected future interest rates on the selection of a bond. Since he firmly believes that interest rates will fall and remain below current levels for several years, he decided to select bond C, the longest term bond that would lock in the current high yields. However, he also decided to consider other bonds to determine what additional returns he could earn for bearing more risk and what the tax implications of his selections were. He noticed that the following ten-year bonds were available:

Bond	Interest per $1,000	Price	Yield to Maturity	Rating
Besttown USA	$ 80	$1,000	8%	AAA
Besttown USA	60	866	8	AAA
U.S. Treasury	$ 80	$1,000	8%	—
WEAK Inc.	$140	$1,000	14%	B
WEAK Inc.	120	896	14	B

To confuse the selection process further, Duesing also learned that the PHONE Company has a preferred stock paying an annual dividend of $4 ($1 each quarter) that is selling for $36 a share.

At this point Duesing was sufficiently frustrated to ask the advice of his stockbroker. If you were his stockbroker, which bond(s) would you recommend? In your advice, specifically explain to Duesing the tax implications (both in terms of income and capital gains) of each bond. Also consider Duesing's willingness to bear risk and the anticipated flow of income both from the bonds and his job. Then construct a portfolio that you believe meets his needs and willingness to bear risk. Assume that the bonds are sold in units of $5,000.

IV Investing in Common Stock

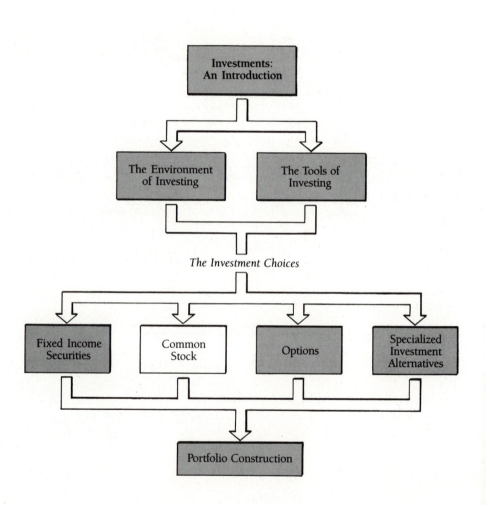

Investments:
An Introduction

The Environment
of Investing

The Tools of
Investing

The Investment Choices

Fixed Income
Securities

Common
Stock

Options

Specialized
Investment
Alternatives

Portfolio Construction

*F*or many individuals the word investing is synonymous with buying and selling common stocks. Although alternatives are certainly available, common stocks are the primary instrument of investing for many people, perhaps because of the considerable exposure individuals have to common stocks. Newspapers report stock transactions, market averages are quoted on the nightly television news, and brokerage firms advertise the attractiveness of such investments.

This section discusses investing in common stocks. To identify the stocks with the greatest earnings potential, various techniques are used to analyze firms and their common stock. In addition, Part Four considers the return earned in the past on investments in common stock.

Unlike bonds, which pay a fixed amount of interest, the dividends paid by common stocks vary. As the economy prospers and corporate earnings grow, dividends and the value of common stocks may also increase. For this reason, common stocks are a good investment for individuals who have less need for current income but desire capital appreciation.

13

Measures of Security Prices

LEARNING OBJECTIVES

After completing this chapter you should be able to

1. Differentiate between a simple price average and a value-weighted average.

2. Illustrate how aggregate measures of stock prices adjust for stock splits.

3. Contrast the Dow Jones averages with other indices of stock prices.

4. Explain the difference among the holding period return, an average rate of return, and the true rate of return.

5. Compare the results of various studies concerning the rates of return earned on investments in common stock.

6. Identify the advantage of "averaging down."

*O*n January 1, 1986, the Dow Jones industrial average stood at 1546, but by January 1, 1987, the Dow Jones industrials had risen to over 1895, for a 22.6 percent increase in one year. While such a bull market does not occur every year, it does illustrate the large return that may be earned in basically conservative stocks.

There is no question that security prices fluctuate and that investors must endure the risk associated with these fluctuations. Those individuals who own stock obviously expect security prices to rise over a period of time. The measurement of stock performance and the returns (or gains) previously earned by stocks are the main focus of this chapter. The first section discusses the construction of aggregate measures of the stock market. These include the Dow Jones averages, Standard & Poor's 500 stock index, and the New York Stock Exchange composite index.

The second section is devoted to the returns earned on investments in securities. It includes an explanation of the methods used to compute the rate of return and the various types of graphs that may be used to plot these values, along with a discussion of the academic studies of the returns earned by investors.

The chapter concludes with a discussion of one strategy that may reduce the impact of price fluctuations. This strategy is to buy stock systematically, which smoothes out the price fluctuations and reduces the average cost of the position (the commitment in a particular stock).

MEASURES OF STOCK PERFORMANCE: AVERAGES AND INDICES

Constructing a measure of security prices may appear to be easy, but there are several possible problems. The first concerns the choice of which securities to include. Although this certainly was a problem before the advent of computers, it is not a major concern today, for a measure may include any number of securities (e.g., all stocks listed on the NYSE may be included).

Which securities to include

A more important problem concerns the weight that should be given to each security. For example, suppose there are two stocks: A sells for $10 and has 1 million shares outstanding, and B sells for $20 and has 10 million shares outstanding. The total market value of A is $10 million, and the total market value of B is $200 million. How should these two securities be weighted? There are basically two choices: to treat each stock's price equally or to adjust for B's larger number of shares.

The problem of weights

The first choice is a simple average of the prices of both stocks. In this case, the two prices are treated equally, giving an average price per share of

$$\$10 + \$20 = \$30,$$
$$\$30/2 = \$15 = \text{Average price.}$$

An average gives equal weight to each stock and does not recognize differences in the number of shares outstanding.

If this technique is used, a problem immediately arises concerning the handling of stock splits. The subject of stock splits is treated in greater detail in Chapter 15. However, since stock splits affect the construction of price measures, let us consider a simple example. The price of a stock adjusts for a split. For example, a two-for-one stock split reduces the price of the stock by half. Since the total value of the stock has not changed, such splits do not affect the value of the firm and should not affect the measure of security prices.

Consider what would happen to the average that was determined earlier if stock B were to split two for one. Its price would become $10, and the number of shares outstanding would increase to 20 million. If the measure of security prices is simply the average of the stock prices, the average price per share is reduced to $10 (i.e., [$10 + $10] ÷ 2). Even though there has been no change in the stockholders' wealth by the two-for-one stock split, there has been a significant decline in the average of stock prices. This decline is misleading; thus, the method of computing the average should be modified.

This problem can be avoided for the simple average by adjusting the denominator for the stock split. This adjustment is best demonstrated by an illustration. Before the stock split, the average was

$$\$20 + \$10 = \$30,$$
$$\$30/2 = \$15 = \text{Average price.}$$

The problem now is to determine what new divisor (or denominator) will yield $15 when the price of B's stock changes as the result of the split. That is,

$$\$10 + \$10 = \$20,$$
$$\$20/X = \$15 = \text{Average price.}$$

Solving this simple equation for X yields 1.333. If the divisor is reduced from 2 to 1.333, the value of the average is not affected (i.e., $\$20 \div 1.33 = \$15$). Such an adjustment, then, erases the problem caused by stock splits and stock dividends.

An alternative way of measuring stock performance is to construct an average that allows for the different number of shares each firm has outstanding. If the preceding example is used, the total value of A and B is

$$
\begin{array}{rcl}
\text{Price} \times \text{Number of shares} & = & \text{Total value} \\
\$10 \times 1,000,000 & = & \$10,000,000 \\
\$20 \times 10,000,000 & = & +\$200,000,000 \\
\hline
 & & \$210,000,000
\end{array}
$$

The average value of a share of stock is then $19.09 ($210,000,000 ÷ 11,000,000). This method obviously places more emphasis on stock B. Its higher price and greater number of shares result in an increase in the average value of a share.

The total value of the two stocks can be used to construct an index. Then all subsequent values may be expressed in terms of this initial total value. For example, suppose the prices of A and B rise to $18 and $22, respectively. The total value is now:

$$
\begin{array}{rcl}
\$18 \times 1,000,000 & = & \$18,000,000 \\
\$22 \times 10,000,000 & = & \$220,000,000 \\
\hline
 & & \$238,000,000
\end{array}
$$

This new value then may be expressed relative to the total value in the first year, which is called the base year:

$$\frac{\$238,000,000}{\$210,000,000} = 1.13.$$

This answer indicates that the current value is 1.13 times the value in the base year. The previous example is an illustration of a *value-weighted index*; that is, the contribution of each stock is weighted for the number of shares a firm has outstanding. Such an index automatically adjusts for stock splits. For example, if stock B splits the shares two for one, the total value is

$$
\begin{array}{rcl}
\$18 \times 1,000,000 & = & \$18,000,000 \\
\$11 \times 20,000,000 & = & \$220,000,000 \\
\hline
 & & \$238,000,000
\end{array}
$$

Thus, there has been no change in the total value. The price has been cut in half, but the number of shares has doubled. Therefore, the index remains

$$\frac{\$238,000,000}{\$210,000,000} = 1.13.$$

The value-weighted index is not affected by stock splits. This fact, along with the emphasis that is placed on the total value of all stocks included in the index, argues strongly for the use of this type of measure.

The Dow Jones Averages

One of the first measures of stock prices was the average developed by Charles Dow.[1] Initially the average consisted of the stock from only 11 companies, but it was later expanded to include more firms. Today this average is called the Dow Jones industrial average, and it is probably the best known and most widely quoted average of stock prices.

The **Dow Jones industrial average** is a simple average. It is computed by summing the prices of the stocks of 30 companies and then dividing that total by an adjusted value. The divisor is not the number of stocks (30) but a value that has been adjusted over the years so that the index is not affected by stock splits and stock dividends in excess of 10 percent. No adjustment is made for cash dividends; hence, the index declines when stocks like AT&T or Exxon go ex-div (pay a dividend) and their prices decline. (The reason a stock's price declines when the firm pays a dividend is explained in Chapter 15.) *The industrials*

The Dow Jones industrial average for the period from 1939 to 1985 is presented in Figure 13.1, which plots the high and low values of the average for each year. As may be seen in the graph, there was a pronounced increase in the average during the 1950s, when the annual high rose from less than 300 to almost 700. During the 1960s and 1970s, the Dow Jones industrial average (and the stock market) was erratic and certainly did not experience the steady growth achieved during the 1950s. In 1970 and in 1974 the Dow Jones industrial average even fell below the highs achieved during 1959. The 1980s, however, have shown a different pattern, as stock prices have soared and the Dow Jones industrial average has reached new highs.

In addition to the industrial average, Dow Jones computes an average for transportation stocks, utility stocks, and a composite of all of the stocks included in the three separate averages. All three averages are composed of a relatively small number of companies. Thirty stocks are included in the industrial average, 20 stocks compose the transportation average, and 15 stocks make up the utilities average. The firms included are among the largest (in terms of sales and total assets) and best known in the nation, as may be seen in Exhibit 13.1. Many firms that have grown into prominence since World War II (e.g., Xerox and Johnson & Johnson), however, are excluded from these averages.

This small number of firms is one source of criticism of the Dow Jones averages. It is argued that the small sample is not indicative of the market as a whole. For this reason, other measures of stock prices that have broader bases, such as the NYSE index or Standard & Poor's 500 stock index, may be better indicators of the general market's performance. *Criticism of these averages*

Other Indices of Stock Prices

Unlike the Dow Jones industrial average, **Standard & Poor's 500 stock index** is a value-weighted index. The base year, 1943, is the time at which the index was 10. Thus, if the index is currently 100, the value of these stocks is ten times their value in 1943. Standard & Poor's also computes an index of 400 industrial stocks and indices of 20 transportation, 40 utility, and 40 financial companies. *S&P's 500*

---

[1] In 1882 Edward Jones joined Charles Dow to form a partnership that grew into Dow, Jones and Company.

Figure 13.1
**Annual Price Range
of the Dow Jones
Industrial Average,
1939–1985**

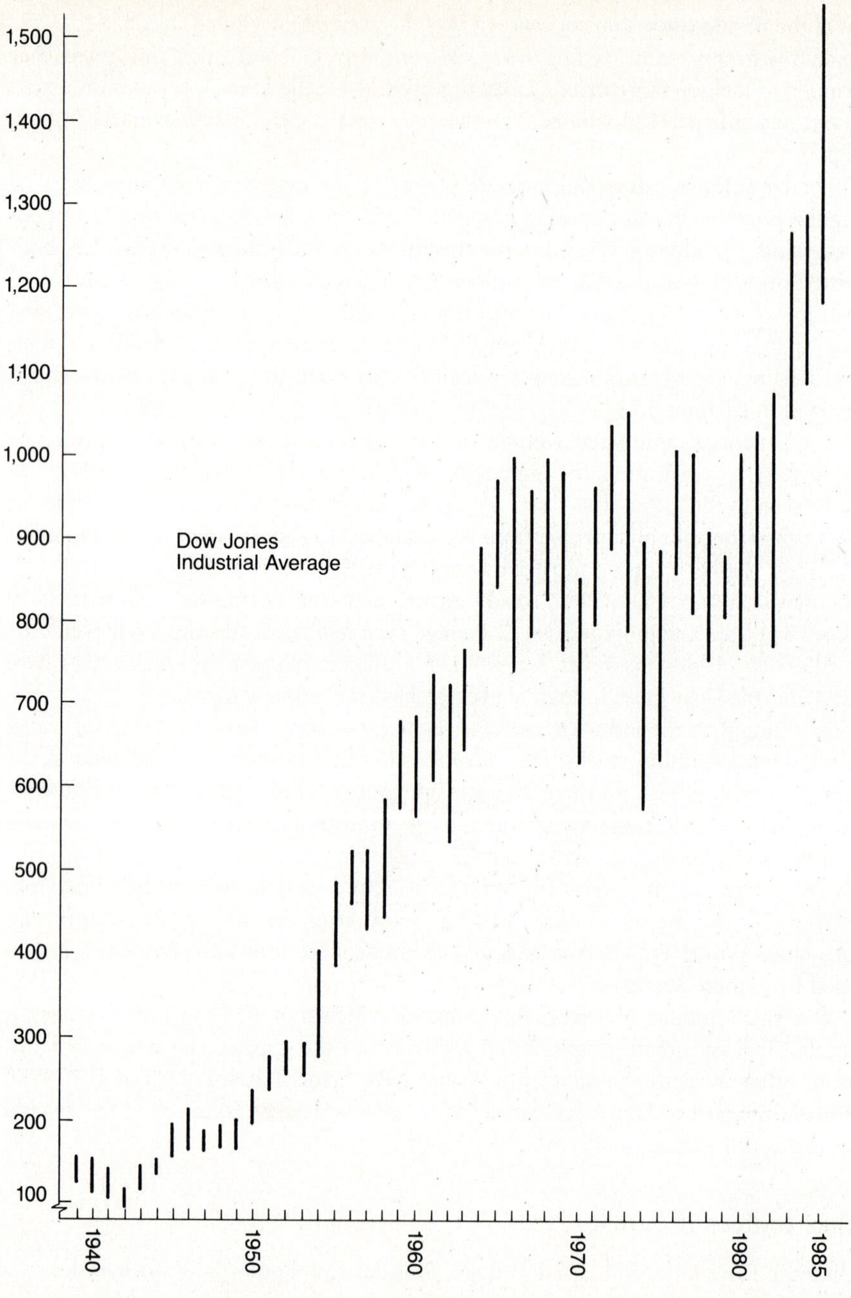

Dow Jones
Industrial Average

The Dow Jones Industrial Stocks

Allied-Signal	International Paper
Aluminum Co. of America	McDonalds
American Can	Merck
American Express	Minnesota Mining and Manufacturing
AT&T	Navistar
Bethlehem Steel	Owens-Illinois
Chevron Corp.	Philip Morris
DuPont	Procter & Gamble
Eastman Kodak	Sears, Roebuck & Co.
Exxon	Texaco
General Electric	Union Carbide
General Motors	United Technologies
Goodyear	USX
IBM	Westinghouse Electric
Inco	Woolworth

The Dow Jones Transportation Stocks

AMR Corp.	Norfolk Southern Corp.
American President	NWA Inc.
Burlington Northern	Pan American Corp.
Canadian Pacific	Piedmont Aviation
Carolina Freight Carriers	Ryder Systems
Consolidated Freight	Santa Fe Southern Pacific
CSX Corp.	TWA
Delta Air Lines	UAL Inc.
Federal Express	Union Pacific Corp.
Leaseway Transportation	USAir Group

The Dow Jones Public Utility Stocks

American Electric Power	Niagara Mohawk Power
Centerior Energy	Pacific Gas & Electric
Columbia Gas System	Panhandle Eastern
Commonwealth Edison	Peoples Energy
Consolidated Edison	Philadelphia Electric
Consolidated Natural Gas	Public Service Enterprises
Detroit Edison	Southern California Edison
Houston Industries	

Exhibit 13.1
Stocks Included in the Dow Jones Averages

Source: The Wall Street Journal.

There is also the **New York Stock Exchange composite index**, which includes all common stocks listed on the NYSE. Like Standard & Poor's averages, the NYSE index is a value-weighted index with a base of 50 as of December 31, 1965. Value Line computes another index of more than 1,700 stocks that includes stocks traded on the New York Stock Exchange, on the American Stock Exchange, and over the counter. Unlike the Dow Jones industrial average, which is a simple average, and the S & P 500, which is a weighted average, the Value Line index is a geometric average.

Other stock indices include those of the American Stock Exchange (AMEX) and over-the-counter (OTC) securities. The AMEX index is a value-weighted index that

NYSE index

encompasses all of the common stocks on that exchange. The National Association of Security Dealers Automatic Quotation System (NASDAQ) index of over-the-counter stocks covers more than 2,000 issues. This index was started in 1971, and since it is relatively new it cannot be used to show long-term trends. The National Association of Security Dealers also publishes nonindustrial OTC indices for banking and insurance.

The differences among simple averages, weighted averages, and geometric averages may be seen in the following example using three stocks. The stocks' prices and number of shares outstanding are as follows:

Stock	A	B	C
Number of shares outstanding	1,000	10,000	3,000
Price as of 1/1/x1	$10	15	25
Price as of 1/1/x2	18	13	25

The simple average of their prices for the two years is

$$(\$10 + 15 + 25)/3 = \$16.67,$$
$$(\$18 + 13 + 25)/3 = \$18.66.$$

The value weighted average is

$$(\$10 \times 1,000 + 15 \times 10,000 + 25 \times 3,000)/14,000 = \$16.78,$$
$$(\$18 \times 1,000 + 13 \times 10,000 + 25 \times 3,000)/14,000 = \$15.93.$$

The geometric average is

$$\sqrt[3]{(\$10 \times 15 \times 25)} = \$15.12,$$
$$\sqrt[3]{(\$18 \times 13 \times 25)} = \$17.50.$$

These examples show that the average value of a share of stock differs in each case. The value of a share of stock rose from $16.67 to $18.66 according to the simple average, but when the weighted average was used, the price of a share decreased from $16.78 to $15.93. The value of a share according to the geometric average rose from $15.12 to $17.50.

There is no answer to the question of which index or method of calculation is best. If there were, there would be fewer indices and all would use the same method of calculation. Aggregate measures of stock prices tend to move together (i.e., they are highly correlated), but there are important differences. The NASDAQ over-the-counter and the AMEX market value indices show more volatility and more rapid growth than the Dow Jones industrials, the Standard & Poor's 500, or the NYSE composite index. This should be expected, since the AMEX and OTC markets are composed of smaller, riskier firms whose stock prices tend to be more volatile than the shares of larger, more stable firms.[2]

Besides indices of stock prices, there are also averages of the bond market. These averages may be expressed in terms of yields, such as the yields used to construct

---

[2] For further discussion of how specific indices are constructed, see Robert C. Radcliffe, *Investment Concepts, Analysis, and Strategy* (Glenview, Ill.: Scott, Foresman, 1982), 459–471.

Ten Public Utilities		
Company	**Coupon**	**Maturity Date**
Alabama Power	9¾%	2004
AT&T	8.80	2005
Commonwealth Edison	8¾	2005
Consolidated Edison	7.95	2001
Consumers Power	9¾	2006
Detroit Edison	9.00	1999
New York Telephone	4½	1991
Pacific Gas & Electric	7¾	2005
Philadelphia Electric	7⅜	2001
Public Service of Indiana	9.60	2005
Ten Industrials		
Bank America	7⅞	2003
Bethlehem Steel	6⅞	1999
Dow Chemical	4.35	1988
Exxon	6.00	1997
Ford Motor	8½	1990
General Motors Acceptance Corp.	4½	1985
NCR	4⅜	1987
Pfizer	9½	2000
Socony	4⅛	1993
Weyhaeuser	5.20	1991

Exhibit 13.2
Bonds Included in the Dow Jones 20-Bond Average

Source: Sumner N. Levine, ed., *Dow Jones-Irwin Business and Investment Almanac, 1985 ed.,* 422.

Figures 9.3, 10.4, and 12.1. In addition there are the Dow Jones bond averages, one of which is the Dow Jones composite corporate bond average, consisting of ten public utility and ten industrial bonds. (See Exhibit 13.2 for the specific bonds included in the average.) The average is expressed as a percentage of the debt's face amount or principal. When the composite of the 20 bonds was 71.52 on January 1, 1983, the average price of the 20 bonds was $715.20.

Price Fluctuations

The fluctuations in stock prices are illustrated in Figure 13.2, which plots the Dow Jones industrial average, Standard & Poor's 500 stock index, and the NYSE index from January 1973 to January 1986. All three aggregate measures document the decline in stock prices that started in January 1973. In two years, the Dow Jones industrial average fell from above 1000 to just above 600, which is a 40 percent decline. Standard & Poor's 500 stock index fell from 117 to under 70 (a 40 percent decline), and the NYSE index declined from 68 to 35, representing a 49 percent fall in prices.

Indices show price fluctuations

Figure 13.2 indicates, as would be expected, that all three measures of stock prices move together. The amount of movement differs, however. From 1973 to 1975, the percentage decline in the Dow Jones industrial average and in the Standard & Poor's index was about 40 percent, but the NYSE index declined by almost 50 percent. In 1976 the Dow Jones industrial average almost reached its former high, while the

Figure 13.2
Aggregate Measures of Stock Prices, 1973–1985

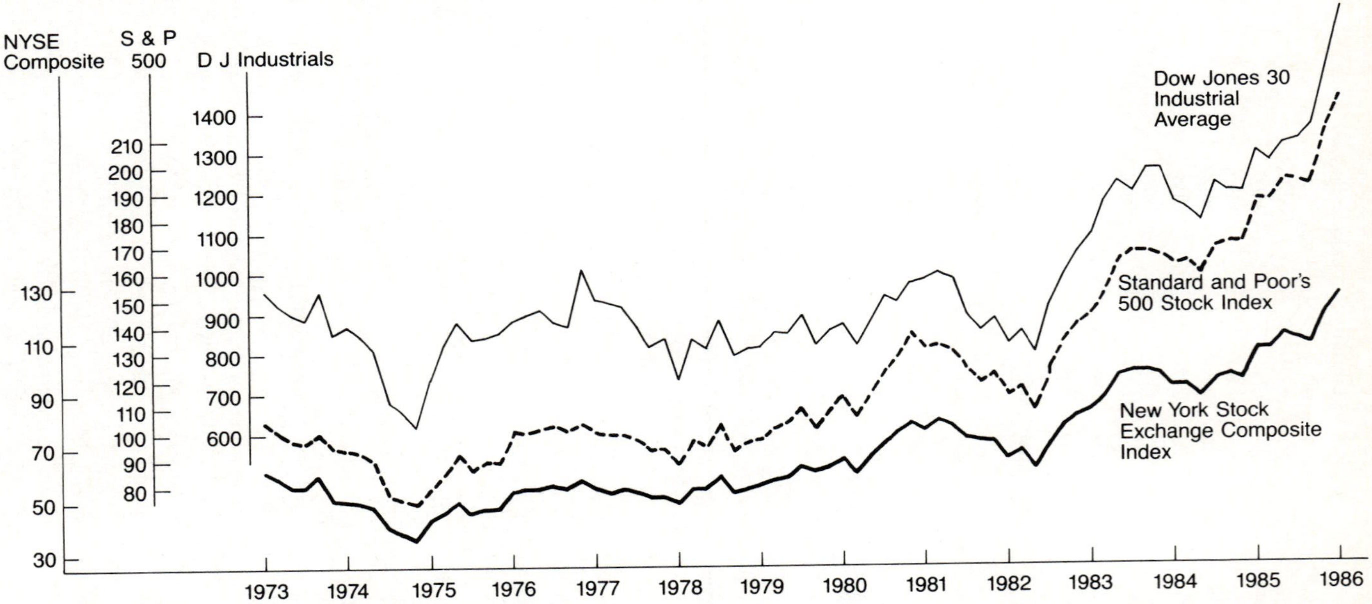

Figure 13.3
Dow Jones Bond Average and Yields on Moody's Aaa-rated Bonds, 1977–1985

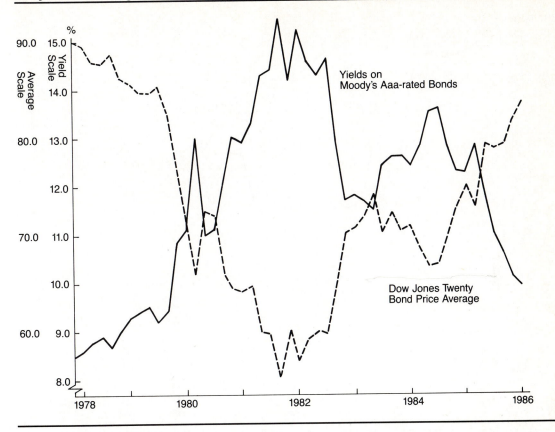

other two indices were considerably below their levels of January 1973. Once again, during 1981, the Dow Jones industrial average reached 1000 and thus approximately matched its highs of 1973 and 1976. However, in 1981 both the Standard & Poor's index and the NYSE index rose *above* their former highs. From January 1979 to January 1981, the broader-based NYSE index rose more than 30 percent, but the Dow Jones industrial average rose by less than 10 percent. From January 1982 to January 1986, the Dow Jones industrial average rose 100 percent while the Standard & Poor's 500 rose 94 percent. These performances give some credibility to the argument that the Dow Jones industrial average is not typical of the market as a whole.

Figure 13.3 illustrates fluctuations in bond prices and presents the Dow Jones 20-bond composite average and the yields on Moody's Aaa-rated bonds from January 1978 through December 1985. The graph vividly illustrates the inverse relationship between bond prices and yields. For example, the bond average fell from 85.4 to 55.4 between January 1979 and September 1981, when interest rates on the Aaa bonds rose from 9.3 to 15.5 percent. However, from May 1984 through 1985, the price of bonds rose as interest rates fell.

Figure 13.4
Dow Jones Industrial Average and Dow Jones Bond Average, 1978–1985

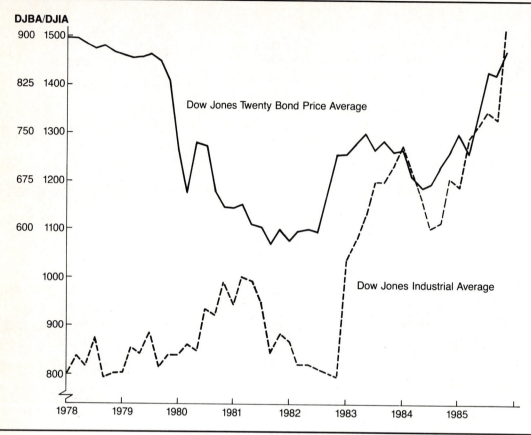

The relationship between bond and stock prices may be seen by comparing Figures 13.2 and 13.3. This is done in Figure 13.4, which combines the Dow Jones industrial average and the Dow Jones composite bond average. As may be seen in the graph, periods of rising bond prices tend to coincide with rising stock prices (e.g., from mid-1982 through 1985), and rising interest rates (falling bond prices) coincide with declining stock prices (e.g., from late 1981 through mid-1982). Figure 13.4 also illustrates a major advantage available to stockholders but not to bondholders. Over time stock values may grow, but bond prices are limited to fluctuations around their principal value. From 1978 to 1986, the Dow Jones industrial average rose from about 800 to over 1500, but the bond average ended 1985 at 84.1, which was slightly lower than where it stood at the beginning of 1978.

Security Prices and Investors' Purchasing Power

Another means to measure security price performance is to compare one of the measures of the market with a general price index. This gives an indication of the losses inflicted on the investing public by inflation. If the general price index rises more

rapidly than the index of security prices, the implication is that stock holders suffer a loss of purchasing power.[3] This loss occurs even if stock prices rise if the increase is at a slower rate than consumer prices.

The loss of purchasing power is illustrated in Figure 13.5. The left half of the figure plots the Dow Jones industrial average from 1965 through 1985 and the Dow Jones average deflated (i.e., divided by the Consumer Price Index). The right half of the graph plots the annual percentage changes in the Dow Jones industrial average and in the Consumer Price Index. As may be seen in both halves of the figure, the Dow Jones industrial average fluctuates. Even though there were years in which the increase in security prices exceeded the increase in consumer prices (e.g., 1975, 1976, 1983, and 1985), investors lost purchasing power throughout the 1970s. Thus, during the 1970s, an investor's real return as measured by the Dow Jones industrial average and deflated by the Consumer Price Index was negative. Only after 1981 did the increase in the Dow Jones industrials consistently offset the increase in the Consumer Price Index, making the real return earned on the investment in common stocks positive.

Inflation reduces investors' real return

The right half of Figure 13.5 also suggests that inflation is detrimental to stock prices. When the rate of inflation started to increase in 1973 and 1974, stock prices fell. Stock prices also fell in 1977, when the inflation rate rose once again. However, once inflation diminished in 1982 to 1985, common stock prices rose dramatically as the Dow Jones increased from 875 at the end of 1981 to over 1540 at the end of 1985.

RATES OF RETURN ON INVESTMENTS IN COMMON STOCK

What returns have been earned on investments in securities? To answer this question, the investor should consider the purchase price of the security, the sale price, the flow of income such as dividends (if any income was received), and how long the investor owned the asset. The easiest (and perhaps the most misleading) return to compute is the **holding period return**. It is derived by dividing the profit (or loss) plus any income by the price paid for the asset. That is,

Holding period return

$$\frac{\text{Sale price} - \text{Purchase price} + \text{Income}}{\text{Purchase price}}.$$

If an investor buys a stock for $10, sells it for $15, and collects $1 in dividends, the holding period return is

$$\text{Holding period return} = \frac{\$15 - \$10 + \$1}{\$10} = 60\%.$$

While the holding period return is easy to compute, it can be misleading. Consider the following example. An investor buys a stock for $10 per share and sells it after ten years for $20. What is the holding period return on the investment? This simple question can produce several misleading answers. The individual may respond by answer-

May be misleading

---

[3] This loss is before considering dividend income which may offset the loss of purchasing power.

Figure 13.5
Purchasing Power of the Dow Jones Industrial Average, 1965–1985

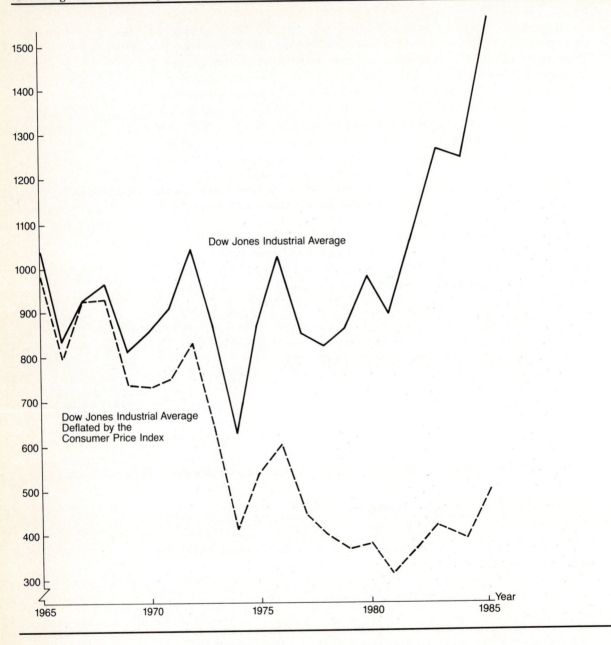

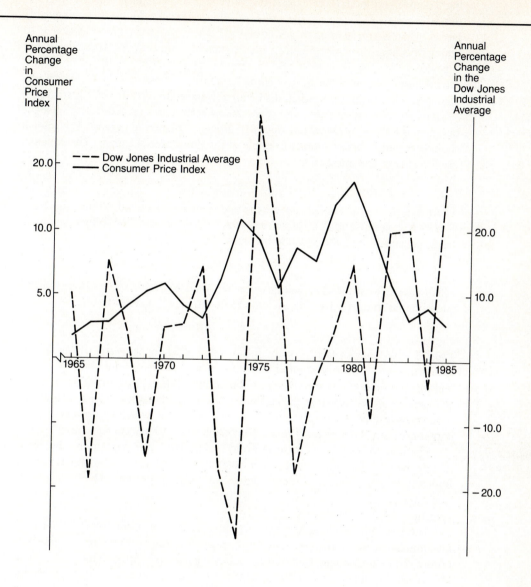

Annual
Percentage
Change
in
Consumer
Price
Index

Annual
Percentage
Change
in the
Dow Jones
Industrial
Average

--- Dow Jones Industrial Average
— Consumer Price Index

Average return

ing "I doubled my money!" or "I made 100 percent!"[4] That certainly sounds impressive, but it completely disregards the *length of time* needed to double the individual's money. The investor may assert that he or she made 10 percent annually (100% ÷ 10 years). This figure is less impressive than the claim that the return is 100 percent, but it is also misleading because it fails to consider compounding. Some of the return earned during the first year in turn earned a return in subsequent years, which was not taken into consideration when the investor averaged the return over the ten years.

Rates of return are another example of the time value of money

The correct way to determine what **rate of return** was earned is to phrase the question as follows: "At what rate does $10 grow to $20 after ten years?" The student should recognize this as another example of the time value of money. The equation used to answer this question is

$$P_0(1 + g)^n = P_n,$$

where P_0 is the cost of the security, g is the rate of return per period, n is the number of periods (e.g. years), and P_n is the price at which the security is sold. When the proper values are substituted, the equation becomes

$$\$10(1 + g)^{10} = \$20,$$

which asks at what rate $10 will grow for ten years to become $20. To answer this question, the student solves the equation to determine the interest factor.

$$(1 + g)^{10} = \$20 \div \$10 = 2.$$

Thus, 2 is the interest factor for the future value of $1 for ten years. If the student locates this factor in the compound value of a dollar table (Appendix A), he or she will find that the value of g is approximately 7 percent.[5] Thus, $10 compounded annually at 7 percent grows to $20 at the end of ten years. The correct rate of return on the investment (excluding any dividend income) is 7 percent, which is considerably less impressive than "I doubled my money!" or "I averaged 10 percent each year."

Averaging positive and negative rates of return

The investor may be tempted to avoid this problem of compounding by determining the rate of return each year. For example, if the price of the stock were to rise from $20 to $22, the annual rate of return would be 10 percent ($2 ÷ $20). If the stock were to fall in price from $20 to $15, the annual rate of return would be −25 percent (−$5 ÷ $20).

There is nothing wrong with this technique until the investor averages the resulting annual percentage changes. Like the average of the ten-year total return, this procedure can be misleading. Consider the following example. An investor buys a stock for $20. At the end of the year it is selling for $25, but the investor holds the stock for a second year and then sells it at cost (i.e., $20). What is the rate of return? Obviously the investor earned nothing and the rate of return should indicate this fact.

If, however, the investor computes the annual rate of return each year, and then averages these annual rates, the investment will have a positive rate of return. In the first

---

[4] The calculation is

$$\frac{\$20 - \$10}{\$10} = 100\%.$$

[5] To find the interest factor 2, look in the future value of a dollar table on the row for ten time periods. When 2 (or close to it) is located, read up the column for the percentage, which in this case is the return, g.

POINTS OF INTEREST
Overstating the Rate of Appreciation in the Value of a House

Holding period returns are frequently used when discussing real estate investments, and because of the long time periods involved they can be very misleading. Their simplest form would include a statement such as, "I bought my house in 1955 for $25,000 and sold it for $125,000 in 1985." The large price increase ($100,000) generates a holding period return of 400 percent ($100,000/$25,000). However, the true annualized rate of return is 5.51 percent. $25,000 deposited in a

bank account that paid 5.51 percent, compounded annually during the same time period, would have grown into $125,000. While this illustration does not consider (1) the use of the house, (2) any expenses associated with upkeep, and (3) any tax advantages associated with home ownership, it does illustrate how misleading holding period returns can be. In the context of this illustration, the house's price appreciation is not particularly impressive.

---

year the stock's price rose from $20 to $25, indicating a 25 percent gain ($5 ÷ $20). During the second year the stock declined from $25 to $20, for a 20 percent loss (−$5 ÷ $25). What is the average rate of return? The answer is

$$25\% - 20\% = 5\%$$
$$5\%/2 = 2.5\% = \text{Average return.}$$

Owing to the magic of numbers, the investor has earned a 2.5 percent average return, even though the investment produced neither a gain nor a loss. This example illustrates how averaging positive and negative numbers can lead to misleading results. The correct method to determine the annual rate of return is to use the future value calculations presented previously. That is,

$$\$20(1 + g)^n = \$20$$
$$(1 + g)^n = \$20/\$20 = 1$$
$$g = 0.$$

The Inclusion of Dividend and Interest Income

Many investments earn income as well as appreciate in price. This income is also part of the total return earned by the investor. Therefore, to determine an investment's rate of return, any income such as interest or dividends must be included in the calculation. For example, if an individual buys a stock for $50, collects a $2.00 dividend in the first year, $2.10 in the second year, and $2.25 in the third year, then sells the stock for $60, the return consists of the dividend payments and the capital gain.

Dividends and interest must be included

To determine the rate of return earned on the investment, the investor could find the growth rate that equates the discounted value of the dividends and the sale price with the cost of the investment. The equation is

$$P_0 = \frac{D_1}{(1 + g)^1} + \cdots + \frac{D_n}{(1 + g)^n} + \frac{P_n}{(1 + g)^n},$$ (13.1)

where P_0 is the cost of the security, g is the rate of return, $D_1 \ldots D_n$ is the flow of income, such as the payment of dividends during the years the investor holds the security, and P_n is the price at which the security is sold. When this equation is applied to the preceding example, the rate of return on the investment may be determined (i.e., the equation is solved for g).

$$\$50 = \frac{\$2}{(1 + g)^1} + \frac{\$2.10}{(1 + g)^2} + \frac{\$2.25}{(1 + g)^3} + \frac{\$60}{(1 + g)^3}.$$

Internal rate of return

These calculations can be tedious unless the individual has access to a computer or a calculator programmed to perform internal rates of return. The rate of return on an investment in stock is calculated in the same way as the rate of return on an investment in plant or equipment. In finance this return is referred to as the **internal rate of return**, which is the rate that equates the present value of the cash flows generated by the investment and its costs.[6] In the case of an investment in stock, the cash flows are the dividend payments and the price for which the stock is sold. Thus, in the above illustration the internal rate of return (i.e., the rate of return on this particular investment) is the rate that equates the dividend payments ($2.00, 2.10, and 2.25) and the sale price ($60) with the cost of the stock ($50). That rate is 10.25 percent, and it includes both the cash dividends and the capital appreciation.

Rates of Return and Graphic Illustrations

Use of semilogarithmic graphs

The investor who reads certain financial publications, such as the *Media General Financial Weekly* or the *Value Line Investment Survey,* will find charts constructed on semilogarithmic paper. This type of graph is used because it gives a truer picture of the *change* in the price of the stock.

This fact may be illustrated by the following monthly range of stock prices and percentage increases:

Month	Price of Stock	Percentage Change in Monthly Highs
January	$10–5	. . .
February	15–10	50
March	20–15	33
April	25–20	25

Even though the monthly price increases are equal ($5), the percentage increments decline. The investor who bought the stock at $10 and sold it for $15 made $5 and earned a return of 50 percent. The investor who bought it at $20 and sold for $25 also made $5, but the return was only 25 percent.

These monthly prices may be plotted on graph paper that uses absolute dollar units for the vertical axis. This is done on the left-hand side of Figure 13.6. Such a graph gives the appearance that equal price movements yield equal returns. However, this is not so, as the preceding illustration demonstrates.

To avoid this problem, **semilogarithmic paper** can be used. This is done in Figure 13.6, and the prices are plotted on the right-hand side. Equal units on the vertical

[6] The same procedure was used to determine the yield to maturity in Chapter 10. The yield to maturity is, in effect, the internal rate of return on an investment in a bond that is purchased today and redeemed at maturity.

axis are in terms of percentage change. Thus, a price movement from $10 to $15 appears to be a greater price movement than one from $20 to $25, because in percentage terms it *is* greater.

The impact of using semilog paper may be seen by comparing Figures 13.1 and 13.7. Both present the annual price range of the Dow Jones industrial average. Figure

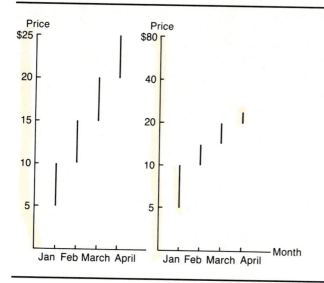

Figure 13.6
Use of Semilogarithmic Paper to Illustrate Stock Price Movements

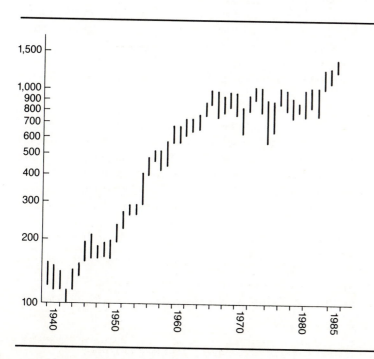

Figure 13.7
Annual Price Range of the Dow Jones Industrial Average, 1939–1985

13.1 uses an absolute scale while Figure 13.7 employs a semilogarithmic scale. The general shape is the same in both cases, but the large absolute increase in the Dow Jones industrial average from 1980 through 1985 is considerably less impressive in Figure 13.7, which expresses the increase in percentage of change instead of absolute numbers. Since absolute price changes are reduced to percentage price changes, graphs such as Figure 13.7 are better indicators of rates of return.

Studies of Investment Returns

Several studies have been conducted by academicians on the returns earned by investments in common stocks; hence, these reports should not contain any bias. Unfortunately, research done by brokerage firms, investment advisory services, or the trust departments of commercial banks may involve a conflict of interest. Although the results may seem valid, one may still be hesitant to accept them as honest appraisals of the returns earned by investors.

Fisher and Lorie's study

Perhaps the most famous (or at least most frequently cited) early study on the rates of return earned by investments in common stocks was done by Fisher and Lorie. They studied the annual rates of return from investments in all common stocks listed on the NYSE from 1926 through 1965 and found that the average annual rate of return was 9.3 percent.[7] The rates of return, of course, varied from year to year and depended on the assumptions made. Fisher and Lorie computed rates of return under three sets of assumptions: (1) that dividends were reinvested in common stocks, (2) that dividends were not reinvested (i.e., the investor pocketed any dividends that were paid), and (3) dividends were ignored. In all three cases, the impact of taxes was not considered (Fisher and Lorie computed before-tax returns).

As would be expected, the failure to include dividends reduced the rates of return, and hence they were not indicative of the total return earned on the investment. In the other two cases, the rates of return were similar. For example, according to the study, the annual rate of return earned on an investment held from December 1935 to December 1965 yielded 12.6 percent when dividends were reinvested and 11.2 percent when they were not.[8] When price change alone was considered, the rate of return was 7.5 percent, which indicates that the dividend yield during that particular time (1935–1965) was in excess of 3 percent.

According to Fisher and Lorie's study, investments in common stocks listed on the NYSE during the period studied earned an excellent return. (The student should remember that an annual return of 9.3 percent means $1,000 will grow to more than $2,000 in eight years.[9]) The rates of return were even higher during the 1950s and early 1960s when the country and the stock market experienced prosperity and rapid growth. During this time the annual rates of return on stocks averaged as high as 15 percent.

These results are impressive, but the student should remember that although this study encompassed all of the common stocks listed on the big board, no investor

[7]Lawrence Fisher and James H. Lorie, "Rates of Return on Investments in Common Stock—The Year-by-Year Record, 1926–1965," *Journal of Business* 40 (July 1968): 1–26.

[8]The difference is the result of compounding.

[9]$1,000 (1 + 0.093)^8 = $2,036.86.

Security	Annual Rate of Return
Common stocks	9.1%
Small stocks	12.1
Long-term corporate bonds	3.6
Long-term government bonds	3.0
Treasury bills	3.0
Rate of inflation	3.0

Exhibit 13.3
**Annual Rates of Return,
1926–1981, Estimated
by Ibbotson and
Sinquefield**

Source: Roger Ibbotson and Rex Sinquefield, *Stocks, Bonds, Bills, and Inflation: The Past and the Future,* 1982 ed. (Charlottesville, Va.: Financial Analysts Research Foundation, 1982).

could have duplicated these results. The individual investor owns a portfolio of se-lected securities and not all stocks. Thus, an aggregate measure of the rate of return does not necessarily apply to a particular individual's portfolio. In fact, one study found that securities selected by individual investors (i.e., nonprofessional money managers) tended to outperform the market (before considering transaction costs).[10]

Studies of the stock market by Holmes and by Brigham and Pappas corroborated the results of Fisher and Lorie.[11] Holmes's study covered the period between 1871 and 1971. The annual rate of return earned for the 100-year period was 7.8 percent. For the years that overlapped with Fisher and Lorie's study, the rate of return was 9.7 percent. This small difference (9.7 versus 9.3 percent) could be attributed to commis-sion costs. Fisher and Lorie included a commission cost for stock purchases, while Holmes's study did not. Hence, one would expect Fisher and Lorie's rates of return to be less.

Brigham and Pappas's study covered the period from 1946 to 1965. They con-cluded that the annual rate of return was about 15 percent. Although this figure is considerably higher than the overall returns in Fisher and Lorie's and in Holmes's studies, it is similar to their returns for the comparable time period.

A more recent study by Ibbotson and Sinquefield has extended the results of pre-vious studies to 1981.[12] Their study was more comprehensive than the previous stud-ies in that it considered not only stocks but also corporate bonds, federal government bonds and bills, and the rate of inflation. A summary of the results is presented in Exhibit 13.3. As may be seen in the exhibit, the annual rate of return for common stocks as measured by the Standard & Poor's 500 common stock index was 9.1%. If smaller stocks were considered, the annual rate of return rose to 12.1 percent. Ibbotson and Sinquefield defined small stocks as the lowest one-fifth of New York Stock Exchange firms with the lowest total value (i.e., price times number of shares outstanding).

*Other studies of
market returns*

[10] See Gary G. Schlarbaum, Wilbur G. Lewellen, and Ronald C. Lease, "Realized Returns on Common Stock Investments: The Experience of Individual Investors," *Journal of Business* 51 (April 1978): 299–325.

[11] See John Russell Holmes, "100 Years of Common Stock Investing," *Financial Analysts Journal* 30 (November–December 1974): 38–45, and Eugene F. Brigham and James L. Pappas, "Rates of Return on Common Stock," *Journal of Business* 42 (July 1969): 302–316.

[12] Roger Ibbotson and Rex Sinquefield, *Stocks, Bonds, Bills, and Inflation: The Past and the Future* (Charlottesville, Va.: Finan-cial Analysts Research Foundation, 1982).

Figure 13.8
NASDAQ, AMEX, and S&P 500 Stock Indices, 1975–1985

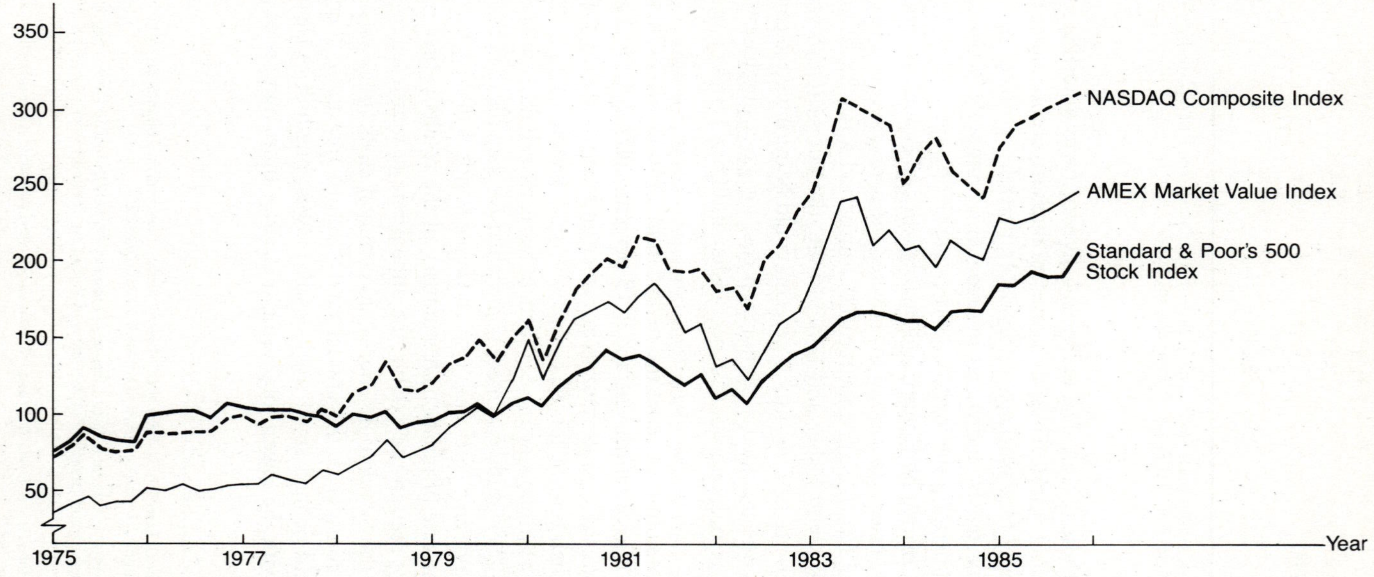

Exhibit 13.3 also gives the annual rate of return earned by long-term corporate debt and federal government securities, as well as the annual rate of inflation. It is interesting to note that the rate earned on treasury bills is exactly the same as the rate of inflation. This suggests that the investor who is concerned with maintaining purchasing power can meet this goal (at least before federal income taxes are considered) by acquiring treasury bills. The exhibit suggests that over time, the yield on stocks tends to be 6 percent above the rate on treasury securities. This information may be important when trying to establish a return necessary to justify purchasing equities. For example, if the current yield on treasury bills is 7.5 percent, that suggests a return of 13.5 percent may be necessary to justify purchasing common stock. This concept will be further developed in Chapter 14, which is concerned with the valuation of common stock.

The investor may ask whether securities traded in a particular market, such as the over-the-counter market or the American Stock Exchange, outperform the securities traded on the New York Stock Exchange. Such a conclusion seems to be indicated by Figure 13.8, which plots the NASDAQ index, the American Stock Exchange index, and the Standard & Poor's 500 stock index. Over the time period, both the NASDAQ and the AMEX indices outperformed the S & P 500 index. This conclusion, however, is not corroborated by a study by Jessup and Upson, who computed returns for OTC stocks. While their study covered an earlier time period (1946–1970), they found that over extended periods of time (five years) the returns were similar for listed and OTC stocks.[13]

These results suggest that OTC stocks are inferior investments. Since the rates of return on listed stocks and OTC stocks are similar, these investments should involve equal risk. However, the study also found that the OTC stocks are more volatile, and because their prices tend to fluctuate more, these stocks are riskier. Presumably, if an investment involves greater risk, it should offer a higher return. If it does not, the investment is inferior, because, given a choice of two portfolios with the same rate of return, the investor will always prefer the portfolio with less risk. For this reason, Jessup and Upson concluded that investments in OTC stocks have resulted in inferior returns.

OTC stocks may have been inferior investments

Before jumping to conclusions as to what an investor in the stock market can earn, the student should realize that studies of investment returns are aggregates and that historical rates of return cannot be taken as indicators of future stock price performance. If this were so, the investor could select a portfolio at random and expect it to earn 9.3 percent annually according to Fisher and Lorie's earlier study or 15 percent according to Brigham and Pappas's study. Obviously, there is a contradiction, because the investor cannot earn both rates of return. A return of 15 percent is obviously greater than the return earned on savings accounts, time deposits, and many other investments. If an investor could randomly buy a portfolio of stocks and earn 15 percent, there would be no need for analysis and investment decisions. Unfortunately, this is not the case.

Past returns may not be indicative of future returns

---

[13] Paul F. Jessup and Roger B. Upson, *Returns in Over-the-Counter Stock Markets* (Minneapolis, Minn.: University of Minnesota Press, 1973).

A portfolio should meet the investor's goals

Nor do all securities meet the investor's specific goals. For example, individuals who are in need of income should select securities whose return consists primarily of dividends or interest. Other investors may desire capital appreciation and therefore should choose stocks whose price is expected to increase. A randomly selected portfolio would not meet either of these specific goals. Thus, even if a 15 percent rate of return is anticipated, investors with different needs would still have to make investment decisions in order to construct portfolios that meet their financial goals.

REDUCING THE IMPACT OF PRICE FLUCTUATIONS: AVERAGING

The systematic purchase of securities

One strategy for accumulating shares and reducing the impact of security price fluctuations is to "average" the position. By buying shares at different times, the investor accumulates the shares at different prices. Such a policy may be achieved through the dividend reinvestment plans that are discussed in Chapter 15. An alternative is for the investor to systematically purchase shares of stock through a broker. There are two basic methods for achieving this averaging: the periodic purchase of shares and the purchase of additional shares if the stock's price falls.

Periodic Purchases

Under the periodic purchase plan, the investor decides to buy additional shares of a stock at regular intervals. For example, the investor may elect to buy $2,000 worth of a stock every quarter or every month. This purchase is made at the appropriate interval, no matter what the price of the stock is.

Periodic purchases

The effect of such a program is illustrated in Exhibit 13.4, which shows the number of shares of EMEC stock purchased at various prices when $2,000 is invested each quarter. The first column gives the dates of purchase, and the second column presents the various prices of the stock; the third and fourth columns list the number of shares purchased and the total number of shares held in the position. The last column presents the average price of the stock held in the position. The student should notice

Exhibit 13.4
Average Position in
EMEC Stock When
$2,000 Worth Is
Purchased Each
Quarter

Date	Price of Stock	Number of Shares Owned	Cumulative Number of Shares Owned	Average Cost of Position
1/1/x0	$25	80	80	$25.00
4/1/x0	28	71	151	26.50
7/1/x0	33	60	211	28.44
10/1/x0	27	74	285	28.07
1/1/x1	21	95	380	26.32
4/1/x1	18	111	491	24.44
7/1/x1	20	100	591	23.69
10/1/x1	25	80	671	23.85

that when the price of the stock rises, $2,000 buys fewer shares. For example, at $33 per share, $2,000 buys only 60 shares, but at $18 per share the investor receives 111 shares. Because more shares are acquired when the price of the stock falls, this has the effect of pulling down the average cost of a share. In this example, after two years the average cost of the stock had fallen to $23.85 and the investor had accumulated 671 shares. If the price of the stock subsequently rises, the investor will earn more profits on the lower priced shares and thus will increase the return on the entire position.

Averaging Down

Some investors find it difficult to purchase stock periodically, especially if the price of the stock has increased. Instead, they prefer to purchase additional shares of the stock only if the price declines. Such investors are following a policy of averaging down. Averaging down is a means by which the investor reduces the cost basis of an investment in a particular security by buying more shares as the price declines so that the average cost of the entire position in the security is reduced. This may be particularly rewarding if the price subsequently rises, because the investor has accumulated shares at decreased prices and earns a gain when the price increases.

Purchases after price declines

There are several methods for averaging down. The investor may **dollar cost average**, which means that the same dollar amount is spent on shares each time a purchase is made. Or the investor may average down by purchasing the same number of shares (i.e., **share average**) every time a purchase is made.

Dollar cost averaging

Exhibit 13.5 illustrates these averaging down strategies. The price of the stock is given in column 1. Column 2 uses the dollar cost averaging method; the investor purchases $1,000 worth of stock every time the price declines by $5. As is readily seen in column 2, the number of shares in each successive purchase is larger. The last entries in the column give the total amount that the investor has spent ($5,000), the total number of shares that have been purchased (289), and the average cost of the shares ($17.30). The average cost of the total position has declined perceptibly below the $30 price of the initial commitment. However, if the price of the stock were to in-

Average cost of the position is reduced

Price of the Stock	Number of Shares Purchased ($1,000 Each Purchase)	Cost of 100 Shares
$30	33	$ 3,000
25	40	2,500
20	50	2,000
15	66	1,500
10	100	1,000
	289 shares	$10,000
	(for a cost of $5,000 and an average cost of $17.30 per share)	(500 shares, for a cost of $10,000 and an average cost of $20 per share)

Exhibit 13.5
Averaging Down
Strategies

crease to $30, the entire position would be worth $8,670. The investor would have made a profit of $3,670 and earned a gain of 73 percent on the entire position.[14]

Column 3 illustrates the share averaging method, which means that the same number of shares are bought every time the investor makes a purchase. When the price declines by $5, the investor buys 100 shares. If the price of the stock were to fall to $10, the investor would have accumulated 500 shares under share averaging, for a total cost of $10,000. If the price of the stock were to return to $30, the entire position would be worth $15,000, and the investor's profit would be $5,000, for a gain of 50 percent.

Share averaging

There is a greater reduction in the average cost of the entire position with dollar cost averaging than with share averaging. When the investor dollar cost averages, the amount spent is held constant and the number of shares purchased varies. When the investor share averages, the number of shares purchased is held constant and the dollar amount varies. Because the investor purchases a fixed number of shares with share averaging regardless of how low their price falls, the average cost of a share in the position is not reduced to the extent that it is with dollar cost averaging.

The preceding discussion and examples explain the essentials of averaging. The investor may choose any number of variations on this basic concept. For example, the investor may choose to average down on declines of any dollar amount in the price of the stock or may select any dollar amount to invest for periodic purchases or for averaging down. The effect is the same, that is, to reduce the average cost basis of the position in that particular security.

Averaging down obviously requires that the investor have the funds to acquire the additional shares once their price has declined. In addition, dollar cost averaging will involve purchasing odd lots (33 shares, for example) or combinations of odd and even lots (such as 133 shares, composed of one round lot of 100 shares and one odd lot of 33 shares). Such purchases may not be cost efficient when considering commissions. Dividend reinvestment plans that permit additional contributions may alleviate the problem of commission costs, but the purchases then cannot be made at a particular desired price.[15] Instead the investor must accept the price on the day the funds are invested.

Depressed stocks may remain depressed

The investor who follows a policy of dollar cost averaging should not assume that such a strategy will lead to a positive return on the investments. Stocks that have a downward price trend may not change course, or many years may pass before the price of the security rises to its previous level. The individual should view the funds spent on the initial investment as a fixed or sunk cost that should not influence the decision to buy additional shares. This type of reasoning is difficult to put into practice. Most individuals will not readily admit that they have made a poor investment. Unfortunately, they then follow a program of averaging down in the belief that it will vindicate their initial investment decision.

The investor should reanalyze the firm

The investor should not automatically follow a policy of averaging down. Before additional purchases are made, the stock should be reanalyzed. If the potential of the

---

[14] Of course, the annual *rate* of return will be different if it takes more or less than a year for this profit to be made.

[15] Corporate dividend reinvestment plans are discussed in Chapter 15. Mutual funds also permit the investor to reinvest dividends.

company has deteriorated (which may be why the price of the stock has fallen), the investor would be wiser to discontinue the policy of averaging down, to sell the stock, and to take a tax loss. If the stock lacks potential, it makes no sense to throw good money (the money used to buy the additional shares) after bad (the money previously invested in the stock). Some questions that the investor should ask are "Does the firm still have potential?" or "Is there a substantive reason for maintaining the current position in the stock?" If the answer is yes, then averaging down and periodic purchase are two means of accumulating shares while reducing their cost basis. Such strategies reduce the impact of security price fluctuations and may produce greater profits if the price of the stock rises subsequently.

SUMMARY

Security prices fluctuate daily. Several measures have been developed to show these price movements. These include the Dow Jones averages, Standard & Poor's indices of stock prices, and the NYSE index. Although the composition of each measure differs, the indices show the same movements in security prices.

Studies have shown that during a certain period, investors in common stock have earned a return in excess of 9.0 percent annually. However, the returns earned during the 1970s were smaller, and the real rate of return was even less when the rate of inflation was considered. These poor results explain in part why investors sought alternative investments to common stocks.

Averaging is one strategy designed to reduce the impact of price fluctuations. The investor either makes periodic purchases or buys additional shares of stock after their price has declined. Such purchases reduce the average cost of the position in the stock and may result in larger gains if the price of the stock rises.

Terms to Remember

Dow Jones industrial average	Internal rate of return
Standard & Poor's 500 stock index	Semilogarithmic paper
NYSE composite index	Dollar cost averaging
Holding period return	Share averaging
Rate of return	

Questions

1. What is a value-weighted average? Why does such an average place more emphasis on firms such as General Motors or Exxon than on other companies?

2. How does the Dow Jones industrial average differ from Standard & Poor's 500 stock index and the NYSE composite index?

3. During the last decade what has happened to the real return (i.e., the return adjusted for price-level changes) earned by investors in common stock?

4. Why may averaging rates of return yield an inaccurate measure of the true rate of return?

5. Historically, what rates of return have investors earned on investments in common stocks?

6. What is the advantage of using semilogarithmic paper to construct graphs of security prices?

7. What is averaging down? What is dollar cost averaging? Why may this strategy result in poor investment decisions?

Problems

1. What is the annual rate of return on a stock that cost $32 and was sold for $99 after ten years?

2. An investor buys a stock for $35 and sells it for $56⅜ (i.e., $56.38) after five years.
     a. What is the holding period return?
     b. What is the true annual rate of return?

3. What is the annual rate of return on a stock that (1) cost $95, (2) paid an annual dividend of $10, and (3) was sold for $100 after three years?

4. A stock costs $80 and pays a $4 dividend each year for three years.
     a. If an investor buys the stock for $80 and expects to sell it for $100 after three years, what is the anticipated rate of return?
     b. What would be the expected rate of return if the purchase price were $75?
     c. What would be the expected rate of return if the dividend was $1 annually and the purchase price was $79 and the sale price was $100?

5. You believe that Xerox stock may be a good investment and decide to buy 100 shares at $40. You subsequently buy an additional $4,000 worth of the stock every time the stock's price declines by an additional $5. If the stock's price declines to $28 and rebounds to $44, at which time you sell your holdings, what is your profit? (Assume that no fractional shares may be purchased.)

6. Given the following information concerning four stocks,

	Price	Number of Shares
Stock A	$10	100,000
Stock B	17	50,000
Stock C	13	150,000
Stock D	20	200,000

     a. Construct a simple price average and a value-weighted average.
     b. What is the percentage increase in each average if the stocks' prices become:
         (1) A: $12, B: $16, C: $20, D: $24;
         (2) A: $15, B: $20, C: $15, D: $20?

Suggested Readings

For material on the returns earned from investments in common stocks, consult:

Brigham, Eugene F., and James L. Pappas. "Rates of Return on Common Stock." *Journal of Business* 42 (July 1969): 302–316.

Fisher, Lawrence, and James H. Lorie. *A Half Century of Returns on Stocks and Bonds.* Chicago: University of Chicago Press, 1977.

Fisher, Lawrence, and James H. Lorie. "Rates of Return on Investments in Common Stock— The Year-by-Year Record, 1926–1965." *Journal of Business* 40 (July 1968): 1–27.

Holmes, John Russell. "100 Years of Common Stock Investing." *Financial Analysts Journal* 30 (November–December 1974): 38–45.

Ibbotson, Roger G., and Rex A. Sinquefield. *Stocks, Bonds, Bills, and Inflation: The Past and The Future.* Charlottesville, Va.: Financial Analysts Research Foundation, 1982.

Jessup, Paul F., and Roger B. Upson. *Returns in Over-the-Counter Stock Markets.* Minneapolis: University of Minnesota Press, 1973.

Lorie, James H., and Mary T. Hamilton. "Stock Market Indexes." In *Modern Developments in Investment Management,* edited by J. H. Lorie and R. A. Brealey. New York: Praeger Publishers, 1972.

Schlarbaum, Gary G., Wilbur G. Lewellen, and Ronald C. Lease. "The Common-Stock-Portfolio Performance Record of Individual Investors: 1964–1970." *The Journal of Finance* 33 (May 1978): 429–441.

Sharpe, William F., and H. B. Sosin. "Risk, Return and Yield on Common Stocks." *Financial Analysts Journal* 32 (March–April 1976): 33–43.

For material on indices and their construction, see:

Cootner, Paul. "Stock Market Indexes—Fallacies and Illusions." *Commercial and Financial Chronicle* (September 29, 1966): 18–19.

Latane, Henry A., Donald L. Tuttle, and William E. Young. "Market Indexes and Their Implications for Portfolio Management." *Financial Analysts Journal* (September–October 1971): 75–85.

Radcliffe, Robert C. *Investment Concepts, Analysis, and Strategy.* Glenview, Ill.: Scott, Foresman, 1982, 459–471.

Reilly, Frank K. "Price Changes in NYSE, AMEX, and OTC Stocks Compared." *Financial Analysts Journal* (March–April 1971): 54–59.

14

The Valuation of Common Stock

LEARNING OBJECTIVES

After completing this chapter you should be able to

1. Name the advantages of the corporate form of business.
2. Identify the components of an investor's required rate of return.
3. Examine the determinants of a stock's price.
4. Calculate the value of a stock using a simple present value model.
5. Explain why debt financing may increase the return on equity.
6. Understand how the use of financial leverage may increase risk.

The valuation of common stock is one of the most elusive and perplexing topics covered in this text. But it is also one of the most crucial, because the investor must estimate the current value of a stock to determine if the security should be purchased. Without such valuation the selection of common stock is based on hunches, intuition, or tips. Conceptually the valuation of stock is the same as the valuation of a bond, as presented in Chapter 10. In both cases the payments that investor receives in the future are discounted back to the present. For debt instruments this process is relatively easy, because a bond pays a fixed amount of interest and matures at a specified date. Common stock, however, does not pay a fixed dividend, nor does it mature. These two facts considerably increase the difficulty of valuing common stock.

Initially in this chapter the features of common stock are described. Then follows a simple model for the valuation of common stock in which discounting future dividends and their anticipated growth back to the present is emphasized. Next a means for adjusting this dividend-growth model for risk is suggested. The dividend-growth model is then related to P/E ratios. The chapter ends with a discussion of the use of debt financing to increase a firm's per-share earnings. Such increases in earnings, however, may not cause the price of the stock to rise, since the use of debt financing may also increase the element of risk.

THE CORPORATE FORM OF BUSINESS

A corporation is an artificial, legal, economic unit. Every corporation must be established by a state. Since there is variation in the laws that establish corporations, some states are more popular than others for the formation of corporations. Under state laws, the firm is issued a **certificate of incorporation** that indicates the name of the corporation, the location of its principal office, its purpose, and the number of shares of stock (shares of ownership) that are authorized (i.e., the number of shares that the firm may issue). Stock (i.e., preferred stock and **common stock**) represents ownership or equity in a corporation. In addition to the certificate of incorporation, the firm receives a **charter** that specifies the relationship between the corporation and the state. At the initial meeting of the stockholders, **bylaws** are established that set the rules by which the firm is governed, including such issues as the voting rights of the stockholders.

Establishing a corporation

The firm issues stock certificates to its owners. These certificates are evidence of ownership in the corporation. An example of a stock certificate is presented in Exhibit 14.1. The face of the certificate identifies the name of the owner, the number of shares, and the bank that serves as the transfer agent. It is the transfer agent that keeps the firm's record of stockholders and transfers the certificates as they are bought and sold.

Stock certificates

The Advantages

In the eyes of the law, a corporation is a legal entity that is separate from its owners. It may enter into contracts and is legally responsible for its obligations. This significantly differentiates corporations from sole proprietorships and partnerships. Once a firm is incorporated, the owners of the corporation are liable only for the amount of their investment in the company. This limited liability is a major advantage of incorporation. Creditors may sue the corporation for payment if it defaults on its obligations, but the creditors cannot sue the stockholders.

Limited liability

For many small, privately held corporations, limited liability may not exist. Creditors may ask the stockholders to pledge their personal assets to secure loans. If the corporation defaults, the creditors may seize the assets that the shareholders have pledged. In this event, the liability of the shareholders is not limited to their initial investment.

Limited liability does apply to investments in publicly held firms. Therefore, an investor knows that if he or she purchases stock in a company such as General Motors, the maximum amount that can be lost is the amount of the investment. If the firm were to go bankrupt, the creditors could not seize the assets of the stockholders.[1] Occasionally, a large corporation (e.g., Baldwin United or Braniff International) does go bankrupt, but owing to limited liability, stockholders cannot be sued by the firm's creditors.

---

[1] Investors in proprietorships and many partnerships do not have this privilege. Their assets may be seized (with court approval) to meet the firm's liabilities.

Exhibit 14.1
CBS Stock Certificate

Source: Reprinted with permission of CBS, Inc.

Ease of transfer of title

A second advantage of the corporate form of business is the ease with which a title of ownership may be transferred from one investor to another. All that is necessary for such transfer is for the investor to sell the shares of stock, endorse the certificates, and have the name of the new owner(s) recorded on the corporation's record of stockholders. Such transfers occur daily through organized security exchanges, such as the New York Stock Exchange (NYSE). The transfer of ownership may be considerably more difficult for small corporations or corporations that are owned by just a few stockholders. Since there is no ready market in the stock of small, privately held corporations, finding a buyer may be very difficult. Although the ease of transferring ownership is an advantage of incorporating, it does not apply equally to all corporations.

Permanence

A third advantage of the corporate form of business is permanence. Since the corporation is established by the laws of the state, it is permanent until dissolved by the state. Proprietorships and partnerships cease when one of the owners dies or goes bankrupt. In order to continue to operate, the proprietorship or partnership must be reconstituted. Corporations, however, continue to exist when one of the owners dies. The stock becomes part of the deceased owner's estate and is transferred to the heirs. The company continues to operate independently of the change in ownership.

Disadvantage of incorporation

There is one major disadvantage of incorporating: the double taxation of earnings that are distributed as cash dividends. As was discussed in Chapter 5, corporate profits are taxed. These earnings are taxed again when they are distributed to stockholders as cash dividends. The earnings of proprietorships and partnerships are taxed only once through the individual owner's share of the firm's profits. The disadvantage of

this double taxation is sufficient to keep many proprietorships and partnerships from incorporating.[2]

The Rights of Stockholders

Since stock represents ownership in a corporation, investors who purchase it obtain all of the rights of ownership. These rights include the option to **vote** the shares. The stockholders elect a board of **directors** that selects the firm's management. Management is then responsible to the board of directors, which in turn is responsible to the firm's stockholders. If the stockholders do not think that the board is doing a competent job, they may elect another board to represent them.

Voting rights

For publicly held corporations, such democracy rarely works. Stockholders are usually widely dispersed, while the firm's management and board of directors generally form a cohesive unit. Rarely does the individual investor's vote mean much.[3] However, there is always the possibility that if the firm does poorly, another firm may offer to buy the outstanding stock held by the public. Once such purchases are made, the stock's new owners may remove the board of directors and establish new management. To some extent this possibility encourages a corporation's board of directors and management to pursue the goal of increasing the value of the firm's stock.

A stockholder generally has one vote for each share owned, but there are two ways to distribute this vote. One system, called **cumulative voting,** gives minority stockholders a means to obtain representation on the firm's board of directors. While cumulative voting is voluntary in most states, it is mandatory in several, including California, Illinois, and Michigan.

Cumulative voting

How cumulative voting works is best explained by an example. Suppose a firm has a board of directors composed of five members. With the traditional voting, each share gives the stockholder the right to vote for one individual for each seat on the board. Since the individual share represents one vote for each seat, that totals five votes. Under cumulative voting, the individual may cast one vote for each seat or as many as five votes for one individual running for one seat. (Of course, then the stockholder cannot vote for anyone running for the remaining four seats.)

A minority group of stockholders can use the cumulative method of voting to elect a representative to the firm's board of directors. By banding together and casting all of their votes for a specific candidate, the minority may be able to win a seat. Although this technique cannot be used to win a majority, it does offer the opportunity for representation that is not possible through the traditional method of distributing votes (i.e., one vote for each elected position). As would be expected, management rarely supports the cumulative voting system.

Since stockholders are owners, they are entitled to the firm's earnings. These earnings may be distributed in the form of cash dividends, or they may be retained by

Earnings are either distributed or retained

---

[2] Small, privately held corporations may elect to be treated as S corporations, in which case earnings are passed through to stockholders. There is no corporate income tax, but the individual stockholders are subject to personal income tax on the earnings even if they are not distributed.

[3] One notable exception occurred in 1981 when Penn Central stockholders voted down a merger with Colt Industries. Management supported the merger but lost the vote: 10,245,440 shares against versus 10,104,220 shares in favor.

the corporation. If they are retained, the individual's investment in the firm is increased (i.e., the stockholder's equity increases). However, for every class of stock, the individual investor's relative position is not altered. Some owners of common stock cannot receive cash dividends, whereas others have their earnings reinvested. For a given class of stock, the distribution or retention of earnings applies equally to all stockholders.[4]

Business risk

Although limited liability is one of the advantages of investing in publicly held corporations, stock ownership does involve risk. As long as the firm prospers, it may be able to pay dividends and grow. However, if earnings fluctuate, dividends and growth may also fluctuate. It is the owners—the stockholders—who bear the business risk associated with these fluctuations. If the firm should default on its debt, it can be taken to court by its creditors to enforce its obligations. If the firm should fail or become bankrupt, the stockholders have the last claim on its assets. Only after all of the creditors have been paid will the stockholders receive any funds. In many cases of bankruptcy, this amounts to nothing. Even if the corporation survives bankruptcy proceedings, the amount received by the stockholders is uncertain.

Preemptive Rights

The right to maintain proportionate ownership

Some stockholders have **preemptive rights**, which is their prerogative to maintain their proportionate ownership in the firm. If the firm wants to sell additional shares to the general public, these new shares must be offered initially to the existing stockholders in a sale called a **rights offering**. If the stockholders wish to maintain their proportionate ownership in the firm, they can exercise their rights by purchasing the new shares. However, if they do not want to take advantage of this offering, they may sell their privilege to whoever wants to purchase the new shares. (The formula for the value of a right is discussed in the appendix to Chapter 19.)

Preemptive rights may be illustrated by a simple example. If a firm has 1,000 shares outstanding and an individual has 100 shares, that individual owns 10 percent of the firm's stock. If the firm wants to sell 400 new shares and the stockholders have preemptive rights, these new shares must be offered to the existing stockholders before they are sold to the general public. The individual who owns 100 shares would have the right to purchase 40, or 10 percent, of the new shares. If the purchase is made, then that stockholder's relative position is maintained, for the stockholder owns 10 percent of the firm both before and after the sale of the new stock.

A decline in the importance of preemptive rights

Although preemptive rights are required in some states for incorporation, their importance has diminished and the number of rights offerings has declined. In 1969 there were 118 public rights offerings, but the number declined to only 51 in 1985.[5] Some firms have tried to have their bylaws changed in order to eliminate preemptive rights. For example, in 1975 AT&T asked its stockholders to relinquish these rights.

---

[4] Some corporations have different classes of stock. For example, Food Lion, Inc. has two classes of common stock, both of which are publicly traded. The class A stock does not have voting power while the class B does. However, if management chooses to pay dividends to the class B stock, it must pay a larger dividend to the class A stock.

[5] *Moody's Dividend Record,* January 1986, 346–348. Of these rights offerings, only 16 involved firms are listed on the NYSE and the AMEX.

The rationale for this request was that issuing new shares through rights offerings was more expensive than selling the shares to the general public through an underwriting. Investors who desired to maintain their relative position could still purchase the new shares, and all stockholders would benefit through the cost savings and the flexibility given to the firm's management. Most stockholders accepted the management's request and voted to relinquish their preemptive rights. Now AT&T does not have to offer any new shares to its current stockholders before it offers them publicly.

Investors' Expected Rate of Return

Investors purchase stock with the anticipation of a **total return** consisting of a dividend yield and a capital gain. The dividend yield is the flow of dividend income paid by the stock. The capital gain is the increase in the value of the stock that is related to the growth in the firm's earnings. If the corporation is consistently able to achieve growth in earnings, then dividends can be increased and the price of the shares will rise. This increase in the shares' value produces a capital gain for the stockholders.

Investors anticipate a total return of dividends and price appreciation

The expected rate of return is expressed algebraically in Equation 14.1.

Expected rate of return = Expected dividend yield + Expected growth in earnings

$$= \frac{D}{P} + g. \tag{14.1}$$

The expected dividend yield is the expected cash dividend (D) divided by the price of the stock (P). The growth rate in earnings (and dividends) is expressed by the symbol g. In this form the model assumes that the firm's earnings and dividends are both growing at the same rate. According to this assumption, the firm's dividend policy does not change over time (i.e., the proportion of earnings distributed by the firm remains constant).

Equation 14.1 is applied in the following example. A firm's earnings are growing annually at the rate of 7 percent, the common stock is expected to pay a dividend of $1 per share during the year,[6] and the stock is currently selling for $25 per share. Thus, the anticipated return on an investment in this stock consists of a 4 percent dividend yield and a 7 percent growth rate.

$$\text{Expected rate of return} = \frac{\$1}{\$25} + 0.07$$

$$= 0.11 = 11\%.$$

For an investment to be attractive, the expected return must be equal to or exceed the investor's required return. (Specification of the required return is deferred until

---

[6] The expected dividend to be received during the year (D_1) is the current dividend (D_0) plus the annual growth in that dividend. That is,

$$D_1 = D_0(1 + g).$$

If the current dividend is $0.944 and grows annually at the rate of 7 percent, then the expected dividend is

$$\$0.944(1 + 0.07) = \$1.$$

later in this chapter.) If an individual requires an 11 percent return on investments in common stock of comparable risk, then this stock meets the investor's requirement. If, however, the investor's required rate of return is in excess of 11 percent, the anticipated yield on this stock is inferior, and the investor will not purchase the shares. Conversely, if the required rate of return on comparable investments in common stock is 10 percent, this particular stock is an excellent purchase because the anticipated return exceeds the required rate of return.

Effect of commissions

In a world of no commission fees, investors should be indifferent to the composition of their return. An investor seeking an 11 percent return should be willing to accept a dividend yield of zero if the capital gain is 11 percent. Conversely, a capital growth rate of zero should be acceptable if the dividend yield is 11 percent. Of course, any combination of growth rate and dividend yield with an 11 percent return should be acceptable.

Because of commissions the investor may be concerned with the composition of the return. To realize the growth in the value of the shares, the investor must sell the security and pay commission fees. This cost suggests a preference for dividend yield. In addition, capital gains occur in the future and may be less certain than the flow of current dividends. The uncertainty of future capital gains versus the likelihood of current dividends also favors dividends over capital appreciation.

Investors have different goals

Since each investor's situation and financial goals are different, it is not surprising that the composition of the required rate of return for various investors is different. Retired people may prefer a dividend yield for the income it provides. Investors with other sources of income who are in the top income tax bracket may prefer growth and capital gains, since the tax is deferred until the shares are sold. And any investor who wishes to reduce risk may prefer dividends to capital growth.

Since the required rates of return differ among investors and since the individual's financial needs and goals change, it is not surprising to find investors making changes in their portfolios. It is the role of security markets to bring these buyers and sellers together so that their portfolio changes can be consummated.

VALUATION AS THE PRESENT VALUE OF DIVIDENDS AND THE GROWTH OF EARNINGS

As with the valuation of debt, the valuation of stock involves bringing future cash flows (e.g., dividends) back to the present at the appropriate discount factor. For the individual investor, that discount factor is the **required rate of return,** which is the return the investor demands to justify purchasing the stock. This return includes what the investor may earn on a risk-free security (e.g., a treasury bill) plus a premium for bearing the risk associated with investments in common stock. The anticipated return must equal or exceed the investor's required rate of return. The process of valuation and security selection is similar to comparing expected and required returns, except the emphasis is placed on determining what the investor believes the security is worth. Future cash flows are discounted back to the present at the required rate of return. The resulting valuation is then compared with the stock's current price to determine if the stock is under- or overvalued.

This process of valuation and security selection is readily illustrated by the simple case in which the stock pays a fixed dividend (D) that is not expected to grow. If the investor's required rate of return is r, then the stock's valuation (V) is

Discounting future cash flows

$$V = \frac{D}{(1+r)^1} + \frac{D}{(1+r)^2} + \cdots + \frac{D}{(1+r)^\infty} \,, \tag{14.2}$$

which simplifies to

$$V = \frac{D}{r} \,. \tag{14.3}$$

If a stock pays a dividend of $1 and the investor's required rate of return is 12 percent, then the valuation is

$$\frac{\$1}{0.12} = \$8.33.$$

Any price greater than $8.33 will result in a yield that is less than 12 percent. Therefore, for this investor to achieve the required rate of return of 12 percent, the price of the stock must not exceed $8.33.

Valuation with fixed dividends

The student has probably recognized that the preceding valuation is identical to the valuation of perpetual debt and preferred stock presented in Chapters 10 and 11. If the common stock's dividend were fixed and expected to be paid indefinitely, then common stock would be the same as preferred stock for the purpose of valuation. Its value would be related only to the dividend and the required rate of return. If the dividend were fixed, the value of the stock would change with fluctuations in the required rate of return (i.e., the rate earned on comparable investments).

However, the dividend for common stock is not fixed. It is the potential for growth, both in value and in dividends, that differentiates common from preferred stock. If the investor expects the dividend to grow at some fixed rate (g) for an indefinite period, the **dividend-growth valuation model** becomes

The valuation model when dividends grow

$$V = \frac{D(1+g)^1}{(1+r)^1} + \frac{D(1+g)^2}{(1+r)^2} + \frac{D(1+g)^3}{(1+r)^3} + \cdots + \frac{D(1+g)^\infty}{(1+r)^\infty} \,, \tag{14.4}$$

which simplifies to

$$V = \frac{D_0(1+g)}{r-g}. \tag{14.5}$$

The stock's intrinsic value is thus related to (1) the current dividend, (2) the growth in earnings and dividends, and (3) the required rate of return.[7] Notice the current dividend is D_0 with the subscript 0 representing the present. The application of this dividend-growth model may be illustrated by a simple example. If the investor's

[7] For a derivation of this equation, see Eugene F. Brigham, *Financial Management—Theory and Practice*, 4th ed. (Hinsdale, Ill.: The Dryden Press, 1985), 175. The model assumes that the required rate of return exceeds the rate of growth (i.e., $r > g$).

required rate of return is 12 percent and the stock is currently paying a $1 per share dividend and is growing at 6 percent annually, the stock's value is

$$V = \frac{\$1(1 + 0.06)}{0.12 - 0.06} = \$17.67.$$

Overvaluation

Any price greater than $17.67 will result in a total yield of less than 12 percent. Conversely, a price of less than $17.67 will produce a return in excess of 12 percent. For example, if the price is $20, according to Equation 14.1 the expected return is

$$\text{Expected return} = \frac{\$1(1 + 0.06)}{\$20} + 0.06$$

$$= 11.3\%.$$

Since this return is less than the 12 percent required by the investor, it is inferior. Therefore, this investor would not buy the stock and would sell it if he or she owned it.

Undervaluation

If the price is $15, the expected return is

$$\text{Expected return} = \frac{\$1(1 + 0.06)}{\$15} + 0.06$$

$$= 13.1\%.$$

This return is greater than the 12 percent required by the investor. Since the security offers a superior return, it is undervalued. This investor then would try to buy it.

Only at a price of $17.67 does the stock offer a return of 12 percent. At that price it equals the rate of return available on alternative investments of the same risk. The investment will yield 12 percent because the dividend yield during the year is 6 percent and the earnings and dividends are growing annually at the rate of 6 percent. These relationships are illustrated in Figure 14.1, which shows the growth in dividends and prices of the stock that will produce a constant yield of 12 percent. After 12 years the dividend will have grown to $2.02, and the price of the stock will be $35.55. The total return on this investment will still be 12 percent. During that year the dividend will grow to $2.14, giving a 6 percent dividend yield, and the price will continue to appreciate annually at the 6 percent growth rate in earnings and dividends.

The student should note that in Figure 14.1 the lines representing the dividend and the price of the stock are curved. The earnings and the price of the stock are growing at the same rate, but they are not growing by the same amount each year. This is another illustration of the time value of money, as the earnings, dividends, and prices of the stock are all compounding annually at 6 percent.

Earnings may fluctuate

A firm's earnings need not grow steadily at this rate. Figure 14.2 illustrates a case in which the firm's earnings grow annually at an average of 6 percent, but the year-to-year changes stray considerably from 6 percent. These fluctuations are not in themselves necessarily reason for concern. The firm does exist within the economic environment, which fluctuates over time. Exogenous factors, such as a strike or an energy curtailment, may also affect earnings during a particular year. If these factors continue to plague the firm, they will obviously play an important role in the valuation of the shares. However, the emphasis in valuation is on the flow of dividends and

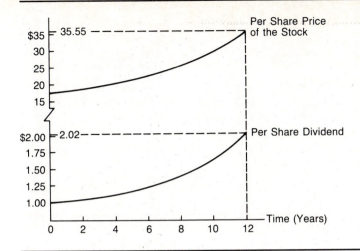

Figure 14.1
Earnings, Dividends, and Price of Stock over Time Yielding 12 Percent Annually

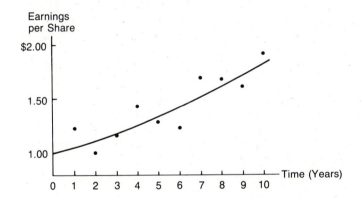

Figure 14.2
Earnings Growth Averaging 6 Percent Annually

the growth in earnings over a period of years. This longer time dimension smooths out temporary fluctuations in earnings and dividends.

Modifications in the dividend growth model

Although the previous model assumes that the firm's earnings will grow indefinitely and that the dividend policy will be maintained, such need not be the case. The model may be modified to encompass a period of increasing or declining growth or one of stable earnings. Many possible variations in growth patterns can be built into the model. Although these variations change the equation and make it appear far more complex, the fundamentals of valuation remain unaltered. Valuation is still the process of discounting future dividends and growth in earnings and dividends back to the present at the appropriate discount rate.

To illustrate such a variation, consider the following pattern of expected earnings and dividends.

Year	Earnings	Yearly Dividends	Change in Earnings and Dividends from Previous Year
1	$1.00	$0.40	. . .
2	1.60	0.64	60%
3	1.94	0.77	21
4	2.20	0.87	12
5	2.29	0.91	4
6	2.38	0.95	4
7	2.47	0.98	4

After the initial period of rapid growth, the firm matures and is expected to grow annually at the rate of 4 percent. Each year the firm pays dividends, which contribute to its current value. However, the simple model summarized in Equation 14.5 cannot be used, because the earnings and dividends are not growing at a constant rate. Equation 14.4 can be used, and when these values, along with a required rate of return of 12 percent, are inserted into the equation, the value of the stock is

$$V = \frac{\$0.40}{(1 + 0.12)^1} + \frac{\$0.64}{(1 + 0.12)^2} + \frac{\$0.77}{(1 + 0.12)^3} + \frac{\$0.87}{(1 + 0.12)^4}$$

$$+ \frac{\$0.91}{(1 + 0.12)^5} + \frac{\$0.95}{(1 + 0.12)^6} + \frac{\$0.98}{(1 + 0.12)^7} + \cdots$$

$$= \$9.16.$$

This answer is derived by dividing the flow of dividends into two periods: a period of super growth (years 1 through 4) and a period of normal growth (from year 5 on). The present value of the dividends in the first four years is

$$V_{1-4} = \frac{\$0.40}{(1 + 0.12)^1} + \frac{\$0.64}{(1 + 0.12)^2} + \frac{\$0.77}{(1 + 0.12)^3} + \frac{\$0.87}{(1 + 0.12)^4}$$

$$= \$0.36 + \$0.51 + 0.55 + \$0.55$$

$$= \$1.97.$$

The dividend growth model is applied to the dividends from year 5 on, so the value of the dividends during normal growth is

$$V_{5-\infty} = \frac{\$0.87(1 + 0.04)}{0.12 - 0.04} = \$11.31.$$

This $11.31 is the value at the end of year 4, so it must be discounted back to the present to determine the current value of this stream of dividend payments. That is,

$$\frac{\$11.31}{(1 + 0.12)^4} = \$11.31(0.636) = \$7.19.$$

The value of the stock, then, is the sum of the two parts[8]:

$$V = V_{1-4} + V_{5-\infty}$$

$$= \$1.97 + 7.19 = \$9.16.$$

As this example illustrates, modifications can be made in this valuation model to account for the different periods of growth and dividends. Adjustments can also be made for differences in risk. The student should realize that the model does not by itself adjust for different degrees of risk. If a security analyst applies the model to several firms to determine which stocks are underpriced, there is the implication that investing in all of the firms involves equal risk. If the analyst uses the same required rate of return for each firm, then no risk adjustment has been made. The element of risk is assumed to be equal for each company.

Assumptions concerning risk

THE INVESTOR'S REQUIRED RETURN, RISK, AND SECURITY VALUATION

The valuation model presented in the preceding section does not explicitly include specification of the required rate of return (r). This required rate of return depends on the return that may be earned on alternative investments and the risk associated with the particular security. Stocks are not equally risky, and presumably the investor will seek a higher return (i.e., a higher r) from those that are riskier.

One means to adjust for risk is to incorporate into the valuation model the beta coefficients presented earlier in Chapter 8. This adjustment is called the **capital asset pricing model** or **CAPM**. In this model, the required return is divided into two components: the risk-free return that the investor could earn on a risk-free security (e.g., a U.S. Treasury bill) and a risk premium. This risk-adjusted required return (r) for a stock is expressed in Equation 14.6.

CAPM

$$r = \text{Risk-free return} + \text{Risk premium}.$$

(14.6)

The risk premium is also composed of two components: (1) the additional return that investing in securities offers above the risk-free rate, and (2) the volatility of the particular security relative to the market as a whole. The volatility of the individual

Risk premium depends on beta coefficient

---

[8] This valuation procedure may be summarized by the following general equation:

$$V = V_s + V_n.$$

V_s is the present value of the dividends during the period of super growth; that is,

$$V_s = \sum_{t=1}^{n} \frac{D_0(1 + g_s)^t}{(1 + r)^t}$$

V_n is the present value of the dividends during the period of normal growth; that is,

$$V_n = \left[\frac{D_n(1 + g)}{r - g}\right]\left(\frac{1}{(1 + r)^n}\right).$$

The value of the stock is the sum of the individual present values; that is,

$$V = \sum_{t=1}^{n} \frac{D_0(1 + g_s)^t}{(1 + r)^t} + \left[\frac{D_n(1 + g)}{r - g}\right]\left(\frac{1}{(1 + r)^n}\right)$$

stock is measured by the beta coefficient (β), and the additional return is measured by the difference between the expected return on the market (R_m) and the risk-free rate (R_f). This differential ($R_m - R_f$) is the risk premium that is required to induce individuals in general to purchase risky securities, and in more advanced literature on investments it is called the "market price of risk."

To induce an investor to purchase a particular security, the risk premium associated with the market must be adjusted by the risk associated with the individual security. This risk is measured by the beta coefficient, which indicates the stock's volatility relative to the market. The total risk adjustment is achieved by multiplying the security's beta coefficient by the difference between the expected return on the market and the risk-free rate. Thus the risk premium for the individual stock is

(14.7) $$\text{Risk premium} = (R_m - R_f)\beta.$$

That is, the risk premium required of a stock is the product of its beta coefficient times the difference between what can be earned by investing in risky securities and what can be earned on a risk-free security such as a treasury bill.

The total return required for investing in a particular stock is found by substituting this risk premium into Equation 14.6, which yields

(14.8) $$r = R_f + (R_m - R_f)\beta.$$

Two examples of return

The following examples show how this equation is employed. The risk-free rate is 9 percent and it is anticipated that the market will rise by 12 percent. Stock A is relatively risky and has a beta coefficient of 1.8, while stock B is relatively safe and has a beta of 0.83. What return is necessary to justify purchasing either stock? Certainly it would not be correct to require a return of 12 percent for either, since that is the expected return on the market. Since stock A is riskier than the market, the required return for A should exceed 12 percent. However, the required return for B should be less than 12 percent because it is less risky than the market as a whole.

Given the above information concerning the risk-free rate and the anticipated return on the market, the required rates of return for stocks A and B are

$$r_A = 9\% + (12\% - 9\%)1.8 = 9\% + 5.4\% = 14.4\%$$

and

$$r_B = 9\% + (12\% - 9\%).83 = 9\% + 2.5\% = 11.5\%.$$

Thus the required rates of return for stocks A and B are 14.4 percent and 11.5 percent, respectively. These required returns are different from each other and from the expected return on the market, because the analysis now explicitly takes into consideration risk (i.e., the volatility of the individual stock relative to the market). Stock A's required rate of return is greater than the expected return on the market (14.4 percent versus 12 percent) because stock A is more volatile than the market. Stock B's required rate of return is less than the return expected for the market (11.5 percent versus 12 percent) because stock B is less volatile than the market as a whole.

Determination of security market line

The relationship between the required rate of return and risk expressed in Equation 14.8 is illustrated in Figure 14.3. The horizontal axis represents risk as measured by the beta coefficient, and the vertical axis measures the required rate of return. Line

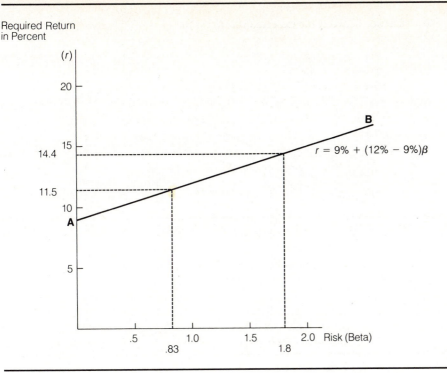

Required Return
in Percent

Figure 14.3
**Relationship between
Risk and Required Rate
of Return**

$r = 9\% + (12\% - 9\%)\beta$

AB represents the required rates of return associated with each level of risk. Line *AB*
uses the information given in the above example: the *y* intercept is the risk-free return
(9 percent), and the slope of the line is the difference between the market return and
the risk-free return (12 percent minus 9 percent). If the beta coefficient were 1.8, the
figure indicates that the required rate of return would be 14.4 percent; if the beta
coefficient were 0.83, the required rate of return would be 11.5 percent.

The security market line will change if the variables that are used to construct it
change. For example, if the expected rate of return on the market were to increase
from 12 percent to 14 percent and there was no simultaneous change in the risk-free
rate, then *AB* would pivot to *AC* in Figure 14.4. At each beta the required rate of return is increased. For example, the required rate of return for a stock with a beta of
1.8 now rises from 14.4 percent to 18 percent, and the required rate of return for a
stock with a beta of 0.83 increases from 11.5 percent to 13.2 percent.

How this risk-adjusted discount rate may be applied to the valuation of a specific
stock is illustrated by the following example. From 1979 through 1984, Continental
Telephone's dividend rose from $1.33 to $1.72. This yields an annual compound
growth rate of approximately 5 percent. According to the *Value Line Investment Survey,*
the stock has a beta of 0.75. As of November 10, 1984, U.S. Treasury bills of six-
month duration offered a risk-free return of 9.4 percent. If an investor anticipated that
the market would rise annually at a compound rate of 15.4 percent (i.e., about 6 per-

*Application of risk-
adjusted required return*

**Figure 14.4
Relationship between
Risk and Required Rate
of Return**

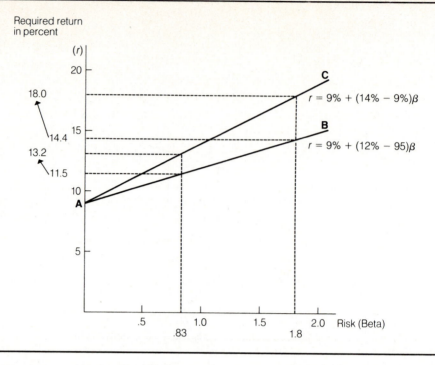

centage points more than the risk-free rate)[9] and that the Continental Telephone dividend growth would continue indefinitely at 5 percent, what would be the maximum price this investor should pay for the stock?

The first step in answering the question is to determine the risk-adjusted required rate of return for Continental Telephone.

$$r = R_f + (R_m - R_f)\beta$$
$$= 0.094 + (0.154 - 0.094)0.75$$
$$= 0.139.$$

Next this risk-adjusted required rate of return is used in the dividend-growth model presented above:

$$V = \frac{D_0(1 + g)}{r - g}$$

$$= \frac{\$1.72(1 + 0.05)}{0.139 - 0.05}$$

$$= \$20.29.$$

[9]Ibbotson and Sinquefield found that over a period of years stocks have yielded a return of 6.1 percent in excess of the return on U.S. Treasury bills. Thus if bills are yielding 13.7 percent, an expected return on the market of 18 percent is not excessive and may even be low. See Roger G. Ibbotson and Rex A. Sinquefield, *Stocks, Bonds, Bills, and Inflation: The Past (1926–1976) and the Future (1977–2000)*. This material is reprinted in J. C. Francis, C. Lee, and D. E. Farrar, eds., *Readings in Investments* (New York: McGraw-Hill, 1980).

POINTS OF INTEREST
Inflation and the Investor's Required Return

While inflation is not explicitly part of the equation for the required rate of return, it is implicitly included. Anticipation of inflation will increase the rate on treasury bills and the required return on the market. Higher rates of inflation will increase the T-bill rate as (1) the Federal Reserve takes steps to reduce inflation and (2) individuals seek to protect themselves by investing only if yields are sufficiently high to compensate them for the anticipated inflation.

A higher T-bill rate will result in an increase in the required return on the market. Investors certainly will not buy risky securities in general if their return declines relative to the T-bill rate. Increases in the T-bill rate must lead to correspond-

ing increases in the required return on the market. The net effect will be to increase the required rate of return on an investment in common stock. For example, suppose the expected rate of inflation rises by 2 percent from 4 to 6 percent, which, in turn, causes the T-bill rate to rise from 6 to 8 percent and the required return on the market to increase from 12 to 14 percent. If a stock has a beta of 1.2, the required return rises from

$$r = 0.06 + (0.12 - 0.06)1.2 = 13.2\%$$

to

$$r = 0.08 + (0.14 - 0.08)1.2 = 15.2\%.$$

As of November 10, 1984, the price of Continental Telephone stock was $21¼. Thus, according to the dividend growth valuation model, the stock was slightly overpriced and should not be bought.

While this procedure does bring a risk adjustment into the valuation model, it should be remembered that the results or conclusions can only be as good as the data employed. This model and others presented in this text are theoretically sound, but their accuracy depends on the data used. The possibility of inaccurate data should be obvious in the valuation model. Any of the estimates (i.e., the growth rate, the expected return on the market, the beta coefficient) may be incorrect, in which case the resulting valuation would be incorrect. For example, if Continental Telephone's expected growth rate were increased from 5 percent to 7 percent, the effect would be to raise the valuation from $20.29 to $26.67. At a valuation of $26.67, the stock appears to be undervalued and would be a good purchase.

The problem of inaccurate data does not mean that the use of models in financial decision making is undesirable. Without such models there would be no means to value an asset. Hunches, intuition, or just plain guessing would then be used to value and select assets. By using theoretical models, the financial manager is forced to identify real economic forces (e.g., earnings and growth rates) and alternatives (e.g., the risk-free rate and the return earned by the market as a whole). Even if the analysis may sometimes be inaccurate, it is still fundamentally sound and should prove better than random guessing or intuitive feelings.

RELATIONSHIP BETWEEN THE VALUATION MODEL AND P/E RATIOS

An alternative means to valuing common stock is to estimate future earnings and then to multiply the estimated earnings by a P/E ratio. For example, suppose the financial analyst determines that the firm will earn $4.50 next year. If the appropriate P/E ratio is 10, then the future price of the stock should be $45. Obviously, if the price of the stock is $35, it would appear to be a good purchase.

The use of a P/E approach to valuation and security selection is often found in the financial press (if not the academic press). The crux of the analysis is (1) the appropriate P/E ratio and (2) the determination of future earnings. Since many stocks tend to trade within a range of P/E ratios, it would seem appropriate to maintain this range. If the stock of Merck has had P/E ratios ranging from 18 to 10, it would be inappropriate to suggest the ratio should be 25 or 7. Unless there has been a fundamental change in the firm, the financial analyst can anticipate the P/E ratio to remain within its historic range.

The second problem is estimating earnings. As will be illustrated in the section on ratio analysis, the financial analyst may compute many ratios based on data found in a firm's financial statements that may help to identify trends and weaknesses within the firm. By combining analysis of the firm's financial statements, its position within its industry, and the direction of the economy, the financial analyst may be able to forecast future earnings. These forecasts are then combined with the P/E ratio to estimate the stock's future price. If, for example, the forecasted earnings are $4.00 and the firm's P/E ratio has ranged from 8 to 12, this suggests that the price of the stock could reach as high as $48 but would not fall below $32.

An alternative method using P/E ratios is to divide the forecasted earnings by the current price to express the P/E ratio in terms of future earnings. For example, suppose the stock was selling for $33 when the estimated earnings were $4.00. The P/E ratio using the estimated earnings is 8.25, which is at the low end of the 8 to 12 range. This suggests that the stock may be undervalued and there is little risk that its price will decline. If the appropriate P/E ratio is believed to be 10, the stock is underpriced in terms of future earnings. As those earnings are achieved, the price should rise from $33 to $40. From this analysis, the stock is undervalued and should be purchased.

While the use of forecasted earnings and P/E ratios seems considerably different from the dividend-growth model presented in the previous section, they are essentially very similar. The dividend-growth model was

$$V = \frac{D_0(1 + g)}{r - g}.$$

Since the firm's current dividend (D_0) is related to its current earnings (E_0) and the proportion of the earnings that are distributed (d), then

$$D_0 = dE_0.$$

When this is substituted back into the dividend-growth model, the model becomes

$$V = \frac{dE_0(1 + g)}{r - g}.$$

POINTS OF INTEREST
Obtaining Earnings Forecasts

To apply P/E ratio analysis, the individual needs forecasts of earnings. It is probably safe to assume that individual investors do not want to construct their own forecasts, so where can these estimates be obtained? There are several answers. Many brokerage firms have estimates for specific companies. The *Value Line Investment Survey* gives esti-

mates for the stocks it covers. Standard & Poor's publishes an earnings forecaster, and *Forbes* periodically publishes earnings estimates that are averages of several earnings forecasts. *Forbes* also gives the number of and the variation in the original estimates from which it compiles its averages.

If both sides of the equation are divided by earnings (E_0), the stock's valuation is expressed as a P/E ratio:

$$\frac{V}{E_0} = \frac{d(1 + g)}{r - g}.$$

From this perspective, a P/E ratio depends on the same fundamental financial variables as the stock's valuation achieved through use of the dividend-growth model.

The use of P/E ratios instead of the dividend-growth model offers one major advantage and one major disadvantage. The advantage is that P/E ratios may be applied to common stocks that are not currently paying cash dividends. The dividend-growth model assumes that the firm will eventually pay cash dividends and that it is these future dividends that give the stock current value. The major weakness of the use of P/E ratios is that these ratios do not tell the analyst if the security is under- or overvalued. Instead the analysis indicates whether the firm's stock is selling near its historic high or low P/E ratio and then draws an inference from this information. The dividend-growth model establishes a value based on the investor's required rate of return, the firm's dividends, and the future growth in those dividends. This valuation is then compared to the actual price to answer the question of whether the stock is under- or overvalued.

THE IMPACT OF FINANCIAL LEVERAGE ON EARNINGS

Financial leverage is the use of another person's money in return for a fixed payment. If a firm borrows funds, it issues debt and must make a fixed interest payment for the use of the money. A company may also obtain financial leverage by paying a fixed dividend on stock. This type of stock is given preference or prior claim on the earnings of the company (i.e., it is preferred stock). Since preferred stock has a fixed dividend, it is similar to debt and is a source of financial leverage.

The use of debt financing

A firm agrees to make fixed interest and dividend payments because it *anticipates* being able to earn more with the borrowed funds than it has to pay in interest to its creditors. This will increase the return on the common stockholders' investment. The creditors are willing to lend the money in return for the fixed payments because they receive a relatively assured flow of income from the loans but do not bear the risk of owning and operating the business. If the creditors had the skills and desired to do so, they would enter the business themselves. There are, however, many people who lack either the skills or the desire to enter a particular business and who are satisfied to let a corporation use their money for the promised fixed return. They are, of course, aware that the firm anticipates earning more with their money than it has agreed to pay.

Management wants to increase the value of the stock

Management wants to increase the value of the firm's stock. Since the use of financial leverage may increase the return on the common stockholders' equity, management may decide to use financial leverage. Its use, however, may also increase the level of risk. Thus, management must try to determine the optimal amount of financial leverage, for the use of insufficient leverage will decrease the stockholders' return on equity but the use of excessive leverage will subject the stockholders to excessive risk.

How Financial Leverage Increases the Rate of Return on Equity

How financial leverage works may be shown by a simple illustration. Firm A needs $100 in capital to operate and may acquire the money from the stockholders (owners) of the firm. Alternatively, it may acquire part of the money from stockholders and part from creditors. If management acquires the total amount from the owners, the firm uses no debt financing (financial leverage) and would have the following simple balance sheet.

The firm without leverage

Assets	Liabilities and Equity
Cash $100	Debt $0
	Equity $100

Once in business, the firm generates the following simplified income statement:

Sales	$100
Expenses	−80
Operating profit	$ 20
Taxes (40%)	− 8
Net profit	$ 12

What is the return that the firm has earned on the owners' investment? The answer is 12 percent, for the investors contributed $100 and the firm earned $12 after taxes. The firm may pay the $12 to the investors in cash dividends or may retain the money to help finance future growth. Either way, however, the stockholders' rate of return on their investment is 12 percent.

By using financial leverage, management may be able to increase the owners' rate of return on their investment. What happens to their rate of return if management is

able to borrow part of the capital needed to operate the firm? The answer to this question depends on (1) the proportion of total capital that is borrowed and (2) the interest rate that must be paid to the creditors. If management is able to borrow 50 percent ($50) of the firm's capital needs at an interest cost of 10 percent, the balance sheet becomes

Assets	Liabilities and Equity
Cash $100	Debt $50
	Equity $50

The firm with leverage

Since the firm borrowed $50, it is now obligated to pay interest. Thus, the firm has a new expense that must be paid before any earnings are available for the common stockholders. The simple income statement becomes

Sales	$100
Expenses	−80
Operating profit	$ 20
Interest expense	− 5
Taxable income	$ 15
Taxes	− 6
Net Profit	$ 9

The use of debt causes the total net profit to decline from $12 to $9 but the owners' return on equity increases from 12 percent to 18 percent. Since the owners invested only $50 and earned $9 on that amount, they made 18 percent on their investment, whereas without the use of leverage they earned only 12 percent on their $100 investment.

There are two sources of this additional return. First, the firm borrowed money and agreed to pay a fixed return of 10 percent. The firm, however, was able to earn more than 10 percent with the money, and this additional earning accrued to the owners of the firm. Second, the entire burden of the interest cost was not borne by the firm. The federal tax laws permit the deduction of interest as an expense before taxable income is determined, and thus this interest expense is shared with the government. The greater the corporate income tax rate, the greater is the portion of interest expense borne by the government. In this case 40 percent, or $2 of the $5 interest expense, was borne by the federal government in lost tax revenues. If the corporate income tax rate were 60 percent, the government would lose $3 in taxes by permitting the deduction of the interest expense.

The impact of taxes

As was seen in the preceding example, a firm's management may increase the owners' return on equity through the use of debt financing, that is, the use of financial leverage. By increasing the proportion of the firm's assets that are financed by debt (by increasing the debt ratio), management is able to increase the return on the owners' equity. Exhibit 14.2 shows various combinations of debt and equity financing, along with the resultant earnings for the firm and the return on the investors' equity. The exhibit is constructed on the assumption that the interest rate is 10 percent regardless of the proportion of the firm's assets financed by debt. As may be seen from Exhibit 14.2, as the proportion of debt financing rises, the return on the owners' equity not

Exhibit 14.2
Relationship Between Debt Financing and the Rate of Return on Equity

Proportion of assets financed by debt (%)	0	20	50	70	90
Amount of debt outstanding ($)	0.00	20.00	50.00	70.00	90.00
Equity ($)	100.00	80.00	50.00	30.00	10.00
Sales ($)	100.00	100.00	100.00	100.00	100.00
Expense ($)	−80.00	−80.00	−80.00	−80.00	−80.00
Operating profit ($)	20.00	20.00	20.00	20.00	20.00
Interest expense ($) (10% interest rate)	0.00	2.00	5.00	7.00	9.00
Taxable income ($)	20.00	18.00	15.00	13.00	11.00
Income tax ($) (40% tax rate)	−8.00	−7.20	−6.00	−5.20	−4.40
Net profit ($)	12.00	10.80	9.00	7.80	6.60
Rate of return on equity (%)	12.00	13.50	18.00	26.00	66.00

only rises but does so at an increasing rate. This indicates dramatically how the use of financial leverage may significantly increase the return on a firm's equity.

Impact on per-share earnings

Besides the possible increase in the return on stockholders' funds, the use of financial leverage may also increase earnings per share. While total earnings declined in the preceding example when the firm borrowed funds, earnings per share would probably rise. This is because the firm is using less equity financing and therefore would have to issue fewer shares. The smaller earnings would be spread over a smaller number of shares, which may cause earnings per share to increase. However, as is subsequently explained, the increased per-share earnings may not necessarily lead to higher stock prices.

Financial Leverage and Risk

The use of financial leverage increases risk

Since the use of financial leverage increases the owners' return on equity, why not use ever-increasing amounts of debt financing? The answer is that as the proportion of debt financing rises, the element of risk increases. This amplification of risk increases (1) the potential for fluctuations in the owners' returns and (2) the interest rate that the creditors charge for the use of their money.

How the use of financial leverage increases the potential risk to the owners is illustrated by employing the simple example presented in the previous section. What happens to the return on the equity if sales decline by 10 percent, from $100 to $90, but expenses remain the same? The income statements for a firm with and a firm without financial leverage become:

	Firm without Leverage (0% Debt)	Firm with Leverage (50% Debt)
Sales	$ 90	$ 90
Expenses	− 80	− 80
Operating profit	$ 10	$ 10
Interest	− 0	− 5
Taxable income	$ 10	$ 5
Taxes	− 4	− 2
Net profit	$ 6	$ 3

POINTS OF INTEREST
A Subtle Means to Hide the Use of Financial Leverage

While the use of financial leverage (debt financing) may increase a firm's per-share earnings, it may also increase risk. Thus management may not wish to show the extent to which the firm has borrowed funds. Some firms are able to hide the use of debt by off-balance sheet financing. For example, Ford Motor Company's sources of financing as reported in its 1985 consolidated balance sheet and their percent of the total were as follows:

Current liabilities (in millions)	$12,777.4	40.4%
Long-term debt	2,157.2	6.8
Other liabilities and deferred taxes	4,400.4	13.9
Equity	12,268.6	38.8

Equity accounted for 38.8 percent, while debt and deferred tax obligations accounted for the remaining 61.2 percent.

Ford Motor owns 100 percent of a subsidiary,

Ford Motor Credit Company, which provides financing to dealers and buyers for installment sales of automobiles and trucks. The credit company's $31.3 billion in assets were primarily financed by $28.7 in debt. Since the subsidiary is wholly owned by Ford Motor Company, the parent must ultimately be responsible for the timely payment of interest and principal.

Ford Motor Company does not consolidate this subsidiary into its accounting statements, so the debt does not appear on the parent company's balance sheet. Instead the information is reported in a footnote. This off-balance sheet financing hides Ford's true use of financial leverage. However, a thorough reading of the financial statements clearly reveals this debt financing. The information is certainly available to the individual who makes the effort to read the footnotes.

The 10 percent decline in sales produces a substantial decline in the earnings and return on the owners' investment in both cases. For the firm without debt financing, the return on equity declines to 6 percent ($6 ÷ $100); for the firm with financial leverage, the return plummets from the 18 percent in the previous example to 6 percent. The decline is greater when financial leverage is used than when it is not.

Earnings may decline more rapidly

The return decreased more for the firm with financial leverage because of the interest payment. When the firm borrowed the capital, it agreed to make a *fixed* interest payment. This fixed interest payment was the source of the increase in the owners' return on equity in the second example when sales were $100, and it is the cause of the larger decline in the owners' return on equity when the firm's sales declined from $100 to $90. If the firm had used leverage to a greater extent (i.e., if it had borrowed more), the decline in the rate of return on the owners' investment would have been even greater. As the proportion of a firm's assets financed by fixed obligations increases, the potential fluctuation in the stockholders' return on equity also increases. Small changes in revenue or costs will produce greater fluctuations in the earnings of a firm with a considerable amount of financial leverage.

Firms that use large amounts of financial leverage are viewed by investors (both creditors and stockholders) as being risky. Creditors may refuse to lend to a firm that uses debt financing extensively, or they may do so only at higher interest rates or

An increase in risk may cause the price of the stock to fall

under more stringent loan conditions. Equity investors will also require a higher return to justify bearing the risk. As is explained in the next section, this increase in the required rate of return may result in a decline in the value of the stock.

Financial Leverage and Valuation

Since financial leverage may increase earnings per share and the return on equity, investors may be willing to pay more for the stock. For example, for a particular required rate of return on an investment, an increase in earnings from $1 to $1.20 per share should increase the value of the stock. If the investor desires a set return and the firm earns more, the investor should be willing to pay more for the stock.

This concept can be illustrated by the use of Equation 14.5. The risk-free rate is 7.0 percent, and the investor expects the market to rise by 13.0 percent. If the beta coefficient is 0.83, the required rate of return is 12.0 percent (i.e., $r = 0.07 + (0.13 - 0.07) 0.83 = 0.12$). If the firm earns $1 before using financial leverage, distributes $0.60, and retains the remaining $0.40 so that it can grow, the value of the stock is

$$V = \frac{\$0.60 \ (1 + 0.05)}{0.12 - 0.05}$$

$$= \$9$$

when the required rate of return is 12 percent and the firm is able to grow annually at the rate of 5 percent.

If the firm now successfully uses financial leverage to increase earnings per share, it can increase its dividend *without* reducing its ability to grow, or it can increase its growth rate without decreasing its cash dividend. If the firm's per-share earnings rise to $1.20 and the additional $0.20 is distributed as cash dividends (i.e., cash dividends rise to $0.80), the value of the stock is

$$V = \frac{\$0.80 \ (1 + 0.05)}{0.12 - 0.05}$$

$$= \$12.$$

Thus, the successful use of financial leverage results in an increase in the value of the stock.

The potential impact on the required rate of return

The use of financial leverage, however, may increase the element of risk because per-share earnings and the return to stockholders become more variable. Therefore, to induce investors to bear this additional risk, the return must be larger. Suppose the beta coefficient rises to 1.17 because earnings are more volatile. The required rate of return rises to 14 percent (i.e., $r = 0.07 + (0.13 - 0.07) 1.17 = 0.14$). The required return, then, has increased as a result of the additional risk, which is attributable to the use of an increased amount of financial leverage.

The potential impact of this increase in the required rate of return may be illustrated by the preceding example. The cash dividends have increased to $0.80 as a result of the use of financial leverage but the required rate of return has increased from 12 percent to 14 percent. The value of the stock becomes

$$P = \frac{\$0.80 \ (1 + 0.05)}{0.14 - 0.05}$$

$$= \$9.33.$$

Although the value of the stock does rise (from $9 to $9.33), the amount of the increase is small. The increase in the required rate of return that occurred when the firm used more financial leverage almost completely offset the increase in value from the higher per-share earnings and higher cash dividends.

The use of financial leverage may not result in an increase in the value of stock. Although more financial leverage may result in higher per-share earnings, it may also cause investors' required rate of return to rise. This increase in the required rate of return will certainly offset part, if not all, of the effect of the increase in per-share earnings. It is even possible that the value of the stock will decline if the required rate of return increases sufficiently.

Management, then, must be concerned with the extent to which the firm uses debt financing. One goal of management is to increase the value of the shares, but the extensive use of financial leverage may have the opposite effect and cause the value of the firm's stock to decline. Therefore, management must determine that combination of debt and equity financing that offers the benefits of financial leverage without unduly increasing the element of risk. Such a capital structure of debt and equity should help to maximize the value of the firm's stock.[10]

Management should strive for the optimal combination of debt and equity financing

Differences in the Amount of Financial Leverage Used by Firms

Although virtually every firm uses financial leverage, there are differences in the extent to which it is used. For some firms, the nature of the business enterprise necessitates the extensive use of financial leverage, and this influences the behavior of the firms in the industry. For example, commercial banks use a large amount of financial leverage because most of their assets are financed by their deposit liabilities (e.g., checking accounts). Slight changes in the revenues of a commercial bank may produce greater fluctuations in the earnings. Bankers are well aware of this effect of financial leverage and are usually not willing to take inordinate risks. The nature of a bank's operations and the high use of financial leverage require bankers to be conservative.

Some industries inherently use a substantial amount of financial leverage

Other firms need large amounts of fixed equipment to operate and may use leverage extensively if this equipment is financed through the issuance of debt. The airlines are an excellent example of an industry that has a large investment in equipment frequently financed by debt. This, in part, explains the large fluctuations in the earnings of airline companies. Exhibit 14.3 presents the earnings per share (EPS) for selected airlines and the proportion of their assets financed by debt. The information in this exhibit indicates that there have been large and sudden fluctuations in the earnings per share of these airlines. These fluctuations are the result of changes in the demand for and in the cost to provide the service, and they are magnified by the use of debt

Management may choose to use a substantial amount of financial leverage

---

[10] For a discussion of a firm's optimal capital structure, see Eugene Brigham, *Financial Management—Theory and Practice*, 4th ed. (Hinsdale, Ill.: The Dryden Press, 1985), 448–472.

Exhibit 14.3
Earnings per Share
(EPS) and Use of Debt
Financing by Selected
Airlines

| | UAL, Inc. | | Eastern Airlines | | Piedmont Aviation | |
| | EPS | Debt as a Proportion of Total Assets | EPS | Debt as a Proportion of Total Assets | EPS | Debt as a Proportion of Total Assets |
Year						
1985	$(2.09)	77.3%	$(0.73)	93.2%	$3.76	66.3%
1984	7.46	63.4	(1.53)	95.1	3.75	71.7
1983	3.88	68.9	(7.19)	95.3	1.82	73.0
1982	1.03	75.6	(3.82)	92.1	2.53	68.4
1981	(2.40)	72.6	(3.46)	88.1	3.43	69.6
1980	0.70	71.2	(1.96)	84.5	2.27	73.4
1979	(2.50)	70.2	2.10	82.0	1.86	79.9
1978	11.93	68.2	2.91	79.4	1.03	80.5
1977	5.41	74.4	1.38	82.9	1.44	82.0
1976	0.52	77.4	1.51	84.8	0.92	74.0

Source: 1985 corporate annual reports.

financing. For example, UAL (United Airlines) finances two-thirds to three-fourths of its assets with debt and has experienced severe fluctuations in earnings that have ranged from profits of $7.46 per share in 1984 to a loss of $2.09 just one year later.

SUMMARY

A corporation is an economic unit created by a state. Ownership in the corporation is represented by stock. Stock certificates may be readily transferred from one individual to another. In addition, investors in publicly held corporations have limited liability.

Investors in common stock anticipate a return in the form of cash dividends and/or capital appreciation. Capital gains taxation laws favor price appreciation over cash dividends: cash dividends are taxed as received, while capital gains receive favorable tax treatment. Such gains are taxed only when realized (i.e., when the stock is sold).

A simple model of stock valuation suggests that this value depends on the firm's earnings, its dividend policy, and investors' required rate of return. According to the model, future dividends should be discounted back to the present to determine a stock's value. The discount factor used depends on returns available on alternative investments and the risk associated with the particular stock. An alternate to the dividend-growth model is the use of P/E ratios and forecasted earnings to determine if the stock should be purchased. Both the dividend-growth model and the use of P/E ratios place emphasis on future earnings and dividends. Since the future is not known with certainty, accurate estimates of future earnings, dividends, and growth rates may be difficult to obtain.

A firm may increase the return earned by its stockholders through the successful use of financial leverage. By borrowing funds and agreeing to pay a fixed rate of interest, the firm may be able to earn more on the funds than it must pay for them. The

difference, then, accrues to the firm's owners. Although the use of debt financing may increase the return on the owners' investment in the firm, it may also increase risk. Such an increase in risk may offset the increment in earnings so that the value of the stock is not enhanced.

Terms to Remember

Certificate of incorporation
Common stock
Charter
Bylaws
Voting rights
Directors
Cumulative voting

Preemptive rights
Rights offering
Total return
Required rate of return
Dividend-growth valuation model
Capital asset pricing model (CAPM)
Financial leverage

Questions

1. What does it mean to say that investors who buy stock in firms such as IBM have limited liability?

2. What are preemptive rights?

3. What are the sources of return to an investor in stock? How do taxes on income and capital gains affect the total return?

4. What variables affect a stock's price according to the dividend-growth valuation model? What role do past earnings play in this model?

5. What is financial leverage? Why may it increase a firm's return on equity and its per-share earnings?

6. Why may the use of financial leverage increase the element of risk?

7. Higher earnings per share may be obtained through the successful use of financial leverage. Why do the increased earnings not necessarily result in a higher stock price?

Problems

1. Given the following data, what should the price of the stock be?

Required rate of return	10%
Present dividend	$1
Growth rate	5%

   a. If the growth rate increases to 6 percent and the dividend remains $1, what should the stock's price be?

   b. If the required rate of return declines to 9 percent and the dividend remains $1, what should the price of the stock be? If the stock is selling for $20, what does that imply?

2. An investor requires a return of 12 percent. A stock sells for $25, it pays a dividend of $1, and the dividends compound annually at 7 percent. Will this investor find the

stock attractive? What is the maximum amount that this investor should pay for the stock?

3. A firm's stock earns $2 per share, and the firm distributes 40 percent of its earnings as cash dividends. Its dividends grow annually at 7 percent.

  a. What is the stock's price if the required rate of return is 10 percent?

  b. The aforementioned firm borrows funds and, as a result, its per-share earnings and dividends increase by 20 percent. What happens to the stock's price if the growth rate and the required rate of return are unaffected? What will the stock's price be if after using financial leverage and increasing the dividend to $1, the required rate of return rises to 12 percent? What may cause this required rate of return to rise?

4. The annual risk-free rate of return is 9 percent and the investor believes that the market will rise annually at 15 percent. If a stock has a beta coefficient of 1.5 and its current dividend is $1, what should be the value of the stock if its earnings and dividends are growing annually at 6 percent?

5. You are considering two stocks. Both pay a dividend of $1, but the beta coefficient of A is 1.5 while the beta coefficient of B is 0.7. Your required rate of return is

$$r = 8\% + (15\% - 8\%)\text{beta}.$$

  a. What is the required return for each stock?

  b. If A is selling for $10 a share, is it a good buy if you expect earnings and dividends to grow at 5 percent?

  c. The earnings and dividends of B are expected to grow annually at 10 percent. Would you buy the stock for $30?

  d. If the earnings and dividends of A were expected to grow annually at 10 percent, would it be a good buy at $30?

6. You are offered two stocks. The beta of A is 1.4 while the beta of B is 0.8. The growth rates of earnings and dividends are 10 percent and 5 percent, respectively. The dividend yields are 5 percent and 7 percent, respectively.

  a. Since A offers higher potential growth, should it be purchased?

  b. Since B offers a higher dividend yield, should it be purchased?

  c. If the risk-free rate of return were 7 percent and the return on the market is expected to be 14 percent, which of these stocks should be bought?

7. Your broker suggests that the stock of QED is a good purchase at $25. You do an analysis of the firm determining that the $1.40 dividend and earnings should continue to grow indefinitely at 8 percent annually. The firm's beta coefficient is 1.34, and the yield on treasury bills is 7.4 percent. If you expect the market to earn a return of 12 percent, should you follow your broker's suggestion?

8. The required rate of return on an investment is 12 percent. You estimate that Firm X's dividends will grow as follows:

Year	Dividend
1	$1.20
2	2.00
3	3.00
4	4.50

For the subsequent years you expect the dividend to grow but at the more modest rate of 7 percent annually. What is the maximum price that you should pay for this stock?

Suggested Readings

The dividend-growth model was developed by Myron Gordon. See:

Gordon, Myron. *The Investment, Financing and Valuation of the Corporation*. Homewood, Ill.: Richard D. Irwin, 1962.

For a practitioner's explanation of the dividend-growth model and other techniques used to value securities, see:

Crowell, Richard A. *Stock Market Strategy*. New York: McGraw-Hill, 1977.

Valuation is a major topic covered in depth in more advanced texts. See, for instance:

Sharpe, William F. *Investments*. 3rd ed. Englewood Cliffs, N.J.: Prentice-Hall, 1985, Chapters 4–8.

Radcliffe, Robert C. *Investment Concepts, Analysis, and Strategy*. Glenview, Ill.: Scott, Foresman, 1982, Chapter 10.

Reilly, Frank K. *Investments*. Hinsdale, Ill.: The Dryden Press, 1982, Chapters 7–8.

15 The Role of Dividends

LEARNING OBJECTIVES

After completing this chapter you should be able to

1. List the important dates for dividend payments.
2. Explain why changes in dividends generally follow changes in earnings.
3. Determine the impact of stock dividends and stock splits on the earning capacity of the firm.
4. Explain the effect of stock splits and stock dividends on the price of a stock.
5. Identify the advantages of dividend reinvestment plans.
6. Analyze the tax implications of stock repurchases and liquidations.

*R*eal estate investment trusts distribute virtually all of their profits as dividends. Many utilities such as Public Service Enterprise Group Inc. of New Jersey distribute more than one half of their earnings as dividends. Other firms such as Toys-R-Us pay no cash dividends. Obviously there can be great diversity in firms' dividend policies.

After a corporation has earned a profit, it must decide what to do with these earnings, which may be either retained or distributed as cash dividends. If the firm retains its earnings, it will put the funds to work by investing in income-earning assets or by retiring debt. The retention of earnings increases the stockholders' equity in the firm and should generate higher earnings and increased dividends in the future.

This chapter is concerned with dividends. Initially the various forms of dividends, which range from the regular quarterly cash dividends to irregular and stock dividends, are described. Then follows a discussion of dividend reinvestment plans, which permit investors to have their cash dividends reinvested in the firm's stock. Earnings retention and growth are then considered, along with the impact of taxes on income and capital gains. The chapter concludes with a discussion of the repurchase of stock and partial liquidations as an alternative to cash dividends.

CASH DIVIDENDS

A **dividend** is a distribution from earnings. Many companies pay cash dividends and have a dividend policy that is known to the investment community. Even if the policy is not explicitly stated by management, the continuation of such practices as paying a quarterly cash dividend implies a specific policy.

Dividend policy

Most American companies that distribute cash dividends pay a **regular dividend** on a quarterly basis. A few companies make monthly distributions (e.g., Winn-Dixie Stores and Wrigley), and some make the distribution semiannually or annually. Frequently in the case of semiannual and annual payments, the dollar amount is small. Instead of paying $0.025 per share quarterly, the company pays $0.10 per share annually, which reduces the expense of distributing the dividend.

Quarterly cash distributions

Although most companies with cash dividend policies pay regular quarterly dividends, there are other types of dividend policies. Some companies pay quarterly dividends plus an additional sum (**extra dividend**). In the past General Motors paid a quarterly dividend but distributed extras twice a year if the company had a profitable year. Such a policy is appropriate for a firm in a cyclical industry because earnings fluctuate over time and the firm may be hard pressed to maintain a higher level of regular quarterly dividends. By having a set cash payment that is supplemented with extras in good years, the firm is able not only to maintain a fixed payment that is relatively assured but also to supplement the cash dividend when the extra is warranted by the earnings.

Extras

Occasionally a firm distributes property as a supplement to or instead of cash dividends. For example, in 1985, Freeport-McMoran adopted a policy of distributing quarterly shares in two of its subsidiaries, Freeport-McMoran Energy Partners, Ltd. and Freeport-McMoran Gold Company. These property distributions are a supplement to the firm's usual quarterly cash dividend. Distributing property (i.e., stock in the subsidiaries) permits the stockholders to benefit directly from the market value of the subsidiaries, both of which are publicly traded, and from any of the subsidiaries' cash dividends. At the time of the declaration of this property dividend, Freeport-McMoran's management announced its intention to continue the policy for five years.

Property distributions

Management may view the dividend policy as the distribution of a certain proportion of the firm's earnings. The ratio of dividends to earnings is the **payout ratio**, which is the proportion of the earnings that the firm is distributing. For some firms this ratio has remained rather stable for a period of time, indicating that management views the best dividend policy in terms of a particular payout ratio.

The payout ratio

Other firms pay cash dividends that are **irregular**: There is no set dividend payment. For example, real estate investment trusts (frequently referred to as REITs) are required by law to distribute their earnings to maintain their favorable tax status.[1] These trusts pay no corporate income tax; instead, their earnings are distributed and the stockholders pay the tax. To ensure this favorable tax treatment, REITs must distribute at least 95 percent of their earnings. Since the earnings of such trusts fluctuate, the cash dividends also fluctuate. The special tax laws pertaining to REITs cause them to have irregular dividend payments.

Irregular dividends

---

[1] For a discussion of REITs, see Chapter 25.

POINTS OF INTEREST
The Longevity of Cash Dividends

The dividend growth model presented in Chapter 14 assumes that firms pay cash dividends indefinitely. Do firms in fact continue to pay cash dividends year after year? For many corporations the answer is "Yes!" Judging by Standard & Poor's *Stock Guide,* over 100 currently publicly traded companies were paying cash dividends in the nineteenth century. Sixty-three have paid a cash dividend every year for more than 100 years, and ten of these firms have paid a cash dividend for over 150 years.

Many of these firms are banks since banking was one of the first important industries to develop. Both the First National of Boston and the Bank of New York started paying dividends in the eighteenth century (1784 and 1785, respectively). Other banks with longevity records include Central Penn National (1828), Chemical New York (1827), Citicorp (1813), First Maryland Bancorporation (1806), First National Bancorporation (1812), Midlantic Banks (1805), and United Bank Corporation of New York (1804).

America's industrial giants developed after the banks, and while their dividend longevity records may not be as impressive as the banks', the accompanying list illustrates the extended period over which industrial firms have maintained cash dividends.

Do dividend payments ever end? Unfortunately the answer is "Yes." The financial difficulty First Pennsylvania experienced in 1980 caused the firm to cease paying cash dividends. Previously the firm had paid a cash dividend every year since 1828.

Firm	Cash Dividends Every Year Since
Amoco	1894
AT&T	1881
Borden, Inc.	1899
Boston Edison	1890
Burroughs	1895
Carter Wallace	1883
Chesebrough-Pond	1883
Cincinnati Gas and Electric	1853
Coca-Cola	1893
Colgate-Palmolive	1890
Consolidated Edison	1885
Continental Corp.	1854
Corning Glass Works	1881
Exxon	1882
General Electric	1899
General Mills	1898
Eli Lilly	1885
Pennwalt	1863
PPG Industries	1899
Procter & Gamble	1891
Rexnord	1894
Singer	1863
Stanley Works	1877
Travelers	1864
UGI	1885
Washington Gas & Light	1852
West Point-Pepperell	1882
Westvaco Corp.	1892

While American firms tend to follow a policy of quarterly dividend distributions, firms in other countries do not. Instead, dividend payments are irregular. Even when the cash payments occur at regular intervals, the dollar amount tends to vary. Of course, part of this variation is the result of fluctuations in the dollar value of each currency. Hence, if the value of the dollar falls relative to the German mark, any dividends that are distributed in marks translate into more dollars when the marks are

Exhibit 15.1
Selected Dividend Payments in 1977 and 1985

Company	1977 Quarter				Indicated Annual Rate	1985 Quarter				Indicated Annual Rate
	1	2	3	4		1	2	3	4	
Dominion Resources	$0.465	$0.465	$0.465	$0.465	$1.86	$0.68	$0.68	$0.68	$0.71	$2.84
General Motors	0.85	1.85	0.85	3.25	3.40	1.25	1.25	1.25	1.25	5.00
Realty ReFund	0.56	0.60	0.59	0.55	None	0.33	0.33	0.34	0.40	None

Source: Standard & Poor's stocks records and annual reports.

converted. The converse is also true. If the dollar value of the mark should fall, the dividend buys fewer dollars when the currency is converted.[2] Americans seeking predictable flows of dividend income are usually advised to purchase American stocks and to avoid foreign securities.

Various dividend policies are illustrated in Exhibit 15.1. Dominion Resources pays a regular quarterly dividend that in 1985 was increased from $0.68 a quarter to $0.71 (i.e., $2.84 annually). General Motors paid a regular quarterly dividend in both 1977 and 1985 but in 1977 paid extra dividends in the second and fourth quarters. The annual rate was $3.40 (i.e., the sum of the regular quarterly payments). The dividend payments of Realty ReFund are erratic. The firm paid $2.30 in 1977 but only $1.40 in 1985, and there is no regular amount that the investor can anticipate receiving each quarter.

Earnings, Growth, and Dividend Increments

As the earnings of a company grow, it is able to increase its cash dividend. Managements, however, may be reluctant to increase the cash dividend immediately when earnings increase because they want to be certain that the higher level of earnings will be maintained. Therefore, dividend increments tend to lag behind increases in earnings. This pattern is particularly well illustrated in Figure 15.1, which presents the quarterly per-share earnings and the quarterly cash dividends that were paid by Emhart from 1974 through 1981. Although there is a pattern of increased earnings, changes from quarter to quarter are erratic. The dividend, however, steadily increases after the earnings reach new highs.

A lag in dividends

The cause of this lag in dividend increments is management's reluctance to reduce dividends if earnings decline. Thus, the large year-end earnings that Emhart reported in 1974 and 1975 did not lead to dividend increments, but the subsequent quarterly declines in earnings did not result in dividend cuts. Instead, a pattern of growing earnings over many quarters leads to dividend increments.

A reluctance to cut dividends

Dividend reductions may be interpreted as a sign of financial weakness. However, a decrease in earnings may not mean the firm's capacity to pay cash dividends is re-

[2] For a discussion of fluctuations in exchange rates, see Chapter 26.

Figure 15.1
Earnings per Share and Cash Dividends of Emhart, 1974–1981

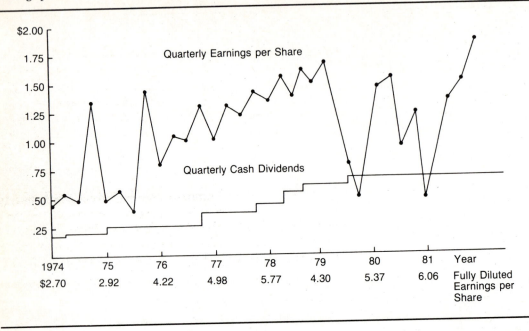

The dividend policy
is often stated

duced. For example, an increased depreciation expense may result in lower earnings but a higher cash flow, which maintains the firm's capacity to pay the dividend.[3]

Most companies announce their dividend policy. Many areas of a firm's operation are unknown to investors and perhaps would not be understood even if they were known. The dividend policy is readily understood and may be a deciding factor in purchasing stock in the firm. Some stockholders need income from their investments and prefer stocks that pay generous cash dividends. These investors will purchase the stock of companies that distribute a large proportion of their earnings in dividends. Other investors prefer capital gains and purchase the stock of companies that retain their earnings to finance future growth. Because investors need to know the dividend policy, it is advisable that firms make this knowledge public, and most companies do.

The Distribution of Dividends

The time dimension of
dividend payments

The process by which dividends are distributed is time-consuming. First, the firm's directors meet. If they declare a dividend, two important dates are established. The first date determines who is to receive the dividend. On the **date of record**, the ownership books of the corporation are closed, and everyone who owns stock in the company at the end of that day receives the dividend. (Exhibit 4.3 illustrated the record date for a CBS dividend.)

---

[3]At least one empirical study has shown that dividends are more highly correlated with cash flow (i.e., earnings plus depreciation) than with earnings. See John A. Brittain, *Corporate Dividend Policy* (Washington, D.C.: The Brookings Institute, 1966): 10–12.

POINTS OF INTEREST
United Telecommunications' Dividend Streak Comes to an End

In 1985, after 26 years in which the cash dividend was increased, a decline in earnings compelled the management of United Telecommunications to forgo the increase in the firm's cash dividend. Prior to 1985, United Telecommunications had risen from $0.31 in 1958 to $1.88 in 1984, and the dividend increments produced an annual growth rate in the dividend of 5.2 percent. The annual cash dividends are illustrated in Figure 15.2. While United Telecommunications' record was exceptional, many firms periodically increase their cash dividends as earnings and financial conditions warrant.

If the stock is purchased after the date of record, the purchaser does not receive the dividend. The stock is traded **ex dividend**, for the price of the stock does not include the dividend payment. This **ex dividend date** is four trading days prior to the date of record, because the settlement date for a stock purchase is five working days after the transaction.

The ex dividend day

In the financial press, transactions in the stock on the ex dividend day are indicated by an *X* before the volume of transactions. The following entry, derived from *The Wall Street Journal,* July 10, 1986, indicates the stock of Trinity traded on that day exclusive of the dividend.

Firm	Dividend	Volume	High	Low	Close	Net Change
Trinity	.50	x551	18¼	18	18	+¼

The $0.125 (i.e., $0.60 ÷ 4) quarterly dividend will be paid to whoever bought the stock on the previous day and will not be paid to investors who purchased the stock on the ex dividend day.

The investor should realize that buying or selling stock on the ex dividend date will not result in a windfall gain or a substantial loss. Generally, the price of the stock falls by the amount of the dividend.[4] If a stock that pays a $0.125 dividend is worth $18 on the day before it goes ex dividend, it cannot be worth $18 on the ex dividend date. If it were worth $18 on both days, investors would purchase the stock for $18 the day before the ex dividend day, sell it for $18 on the ex dividend day, and collect the $0.125 dividend. If investors could do this, the price would exceed $18 on the day preceding the ex dividend date and would be less than $18 on the ex dividend date. In effect, this price pattern does occur because this stock would sell for $18 and then be worth $18 minus $0.125 on the ex dividend date.

The price adjusts for the dividend

---

[4]Some empirical work suggests that the prices of stocks with high dividend yields tend to fall *more* than the amount of the dividend. See John D. Finnerty, "The Behavior of Electric Utility Common Stock Prices Near the Ex-Dividend Date," *Financial Management* (Winter 1981): 59–69.

Figure 15.2
Annual Cash Dividends
Paid by United
Telecommunications,
1957–1984

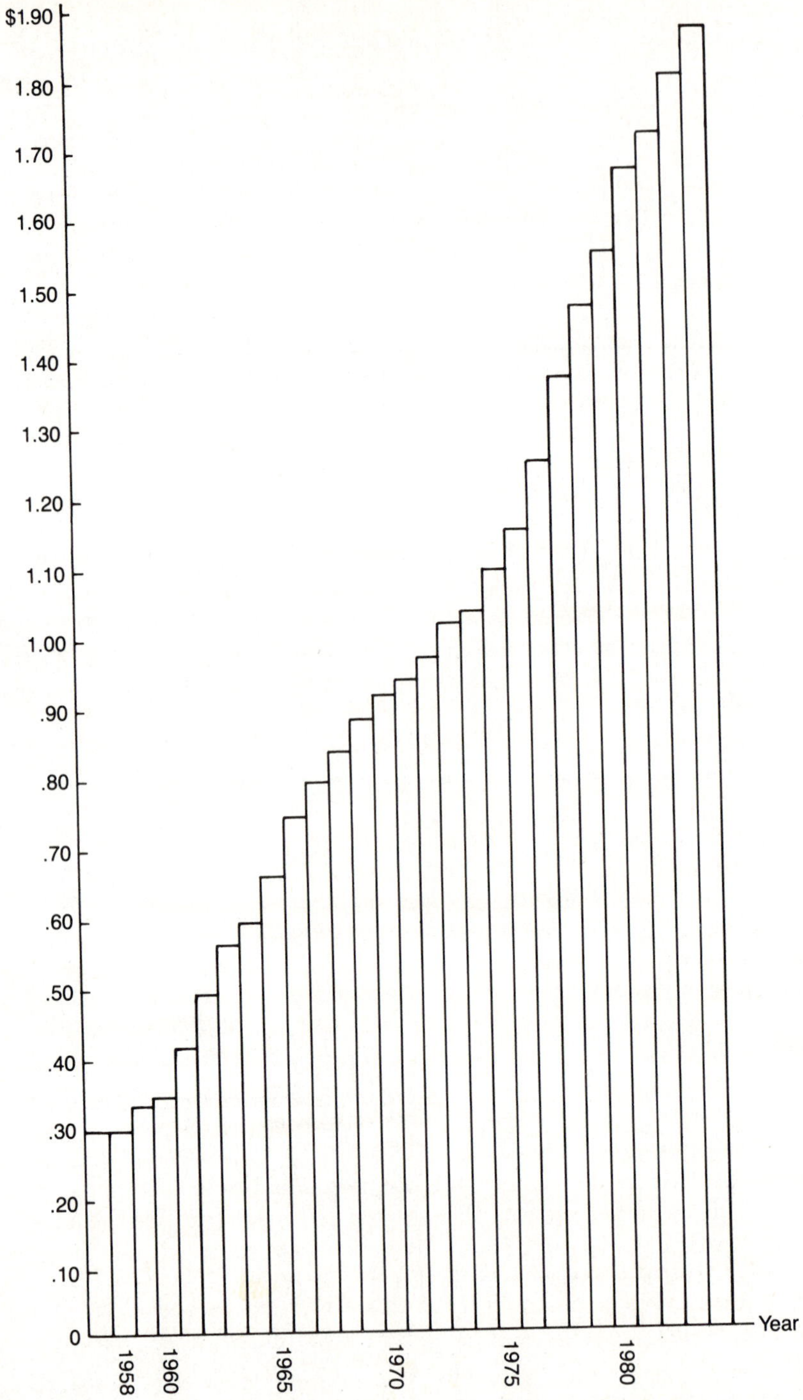

This price change is illustrated in the previous example from *The Wall Street Journal*. There was a net change of ¼ point in the price of Trinity stock for the ex dividend day. This indicates that the closing price on the previous day was $17⅞ and not $17¾, as might be expected from the increase of ¼ point for the day. Since the current buyers will not receive the dividend, the net change in the price of the stock is reduced for the dividend. The net change is figured from the adjusted price (i.e., $17⅞ minus the $0.125 dividend).

The second important date established when a dividend is declared is the day on which the dividend is paid, or the **distribution date.** The distribution date may be several weeks after the date of record, as the company must determine who the owners were as of the date of record and process the dividend checks. The company may not perform this task itself; instead, it may use the services of its commercial bank, for which the bank charges a fee. The day that the dividend is received by the stockholder is thus likely to be many weeks after the board of directors announces the dividend payment. For example, the distribution date for the CBS dividend in Exhibit 4.3 was September 12, which was about three weeks after the date of record, August 27.

The distribution date

Many firms try to maintain consistency in their dividend payment dates. For example, Xerox makes payments on the first business day of January, April, July, and October. Public Service Electric & Gas pays its dividends on the last day of March, June, September, and December. Such consistency in payments is beneficial to investors and the firm, as both can plan for this receipt and disbursement.

STOCK DIVIDENDS

Some firms make a practice of paying stock dividends in addition to or in lieu of cash dividends. **Stock dividends** are a form of **recapitalization** and do *not* affect the assets or liabilities of the firm. Since the assets and their management produce income for the firm, a stock dividend does not by itself increase the potential earning power of the company. Some investors, however, may believe that stock dividends will enhance the earning capacity of the firm and consequently the value of the stock. They mistakenly believe that the stock dividend increases the firm's assets.

The following balance sheet demonstrates the transactions that occur when a firm issues a stock dividend:

Assets		Liabilities and Equity	
Total assets	$10,000,000	Total liabilities	$2,500,000
		Equity: $2 par common stock (2,000,000 shares authorized; 1,000,000 outstanding)	2,000,000
		Additional paid-in capital	500,000
		Retained earnings	5,000,000

Since a stock dividend is only a recapitalization, the assets and the liabilities are not affected by the declaration and payment of the stock dividend. However, the entries in the equity section of the balance sheet are affected. The stock dividend transfers amounts from retained earnings to common stock and additional paid-in capital. The amount transferred depends on (1) the number of new shares issued through the stock dividend and (2) the market price of the stock.

Assets and liabilities are not affected

If the company in the preceding example issued a 10 percent stock dividend when the price of the common stock was $20 per share, 100,000 shares would be issued with a market value of $2,000,000. This amount is subtracted from retained earnings and transferred to common stock and additional paid-in capital. The amount transferred to common stock will be 100,000 times the par value of the stock ($2 × 100,000 = $200,000). The remaining amount ($1,800,000) is transferred to additional paid-in capital. The balance sheet then becomes:

Assets		Liabilities and Equity	
Total assets	$10,000,000	Total liabilities	$2,500,000
		Equity: $2 par common stock (2,000,000 shares authorized; 1,100,000 outstanding)	2,200,000
		Additional paid-in capital	2,300,000
		Retained earnings	3,000,000

The number of shares is increased

The student should note that no funds (or money) have been transferred. While there has been an increase in the number of shares outstanding, there has been no increase in cash and no increase in assets that may be used to earn profits. All that has happened is a recapitalization: The equity entries have been altered.

A firm's earning capacity is not increased

The major misconception concerning the stock dividend is that it increases the ability of the firm to grow. If the stock dividend is a substitute for a cash dividend, then this belief may be partially true, because the firm still has the asset cash that would have been paid to stockholders if a cash dividend had been declared. However, the firm will still have the cash even if it does not pay the stock dividend because a firm may retain its earnings. Hence, the decision to pay the stock dividend does not increase the amount of cash; it is the decision *not to pay* the cash dividend that conserves the money. When a stock dividend is paid in lieu of cash, it may even be interpreted as a screen: The stock dividend is hiding the firm's reluctance to pay cash dividends.

The wealth of the stockholder is not increased

Although the stock dividend does not increase the wealth of the stockholder, it does increase the number of shares owned. In the previous example, a stockholder who owned 100 shares before the stock dividend had $2,000 worth of stock. After the stock dividend is distributed, this stockholder owns 110 shares that are also worth $2,000, for the price of the stock falls from $20 to $18.18. The price of the stock declines because there are 10 percent more shares outstanding, but there has been no increase in the firm's assets and earning power. The old shares have been diluted, and hence the price of the stock must decline to indicate this **dilution**.

If the price of the stock did not fall to adjust for the stock dividend, all companies could make their stockholders wealthier by declaring stock dividends. However, because the stock dividend does not increase the assets or earning power of the firm, investors are not willing to pay the former price for a larger number of shares; hence, the market price must fall to adjust for the dilution of the old shares.

Disadvantages of stock dividends

There are some significant disadvantages associated with stock dividends. The primary disadvantage is the expense. The costs associated with these dividends include the expense of issuing new certificates, payments for any fractional shares, any taxes or listing fees on the new shares, and the revision of the firm's record of stockholders. These costs are indirectly borne by the stockholders. There are also costs that

fall directly on the stockholders, including increased transfer fees and commissions (if the new securities are sold), additional odd lot differentials, and the cost of storage.[5]

Perhaps the primary advantage of the stock dividend is that it brings to the current stockholders' attention the fact that the firm is retaining its cash in order to grow. The stockholders may subsequently be rewarded through the firm's retention of assets and its increased earning capacity. By retaining its assets, the firm may be able to earn more than the stockholders could if the funds were distributed. This should increase the price of the stock in the future. However, this same result may be achieved without the expenses associated with the stock dividend.

Advantage of stock dividends

THE STOCK SPLIT

After the price of a stock has risen substantially, management may decide to split the stock. The rationale for the **stock split** is that it lowers the price of the stock and makes it more accessible to investors. For example, when United Jersey Banks split its stock three for two, management stated that the split would put the stock in a "more affordable price range for investors and should improve the stock's marketability and liquidity."[6] Implicit in this reasoning are the beliefs that investors prefer lower priced shares and that reducing the price of the stock benefits the current stockholders by widening the market for their stock.

Like the stock dividend, the stock split is a recapitalization. It does not affect the assets or liabilities of the firm, nor does it increase its earning power. The wealth of the stockholder is increased only if investors prefer lower priced stocks, which will increase the demand for this stock.

No change in assets or liabilities

The balance sheet used previously for illustrating the stock dividend may also be used to illustrate a two-for-one stock split. In a two-for-one stock split, one old share becomes two new shares, and the par value of the old stock is halved. There are no changes in the additional paid-in capital or retained earnings. The new balance sheet becomes:

Assets		Liabilities and Equity	
Total assets	$10,000,000	Total liabilities	$2,500,000
		Equity: $1 par common stock (2,000,000 shares authorized; 2,000,000 shares outstanding)	2,000,000
		Additional paid-in capital	500,000
		Retained earnings	5,000,000

There are now twice as many shares outstanding, and each new share is worth half as much as one old share. If the stock had sold for $80 before the split, each share becomes worth $40. The stockholder with 100 old shares worth $8,000 now owns 200 shares worth $8,000 (i.e., $40 × 200).

An easy way to find the price of the stock after the split is to multiply the stock's price before the split by the reciprocal of the terms of the split. For example, if a stock

The price adjusts for the split

---

[5] See Stephen H. Sosnick, "Stock Dividends Are Lemons, Not Melons," *California Management Review* III (Winter 1961): 61–70.

[6] United Jersey Banks, *Third Quarter Report, 1985* (Princeton, NJ: United Jersey Banks, 1985), 4.

Exhibit 15.2
**Selected Stock Splits
Declared or Distributed
in 1986**

Subaru of America	8 for 1
Coca Cola	3 for 1
Bell Atlantic	2 for 1
Boston Edison	2 for 1
Digital Equipment	2 for 1
Liz Claiborne	2 for 1
Borden Inc.	3 for 2
Standard Pacific	3 for 2
Dow Jones	3 for 2
Analog Devices	4 for 3
Jim Walter, Corp.	5 for 4

is selling for $54 per share and is split three for two, then the price of the stock after the split will be $54 × ⅔ = $36. Such price adjustments must occur because the old shares are diluted and the earning capacity of the firm is not increased.

Stock splits may be any combination of terms. Exhibit 15.2 illustrates the terms of several stock splits in 1986. Although two-for-one splits are the most common, there can be unusual terms, such as the five-for-four split of Jim Walter, Corp. There is no obvious explanation for such terms except that management wanted to reduce the stock's price to a particular level and selected the terms that would achieve the desired price.

The reverse split

Occasionally there is a reverse split, such as the 1984 Keystone Camera Products one-for-twenty split. A reverse split reduces the number of shares and raises the price of the stock. The purpose of such a split is to add respectability to the stock (i.e., to raise the price above the level of the "cats and dogs"). Since some investors will not buy low-priced stock and since commissions on such purchases are higher, it may be in the best interest of all stockholders to raise the stock's price through a reverse split.

Stock splits, like stock dividends, do not by themselves increase the wealth of the stockholder, for the split does not increase the assets or earning capacity of the firm. The split does decrease the price of the stock and thereby may increase its marketability. Thus, the split stock may be more widely distributed, which increases investor interest in the company. This wider distribution may increase the wealth of the current stockholders over time.

Academic studies, however, have not been able to demonstrate that stock splits or stock dividends increase the value of stock.[7] Instead, these studies consistently show that other factors, such as increased earnings, increased cash dividends, or a rise in the general market, result in higher prices for individual stocks. The stock dividends and stock splits do not by themselves affect the value of the stock. In fact, stock splits generally occur *after* the price of the stock has risen. Instead of being a harbinger of good news, they mirror an increase in the firm's earnings and growth.

*Splits do not increase the
wealth of the stockholder*

From the investor's point of view, there is little difference between a stock split and a stock dividend. In both cases the stockholders receive additional shares, but

---

[7] See, for instance, W. H. Hausman, R. R. West, and J. A. Largay, "Stock Splits, Price Changes and Trading Profits: A Synthesis," *Journal of Business* 44 (January 1971): 69–77, and E. F. Fama, L. Fisher, M. Jensen, and R. Roll, "The Adjustment of Stock Prices to New Information," *International Economic Review* (February 1969): 1–21.

their proportionate ownership in the firm is unaltered. In addition, the price of the stock adjusts for the dilution of per-share earnings caused by the new shares.

Accountants, however, do differentiate between stock splits and stock dividends. Stock dividends are generally less than 20 to 25 percent. A stock dividend of 50 percent would be treated as a three-for-two stock split. Only the par value and the number of shares that the firm has outstanding would be affected. There would be no change in the firm's retained earnings. A stock split of 11 for 10 would be treated as a 10 percent stock dividend. In this case, retained earnings would be reduced, and the amount would be transferred to the other accounts (i.e., common stock and paid-in capital accounts). Total equity, however, would not be affected.

DIVIDEND REINVESTMENT PLANS

Many corporations that pay cash dividends also have **dividend reinvestment plans** in which the cash dividends are used to purchase additional shares of stock. Dividend reinvestment programs started in the 1960s, but the expansion of the programs occurred in the early 1970s. By 1980, more than 1,000 companies offered some version of the dividend reinvestment plan.[8]

Types of Dividend Reinvestment Plans

There are two general types of dividend reinvestment programs. In most plans a bank acts on behalf of the corporation and its stockholders. The bank collects the cash dividends for the stockholders and in some plans offers the stockholders the option of making additional cash contributions. The bank pools all of the funds and purchases the stock on the open market. Since the bank is able to purchase a larger block of shares, it receives a substantial reduction in the per-share commission cost of the purchase. This reduced brokerage fee applies to all of the shares purchased by the bank. Thus, all investors, ranging from the smallest to the largest, receive this advantage. The bank does charge a fee for its service, but this fee is usually modest and does not offset the savings in brokerage fees.

Funds are pooled and existing shares are purchased

In the second type of reinvestment plan, the company issues new shares of stock for the cash dividend, and the money is directly rechanneled to the company. The investor may also have the option of making additional cash contributions. This type of plan offers the investor an additional advantage in that the brokerage fees are completely circumvented. The entire amount of the cash dividend is used to purchase shares, with the cost of issuing the new shares being paid by the company. This type of reinvestment plan is offered primarily by utilities, such as telephone, electric, and gas companies. Utilities need continual sources of new equity funds, and dividend reinvestment plans are one means of raising this capital.

New shares of stock are issued

Advantages of Dividend Reinvestment Plans

Dividend reinvestment plans offer advantages to both firms and investors. For stockholders the advantages include the purchase of shares at a substantial reduction in

A reduction in commission

---

[8] Moody's *Dividend Record* lists the firms traded on the NYSE and Amex that offer dividend reinvestment plans. See, for instance, the January 1, 1986, issue, pages 344–345.

commissions. Even reinvestment plans in which the fees are paid by the stockholder offer this savings. Both types of plan are particularly attractive to the small investor, for few brokerage firms are interested or willing to buy $100 worth of stock, and substantial commissions are charged on such small transactions.

Forced savings

Perhaps the most important advantage to investors is the fact that the plans are automatic. The investor does not receive the dividends, for the proceeds are automatically reinvested. The plans are a means to force the individual to save.[9] For any investor who lacks the discipline to save, such forced saving may be a means to systematically accumulate shares.

An incentive not to cut dividends

There may also be an advantage to income-oriented stockholders if these plans encourage the company to distribute cash dividends. A dividend reinvestment plan, especially one that results in the issue of new shares, may be an incentive for the company to maintain cash dividends. Even if the company desires to cut dividends in order to build its equity base, such a move reduces the funds that are available through reinvested dividends. If the company's reinvestment plan involves the issue of new shares, the increase in the equity base that is achieved through cutting the dividend is partially offset by the reduction in reinvested dividends and cash contributions. Hence, the reinvestment plans may result in fewer dividend cuts and perhaps more dividend increments.[10]

Goodwill

For the firm the primary advantages are the goodwill that is achieved by providing another service for its stockholders and some cost savings in the delivery of dividend checks. The plans that involve the issue of new shares also raise new equity capital. Firms that frequently must raise large amounts of externally generated funds may find the dividend reinvestment plan to be a major source of new capital. For example, AT&T stated in its 1985 annual report that its plan resulted in the issue of 11.9 million shares, which raised over $245.8 million in equity capital. This automatic flow of new equity reduced the need for the sale of shares through underwriters.

The dividends are still subject to income tax

The Internal Revenue Service considers dividends that are reinvested to be no different from cash dividends that are received. Such dividends are subject to federal income taxation. The exclusion of dividend income that is reinvested from federal income taxation has been considered as one possible change in the tax code, but there is little chance of passage since Congress has been closing, rather than opening, loopholes.

EARNINGS RETENTION AND GROWTH

Alternative uses of funds

Since management seeks to maximize the wealth of the stockholders, the dividend decision should depend on who can put the funds to better use, the stockholders or the firm. Management, however, probably does not know the stockholders' alternative uses for the funds and thus pursues a policy that it believes is in the stockholders' best interests. Stockholders who do not like the dividend policy of the firm may sell their

---

[9] See K. Larry Hasties's Comment on "Automatic Dividend Reinvestment Plans of Nonfinancial Corporations," *Financial Management* 3 (Spring 1974): 26.

[10] At present there is no evidence that such plans do affect firms' dividend policies. See Richard H. Pettway and R. Phil Malone, "Automatic Dividend Reinvestment Plans of Nonfinancial Corporations," *Financial Management* 2 (Winter 1973): 11–17.

shares. If sellers exceed buyers, the price of the stock will be depressed, and management will be made aware of the investors' attitude toward the dividend policy.

Earnings Retention and Security Prices

In the 1960s dividend policy was not a major concern of management. During this period the emphasis was on growth and the retention of earnings to finance that growth. Management retained as much of the earnings as it believed necessary to finance growth, and any residual was paid to stockholders. It was a period of spectacular growth by major firms, such as IBM, Xerox, and Johnson & Johnson. For example, during the years between 1964 and 1972, IBM's earnings and stock price increased at an annual rate of 14 percent. Investors in these growth-oriented companies were rewarded as the price of the stocks rose. Obviously, the best use of corporate funds was to finance growth, for few investors could have earned a comparable return through alternative uses of the money. These stockholders were well rewarded for forgoing current dividend income.

Retained earnings may produce growth

With the onset of inflation in the 1970s and the increase in interest rates, dividend policy became more important. Investors had several potential uses for funds, such as the purchase of material goods whose price investors anticipated would continue to rise. Bonds, which were yielding historically high interest rates, were an attractive investment. Since investors had more obvious alternative uses for the money earned by companies, the dividend policy of the firm became more important to them as they viewed the return on their investments to include not only growth in the value of the shares but also the dividend return.

During the 1970s and 1980s earnings and dividend growth were rewarded by higher security prices. The companies that experienced growth tended to be smaller, and the growth in their earnings and stock prices were less well publicized than the success stories of the 1960s. Such a case is Teledyne, whose growth in earnings per share and stock price is illustrated in Exhibit 15.3. While Teledyne has not achieved the publicity of IBM or Johnson & Johnson, its earnings per share grew annually at

Higher earnings should lead to higher stock prices

Year	Number of Shares Outstanding (in Millions)	Percent Earned on Equity	Earnings per Share	High-Low Stock Prices
1982	20.7	13.8%	$12.62	$143–69
1981	20.6	26.5	19.96	174–118
1980	20.7	28.1	15.24	153–61
1979	25.8	35.1	14.71	82–47
1978	25.8	32.8	9.40	59–26
1977	26.4	33.7	7.09	33–21
1976	26.3	31.2	4.56	35–9
1975	32.3	24.8	2.57	11–4
1974	45.0	6.5	0.54	6–3
1973	58.5	12.9	1.00	8–4
1972	59.6	11.5	0.64	11–6

Exhibit 15.3
Teledyne's Earnings per Share and High-Low Stock Prices

Source: Standard & Poor's *Stock Reports,* various issues.

about 50 percent from 1972 through 1980, and the price of the stock rose considerably during that period.

REPURCHASES OF STOCK AND LIQUIDATIONS

A firm with excess cash may choose to repurchase some of its outstanding shares of stock or to liquidate the corporation. This section briefly covers **stock repurchases** and **liquidations**. A repurchase is in effect a partial liquidation, as it decreases the number of shares outstanding. This reduction should increase the earnings per share because the earnings are spread over fewer shares.

Repurchase as an alternative to cash dividends

While the repurchase of shares is a partial liquidation, it may also be viewed as an alternative to the payment of cash dividends. Instead of distributing the money as cash dividends, the firm offers to purchase shares from stockholders. If the stockholders believe that the firm's potential is sufficient to warrant the retention of the shares, they do not have to sell them. If the shares are sold back to the company, any resulting profits will be taxed as capital gains.

Recapitalization reduces the number of shares outstanding

One company that has followed a policy of retiring shares is Teledyne. Prior to 1987, Teledyne did not pay cash dividends but either offered stockholders the option to exchange their shares for debt issued by the company or repurchased stock.[11] The result of these recapitalizations has been to reduce the number of shares outstanding from 59.6 million in 1972 to 11.7 million in 1986. This reduced number of shares plus an excellent growth in earnings has resulted in a substantial increase in Teledyne's per-share earnings. As may be seen in Exhibit 15.3, the price of the stock has risen, which has certainly benefited the remaining stockholders. Even those stockholders who sold their shares cannot complain, because they were not forced to sell. These investors sold their shares presumably because they thought that selling was better than continuing to hold the shares.

Occasionally a firm is liquidated. The final distribution of the firm's assets is called a liquidating dividend. The use of the term *dividend* is a bit misleading, because the distribution is not really a dividend. It is treated for tax purposes as a distribution of capital and is taxed at the appropriate capital gains tax rate. Thus, liquidating dividends are treated in the same manner as realized sales for federal income tax purposes.

A liquidation dividend in cash

A simple example may illustrate how such a dividend works. A firm decides to liquidate and sells all of its assets for cash. The stockholders then receive the cash. If the sales raise $25 in cash per share, a stockholder surrenders the stock certificate and receives $25 in cash. The capital gain is then determined by subtracting the stockholder's cost basis of the share from the $25. If the stockholder paid $10 for the share, the capital gain would be $15. The stockholder then pays the appropriate capital gains tax. If the cost basis were $40, the investor would suffer a capital loss of $15, which may be used for tax purposes to offset other capital gains or income. In either case, this is no different than if the stockholder had sold the shares. However, in a sale the stockholder does have the option to refuse to sell and thus may postpone any capital gains tax. In a liquidation the stockholder must realize the gain or loss. Once the firm has adopted a plan of liquidation, it must execute it or face penalties. When a firm liquidates, the stockholder cannot postpone the capital gains tax.

---

[11] Teledyne's largest single purchase occurred in May 1984, when it repurchased 8.7 million shares at a cost of $1.74 billion.

In the preceding example, the liquidating dividend was cash. However, the dividend need not be cash but may be property. For example, a real estate holding company could distribute the property it owns. Or a company that has accumulated stock in other companies could distribute the stock instead of selling it. Such distributions may be desirable if the stockholders want the particular assets being distributed. However, if the stockholders want or need cash (perhaps to pay the capital gains tax), then the burden of liquidating the assets is passed on to them.

A liquidation dividend in property

An example of a firm that did liquidate is Tishman Realty. The stockholders adopted a plan of liquidation; the firm then sold most of its assets to Equitable Life Assurance for $200 million. The company paid an initial $11 per share liquidating dividend. After additional cash distributions were made, a partnership was established to hold the remaining assets, which consisted primarily of mortgages on properties sold. These partnership shares were then distributed to stockholders to complete the liquidation.

SUMMARY

After a firm has earned profits, it may either retain them or distribute them in the form of cash dividends. Many publicly held corporations follow a stated dividend policy and distribute quarterly cash dividends. A few firms supplement this dividend with extra dividends if earnings warrant the additional distribution. Some firms pay irregular dividends that vary in amount from quarter to quarter.

Dividends are related to the firm's capacity to pay them. As earnings rise, dividends also tend to increase, but there is usually a lag between higher earnings and increased dividends. Most managements are reluctant to cut dividends and thus do not raise the dividend until they believe that the higher level of earnings can be sustained.

In addition to cash dividends, some firms distribute stock dividends. These dividends and stock splits do not increase the earning capacity of the firm. Instead, they are recapitalizations that alter the number of shares the firm has outstanding. Since stock dividends and stock splits do not alter the firm's earning capacity, they do not increase the wealth of the stockholders. The price of the stock adjusts for the change in the number of shares that results from stock dividends and stock splits.

The retention or distribution of earnings should be a question of who can put the funds to better use—the firm or its stockholders. If a firm retains earnings, it should grow and the value of the shares should increase. When this occurs, the stockholders may be able to sell their shares for a profit.

Many firms offer their stockholders the option of having their dividends reinvested in the firm's stock. This is achieved either through the firm's issuing new shares or purchasing existing shares. Dividend reinvestment plans offer the stockholders the advantages of forced savings and a reduction in brokerage fees.

Instead of paying cash dividends, a firm may offer to repurchase some of its existing shares. Such repurchases reduce the number of shares outstanding and may enhance the growth in the firm's per-share earnings because there will be fewer shares outstanding. Any profits earned on such repurchases are taxed as capital gains, as are liquidating dividends that occur when a corporation is disbanded and its assets are distributed to the stockholders.

Terms to Remember

Dividend

Regular dividend

Extra dividend

Payout ratio

Irregular dividends

Date of record

Ex dividend

Ex dividend date

Distribution date

Stock dividend

Recapitalization

Dilution

Stock split

Dividend reinvestment plan

Stock repurchase

Liquidation

Questions

1. Why may a firm distribute dividends even though earnings decline?

2. Why may a dividend increment lag after an increase in earnings?

3. Define *ex dividend date, date of record,* and *distribution date.*

4. Explain the differences between the following dividend policies: (a) regular quarterly dividends; (b) regular quarterly dividends plus extras; and (c) irregular dividends.

5. How are stock dividends and stock splits similar?

6. What are the advantages to stockholders of dividend reinvestment plans?

7. What tax advantages apply to stock repurchases that do not apply to cash dividend distributions?

8. Why should dividend policy be a question of who can put the funds to better use, the firm or its stockholders?

Problems

1. A firm has the following items on its balance sheet:

Cash	$ 20,000,000
Inventory	134,000,000
Notes payable to bank	31,500,000
Common stock (1,000,000 shares, $10 par)	10,000,000
Retained earnings	98,500,000

How would each of these accounts appear after:
  a. a cash dividend of $1 per share;
  b. a 10 percent stock dividend (fair market value of stock is $13 per share);
  c. a three-for-one stock split;
  d. a one-for-two reverse stock split;
  e. a repurchase of 100,000 shares for $13 per share?

2. A company whose stock is selling for $60 has the following balance sheet:

Assets	$30,000,000	Liabilities	$14,000,000
		Preferred stock	1,000,000
		Common stock ($12 par; 100,000 shares outstanding)	1,200,000
		Paid-in capital	1,800,000
		Retained earnings	12,000,000

a. Construct a new balance sheet showing the effects of a three-for-one stock split. What is the new price of the stock?

b. Construct a new balance sheet showing the effects of a 10 percent stock dividend. What will be the approximate new price of the stock?

3. An investor who buys 100 shares of a stock for $40 a share that pays a per-share dividend of $2.00 annually signs up for the dividend reinvestment plan. If neither the price of the stock nor the dividend is changed, how many shares will the investor have at the end of ten years?

Suggested Readings

Cash dividends may depend on cash flow (earnings plus depreciation) more than on earnings. See, for instance:

Brittain, John A. *Corporate Dividend Policy.* Washington, D.C.: The Brookings Institution, 1966.

Whether or not the distribution of cash dividends increases stockholder wealth is subject to debate. See, for instance:

Black, Fischer. "The Dividend Puzzle." *Journal of Portfolio Management* (Winter 1976): 5–8.

Hayes, Linda S. "Fresh Evidence That Dividends Don't Matter." *Fortune,* May 4, 1981.

A survey of corporate financial managers suggests that management (1) is concerned with dividend continuity, (2) believes dividends help maintain or increase stock prices, and (3) believes dividend payments indicate the future prospects of the firm. These results are reported in:

Baker, H. Kent, Gail E. Farrelly, and Richard B. Edelman. "A Survey of Management Views on Dividend Policy." *Financial Management* (Autumn 1985): 78–84.

Even though the finance literature attributes no value to stock dividends and stock splits, the following articles identify why some corporate managements still declare them.

Eisemann, Peter C., and Edward A. Moses. "Stock Dividends: Management's View." *Financial Analysts Journal* (July–August 1979): 77–80.

Baker, W. Kent, and Patricia L. Gallagher. "Management's View of Stock Splits." *Financial Management* (Summer 1980): 73–77.

For an enumeration of the negative implications of stock dividends, see:

Sosnick, Stephen H. "Stock Dividends Are Lemons, Not Melons." *California Management Review* (Winter 1961): 61–70.

Reverse stock splits are relatively rare and may be a harbinger of future declines in the stock's price. See:

Woolridge, J. R., and D. R. Chambers. "Reverse Splits and Shareholder Wealth." *Financial Management* (Autumn 1983): 5–15.

Spudeck, R. E., and R. Charles Moyer. "Reverse Splits and Shareholder Wealth: The Impact of Commissions." *Financial Management* (Winter 1985): 52–56.

Stock repurchases have become common. For the characteristics of firms that repurchase their own stock, consult:

Finnerty, Joseph E. "Corporate Stock Issue and Repurchase." *Financial Management* (October 1975): 62–66.

16

The Fundamental Approach to the Selection of Stock

LEARNING OBJECTIVES

After completing this chapter you should be able to

1. Explain the relationship between economic activity and security prices.
2. Describe the tools of monetary policy and the mechanics of open market operations.
3. Explain how monetary and fiscal policy may affect security prices.
4. Contrast measures of the supply of money.
5. Identify the sources of funds to finance the federal government's deficit.
6. Differentiate cyclical and stable industries.
7. Identify factors that may affect the performance of an industry.

*T*wo methods other than random choice or "hot tips" used by investors to select securities are the fundamental approach and the technical approach. The fundamental approach stresses economic conditions, such as the level of employment and economic growth, and financial conditions, such as the level and direction of changes in interest rates. This approach also examines a firm's earning capacity, its growth potential, and its sources of finance. Financial analysts who use this method compare firms within an industry to identify those with the greatest potential and strongest financial position. Emphasis is placed on a firm's economic performance and the potential to improve its relative position within its industry. Ratios, financial data, and astute observation are the primary tools of fundamental analysis.

The technical approach is based on the past market performance of a firm's securities. It attempts to identify superior investments by analyzing the price performance and the volume of transactions in the firm's stock. This type of analysis emphasizes price trends and deviations from these trends. For example, stocks that are rising in price may continue to do so. When the technical analyst perceives that this trend is coming to a halt, it is time to

liquidate the position in that security, even if the firm has superior management, excellent growth potential, and a strong balance sheet.

Although both methods attempt to identify superior securities for purchase, the two approaches are significantly different. Fundamental analysis is based on the premise that real factors, such as the firm's productivity and profitability, will ultimately govern the stock's price. Technical analysis, however, stresses market factors and suggests that future stock prices are related to past market behavior.

This and the following chapters will explore these techniques. Chapters 16 and 17 focus on fundamental analysis. The first section in Chapter 16 discusses the general economic environment. The impact of the Federal Reserve's monetary policy on interest rates is explained next. The chapter then considers the federal government's fiscal policy and analysis of a firm in relation to its industry. Chapter 16 ends with a discussion of the expected economic environment and investment strategies. The bulk of the next chapter is devoted to financial analysis of the firm. Particular emphasis is placed on the various ratios used in this type of analysis. Chapter 18 discusses technical analysis and illustrates several techniques that are used by advocates of this approach. The student should realize that these three chapters cannot cover these important topics in depth; entire books have been written on each topic alone. This text includes only basic methods used in fundamental and technical analysis.

THE ECONOMIC ENVIRONMENT

All firms work within the economic environment. Their survival may depend on how the economy as a whole is faring. During periods of economic prosperity, the demand for the goods and services of firms may result in increased sales and higher profits. Even financially weak or incompetently managed firms may experience increased sales and earnings if they are swept up in the general economic prosperity.

Hard times or periods of **recession** (i.e., periods of rising unemployment) may have the opposite impact. Financially weak firms may fail, and even the financially strong may feel the effects of poor economic conditions. Recession leads to a general decline in economic activity, which in turn results in a lessening of demand for the output of virtually all firms. Sales become sluggish or even decline, and earnings tend to diminish even more rapidly because certain fixed costs (such as interest) must still be met, which may severely reduce profit margins.

Recession may cause earnings to decline

During periods of prosperity, security prices as a whole tend to rise. Thus, even poor investment decisions may produce acceptable or even superior results. Conversely, during periods of economic downturn, even excellent security analysis may not protect the investor from declining security prices. For these reasons, the ability to forecast the future economic environment may be even more important than the purchase of specific securities.[1] Unfortunately such **forecasting** is virtually impossible for the individual investor. Even access to sophisticated techniques, computers, and more complete data does not guarantee accurate forecasts. Certainly, if various economic groups such as the Council of Economic Advisors (to the president) have diffi-

---

[1] Frank K. Reilly, "The Misdirected Emphasis in Security Valuation," *Financial Analysts Journal* (January–February 1973): 54–56.

culty predicting the economy, the individual investor cannot expect to do what those trained analysts are unable to do.

The individual investor, however, does have access to the predictions of the various forecasting services, which are reported in the financial press. For example, *Fortune* and *Financial World* publish annual forecasts at the beginning of the calendar year. These predictions include the growth in gross national product, which measures the nation's final output of goods and services for the year; the level of unemployment; and the rate of inflation, that is, the rate of increase in the level of prices. Although the various forecasts are different, they vary only in degree, since all analysts are working with essentially the same information.

The importance of direction of change

The importance of these forecasts to investors is not so much the actual predicted numbers but the direction and amount of change. Since profits are related to economic activity, forecasts of such activity may be helpful in predicting the level of a firm's earnings. However, the investor should realize that changes in stock prices frequently precede changes in economic activity. Thus, estimates of economic growth may be too late to help investors if stock prices have already risen. The investor should also realize that not all companies benefit from periods of economic growth. Analysis of the financial condition and the growth potential of the individual firm is still warranted.

THE FEDERAL RESERVE

The central bank

In addition to forecasts of aggregate economic activity, the investor should be concerned with the monetary policy of the **Federal Reserve** (the "Fed"). The Federal Reserve is the country's central bank. Although in many countries the treasury and the central bank are one and the same, in the United States they are independent of each other. Such independence is an example of the checks and balances of the country's political system. However, both the U.S. Treasury and the Federal Reserve have the

Economic goals

same general economic goals of full employment, stable prices, and economic growth.

The Federal Reserve pursues these economic goals through the regulation of the supply of credit and money. Monetary policy refers to changes in the supply of money and credit. When the Federal Reserve wants to increase the supply of money and credit to help expand the level of income and employment, it follows an "easy" monetary policy. When it desires to contract the supply of money and credit to help fight inflation, it pursues a "tight" monetary policy.

Tools of monetary policy

The Federal Reserve has several tools by which it may affect the supply of money and the availability of credit. These tools work primarily by altering the ability of commercial banks to grant loans, thereby expanding or contracting the money supply. Commercial banks must hold **reserves**, which are assets held against their deposit liabilities. The amount of the **reserve requirement** is established by the Federal Reserve. Any reserves in excess of those required may be lent. By lowering the reserve requirement, the Fed increases the banks' excess reserves and thus increases their capacity to lend. When the banks do make new loans, they expand the supply of money. By raising the reserve requirement and hence reducing the excess reserves of banks, the Fed decreases the banks' capacity to lend and may cause them to contract their outstanding loans, which reduces the supply of money and credit.

The discount rate

In addition to reserve requirements, the other two major tools of monetary policy are the discount rate and open market operations. The **discount rate** is the rate of

interest charged by the Fed when banks borrow reserves. If the Fed seeks to expand the money supply, it lowers the discount rate, which encourages the banks to borrow reserves from the Fed. When the banks in turn lend the funds acquired from the Fed, the money supply is expanded. The converse occurs when the Fed seeks to reduce the supply of money. It raises the discount rate, which discourages banks from borrowing reserves from the Federal Reserve.

Of the major tools of monetary policy, by far the most important is **open market operations**, which refers to the purchase or sale of government securities (especially treasury bills) by the Federal Reserve. By buying and selling these securities, the Federal Reserve is able to alter both the supply of money in circulation and the reserves of the commercial banking system. The Federal Reserve may buy and sell securities at any time and in any volume and thus is able to affect the supply of money and credit whenever it chooses to do so.

Open market operations

When the Federal Reserve wants to increase the money supply and the reserves of the banking system, it purchases securities. Ownership of the securities is transferred to the Federal Reserve, and the Federal Reserve pays for the securities by writing checks drawn on itself, which the sellers deposit in commercial banks. The banks clear the checks and receive reserves from the Federal Reserve.

Increasing the supply of money

These transactions have the following effect on each participant's balance sheet.

Federal Reserve		Commercial Banks		General Public	
Government securities ↑	Reserves of commercial banks ↑	Reserves ↑	Demand deposits ↑	Government securities ↓ Demand deposits ↑ (money)	

The general public has sold securities and received payment. In effect, it traded one asset (the government securities) for another (the demand deposits). The banks, however, have received a new liability (the new checking account) and a new asset (the reserves). The Federal Reserve acquired a new asset (the government securities) and paid for the securities by issuing a new liability on itself (the reserves of the commercial banks).

The total effect of the transaction is (1) to increase the supply of money by increasing demand deposits and (2) to increase the reserves of the banking system. While the required reserves of the banks rise (because the deposit liabilities of the commercial bank have risen), only a fraction of the increase in reserves will be required reserves. This increase in excess reserves means that the capacity of the commercial banking system to expand the supply of money and to issue more credit has risen. The purchase of government securities by the Federal Reserve from the general public brings about not only an increase in the supply of money but also the potential for additional increases through an increase in the excess reserves of commercial banks.

When the Federal Reserve desires to contract the money supply, it sells government securities. Once again it is the payment for the purchased securities that alters

Contracting the supply of money

the money supply and the capacity of commercial banks to lend. If the public buys the securities, demand deposits decrease along with the money supply and the reserves of commercial banks. The sale of securities by the Federal Reserve affects the balance sheets of the Federal Reserve, commercial banks, and the public as follows:

Federal Reserve		Commercial Banks		General Public	
Government securities ↓	Reserves of commercial banks ↓	Reserves ↓	Demand deposits ↓	Demand deposits ↓ Government securities ↑	

The general public has traded one asset (the demand deposit) for another (the government securities). Commercial banks lose demand deposits, and when the check clears and payment is made to the Federal Reserve, the reserves of commercial banks on deposit at the Federal Reserve are reduced. The Federal Reserve loses an asset (the government securities) and a liability (the reserves). It has, in effect, retired a liability by giving up an asset.

The total effect of this transaction is (1) to decrease the money supply because demand deposits have decreased and (2) to decrease the total reserves of the banking system because commercial banks have fewer reserves on deposit at the Federal Reserve. Since only a percentage of these reserves is required against deposit liabilities, the banks' excess reserves also decrease. Thus, by selling securities in the open market, the Federal Reserve decreases the supply of money and decreases the excess reserves of commercial banks. The decrease in excess reserves reduces the ability of the commercial banking system to lend and to issue credit.

THE IMPACT OF MONETARY POLICY ON SECURITY PRICES

Open market operations affect security prices

The importance of open market operations for investment analysis is two-fold. First, the buying and selling of government securities have an immediate impact on interest rates and bond prices. Second, there is an indirect effect on security prices that results from the impact of monetary policy on a firm's earning capacity.

When the Federal Reserve buys treasury securities, it bids up their prices and causes yields to decline. The rate differential between treasury debt and corporate debt widens, and as a result investors purchase corporate securities. This causes their prices to rise and their yields to decline, and the effect on yields of the open market purchases by the Federal Reserve is transferred to other debt instruments.

The converse happens when the Federal Reserve sells government securities. This depresses their prices and increases interest rates. The rate differential between corporate and federal government debt is reduced, and investors move from corporate to government securities. This reduces the price of corporate bonds and increases their

yield. Thus, the effect of the sale of government securities by the Federal Reserve is transferred to corporate and all other forms of debt.

The second source of the impact of monetary policy is the effect of changes in monetary conditions on the earning capacity of a firm. Since all assets must be financed, any change in monetary policy affects the cost of a firm's financing. Tightening credit will increase the cost of financing, which by itself will result in lower earnings. The increased cost of credit will be reflected in the prices charged by the firm, which should dampen the demand for the company's output. Its buyers will find their credit more expensive, which may result in individuals, governments, and firms buying fewer goods and services. This reduced demand will reinforce the increased cost of financing and cause earnings to decline.

The cost of credit is altered

In addition to the impact on earnings, the tighter monetary policy will result in individuals increasing their required rate of return on equity investments. If investors can earn more on debt instruments than was possible before the increase in interest rates, they will require higher returns on equity investments. Higher returns are possible if stock prices fall. Thus, there is pressure from two sources on stock prices to fall. The higher interest rates will probably result in lower earnings and in higher required rates of return. Both of these will depress stock prices.

Investor's required rate of return may increase

This argument can be expressed in more formal terms by using the dividend-growth valuation model that was presented in Chapter 14. That model is

Impact of monetary policy on stock prices

$$V = \frac{D_0 (1 + g)}{r - g},$$

where V is the value of the stock, D_0 the dividend that is currently being paid, r the investors' required rate of return on stock, and g the firm's growth rate in earnings and dividends. A tightening of credit by the Federal Reserve may reduce the firm's growth rate and its capacity to pay dividends. Therefore, the value of D or g or both will decline, which will cause the price of the stock to decline. In addition, the required rate of return (r) will rise. This increases the denominator and causes the price of the stock to fall. Thus, tighter credit and higher interest rates generally indicate that the value of stock will decline. In terms of the constant growth valuation model, tight money reduces the numerator and increases the denominator, which puts downward pressure on the value of the stock.

This impact of monetary policy on security prices is illustrated in Figure 16.1. The figure relates the lending capacity of commercial banks to security prices for 1971 through 1981. The capacity of commercial banks to lend is measured by their free reserves, which are the excess reserves of commercial banks minus their borrowings of reserves from the Federal Reserve. These free reserves increase when credit is easy but decline and become negative when credit is tight. As may be seen from the figure, there is a definite relationship between commercial banks' capacity to lend and the level of stock prices. This figure strongly suggests that if the investor can anticipate changes in monetary policy, he or she should adopt a strategy of converting securities into cash or short-term assets as money gets tighter to produce positive investment results. The reverse strategy should be implemented when credit becomes easier.

The problem, of course, lies in determining which monetary policy is currently being followed by the Federal Reserve. This is best perceived through changes in the nation's stock of money and the reserves of commercial banks and through the policy

Figure 16.1
The Dow Jones Industrial Average and the Free Reserves of Commercial Banks (1971–1981)

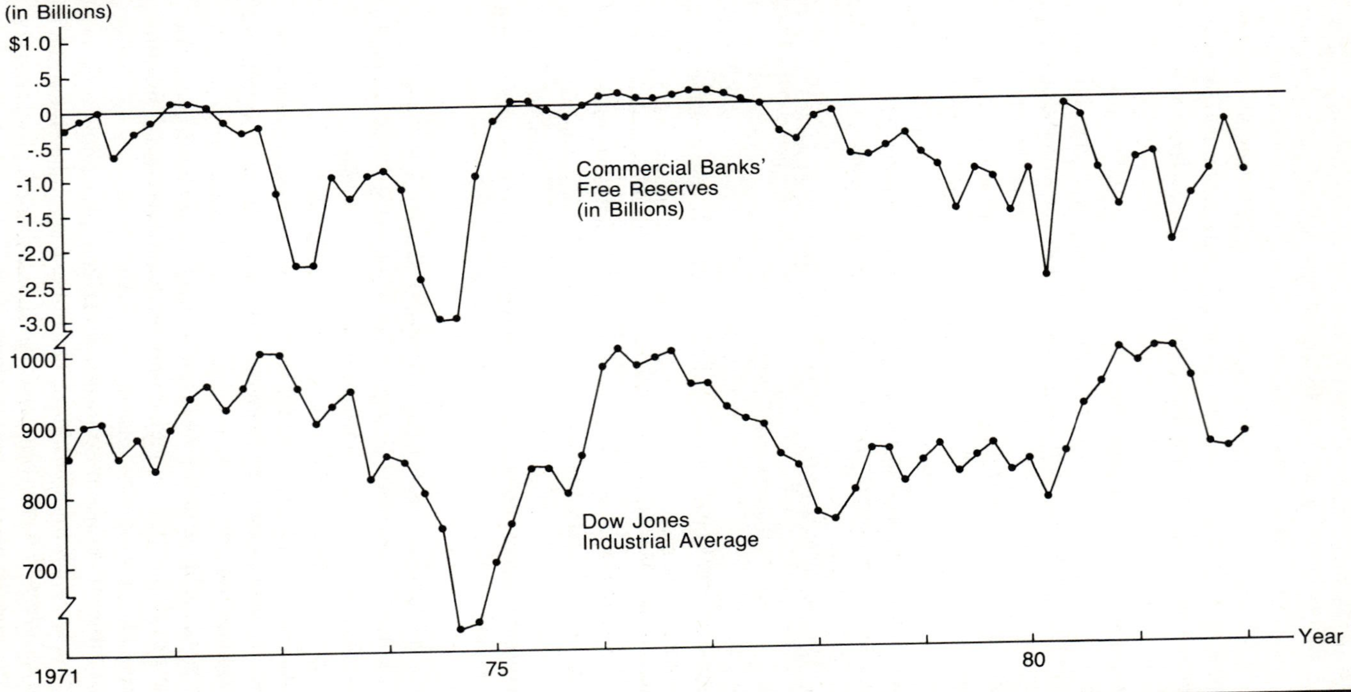

statements of the leaders of the Federal Reserve (i.e., the board of governors). The first two factors are reported weekly in the financial press. Data for several time periods are reported monthly in the *Federal Reserve Bulletin,* which may be readily obtained by subscription or in libraries. Policy statements are published in the financial press but are not neatly collected in one volume or publication for easy access.

Unfortunately, monetary statistics may not clearly indicate the monetary policy of the Federal Reserve. For example, the Federal Reserve's purpose is to control the money supply to stimulate economic growth and to maintain stable prices and full employment, but there is disagreement as to the composition of the money supply. The simplest definition of the **supply of money** (commonly referred to as **M-1**) is the sum of cash, coin, and checking accounts (including interest-bearing NOW accounts) in the hands of the general public. A broader definition (called **M-2**) adds savings accounts to the above definition. Thus if individuals shift funds from savings accounts to checking accounts, the money supply is increased under the narrow definition (M-1) but is unaffected if the broader definition (M-2) is employed.

The growth rate in the money supply will depend on the definition used by the analyst. Figure 16.2 plots M-1 and M-2 for the period 1980 through 1985. Over the entire time period, M-1 rose 8.64 percent annually while M-2 rose 9.02 percent. There were periods in which the rates of growth in M-1 and M-2 differed considerably. For example, during part of 1981, M-2 grew by 3.8 percent while M-1 grew by only 1.0 percent. There were even periods (such as early in 1984) when M-1 declined (by 1.3 percent) while M-2 rose (by about 1.0 percent).

While M-1 and M-2 may give conflicting signals, there is still a concensus that the Federal Reserve systematically expands the money supply over time to maintain economic growth. While the Federal Reserve cannot exactly control the week-to-week changes in M-1 or M-2, it can maintain growth in the money supply over a period of time within defined targets. These targets are established within the bounds the Fed believes will maintain economic growth without increasing inflationary pressure.

For illustrative purposes, assume that these targets range from a high of 6.0 percent to a low of 4.0 percent annual growth in the money supply. As long as the money supply is expanding within these targets, there may be little reason for the Federal Reserve to change its current monetary policy. However, if the rate of growth begins to exceed the upper limit (e.g., is 7.2 percent), the Fed may then take action to reduce the growth rate in the supply of money. Conversely, if the supply of money is expanding at a slower rate, such as 3.0 percent, the Fed may take action to increase the rate of growth in the money supply.

Such target growth in the money supply is illustrated in Figure 16.3, in which the vertical axis measures the money supply while the horizontal axis measures time. As of the present (t_0), the money supply is some amount X. If this amount grows at the upper limit of 6.0 percent, it will follow line XU. If, however, the growth rate in the supply of money is the lower limit of 4.0 percent, the money supply will follow line XL. The actual money supply may fluctuate between the two targets, as is illustrated during the time period $t_0 t_1$.

If the rate of growth were to increase and exceed the 6.0 percent target growth rate, the money supply would break the upper limit (e.g., t_2 in Figure 16.3). Since this excessive expansion in the money supply is inflationary, the Federal Reserve

Figure 16.2
Money Supply (M-1 and M-2), January 1980–December 1985

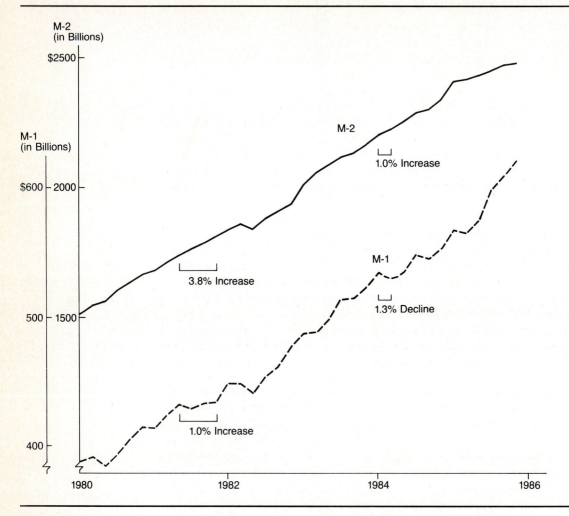

would probably take steps to reduce the money supply's growth. The financial analyst would then expect monetary policy to tighten, which would cause interest rates to increase. This then suggests that the investor should liquidate long-term holdings and move into short-term, liquid securities.

Conversely, if the rate of growth in the money supply were to decline below the 4.0 percent target growth rate, the money supply would break the lower limit, t_3 in Figure 16.3. Since this reduction in the money supply would retard economic growth, the Federal Reserve would probably take steps to increase the growth rate in the money supply. The financial analyst would then expect monetary policy to ease credit, which would cause interest rates to fall. Such a scenario suggests that investors should move out of short-term investments into longer-term securities.

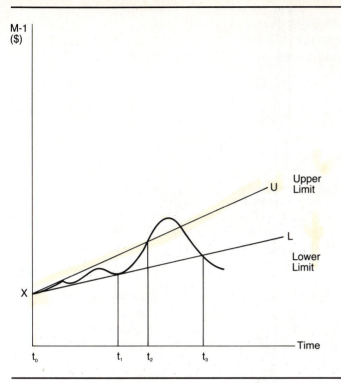

Figure 16.3
Upper and Lower Limits in the Growth of the Money Supply

It should be noted that the investor is not concerned with the absolute level of the money supply but with the trend (i.e., the rate of growth) and changes in the trend. Emphasis may be placed on anticipating changes in the Federal Reserve's policy. Thus a decrease in the money supply, which could be interpreted as an attempt by the Federal Reserve to tighten credit, may actually be taken as a bullish sign. The current decrease in the supply of money may suggest that the Federal Reserve will ease credit and increase the money supply in the future. Such anticipation of future expansionary monetary policy may imply that interest rates will decline in the future and now is the time to acquire interest-sensitive securities.

FISCAL POLICY

In addition to the monetary policy of the Federal Reserve, the fiscal policy of the federal government can play an important role in the security markets. **Fiscal policy** is taxation, expenditures, and debt management by the federal government. Like monetary policy, fiscal policy may be used to pursue the economic goals of price stability, full employment, and economic growth.

Obviously taxation can have an impact on security prices. Corporate income taxes reduce corporate earnings and hence reduce firms' capacity to pay dividends

and to retain earnings for growth. Personal income taxes reduce disposable income. This reduces demand for goods and services as well as savings that would be invested in some asset. Federal taxes also affect the demand for specific securities, such as tax-exempt bonds. Thus the tax policies may affect not only the level of security prices but also relative prices, as certain types of assets receive favorable tax treatment.

The potential impact of the federal government's fiscal policy is not limited to taxation. Expenditures can also affect security prices. This should be obvious with regard to the specific products bought by the government. Such purchases may increase a particular firm's earnings and help enhance its stock's price. However, expenditures in general, especially **deficit spending,** can affect the financial markets and security prices.

Expenditures exceed revenues

When the federal government's expenditures exceed revenues, it runs a deficit. The federal government may obtain funds to finance this deficit from three sources: (1) the general public, (2) banks, and (3) the Federal Reserve. When the federal government sells securities to the general public to finance the deficit, these securities compete directly with all other securities for the funds of savers. This increased supply of federal government securities will tend to decrease security prices and increase their yields.

A similar conclusion applies to sales of treasury securities to banks. If the banks lend money to the federal government, they cannot lend these funds to individuals and businesses. The effect will be to raise the cost of loans as the banks ration their supply of loanable funds. Higher borrowing costs should tend to reduce security prices for several reasons. First, higher costs should reduce corporate earnings, which will have an impact on dividends and growth rates. Second, higher borrowing costs should reduce the attractiveness of buying securities on credit (i.e., margin) and thus reduce the demand for securities. Third, the higher costs of borrowing will probably encourage banks to raise the rates they pay depositors. Especially, the rates on negotiable certificates of deposit should rise as the banks attempt to attract funds. Since all short-term rates are highly correlated, increases in one rate will be transferred to other rates. Once again the higher interest rates in general produce lower security prices.

If the Federal Reserve were to finance the federal government's deficit, the impact would be the same as if the Fed had purchased securities through open market operations. In either case the money supply would be expanded. In effect when the Fed buys the securities issued to finance the federal government's deficit, the Fed is monetizing the debt because new money is created. This new money may initially cause security prices to rise; however, the longer term impact may be to cause security prices to fall. If the public perceives this newly created money as inflationary, required rates of return will rise. Investors will seek higher returns to compensate them for the loss of purchasing power caused by the inflation. The higher required rates of return will drive down security prices.

Thus the security markets are not immune to the fiscal policy of the federal government. As with monetary policy, if the investor could anticipate changes, then he or she could take steps now to profit by the changes in fiscal policy. It is for this reason that investors are so concerned with the policies of both the Federal Reserve and the federal government, since policy actions by either can have a substantial impact on security prices.

INDUSTRY ANALYSIS

Firms are not unique unto themselves but exist within the framework of a specific   *Cyclical industries*
industry. Some industries tend to be very cyclical and move with the economy. Examples of **cyclical industries** include the automobile and building industries. Since
consumers can defer such high-priced items from one year to the next, sales in these
industries tend to be exaggerated by economic fluctuations. Car sales and housing
starts can vary significantly from year to year, and, as would be expected, earnings of
firms in these industries also tend to fluctuate.

The fluctuations in revenues and earnings of a cyclical firm are illustrated in Figure 16.4. The firm, Lone Star Industries, produces cement and related building materials, so its sales and earnings fluctuate with the fortunes of the construction industry.

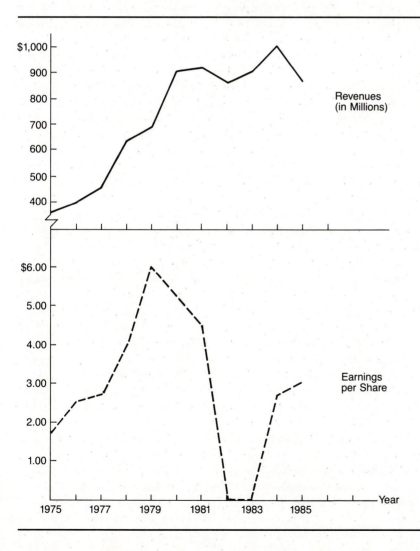

Figure 16.4
Cyclical Sales and
Earnings: Lone Star
Industries

This may be seen in the figure during 1980 to 1983. Housing and construction were particularly hard hit by the high interest rates of the period, which precipitated a large decline in Lone Star Industries' earnings from a high of $5.95 in 1979 to a low of $0.05 and $0.07 in 1982 and 1983, respectively.

The investor should also note that earnings tend to fluctuate more than revenues, as firms have fixed costs that cannot be deferred. Although some costs vary with the level of sales, fixed costs do not. Even when sales decline, these costs still exist and must be met, which causes greater variations in earnings than in revenues.

Stable industries

While some industries are cyclical, others are not. Some are quite stable even though the economy may be in a recession. These industries include food processing and retailing. Such purchases must be made on a continual basis by consumers. People have to eat, and such purchases cannot be deferred. Figure 16.5 illustrates a firm that is representative of these industries. The sales and earnings per share of Campbell Soups do not fluctuate as much as the sales and earnings of Lone Star Industries, as shown in Figure 16.4. The earnings of Campbell Soups rose almost consistently during the same period.

The fact that some firms are in cyclical industries while others are in more stable industries does not imply that investors should purchase securities in the latter group to the exclusion of those in the former. Security markets tend to smooth out the fluctuations in earnings so the firm's value is related to its performance over a period of time. As the valuation models presented in Chapter 14 indicated, the flow of dividend income and the growth in the firm's earnings over many years (all properly discounted back to the present) ultimately determine the value of the shares. The fact that a firm is in a cyclical industry does not by itself imply that the firm's securities are inferior investments. It indicates that such investments are riskier. Nor does the fact that a firm is in a more stable industry mean that the firm's securities are superior investments. These securities tend to be less risky.

Growth industries

Perhaps the ideal investment is in a firm in a growing industry. Demand for the firm's output can be anticipated to grow, and even if more companies enter the market the expansion of the market itself will permit the firm to maintain its profits in the face of increased competition. Identifying such industries is not easy. Airlines were considered a growth industry in the 1960s but fell on hard times in the 1970s. Other technologically oriented industries, such as those that produce copiers, semiconductors, and computers, have provided excellent examples of past growth. Perhaps home computers will be tomorrow's growth industry. Even industries that were once considered mature may regain their former growth.

While many previous growth industries were based on technological change, future growth need not necessarily be built on technology. Consumer tastes change, and, as incomes increase, consumers may buy different types of products. More income may be spent on services, travel, or fine-quality consumer durable goods, such as crystal instead of glass. Companies in these industries may become the next generation of growth firms. The best investments, then, should prove to be in the securities of firms that are able either to capitalize on technological change or to expand and take advantage of shifts in demand.

In addition to studying the type of industry, the financial analyst will consider such factors as government regulations, labor conditions, and the financing requirements of the industry. While all industries are subject to regulation, some are more

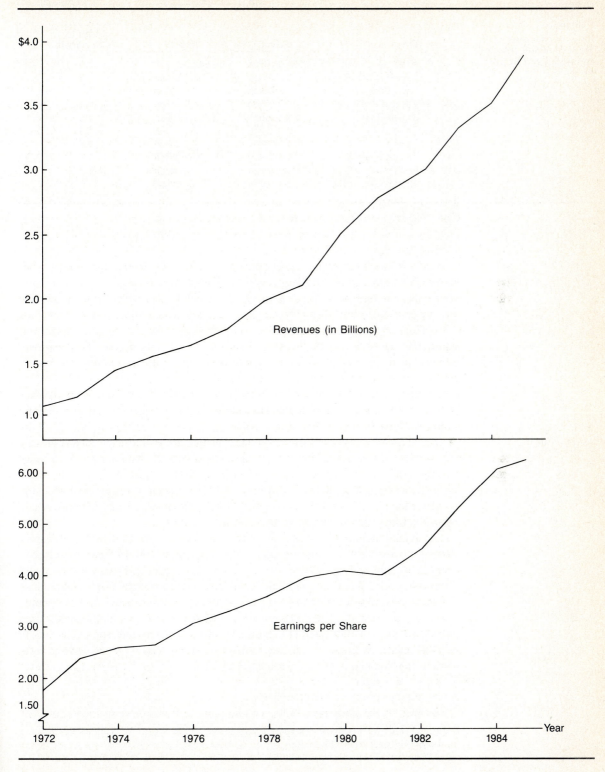

Figure 16.5
Noncyclical Sales and Earnings: Campbell Soups, 1972–1985

Exhibit 16.1
Ratio of Revenues to
Total Assets of Selected
Industrial and Retail
Firms

Firm	Sales	Assets	Sales to Total Assets
AT&T	$34.9 billion	$45.0 billion	0.9
Reynolds Metals	3.4 billion	3.6 billion	0.9
Coca-Cola	7.9 billion	6.9 billion	1.1
Georgia-Pacific	6.7 billion	4.9 billion	1.4
James River	2.5 billion	1.7 billion	1.5
Philip Morris	13.8 billion	9.3 billion	1.5
Fluor	4.2 billion	2.8 billion	1.5
VF (Lee Jeans)	1.4 billion	0.9 billion	1.7
Best Products	2.2 billion	1.3 billion	1.7
The Limited	2.4 billion	1.2 billion	2.0

Source: Annual reports for 1985 fiscal year.

heavily regulated than others. For example, utilities such as electric, gas, and telecommunications are subject to a large amount of regulation as to the price firms may charge and the returns they may earn for their stockholders. This regulatory climate varies from state to state. If a utility operates in a state whose utility commission tends to be more stringent, that utility will often experience lower returns on assets and equity. This tends to result in lower dividends and a lower stock price. Any improvement in the firm's regulatory climate may increase the stock's price as investors anticipate higher earnings and dividends.

Labor conditions also affect the analysis of an industry. The presence of labor unions or the industry's need for skilled labor can have an impact on earnings. Strong unions such as those that exist in airlines (e.g., the pilots' union) or mining (e.g., the United Mine Workers) can affect earnings through strikes and expensive contracts. The need for specialized labor such as engineers can also have an impact on earnings as firms pay generous salaries in an effort to bid away skilled workers from other firms. An analysis of the history of strikes and previous labor negotiations or an analysis of the supply of available skilled labor can give the financial analyst considerable insight into the risk associated with the industry as a whole.

Financing requirements also can have an impact on firms' earnings. Industries that are growing or use a large amount of plant and equipment need more funds than more stable and less capital intensive industries. For example, firms with oil operations need a substantial amount of plant and equipment, since drilling for oil requires investments in rigs, completed wells require transportation systems, and oil refining requires investment in plant and equipment. Differences in the amount of assets used to generate sales are illustrated in Exhibit 16.1, which presents the ratio of revenues to total assets for ten firms. AT&T uses more than $1 in assets to generate $1 in revenues, while The Limited (a retailer) generates $2 in revenues for every $1 in assets.[2]

---

[2] These numbers may be somewhat misleading since a firm may have lease obligations that are not on the balance sheet. Leases are an alternative to debt financing, and under some circumstances must be "capitalized," which means that the present value of the obligation is stated as an asset and the lease obligation as a liability. The asset is then reduced as the lease payments are made. If a firm has uncapitalized leases (and these would have to be given in a footnote to the financial statements), that would imply its assets are understated, which artificially increases the ratio of revenues to total assets.

The larger the amount of assets needed to generate sales, the larger is the potential impact on earnings. All assets necessitate a source of funds. Debt financing requires servicing (interest and principal repayment), and additional equity financing spreads earnings over more shares, which may decrease earnings per share. Thus, this need for funds to finance plant and equipment can have an impact on the valuation of an individual firm's stock because such financing can have an impact on the firm's earnings.

THE ANTICIPATED ECONOMIC ENVIRONMENT AND INVESTMENT STRATEGIES

Investing would certainly be easier if there were an identifiable relationship between a specific asset's return and the general economy. Then changes in the economy would lead to predictable changes in the asset's price and its return. In some cases such relationships do exist. For example, real estate values tend to increase with higher prices in general, and bond prices are responsive to changes in interest rates.

However, for many assets, especially common stocks, the linkage between an asset's price (i.e., the return it offers) and the general economy is very complex. An expanding economy may increase the demand for a firm's product, which leads to higher earnings. The higher earnings may permit increased dividends or growth, since the firm has more funds to reinvest. If other factors are held constant, the expanding economy should lead to higher stock prices. Unfortunately, those factors cannot be relied on to remain constant. The expanding economy may result in higher wages and salaries, higher interest rates, increased competition, the deterioration of the value of the dollar in regard to other currencies, higher taxes, and rising prices. All of these factors may have an adverse effect on the firm. The other factors may offset the positive impact of the higher earnings or may even cause the increase in earnings to never materialize.

Expanding economy may lead to higher earnings

The relationship between the economy and investment selection is made more difficult when one realizes that security prices are a harbinger of economic activity and not a mirror. Changes in security prices tend to precede changes in economic activity. If an investor waits until the economy has changed before executing a particular strategy based on that economy, the action is often too late. Security prices may have already incorporated the economic change.

Stock prices are a leading indicator

While this discussion suggests that it is not simple to link the economy to investing and security selection, there still are strategies the individual investor may follow. For example, changes in interest rates, changes in the rate of inflation or deflation, increased unemployment and recession, and continued economic growth may each suggest a particular strategy that is more desirable and should be followed.

Changes in Interest Rates

Those securities whose return primarily consists of a fixed flow of income, such as long-term bonds, preferred stock, and the common stocks of public utility companies, are particularly sensitive to changes in interest rates. In addition, the common stocks of financial institutions and firms in cyclical industries such as building supplies are considered sensitive to interest rate changes.

Most long-term bonds pay a fixed dollar amount of interest each year. As yields rise elsewhere, this fixed flow of income is no longer competitive with other investments whose flow of income is not fixed. Therefore, investors may seek to sell long-term bonds and place the funds in money market mutual funds and other liquid assets whose flow of income will increase with the higher level of interest rates. This selling pressure drives down the prices of long-term, fixed-income securities. Thus, anticipation of higher interest rates certainly implies that the investor should seek to move out of long-term, fixed-income securities. Conversely, anticipation of lower interest rates implies that such securities should be acquired. Purchases of long-term bonds lock in the fixed flow of interest income, and the prices of these bonds will rise when interest rates fall.

Changes in interest rates may affect stock prices

The common stock of some firms is also very sensitive to changing interest rates. For example, the prices of public utility stocks, especially power companies, fluctuate with changes in interest rates. Many of these companies distribute a large proportion of their earnings. Since much of the return the investor can anticipate is the flow of dividend income, the common stocks of public utilities are similar to long-term bonds. Unless the dividends increase to offset rising interest rates, the prices of public utility stocks will decline (the stocks' prices move inversely with changes in interest rates).

The common stocks of financial institutions such as commercial banks and savings and loan institutions are also sensitive to changes in interest rates because higher interest rates increase banks' cost of funds. Since their primary sources of funds are the various types of deposit accounts they offer, higher interest rates will require banks to make higher interest payments to depositors. While lending institutions will certainly attempt to pass along their higher interest costs when they make loans, the differential between what they receive and what they pay for deposit funds tends to decline during a period of higher interest rates. This reduces profitability and lowers the prices of their common stock. Thus the anticipation of higher interest rates suggests that investors shift funds from the common stocks of financial institutions into other investments.

Cyclical firms affected by changing interest rates

Cyclical firms produce goods such as houses, automobiles, and other consumer durables that require a large expenditure by the consumer. The purchase of a new car or durable good may be deferred. The purchase of a house may even be postponed indefinitely if the higher interest rates make mortgage payments more than the individual can afford to service.

The ability of consumers to postpone purchases of durables suggests that the demand for these products will fluctuate with changes in interest rates. Periods of high interest rates reduce demand, which, in turn, leads to lower sales and lower profits for firms in cyclical industries. The lower profits make cyclical firms less attractive to investors, as the capacity to pay dividends and retain earnings to finance future growth is reduced. Anticipation of higher interest rates suggests that the common stocks of cyclical firms should be sold. Conversely, expectations of lower interest rates imply that these stocks should be purchased. Cyclical firms may be among the best performing investments when lower interest rates and economic growth occur.

Anticipation of higher interest rates

As the above discussion implies, the anticipation of higher interest rates suggests that investors avoid (1) fixed-income investments, (2) firms, such as utilities or banks, whose cost of funds is sensitive to changes in interest rates and who are unable to pass on the increased cost, and (3) firms in cyclical industries whose product demand is

affected by changes in interest rates. Of course, the opposite would hold for expectations of declining interest rates. These investments may prove to be among the most profitable if the investor is correct and interest rates do fall.

While the anticipation of higher interest rates implies that the individual should avoid many assets, that does not answer the question of which assets should be acquired. If the investor anticipates higher interest rates (and correspondingly lower security prices), he or she should acquire more liquid investments and debt instruments with short maturities, such as treasury bills, shares of money market mutual funds, and certificates of deposit. The yields on these assets will tend to increase with any increase in interest rates, and the principal is relatively safe. These short-term debt instruments frequently mature, providing an opportunity to reinvest the funds at the then current rates. Thus if interest rates continue to increase, the investor is in the position to take advantage of the higher rates.

Liquid investments

If the investor anticipates that interest rates will fall, a bullish position is established by purchasing interest-sensitive securities such as long-term bonds. If the investor wants to follow a more aggressive strategy, that individual may purchase bonds with long terms to maturity or with poorer quality ratings, since such bonds' prices will tend to rise more during periods of declining interest rates.

Anticipation of lower interest rates

Inflation

The anticipation of inflation (i.e., expectation of higher prices of goods and services) will also imply an expectation of higher interest rates for several reasons. In an attempt to slow inflation, the Federal Reserve will tighten credit to reduce the supply of money and credit. Monetary policy will also reduce the supply of available credit. In addition, creditors, being aware that inflation reduces the purchasing power of the funds they lend, will protect this purchasing power by demanding a higher return for the use of their funds. All of these actions will also drive up interest rates.

Inflation associated with higher interest rates

Several of the previously discussed strategies appropriate during periods of higher interest are also appropriate during a period of inflation. In particular, investors should avoid interest-sensitive securities and long-term debt instruments that pay fixed amounts of interest and should acquire short-term instruments (e.g., U.S. Treasury bills) whose yields will increase with the rate of inflation.

However, the anticipation of inflation requires more than a passive strategy of holding short-term liquid assets. The investor should also acquire those assets that will benefit from the inflationary environment. The prices of real estate and other physical assets tend to increase during a period of inflation. Thus, the investor may seek to move out of financial assets into tangible assets.

Selected assets benefit through inflation

The common stocks of selected firms may also do well in an inflationary environment. Companies that own substantial amounts of physical resources (e.g., oil, metals, land) tend to prosper during inflation, as their assets' value increases with the general rise in prices. The real value of these assets is usually hidden from investors, as firms carry the assets on their balance sheets at cost rather than at current market value. However, the prices of the common stocks of firms with such "hidden assets" may rise as the replacement cost of these assets increases. In general, any firm with a rich asset base such as metals or real estate may experience rapid growth in earnings that is directly attributable to higher prices (i.e., the inflationary environment).

Understated or "hidden" assets

The expectation of an inflationary environment thus suggests that the investor should stress liquid assets, tangible assets, and the common stocks of firms whose asset base will be enhanced by increased asset values. Correspondingly, the investor should not acquire fixed-income instruments, long-term debt obligations, and the common stocks of firms lacking assets whose prices will rise with inflation. In a sense the strategy is more defensive than offensive, as it is built around retaining and protecting the investor's current purchasing power and the real (deflated) value of assets held.

Deflation

Declining prices

Deflation, the opposite of inflation, is a period of declining prices. Thus, the prices of tangible assets such as real estate, collectibles, and precious metals will fall during a period of deflation. The anticipation of deflation strongly suggests that the investor should acquire those financial assets whose value will appreciate; then the individual can acquire the tangible assets once their prices have fallen.

The safest strategy is to acquire short-term liquid assets such as bank deposits. Since deflation increases the purchasing power of money, the investor will want to hold money (e.g., NOW accounts) and other liquid assets. However, deflation should also be accompanied by declining interest rates and rising bond prices. A deflationary environment should make long-term debt obligations exceptionally good investments.

Importance of quality

If the individual does acquire long-term bonds, he or she should purchase only bonds of excellent quality. Deflation may be accompanied by many bankruptcies as firms become unable to meet their financial obligations. The safest strategy for investors, then, may be to acquire only the bonds issued by the federal government and large industrial firms, major utilities (especially the regulated phone companies), and firms with strong financial statements. The investor should limit purchases to quality fixed-income securities because the bonds' value is primarily related to the ability of the debtor firms to service the debt. If these firms are able to maintain timely interest and principal payments, the value of the bonds will appreciate as falling interest rates accompany the deflation.

The same stress on quality also applies to investments in common stocks. However, since many firms will experience falling demand for their products, difficulty in collecting accounts receivable, and declining profit margins, many firms' stocks may prove to be poor investments during a deflationary period. However, the deflation may create excellent buying opportunities should stock prices be driven down sufficiently.

Recession and Economic Stagnation

Rising unemployment

Periods of recession and economic stagnation will require different strategies. Recession is a period of rising unemployment (which may or may not be accompanied by deflation). During a recession, the Federal Reserve will put money into circulation and expand the supply of credit. This expansion will at least initially decrease interest rates until the stimulus increases the level of economic activity.

The federal government will adopt an expansionary fiscal policy. Lower taxes and increased government expenditures will increase aggregate demand for goods and services. This increased demand is designed to stimulate economic activity, which, in turn, should reduce the level of unemployment.

To take advantage of the economic stimulus, the investor will seek to move out of short-term money market instruments into financial assets, especially the common stocks of firms that will benefit from the expansionary monetary and fiscal policy. Firms that produce consumer goods or durables such as automobiles and housing may profit from the expansion in the economy. Retailing firms and firms that produce leisure goods or provide services will prosper as the economy moves from the period of economic stagnation and recession toward expansion and economic growth. Increased business activity should also generate increased investment in plant and equipment. Manufacturers of capital goods, machine tools, and other inputs necessary for the production of consumer goods and services will experience increased demand, which may result in increased profits.

Economic stimulus

The investor, however, should realize that not all firms will perform equally well during a period of induced expansion. Expansionary monetary and fiscal policy does not imply that all firms will prosper. In addition, some forms of stimulatory policy are not general in their effect. The investment tax credit and more generous accelerated depreciation allowances, which have been used to stimulate economic expansion, favor firms that make substantial investments in plant and equipment. Firms that provide services may not require as much of an investment in long-term physical assets to generate sales. Thus these firms will not be helped as much as the firms that are able to take advantage of changes in the tax codes.

Impact may not be general

Once the investor identifies the firms most likely to benefit from the expansionary monetary and fiscal policy, he or she may adopt any of a number of individual strategies, ranging from conservative to very aggressive. A conservative strategy may include convertible securities (i.e., convertible bonds and preferred stock, discussed in Chapter 21) and common stocks of firms with low beta coefficients. Fixed-income securities may be purchased in anticipation of lower interest rates. But the investor must be willing to rapidly move out of fixed-income securities, because they do not benefit from economic expansion per se and may be hurt if the expansion leads to higher interest rates.

A more aggressive strategy designed to take advantage of expansionary fiscal and monetary policy will stress less current income (i.e., no fixed-income securities) and more potential for capital gains. The investor will then primarily purchase common stocks of firms with low payout ratios that retain earnings to finance expansion. Such common stocks have the best possibility of generating capital appreciation during an expansionary period.[3]

Economic Growth

A period of sustained economic growth differs from a period of expansion generated through the use of stimulatory monetary and fiscal policy. Monetary policy is often designed to thwart a return of inflation and may be only mildly stimulatory. Interest rates may be stable and higher than would be necessary to stimulate the economy. Fiscal policy may also not be designed to generate demand other than for those goods

Sustained economic growth

---

[3] The investor could adopt a very aggressive strategy through the use of options and futures contracts, which are discussed in Chapters 19, 20, and 23. He or she would purchase call options or sell put options for the common stocks that were expected to increase in price. Stock index futures or stock market options could be purchased, since the prices of these contracts will increase if the expansionary fiscal and monetary policy increases security prices in general.

and services that are a necessary component of operating the government. New tax laws designed to stimulate the economy may not be forthcoming.

During such a period, the investor cannot rely on lower interest rates or expansionist government policy to boost security prices, but instead must rely on economic growth to generate returns. Possible investments may include the common stocks of firms with good financial positions and records of sustained earnings and dividend growth. The prospect for continued, sustainable growth is crucial to generate a return during a period of economic growth with neutral expansionary and monetary policy.

Intermediate- and long-term bonds may be acquired during this period by investors seeking current income. There is less need for liquidity to take advantage of anticipated lower prices of tangible assets or securities. Thus investors may be more willing to acquire these long-term investments. However, these individuals must be willing to change such a strategy rapidly should the period of economic growth start to increase the inflation rate.

An aggressive investor may purchase common stocks with an emphasis on growth potential. However, the investor must realize that while a rising stock market will tend to increase the value of most stocks, some will lag behind. Obviously if the investor purchases those laggards, he or she will not participate in the rally.

Active portfolio management

Portfolio management and asset selection can be designed to meet the investor's expectations of higher or lower interest rates, inflation or deflation, recession or economic growth. Such portfolio construction requires active decision making. If the investor does not want to devote the time and effort to active portfolio management, that

Mutual fund shares

individual may buy the shares of investment companies, such as mutual funds. As is discussed in Chapter 22, each mutual fund identifies the strategies and goals (e.g., growth or income) that it follows. The investor then selects the funds whose strategies and goals are consistent with his or her own. For example, if the investor anticipates inflation and wants a position in gold, he or she may purchase shares in a gold fund. Anticipation of lower interest rates suggests purchasing the shares on a bond fund.

Since more than one fund pursues a particular strategy, the individual must choose among the various funds. However, the investor is relieved of the decision as to which individual securities to acquire.

SUMMARY

Fundamental financial analysis selects stocks by identifying the strongest firms within an industry. The analysis starts by considering the direction of the aggregate economy, since security prices respond to economic activity. During periods of prosperity, stock prices tend to rise. Conversely, stock prices will fall when investors anticipate recession and sluggish economic growth.

The aggregate economy is affected by many factors, but the monetary policy of the Federal Reserve and the fiscal policy of the federal government are particularly important. Both the Fed and the federal government pursue the general economic goals of full employment, stable prices, and economic growth. The Federal Reserve affects economic activity through its impact on the supply of money and credit. The federal government affects the economy through taxation, expenditures, and how its deficit is financed. Both monetary and fiscal policy can alter security prices through

their impact on interest rates and their impact on firms' earnings (and hence on dividends and growth rates).

Firms exist within an industry. Factors that affect an industry also have an impact on the individual firm. Government regulations, the existence of labor unions, skilled labor requirements, technological changes, and cyclical demand for an industry's output can and do alter the earnings of a firm. The financial analyst thus considers those characteristics of an industry that play an important role in determining the capacity of the individual firm to succeed and grow within its industry.

Investment strategies are affected by the economic environment. During a period of rising interest rates, the investor should seek liquid, short-term investments and avoid long-term, fixed-income securities. Expectations of increasing inflation also call for avoiding long-term investments, as well as for acquiring those tangible assets whose value will increase with the rate of inflation, such as real estate and precious metals. Expectation of deflation suggests that these assets should be avoided.

During a period of recession, the investor should acquire assets such as the common stocks of firms that will benefit from expansionary monetary and fiscal policy. While in a period of sustained economic growth, the individual may prefer long-term investments in firms whose position is sufficiently strong to sustain and finance growth.

None of these economic scenarios has one simple strategy. There are so many possible investments, ranging from extremely conservative to extremely risky and volatile, that may be appropriate for a particular investment strategy. Also, some alternatives may not be appropriate for a particular investor whose willingness to bear risk differs from the risk exposure generated by the particular asset. However, these same assets may be combined in ways that will suit another investor's strategy and willingness to bear risk.

Active management of a portfolio based on moves in the economy requires portfolio shifts before the economy changes. The individual must anticipate when interest rates will rise or fall in order to take advantage of the price changes in fixed-income securities. The investor must anticipate inflation in order to purchase real assets before the inflation occurs. To take advantage of sustained economic growth, the investor must anticipate when that growth will occur and which firms will benefit. Once economic change has occurred, it will be too late, as security prices will have already changed.

It is not sufficient to base portfolio decisions on today's economy. It is the future economic environment that is crucial, which helps explain why portfolio decisions based on the anticipated economy are among the most difficult decisions facing the individual investor.

Terms to Remember

Recession
Forecasting
Federal Reserve
Reserves
Reserve requirements
Discount rate

Open market operations
Supply of money: M-1 and M-2
Fiscal policy
Deficit spending
Cyclical industry

Questions

1. Where can the investor find economic forecasts?

2. What is the Federal Reserve? What are its economic goals? How may the Fed pursue its economic goals?

3. What are open market operations? How may they affect security prices?

4. What are M-1 and M-2? How may the Federal Reserve alter M-1 or M-2?

5. What are the differences between monetary policy and fiscal policy?

6. If the federal government runs a deficit, where do the funds come from that finance this deficit?

7. What is a "cyclical" industry? Is it undesirable to invest in firms in cyclical industries?

8. Classify the following firms as either cyclical, growth, or stable (based on the nature of their respective industries).
   - Apple Computer
   - U.S. Homes
   - Philadelphia Electric
   - MCI Communications
   - Reynolds Metals

9. If an investor expects interest rates and prices to decline, what types of financial assets should be acquired?

10. What are the linkages between higher interest rates and stock prices?

11. Should economic stimulus by the federal government generate higher or lower earnings? What types of industries will benefit from higher depreciation allowances? Why will an expansionary monetary policy encourage investments in long-term financial assets?

12. Which is more important from an investment perspective—current earnings or anticipated earnings?

Suggested Readings

In addition to the readings at the end of Chapter 2, material on the economic and financial environment may be found in:

Board of Governors. *The Federal Reserve System—Purposes and Functions.* Washington, D.C.: Government Printing Office, 1974.
This is a concise introduction to the structure and role of the Federal Reserve.
Federal Reserve Bulletin.
This monthly publication reports financial data including interest rates, employment, gross national product, and the money supply.
U.S. President's Council of Economic Advisors. *Economic Report of the President.*
This annual publication reports the fiscal policy (i.e., taxation and expenditures) of the federal government.

For a discussion of using past money supply data to forecast future stock prices, see:

Rozeff, Michael. "The Money Supply and the Stock Market." *Financial Analysts Journal* (September–October 1975): 18–26.

Evidence from previous business cycles suggests that stock prices lead business activity, which implies that stock purchases should precede economic expansion and that sales should occur while the economy is still expanding (i.e., before recession starts). See:

Piccini, Raymond. "Stock Market Behavior Around Business Cycle Peaks." *Financial Analysts Journal* (July–August 1980): 55–57.

Several advanced textbooks on investments cover at length the relationships between the aggregate economy and security markets. See, for instance:

Cohen, Jerome B., Edward D. Zinbarg, and Arthur Zeikel. *Investment Analysis and Portfolio Management.* 4th ed. Homewood, Ill.: Richard D. Irwin, 1982, 247–293 and 412–443.

Kolb, Robert W. *Investments.* Glenview, Ill.: Scott, Foresman, 1986, 265–293.

17 Security Selection: Analysis of Financial Statements

LEARNING OBJECTIVES

After completing this chapter you should be able to

1. Differentiate between (a) the current ratio and the quick ratio, (b) accounts receivable turnover and the average collection period, and (c) gross profit margin, operating profit margin, and net profit margin.

2. Identify which ratios are a primary interest to short-term creditors, long-term creditors, and stockholders.

3. Apply ratios to analyze the financial statements of a firm.

4. Compare a firm's ratios with other firms in its industry.

5. Be able to trace the effect of a change in a firm's financial statements on the analysis of the statements.

The preceding chapter considered the aggregate economic picture and how expected changes in the economy may affect investment strategy. However, after deciding on a strategy, the individual still must decide which specific securities to buy. The investor cannot buy every bond or stock but must choose among an almost unlimited number of possibilities. This chapter helps in security selection by focusing on the financial condition of the firm.

Most of the chapter is devoted to ratios that are used to analyze a firm's financial statements. The analysis may cover a period of time to determine trends, or one firm may be compared with similar firms or with industry averages to ascertain the firm's position within its industry.

There are many ratios that the financial analyst may compute, but they all may be classified into one of four groups. These include (1) liquidity ratios, which seek to determine if a firm can meet its financial obligations as they come due; (2) activity ratios, which tell how rapidly assets flow through the firm; (3) profitability ratios, which measure performance; and (4) leverage ratios, which measure the extent to which a firm uses debt financing.

Since the data used in this analysis is taken from the firm's financial statements, an understanding of the components of these statements is a prerequisite for understanding ratio analysis.

At the beginning of this chapter, each ratio is defined, explained, and illustrated. Next follows a discussion of which ratios are the most appropriate for bondholders and which are the most important from the stockholder's perspective. The final section ties together ratio analysis and valuation, presented earlier in Chapter 14. The ratio analysis indicates the firm's financial condition and performance while valuation determines how much the investor is willing to pay for the stock. Together these tools help determine if the firm's stock is under- or overvalued.

RATIO ANALYSIS

Ratios, which are probably the most frequently used tool to analyze a company, are popular because they are readily understood and can be computed with ease. In addition, the information used in ratio analysis is easy to obtain, for many ratios employ data available in a firm's annual and quarterly reports. Ratios are used not only by investors but also by a firm's management and its creditors. Management may use ratio analysis to plan, to control, and to identify weaknesses within the firm. Creditors use the analysis to establish the ability of the borrower to pay interest and retire debt. Stockholders are primarily concerned with performance and employ ratio analysis to measure profitability.

Although a variety of people use ratio analysis, they should select those ratios that are best suited to their specific purposes. As is illustrated later in this chapter, a bondholder is concerned primarily with the firm's ability to pay interest and repay principal and is less concerned with the rate at which the firm's inventory is sold. While the rate at which fixed assets turn over may affect the ability of the company to pay the interest and principal, the typical bondholder is more concerned with the firm's capacity to generate cash.

A need to select appropriate ratios

The investor may find that a specific industry requires additional ratios or more sophisticated versions of a particular ratio. For example, the ratios used to analyze public utilities are considerably different from those used to analyze railroads. Although both are highly regulated and have many similarities, such as large investments in plant and equipment, the natures of the industries are quite different, including factors such as the labor requirements, the element of competition, and the demand for each service. Emphasis, then, is placed on different factors, such as miles traveled per ton of freight for railroads versus the peak load requirements relative to the average demand for electricity for an electric utility.

Ratios may be computed and interpreted from two perspectives. They may be compiled for a number of years to perceive trends, which is called **time-series analysis.** Or they may be compared at a given time for several firms within the same industry, known as **cross-sectional analysis.** Time-series and cross-sectional analysis may be used together, as the analyst will compare the firm to its industry over a period of years.

Exhibit 17.1
**Chesapeake Corporation
Consolidated Balance
Sheet**

Consolidated Balance Sheet

Assets

	December 31, 1985	December 30, 1984
	(In millions)	
Current assets:		
Cash	$ 2.8	$ 2.7
Accounts receivable, net	44.3	31.0
Refundable income taxes	4.6	—
Inventories	61.2	37.8
Other	2.3	3.7
Total current assets	115.2	75.2
Property, plant and equipment:		
Plant sites and buildings	69.2	31.2
Machinery and equipment	537.2	322.4
Construction in progress	6.4	20.0
	612.8	373.6
Less accumulated depreciation	196.3	169.9
	416.5	203.7
Timber and timberlands, net	38.2	39.1
Net property, plant and equipment	454.7	242.8
Goodwill, net	37.8	3.3
Other assets	10.1	9.6
	$617.8	$330.9

Liabilities and Stockholders' Equity

	December 31, 1985	December 30, 1984
Current liabilities:		
Accounts payable and accrued expenses	$ 43.3	$ 21.9
Current maturities of long-term debt	2.6	2.2
Notes payable – timber properties	.5	.7
Dividends payable	2.1	2.1
Income taxes	3.3	2.1
Total current liabilities	51.8	29.0
Long-term debt	308.8	60.7
Other liabilities	5.3	4.0
Deferred income taxes	44.9	40.0
Stockholders' equity:		
Common stock, $1 par value: authorized, 30,000,000 shares: outstanding, 6,686,201 and 6,613,186 shares	6.7	6.6
Additional paid-in capital	42.1	39.8
Retained earnings	158.2	150.8
	207.0	197.2
	$617.8	$330.9

The accompanying Notes to Consolidated Financial Statements are part of the financial statements.

Source: Chesapeake Corporation, *1985 Annual Report.* Reprinted with permission.

One ratio by itself means little, but several ratios together may give a clear picture of a firm's strengths and weaknesses. Rarely will all the ratios indicate the same general tendency. However, when they are taken as a group, the ratios often give the investigator an indication of the direction in which the firm is moving and its financial position in comparison to other firms in its industry.

The subsequent sections of this chapter cover a variety of ratios. The illustrations of these ratios employ data taken from the balance sheet and income statements of

Consolidated Statement of Income and Retained Earnings

	For the years ended		
	December 31, 1985	December 30, 1984	January 1, 1984
	(In millions except per share data)		
Income:			
Net sales	$454.1	$350.2	$273.8
Costs and expenses:			
Cost of products sold	350.1	262.0	215.9
Depreciation and cost of timber harvested	31.3	24.0	20.9
Selling, general and administrative expenses	41.0	28.8	21.3
Income from operations	31.7	35.4	15.7
Other income (expense), net	(.3)	3.1	2.5
Interest expense	(14.3)	(4.9)	(5.6)
Income before taxes and extraordinary item	17.1	33.6	12.6
Income taxes	1.4	11.5	4.1
Income before extraordinary item	15.7	22.1	8.5
Extraordinary item	–	–	4.0
Net income	$ 15.7	$ 22.1	$ 12.5
Earnings per share:			
Income before extraordinary item	$ 2.36	$ 3.35	$ 1.33
Extraordinary item	–	–	.63
Net income	$ 2.36	$ 3.35	$ 1.96
Retained earnings:			
Balance, beginning of year	$150.8	$136.4	$131.1
Net income	15.7	22.1	12.5
Cash dividends declared, $1.24, $1.18 and $1.12 per share	(8.3)	(7.7)	(7.2)
Balance, end of year	$158.2	$150.8	$136.4

The accompanying Notes to Consolidated Financial Statements are part of the financial statements.

Exhibit 17.2
Chesapeake Corporation Income Statement

Source: Chesapeake Corporation, *1985 Annual Report.* Reprinted with permission.

Chesapeake Corporation (CSK—the NYSE trading symbol), an integrated paper and forest products company. Its products include paperboard and paper, corrugated containers, commercial and industrial tissue products, and bleached hardwood pulp. Chesapeake's balance sheet and income statement for 1984 and 1985 are given in Exhibits 17.1 and 17.2. The 1985 data is used to illustrate the ratios, and both years plus several additional years' data are employed later in the chapter to illustrate the use of ratios in time-series analysis.

LIQUIDITY RATIOS

Liquidity is the "moneyness" of the asset

Liquidity is the ease with which assets may be quickly converted into cash without the firm's incurring a loss. If a firm has a high degree of liquidity, it will be able to meet its debt obligations as they become due. Therefore, liquidity ratios are a useful tool for the firm's creditors, who are concerned with being paid. Liquidity ratios are so called because they indicate the degree of liquidity or "moneyness" of the company's assets.

The Current Ratio

The **current ratio** is the ratio of current assets to current liabilities.

$$\text{Current ratio} = \frac{\text{Current assets}}{\text{Current liabilities}}.$$

It indicates the extent to which the current liabilities, which must be paid within a year, are "covered" by current assets. For CSK the current ratio as of December 31, 1985, was

$$\frac{\$115.2}{\$51.8} = 2.22,$$

which indicates that for every $1 that the firm had to pay within the year, there was $2.22 in the form of either cash or an asset that was to be converted into cash within the year. (Dollar amounts are in millions.)

It is desirable to have current assets exceed current liabilities

For most industries, it is desirable to have more current assets than current liabilities. It is sometimes asserted that a firm should have at least $2 in current assets for every $1 in current liabilities or a current ratio of at least 2 : 1. If the current ratio is 2 : 1, then the firm's current assets could deteriorate in value by 50 percent and the firm would still be able to meet its short-term liabilities.

Utilities may be an exception

Although such rules of thumb are convenient, they need not apply to all industries. For example, electric utilities usually have current liabilities that exceed their current assets (i.e., a current ratio of less than 1 : 1). Does this worry short-term creditors? No, because the short-term assets are primarily accounts receivable from electricity users and are of high quality. Should a customer fail to pay an electricity bill, the company threatens to cut off service, and this threat is usually sufficient to induce payment. The higher the quality of the current assets (i.e., the greater the probability that these assets can be converted to cash at their stated value), the less vital it is for the current ratio to exceed 1 : 1. The reason, then, for selecting a rule of thumb such as a current ratio of at least 2 : 1 is for the protection of the creditors, who are aware that not all current assets will, in fact, be converted into cash.

A high current ratio may also be undesirable

Both creditors and investors want to know if the firm has sufficient liquid assets to meet its bills. Obviously, a low current ratio is undesirable because it indicates financial weakness, but a high current ratio may also be undesirable. A high current ratio may imply that the firm is not using its funds to best advantage. For example, the company may have issued long-term debt and used it to finance an excessive amount of inventory or accounts receivable. The high current ratio may also indicate that the firm is not taking advantage of available short-term financing or is mismanaging its current assets, which reduces its profitability. A high or low numerical value for the current ratio may be a signal to creditors and stockholders that the management of short-term assets and liabilities should be revised.

The Acid Test or Quick Ratio

The current ratio gives an indication of the company's ability to meet its current liabilities as they become due, but it has a major weakness. It is an aggregate measure of liquidity that does not differentiate between the degrees of liquidity of the various types of current assets, which may be in the form of cash, accounts receivable, or inventory. Cash is a liquid asset, but it may take many months before inventory is sold and turned into cash. This failure of the current ratio to distinguish between the degrees of liquidity has led to the development of the quick ratio, which omits inventory from the calculation. The **acid test** or **quick ratio** (both names are used) is determined as follows:

The acid test excludes inventory

$$\text{Acid test ratio} = \frac{\text{Current assets} - \text{Inventory}}{\text{Current liabilities}}.$$

For CSK the acid test ratio is

$$\frac{\$115.2 - \$61.2}{\$51.8} = 1.04,$$

which is lower than the current ratio of 2.22. The difference lies, of course, in the inventory that the company is carrying, which is excluded from the acid test.

A low acid test ratio implies that the firm may have difficulty meeting its current liabilities as they become due if it must rely on converting inventory into cash. However, a low acid test value does not indicate that the firm will fail to pay its bills. The ability to meet liabilities is influenced by such factors as (1) the rate at which cash flows into the firm, (2) the time at which bills become due, (3) the relationship between the company and its creditors and their willingness to roll over debt, and (4) the firm's ability to raise additional capital. The acid test merely indicates how well the current liabilities are covered by cash and by highly liquid assets that may be converted into cash relatively quickly. Because this test takes into account that not all current assets are equally liquid, it is a more precise measure of liquidity than is the current ratio.

The ability to pay is also affected by other factors

The Components of Current Assets

Another approach to analyzing liquidity is to rank current assets with regard to their degree of liquidity and to determine the proportion of each asset in relation to total current assets. The most liquid current asset is cash, followed by marketable securities (i.e., cash equivalents) such as treasury bills or certificates of deposit, accounts receivable, and finally inventory. For CSK the proportion of each asset to total current assets is

Current assets may be ranked according to liquidity

Current Assets	Proportion of Total Current Assets
Cash and cash equivalents	2.4%
Accounts receivable	38.5
Inventory	53.1
Other current assets	6.0
	100.0%

Since this technique ranks current assets from the most liquid to the least liquid, it gives an indication of the degree of liquidity of the firm's current assets. If a large proportion of total current assets is inventory, the company is not very liquid. CSK appears to be reasonably liquid, as almost 41 percent of its current assets are cash, cash equivalents, and accounts receivable.

This method of separating total current assets into their components and then ranking them according to their degree of liquidity gives management, creditors, and investors a better measure of the firm's ability to meet its current liabilities than does the current ratio. When used with the acid test, these two measures supplement the current ratio and should be used to analyze the liquidity of any firm that carries a significant amount of inventory in its operations.

ACTIVITY RATIOS

Activity ratios measure the speed of conversion to cash

Activity ratios indicate at what rate the firm is turning its inventory and accounts receivable into cash. The more rapidly the firm turns over its inventory and receivables, the more quickly it acquires cash. High turnover indicates that the firm is rapidly receiving cash and is in a better position to pay its liabilities as they become due. Such high turnover, however, need not imply that the firm is maximizing profits. For example, high inventory turnover may indicate that the firm is selling items for too low a price in order to induce quicker sales. A high receivables turnover may be an indication that the firm is too stringent in extending credit to buyers, and this may reduce sales and result in lower profits.

Inventory Turnover

Inventory turnover is defined as annual sales divided by average inventory. That is,

$$\text{Inventory turnover} = \frac{\text{Sales}}{\text{Average inventory}}.$$

Two views of inventory turnover

This ratio uses average inventory throughout the year. Such an average reduces the impact of fluctuations in the level of inventory. If only year-end inventory were used and it was abnormally high at the end of the fiscal year, the turnover would appear to be slower. Conversely, if inventory was lower than normal at the year's end, the turnover would appear faster than in fact it was. Averaging the inventory reduces the impact of these fluctuations. Management may use any number of observations (e.g., monthly or weekly) to determine the average inventory. The information available to investors, however, may be limited to the level of inventory given in the firm's annual reports.

For CSK the level of inventory was $61.2 in 1985 and $37.8 in 1984. The average for the two years was

$$\frac{\$61.2 + \$37.8}{2} = \$49.5.$$

Thus, for CSK inventory turnover was

$$\frac{\text{Sales}}{\text{Average inventory}} = \frac{\$454.1}{\$49.5} = 9.17.$$

This indicates that annual sales are nine times the level of inventory. Inventory thus turns over nine times a year or about once every six weeks.

Inventory turnover may also be defined as the cost of goods sold divided by the inventory. That is,

$$\text{Inventory turnover} = \frac{\text{Cost of goods sold}}{\text{Average inventory}}.$$

If this definition is used, CSK's inventory turnover is

$$\frac{\$350.1}{\$49.5} = 7.07.$$

This definition places more emphasis on recouping the cost of the goods. However, creditors may prefer to use sales, since sales produce the funds to service the debt. Dun and Bradstreet uses sales in its industry averages, and any creditors or bond-holders who use Dun and Bradstreet data as a source of comparison must remember to use sales instead of cost of goods sold to be consistent.

Average Collection Period

The **average collection period** measures how long it takes a firm to collect its ac-counts receivable. The faster the company collects its receivables, the more rapidly it receives cash and hence can pay its obligations, such as its interest expense. The aver-age collection period (ACP) is determined as follows:

How long it takes to collect receivables

$$\text{ACP} = \frac{\text{Receivables}}{\text{Sales per day}}.$$

Sales per day are total sales divided by 360 (or 365) days. For CSK the average collec-tion period is

$$\frac{\$44.3}{\$454.1 \div 360} = 35.1.$$

This indicates that the firm takes 35.1 days to convert its receivables into money.

Receivables turnover, which is another way of viewing the average collec-tion period, may be defined as annual credit sales divided by receivables.[1] By this definition,

Alternative definitions of receivables turnover

$$\text{Receivables turnover} = \frac{\text{Annual credit sales}}{\text{Accounts receivable}}.$$

An alternative definition of receivables turnover substitutes annual sales for annual credit sales. That is,

$$\text{Receivables turnover} = \frac{\text{Annual sales}}{\text{Accounts receivable}}.$$

Either definition is acceptable as long as it is applied consistently. Although manage-ment has access to the information used in both formulas, investors may be limited to

---

[1] Some analysts may prefer to average the accounts receivable in the same way that inventory was averaged for the inventory turnover ratio.

the data provided by the firm. If annual credit sales are not reported by the firm, the investor will have no choice but to use annual sales.

Since the CSK income statement does not give annual credit sales, the first definition cannot be used; hence, for CSK,

$$\text{Receivables turnover} = \frac{\$454.1}{\$44.3} = 10.3.$$

This indicates that annual sales are 10.3 times the amount of receivables. The larger the ratio, the more rapidly the firm turns its credit sales into cash. A turnover of 10.3 times per year indicates that receivables are paid off on the average of every 1.2 months. This is the same information that was derived by computing the average collection period, since 35 days is approximately 1.2 months.

There is a need for caution in interpreting the results

All of the previously mentioned turnover ratios need to be interpreted with much caution. These ratios are static, for they use information derived at a given time (i.e., the year-end figures on the balance sheet). The ratios, however, are dealing with dynamic events, for they are concerned with the length of time it takes for an event to occur. Because of this problem with time, these turnover ratios, which are based on year-end figures, may be misleading if the firm has (1) seasonal sales, (2) sporadic sales during the fiscal year, or (3) any growth in inventory and sales during the fiscal year. Creditors and bondholders need to be aware of these potential problems, since they can lead to incorrect conclusions concerning the firm's capacity to service its debt.

Fixed Asset Turnover

Inventory and accounts receivable turnover stress the speed with which current assets flow up the balance sheet. Rapid inventory turnover means inventory is quickly sold and converted into either cash or an account receivable. The average collection period tells how long it takes the firm to collect the account (i.e., how long it takes to receive cash from a credit sale).

Turnover ratios may also be constructed for long-term assets. Such a ratio is the **fixed asset turnover.**

$$\text{Fixed asset turnover} = \frac{\text{Annual sales}}{\text{Fixed assets}}.$$

Fixed assets are the firm's plant and equipment, and this ratio indicates the amount of plant and equipment that were used to generate the firm's sales. For CSK the fixed asset turnover was

$$\text{Fixed asset turnover} = \frac{\$454.1}{\$454.7} = 0.99.$$

This indicates that CSK generated $0.99 in sales for every $1 invested in plant and equipment (i.e., fixed assets).

Many firms (such as utilities) must have substantial investment in plant and equipment to produce the output they sell. Other firms, especially those providing services, need only modest amounts of fixed assets. The more rapidly fixed assets turn over, the smaller the amount of plant and equipment the firm is employing. While the ratio is obviously sensitive to the firm's industry, it does help measure the efficiency with which management is using its long-term assets.

PROFITABILITY RATIOS

The amount that a firm earns is particularly important to investors. Earnings accrue to stockholders and either are distributed to them as dividends or are retained. Retained earnings represent an additional investment in the corporation by stockholders. Obviously a firm's performance is a crucial element in fundamental analysis.

Earnings to sales

Profitability ratios are measures of performance that indicate the amount the firm is earning relative to some base, such as sales, assets, or equity. The **operating profit margin** is operating income (i.e., earnings before interest and taxes) divided by sales, and the **net profit margin** is the ratio of profits after taxes to sales. That is,

$$\text{Operating profit margin} = \frac{\text{Earnings before interest and taxes}}{\text{Sales}};$$

$$\text{Net profit margin} = \frac{\text{Earnings after taxes}}{\text{Sales}}.$$

For CSK, the operating profit margin for 1985 was

$$\text{Operating profit margin} = \frac{\$31.7}{\$454.1} = 6.98\%,$$

and the net profit margin was

$$\text{Net profit margin} = \frac{\$15.7}{\$454.1} = 3.46\%.$$

These ratios indicate that the company earned $0.0698 before interest and taxes on every $1 of sales and $0.0346 after interest and taxes on every $1 of sales.

The impact of taxes

The computation of both these ratios may seem unnecessary, but interest (either earned or an expense), extraordinary items, and taxes can have an impact on a firm's profitability. For example, if the investor computes only the net profit margin, an increase in tax rates will decrease the profit margin even though there has been no internal deterioration in the profitability of the company.

Earnings on assets

Other profitability ratios measure the **return on assets** and the **return on equity**. The return on assets is net earnings divided by assets. That is,

$$\text{Return on assets} = \frac{\text{Earnings after taxes}}{\text{Total assets}}.$$

For CSK, the return on assets was

$$\frac{\$15.7}{\$617.8} = 2.54\%.$$

Thus, CSK earned $0.0254 on every $1 of assets. This ratio measures the return on the firm's resources (i.e., its assets). It is an all-encompassing measure of performance that indicates the total that management is able to achieve on all the firm's assets. This return on assets takes into account the profit margins and the rate at which the assets are turned over (e.g., the rate at which the firm collects its accounts receivable and sells its inventory), as well as taxes and extraordinary items.

Earnings on equity

Although return on assets gives an aggregate measure of the firm's performance, it does not tell how the management is performing for the stockholders. This is indi-

POINTS OF INTEREST
When Is an Increase in Earnings a Loss?

Financial analysis may be more concerned with a firm's operating income than with the bottom line or net income. Analysts will determine how that net income was achieved. Sometimes a firm's income from operations may have declined or the firm may have even operated at a loss, but as the result of other sources of income, such as interest, capital gains, or tax benefits, the firm is able to report an increase in net income.

Consider the following abridged income statements for McDermott International, Inc.

While sales rose during 1986, McDermott operated at a loss. However, the firm was able to report an increase in net income and earnings per share because of interest income, capital gains, and tax benefits. Many of these income-producing items are nonrecurring. For example, the firm may report the benefit of tax credits in the year in which they occur, but such deductions will not necessarily occur every year. Thus the financial

analyst may place more emphasis on the operating loss than on the net income as an indicator of the true earning capacity of McDermott.

Years Ended March 31	1986	1985
Revenues (in millions)	$3,257	$3,223
Costs of operations	2,879	2,892
Gross profit	378	331
Depreciation	158	149
Selling and administrative expenses	308	301
Operating income	(88)	(109)
Other income (interest, capital gains)	88	53
Tax benefits (e.g., investment tax credits)	71	90
Extraordinary items and minority dividends (net)	(12)	(3)
Net income	$ 59	$ 31
Earnings per share	$1.60	$0.83

cated by the return on equity, which is earnings available to common stockholders divided by the equity, or the net worth, of the firm. That is,

$$\text{Return on equity} = \frac{\text{Earnings after taxes}}{\text{Equity}}.$$

Equity is the sum of common stock, additional paid-in capital (if any), and retained earnings (if any). The return on equity measures the amount that the firm is earning on the common stockholders' investment.

Adjustments for preferred stock

Many stockholders may be concerned not with the return on the firm's total equity but with the return earned on the equity attributable to the common stock. To determine this return on common stock, adjustments must be made for any preferred stock the firm has outstanding. First, the dividends paid to preferred stockholders must be subtracted from earnings to obtain earnings available to common stockholders. Second, the contribution of the preferred stock to the firm's equity must be subtracted to obtain the investment in the firm by the common stockholders. Thus, the return to common stockholders is

$$\text{Return on common equity} = \frac{\text{Earnings after taxes} - \text{Preferred stock dividends}}{\text{Equity} - \text{Preferred stock}}.$$

Of course, if the firm has no preferred stock, the return on equity and the return on the common equity are identical.

For CSK, the return on equity for 1985 was

$$\text{Return on equity} = \frac{\$15.7 - 0}{\$207.0 - 0} = 7.58\%.$$

The ratio indicates that CSK earned a return of $0.0758 for every $1 invested by stockholders. Thus, while CSK achieved only 2.54 percent on its total assets, it was able to earn 7.58 percent on the stockholders' investment.

LEVERAGE OR CAPITALIZATION RATIOS

How can a firm magnify the return on the stockholders' investment? One method, which was discussed in Chapter 14, is the use of financial leverage. By successfully using debt financing instead of equity financing, management is able to increase the return to the residual: the common stockholder. This use of financial leverage may be measured by capitalization ratios, which indicate the extent to which the firm finances its assets by debt. These ratios are also referred to as **debt ratios**.

Since debt financing can have such impact on the firm, each of these ratios is *Debt ratios* extremely valuable in analyzing the financial position of the firm. The most commonly used capitalization ratios are (1) the debt-to-equity ratio and (2) the debt-to-total assets ratio. These ratios are

$$\frac{\text{Debt}}{\text{Equity}} \qquad \frac{\text{Debt}}{\text{Total assets}}.$$

For CSK, the values for these ratios for 1985 were as follows:[2]

$$\frac{\text{Debt}}{\text{Equity}} = \frac{\$365.9}{\$207.0} = 1.77.$$

$$\frac{\text{Debt}}{\text{Total assets}} = \frac{\$365.9}{\$617.8} = 59.2\%.$$

For CSK, the debt-to-equity ratio indicates that there was $1.77 in debt for every $1 of stock. The ratio of debt to total assets indicates that debt was used to finance 59.2 percent of the firm's assets.

Since these ratios measure the same thing (i.e., the use of debt financing), the student may wonder which is preferred. Actually, either is acceptable, and preference is a matter of choice. The debt-to-equity ratio expresses debt in terms of equity, while the debt-to-total assets ratio gives the proportion of the firm's total assets that are financed by debt. Financial analysts or students should choose the one they feel most comfortable working with.

These capitalization ratios are aggregate measures. They both use *total* debt and *Debt ratios are* hence do not differentiate between short-term and long-term debt. The debt-to-equity *aggregates* ratio uses total equity and therefore does not differentiate between the financing pro-

---

[2] Debt = Current liabilities + Long-term debt + Other liabilities = $51.8 + $308.8 + $5.3 = $365.9.

vided by preferred and common stock. The debt-to-total assets ratio uses total assets and hence does not differentiate between current and long-term assets.

Financial leverage and declines in the value of assets

The fact that these ratios are aggregate measures does not present a problem, for they measure the extent to which total assets (both short-term and long-term) are financed by creditors. The smaller the proportion of total assets financed by creditors, the larger the decline in the value of assets that may occur without threatening the creditors' position. Capitalization ratios thus give an indication of risk. Firms that have a small amount of equity capital are considered to involve greater risk because there is less cushion to protect creditors if the value of the assets deteriorates. For example, the ratio of debt to total assets for CSK was 59.2 percent. This indicates that the value of the assets may decline by 40.8 percent (100% − 59.2%) before only enough assets remain to pay off the debt. If the debt ratio had been 70 percent, a decline of only 30 percent in the value of the assets would endanger the creditors' position.

Risk

Capitalization ratios indicate risk as much to investors as they do to creditors, for firms with a high degree of financial leverage are riskier investments. If the value of the assets declines or if the firm experiences declining sales and losses, the equity deteriorates more quickly for firms that use financial leverage than for those that do not use debt financing. Hence, debt ratios are an important measure of risk for both investors and creditors.

Debt ratios differ among firms

Capitalization ratios differ significantly among firms. In Exhibit 17.3 the debt ratios for seven large industrial firms are presented. Several of these firms use a substantial amount of debt financing. For example, Fluor has acquired over 60 percent of its assets through debt financing, while VF Corp. has financed 65 percent of its assets through equity.

Exhibit 17.4 presents the debt ratio for five telephone utilities. This exhibit is arranged in descending order from the firm that uses the greatest amount of debt financing to the firm that uses the least. As may be seen from Exhibits 17.3 and 17.4, the proportion of a firm's total assets financed by debt varies not only from industry to industry but also within an industry. The debt ratios of the telephone companies do, however, have less variation than those of the selected industrial firms.

The optimal combination of debt to equity

Financial theory suggests there is an optimal combination of debt and equity financing that maximizes the value of a firm. The optimal use of financial leverage may significantly benefit the common stockholder by increasing the per-share earnings of

---

Exhibit 17.3
Ratio of Debt to Total Assets for Selected Industrial Firms as of December 1985

Firm	Debt Ratio
Reynolds Metals	68.4%
Fluor	63.0
Greyhound	59.3
Exxon	54.4
Georgia-Pacific	52.7
Coca-Cola	46.9
VF (Vanity Fair)	35.6

Source: 1985 annual reports.

Utility	Debt Ratio	Exhibit 17.4
General Telephone and Electronics (GTE)	55.0%	Ratio of Debt to Total Assets for Five Telephone Utilities as of December 1985
United Telecom	54.8	
Contel	54.4	
Pacific Telesis	40.9	
BellSouth	39.8	

Source: 1985 annual reports.

the company and by permitting faster growth and larger dividends. If, however, the firm uses too much financial leverage or is **undercapitalized**, creditors may require a higher interest rate to compensate them for the increased risk. Investors may also be willing to invest their funds in a corporation with a high usage of financial leverage only if the anticipated return is higher. Thus, the debt ratio, which measures the extent to which a firm uses financial leverage, is one of the most important ratios that managers, creditors, and investors may calculate.

Coverage Ratios

Leverage ratios also include measures of the firm's ability to service its debt. These ratios indicate to creditors and management how much the firm is earning from operations relative to what is owed. The coverage for interest payments is called **times-interest-earned**. Times-interest-earned is the ratio of earnings that are available to pay the interest (i.e., operating income) divided by the amount of interest. That is,

$$\text{Times-interest-earned} = \frac{\text{Earnings before interest and taxes}}{\text{Annual interest charges}}.$$

A ratio of 2 indicates that the firm has $2 after meeting other expenses to pay $1 of interest charges. The larger the times-interest-earned ratio, the more likely it is that the firm will be able to meet its interest payments.

For CSK, times-interest-earned is

$$\text{Times-interest-earned} = \frac{\$31.7}{\$14.3} = 2.2,$$

which indicates the firm has operating income of $2.2 for every $1 of interest expense.

The ability to cover the interest expense is important, for failure to meet interest payments as they become due may throw the firm into bankruptcy. A decline in the times-interest-earned ratio may serve as an early warning to creditors and investors, as well as to management, of a deteriorating financial position and the increased probability of default on interest payments.

In the previous equation, the times-interest-earned ratio is an aggregate value that lumps together all interest payments. Some debt issues may be subordinated to other debt issues and are paid only after senior debt issues are redeemed. Thus, it is possible to pay the senior debt issues in full and to have no funds left with which to pay the interest on the subordinate debt. When this subordination exists, the times-interest-

There is a need to adjust for subordination

earned statistic may be altered to acknowledge it. For example, consider a company with $2,000 in earnings before interest and taxes and $10,000 in debt consisting of two issues. Issue A has a principal amount of $8,000 and carries an interest rate of 10 percent. Issue B has a principal amount of $2,000 and carries an interest rate of 14 percent. Issue B is subordinate to issue A. The subordination may explain why the second issue has the higher interest rate, for creditors usually demand higher rates in return for debt issues involving greater risk.

The times-interest-earned ratio for each debt issue is computed as follows. The firm has two debt issues (A and B) and $2,000 in earnings before interest and taxes. The interest on issue A is $800 and on issue B is $280. For issue A there is $2,000 available to pay the $800 in interest expense, and thus the coverage ratio is

$$\frac{\$2,000}{\$800} = 2.50.$$

For issue B there is $2,000 to cover the interest on A and B. Thus, for issue B the coverage ratio is

$$\frac{\$2,000}{\$800 + \$280} = 1.85.$$

It would be misleading to suggest that the coverage for issue B is the amount available after issue A was paid. In such a case that would indicate a coverage of

$$\frac{\$1,200}{\$280} = 4.29,$$

which is incorrect. Issue B would then have the higher coverage ratio and would appear to be safer than the senior debt. The proper way to adjust for subordination is to add the interest charges to the denominator and *not* to subtract the interest paid to the senior debt issue from the numerator. For successive issues of subordinated debt, the interest payments would be added to the denominator. Since the total amount of earnings available before taxes to pay the interest is spread out over ever-increasing interest payments, the coverage ratio declines and hence gives the true indication of the actual coverage of the subordinated debt.

RATIO ANALYSIS FOR SPECIFIC INVESTORS

An investor may not need to compute many ratios; a few selected ratios will probably provide sufficient information concerning the financial condition of the firm. The ratios that should be selected depend on the investor's need, which varies with the type of investment. Bondholders are concerned with the firm's capacity to service its debt (i.e., pay the interest and retire the principal) as well as the extent to which the firm is financially leveraged. Stockholders, however, are more concerned with performance (i.e., earnings, dividends, growth, and valuation). While bondholders and stockholders are both concerned with the financial condition of the firm, their emphasis differs. Hence, they may compute different ratios to determine the firm's financial position as it applies to their specific investments.

Ratio Analysis for Bondholders

Bondholders are concerned with the firm's use of debt and its capacity to pay interest and retire its debt obligations as they come due. Debt financing may increase the return the firm is able to earn for its stockholders but also adds to the financial obligations of the firm, thus increasing the firm's financial risk. Bondholders would prefer that the firm use less debt financing, since equity financing increases the safety of the firm's existing debt obligations.

The extent to which a firm uses debt financing is measured by the debt-to-total assets ratio or debt-to-equity ratio. The greater the proportion of the firm's assets financed with debt, the larger both ratios will be. Bondholders may compute these ratios to ascertain the extent to which the firm uses debt financing and thereby may perceive the financial risk associated with the firm's sources of finance.

While bondholders are concerned with the firm's sources of financing, they are even more concerned with the firm's liquidity position and its ability to generate cash to service the debt. The capacity of the firm to pay current interest obligations is measured by liquidity ratios (e.g., the current ratio and the quick ratio), selected activity ratios (e.g., inventory turnover and the average collection period), and the coverage ratio, times-interest-earned.

The liquidity ratios indicate the extent to which a firm has current assets relative to current liabilities. Since interest owed during the year is a current liability, the more current assets the firm has relative to current liabilities, the greater is the probability that the interest payment will be made. A high current ratio or high quick ratio implies that bondholders will be paid their interest when due.

The current and quick ratios do not indicate the firm's capacity to generate cash. They only indicate the firm's current assets relative to current liabilities. For most firms a large percentage of the current assets will be inventory and accounts receivable. Since these assets must be converted into cash before interest can be paid, the bondholder may wish to analyze inventory turnover and the average collection period. These ratios indicate how rapidly inventory and accounts receivable flow up the balance sheet. The more rapidly inventory turns over, the more quickly the firm generates sales. These sales will be either for cash or on credit. The more rapidly the firm collects its accounts receivable, the more rapidly it is receiving cash. Rapid turnover of both inventory and accounts receivable is desirable from the bondholder's viewpoint because it indicates that the firm is generating the funds with which it can make interest payments.

The bondholder should also compute the coverage ratio, times-interest-earned, to determine if the firm is generating sufficient operating income to pay its interest obligations. Individually this is one of the most important ratios, because times-interest-earned measures the extent to which operating income (i.e., earnings before interest and taxes) covers interest expense. Since bondholders are paid after operating expenses are met but before income taxes, they must be concerned with the operating income generated by the firm. Ultimately interest payments must be generated by operations. If the firm's operations cannot generate sufficient income to meet its interest expense, the bondholders' position is tenuous.

The bondholder is not concerned with net earnings, which are earnings after interest and taxes. It is the stockholders who are concerned with the net income that

remains after interest and taxes are paid. This net income is the source of cash dividends and retained earnings, which will finance the firm's future growth and generate capital gains for the stockholders.

Any ratio by itself probably does not tell the bondholder very much. A firm could be generating profitable sales but still not have cash. If a firm sells $100 worth of inventory for $120, that is a profitable sale. If the sale is for credit, the firm acquires an account receivable and not cash. Obviously the firm is operating profitably, but until the account receivable is collected, the creditors cannot be paid. It is by combining several ratios (e.g., leverage, liquidity, and the turnover of short-term assets) that bondholders perceive the safety of their current interest payments. The more rapidly the firm turns over inventory and accounts receivable, the more liquid its current position, and the higher the coverage of interest owed, the safer should be the bondholder's interest payment.

Cash flow from operations = EBIT + depreciation

In addition to interest payments, bondholders are also concerned with the repayment of their principal, which comes from the capacity of the firm to generate sufficient cash flow. This capacity may not be indicated by the firm's balance sheet or income statement. A firm could be operating at a profit but not be generating cash, and a firm could be reporting an accounting loss but still be generating cash.

Since the income statement does not tell if the firm is generating cash, bondholders should study the firm's statement of changes in financial position. This statement enumerates the firm's sources and uses of funds. It adjusts earnings that the firm reports but for which the firm did not receive cash (e.g., equity earnings in another firm's profits from which no cash was received). The statement of changes in financial position also adds back to earnings those expenses that did not involve an outlay of cash (e.g., depreciation). A firm with large depreciation expenses could be operating with little profit or even at a loss and still have the funds to retire its bonds as they mature.

The capacity of the firm to meet both the interest and principal repayment may be indicated by the following expanded coverage ratio, which includes interest, principal repayment, operating income, and depreciation expense:

$$\frac{\text{Earnings before interest and taxes} + \text{Depreciation}}{\text{Interest expense} + \dfrac{\text{Principal repayment}}{(1 - \text{Firm's income tax rate})}}$$

For CSK this ratio is

$$\frac{\$53.1}{\$14.3 + \dfrac{2.6}{1 - 0.34}} = 2.91.$$

The current portion of long-term debt due within the year is $2.6, and 0.34 (34 percent) is the firm's average federal and state income tax rate in 1984.[3] The ratio indicates that CSK generates sufficient cash flow to cover not only its interest payments but also the principal repayments.

---

[3] The 1985 tax rate was abnormally low as a result of accounting adjustments and the investment tax credit. Since 1985 does not appear to be a typical year for CSK, the 1984 average income tax rate was used. The funds from operations, $53.1, were given in the annual report.

Depreciation expense is added to earnings before interest and taxes (EBIT) in the numerator to determine cash flow from operations. (Other applicable non-cash expenses such as depletion and amortization should also be added to EBIT.) The principal repayment is added to interest expense in the denominator. Since principal repayment is not a tax deductible expense, the amount of the payment must be expressed before tax. This adjustment is achieved by dividing the principal repayment by 1 minus the firm's tax rate. As with times-interest-earned, the larger the ratio, the safer should be the bondholder's position, because the larger the ratio, the greater is the firm's capacity to pay the interest and repay the principal.

Ratio Analysis for Stockholders

Stockholders, like bondholders, are investors, but stockholders earn their return not through interest payments but through dividends and growth in the value of the shares. Thus stockholders are primarily concerned with performance (i.e., the capacity of the firm to generate earnings). Performance is measured by such ratios as the profit margin on sales, return on assets, and return on equity. Stockholders are also concerned with the source of the return on their individual investments (i.e., dividends and capital gains). Measures of the distribution of earnings, growth in earnings and dividends, and the market's valuation of the stock are also important to the individual stockholder. Thus, in addition to profitability ratios, stockholders are concerned with the payout ratio, measures of growth, and the P/E ratio.

Sales are the firm's source of revenues and profits. Unless the firm earns its revenues from an investment portfolio, the ability to generate profitable sales is ultimately the source of the return earned by the firm for its stockholders. The ability to generate profitable sales is indicated by profitability ratios, especially the net profit margin (i.e., net earnings to sales). Firms with a high net profit margin or whose net profit margins exceed their industry's averages may be attractive investments.

The gross profit margin (i.e., sales minus cost of goods sold quantity divided by sales) and the operating profit margin (i.e., earnings before interest and taxes quantity divided by sales) are also important, for they may indicate a specific area in which the firm excels or is having problems. For example, a firm may have a large gross profit margin but its operating and net income may be small if the firm has high operating expenses (e.g., selling and administrative expenses). In this case the operating profit margin will be low. A small change in the firm's administrative cost controls could have a magnified effect on the operating profit margin. Since the analysis indicated an acceptable gross profit margin, the firm may prove to be a good investment if the operating expenses can be reduced.

Computing the gross profit margin, operating profit margin, and net profit margin may isolate why the firm's net profit is low (or high). If the investor believes that such problems may be corrected (or if they are the result of a temporary event such as a strike or an extraordinary item such as a fire), the stock may still be a good investment. While emphasis is often placed on the bottom line (e.g., net profit margin), analysis of gross and operating profit margins may indicate that net profits are artificially under- or overstated.

The return on assets (earnings divided by total assets) indicates what the firm has earned on its resources. The ratio does not indicate what the firm earned on the stock-

holders' funds. Thus for stockholders the return on equity (earnings divided by equity) is exceedingly important, because it indicates what management has earned on the stockholders' investment in the firm. A high return on equity indicates that the management has achieved high earnings for the stockholders relative to the funds they have invested in the firm.

A high return on equity is by itself not necessarily desirable. Successful use of debt financing (i.e., earning more on the assets acquired through the use of debt financing than must be paid in interest) will magnify the return on equity. If the firm employs a substantial amount of debt financing to acquire assets, this may magnify the return on equity. However, if the firm were to operate at a loss, the use of financial leverage would magnify the loss to the stockholders. Thus stockholders, like bondholders, are concerned with the extent to which the firm uses debt financing. The debt ratios indicate the use of debt financing and hence measure the financial risk associated with the firm.

If a firm has both a high return on equity and a high debt ratio, the return on equity may be the result of successfully using financial leverage to magnify the return on the stockholders' funds. If the firm has a high return on equity but a low debt ratio, that indicates the firm has profitable operations and is not using debt financing as a major source of the return to its stockholders. The latter situation is less risky, as the profits are the result of operating decisions and not financing decisions. Small changes in sales or expenses should not have a large impact on earnings.

Since earnings are either distributed or retained, stockholders are concerned with the payout ratio.

$$\text{Payout ratio} = \frac{\text{Dividends}}{\text{Earnings}}.$$

For CSK the per-share payout ratio in 1985 was

$$\text{Payout ratio} = \frac{\$1.24}{\$2.36} = 0.525 = 52.5\%.$$

This indicates that management distributed half of the firm's earnings. The distribution of earnings is a prerogative of the board of directors. Some managements prefer to retain earnings to finance future growth.

If an investor is primarily concerned with the flow of dividend income, a high payout ratio is desirable. Stockholders who seek growth and capital gains will prefer a lower payout ratio, which indicates that a larger proportion of earnings are being retained to finance future operations. Of course, even investors who seek income will not desire a payout ratio of 100 percent, since even modest growth in the dividends will require some retention of earnings.

The capacity of the firm to grow by internally generated funds depends on its return on equity and the distribution of its earnings. For example, consider a firm with $100 in equity that earns $10. The return on equity is 10 percent ($10/$100). If the firm distributes $10, the equity cannot internally grow. If the $100 is retained, the equity grows from $100 to $110, a 10 percent increase. If 40 percent of the earnings are distributed (0.4 × $10 = $4), only $6 are retained and the equity grows by 6 percent, from $100 to $106. The firm cannot increase its equity more than 6 per-

cent and maintain the dividend unless it increases its profitability (i.e., increases the return on equity). Thus the larger the return on equity and the smaller the payout ratio, the greater the firm's internal growth will be.

Stockholders who seek capital gains should be particularly interested in the payout ratio. The value of the shares will not appreciate over time unless earnings and dividends grow. The product of the payout ratio and the return on equity provides the investor with a measure of internal growth (i.e., $(0.4)(0.1) = 0.06 = 6\%$ rate of growth in equity). The payout ratio combined with the return on equity indicates the capacity of the firm to grow internally without (1) using additional debt financing, which may increase financial risk, or (2) selling additional shares, which may dilute the existing stockholders' equity and earnings.

Stockholders are concerned not only with the firm's earnings and how they are distributed but also with what the market believes the earnings are worth. In Chapter 14 the price/earnings (P/E) ratio and the dividend-growth model were used to value common stock. Firms with the potential for higher growth in earnings and dividends achieve higher valuations. A higher P/E ratio indicates that the market is currently willing to pay more for $1 worth of the firm's current earnings. Since the P/E ratio is reported daily in the financial press, it is readily available and may be easily used to compare firms.

An alternative valuation ratio that has recently achieved some prominence is the ratio of the stock's price to sales.[4] The ratio of per-share price to per-share sales offers one particular advantage over the P/E ratio. If a firm has no earnings, the P/E ratio has no meaning, in which case the P/E ratio as a tool for valuation and comparison breaks down. The ratio of price to sales, however, can be computed even if the firm is operating at a loss, thus permitting comparisons of all firms, including those that are unprofitable.

Even if the firm has earnings and thus has a positive P/E ratio, the ratio of price to sales is still a useful tool. Since profits are ultimately related to sales, the larger the firm's sales per share, the greater is the potential for profit. A low stock price to per-share sales indicates a low market valuation, which may suggest the stock is undervalued. If the firm is operating at a loss, a low price-to-sales ratio may indicate a potentially profitable investment. If the firm were to return to profitability, it would produce higher earnings per share if sales per share were large. Thus, a low price-to-sales ratio may indicate the unprofitable firm has substantial potential if and when it returns to profitability.

The Need for Comparisons but Problems with Interpretation

While bondholders and stockholders may emphasize different ratios that analyze a firm's financial statements, both should realize that one ratio by itself can be misleading. The usefulness of ratio analysis is the general picture derived from the ratios. While individual ratios may be contradictory, the total analysis should provide any investor with an indication of the financial position of the firm.

---

[4]See, for instance, Lawrence Minard, "The Case Against Price/Earnings Ratios," *Forbes*, February 13, 1984.

Exhibit 17.5
Selected Ratios for
Chesapeake Corporation
and Industry Averages

Ratio	Chesapeake	Almanac of Business Ratios*	RMA Annual Statement Studies†
Current ratio	2.2	1.4	1.8
Quick ratio	1.0	0.8	0.9
Return on equity	7.6%	6.5%	Not given
Payout ratio	53.0%	78.2%	Not given
Debt/equity	1.8	Not given	1.3
Times-interest-earned	2.2	Not given	3.7

*Almanac of Business and Industrial Financial Ratios—1985 edition, 78.

†RMA Annual Statement Studies—1985 edition, 150.

Just as an individual ratio may be meaningless, so may be a set of ratios for a given firm if there is no benchmark with which to compare them. Thus the investor should either (1) compare individual ratios for a firm over a period of time to establish norms for the firm or (2) compare the individual firm's ratios to an industry average. Such comparisons, however, are not easy to interpret. Many firms have a variety of product lines and may not be readily classified into a particular industry. In addition, industry averages may be dated. Material on industry averages published in the current year must be based on financial statements that are at least one year old. There may be inconsistencies comparing this year's financial statements with previous years' industry averages. Such comparisons will have meaning only if the industry averages are stable over time.

The problem of defining the industry may be illustrated by comparing selected ratios in Exhibit 17.5 for CSK with industry averages for building and forest products published in the *Almanac of Business and Industrial Financial Ratios—1985 edition* or the *RMA Annual Statement Studies, 1985*. While Chesapeake Corporation may be classified in this industry, it does make products (e.g., tissue paper) that could be classified as consumer products. Hence the financial ratios for CSK may not be comparable to any industry average because the firm does not neatly fit into one industry classification.

Another problem immediately becomes apparent: the sources only publish some of the ratios the individual may wish to use to analyze Chesapeake's financial statements, and even those that are available can have different values. Consider the current ratio reported in Exhibit 17.5. The industry averages differ, so the individual investor is left with the problem of deciding which industry average to use as the standard. Of course, investors can overcome this problem by computing industry averages for themselves. Such calculations will require access to financial statements that the investors may obtain directly from each firm or through the use of a computer data base.

Problems concerning the use of ratio analysis are not limited to the availability and comparability of industry averages. Differences in accounting practices may also alter a firm's financial statements and thus affect ratio analysis. For example, the use of LIFO (last in, first out) for inventory valuation instead of FIFO (first in, first out) can have an impact on the inventory carried on the balance sheet and on the cost of goods

sold. During a period of inflation, many firms will choose to use LIFO instead of FIFO. This choice results in their selling the last (and presumably most costly) inventory first. The firm's cost of goods sold is higher, which reduces the firm's earnings and taxes. The cost of the inventory still held is lower, because the more costly inventory was sold first. Any ratio that uses inventory or earnings will be affected by the choice of LIFO instead of FIFO. If a financial analysis is comparing two firms, one of which uses LIFO and the other FIFO, the analysis will be biased. The firm using LIFO will appear to be less profitable. However, since its level of inventory is lower, it will have higher inventory turnover. In actuality there may be little substantive difference between the two firms.

Other accounting choices may also alter the results of ratio analysis. The choice of leasing instead of buying, the expensing of research and development costs instead of capitalizing them, larger allowances for doubtful accounts, or the accounting for pension liabilities may have an impact on a firm's financial statements. While the accounting profession seeks to standardize the construction of financial statements, differences among firms can and do exist, which may raise questions concerning the use of ratio analysis to compare firms.

Even a trend analysis of a firm's financial statements may be suspect. The problems mentioned before also apply to a ratio analysis of one firm over time if it has made accounting changes from one accounting period to the next. While such changes will be noted in the financial statements, they do raise questions concerning the comparability of ratios computed over a number of years.[5]

While there can be weaknesses in the use of ratios to analyze a firm's financial statements, the technique is still an excellent starting point to analyze a firm's financial position. The limitations of the data do not necessarily negate the technique. Instead, the analyst needs to be aware of the weaknesses so that appropriate adjustments can be made in either the construction of the ratios or the interpretation of the results.

FINANCIAL RATIOS AND STOCK VALUATION

Many ratios have been presented throughout this chapter. In this section several ratios are used to analyze the financial position of Chesapeake Corporation. Then the valuation model presented in Chapter 14 is applied to determine the value of the firm's stock. The ratios provide background evidence for the application of the valuation model.

Figure 17.1 presents Chesapeake's revenues, earnings per share, and per-share dividends for the period 1975 through 1985. As may be seen in the figure, revenues and per-share dividends have grown over time. Earnings per share, however, have been very erratic. Many of Chesapeake's products are tied to the business cycle (it is considered a cyclical firm), so large fluctuations, such as occurred in 1982, are to be expected.

---

[5] If possible, the financial analysts should recompute previous years' ratios using the firm's current accounting practices.

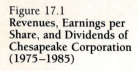

Figure 17.1
Revenues, Earnings per Share, and Dividends of Chesapeake Corporation (1975–1985)

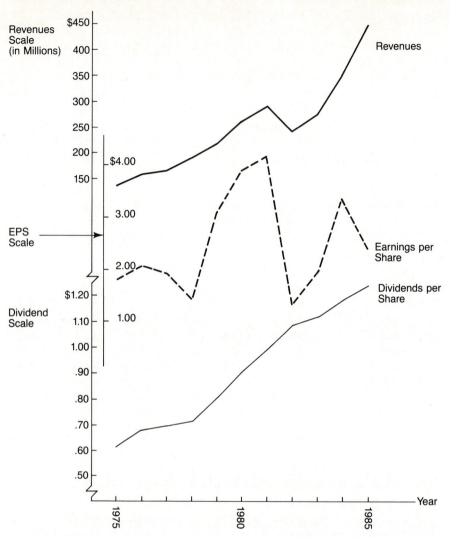

Exhibit 17.6 reports a ratio analysis of the firm for the period 1978 through 1985, and Figure 17.2 presents the same material in graphic form, clearly showing the patterns in each of the ratios. Several of the ratios have been relatively stable. For example, the current ratio only ranged from 2.2 to 2.7 during the eight-year period, but there is no discernible trend in the ratio. The same conclusion holds for the average collection period. Before 1984, the quick ratio had been very stable, but starting in 1984 this ratio deteriorated somewhat, and this decline is mirrored in both inventory turnover ratios. However, inventory still turns over nine times a year (using sales), which is about every 40 days. Fixed asset turnover has also declined, for in

Exhibit 17.6
Ratio Analysis of Chesapeake Corporation, 1978–1985

	1985	1984	1983	1982	1981	1980	1979	1978
Liquidity Ratios								
Current ratio	2.2	2.6	2.5	2.8	2.6	2.4	2.2	2.7
Quick ratio	1.0	1.3	1.6	1.7	1.6	1.7	1.6	1.7
Activity Ratios								
Average collection period (days)	35.1	32.3	36.5	34.7	34.5	35.0	32.1	38.4
Inventory turnover (sales/average inventory)	9.2	11.2	10.8	9.2	12.0	13.0	12.7	10.9
Inventory turnover (cost of goods sold/average inventory)	7.1	8.4	8.6	7.3	9.1	9.3	9.2	8.3
Fixed asset turnover	1.0	1.4	1.3	1.1	1.5	1.7	1.8	1.5
Profitability Ratios								
Operating profit margin	7%	10	6	5	12	16	15	17
Net profit margin	3.5%	6.3	4.6	2.8	9.3	9.1	8.1	4.6
Return on assets	2.5%	6.7	4.2	2.4	10.4	10.4	9.1	4.7
Return on equity	7.6	11.2	6.9	4.1	15.9	16.5	15.3	7.9
Leverage Ratios								
Debt/equity	1.77	0.69	0.62	0.72	0.69	0.59	0.67	0.66
Debt ratio (debt/total assets)	59.2%	40.8	38.3	41.9	40.8	37.1	40.1	39.8
Times-interest-earned	2.2	7.2	2.8	2.1	12.0	13.1	10.6	3.9
Other Ratios								
Payout ratio	53%	35	58	84	23	24	26	47
P/E ratio (year-end price)	14.7	12.2	24.8	18.5	7.3	6.1	6.7	12.9

1985 approximately $1 in fixed assets was used to generate $1 in sales. In 1980 to 1981, only $0.57 in fixed assets was used to generate $1 in sales.

Chesapeake is a cyclical firm, so an analyst can anticipate fluctuations in the profitability ratios. The economic downturn of the early 1980s is clearly shown in the low turnover and profitability ratios for 1982 (which have been highlighted in Figure 17.2). However, the profitability ratios were weak in 1985, which was not a period of recession. As with the decline in the inventory and fixed asset turnover ratios, the deterioration in the 1985 profitability ratios may be some cause for concern.

The leverage ratios for 1985 show the most dramatic change. Debt to total assets and debt to equity both rose dramatically. The increased use of debt with its resulting increase in interest expense also produced a large decline in the times-interest-earned ratio. No doubt the large increase in interest expense, from $4.9 million in 1984 to $14.3 million in 1985, contributed to the decline in the firm's profitability. This increased use of debt financing must be significant, and in this case Chesapeake made a major acquisition during the year that was financed through the use of long-term debt. (The balance sheet indicates that long-term debt rose from $60.7 million in 1984 to $308.8 million in 1985.)

This acquisition has to be of major concern, since it perceptibly increases the size of the firm from total assets of $330.9 million in 1984 to $617.8 million in 1985.

Figure 17.2
Ratio Analysis for Chesapeake Corporation (1978–1985)

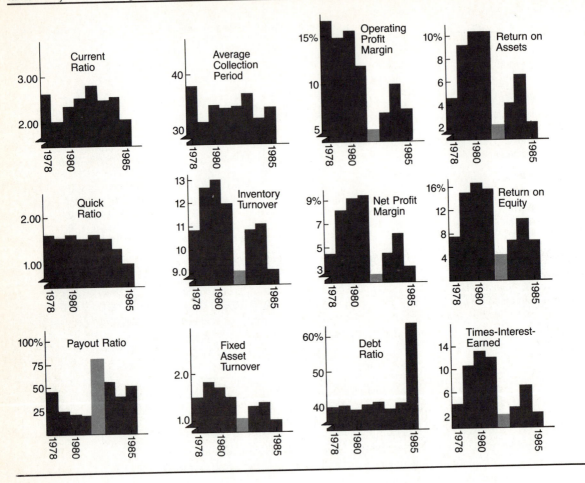

Since the acquisition occurred during 1985, the balance sheet shows the acquisition but the income statement only includes it from date of purchase. Hence any of the ratios that use information from the income statement may be misleading.[6] For example, earnings may be artificially lowered since the acquisition's contribution is for only part of the year. Hence, the returns on sales, assets, and equity may be understated. (This illustration points out the problem of computing only a single year's ratios and explains why the analyst should compute the ratios over a period of time, since a given year may not be representative of the firm's financial condition.)

---

[6] It would be desirable to restate the firm's financial statements for the past years to include the acquisition. However, data for such reconstructions may not be available to the financial analyst.

In order to use the dividend-growth model to value Chesapeake's common stock, the growth rate in dividends must be determined. The per-share dividends and their annual percentage change were as follows:

Year	Dividends per Share	Percentage Change
1975	$0.61	—
1976	0.67	9.8%
1977	0.69	2.9
1978	0.71	2.8
1979	0.80	12.7
1980	0.90	12.5
1981	0.99	10.0
1982	1.08	9.1
1983	1.12	3.7
1984	1.18	5.1
1985	1.24	5.1
	Average percentage change =	8.2%

These percentage changes could be averaged and this average then used as the growth rate. By this method, the annual rate of growth in Chesapeake Corporation's dividend is 8.2%.

However, the discussion in Chapter 13 suggested that averaging percentage changes could overstate the growth rate. An alternative method to determine growth uses the future value formulas presented in Chapter 6. The question to be solved is: At what annual rate did Chesapeake's dividend grow from $0.61 in 1975 to $1.24 in 1985?

Using future value

$$\$0.61(1 + g)^{10} = \$1.24$$
$$(1 + g)^{10} = 1.24/0.61 = 2.033.$$

The interest factor for the future value of $1 for ten years is 2.033. This yields (according to Appendix A) an annual growth rate between 7 and 8 percent, with the correct rate being 7.35 percent.[7]

This calculation uses only two observations, the first and the last years. An alternative approach for the determination of the growth rate uses all the data and estimates an equation that summarizes the points relating dividends and time. Such an equation in effect estimates the annual growth rate in the dividend. This estimation technique is least-squares regression analysis, and it is illustrated in the appendix to this chapter. Using this technique yields an annual growth rate of 7.85 percent.

Estimating equations

Which growth rate should be used in the valuation model—the average percent change (8.2 percent), the rate using the future value (7.35 percent), or the rate determined by regression analysis (7.85 percent)? The answer requires judgment on the part of the analyst because the results will differ depending on the choice. In this case the future value provides the lowest rate and would seem to be the most conservative choice. Such a choice may be appropriate for a cyclical firm that has just made a major acquisition that may temporarily retard the firm's growth. (Of course, the ac-

---

[7] $g = \sqrt[10]{2.033} - 1 = 1.0735 - 1 = 7.35\%$

quisition may stabilize the firm's earnings so that it is no longer a cyclical firm and thus can achieve higher and steadier growth.)

In addition to the determination of the dividend growth rate, the analyst must determine the required rate of return. As was explained previously, the required rate of return depends on the risk-free rate, the return on the market, and the firm's beta coefficient. As of July 1986, the yield on six-month treasury bills was approximately 5.9 percent. If the Ibbotson-Sinquefield study is used, then the return on the market should be 11.9 percent, which is 6 percent greater than the treasury bill rate. According to the *Value Line Investment Survey,* Chesapeake Corporation's beta is 0.9. Thus the required rate of return (r) is

$$r = R_f + (R_m - R_f)\beta$$
$$= 0.059 + (0.119 - 0.059)0.9$$
$$= 0.104 = 10.4\%.$$

Since the required rate of return has been determined, the valuation model may be applied. In this illustration the value of Chesapeake Corporation's stock is

$$V = \frac{D_0(1 + g)}{r - g}$$

$$= \frac{\$1.24(1 + 0.0735)}{0.104 - 0.0735}$$

$$= \$43.64$$

On July 9, 1985, the stock was selling for $41⅜, which indicates the stock is slightly undervalued.[8]

If the valuation model generates a large divergence between the valuation and the market price, the estimates used in the model may be incorrect. A large divergence would indicate that the stock is either well undervalued or overvalued. Such mispricing should be rare for, as is discussed in several places in this text, security markets are competitive and efficient. If a security were undervalued, investors would seek to buy it, which would drive up the price. If a security were overvalued, investors would seek to sell it, which would drive down the price. Thus if the dividend-growth model indicates a large divergence between the estimated value and the current market price, it would be advisable for the analyst to determine if the data used in the model is inaccurate.

ALTERNATIVE STRATEGIES FOR SELECTING COMMON STOCKS

Besides the valuation model, other techniques may be used to identify possible stocks for purchase. These include the ratio of price to book value, low P/E stocks, small capitalization stocks, stocks followed by few professional analysts, and screening tech-

---

[8] If the regression estimate of the growth rate had been used, the valuation of the stock would have been $52.44. Since the market price was $41⅜, this valuation indicated that the stock was undervalued by more than 20 percent and that Chesapeake's shares should be purchased. It is interesting to note that the stock reached a high of $52½ in less than six months after this valuation was completed.

niques. These techniques are not necessarily a substitute for analysis of financial statements and valuations but may be used in conjunction with them.

The ratio of price to book value suggests that the investor should limit purchases to those stocks selling for less than their book value. For example, in July 1986, Kerr-McGee Corporation was selling for $27 a share but its book value per share exceeded $32. By implication Kerr-McGee would be an attractive investment. By the same reasoning, since Chesapeake Corporation's book value was $31 and the stock was selling for approximately $42, the stock would not be a good purchase.

Discount from book value

The simplicity of this technique is very appealing, but unfortunately it does not answer the question "Why is the stock selling below its book value?" The answer could indicate several negative considerations, such as declining earnings (in which case the firm could cut its dividends or be unable to sustain future growth). Kerr-McGee is a large producer of crude oil and natural gas with a wide range of petroleum refining and chemical manufacturing products. However, the rapid decline in oil prices during 1986 clouded the firm's potential, so it should not be surprising that the stock sold for a discount below book value. It does not follow that the stock is a good purchase.

Buying low P/E stocks is a similar strategy in which the investor limits purchases to stocks with low price-earnings multiples or those whose current P/E ratio is near the low end of its historical range. Consider in Exhibit 17.7 the price-earnings ratios over a ten-year period for Bristol-Myers. On the average the P/E has ranged from 14.3 to 10.4. Unless there has been a change in the composition of the firm (such as AT&T's divestiture), there is little reason for a stock that has traded with a P/E between 14.3 and 10.4 to start selling for a P/E of 30. Instead a P/E of 30 would indicate that the stock is overpriced and should be avoided. A P/E of 5 would indicate the opposite.

Low P/E ratios

While the previous illustration of a P/E = 30 or 5 is an exaggeration, if a stock sells for a P/E near the end of its historic range, that may suggest a specific strategy. If Bristol-Myer's stock is selling for a P/E of 10 (i.e., near the low end of its historic P/E), that would suggest the stock may be considered for purchase. Conversely, when it sells near its historic high P/E, the stock is not a good purchase and may be a candidate for sale if the investor owns it.

	High	Low
1985	18	13
1984	15	12
1983	16	10
1982	14	10
1981	13	10
1980	13	7
1979	11	9
1978	13	9
1977	13	11
1976	17	13
Average	14.3	10.4

Exhibit 17.7
Price/Earnings Ratios for Bristol-Myers

Exhibit 17.8
Market Capitalization
of Selected Stocks

Firm	Number of Shares Outstanding*	Price (7/11/1986)	Market Value of Stock
Ampad	4,061,000	$17	$ 69,037,000
Chesapeake Corporation	6,631,000	42¼	280,159,750
Apple Computer	62,650,000	37⅛	2,325,881,250
Georgia-Pacific	103,225,000	31⅝	3,264,490,625
AT&T	1,069,333,000	24½	26,198,658,500

*Source: Information regarding number of shares is taken from *Standard & Poor's Stock Guide,* April 1986.

Low capitalization stocks

Instead of analyzing the ratio of a firm's stock price to its book value or its per-share earnings, the individual may prefer to invest in firms that are small or that are not well followed by professional financial analysts. This group of stocks is referred to as small capitalization ("small cap") stocks, which means that the total market value of the company's equity is modest. The total market value of the equity is the number of shares outstanding times the stock's price. Exhibit 17.8 presents the capitalization (i.e., number of shares outstanding, price per share, and total market value) for selected stocks. The exhibit is constructed so the smallest cap stocks are listed first. Obviously AT&T is a large firm whose stock is, in the aggregate, worth much more than the stock of Chesapeake Corporation, which in turn has a market capitalization that is considerably larger than Ampad.

Lack of coverage

Small capitalization stocks may lack a following on Wall Street. Analysts often work for large financial institutions such as life insurance companies or the trust departments of banks. These financial institutions tend to avoid investing in the stocks of small companies, so their analysts do not cover them. This lack of coverage by financial analysts suggests that small companies may offer the individual excellent investment opportunities. It should be pointed out that a strategy of investing in small capitalization stocks is based on the belief that the market for large companies is very efficient but the market for small companies is less efficient. It may be possible to identify a specific small company that is currently undervalued and hence is a good investment.

Use of screens

Screening techniques are another means designed to identify undervalued securities. The investor identifies specific criteria that must be met (e.g., return on equity of at least 20 percent, dividend yield of at least 5 percent, and a P/E ratio of less than 10). Through the use of a computer and a data base, the investor is able to identify all firms that meet the specified conditions. If the number of firms is large, the criteria may be made more stringent or additional criteria may be added to the screening process. The purpose of the screening technique is to limit the number of possible investments and to select among those stocks that meet the criteria the individual believes to be most important.

All of the techniques described above use financial information (e.g., book value, earnings per share, number of shares outstanding, and current market price of the stock). The difference between them and the valuation model presented in Chapter 14 is more of degree than of fundamental differences. However, no matter what technique to used to select specific stocks, all investment decisions are ultimately made in very efficient financial markets. Thus, it may be impossible for any technique to gen-

erate consistently superior investment decisions. In general, empirical evidence supports this conclusion—it is very difficult to consistently outperform the market. However, some of these techniques may prove to be beneficial to the individual making investment decisions.

SUMMARY

Ratio analysis is frequently used to analyze a firm's financial position. These ratios are easy to compute and employ data that are readily available on a firm's financial statements. The ratios include those designed to measure liquidity, activity, profitability, and capitalization (leverage). A summary of the ratio definitions follows.

While an investor may compute many ratios, it may be wise to select those ratios pertinent to the analysis. Creditors and investors in bonds are primarily concerned with determining the firm's capacity to meet its debt obligations as they come due, while investors who purchase stock may stress profitability and growth.

Ratios facilitate comparisons. A firm's current financial condition may be compared with previous years, and trends in the financial position may be identified. In addition, the firm may be compared with other firms within its industry. There are different definitions of some ratios, so the analyst must be sure when comparing his or her analysis with industry averages from other sources that the same ratio definitions are employed.

Ratio analysis may be used in conjunction with the dividend-growth model to help identify under- or overvalued stocks. Other selection methods also use financial information to help in the process of security selection. These techniques include (1) the analysis of the ratios of price to book value and price to earnings, (2) the total market value of the firm's stock, and (3) various screening techniques designed to identify superior stocks for possible investments.

Summary of Ratio Definitions

1. Liquidity Ratios

   a. Current ratio $= \dfrac{\text{Current assets}}{\text{Current liabilities}}$

   b. Acid test $= \dfrac{\text{Current assets} - \text{Inventory}}{\text{Current liabilities}}$

2. Activity Ratios

   a. Inventory turnover $= \dfrac{\text{Sales}}{\text{Average inventory}}$ or $= \dfrac{\text{Cost of goods sold}}{\text{Average inventory}}$

   b. Average collection period $= \dfrac{\text{Receivables}}{\text{Sales per day}}$

   c. Receivables turnover $= \dfrac{\text{Annual credit sales}}{\text{Accounts receivable}}$ or $= \dfrac{\text{Annual sales}}{\text{Accounts receivable}}$

   d. Fixed asset turnover $= \dfrac{\text{Annual sales}}{\text{Fixed assets}}$

3. Profitability Ratios

   a. Operating profit margin $= \dfrac{\text{Earnings before interest and taxes}}{\text{Sales}}$

   b. Net profit margin $= \dfrac{\text{Earnings after taxes}}{\text{Sales}}$

   c. Return on assets $= \dfrac{\text{Earnings after taxes}}{\text{Total assets}}$

   d. Return on equity $= \dfrac{\text{Earnings after taxes}}{\text{Equity}}$

   e. Return on common equity

$$= \dfrac{\text{Earnings after taxes} - \text{Preferred dividends}}{\text{Equity} - \text{Preferred stock}}$$

4. Leverage Ratios

   a. Debt ratios $= \dfrac{\text{Debt}}{\text{Equity}}$ or $= \dfrac{\text{Debt}}{\text{Total assets}}$

   b. Coverage ratio:

      Times-interest-earned $= \dfrac{\text{Earnings before interest and taxes}}{\text{Annual interest expense}}$

5. Miscellaneous Ratios

   a. Earnings per common share

$$= \dfrac{\text{Earnings} - \text{Preferred dividends}}{\text{Number of common shares outstanding}}$$

   b. Payout ratio $= \dfrac{\text{Dividends}}{\text{Earnings}}$

   c. P/E ratio $= \dfrac{\text{Price of stock}}{\text{Earnings per share}}$

   d. Price/Sales ratio $= \dfrac{\text{Price of stock}}{\text{Sales per share}}$

Terms to Remember

Time-series analysis

Cross-sectional analysis

Current ratio

Acid test (quick ratio)

Inventory turnover

Average collection period

Receivables turnover

Fixed asset turnover

Operating profit margin

Net profit margin

Return on assets

Return on equity

Debt ratio

Undercapitalized

Times-interest-earned

Questions

1. What is the difference between the current ratio and the acid test?

2. If accounts receivable increase, what effect will this have on the average collection period?

3. What is the difference between liquidity ratios and activity ratios?

4. What is times-interest-earned and what does it add to the analyst's knowledge of the firm? Would this ratio be of interest to a creditor?

5. What is the difference between the operating and net profit margins?

6. What does the debt ratio measure? Do all firms within an industry use the same proportion of debt financing?

7. Why may the return on equity exceed the return on a firm's total assets?

8. Given the following ratios, has the firm's financial position deteriorated?

	19x6	19x5	19x4	19x3	19x2	19x1	19x0
Current ratio	3.6	3.4	3.0	3.2	3.1	3.1	3.3
Quick ratio	2.2	2.2	2.1	2.2	1.7	1.8	2.0
Average collection period (days)	78	84	83	85	106	105	110
Inventory turnover (sales/average inventory)	4.4	4.5	4.5	4.9	4.6	4.7	4.7
Fixed asset turnover	6.4	6.4	8.6	9.0	9.0	9.6	10.0
Operating profit margin (%)	11.9	13.3	13.2	14.2	14.7	14.9	13.7
Net profit margin (%)	6.1	6.8	6.9	7.3	7.7	7.7	7.9
Return on assets (%)	8.8	10.0	10.4	11.4	11.1	11.1	11.5
Return on equity (%)	13.7	15.2	15.5	16.5	16.7	16.6	16.3
Debt ratio (%) (debt/total assets)	35.5	34.1	32.8	30.1	33.1	33.0	31.5
Times-interest-earned	9.3	14.2	14.5	14.2	11.8	10.7	11.5
Payout ratio (%)	41.4	37.6	35.9	33.5	34.2	34.7	35.3

Problems

1. Using the income statement and balance sheet presented below, compute the following ratios. Compare your results with the industry averages. What strengths and weaknesses are apparent?

Ratio	Industry Average
Current ratio	2:1
Acid test (quick ratio)	1:1
Inventory turnover	
a. Annual sales	4.0×
b. Cost of goods sold	2.3×
Receivables turnover	
a. Annual credit sales	5.0×
b. Annual sales	6.0×
c. Average collection period	2.5 months
Operating profit margin	26%
Net profit margin	19%
Return on assets	10%
Return on equity	15%
Debt ratio	
a. Debt/equity	33%
b. Debt/total assets	25%
Times-interest-earned	7.1×

Income Statement for XYZ
for the period ending December 31, 19xx

Sales	$100,000
Cost of goods sold	60,000
Gross profit	40,000
Selling and administrative expense	15,000
Operating profit	25,000
Interest expense	5,000
Interest earned	(2,400)
Earnings before taxes	22,400
Taxes	5,600
Earnings available to stockholders	$ 16,800
Number of shares outstanding	10,000
Earnings per share	$1.68

(To compute the inventory turnover, assume
that the prior year's inventory was $40,000.)

Firm XYZ
Balance Sheet as of December 31, 19xx
Assets

Current assets		
Cash and marketable securities		$ 10,000
Accounts receivable	$ 32,000	
Less allowance for doubtful accounts	2,000	30,000
Inventory		
Finished goods	30,000	
Work in progress	5,000	
Raw materials	7,000	42,000
Total current assets		$ 82,000
Investments		$ 10,000
Long-term assets		
Plant and equipment	100,000	
Less accumulated depreciation	30,000	70,000
Land		10,000
Total long-term assets		$ 80,000
Total assets		$172,000

Liabilities & Stockholders' Equity

Current liabilities		
Accounts payable		$ 10,000
Accrued wages		11,000
Bank notes		15,000
Accrued interest payable		4,000
Accrued taxes		1,000
Total current liabilities		$ 41,000
Long-term debt		$ 15,000
Total liabilities		$ 56,000
Stockholders' equity		
Common stock ($1 par value; 20,000 shares authorized; 10,000 shares outstanding)		$ 10,000
Additional paid-in capital		20,000
Retained earnings		86,000
Total stockholders' equity		$116,000
Total liabilities and equity		$172,000

2. You have taken the following information from a firm's financial statements. As an investor in the firm's debt instruments, you are concerned with its liquidity position and its use of financial leverage. What conclusions can you draw from this information?

	19x0	19x1	19x2
Sales	$1,000,000	$1,500,000	1,700,000
Cash	5,000	7,000	18,000
Accounts receivable	125,000	130,000	152,000
Inventory	200,000	190,000	200,000
Current liabilities	175,000	210,000	225,000
Operating income	90,000	145,000	170,000
Interest expense	20,000	23,000	27,000
Taxes	25,000	45,000	53,000
Net income	45,000	77,000	90,000
Debt	200,000	250,000	260,000
Equity	200,000	300,000	330,000

3. What is the debt/net worth ratio and the debt ratio for a firm with total debt of $700,000 and equity of $300,000?

4. A firm with sales of $500,000 has average inventory of $200,000. The industry average for inventory turnover is four times a year. What would be the reduction in inventory if this firm were to achieve a turnover comparable to the industry average?

5. Company A has three debt issues of $3,000 each. The interest rate of issue A is 4 percent, on B the rate is 6 percent, and on C the rate is 8 percent. Issue B is subordinate to A, and issue C is subordinate to both A and B. The firm's operating income (EBIT) is $500. Compute the times-interest-earned ratio for issue C. What does the answer imply? Does the answer mean that the interest will not be paid?

6. If a firm has sales of $42,791,000 a year, and the average collection period for the industry is 40 days, what should this firm's accounts receivable be if the firm is comparable to the industry?

7. Two firms have sales of $1 million each. Other financial information is as follows:

Firm	A	B
EBIT	$150,000	$150,000
Interest expense	20,000	75,000
Income tax	50,000	30,000

What are the operating profit margins and the net profit margins for these two firms? Why are they different? If total assets are the same for each firm, what can you conclude about their respective uses of debt financing?

Suggested Readings

The father of conservative financial analysis is Benjamin Graham. His text is a classic that employs many of the ratios described in this chapter.

Graham, Benjamin, David L. Dodd, Sidney Cottle, and Charles Tatham. *Security Analysis: Principles and Techniques.* 4th ed. New York: McGraw-Hill, 1962.
See especially Part 4, "The Valuation of Common Stock," for the conservative financial approach to the analysis of common stock.

For Graham's more recent thoughts on security analysis, see:

"A Conversation With Benjamin Graham." *Financial Analysts Journal* (September–October 1976): 20–23.

For additional material on ratio analysis, consult:

Bernstein, Leopold A. *The Analysis of Financial Statements.* Revised ed. Homewood, Ill.: Dow Jones-Irwin, 1984.
This book develops the ratios presented in this chapter and places special emphasis on accounting subtleties that may bias the results of the ratio analysis.
Horrigan, James C. "A Short History of Financial Ratio Analysis." *Accounting Review* (April 1968): 284–294.
This article traces the development of ratio analysis from the 1900s through the late 1960s.

Ratio analysis has been employed as a tool to help predict corporate bankruptcy. See, for instance:

Altman, Edward E. "Financial Ratios, Discriminant Analysis, and the Prediction of Corporate Bankruptcy." *Journal of Finance* (September 1968): 589–610.
Murray, Roger. "Lessons for Financial Analysis." *Journal of Finance* (May 1971): 327–332.
Gentry, James A., Paul Newbold, and David T. Whitford. "Predicting Bankruptcy: If Cash Flow's Not the Bottom Line, What Is?" *Financial Analysts Journal* (September–October 1985): 47–58.

A survey of more than 100 firms found that ratio analysis is an important tool used by management and that profitability ratios are the most important for judging performance. See:

Gibson, Charles H. "How Industry Perceives Financial Ratios." *Management Accounting* (April 1982): 13–19.

A survey of 2,000 members of the Financial Analysts Federation found that analysts emphasize expected changes in return on equity, expected changes in earnings per share, prospects for the industry, and the general economic conditions. Importance is also given to qualitative factors such as quality of management and strategic planning, but the former is hard to measure and it is difficult to obtain good information on the latter. See:

Chugh, Lal C., and Joseph W. Meador. "The Stock Valuation Process: The Analyst's View." *Financial Analysts Journal,* (November–December 1984): 41–48.

Appendix

Use of Regression Analysis to Estimate Growth Rates

In the appendix to Chapter 8 regression analysis was used to estimate beta coefficients. In this appendix it is used to estimate growth rates. The equation to be estimated is

$$D_0 (1 + g)^n = D_n.$$

This equation states that the initial dividend (D_0) will grow at some rate (g) for some time period (n) into the future dividend (D_n). This equation may be expressed in the following general form:

$$Y = (a)(b)^x,$$

in which $Y = D_n$, $a = D_0$, $b = (1 + g)$, and $x = n$.

The above equation is exponential, which is difficult to estimate, but it may be restated in log-linear form as:

$$\log Y = \log a + (\log b)X.$$

In this form, least-squares method of regression may be used to estimate a and b. This procedure using Chesapeake Corporation's dividends (Y) and time (X) is as follows:

	Year (X)	Dividend (Y)	log Y	X²	X (log Y)
1975	1	0.61	−0.21467	1	−0.21467
1976	2	0.67	−0.17392	4	−0.34785
1977	3	0.69	−0.16115	9	−0.48345
1978	4	0.71	−0.14874	16	−0.59496
1979	5	0.80	−0.09691	25	−0.48455
1980	6	0.90	−0.04575	36	−0.27454
1981	7	0.99	−0.00436	49	−0.03055
1982	8	1.08	0.03342	64	0.26739
1983	9	1.12	0.04922	81	0.44296
1984	10	1.18	0.07188	100	0.71882
1985	11	1.24	0.09342	121	1.02764
	Σ = 66	= 9.99	= −0.59757	= 506	= 0.026222

$$\log b = \frac{(n)\Sigma X(\log Y) - (\Sigma \log Y)(\Sigma X)}{(n)\Sigma X^2 - (\Sigma X)^2}$$

$$= \frac{(11)(0.02622) - (-0.59757)(66)}{(11)(506) - (66)^2}$$

$$= \frac{39.72837}{1210} = 0.032833.$$

$$\log a = \frac{\Sigma \log Y}{n} - \frac{(\log b)\Sigma X}{n}$$

$$= \frac{-0.59757}{11} - (0.032833)(66/11)$$

$$= -0.05432 - 0.197000$$

$$= -0.25132.$$

The estimated equation is

$$\log Y = -0.25132 + 0.032833X.$$

Figure 17.3
Dividends, Estimated
Regression Line, and
Forecasted Dividends
of Chesapeake
Corporation,
(1975–1988)

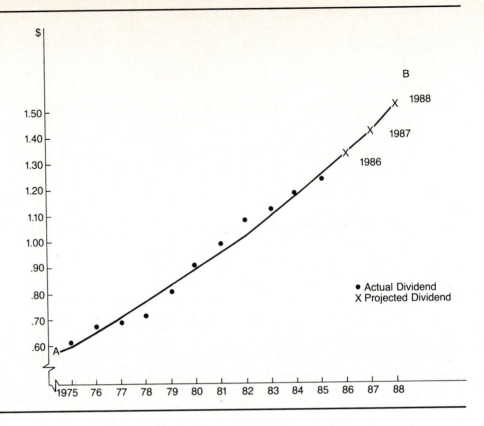

The equation in exponential form is[9]

$$Y = (0.560634)(1.078531)^x,$$

and the growth rate is

$$g = 1.078531 - 1 = 7.8531\%.$$

Figure 17.3 plots Chesapeake Corporation's cash dividends over time as well as the estimated equation (line AB). While the observations lie both above and below the estimated line, they tend to follow the contour of the line very closely. The projected dividends using the equation for the next three years (1986, 1987, and 1988) are also shown on the graph.[10]

---

[9] $10^{-0.25132} = 0.560634$ and $10^{0.032833} = 1.078531$.

[10] The projections are

$$\text{Dividend}_{1986} = (0.560634)(1.078531)^{12} = \$1.389,$$
$$\text{Dividend}_{1987} = (0.560634)(1.078531)^{13} = \$1.498,$$
$$\text{Dividend}_{1988} = (0.560634)(1.078531)^{14} = \$1.614.$$

A SHORT CASE STUDY FOR CHAPTERS 14–17
The Determination of Fundamental Values

Roger Coulson often observed that the clothes worn by his daughters and their friends were made of denim. No matter what the style, blue jeans and other clothes made of denim were popular. While certain styles would remain popular for only brief periods of time, the use of denim continued year after year. Coulson reasoned that the manufacturers of denim may be potentially attractive investments, as there appeared to him to be little fluctuation in the demand for denim.

Coulson discovered that the primary manufacturer of denim was Dentex, a textile mill in North Carolina. Dentex specializes in denim and produces only a modest amount of other types of cloth. Its sales of denim account for one-third of the total denim market, both domestic and abroad. Dentex's balance sheets and income statements for the last two years are presented in Exhibit 1. Dentex's per-share earnings and dividends are given in Exhibit 2. With the exception of 19x1 and 19y8, per-share earnings have steadily increased, and dividends have risen every year for the last ten years. This pattern of earnings and dividend growth impressed Coulson, who tended to think of textiles as a dull industry with little growth potential.

Coulson realized that for the firm to be a good investment, it should have strong fundamentals and be financially sound. So he decided to use ratios to analyze the firm's financial statements. From other sources, he found the industry averages given in Exhibit 3.

Currently Dentex's stock sells for $28. Coulson could invest in U.S. Treasury bills that yield 8.3 percent, but he believes that the stock market may offer a return over a period of years of 14.3 percent. Should he buy the stock of Dentex? To help answer that question, answer the following questions.

1. What conclusion(s) are indicated by the ratio analysis?

2. What is the annual growth rate in per-share earnings and dividends? Currently what is the dividend yield on Dentex stock? Can the dividend growth be sustained?

3. Is there any reason to conclude that the firm has changed its dividend policy?

4. Risk may be affected by many factors. How may each of the following affect the unsystematic risk associated with Dentex?
   a. The location of the firm
   b. Its use of debt financing
   c. Its product line

5. What may the P/E ratio indicate?

6. The current dividend growth rate cannot be maintained indefinitely, but Coulson believes that a 7 percent dividend growth rate is sustainable. Is the stock a good purchase if Coulson wants a 14.3 percent annual return?

7. If Dentex's beta coefficient was 0.8 and the sustainable growth rate was assumed to be 7 percent, what would be the value of the stock? What should Coulson do given this valuation?

Exhibit 1
Financial Statements
of Dentex

**Consolidated Statement of Income, Dentex Corporation
(for the years ending)**

	19x1	19x0
Sales (in thousands)	$668,000	$730,000
Cost of goods sold	531,000	571,000
Selling and administrative expense	54,000	52,000
Depreciation	24,000	22,000
Interest expense (net)	3,000	3,000
	612,000	648,000
Income before taxes	56,000	82,000
Income taxes	24,000	35,000
Net income	$ 32,000	$ 47,000
Earnings per share	$5.87	$8.82
Dividends per share	2.20	2.00

**Consolidated Balance Sheet, Dentex Corporation
(as of December 31)**

	19x1	19x0
Assets (in thousands)		
Current assets		
Cash and short-term investments	$ 23,000	$ 5,000
Accounts receivable	80,000	114,000
Inventory	120,000	118,000
Total current assets	223,000	237,000
Property, plant and equipment		
Land	3,000	3,000
Buildings and equipment	177,000	156,000
Other	20,000	17,000
	200,000	176,000
Total Assets	$423,000	$413,000

Liabilities and Stockholders' Equity

	19x1	19x0
Liabilities		
Current liabilities		
Long-term debt due within a year	$ 6,000	$ 4,000
Accounts payable	22,000	22,000
Accrued expenses	30,000	35,000
Income taxes owed	3,000	10,000
Total current liabilities	61,000	71,000
Long-term debt	20,000	22,000
Stockholders' equity		
Common stock	57,000	57,000
Paid-in capital	5,000	5,000
Retained earnings	280,000	258,000
Total stockholders' equity	342,000	320,000
Total Liabilities and Stockholders' Equity	$423,000	$413,000

	Earnings per Share	Dividends
19x1	$5.87	$2.20
19x0	8.82	2.00
19y9	7.49	1.80
19y8	6.21	1.60
19y7	6.75	1.35
19y6	4.90	0.95
19y5	3.97	0.75
19y4	2.51	0.70
19y3	1.58	0.55
19y2	1.33	0.51
19y1	1.00	0.50

Exhibit 2
Earnings per Share and Dividends of Dentex

Current ratio	3.2:1
Quick ratio	1.6:1
Average collection period	55 days
Inventory turnover (sales/average inventory)	3.7 a year
Fixed asset turnover	4.5 a year
Debt ratio (debt/total assets)	33%
Times-interest-earned	10×
Net profit margin	3.3%
Return on assets	4.5%
Return on equity	7.0%

Exhibit 3
Industry Averages for Selected Ratios

18 Technical Analysis

LEARNING OBJECTIVES

After completing this chapter you should be able to

1. State the purpose of technical analysis.
2. Differentiate between the various technical approaches to security selection.
3. Construct X–O charts and bar graphs.
4. Calculate a moving average.
5. Explain why studying insider activity may result in the selection of superior securities.
6. Explain why the technical approach has little support from many investors.

Investing would be much simpler if a trading rule could be found that told the investor when to buy or sell. Then the individual would not have to perform the analysis described in the previous chapters. The technical approach to security selection purports to do just that. By analyzing how the market (or a specific stock) has performed in the past, the investor may forecast how the market (or a specific stock) will perform in the future. Studying historical data concerning prices or the volume of transactions is substituted for analysis of financial statements and forecasts of future dividends and the growth in earnings.

Technical analysis is a very broad topic, because there are so many different varieties of this type of analysis. This chapter covers several popular technical approaches to the market and security selection. These include the Dow theory, odd lot purchases and sales, point-and-figure charts, and moving averages. Since these techniques accumulate and summarize data in a variety of charts and graphs, investors who use these techniques are often referred to as chartists.

The discussion in this chapter is primarily descriptive. After presenting the various technical approaches, the chapter ends with a consideration of the empirical studies that seek

to verify the techniques. The results of these studies strongly suggest that technical analysis does not lead to superior investment results. *However, this lack of empirical support has not stopped the use of technical analysis, and some of its jargon is commonly used by both professional and lay investors.*

THE PURPOSE OF THE TECHNICAL APPROACH

Technical analysis attempts to predict future stock prices by analyzing past stock prices. In effect, it asserts that tomorrow's stock price is influenced by today's price. That is a very appealing assertion, because it eliminates the need to perform fundamental analysis. No longer does the investor have to be concerned with ratios, financial leverage, and appropriate discount rates. Instead, he or she keeps a record of specific market factors, such as who is buying and selling the stock, and of specific information on individual stocks, such as the closing price and the volume of transactions. This information is then summarized in a variety of forms, such as charts and graphs, which in turn tell the investor when to buy and sell the securities.

The importance of the past

There are many different technical approaches to the selection of securities. Only a few will be discussed in this chapter. These are classified into two groups. The first techniques are designed to indicate the general direction of the market. Since security prices move together, the direction of the market is the overriding factor in the decision to buy and sell securities. In fact, it is the single most important factor in these technical approaches. This first group of techniques includes the Dow theory (which is perhaps the oldest of all the technical approaches to the market), Barron's confidence index, and odd lot purchases versus odd lot sales. These three approaches may be constructed from information reported in the financial press. For practical purposes, the investor may consider these sources of information as virtually free.

Market indicators

The second group of technical approaches discussed in this chapter is designed not only to discern the direction of the market but also to decide when to buy or sell specific securities. These include point-and-figure charts, bar graphs, moving averages of stock prices, and insider transactions. The information necessary to perform this analysis is also readily available in the financial press. Thus, the investor may either perform the analysis or purchase advisory services that perform the analysis.

Specific security indicators

Before reading further, the student should be forewarned that the presentations of the various approaches make their application appear to be easy. Also, the examples have been constructed to illustrate the techniques. In actual practice the buy and sell signals indicated by technical analysis may frequently be less obvious than the illustrations used in the text. Furthermore, one technical indicator may contradict another. Thus, if the investor follows several technical indicators, they rarely give clear buy or sell signals as a group.

A warning

Even if the technical indicators did give unambiguous signals, the investor should realize that frequent buying and selling becomes costly as commissions are generated for the broker. Scientific studies have found that a strategy of buy and hold may produce equal or better investment results than the trading of securities associated with technical analysis.

MARKET INDICATORS

The **Dow theory** is one of the oldest technical methods for analyzing security prices. It is an aggregate measure of security prices and hence does not predict the direction of change in individual stock prices. What it purports to show is the direction that the market will take. Thus, it is a method that identifies the top of a bull market and the bottom of a bear market.

Price movements

The Dow theory developed from the work of Charles Dow, who founded Dow Jones and Company and was the first editor of *The Wall Street Journal*.[1] Dow identified three movements in security prices: primary, secondary, and tertiary. Primary price movements are related to the security's intrinsic value. Such values depend on the earning capacity of the firm and the distribution of dividends. Secondary price movements, or "swings," are governed by current events that temporarily affect value and by the manipulation of stock prices. These price swings may persist for several weeks and even months. Tertiary price movements are daily price fluctuations to which Dow attributed no significance.

Dow theory evolved into a technical approach

Although Charles Dow believed in fundamental analysis, the Dow theory has evolved into a primarily technical approach to the stock market. It asserts that stock prices demonstrate patterns over four to five years and that these patterns are mirrored by indices of stock prices. The Dow theory employs two of the Dow Jones averages, the industrial average and the transportation average. The utility average is generally ignored.

Stock prices move together

The Dow theory is built upon the assertion that measures of stock prices tend to move together. If the Dow Jones industrial average is rising, then the transportation average should also be rising. Such simultaneous price movements suggest a strong bull market. Conversely, a decline in both the industrial and transportation averages suggests a strong bear market. However, if the averages are moving in opposite directions, the market is uncertain as to the direction of future stock prices.

When averages move in opposite directions, that is a buy or sell signal

If one of the averages starts to decline after a period of rising stock prices, the two are at odds. For example, the industrial average may be rising while the transportation average is falling. This suggests that the industrials may not continue to rise but may soon start to fall. Hence, the smart investor will use this signal to sell securities and convert to cash.

The converse occurs when, after a period of falling security prices, one of the averages starts to rise while the other continues to fall. According to the Dow theory, this divergence suggests that the bear market is over and that security prices in general will soon start to rise. The astute investor will then purchase securities in anticipation of the price increase.

The Dow theory does not explain why prices move

There are several problems with the Dow theory. The first is that it is not a theory but an interpretation of known data. It does not explain why the two averages should be able to forecast future stock prices. In addition, there may be a considerable lag between actual turning points and those indicated by the forecast. It may be months before the two averages confirm each other, during which time individual stocks may show substantial price changes.

---

[1] See George W. Bishop, Jr., *Charles H. Dow and the Dow Theory* (New York: Appleton-Century-Crofts, 1960), 225–228.

The accuracy of the Dow theory and its predictive power have been the subject of much criticism. Greiner and Whitcomb assert that "the Dow Theory provides a time-tested method of reading the stock market barometer."[2] However, between 1929 and 1960 the Dow theory made only 9 correct predictions out of 24 buy or sell signals.[3] Such results are less accurate than the investor may obtain by flipping a coin and have considerably diminished support for the technique.

The Dow theory may not be accurate

Barron's Confidence Index

Barron's confidence index is based on the belief that the differential between the returns on quality bonds and bonds of lesser quality will forecast future price movements. During periods of optimism, investors will be more willing to bear risk and thus will move from investments in higher quality debt to more speculative but higher yielding, lower quality debt. This selling of higher quality debt will depress its price and raise its yield. Simultaneously, the purchase of poor-quality debt should drive up its price and lower the yield. Thus, the difference between the two yields will diminish.

It compares yields on poor- and high-quality debt

The opposite occurs when sentiment turns bearish. The investors and especially those who "know" what the market will do in the future will sell poor-quality debt and purchase higher quality debt. This will have the effect of increasing the spread between the yields, as the price of poor-quality debt falls relative to that of the higher quality debt.

Barron's confidence index is constructed by using Barron's index of yields on higher and lower quality bonds. When the yield differential is small (i.e., when the yields on high-quality debt approach those that can be earned on poor-quality debt), the ratio rises. This is interpreted as showing investor confidence. Such confidence means that security prices will tend to rise. Conversely, when the index declines, that is an indication that security prices will fall.

Like the other technical approaches, Barron's confidence index has been subjected to scrutiny. Although it may indicate a tendency, it does not give conclusive signals. Since the signals of the Barron's confidence index are often ambiguous or there is a considerable time lag between the signal and the change forecasted, the index can be of only modest use for investors. Like many technical indicators it may point to the direction that security prices will follow, but it is not a totally reliable predictor of future stock prices.

Purchase and Sales of Odd Lots

Another technical indicator of the market is the **odd lot theory,** which concerns the purchase and sale of securities by small investors. These investors buy in small quantities (i.e., odd lots or less than 100 shares). The volume of such odd lot purchases and sales is reported in the financial press along with other financial data. The ratio of

[2] Perry P. Greiner and Hale C. Whitcomb, *The Dow Theory and the Seventy-Year Record* (Larchmont, N.Y.: Investors Intelligence, Inc., 1969), 130.

[3] See Leonard T. Wright, *Principles of Investments—Text and Cases.* 2d ed. (Columbus, Ohio: Grid, Inc., 1977), 312–317.

these odd lot purchases to odd lot sales is taken by some technicians as an indicator of the direction of future prices.

Small investors may be wrong

The rationale behind the use of the ratio of odd lot purchases to sales is that small investors are frequently wrong, especially just prior to a change in the direction of the market. Such investors will get caught up in the enthusiasm of a bull market and expand their purchases just as the market is reaching the top. The converse occurs at the market bottom. During declining markets, small investors become depressed about the market. After experiencing losses, they sell out as the market reaches its bottom. Such sales are frequently referred to as the passing of securities from "weak" hands to "strong" hands. The weak hands are, of course, the small investors who are misjudging the market, and the strong hands are the large investors who are more informed and capable of making correct investment decisions.

The weak and strong hands

Generally, the ratio of odd lot purchases to odd lot sales ranges from 1.4 to 0.6.[4] If the ratio approaches 1.25 to 1.30, that means the small investors are increasing their purchases relative to sales, which is a very bearish signal. According to the odd lot theory, such purchases forecast a decline in stock prices. If the ratio approaches 0.7 to 0.65, odd lot sales exceed purchases, indicating that the small investor is bearish. Such bearishness on the part of the small investor is then taken as a bullish sign by believers in the odd lot theory.

The prediction of future prices has not been verified

Empirical work has not been able to verify that odd lot purchases and sales are a good predictor of future prices.[5] These studies indicate that during rising markets, purchases do tend to exceed sales. Conversely, during periods of declining markets the odd lot sales increase. Like the Dow theory and Barron's confidence index, the odd lot theory illustrates a tendency, but there is also little concrete evidence of its ability to forecast accurately when the market will change. It assumes that purchasers of odd lots make inferior investment decisions, but it should be remembered that many large investors are also sellers at the market bottom and buyers at the market top. Incorrect investment decisions are not the monopoly of small investors!

Investment Advisory Opinions

While the odd lot theory suggests that the small investor is often wrong, the advisory opinion theory suggests that financial advisors are often wrong. This approach is often referred to as a "contrarian" view, since it takes the opposite side of most financial advisors. The theory suggests that when most financial advisors and financial services become bearish and forecast declining security prices, that is the time to purchase securities. When the majority of financial advisors become bullish and forecast rising security prices, the wise investor liquidates (i.e., sells securities). This technical indicator seems perverse, as it suggests that those most likely to know are unable to forecast the direction of security prices accurately. However, there is some evidence to support the theory.[6]

---

[4]See Frank K. Reilly, *Investments* (Hinsdale, Ill.: The Dryden Press, 1982), 334.

[5]See Richard A. Brealey, *An Introduction to Risk and Return From Common Stocks* (Cambridge, Mass.: M.I.T. Press, 1969), 129–140.

[6]See A. W. Cohen, "A Contrary Opinion Indicator," *Investors Intelligence* (October 1975), 1.

Advances/Declines

An alternative to the odd lot theory and the opinions of investment advisory services is the advance-decline cumulative series. This indicator is based on the cumulative net difference between the number of stocks that rose in price relative to the number that declined. Consider the following summaries of daily trading on the New York Stock Exchange:

Issued advancing	1,200	820	480	210
Issues declining	400	760	950	1,190
Issues unchanged	200	220	370	400
Net advances (declines)	800	60	(470)	(980)
Cumulative net advances (declines)	800	860	390	(590)

During the first day, 800 more stocks rose than declined. While this pattern continued during the second day, the number of stocks rising was considerably less than during the previous day, so the cumulative total registered only a small increment. During the third day, the market weakened, and the prices of more stocks fell than rose. However, the cumulative total still remained positive. During the fourth day, the number of stocks that declined rose further, so that the cumulative total now became negative.

Importance of changes in the cumulative total

According to technical analysis, the cumulative total of net advances gives an indication of the general direction of the market. If the market is rising, the net cumulative total will be positive and expanding; however, when the market changes direction, the cumulative total will start to diminish and will become negative as prices continue to decline. Of course, the converse applies at market bottoms. When the market declines, the net advances fall (i.e., the negative cumulative total increases). Once the bottom in the market has been reached and security prices start to rise, the number of advances will start to exceed the number of declines, which will cause the net advances to increase. Changes in the direction of advances/declines becomes a barometer of the trend in the market. (This technique is similar to moving averages, which are discussed later in this chapter and which are used to measure both the direction of prices in individual stocks and in the market as a whole.)

SPECIFIC STOCK INDICATORS

The preceding section discussed several technical approaches to the market as a whole. This section considers several techniques that may be applied to either the market or individual securities. When applied to the market, their purpose is to identify the general trend. When applied to individual securities, these techniques attempt to inform the investor when to buy, when to sell, or when to maintain current positions in a specific security.

Point-and-Figure Charts (The X–O Chart)

Most technical analysis has an underlying basis (or perhaps rationalization) in economics. In effect, these analytical techniques seek to measure supply and demand. Since an increase in demand will lead to higher prices and an increase in supply will

lead to lower prices, an analysis that captures shifts in supply and demand will be able to forecast future price movements. **Point-and-figure charts**, which are also called **X–O charts**, seek to identify changes in supply and demand by watching changes in security prices.

*Changes in supply
or demand*

If a stock's price goes up, that movement is caused by demand exceeding supply. If a stock's price falls, then supply exceeds demand. If a stock's price is stable and trades within a narrow range, the supply of the stock coming onto the market just offsets the current demand. However, when the stock's price breaks this stable pattern of price movements, there has been a fundamental shift in demand and/or supply. Thus a movement upwards suggests a change in demand relative to supply, while a movement downwards suggests the opposite.

Point-and-figure charts seek to identify these fundamental changes through the construction of graphs employing Xs and Os. Such an X–O chart is constructed by placing an X on the chart when the price of the stock rises by some amount, such as $1 or $2, and an O on the chart when it declines by that amount. Such a chart requires following the stock on a daily basis and noting the price at the end of the day. If the price has changed by the specified amount, an entry is made on the chart.

This procedure is best explained by an illustration. Suppose the price of a stock had the following day-to-day price changes and the investor wanted to construct an X–O chart for price movements of $2. The procedure is illustrated in Figure 18.1.

Daily Closing Prices for January

Date	Prices				
1/1–1/5	$50⅛	$51⅜	$51¾	$52⅛	$54½
1/8–1/12	53½	53⅛	52½	51⅞	51⅛
1/15–1/19	49½	49¾	47⅛	48¾	47⅞
1/22–1/26	49¾	46⅞	46⅛	45⅞	44⅞

Figure 18.1 is divided into four quadrants, which illustrate the four steps necessary to create the chart.

Construction of the chart

The first quadrant (A) sets up the axes—time on the horizontal axis and dollars on the vertical axis. The dollar unit that is selected depends on the prices of the stock. For lower priced stocks the units should be $1, but for higher priced stocks the units may be larger, such as $2 or $3. Since a movement from $40 to $42 is the same percentage increase as a price movement from $20 to $21, the use of the large increments for higher priced stocks does not reduce the quality of the X–O chart. In addition, the use of larger units will reduce the number of entries necessary to create the chart. Since the price of the stock in question is in the $50 range, a $2 interval is selected, and the vertical axis shows the increments in $2 units.

The second quadrant (B) plots the price of the stock on the first day of observation. Since the price of the stock is rising, the chartist enters an X at $50 on the chart. Additional Xs are entered only after the price of the stock rises by $2 (e.g., $50 to $52). All small movements in price both up and down are ignored, and only after the price has risen by $2 is a second X entered on the chart. Thus, although the price of the stock rose during the first three days, no entry is made. The effect of such omissions is both to reduce the work required to construct the chart and to minimize the effect of small daily price fluctuations.

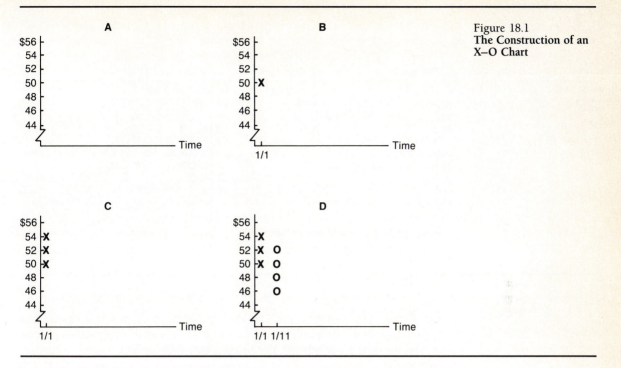

Figure 18.1
The Construction of an X–O Chart

The third quadrant (C) plots the price increases that occurred on days 4 and 5. The price closed above $52 on day 4, so an X is placed on the chart. The same applies to day 5, when the stock closed above $54.

After reaching a high of $54½, the price of the stock starts to fall. The chartist now uses only Os instead of Xs to indicate the declining price. Once again the price must fall by $2 before an entry is made (i.e., the stock must sell for $52 or less, since $54 was the highest X entry). The date on which Os began to be recorded on the chart is noted on the horizontal axis. The analyst will continue to place Os on the chart until the present downward trend is reversed and the price of the stock rises by the necessary $2. Then the analyst will start a new column and enter an X to indicate an increase in the stock's price.

The fourth quadrant (D) illustrates the decline in the stock's price. After the initial price rise illustrated in quadrant C, the price falls. Once it reaches $52, an O is placed on the chart. This occurs on January 11. The price of the stock now appears to be declining. Should the price fall to $50 or below, another O will be placed on the chart. If, however, the price again reaches $54 an X will be placed in the next column and the date will be recorded to indicate the change in the direction of the price.

In this case the price of the stock continues to decline. Each time the stock breaks the two-point barrier, another O is placed on the chart. If the price continues to decline, the column will fill up with Os. If the stock's price stabilizes, no entries will be made until a two-point movement occurs.

After a period of stable prices, a deviation signals the direction of future price changes. Such signals are illustrated in Figure 18.2. On the left-hand side (A), after a   *Signals of future prices*

Figure 18.2
Buy and Sell Signals

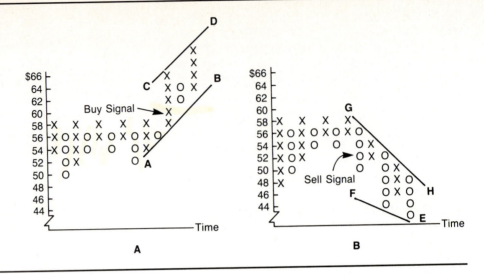

A

B

period of trading between $52 and $58, the price of the stock rises to a new high of $60. This suggests that a new upward price trend is being established, which is a buy signal. On the right-hand side (B), the opposite case is illustrated. The price declines below $52, which suggests that a new downward price trend is being established. If the investor owns the stock, the shares should be sold.

It is interesting to note that in both cases illustrated in Figure 18.2, the purchases and sales appear to be made at the wrong time. In the case of the purchase, it is made after the stock has already increased in price. Conversely, the sale is made after the stock has declined in price. Thus, purchases are not made at the lows, and sales are not made at the highs. Instead, the purchases appear to be made when the stock is reaching new highs, and the sales are made when the stock is reaching new lows. The rationale for this behavior rests primarily on the belief that the charts indicate new trends. Despite the fact that the investor missed the high prices for the sale and the low prices for the purchase, if the price change that is being forecasted proves accurate, then the investor will have made the correct investment decision even though the purchases and sales were not made at the exact turning points.

Signals for possible trading strategies

Besides indicating the buy or sell signals when trends are being established, these charts suggest possible trading strategies during the trends, which are also illustrated in Figure 18.2. While the left-hand side shows a price that is obviously rising, the price is still fluctuating. The right-hand side illustrates a downward trend, but the price is also fluctuating. During the upward trend, which is illustrated in Figure 18.2, part A, each high is higher than the preceding high price, and each low is higher than the preceding low price. Obviously, if an investor buys this stock and holds it, the return will be positive over this period. However, the return may be increased by judiciously buying at each low, selling at each high, and repeating the process when the cycle within the trend is repeated.

"Support"

In order to isolate these opportunities, a set of lines has been drawn in Figure 18.2 connecting the high and the low prices that the stock is achieving. These lines are

believed to have special significance because they indicate when to make the buy and sell decisions. The bottom lines (*AB* and *EF*), which connect the lowest prices, suggest a price level that generates "support" for the stock. Technical analysis asserts that when the price of the stock approaches a support line, the number of purchases will increase, which will stop further price declines. Hence, the approach of a stock's price toward a support line suggests that a buying opportunity is developing. Should the price reach the line and start back up, then the investor should buy the stock.

    The opposite occurs at the top line (*CD* and *GH* in Figure 18.2, parts A and B), which represents "resistance." Since the price of the stock has risen to that level, more investors will want to sell their stock, which will thwart further price advances. Accordingly, the investor should sell the stock when the price reaches a line of resistance. After the stock has been sold, the investor then waits for the price to decline to the level of price support.

"Resistance"

Bar Graphs

Bar graphs are similar to point-and-figure charts. Like the X–O charts, they require a day-to-day compilation of data, and they use essentially the same information. Preference for one over the other is a matter of choice, and while the investor could construct both, such work would seem redundant.

    A bar graph is constructed by using three price observations—the high, the low, and the closing price for the day. If the prices were

Construction of bar graphs

Price	Monday	Tuesday	Wednesday	Thursday	Friday
High	$10	$9½	$9⅞	$10½	$12
Low	9	9	9¼	9⅞	10⅛
Close	9	9⅜	9⅞	10	11½

the bar graphs for each day would be

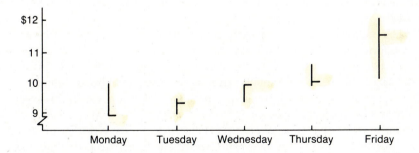

The vertical lines represent the range of the stock's price (i.e., the high and the low prices), and the horizontal lines represent the closing price.

    It is obvious that such a chart is easy to construct, but it does require a substantial amount of work to keep several of these charts up to date on a daily basis. Each stock requires 15 price observations per week, which means 150 observations for just ten stocks per week. Since an entry is made on an X–O chart only if the price of the stock

Figure 18.3
Head-and-Shoulder
Pattern

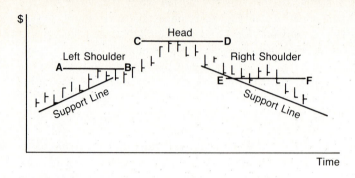

Patterns of stock prices

has moved to the next interval, less work is required to construct such a chart, and it may be preferred to the bar graph for this reason alone.

As with the X–O chart, the bar graph is supposed to indicate future price movements in the stock by the pattern that emerges. There are several possible patterns. For example, one brief paperback book on charting identifies at least ten patterns, each with a descriptive name such as head and shoulder, wedge, flag, or pennant.[7] Space limits this discussion to only one pattern: the head and shoulder. The student who is interested in the variety of patterns should consult a book that explains the different patterns and how they are used to predict future stock prices.

The head-and-shoulder pattern

A **head-and-shoulder pattern** does just what its name implies: The graph forms a pattern that resembles a head and shoulders. Such a pattern is illustrated in Figure 18.3. Initially, the price of the stock rises. Then it levels off before rising to a new high, after which the price declines, levels off, and then starts to fall. To illustrate the head-and-shoulder pattern, several lines have been imposed on the graph. These lines are similar to the lines of resistance and support found on the X–O charts. Line *AB* shows the left shoulder and also represents a line of resistance. However, once it is penetrated, the price of the stock rises to a new high, where it meets new resistance (line *CD*).

When the stock is unable to penetrate this new resistance, the price starts to decline and forms the head. However, after this initial decline in price the stock reaches a new level of support, which forms the right shoulder (line *EF*). When the price falls below line *EF*, the head-and-shoulder pattern is completed. This is interpreted to mean that the stock's price will continue to fall and is taken as a very bearish sign by followers of this type of analysis.

While the head-and-shoulder pattern in Figure 18.3 indicates that the price of the stock will subsequently fall, the same pattern upside down implies the exact opposite. In this case, penetration of the right shoulder indicates that the price of the stock will rise and is taken as a very bullish sign by those who use bar graphs.

---

[7]See Anthony J. Lerro and Charles B. Swayne, Jr., *Selection of Securities: Technical Analysis of Stock Market Prices* (Morristown, N.J.: General Learning Corporation, 1971).

Moving Averages

A **moving average** is an average computed over time. For example, in 1985 the closing monthly values for the Dow Jones industrial average were as follows:

Averages over time

January	1287	April	1258	July	1347	October	1374
February	1284	May	1315	August	1334	November	1472
March	1267	June	1335	September	1328	December	1547

A six-month moving average of the Dow Jones industrials would be computed as follows. The average for the first six months is computed first.

How a moving average is computed

$$\frac{1287 + 1284 + 1267 + 1258 + 1315 + 1335}{6}$$

$$= \frac{7746}{6} = 1291.$$

Then the average is computed again, but the entry for July (1347) is added in and the entry for January (1287) is deleted:

$$\frac{1284 + 1267 + 1258 + 1315 + 1335 + 1347}{6}$$

$$= \frac{7806}{6} = 1301.$$

The average is thus 1301, which is greater than the average for the preceding six months (1291).

To obtain the next entry, the average is computed again, with August being added and February being dropped. The average in this case becomes 1309. By continuing this method of adding the most recent entry and dropping the oldest entry, the averages move through time.

Figure 18.4 presents both the Dow Jones industrial average for 1982 through 1985 and the six-month moving average. As may be seen from the figure, the moving average follows the Dow Jones industrials. However, when the Dow Jones industrials are declining, the moving average is greater than the industrial average. The converse is true when the Dow Jones industrial average is rising: the moving average is less than the industrial average. At one point the two are equal (where the two lines cross). In this example, the Dow Jones industrial average and the six-month moving average are equal in December 1983. Technicians place emphasis on such a crossover, for they believe that it is indicative of a change in the direction of the market. (It may also indicate a change in a specific security's price when the moving average is computed for a particular stock.) In this illustration, there appears to be some validity to the claim of the predictive power of the 200-day moving average, as the market rose after both buy signals and fell after the sole sell signal.

The moving average for the Dow Jones industrials

The average that is most frequently used is a 200-day moving average. Thus, for a specific stock, the investor must keep a daily tabulation of 200 stock prices and recompute the average daily! Such calculations are obviously tedious if a significant number of stocks are included. However, a 200-day average may be approximated by

Figure 18.4
Dow Jones Industrial Average and a Six-month Moving Average of the Dow Jones Industrials

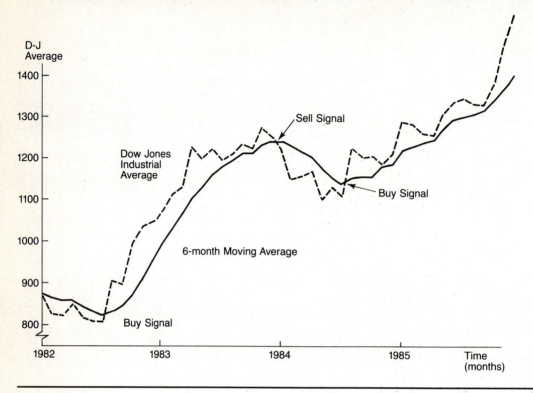

using weekly prices for 35 to 40 weeks, and the investor may obtain 200-day moving averages from Trendline, 345 Hudson Street, New York, NY 10014. In addition, the investor should realize there is no evidence that using moving averages of different durations produces results inferior (or superior) to the 200-day moving average.[8]

Volume

The preceding techniques emphasized price movements as measured by point-and-figure charts, bar graphs, and moving averages. Technical analysts also place emphasis on the volume of transactions and deviations from the normal volume of trading in a specific stock. A large deviation from normal volume is interpreted to mean a change in the demand for or supply of the stock.

   Since a price change can occur on small volume or on large volume, the price change itself says nothing concerning the breadth of the change in demand or supply.

---

[8]A study by Van Horne and Parker suggests that the use of moving averages does not increase investment results. See James C. Van Horne and G. G. C. Parker, "The Random Walk Theory: An Empirical Test," *Financial Analysts Journal* (November–December 1967).

A price increase on small volume is not as bullish as one accompanied by heavy trading. Conversely, a price decline on small volume is not as bearish as a decline accompanied by a large increase in the number of shares traded. When a price decline occurs on small volume, that indicates only a modest increase in the supply of the stock was offered for sale relative to the demand. However, if the price decline were to occur on a large increase in volume, that would indicate many investors were seeking to sell the stock and would be considered bearish.

Insider Transactions

In Chapter 4 we learned that insiders, such as officers, directors, and very large stockholders, cannot legally use inside information for personal gain (e.g., buy the stock prior to an important announcement and subsequently sell it after the price has risen). However, they can and often do purchase and sell the stock of the firm in which they have access to privileged information. Such transactions are legal if they are reported to the SEC.[9] Since insiders may have the best picture of how the firm is faring, some devotees of technical analysis feel that these inside transactions offer a clue to future earnings, dividends, and stock price performance. A greater number of purchases than sales is believed to be a bullish indicator, and more sales transactions than purchases imply that the stock's price will fall.

Insider purchases and sales

The hypothesis that insider activity may be indicative of future stock prices has received some support in the academic literature. As is discussed in the following section on the verification of technical analysis, very little support has been found for the various technical approaches to security selection. However, several reports do suggest that the study of insider activity may indeed lead to the selection of superior securities. For example, Martin Zweig reported that from June 1974 to April 1976 more than 60 percent of stocks with significant insider purchases outperformed the market, but only 37 percent of stocks with significant insider sales outperformed the market.[10] This study and others reported in the academic literature give some credence to this particular method of technical analysis that is lacking in the other techniques previously discussed.[11] Thus, the individual investor would be well advised to keep track of insider activity in those securities of particular interest.[12]

Insider activity may predict future price behavior

Short Sales By Specialists

While purchases and sales by insiders may indicate their perception of the firm's future prospects, short sales by specialists may indicate the stock's future price performance. Hence technical analysts may follow both activities. As was explained in

---

[9] The *Insiders Chronicle* reports these transactions weekly. This publication is devoted almost exclusively to reporting transactions by insiders.

[10] See Martin E. Zweig, "Canny Insiders," *Barron's* (June 21, 1976): 5.

[11] These studies include Jeffrey F. Jaffe, "Special Information and Insider Trading," *Journal of Business* (July 1974), and James H. Lorie and Victor Niederhoffer, "Predictive and Statistical Properties of Insider Trading," *Journal of Law and Economics* 11 (April 1968): 35–53.

[12] The ratio of insider sales to insider purchases may be obtained from Stock Research Corp., 50 Broadway, New York, NY 10004.

Chapter 2, specialists make a market in securities listed on the organized exchanges (i.e., they offer to buy and sell securities for their own accounts). While short sales are explained in the next chapter, all that is needed for this discussion is the realization that short sellers profit when security prices fall.

In order to make a market, specialists must be abreast of the events affecting securities. They continually adjust their portfolios in response to the flow of securities onto and off of the market. It is through this process that they continue to make the market in the individual securities. If they misjudge demand and supply and subsequent price changes, they could suffer large losses.

Specialists' short sales relative to total short sales

If specialists believe that the supply of stock coming to the market will increase and drive down a stock's price, they take short positions in the stock in anticipation of the price decline. Total short sales and specialists' short sales must be reported to the SEC and the NYSE. Generally about half of all short sales are made by the specialists. If, however, the proportion of specialists' short sales to total short sales rises to above 65 percent, technical analysts believe this is a bearish indicator. The high ratio of specialists' short sales indicates that those who may be best able to perceive changes in supply and demand are anticipating price declines. If the ratio of specialists' short sales to total short sales falls to 40 percent, technical analysts interpret that as a bullish sign, indicative of rising future stock prices.[13]

THE VERIFICATION OF TECHNICAL ANALYSIS

At first glance technical analysis seems so very appealing. One needs only to construct a set of charts or compute some simple ratios (e.g., insider sales to insider purchases) and then follow the signals given by the analysis. Such simple rules for investing literally beg for verification to ascertain if they are, in fact, good predictors.

Several studies have sought to test the validity of technical analysis. The use of computers has eased calculations and made it possible to test several variations of the technical approach. For example, the investigator may have the computer calculate various moving averages (e.g., 200-day, 100-day, or 50-day averages) to determine if one is the best predictor.

There is little empirical evidence to support the technical approach

The majority of this research has failed to verify the various technical approaches to investing.[14] This conclusion is the basis for the weak form of the efficient market hypothesis discussed in Chapter 8. The large body of empirical evidence has convinced many investors to believe that the technical approach does not lead to superior investment performance and that the investor would do just as well to buy a randomly selected portfolio and hold it. When commissions are included, the return from fol-

---

[13] See Frank K. Reilly, *Investments* (Hinsdale, Ill.: The Dryden Press, 1982), 336–337.

[14] For example, see Michael C. Jensen and George A. Bennington, "Random Walks and Technical Theories: Some Additional Evidence," *The Journal of Finance* 25 (May 1970): 469–482; Eugene Fama, "The Behavior of Stock-Market Prices," *Journal of Business* 37 (January 1965): 34–105; F. E. James, Jr., "Monthly Moving Averages—An Effective Investment Tool?" *Journal of Financial and Quantitative Analysis* (September 1968): 315–326; and J. C. Van Horne and G. G. C. Parker, "The Random Walk Theory: An Empirical Test," *Financial Analysts Journal* (November–December 1967): 87–92. (The student should be warned that most of this material may be difficult to comprehend.) Empirical support for technical analysis may be found in Robert A. Levy, "Random Walks: Reality or Myth," *Financial Analysts Journal* (November–December 1967): 69–77.

POINTS OF INTEREST
The Elves of Wall Street

"Wall Street Week" is a popular TV program aired through the public broadcasting network. Each week the program discusses recent events in the financial markets and a guest analyst talks about a facet of investing, such as airline stocks or the bond market.

A segment of the program is devoted to technical analysis. Ten technical indicators—called "the elves of Wall Street"—suggest the direction that the market will take. Unfortunately their signals are frequently ambiguous. For example, three will indicate a rising market (+3), four will point to a downward market (−4), and three will be neutral (0). In this example the net score is −1

(+3, −4, 0) which is interpreted as neutral. A net score of +5 or −5 indicates that the technical indicators are extremely bullish or bearish, respectively. Thus if six indicators are positive (+6), one is negative (−1), and three are neutral (0), the net score is +5, which is a very bullish technical forecast.

The technical indicators used include moving averages, analysis of the volume of shares traded, insider transactions, and the price performance of long-term government bonds. For information on the specific technical indicators and how they are interpreted, write Butcher & Singer, Inc., Box 957, Philadelphia, PA 19105.

lowing the technical approach may be even less than that earned on a randomly selected portfolio. These conclusions have resulted in a general rejection of technical analysis by many academically trained teachers of finance.

The primary cause for the inability of the technical approach to select securities that outperform the market is that the market is very efficient. Information is readily disseminated among the investors, and prices adjust accordingly. Thus, if an investor were to develop an approach that outperformed the market, it would be a matter of time before the technique would be learned by others. The method would no longer achieve the initial results as the mass of investors applied it. A system that works (if one can be found) can succeed only if it is not known by many investors. Thus, it is naive for an investor to believe that he or she can use a known technical approach to beat the market. A new and unknown system is needed. However, when one realizes that many investors are looking for and testing various approaches, it is hard to believe that the individual investor will find a technical approach that can beat the market.

Although the technical approach lacks verification, it is still used by some portfolio managers as a supplement to fundamental analysis to help the timing of purchases and sales. The primary users of technical analysis are individuals and advisory services. One frequently sees advertisements in the financial press for advisory services that employ various technical approaches. Perhaps the investor should ask why the service is being sold and not being applied exclusively by those who know the "secret." Certainly if one knows how to beat the market, one should be able to earn a substantial return on investments and should not need to sell the secret for monetary gain.

SUMMARY

Technical analysis seeks to identify superior investments by examining the past behavior of the market and of individual securities. Technical analysts, or "chartists," stress the past as a means to predict the future. This approach is diametrically opposed to the fundamental approach, which stresses future earnings and dividends appropriately discounted back to the present.

Several technical approaches (the Dow theory, Barron's confidence index, and odd lot purchases versus odd lot sales) attempt to identify changes in the direction of the market. Since individual security prices move together, the determination of a change in the direction of the market should identify the future movement of individual security prices.

Other technical approaches (X–O charts, bar graphs, moving averages, and analysis of insider activity) may be applied to individual securities. By constructing various charts and graphs, the technical analyst determines when specific securities should be bought or sold.

Whether or not the technical approach leads to superior investment results is open to debate. However, with the exception of insider activity, little support has been found to verify technical analysis. The results of these studies imply that the investor may achieve similar results by purchasing a random selection of securities.

Terms to Remember

Technical analysis	Point-and-figure chart (X–O chart)
Dow theory	Bar graph
Barron's confidence index	Head-and-shoulder pattern
Odd lot theory	Moving average

Questions

1. What is the purpose of technical analysis?

2. Why are those who use technical analysis sometimes referred to as chartists?

3. What changes represent a sell signal in the Dow theory, Barron's confidence index, and the odd lot theory?

4. What is a moving average? What is the significance when a stock's price equals a moving average of that price?

5. Why may technical analysis produce self-fulfilling predictions?

6. Why may the construction of some charts or graphs used in technical analysis be tedious and time consuming?

7. What is the problem with time lags in technical analysis?

8. Why does technical analysis receive little support from academically oriented students of investments?

9. Which technical approach may be the best?

Suggested Readings

Descriptions of various technical approaches may be found in

Bishop, George W., Jr. *Charles Dow and the Dow Theory.* New York: Appleton-Century-Crofts, 1960.

Cohen, A. W. *Point and Figure Stock Market Trading.* Larchmont, N.Y.: Chartcraft, 1968.

Granville, Joseph E. *Granville's New Strategy of Daily Stock Market Timing for Maximum Profit.* Englewood Cliffs, N.J.: Prentice Hall, 1976.

Lerro, Anthony J., and Charles B. Swayne, Jr. *Selection of Securities: Technical Analysis of Stock Market Prices.* Morristown, N.J.: General Learning Press, 1971.

Rhea, Robert. *The Dow Theory.* New York: Barron's Publishing Co., 1932.

Zahorchak, Michael G. *The Art of Low Risk Investing.* New York: Van Nostrand Reinhold, 1972.

Summaries of the empirical evidence that generally refute technical analysis are given in

Brealey, Richard A. *An Introduction to Risk and Return From Common Stocks.* Cambridge, Mass.: M.I.T. Press, 1969.

Ehrbar, A. F. "Technical Analysis Refuses to Die." *Fortune* 92, August 1975, 99.

Fama, Eugene F., and Marshall E. Blume. "Filter Rules and Stock Market Trading." *Journal of Business* (January 1966): 226–241.

Greiner, Perry P., and Hale C. Whitcomb. *The Dow Theory and the Seventy-Year Record.* Larchmont, N.Y.: Investors Intelligence, Inc., 1969.

Kerrigan, Thomas J. "The Short Interest Ratio and Its Component Parts." *Financial Analysts Journal* (November–December 1974): 45–49.

Lorie, James H., and Mary T. Hamilton. *The Stock Market: Theories and Evidence.* Homewood, Ill.: Richard D. Irwin, 1973.

Malkiel, Burton G. *A Random Walk Down Wall Street.* New York: W. W. Norton & Co., 1973.

A large amount of data used in technical analysis is presented weekly in *Barron's*. For a guide to this material, consult:

Zweig, Martin E. *Understanding Technical Forecasting—How To Use Barron's Laboratory Pages.* Princeton, N.J.: Dow Jones & Co., 1980.

The large body of evidence that does not support the use of technical analysis has caused many instructors to slight and even omit technical analysis. One text that does present a sympathetic coverage of technical analysis is

Cohen, Jerome B., Edward D. Zinbarg, and Arthur Zeikel. *Investment Analysis and Portfolio Management.* 4th ed. Homewood, Ill.: Richard D. Irwin, 1982, Chapter 8.

For an integration of fundamental and technical analysis, see:

Stein, Lawrence. *The Fundamental Stock Market Technician.* Chicago: Probus Publishing, 1986.

V Investing in Options

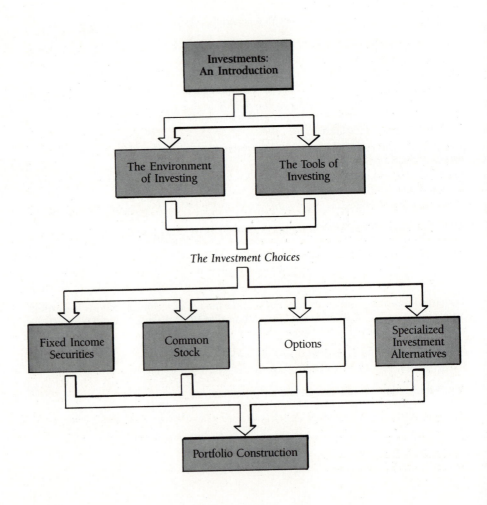

Investments:
An Introduction

The Environment
of Investing

The Tools of
Investing

The Investment Choices

Fixed Income
Securities

Common
Stock

Options

Specialized
Investment
Alternatives

Portfolio Construction

*P*arts Five and Six are devoted to alternatives to stocks and bonds. While some of these assets are very speculative, others, such as home ownership, are conservative forms of investment.

Part Five is devoted to options. An option is a contract that gives the holder the right to buy or sell a security at a specified price within a specified time period. Many options (warrants, calls, and puts) may be considered speculative investments. Only those investors who are willing and able to bear substantial risk should consider purchasing them. However, these options do offer the possibility of a large return. Those investors who are willing to bear the risk for the potential return may find the next two chapters to be the most fascinating in the text.

Chapter 21 is devoted to convertible bonds, which are a hybrid type of security that combines features of both debt and stock. Since the bondholder has the option to convert the bond into stock, this type of bond is included in this section on options. A convertible bond is, however, a considerably safer investment than the other securities discussed in Part Five.

19 Introduction to Options*

LEARNING OBJECTIVES

After completing this chapter you should be able to

1. Explain short selling.
2. Determine the source of profits and losses from short selling.
3. Define the word "option" as it applies to securities.
4. Differentiate between an option's market value and its intrinsic value.
5. Understand how options offer leverage.
6. Identify the factors affecting an option's time premium.
7. Demonstrate how hedging with warrants may yield a profit regardless of whether the price of the stock rises or falls.

*A*n option is the right to do something. In the security markets an option is the right to buy or sell stock at a specified price within a specified time period. Options take various forms, including warrants, calls, puts, convertible bonds, and convertible preferred stock. Part Five is devoted to these securities. This chapter serves as a general introduction to investing in options. It covers features that apply to all types of options: their intrinsic value, the leverage they offer, and the premium paid for an option. A specific option, the warrant, is used to illustrate these concepts.

The next chapter discusses the speculative options—puts and calls. Owners of these options do not receive the benefits offered by common stock, but some investors buy them because their anticipated return is greater and hence it is worth taking the greater risk associated with the options. These investors expect the price of the option to rise or fall more

---

* This and the subsequent chapter use material from Herbert B. Mayo, *Using the Leverage in Warrants and Calls to Build a Successful Investment Program* (Larchmont, N.Y.: Investors Intelligence, 1974). Permission to use this material has been graciously given by the publisher.

rapidly than the price of the stock, another illustration of the use of leverage. Without the possibility of such leverage, investors would not buy speculative options.

The third chapter in Part Five covers convertible bonds and convertible preferred stock. These securities do not offer investors potential leverage, but they do offer modest returns with some potential for growth in value. In addition, convertible bonds and convertible preferred stocks are less risky investments than common stock but are more risky than most investments in nonconvertible bonds (i.e., the bonds described in Part Three).

This chapter commences with a discussion of the short sale. Before one can discuss options, it is necessary to understand both the long and short positions (i.e., the short sale) because some option positions are alternatives to short sales. After the mechanics of short selling are covered, an explanation of an option's intrinsic value, and the potential leverage available through options, and the time premium (or time value) paid for the option follows. The chapter ends with a discussion of warrants and how they are used to reduce risk through the construction of hedge positions.

THE SHORT SALE

How does an investor make money in the security markets? The obvious answer is to buy at low prices and to sell at high prices. For most people this implies that the investor first buys the security and then sells it at some later date. This is called the **long position** and was discussed in Chapter 3. Can the investor sell the security first and buy it back later at a lower price? The answer is yes, for a **short sale** reverses the order. The investor sells the security first with the intention of purchasing it in the future at a lower price.

Since the sale precedes the purchase, the investor does not own the securities that are being sold short. Selling something that a person does not own may sound illegal, but there are many examples of such short selling in normal business relationships. A magazine publisher who sells a subscription, a professional such as a lawyer, engineer, or teacher who signs a contract for future services, and a manufacturer who signs a contract for future delivery are all making short sales.[1] If the cost of fulfilling the contract increases, the short seller loses. If the cost declines, the short seller profits. Selling securities short is essentially no different: It is a current sale with a contract for future delivery. If the securities are subsequently purchased at a lower price, the short seller will profit. However, if the cost of the securities rises in the future, the short seller will suffer a loss.

Selling what one does not own

The mechanics of the short sale can be illustrated by a simple example employing the stock of XYZ, Inc. If the current price of the stock is $50 per share, the investor may buy 100 shares at $50 per share for a total cost of $5,000. Such a purchase represents taking a long position in the stock. If the price subsequently rises to $75 per share and the stock is sold, the investor will earn a profit of $2,500 ($7,500 − $5,000).

An illustration of the short sale

The short position reverses this procedure: The investor sells the stock first and buys it back at some time in the future. For example, an investor sells 100 shares of XYZ short at $50 ($5,000). Such a sale is made because the investor believes that the

Sell short when anticipating a price decline

---

[1] See Mark Weaver, *The Technique of Short Selling* (Palisades Park, N.J.: Investors' Press, 1963), 2. When your school collected the semester's tuition, it established a short position. It contracted for the future delivery of educational services.

stock is *overpriced* and that the price of the stock will *fall*. In a short sale the investor does not own the 100 shares sold. The buyer of the shares, however, certainly expects delivery of the stock certificate. (Actually, the buyer does not know if the shares come from an investor who is selling short or an investor who is liquidating a position in the security.) The short seller has to *borrow* 100 shares to deliver to the buyer. The shares are usually borrowed from a broker, who in turn probably borrows them from clients who have left their securities with him or her. (Shares held in a margin account may be used by the broker, and one such possible use is to lend the shares to a short seller. However, shares left with the broker in a cash account cannot be lent to a short seller.)

The proceeds of sale are held by the broker

The short seller must put up collateral

Although the investor has sold the securities, the proceeds of the sale are not delivered to the seller but are held by the broker. These proceeds will be subsequently used to repurchase the shares. (In the jargon of security markets such repurchases are referred to as **covering the short sale.**) In addition, the short seller must deposit with the broker an amount of money equal to the margin requirement for the purchase of the stock. Thus, if the margin requirement is 60 percent, the short seller in the above illustration must deposit $3,000 ($5,000 × 0.6) with the broker. This money protects the broker (i.e., it is the short seller's collateral) and is returned to the short seller plus any profits or minus any losses when he or she buys the shares and returns them to the broker. This flow of certificates and money is illustrated in Figure 19.1. The broker receives the money from the short seller (the $3,000 collateral) and from the buyer of the stock (the $5,000 in proceeds from the sale). The investor who sells the stock short receives nothing, but the borrowed securities flow through this investor's account en route to the buyer. The buyer then receives the securities and remits the funds to pay for them.

What occurs if the price of the stock falls

If the price of a share declines to $40, the short seller can buy the stock for $4,000. This purchase is no different from any purchase made on an exchange or in the over-the-counter market. The stock is then returned to the broker, and the loan of the stock is repaid. The short seller will have made a profit of $1,000 because the shares were purchased for $4,000 and sold for $5,000. The investor's collateral is then returned by the broker plus the $1,000 profit. These events are illustrated in Figure 19.2. The 100 shares of XYZ stock are purchased for $4,000 by the short seller. When the certificate for the 100 shares is received, it is returned by the short seller to the broker (who, in turn, returns the shares to whomever they were borrowed from). The broker returns the investor's $3,000 that was put up for collateral. Since the in-

Figure 19.1
The Flow of Money and Certificates in a Short Sale

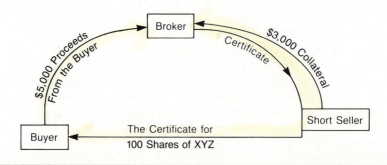

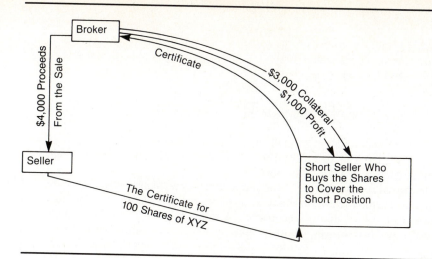

Figure 19.2
The Flow of Money and Certificates When Covering a Profitable Short Sale

vestor uses only $4,000 of the $5,000 in proceeds from the short sale to purchase the stock, the broker sends the investor the remainder of the proceeds (the $1,000 profit).

If the price of the stock had risen to $60 per share and the short seller had purchased the shares and returned them to the broker, the short position would have resulted in a $1,000 loss. The proceeds from the short sale would have been insufficient to purchase the shares. One thousand dollars of the collateral would have had to be used in addition to the proceeds to buy the stock and cover the short position. The broker would owe the short seller only what was left of the collateral ($2,000) after the transactions had been completed.

What occurs if the price of the stock rises

Although the previous transactions may sound complicated, they really are not. All that has occurred is that an investor has bought and sold a security. Instead of the investor's first purchasing the security and then selling it, the investor initially sold the security and subsequently purchased the shares to cover the short position. Because the sale occurred first, there is additional bookkeeping to account for the borrowed securities, but the transaction itself is not complicated.

Unfortunately, there is a belief among many investors that short selling is gambling. They believe that if investors sell short and the price of the stock rises substantially, the losses could result in financial ruin. However, short sellers can protect themselves by placing stop loss purchase orders to cover the short position if the stock's price rises to a particular level.[2] Furthermore, if these investors fail to place stop loss orders, the brokers will cover the position for them once their collateral has shrunk and can no longer support the short position. Thus the amount that an investor can lose is limited to the collateral. Short selling really involves no greater risk than purchasing securities, for when investors buy securities, they can lose all of their invested funds.

Short selling is not gambling

Actually, short selling is consistent with a rational approach to the selection of securities. If an investor analyzes a company and finds that its securities are over-

Sell short when securities are overpriced

---

[2] For a discussion of a stop-loss order, see Chapter 3, p. 48.

431

priced, he or she will certainly not buy the securities. Instead, any that are currently owned should be sold. In addition, if the individual has confidence in the analysis and believes that the price will decline, the investor may sell short. The short sale, then, is the logical strategy given the basic analysis. Securities that are overpriced should be considered for short sales, just as securities that the investor believes are undervalued are the logical choice for purchase.

Market makers may also sell short

Short selling is not limited to individual investors, as market makers may also sell short. If there is an influx of orders to buy, the market makers may partially satisfy this demand by selling short. They will then repurchase the shares in the future to cover the short position after the influx of orders has subsided. Frequently this transaction can be profitable. After the speculative increase in price that results from the increased demand, the price of the security may decline. When this occurs, the market makers profit because they sell short when the price rises but cover their positions after the price subsequently falls.[3]

THE INTRINSIC VALUE OF AN OPTION

An **option** is the right to buy or sell stock at a specified price within a specified time period. At the end of the time period, the option expires on its **expiration date**. The minimum price that an option will command is its **intrinsic value** as an option. For

---

[3] For a stinging criticism of market makers' capacity to profit from short sales, see Richard Ney, *The Wall Street Jungle* (New York: Grove Press, 1970).

an option to buy stock, this intrinsic value is the difference between the price of the stock and the per-share **exercise price (strike price)** of the option. The market price of an option is frequently referred to as the **premium.** If an option is the right to buy stock at $30 a share and the stock is selling for $40, then the intrinsic value is $10 ($40 − 30 = $10).

If the stock is selling for a price greater than the per-share exercise price, the option has positive intrinsic value. This may be referred to as the option's being "in the money." If the common stock is selling for a price that equals the strike price, the option is "at the money." And if the price of the stock is less than the strike price, the option has no intrinsic value. The option is "out of the money." No one would purchase and exercise an option to buy stock when the stock could be purchased for a price that is less than the strike price of the option. However, as is explained subsequently, such options may still trade.

"In, out, and at" the money

The relationships among the price of a stock, the strike price (i.e., the exercise price of an option), and the option's intrinsic value are illustrated in Exhibit 19.1 and Figure 19.3. In this example, the option is the right to buy the stock at $50 per share. The first column of the exhibit (the horizontal axis on the graph) gives various prices of the stock. The second column presents the strike price of the option ($50), and the last column gives the intrinsic value of the option (i.e., the difference between the values in the first and second columns). The values in this third column are illustrated in the figure by line *ABC,* which shows the relationship between the price of the stock and the option's intrinsic value. It is evident from both the exhibit and the figure that as the price of the stock rises, the intrinsic value of the option also rises. However, for all stock prices below $50, the intrinsic value is zero, since security prices are never negative. Only after the stock's price has risen above $50 does the option's intrinsic value become positive.

The relationship between the price of a stock and the intrinsic value of the option

The intrinsic value is one of the most important aspects of analyzing options. First, the market price of an option must approach its intrinsic value as the option approaches its expiration date. On the day that the option is to expire, the market price can be only what the option is worth as stock. It can be worth only the difference between the market price of the stock and the exercise price of the option. This fact means that the investor may use the intrinsic value of an option as an indication of the

The importance of the intrinsic value

Price of the Stock	minus	Per-Share Strike Price of the Option	equals	Intrinsic Value of the Option
$ 0		$50		$ 0
10		50		0
20		50		0
30		50		0
40		50		0
50		50		0
60		50		10
70		50		20
80		50		30
90		50		40

Exhibit 19.1
The Price of a Stock and the Intrinsic Value of an Option to Buy the Stock at $50 per Share

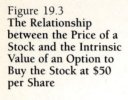

Figure 19.3
The Relationship between the Price of a Stock and the Intrinsic Value of an Option to Buy the Stock at $50 per Share

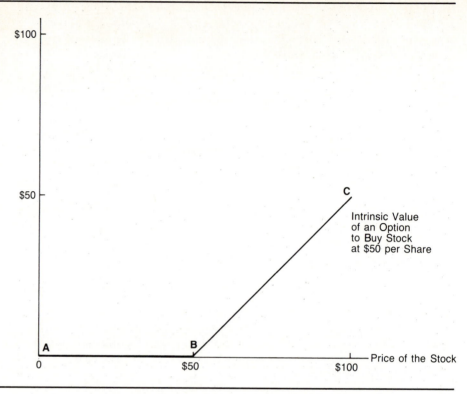

Arbitrage

option's future price, for the investor knows that the market price of the option must approach its intrinsic value as the option approaches expiration.

Second, because of arbitrage, the intrinsic value of an option sets the minimum price that the security will command. **Arbitrage** is the act of simultaneously buying and selling a commodity or security in two different markets to make a profit from the different prices offered by the markets. In the case of an option, the two markets are the market for the stock and the market for the option. The essence of the arbitrage position is a short sale in the stock and a long position (i.e., a purchase) in the option. After these transactions are effected, the arbitrageur will exercise the option. Then the shares acquired by exercising the option will be used to cover the short position in the stock.

An illustration of arbitrage

This act of arbitrage may be clarified by using the simple example presented in Exhibit 19.2. If the price of the stock is $60 and the strike price of the option is $50, the option's intrinsic value is $10. If the current market price of the option were $6, an investor could buy the option and exercise it to acquire the stock. By doing so the investor saves $4, for the total cost of the stock is $56 (i.e., $6 for the option and $50 to exercise the option). The investor then would own stock that has a market value of $60.

If the investor continues to hold the stock, the $4 saving could evaporate if the stock's price falls. However, if the investor were to simultaneously buy the option and sell the stock short, the $4 profit would be guaranteed. In other words, the investor

Exhibit 19.2
**The Steps Required
for Arbitrage**

Givens

Price of the stock	$60
Per-share strike price of the option	50
Price of the option	6

Step 1
Buy the option for $6
Sell the stock short for $60

Step 2
Exercise the option, thereby acquiring the stock for $50

Step 3
After acquiring the stock, cover the short position

Determination of profit or loss

Proceeds from the sale of the stock		$60
Cost of the stock		
Cost of the option	$ 6	
Cost to exercise the option	50	
Total cost		56
Net profit		$ 4

uses arbitrage, the required steps for which are presented in Exhibit 19.2. The investor sells the stock short at $60 and purchases the option for $6 (step 1). The stock
certificate is borrowed from the broker and delivered to the buyer. Then the investor
exercises the option (step 2). After receiving the stock certificate acquired by exercising the option, the investor covers the short position by giving the certificate to the
broker (step 3). This set of transactions locks in the $4 profit, because the investor
sells the stock short at $60 per share and simultaneously purchases and exercises the
option for a combined cost of $56 per share. By selling the stock short and purchasing
the option at the same time, the investor ensures that he or she will gain the difference
between the intrinsic value of the option and its price. Through arbitrage the investor
guarantees the profit.

Of course, the act of buying the option and selling the stock short will drive up
the option's price and put pressure on the price of the stock to fall. Thus, the opportunity to arbitrage will disappear, because arbitrageurs will bid up the price of the
option to at least its intrinsic value. Once the price of the option has risen to its intrinsic value, the opportunity for a profitable arbitrage disappears. However, if the price
of the option were to fall again below its intrinsic value, the opportunity for arbitrage
would reappear, and the process would be repeated. Thus, the intrinsic value of an
option becomes the minimum price that the option must command, for arbitrageurs
will enter the market as soon as the price of an option falls below its intrinsic value as
an option.

If the price of the option were to exceed its intrinsic value, arbitrage would offer
no profit, nor would an investor exercise the option. If the option to buy the stock in
the previous examples were to sell for $5 when the price of the common stock was
$50, no one would exercise the option. The cost of the stock acquired by exercising
the option would be $55 (i.e., $50 + $5). The investor would be better off buying the
stock outright than purchasing the option and exercising it. The opportunity for ar-

*Arbitrage causes prices
to change*

bitrage thus occurs only when the price of the option is less than the option's intrinsic value. The option would not be purchased or exercised when its price exceeded its intrinsic value.

The opportunity to execute arbitrage is rare

Actually, the opportunity for the typical investor to execute a profitable arbitrage is rare. Market makers are cognizant of the possible gains from arbitrage and are in the best possible position to take advantage of any profitable opportunities that may emerge. Hence, if the opportunity to purchase the option for a price less than its intrinsic value existed, the purchases would be made by the market makers, and the opportunity to arbitrage would not become available to the general public. For the general investor the importance of arbitrage is not the opportunity for profit that it offers but the fact that it sets a *floor* on the price of an option, and that floor is the minimum or intrinsic value.

LEVERAGE

Options offer leverage

Some options offer investors the advantage of **leverage**. The potential return on an investment in an option may exceed the potential return on an investment in the underlying stock (i.e., the stock that the option represents the right to purchase). Like the use of margin, this magnification of the potential gain is an example of leverage. Unless these options offer investors leverage, there is no reason to purchase them in preference to the stock.

An illustration of the potential leverage

Exhibit 19.3, which illustrates the relationship between the price of a stock and an option's intrinsic value, also demonstrates the potential leverage that options offer. For example, if the price of the stock rose from $60 to $70, the intrinsic value of the option would rise from $10 to $20. The percentage increase in the price of the stock is 16.67 percent ([$70 − $60] ÷ $60), whereas the percentage increase in the intrinsic value of the option is 100 percent ([$20 − $10] ÷ $10). The percentage increase in the intrinsic value of the option exceeds the percentage increase in the price of the stock. If the investor purchased the option for its intrinsic value and the price of the stock then rose, the return on the investment in the option would exceed the return on the investment in the stock.

Exhibit 19.3
The Relationship between the Price of Stock, the Value of an Option, and the Hypothetical Market Price of the Option

Price of the Common Stock	Per-Share Strike Price	Option Intrinsic Value	Option Hypothetical Market Price
$ 10	$50	$ 0	$ 1
20	50	0	5
30	50	0	9
40	50	0	13
50	50	0	18
60	50	10	22
70	50	20	27
80	50	30	34
90	50	40	42
100	50	50	51

Leverage, however, works in both directions. Although it may increase the investor's potential return, it may also increase the potential loss if the price of the stock declines. For example, if the price of the stock in Exhibit 19.3 fell from $70 to $60 for a 14.2 percent decline, the intrinsic value of the option would fall from $20 to $10 for a 50 percent decline. As with any investment, the investor must decide if the increase in the potential return offered by leverage is worth the increased risk.

THE TIME PREMIUM PAID FOR AN OPTION

If an option offers a greater potential return than does the stock, investors may prefer to buy the option. In an effort to purchase the option, investors will bid up its price, so the market price will exceed the option's intrinsic value. Since the market price of an option is frequently referred to as the "premium," the extent to which this price exceeds the option's intrinsic value is referred to as the **time premium** or time value. Investors are willing to pay this time premium for the potential leverage the option offers. This time premium, however, reduces the potential return and increases the potential loss.

Time value of an option

The time premium is illustrated in Exhibit 19.3, which adds to Exhibit 19.1 a hypothetical set of option prices in column 4. The hypothetical market prices are greater than the intrinsic values of the option because investors have bid up the prices. To purchase the option, an investor must pay the market price and not the intrinsic value. Thus, in this example when the market price of the stock is $60 and the intrinsic value of the option is $10, the market price of the option is $22. The investor must pay $22 to purchase the option, which is $12 more than the option's intrinsic value.

Time value illustrated

The relationships in Exhibit 19.3 among the price of the stock, the intrinsic value of the option, and the hypothetical price of the option are illustrated in Figure 19.4. The time premium paid for the option over its intrinsic value is easily seen in the graph, for it is the shaded area that is the difference between the line representing the market price of the option (line DE) and the line representing its intrinsic value (line ABC). Thus, when the price of the stock and option are $60 and $22 respectively, the time premium is $12 (the price of the option, $22, minus its intrinsic value, $10).

As may be seen in the figure, the amount of the time value varies at the different price levels of the stock. However, the amount of the time premium declines as the price of the stock rises above the option's strike price. Once the price of the stock has risen considerably, the option may command virtually no time premium over its intrinsic value. At $100 per share, the option is selling at approximately its intrinsic value of $50. The primary reason for this decline in the time premium is that as the price of the stock and the intrinsic value of the option rise, the potential leverage is reduced. In addition, at higher prices the potential price decline in the option is greater if the price of the stock falls. For these reasons investors become less willing to bid up the price of the option as the price of the stock rises, and hence the amount of the time premium diminishes.

The time premium varies

The time premium decreases the potential leverage and return from investing in options. If, for example, this stock's price rose from $60 to $70 for a 16.7 percent gain, the option's price would rise from $22 to $27 for a 22.7 percent gain. The percentage increase in the price of the option still exceeds the percentage increase in the price of the stock; however, the difference between the two percentage increases is

The time premium reduces the potential leverage

Figure 19.4
The Relationships among the Price of the Stock, the Intrinsic Value of the Option, and the Hypothetical Price of the Option

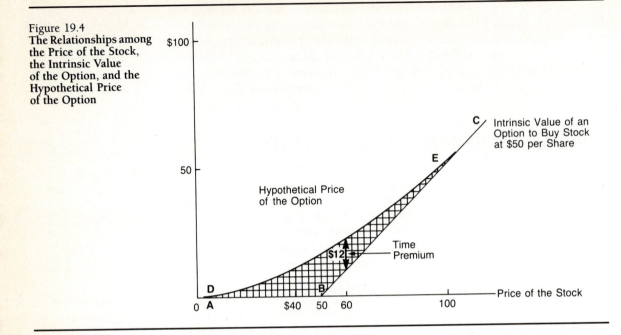

smaller, since the option sells for more than its intrinsic value. The time premium has substantially reduced the potential leverage that the option offers investors.

Investors who are considering purchasing options should ask themselves what price increase they can expect in the option if the price of the underlying stock should rise. For the option to be attractive, its anticipated percentage increase in price must exceed the anticipated percentage increase in the price of the stock. The option must offer the investor leverage to justify the additional risk. Obviously an investor should not purchase the option if the stock's price is expected to appreciate in value more rapidly than the option's price. The previous example illustrates that the time premium paid for an option may substantially decrease the potential leverage. Thus, recognition of the time premium that an option commands over its intrinsic value is one of the most important considerations in the selection of an option for investment.

WARRANTS

The preceding section considered options in general; the remainder of this chapter is devoted to a specific option, the warrant. A **warrant** is an option issued by a company to buy its stock at a specified price within a specified time period. This definition includes the essential elements of all warrants, but there can be subtle differences. For example, the specified exercise price may rise at predetermined intervals (e.g., every five years) or the firm may have the right to extend the expiration date of the warrant.

An example of a warrant is the one issued by McDermott International, which offers the right to purchase one share of McDermott common stock for $25 per share through April 1, 1990. If this option is not exercised by April 1, 1990, it will expire

and become worthless. Thus, unlike stock, which is perpetual (i.e., continues in existence until the company is liquidated or merged into another company), most warrants have a finite life. Very few are perpetual.[4]

Most warrants are an option, or right, to buy one share of common stock. Some *Conversion to per-share* warrants, however, are the option to buy more or less than one share. Such terms may be the result of stock dividends, stock splits, or a merger. For example, a warrant that is the option to buy 0.4 share may have evolved through a merger. The warrant initially represented the option to purchase one share of the company. However, when the company subsequently merged into another firm, the terms of the merger were 0.4 share of the acquiring firm (i.e., the surviving company) for each share of the company being acquired. The warrant then became an option to buy one share that had been converted into 0.4 share of the surviving company.

If a warrant is an option to buy more or less than one share, the strike price and the market price of the warrant can be readily converted to a per-share basis. Such conversion is desirable to facilitate comparisons among warrants. Consider, for example, an option that gives the right to buy 0.4 share at $10 and is currently selling for $4. The warrant's strike price and market price are divided by the number of shares that the warrant is an option to buy. Thus, the per-share strike price is $25 ($10 ÷ 0.4), and the per-share market price is $10 ($4 ÷ 0.4). Stated differently, 2.5 warrants are necessary to buy one share for $25.

Warrants are usually issued by firms in conjunction with other financing. They *Warrants are sweeteners* are attached to other securities, such as debentures or preferred stock, and are a sweetener to induce investors to purchase the securities. For example, in July 1978, Chrysler Corporation issued preferred stock with warrants attached. The warrants were an added inducement to purchase the stock.

When a warrant is exercised, the firm issues new stock and receives the proceeds. *The impact of finite life* For this reason, most warrants usually have a finite life. The expiration date ultimately forces the holder to exercise the option if the strike price is less than the current market price of the stock. However, if the strike price exceeds the stock's price at expiration (i.e., if the warrant has no intrinsic value), the warrant will not be exercised and will expire. After the expiration date, the warrant is worthless. This was the case with the Gulf and Western warrant that expired on January 31, 1978: The warrant was not exercised because it had no intrinsic value as an option. On that day the price of the stock was $11, but the exercise price of the warrant was $19.37. No one would exercise the warrant to buy stock at $19.37 when the stock could be purchased for $11 on the New York Stock Exchange.

Exhibit 19.4 presents selected warrants and their strike price, market price, and intrinsic value, along with the market price of the stock, the expiration date of the warrants, and the time premium paid for each warrant. As may be seen in the exhibit, all of the warrants sell for a time premium (i.e., the market price exceeds the intrinsic value). Three of these warrants have strike prices that exceed the price of the stock. These warrants have no intrinsic value.

As is evident in the last column, there is variation in the time premiums, which *Determinants of the* range from only $0.25 for the Hotel Properties warrant to $4.125 for the General *time premium* Development warrant. What accounts for this variation? Obviously as the warrant ap-

---

[4]One exception is the Alleghany Corporation warrant, which has no time limitation.

Exhibit 19.4
The Terms and Time
Premiums Paid for
Selected Warrants as
of January 1, 1986

Company	Price of the Stock	Per-Share Strike Price	Warrant Expiration Date	Warrant Market Price	Warrant Intrinsic Value	Warrant Time Premium
General Development	$15½	$14	9-20-90	$5⅝	$1.50	$4.125
Hotel Properties	19¼	13	4-30-89	6½	6.25	0.25
Kiddie Inc.	34¾	40	3-20-90	3⅛	0	3.125
McDermott International	18¼	25	4-1-90	2⅞	0	2.875
Western Air Lines	6⅞	9.50	6-15-93	2⅜	0	2.375

Source: Standard & Poor's Stock Guide, January 1986.

1. Time to expiration

proaches expiration, its market price will approach the option's intrinsic value. On the expiration date, the warrant cannot command a price greater than its true value. Thus, as the warrant nears expiration, it will sell for a lower time premium. While the time to the expiration date of the option is an important determinant of the observed differences in time premiums, cash dividends and the volatility of the common stock also affect the amount of the time premium.

2. Dividends

Warrants of companies that pay cash dividends tend to sell for lower time premiums. There may be two explanations for this relationship. Companies that do not distribute earnings but retain them will have more funds available for investments. By retaining and reinvesting their earnings, the companies may grow more rapidly. This growth may be reflected in the price of their stock, and hence the potential gain in the price of the warrant may be greater if the firm retains its earnings and does not pay a dividend. A second explanation is that if the company pays a cash dividend, the holder of the warrant does not receive the cash payment. The warrant will be less attractive relative to the common stock, for the owner of the warrant must forgo the dividend. Therefore, investors will not be as willing to pay as much for the warrant, and it will sell for a lower time premium.

3. The price volatility of the stock

A third factor that may influence the time premium paid for a warrant is the volatility of the price of the common stock. If the stock's price fluctuates substantially, the warrant may be more attractive and hence may command a higher time premium. Since the price of the warrant follows the price of the common stock, fluctuations in the price of the stock will be reflected in the warrant's price. The more volatile the price of the stock, the more opportunity the warrant offers speculators. Thus, the warrants of volatile common stocks may be more attractive (especially to speculators), and hence the time premium commanded by these warrants will tend to be greater than that commanded by warrants of less volatile stocks.

How have investments in warrants fared? The answer depends on the warrant selected and time period. Figure 19.5 illustrates two opposite results involving the stock and warrant of Mattel. As may be seen in the figure, the prices of the stock and the warrant follow each other very closely. When the price of the stock fell during 1979 and 1983, the price of the warrant also declined. An investment in either the stock or the warrant produced a loss.

Figure 19.5 also illustrates the potential for profit offered by an investment in a warrant when the price of the underlying stock rises. From July 1981 to April 1982,

POINTS OF INTEREST
Finding Information on Warrants

Finding information on warrants requires some effort on the part of the investor. Firms with warrants outstanding must detail the option's terms in their annual reports. Since this material is reported in Standard & Poor's *Corporation Records* and in the various Moody's manuals, these two references may be the most efficient sources of general information, such as the warrant's expiration date and strike price. For warrants listed on the NYSE and AMEX, some of the same information is also available in Standard & Poor's *Stock Guide.* For investment advice, the individual may subscribe to *R. H. M. Survey of Warrants, Options and Low-Priced Stocks,* R. H. M. Associates, 417 Northern Boulevard, Great Neck, NY 11021.

Figure 19.5
Prices of the Stock and Warrant of Mattel, July 1978–December 1985

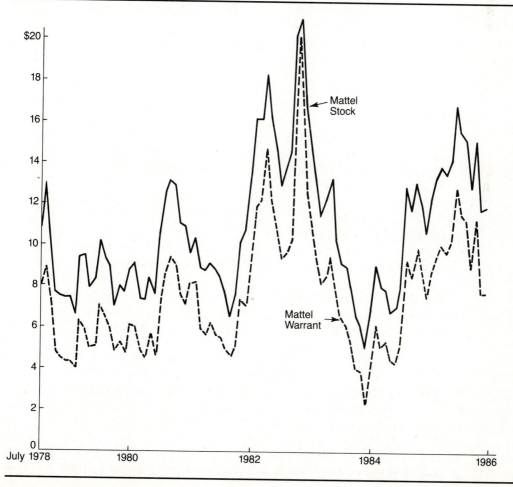

the price of Mattel stock rose from 8½ to 18½ for a 118 percent increase. The warrant, however, rose from 5⅝ to 14⅝ for a 161 percent increase, illustrating the potential leverage offered by an investment in a warrant. It is the possibility of this magnified return that induces those investors with a desire to speculate to purchase warrants.

HEDGING WITH WARRANTS

Hedging can be used to reduce risk

Although warrants are speculative investments, they can be used in **hedge** positions to reduce risk. A hedge position offers the investor a modest gain in return for this reduction in risk. Before executing a hedge position, the investor must determine whether the reduction in risk is worth the loss in potential profit.

Sell the warrant short and buy the stock

Hedging with warrants means that the investor simultaneously takes a long position and a short position.[5] In the usual hedge position, the investor sells the warrant short and purchases the stock that the warrant is an option to buy. The investor may also reverse this traditional hedge by selling the stock short and purchasing the warrant. The conditions under which such a reverse hedge would be profitable are rarer. Thus, the main concern of this section will be the usual hedge—a short position in the warrant and a long position in the stock.

To determine if a hedge will be profitable, the investor needs an indication of the potential gain or loss from the position. The current market price of the warrant, the current market price of the stock, and the per-share exercise price of the warrant are known. The investor also knows when the warrant will expire and that as the warrant approaches expiration, its market price must approach its intrinsic value. No one will pay more than the intrinsic value of the warrant on the option's expiration date. Thus, on the expiration date the warrant must be worth its value as stock, which is the difference between the market price of the stock and the strike price (i.e., the per-share exercise price of the warrant). This information permits the investor to calculate the possible gain from a hedge position at various prices of the stock.

An illustration of the potential profit

The possible gain from a hedge position may be seen in Exhibit 19.5. In this example the current market price of the stock and of the warrant are $30 and $20, respectively. The warrant is an option to buy the common stock at $15 per share expiring after one year. Its minimum value is $15 (i.e., $30 − $15), and thus the warrant is selling at a time premium of $5 (i.e., $20 − $15) over its intrinsic value. This time premium must diminish until it is zero on the expiration date of the warrant, for on that day no one would be willing to pay more than the value of the warrant as an option.

Column 1 in Exhibit 19.5 gives various prices of the stock on the expiration date of the warrant. Column 2 gives the profit or loss on the long position in the stock (i.e., the profit or loss from purchasing the stock at $30 now and holding it until the warrant expires a year from now). Column 3 gives the value of the warrant on the expiration date at various stock prices. Since the price of the warrant approaches its intrinsic value as the expiration date nears, this value can be used to estimate the price of the warrant as it approaches expiration.

---

[5] Hedging with warrants is similar to writing covered call options, which is explained in the next chapter.

Price of the Common Stock	Profit or Loss on the Common Stock Bought Long	Value of the Warrant at Expiration	Profit or Loss on the Warrant Sold Short	Net Profit*
$ 5	$-25	$ 0	$ 20	$-5
10	-20	0	20	0
15	-15	0	20	5
20	-10	5	15	5
25	- 5	10	10	5
30	0	15	5	5
35	5	20	0	5
40	10	25	- 5	5
45	15	30	-10	5
50	20	35	-15	5

Exhibit
Net Pro
Hypoth
Position
Current
$30, the ____ price
of the Warrant is $20,
and the Exercise Price
of the Warrant is $15

*The net profit is determined by adding the profit or loss on the common stock bought long and the profit or loss on the warrant sold short.

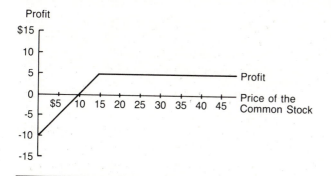

Figure 19.6
Relationship between the Price of the Common Stock and the Profit on a Hypothetical Hedge Position

The profit or loss on a short position in the warrant at different hypothetical prices of the stock is presented in column 4. This is the difference between the purchase and sales prices. The warrant would be sold short today for $20 and would be purchased to cover the short position near its expiration date. The value of the warrant in column 3 indicates the price that the investor will pay when the warrant is purchased in the future to cover the short position.

The net profit or loss on the entire hedge position is presented in column 5. This profit is the sum of the profits (or losses) on the long position in the stock (column 2) and on the short position in the warrant (column 4). The information given in column 5 is plotted in Figure 19.6. As can be seen from either Exhibit 19.5 or Figure 19.6, a hedge position established at a price of $30 for the stock and $20 for the warrant yields a profit for all prices of the stock above $10 per share. The hedge position would be profitable even if the price of the common stock were to *fall* from $30 to $10 a share. Such a hedge position substantially reduces the risk of loss, for the investor earns a profit even if the price of the common stock declines. The investor need not be concerned with the direction of change in the stock's price. A fall in the price of the stock guarantees a profit on the short position in the warrant. A rise in the price of

The net profit or loss

the stock guarantees a profit on the long position in the common stock. As long as the price of the common stock stays within the profitable range (in this case above $10 per share), the investor cannot lose money. However, it should also be noted that the potential profit is modest. In this example, the maximum possible profit before commissions is only $5 for each warrant sold short and each share purchased.

Other Possible Hedges with Warrants [6]

A hedge position need not be limited to a ratio of one share purchased to one warrant sold short. Any ratio of shares to warrants is possible. Altering the mix, however, alters (1) the range of stock prices that yields a profit on the hedge position and (2) the potential return on the hedge position. Exhibit 19.6 illustrates the possible gains from two other hedge positions of different combinations of the warrants and stock that were presented in Exhibit 19.5. The top section gives the potential profit from a hedge of one share purchased to two warrants sold short. The bottom section gives the potential profit from one share purchased to three warrants sold short. The profit potential of these hedges is summarized in Figure 19.7, which reproduces Figure 19.6 and adds the relationship between the price of the stock and the profit from these additional hedge positions.

More warrants sold short places emphasis on a decline in the price of the stock

Both of these hedge positions offer a range of stock prices that yield a net profit on the entire position. For example, a hedge position of three warrants sold short to one share of stock purchased will yield a profit for all prices of the stock below $37.50 per share. As can be seen from Figure 19.7, as the proportion of warrants sold short to shares of common stock purchased long is increased, (1) the range of prices of the stock that yield a profit is narrowed and (2) the potential gain on the hedge position is increased. Thus, the net profit will be larger if the price of the common stock falls, and the loss will be greater if the price of the stock rises. As the investor sells more warrants short, more emphasis is placed on the price of the stock remaining stable or falling. The investor has weighted the hedge position on the short side in the warrant. The potential gain is realized if the price of the common stock, and hence the intrinsic value of the warrant, does not rise. The investor is also increasing the potential risk of loss, for the emphasis is now on a decline in the price of the stock.

The ratio of warrants sold short to shares purchased is a major consideration in establishing a hedge position. This ratio depends on the investor's view of the potential for the stock. The more pessimistic or bearish the investor is with regard to the stock's potential, the larger the proportion of warrants sold short to shares purchased should be. If the investor is relatively bullish or optimistic about the company, the proportion of shares purchased to warrants sold short should be greater. Of course, the investor may decide to dispense with the hedge entirely and buy either the stock or the warrant. The investor then bears the risk of loss if the security's price falls.

An investor who is contemplating a hedge position must also consider when the hedge position should be established. An investor does not want a hedge position for the life of the warrant. The profit from the hedge position arises from the warrant's time premium ceasing to exist when the warrant expires. Thus, the investor estab-

---

[6] This section may be omitted without loss of continuity.

Exhibit 19.6
Profit and Loss on
Hedge Positions With
Various Ratios of
Warrants Sold Short
to Common Shares
Purchased Long

Price of the Stock	Profit on the Stock	Value of the Warrants at Expiration	Profit on the Warrants	Net Profit
One share of stock purchased at $30; two warrants sold short at $20 each (exercise price = $15)				
$ 0	$−30	$ 0	$ 40	$ 10
5	−25	0	40	15
10	−20	0	40	20
15	−15	0	40	25
20	−10	10	30	20
25	− 5	20	20	15
30	0	30	10	10
35	5	40	0	5
40	10	50	−10	0
45	15	60	−20	− 5
One share of stock purchased at $30; three warrants sold short at $20 each (exercise price = $15)				
$ 0	$−30	$ 0	$ 60	$ 30
5	−25	0	60	35
10	−20	0	60	40
15	−15	0	60	45
20	−10	15	45	35
25	− 5	30	30	25
30	0	45	15	15
35	5	60	0	5
40	10	75	−15	− 5
45	15	90	−30	−15

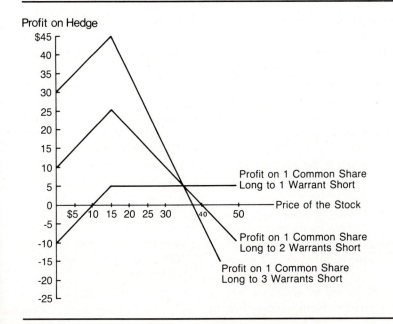

Profit on Hedge

Profit on 1 Common Share Long to 1 Warrant Short

Price of the Stock

Profit on 1 Common Share Long to 2 Warrants Short

Profit on 1 Common Share Long to 3 Warrants Short

Figure 19.7
Profit Potential of
Various Hedge Positions

lishes the hedge position as the warrant approaches expiration and only if the warrant sells for a time premium over its intrinsic value. If the position is established many years before the warrant expires, the long wait to realize the gain will substantially reduce the annual percentage return. The yield on a hedge position may be respectable, but it is not large. If this yield is spread over many years, the rate of return will be insufficient to justify such a use of the money. Other investments offer a superior return without an increase in risk.

The hedge position is established as the warrant approaches expiration

Conversely, if an investor chooses to wait until a few months before the expiration date of the warrant, he or she may not be able to establish a hedge position. The Board of Governors of the SEC, which regulates trading on the exchanges, will ban short sales in the warrant as it approaches expiration. The purpose of this ban is to reduce undue speculation during the last few months of the warrant's existence. Thus, the establishment of a hedge position will require that the investor act before the ban on short sales. Such action may be necessary one year before the expiration date of the warrant.

A need to reevaluate the position

Even after a hedge position has been established and time has elapsed, the investor should reevaluate and perhaps alter the position. For example, if the price of the stock has fallen along with the price of the warrant, the investor may decide to increase the ratio of warrants sold short to shares purchased. The decline in the price of the stock and the lapse of time may indicate that the warrant's potential for a price increase has been reduced. The investor may take advantage of this additional information and alter the proportion of warrants sold short. Hedge positions, like all investments, need to be reevaluated periodically so that changes that are consistent with the investor's goals can be made.

SUMMARY

Individuals who expect security prices to rise take long positions in stocks in anticipation of the price increases. Individuals who expect falling prices take short positions in stock. To execute a short sale, the investor sells borrowed stock and anticipates repaying the loan after purchasing the stock in the future at the lower price. If, however, the price of the stock rises, the investor sustains a loss when the stock is purchased and the loan repaid.

Long and short positions in securities may also be achieved through the use of options: warrants, puts, and calls. Options are rights to buy or sell stock at specified prices within specified time periods. The main reason for purchasing an option is the potential leverage it offers: the returns on an option may be greater than the comparable return in the underlying security.

Options may have an intrinsic value, which for an option to buy stock is the difference between the stock's price and the option's exercise (strike) price. The intrinsic value sets the minimum price for which an option can sell. If an option were to sell for less than its intrinsic value, a risk-free opportunity for profit would exist. Investors could simultaneously buy the option, exercise it, and sell the stock, thereby assuring the profit.

Generally options sell for more than their intrinsic value; they command a "time premium." This time premium works against the holder of an option because it re-

duces the option's potential leverage. On the expiration day, the time premium disappears; the option must then sell for its intrinsic value since no individual would be willing to pay a time premium for the option. Unless the stock's price has risen sufficiently to increase the option's intrinsic value, the disappearance of the time premium inflicts a loss on the investor who purchased the option.

A warrant is a type of option issued by a firm that permits the investor to buy stock at a specified price within a specified time period. When a warrant is exercised, the firm issues new stock and receives the proceeds of the sale. Warrants are purchased by individuals to obtain potential leverage. If the value of the stock rises (or falls), the price of the warrant will tend to increase (or decline) more rapidly. However, the price of the warrant will tend to decline more rapidly than the price of the stock. This increased price volatility means that the warrant is more risky than the stock. Warrants may also be used in conjunction with stock to construct hedge positions that reduce the investor's risk exposure but also limit the potential return.

Terms to Remember

Long position	Premium
Short sale	Arbitrage
Covering (a short position)	Leverage
Option	Time premium
Intrinsic value	Warrant
Expiration date	Hedge
Exercise price (strike price)	

Questions

1. When should an investor sell short? How can an investor sell something he or she does not own? What is the source of profit in a short sale?

2. What is an option? How is an option's minimum (or intrinsic) value determined?

3. How does arbitrage assure that the price of an option will not be less than the option's intrinsic value?

4. What advantages do options offer investors? Why are options considered to be speculative investments?

5. What does it mean to say that an option sells for a premium? What effect does this premium have on the potential leverage offered by an option?

6. If you saw that the selling price of a share of stock was $20, the exercise price of an option to buy the share was $10, and the price of the option was $5, what would you do?

Problems

1. An investor sells a stock short for $36 a share. A year later, the investor covers the position at $30 a share. If the margin requirement is 60 percent, what is the percentage earned on the investment? Redo the calculations, assuming the price of the stock is $42 when the investor closes the position.

2. A warrant with an expiration date of two years is an option to buy stock at $24. The current market price of the stock is $35, and the market price of the warrant is $15.

    a. What is the warrant's intrinsic value?

    b. What is the time premium paid for the warrant?

    c. If after two years the stock is selling for $50, what will be the price of the warrant? What is the percentage increase in the value of the stock and in the value of the warrant?

    d. Why does the warrant's time premium disappear?

    e. If after two years the stock is selling for $22, what will be the price of the warrant? What is the percentage increase in the value of the stock and in the value of the warrant?

3. A warrant has the following terms: It gives the option to buy stock at $10 per share, expires after nine months, and is currently selling for $8. The stock that it is an option to buy is selling for $15. Construct a hedge position showing the potential profit for (1) one warrant sold short to one share purchased and (2) three warrants sold short to one share purchased. Compare the risks and potential profits from these two hedges.

4. A warrant is the option to buy stock at $20 per share and expires in one year. Currently the price of the stock is $25, and the price of the warrant is $9. Determine the range of stock prices that will produce a profit for the following hedge positions:

    a. One warrant sold short for every share purchased.

    b. Two warrants sold short for every share purchased.

    c. One warrant purchased for every share sold short.

Suggested Readings

There are several excellent books on options and their use in portfolios. These include:

Clasing, Henry K., Jr. *The Dow Jones Guide to Put and Call Options.* Revised ed. Homewood, Ill.: Dow Jones-Irwin, 1978.

Gastineau, Gary L. *The Stock Options Manual.* 2d ed. New York: McGraw-Hill, 1979.

McMillan, Lawrence G. *Options as a Strategic Investment.* 2d ed. New York: New York Institute of Finance, 1986.

For a more technical discussion of options, see:

Technican, Michael. *Convertible Debentures and Related Securities.* Cambridge, Mass.: Harvard University Press, 1975.

For a brief discussion of when to sell short, see:

Weaver, Mark. *The Technique of Selling Short.* Palisades Park, N.J.: Investors' Press Inc., 1963.

Additional readings on options are given at the conclusion of the next chapter.

Rights Offerings

Appendix

As was explained in Chapter 14, some stockholders have preemptive rights that enable them to maintain their proportionate ownership in the corporation. If the firm wants to raise additional equity capital by issuing more shares of stock, it must first offer these shares to its current stockholders. The stockholders are not required to buy the new shares, but they do have the privilege of purchasing or refusing them. If the stockholders do purchase the new shares to which they are entitled, they maintain their proportional ownership in the firm.

Preemptive rights

Firms that have granted preemptive rights present a *rights offering*[7] when they issue new stock. This offering gives the stockholder the option to purchase the additional shares at a predetermined price. Evidence of this option is called a *right,* and one right is issued for every existing share of stock. This right specifies the exercise price of the right, the expiration date, and the number of shares that the right is an option to buy.

The sale of securities to existing stockholders

For example, suppose a company has 1,000,000 shares outstanding and wants to raise $12,500,000. The price of its stock is currently $60, and management believes that it can sell additional shares to its current stockholders at $50. The firm then will have to issue 250,000 new shares at $50 each to raise the $12,500,000. These 250,000 new shares will increase the number of shares outstanding by 25 percent. The firm offers its current stockholders the right to buy additional shares. Each existing share receives a right to buy one quarter of a new share at $50 per share. Thus, it takes four rights to buy an additional share. If the stockholder has 100 shares, he or she may purchase 25 additional shares for $1,250 (25 × $50). If the stockholder does buy the new shares, the individual's proportionate ownership in the firm is unaltered. The stockholder then owns 125 shares of the 1,250,000 shares outstanding, whereas before the rights offering that stockholder owned 100 of the 1,000,000 shares outstanding.

An illustration of a rights offering

The issuing of rights, like the declaration and distribution of dividends, occurs over time. The following series of dates illustrate the time frame of a rights offering. On January 1 stockholders have no knowledge of a rights offering. On January 10 the firm announces that a rights offering will be made and that stockholders owning shares at the close of the business day on January 31 will receive the rights to purchase the new shares. From January 10 through January 31 the stock continues to trade on the open market, and anyone who purchases the stock during that period and holds the stock until February will receive the rights to purchase the new shares. During this time the price of the stock includes the value of the right. The stock trades with the *rights on* (i.e., the stock still confers the rights).

A rights offering occurs over time

On February 1 purchasers of the stock no longer receive the rights, and the stock trades exclusive of the rights, or *ex rights*. Purchasing the stock after January 31 means the purchaser may not participate in the rights offering. However, the price paid for

Ex rights

---

[7]The number of rights offerings has diminished so that in 1985 only ten firms listed on the NYSE and six listed on the AMEX issued new stock through a rights offering. (See *Moody's Dividend Record, 1986:* 346–348.) This appendix facilitates the coverage of a rights offering but may be omitted without loss of continuity.

the stock will be lower because the existing shares have been diluted. As with the distribution of cash dividends, stock dividends, or stock splits, the price of the stock must decline on February 1 to account for the dilution of the existing shares.

The stockholders who own the shares on January 31 receive their rights from the company. These stockholders may exercise the rights or sell them in the open market. The rights now trade independently of the common stock. The only constraint on these stockholders is that they act (i.e., exercise or sell the rights) by the expiration date of the right, which is usually about four weeks after the rights are issued (in this case March 1). The market price of the right may rise or fall. If speculators anticipate that the price of the stock will rise, they will seek to buy the right and may even bid up the price so that it sells for a premium over its value as stock. If the stock's price does subsequently rise, these speculators will realize a profit because the value of the rights must also increase.

The value of a right   The value of a right, like the value of any option, is related to the market price of the stock, the exercise (or subscription) price of the right, and the number of rights necessary to purchase a new share. When the firm offers the rights to stockholders it must fix (1) the number of rights necessary to purchase a new share and (2) the exercise price of the rights. The market price of the stock, however, may continue to fluctuate, which will cause the value of the right to fluctuate.

How is the value of a right determined? The answer depends on whether the individual wants the value of the right when it is still affixed to the stock (i.e., when the *Rights-on value*   stock is trading "rights on") or after the right has been issued and is trading independently of the stock. There is a simple formula for determining the value of the right as an option in either case. If the stockholder wants the rights-on value of the option (i.e., the value of the rights before they trade independently of the stock), the simple formula is

(19A.1)
$$V = \frac{P_0 - P_e}{n + 1},$$

where V indicates the value of the right; P_0, the current market price of the stock including the rights; P_e, the exercise price of the right (which is also referred to as the subscription price); and n, the number of rights necessary to purchase one share. If the investor applies this formula to the example presented previously, the value of the right is

$$V = \frac{\$60 - \$50}{4 + 1}$$

$$= \frac{\$10}{5}$$

$$= \$2.$$

The effect of dilution   This formula helps to illustrate the dilution that occurs when additional shares are issued. The "$n + 1$" in the denominator adjusts for the dilution that will occur when the stock trades ex rights. The "$+ 1$" represents the new share that will come into existence for every n number of shares the firm currently has. In this case the firm issues one new share for every four shares currently outstanding.

After the stock goes ex rights, its price declines by the value of the right. Thus, in *Rights-off value* this case the market price of stock declines by $2, from $60 to $58. The rights are now traded independently of the stock (i.e., traded "rights off"). The formula for the value of a right after the stock trades ex rights is

$$V = \frac{P_1 - P_e}{n}.$$

(19A.2)

The differences between the two formulas are the price of the stock (P_1), which now excludes the value of the rights, and the "+ 1." Since the price of the stock has already been adjusted for the dilution, the "+ 1" is no longer necessary. Now the value of the right is

$$V = \frac{\$58 - \$50}{4}$$

$$= \$2.$$

Notice that the market price of the stock is lower as a result of the dilution, but the value of the right is unaltered. The terms of the option have not been changed, but the increase in the total number of shares that will occur when the new shares are issued has caused a dilution of the old shares, and this dilution caused the price of the stock to decline by the value of the right.

These rights are an example of an option and as such may attract speculative in- *These rights may* terest. Should the price of the stock rise, the value of the right will tend to rise more *attract speculators* rapidly because the rights offer potential leverage. If this occurs, speculators may be rewarded for purchasing the right from those stockholders who did not wish to exercise the option. For example, consider the impact of a four-point increase in the price of the preceding stock from $58 to $62. What effect does that have on the value of the right? The answer is

$$V = \frac{\$62 - \$50}{4}$$

$$= \$3.$$

The small increase in the price of the stock causes the value of the right to rise by 50 percent ([$3 − $2] ÷ $2).

Such potential leverage may attract speculators who anticipate an increase in the price of the stock. Of course, if the price of the stock declines, then the value of the right will decline. Leverage works both ways, and speculators who purchase rights for the potential increase in value must also bear the risk of loss that will occur if the price of the stock falls.

20 Options: Puts and Calls

LEARNING OBJECTIVES

After completing this chapter you should be able to

1. Identify the risks and rewards associated with buying a call option.
2. Explain why an investor may write a call option.
3. Distinguish a call from a warrant.
4. Differentiate the potential profit and loss from writing a covered call option versus a naked call option.
5. Explain the relationship between the price of a stock and a put option to sell the stock.
6. Compare buying a put with selling short.
7. Perceive the advantages offered by stock-index options.

In the spring of 1973, a new type of option was introduced that revolutionized the options market. This was a call option traded on an organized exchange. While puts and calls had existed for years, there was no secondary market in which to trade them. In 1973, the Chicago Board Options Exchange (CBOE) was created solely for the purpose of trading in put and call options. The initial success of the CBOE led to the trading of options on other exchanges and to the creation of new types of options.

This chapter is devoted to put and call options traded on the CBOE and other exchanges. First the chapter describes call options, explains how they come into existence, and considers the risk exposure of those who buy and those who create these options. Emphasis is also given to the potential returns for those who buy and those who create call options. A discussion of put options follows. The chapter ends with a description of a new type of option—the stock index option—which is not based on a specific company's securities but on an index of the market as a whole.

CALLS

Although warrants were the popular speculative option during the 1960s, they were displaced in popularity in the 1970s by the call. A **call option** is an option to buy a specified number of shares of stock (usually 100) at a specified price (which is frequently referred to as the "strike" price) within a specified time period.[1] The owner of a call has the right *to call forth* the shares of stock and to purchase the shares at the specified price. (There is also the opposite type of option, which is called a put. A put is an option to sell a specified number of shares [usually 100] at a specified price within a specified time period. A put, then, is an option *to place or put* with someone else shares owned by the holder of the option. Puts are discussed later in this chapter.)

Calls are very similar to warrants (their definitions are essentially identical), but they have several distinguishing features. Warrants are issued by companies. Calls are issued by individuals and are sold to other individuals. This ability of the individual investor to write calls is a very important difference between calls and warrants, for the investor may be either a buyer *or* an issuer of call options. By enabling individuals to write options, calls offer investors opportunities for profit that are not available with warrants.

Calls differ from warrants

Calls are issued by individuals

A second distinction between warrants and calls is the duration of the option. When warrants are issued their expiration date is set. It is generally several years into the future (e.g., five years), and a few warrants are perpetual. Calls are of relatively short duration: three, six, or nine months.

Calls are of short duration

The third distinguishing feature of calls becomes evident when they are exercised. When a warrant is exercised, the firm issues new stock and receives the proceeds. The seller of a call, however, cannot issue new stock when the call is exercised but must either purchase the stock on the open market or surrender the stock from personal holdings. When the stock is supplied for the exercised call option, the option writer and not the firm receives the proceeds.

No new stock is issued with calls

The Chicago Board Options Exchange

Prior to the formation of the **Chicago Board Options Exchange (CBOE)**, calls were purchased only in the over-the-counter market. If an investor wanted to buy a call option, it was obtained from an options dealer. Each option sold was different, because the exercise price and the expiration date were negotiated with each sale. Once the option was purchased, the investor who desired to sell it had difficulty, because there was no secondary market in options.

OTC trading

With the advent of the CBOE, an organized market in call options on selected securities was created. For the first time investors could buy and sell call options through an organized exchange (i.e., an organized secondary market). An investor purchasing a call on the CBOE knew that there would be a market for that option in the future. This ability to sell options that had been previously purchased gave a degree of marketability to call options that had not existed earlier.

CBOE provided a secondary market

---

[1] Actually, call options are not new. They have existed as early as the 1630s, when options on tulip bulbs played a role in the speculative tulip bulb craze that swept Holland. See Burton G. Malkiel, *A Random Walk Down Wall Street* (New York: W. W. Norton, 1973), 28–45, for a fascinating portrait of such speculative periods.

Exhibit 20.1
Listing of Selected Options Traded on the CBOE, June 11, 1986

LISTED OPTIONS QUOTATIONS

Wednesday, June 11, 1986

Closing prices of all options. Sales unit usually is 100 shares.
Stock close is New York or American exchange final price.

CHICAGO BOARD

Option & NY Close	Strike Price	Calls–Last			Puts–Last		
		Jun	Jul	Oct	Jun	Jul	Oct
Amrtch	120	r	4 5/8	7 7/8	r	r	r
124 1/8	125	1	2	4 5/8	r	r	r
124 1/8	130	r	3/4	r	r	r	r
Atl R	50	r	4 5/8	r	1/16	5/16	r
53 5/8	55	3/8	1 1/4	2 3/4	r	2	r
53 5/8	60	r	5/16	1	r	r	r
BankAm	10	s	6 1/8	s	s	r	s
16 1/4	12 1/2	s	4 1/4	r	s	r	1/8
16 1/4	15	1	1 1/4	2	1/16	5/16	3/4
16 1/4	17 1/2	1/16	3/8	1	1 5/16	1 3/4	2
16 1/4	20	r	1/8	7/16	r	r	r
BellAtl	62 1/2	s	4	r	s	r	r
66 1/4	65	r	r	3 1/2	r	1	r
Citicp	50	r	9 3/8	r	r	r	r
58 3/4	55	r	4 1/2	5 5/8	1/8	7/16	1 1/2
58 3/4	60	1/2	1 1/2	2 7/8	1 1/2	2	3 1/4
58 3/4	65	r	5/16	1 1/4	r	r	r
Tex In	110	s	r	r	s	5/8	1 3/4
129 1/4	115	s	r	r	s	11/16	r
129 1/4	120	9 3/4	9 3/4	r	1/8	1	4 1/2
129 1/4	125	5 1/2	7 3/4	11 3/4	7/8	2 5/8	6
129 1/4	130	2	5 1/2	10	2 1/2	5 1/2	8 1/2
129 1/4	135	15/16	3 1/4	7 1/2	6 3/4	9	r
129 1/4	140	1/4	2 1/8	5 3/4	11	12 1/2	r
129 1/4	145	1/16	3/4	4	18	17	17 3/4
129 1/4	150	r	1/2	3	r	r	r
129 1/4	155	r	5/16	r	r	r	r
Winnbg	12 1/2	r	r	3	r	3/16	1/2
14 1/2	15	3/16	7/8	1 1/2	1/2	1	1 3/4
14 1/2	17 1/2	r	1/4	7/8	3	3 1/4	3 1/4
14 1/2	20	1/16	1/16	1/2	r	r	5 3/4
Xerox	55	2 1/8	3 1/2	5 1/8	r	3/4	r
57 1/4	60	5/16	1 1/16	2 1/2	3 1/4	3 1/2	4 1/2
57 1/4	65	r	1/4	1 1/8	r	r	8 3/8
57 1/4	70	r	1/16	9/16	r	r	r
57 1/4	75	s	r	5/16	s	r	r
Zayre	70	9	r	r	r	r	r
79 3/8	80	r	r	5 3/8	r	r	r
79 3/8	85	r	r	3 1/2	6	r	r

Source: The Wall Street Journal, June 12, 1986. Reprinted by permission of *The Wall Street Journal,* © Dow Jones & Company, Inc., 1986. All Rights Reserved.

Transactions are reported in the financial press

There are several features of the CBOE that are conducive to the development of secondary markets for the calls. First, transactions are continuously reported, and daily summaries of transactions appear in leading newspapers. Exhibit 20.1 presents a clipping of selected calls and puts traded on the CBOE on June 11, 1986, as reported in *The Wall Street Journal*. As may be seen from the exhibit, there are several options traded on each of the securities. The company and its closing stock price are given on the left. Then the "strike" price (exercise price) is given. For Xerox the strike prices of the options are 55, 60, 65, 70, and 75. The next three columns are devoted to call options and the last three columns are devoted to put options. These six columns report the closing prices of the options. If no options were traded during the day, an *r* is listed. If no options were offered, an *s* is listed. The months that each of the options expire is given at the top of the columns. Thus from these listings an investor learns that the closing price of Xerox was 57 1/4 and that the July call and put options with an exercise price of $60 closed at 1 1/16 and 3 1/2, respectively.

The clearing house

Second, a clearinghouse was established for the CBOE that maintains a daily record of options issued in the accounts of its members. The members are required to

keep a continuous record of their respective customers' positions in options. No actual options certificates are issued; only the bookkeeping is maintained by the clearinghouse. A centralized clearinghouse greatly facilitates trading in the options, for it serves as the intermediary through which purchases and sales of the calls are recorded.

Third, the CBOE is self-regulated. It has the power to impose requirements that must be met before calls may be traded on the exchange, and options on only a selected number of securities have been accepted for trading on the exchange. Investors must be approved before they can purchase and sell through the CBOE, and there is a limit to the number of options on a single stock that an investor may own. Brokers on the floor of the exchange must have a minimum amount of capital. Although such self-regulation does not guarantee the absence of illegal transactions, it is conducive to the development of organized security markets.

The CBOE is self-regulated

The initial success of the CBOE exceeded expectations. Soon after its formation, other exchanges started to list call options. Currently, call options are traded not only on the CBOE but also on the New York, American, Pacific, and Philadelphia exchanges. While all companies do not meet the criteria for having options listed, several hundred firms are eligible to have the call options traded on their stock listed.[2]

Other secondary markets

The Pricing of Calls

The price that the investor pays for a call traded on the CBOE or any other exchange is determined by the demand for and the supply of the option. The price of a call is referred to as the *premium*. To some extent this term is a misnomer, for the price may include some intrinsic value as an option.

The minimum price of a call, like the minimum price of any option, is set by the option's intrinsic value. The price of a call cannot fall (for any significant length of time) below the difference between the price of the common stock and the per-share exercise price of the call. If the price of the call were to fall below its true value as an option, arbitrageurs would purchase calls, exercise them, and simultaneously sell the stock. These actions would bid up the price of the call and put downward pressure on the price of the stock until the option's price equaled or exceeded its intrinsic value.

The minimum price of a call

The actual price investors pay for a call traded on the CBOE or other exchanges depends on their willingness to bid for the options and the willingness of other investors to supply the options. Through supply and demand, a single price is determined for each option.[3] Several of the variables that influence the demand for options include (1) the potential leverage the option offers, (2) the duration of the option, and (3) the potential for an increase in the price of the common stock in the immediate future. The long-term potential growth of the company is of little significance in the decision to purchase a CBOE call, for the growth may occur too far in the future. Since the call has a short life span, the emphasis is primarily on short-term increases in the market price of the stock, not on the company's long-term growth potential.

The price of a call

---

[2] The criteria for having call options listed on an exchange include the following: The firm must have at least 8,000,000 shares outstanding, 10,000 shareholders, and an annual turnover of 2,000,000 shares for the last two years.

[3] As with stocks and bonds, option dealers quote bid and ask prices at which they are willing to buy and sell for their own accounts.

Exhibit 20.2
Potential Leverage
Offered by CBOE Call to
Buy XYZ Stock at $60

Price of XYZ Stock	minus	Strike Price of the Call	equals	Intrinsic Value of the Call	Hypothetical Price of the Call	Percentage Change in the Price of the Stock	Percentage Change in the Price of the Call
$50		$60		$ 0	$ ¼	. . .	. . .
55		60		0	1	10.0%	300%
60		60		0	3	9.1	200
65		60		5	6	8.3	100
70		60		10	10½	7.7	75

The Advantage of Purchasing Calls: Leverage

Warrants and calls are similar in many ways. Both represent the right to buy stock at a specified price within a specified time period. The reason for purchasing either warrants or calls is the potential leverage that they offer the investor. Calls, however, tend to offer greater leverage than warrants, since they sell for a smaller time premium above their intrinsic value. Because of the short duration of the call option, the time premium paid is less than that paid for a warrant, which is of longer duration.

The potential leverage

The considerable potential leverage offered by a call to buy XYZ stock at $60 is shown in Exhibit 20.2. This exhibit presents the price of the XYZ stock (column 1); the strike price of the call (column 2); the intrinsic value of the call, that is, the difference between the price of the common stock and the per-share strike price of the call (column 3); and some hypothetical market prices of the call (column 4). The exhibit also includes the percentage change in the price of the common stock for successive increments of $5 (column 5) and the percentage change in the hypothetical price of the call (column 6). As may be seen in the exhibit, if the price of XYZ's common stock rose from $60 to $65 (an 8.3 percent increase), the hypothetical price of this call would rise from $3 to $6 (a 100 percent increase). If equal amounts were invested in the common stock and the call, the call would have the potential to yield much more profit.

A high degree of risk

Although the potential leverage that calls offer is the primary reason for purchasing them, the investor does accept substantial risk.[4] On its expiration date the call can be worth only its intrinsic value. The call will be worthless if the price of XYZ stock is less than the strike price (i.e., below $60). This call will prove to be a profitable investment only if the price of the common stock rises. Thus, for a call to be profitable, the price of the common stock must increase during the call's relatively short life span.

The Advantage of Issuing Calls: Income

The preceding section considered the reason for purchasing calls; this section will consider the advantages of issuing them. While buying calls gives the investor an op-

---

[4]Calls may be combined with other securities such as U.S. Treasury bills so that risk is less than holding only the stock. See problem 9 at the end of this chapter.

portunity to profit from the leverage that call options offer, issuing calls produces revenue from their sale. The selling of options may also offer the investor an opportunity to earn a respectable return when the option is used in conjunction with stock already owned. In this case issuing options is similar to hedging with warrants. Both offer modest returns and a reduction in risk.

There are two ways to write (i.e., sell) options. The first is the more conservative method, which is called **covered option writing**. The investor buys the stock and then sells an option to buy that stock. If the option is exercised, the investor supplies the stock that was previously purchased (i.e., "covers" the option with the stock). The second method entails selling the call without owning the stock. This is referred to as **naked option writing**, for the investor is exposed to considerable risk. If the price of the stock rises and the call is exercised, the option writer must buy the stock at the higher market price in order to supply it to the buyer. With naked option writing the potential for loss is considerably greater than with covered option writing.

Covered options

Naked options

The reason for writing options is the income to be gained from their sale. The potential profit from writing a covered option may be seen in Exhibit 20.3. In this example the investor purchases the common stock of XYZ at the current market price of $50 per share and simultaneously sells for $5 a call to buy the shares at the strike price of $50. Thus, the investor sells the call for $500 (i.e., $5 × 100 shares). The possible future prices for XYZ stock at the expiration of the call are given in column 1. Column 2 presents the net profit to the investor from the purchase of the stock. Column 3 gives the value of the call at expiration, and column 4 presents the profit to the investor from the sale of the call. As may be seen in column 4, the sale of the call is profitable to the investor as long as the price of the common stock remains below $55 per share. The last column gives the net profit on the entire position. As long as the price of the common stock stays above $45 per share, the entire position will yield a profit before commission fees. The maximum amount of this profit, however, is limited to $500. Thus, by selling the call the investor forgoes the possibility of large gains. For example, if the price of the stock were to rise to $70 per share, the holder of the call would exercise it and purchase the 100 shares from the seller at $50 per share. The seller would then make only the $500 that was received from the sale of the call.

The potential profit

Price of XYZ Stock at Expiration of the Call	Net Profit on the Stock	Value of the Call at Expiration	Net Profit on the Sale of the Call	Net Profit on the Position
$42	$-800	$ 0	$500	$-300
44	-600	0	500	-100
46	-400	0	500	100
48	-200	0	500	300
50	0	0	500	500
52	200	200	300	500
54	400	400	100	500
56	600	600	-100	500
58	800	800	-300	500
60	1000	1000	-500	500

Exhibit 20.3
Profit on a Hedge Position Consisting of the Purchase of 100 Shares of XYZ Stock and the Sale of One Call to Buy 100 Shares of XYZ at $50 a Share

**Figure 20.1
Profit or Loss on Selling
a Covered Call**

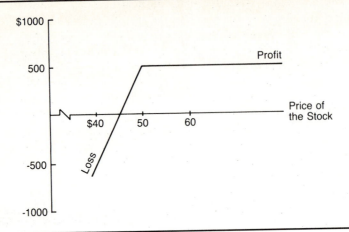

The potential loss

    If the price of the stock were to fall below $45, the entire position would result in a loss to the seller. For example, if the price of the common stock fell to $40, the investor would lose $1,000 on the purchase of the stock. However, $500 has been received from the sale of the call. Thus, the net loss is only $500. The investor still owns the stock and may now write another call on that stock. As long as the investor owns the stock, the same 100 shares may be used over and over to cover the writing of options. Thus, even if the price of the stock does fall, the investor may continue to use it to write more options. The more options that can be written, the more profitable the shares become. For individuals who write options, the best possible situation would be for the stock's price to remain stable. In that case the investors would receive the income from writing the options and never suffer a capital loss from a decline in the price of the stock on which the option is being written.

    The relationship between the price of the stock and the profit or loss on writing a covered call is illustrated in Figure 20.1, which plots the first and fifth columns of Exhibit 20.3. As may be seen from the figure, the sale of the covered option produces a profit (before commissions) for all prices of the stock above $45. However, the maximum profit (before commissions) is only $500.

*The potential profit
from naked calls*

    Option writers do not have to own the common stock on which they write calls. Although such naked or uncovered option writing exposes the investor to a large amount of risk, the returns may be considerable. If the writer of the XYZ option given in Exhibit 20.3 had not owned the stock and had sold the option for $500, the position would have been profitable as long as the price of the common stock remained below $55 per share at the expiration of the call. The potential loss, however, is theoretically infinite, for the naked option loses $100 for every $1 increase in the price of the stock above the call's exercise price. For example, if the price of the stock were to rise to $70 per share, the call would be worth $2,000. The owner of the call would exercise it and purchase the 100 shares for $5,000. The writer of the call would then have to purchase the shares on the open market for $7,000. Since the writer received only $500 when the call was sold and $5,000 when the call was exercised, the loss

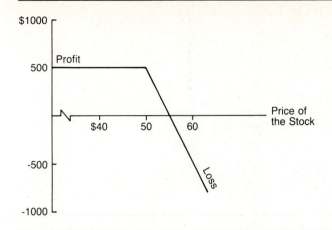

Figure 20.2
**Profit or Loss on Selling
a Naked Call**

would be $1,500. Therefore, uncovered option writing exposes the writer to considerable risk if the price of the stock rises.[5]

The relationship between the price of the stock and the profit or loss on writing a naked call option is illustrated in Figure 20.2. In this case the option writer earns a profit (before commissions) as long as the price of the stock does not exceed $55 at the expiration of the call. Notice that the investor earns the entire $500 if the stock's price falls below $50. However, the potential for loss is considerable if the price of the stock increases.

Investors should write naked call options only if they anticipate a decline (or at least no increase in) the price of the stock. These investors may write covered call options if they believe the price of the stock may rise but are not certain of the price increase. And they may purchase the stock (or the option) and not write calls if they believe there is substantial potential for a price increase.

A Comparison of Selling Calls and Hedging with Warrants

Selling covered options and hedging with warrants is very similar. Selling a covered call option is like buying stock and selling the warrant short. In both cases the potential profit from an increase in the price is limited. However, if the price of the stock declines, the sale prices of the call and the warrant protect the investor from loss.

Selling covered call options is like hedging with warrants

This similarity may be seen by comparing Figures 19.6 and 20.1. In both cases the profit is limited, and in both cases the investor gains even if the price of the stock declines. Thus, there exists potential profit if the price of the stock rises or falls, but the gain is small. This is exactly the reason for hedging—to reduce the risk of loss from price movements. Hedging with warrants or selling covered options does just

[5]This risk may be reduced by a stop loss order to purchase the stock at $55. If the price of the stock rises, the stop loss order is executed so that the option writer buys the stock.

POINTS OF INTEREST
Big Profits; Big Losses

Profits and losses can be sustained very rapidly in option trading. Combine options with corporate takeovers and the possible price movements are magnified. Consider the attempted takeover of Cities Service by Gulf Oil. On Wednesday, June 16, 1982, the following options on Cities Service were traded when the stock sold for $37¾.

June Option Exercise Price	Option's Closing Price (6/16/82)
$20	$17⅛
25	12
30	7⅜
35	2
40	⁷⁄₁₆
45	⅛
50	¹⁄₁₆
55	¹⁄₁₆

On Thursday, June 17, 1982, there was no trading in Cities Service stock pending an announcement. The announcement turned out to be that Gulf Oil would buy Cities Service for $63 a share. When trading resumed on Friday, June 18, 1982, Cities Service stock rose to $53⅛. The options' prices rose (and the percentage increases from the previous closing prices) as follows:

June Option Exercise Price	Option's Closing Price (6/18/82)	Percentage Increase in Price
$20	$33¼	94.2%
25	28½	137.5
30	22⅞	210.2
35	18	800.0
40	13⅛	2,900.0
45	9½	7,500.0
50	3½	5,500.0
55	¹⁄₁₆	—

The irony of this incident is that the options were to expire on June 18, 1982. Thus the individual who bought the 40s at ⁷⁄₁₆ ($43.75) with only *two days to expiration* would normally have lost this money. But as a result of the attempted takeover, this speculator earned a return of 2,900 percent in two days!

While few investors earned such a return, the *New York Times* (June 19, 1982, 33) reported that several traders who had sold these options without owning the stock (i.e., had sold the options naked) had sustained heavy losses. If a trader had sold 100 contracts at 40 for ⁷⁄₁₆ ($43.75) per contract on Wednesday, those options were worth $4,375 (100 contracts times $43.75 per contract = $4,375). On Friday those calls were worth $131,250 (100 × $1,312.50 = $131,250). The loss to the naked call writer would be $126,875 ($4,375 − $131,250). Thus naked call writers of Cities Service stock suffered large losses as the unexpected happened and gave value to options that normally would have been worthless at expiration.

that. For accepting a smaller return, the investor reduces the risk of loss from fluctuations in the price of the stock. However, since there are many calls traded (in Exhibit 20.1 there were 11 calls traded on Xerox's stock), there are many possible hedging strategies. Problems 5 through 9 at the end of this chapter cover several of these strategies.

Strike Price	minus	Price of the Stock	equals	Intrinsic Value of the Put
$30		$15		$15
30		20		10
30		25		5
30		30		0
30		35		0
30		40		0

Exhibit 20.4
The Relationship between the Price of a Stock and the Intrinsic Value of a Put

PUTS

At first, only call options were traded on the CBOE and other exchanges, but as of May 31, 1977, put options were admitted for trading. A **put option** is an option to *sell* stock (usually 100 shares) at a specified price within a specified time period. As with calls, the time period is short—three, six, or nine months. Like all options, a put has an intrinsic value, which is the difference between the strike price of the put and the price of the stock.[6] The relationship between the price of a stock and the intrinsic value of a put is illustrated in Exhibit 20.4. This put is an option to sell 100 shares at $30 per share. The first column gives the strike price of the put, the second column presents the hypothetical prices of the stock, and the third column gives the intrinsic value of the put (i.e., the strike price minus the price of the stock).

Puts—the option to sell

If the price of the stock is less than the strike price, the put has a positive intrinsic value and is said to be "in the money." If the price of the stock is greater than the strike price, the put has no intrinsic value and is said to be "out of the money." If the price of the stock equals the strike price, the put is "at the money." As with call options, the market price of a put is called "the premium."

As may be seen in Exhibit 20.4, when the price of the stock declines the intrinsic value of the put rises. Since the owner of the put may sell the stock at the price specified in the option agreement, the value of the option rises as the price of the stock falls. Thus, if the price of the stock is $15 and the exercise price of the put is $30, the put's intrinsic value as an option must be $1,500 (for 100 shares). The investor can purchase the 100 shares of stock for $1,500 on the stock market and sell them for $3,000 to the person who issued the put. The put, then, must be worth the $1,500 difference between the purchase and sale prices.

The value of a put rises as the price of the stock declines

Why should an investor purchase a put? The reason is the same for puts as it is for other speculative options: The put offers potential leverage to the investor. Such leverage may be seen in the example presented in Exhibit 20.4. When the price of the stock declines from $25 to $20 (a 20 percent decrease), the intrinsic value of the put rises from $5 to $10 (a 100 percent increase). In this example a 20 percent decline in the price of the stock produces a larger percentage increase in the intrinsic value of the put. It is this potential leverage that makes put options attractive to investors.

The potential leverage

[6] Note that the intrinsic value of a put is the reverse of the intrinsic value of an option to buy (e.g., a call). Compare Exhibits 19.1 and 20.4.

Strike Price of the Put	Price of the Stock	Intrinsic Value of the Put	Hypothetical Price of the Put
$30	$15	$15	$15¼
30	20	10	12
30	25	5	8
30	30	0	6
30	35	0	3½
30	40	0	1
30	50	0	—

As with other options, investors are willing to pay a price that is greater than the put's intrinsic value: The put commands a time premium above its intrinsic value as an option. As with warrants and calls, the amount of this time premium depends on such factors as the volatility of the stock's price, the duration of the put, and the potential for *decline* in the price of the stock.

The relationships among the price of the stock, the strike price of the put, and the hypothetical prices for the put are illustrated in Exhibit 20.5. The first three columns are identical to those in Exhibit 20.4. The first column gives the strike price of the put, the second column gives the price of the stock, and the third column gives the put's intrinsic value as an option. The fourth column presents hypothetical prices for the put. As may be seen in Exhibit 20.5, the hypothetical price of the put exceeds the intrinsic value, for it commands a time premium over its intrinsic value as an option.

Figure 20.3 illustrates the relationships among the price of the common stock, the intrinsic value of the put, and the hypothetical market value of the put that were presented in Exhibit 20.5. This figure shows the inverse relationship between the price of the stock and the put's intrinsic value. As the price of the stock declines, the intrinsic value of the put increases (e.g., from $5 to $10 when the stock's price declines from $25 to $20). The figure also readily shows the time premium paid for the option, which is the difference between the price of the put and the option's intrinsic value. If the price of the put is $8 and the intrinsic value is $5, the time premium is $3.

As may be seen in both Exhibit 20.5 and Figure 20.3, the hypothetical market price of the put converges with the put's intrinsic value as the price of the stock declines. If the price of the stock is sufficiently high (e.g., $50 in Exhibit 20.5), the put will not have any market value because the price of the stock must decline substantially for the put to have any intrinsic value. At the other extreme, when the price of the stock is low (e.g., $15), the price of the put is equal to the put's intrinsic value as an option. There are two reasons for this convergence. First, if the price of the stock rises, the investor may lose the funds invested in the put. As the price of the stock declines below the strike price of the put, the potential risk to the investor if the price of the stock should start to rise becomes greater. Thus, put buyers are less willing to pay a time premium above the put's intrinsic value. Second, as the intrinsic value of a put rises when the price of the stock declines, the investor must spend more to buy the put; therefore, the potential return on the investment is less. As the potential return declines, the willingness to pay a time premium diminishes.

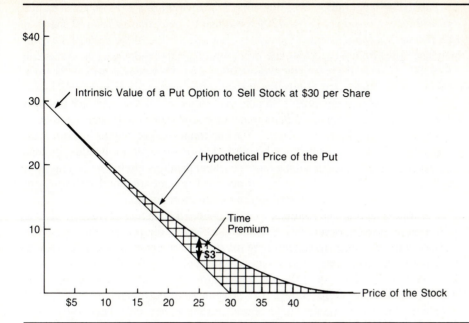

Figure 20.3
The Relationships among the Price of the Stock, the Intrinsic Value of a Put Option, and the Hypothetical Price of the Option

Puts Compared with Short Sales

Investors purchase put options when they believe that the price of the stock is going to decline. Purchasing puts, however, is not the only method investors can use to profit from falling security prices. As was explained in Chapter 19, an investor who believes that the price of a stock is going to fall may profit from such a decline by selling short. Buying a put is another form of a short position. However, the put option offers the investor two major advantages over selling short. First, the amount of potential loss is less; second, puts may offer a greater return on the investor's capital because of their leverage.

In order to execute a short position, the investor must sell the stock, deliver the borrowed stock, and later purchase the stock to cover the position. The profit or loss is the difference between the price at which the borrowed stock was sold and the price at which the stock is purchased to repay the loan. If the price of the stock declines, the investor reaps a profit, but if the price of the stock rises, the investor suffers a loss. This loss may be substantial if the stock's price rises significantly. For example, if 100 shares are sold short at $30 and later purchased at $50, the investor loses $2,000 plus commissions on the investment. The higher the price of the stock rises, the greater is the loss that the short position inflicts on the investor.[7]

Puts are an alternative to selling short

---

[7] Once again the investor may limit this potential loss by establishing a stop loss order to purchase the stock should the price rise to some predetermined level.

requires

Purchasing a put option does not subject the investor to a large potential capital loss. If the investor purchases for $300 a put that is the option to sell 100 shares at $30, the maximum amount that the investor can lose is $300. If the price of the common stock rises from $30 to $50, the maximum that can be lost with the put is still only $300. However, the loss on the short position is $2,000 when the price of the stock rises from $30 to $50. Puts reduce the absolute amount that the investor may lose.

Besides subjecting the investor to potentially large losses, the short sale ties up a substantial amount of capital. When the investor sells short, the broker will require that he or she put up funds as collateral. The minimum amount that the investor must remit is the margin requirement set by the Federal Reserve, and individual brokers may require that the investor supply more collateral than this minimum. Selling short thus requires the investor to tie up capital, and the larger the amount that the investor must remit, the smaller the potential return on the short position.

Less capital is required to invest in a put. While the amount of margin varies at different time periods, it certainly will not be as low as the price of the put. Thus, purchasing the put instead of establishing the short position ties up a smaller amount of the investor's funds. The potential return is greater if the price of the stock declines sufficiently to cover the cost of the put, because the amount invested is smaller. Puts thus offer the investor more leverage than does the short position.

Short sales, however, offer one important advantage over puts. Puts expire, but a short position can be maintained indefinitely. If an investor anticipates a price decline, it must occur during the put's short life for the investment to be profitable. With a short sale, the investor does not have this time constraint and may maintain the position indefinitely.

The short position may be maintained indefinitely

Returns from Investments in Puts and Calls

Returns from investments in puts and calls are sensitive to the period selected and the volatility of the underlying stock. This is illustrated in Figures 20.4 and 20.5 for puts and calls on United States Steel (now USX) and Teledyne. Figure 20.4 clearly illustrates the impact of the decline in United States Steel's stock price. The stock continuously declined during the time period, causing the price of the call to fall while the price of the put rose. The call, which initially traded for $2½, was worthless at expiration, but during the same time period the price of the put rose from less than $1 to $5.

Figure 20.5 illustrates the impact of a volatile stock on the prices of puts and calls. In January 1986, Teledyne's stock was $340. During the next three and a half months it fell to below $310, then rose to $360, and at the options' expiration was trading for $350. As may be seen in the figure, the price of the put rose rapidly at first (i.e., its price doubled in January); however, the price fell almost as rapidly in February, and the option was worthless at expiration. The price of the call initially fell rapidly from $21½ to $8 in two weeks. Then its price rose dramatically in late February in response to the large increase in the stock's price. However, in late March the price of the call fell even more drastically, from over $26 to about $5. The price did recover somewhat, so at expiration the call sold for its intrinsic value of $10.

Perhaps what is most striking about Figure 20.5 is the fact that the ending price of Teledyne's stock was only $10 above the starting price. This small percentage increase

Figure 20.4
Prices of U.S. Steel (USX) Stock and April Put and Call at $25

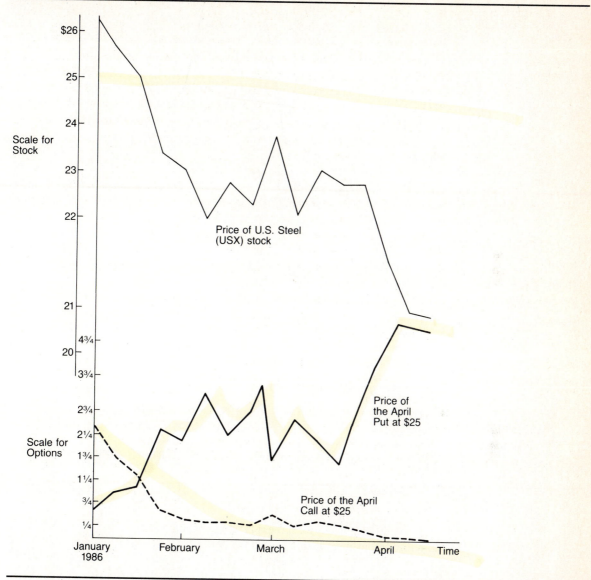

of less than 3 percent from January to mid-April caused the value of the put to fall from $14½ to $0, for a 100 percent decline, and caused the value of the call to fall from $21½ to $10, for a 53.5 percent decline. Even though the price of the stock did rise, the increase was insufficient to offset the time premium the call initially commanded, so the price of the call fell.

Figure 20.5
**Prices of Teledyne Stock
and April Put and Call
at $340**

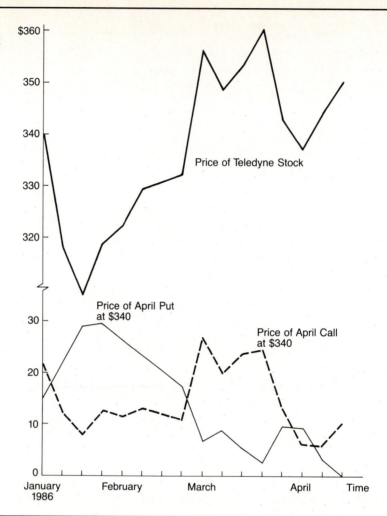

It should be obvious from these illustrations that there can be large variations in the returns from investments in options. Since there are many options for a given stock (Exhibit 20.1 gave the prices for eleven call options and five put options on Xerox), the investor has a mind-boggling array of possible strategies.[8] No particular strategy can be expected to yield consistently superior results. If such a strategy existed, many investors would seek to use it, which would reduce the strategy's potential for profit. As with investments in other securities (such as stocks and bonds), profits from investments in options should not tend to exceed the return consistent with the risk borne by the investor.

[8] See the references at the end of this chapter for readings that explore many of the strategies for using options.

The Option	Where Traded
S&P 100 Index	Chicago Board Options Exchange
S&P 500 Index	Chicago Board Options Exchange
Major Market Index	American Stock Exchange
AMEX Market Value Index	American Stock Exchange
Computer Technology Index	American Stock Exchange
Oil Index	American Stock Exchange
Airline Index	American Stock Exchange
Value Line Index	Philadelphia Exchange
National O-T-C Index	Philadelphia Exchange
Technology Index	Pacific Exchange
NYSE Options Index	New York Stock Exchange

Exhibit 20.6
Index Options and
Where They Are Traded

STOCK INDEX OPTIONS

While put and call options were initially created for individual stocks, **stock index options** have developed. (As is explained in Chapter 23, there are also stock index futures.) These stock index options are similar to options based on individual stocks, but the index option is based on an aggregate measure of the market, such as the Standard & Poor's 500 stock index. In addition to puts and calls based on the aggregate market, there are options based on subsets of the market, such as computer technology stocks or oil stocks. A listing of these index options and where they are traded is given in Exhibit 20.6. Stock index options have proved to be particularly popular and account for a substantial proportion of the daily transactions in options.

Options based on an index

These options are popular because they permit the investor to take a position in the market or in a group of companies without having to select specific securities. For example, suppose an investor anticipates that the stock market will rise. What does this individual do? He or she cannot buy every stock but must select individual stocks.[9] Remember from the discussion of risk in Chapter 8 that there are two sources of risk associated with the individual stock: systematic risk and unsystematic risk. Systematic risk refers to the tendency of a stock's price to move with the market. Unsystematic risk refers to price movements generated by the security that are independent of the market (e.g., a take-over announcement, dividend cut, or large increase in earnings).

No need to select individual securities

If the investor buys a particular stock on the expectation of a rising market, it does not necessarily follow that the individual stock's price will increase when the market rises. Investors construct diversified portfolios to reduce the unsystematic risk associated with the individual asset. As the portfolio becomes more diversified, unsystematic risk is reduced further and the return on the portfolio mirrors the return on the market. (Whether or not the return on the portfolio exceeds the market de-

[9]As is explained in Chapter 22, the investor could buy an index mutual fund. Such funds construct portfolios that mirror aggregate measures of the stock market.

pends on the portfolio's beta. If the individual selects stocks with high betas, the diversified portfolio should tend to outperform the market as a whole in rising markets but underperform the market in declining markets.)

Immediate diversification

Index options offer the investor an alternative to creating diversified portfolios as a means to earn the return associated with movements in the market. For example, if the investor anticipates that the market will rise in the near future, he or she may purchase a call option based on an index of the market as a whole (such as the Standard & Poor's 500 stock index). If the market does rise, the value of the call option also increases. The investor has avoided the unsystematic risk associated with the in-

Avoid unsystematic risk

dividual stock. In addition, the investor has avoided the large commission costs necessary to construct a diversified portfolio.

If the investor anticipates the market will decline, he or she will purchase a stock index put. If the investor is correct and the market as a whole does fall, the value of the stock index put rises. Of course, if the market does not decline but rises instead, the investor loses the amount invested in the put option. Here, however, is another

Potential loss is limited to the cost of the option

major advantage offered by stock index options—*the maximum that the investor can lose is the cost of the option.* If the investor had sold stocks short instead of purchasing stock index put options, that individual may have been exposed to a large loss if stocks' prices rose.

Use in hedges

Stock index options also give investors a means to hedge their existing portfolios. This is particularly important for portfolio managers with large holdings or individuals who want to improve the tax management of these holdings. Consider a substantial stock portfolio that has appreciated in value. If the investor anticipates declining stock prices and sells the shares, this is a taxable transaction. Instead of selling the stocks, the investor may sell stock index calls or purchase stock index puts. Then if the market declines, profits in these positions will help offset the losses on the individual stocks.

If the investor were to sell stock index call options, the value of these options would decline as the market decreased. The gain on the sale would then offset the loss in the individual stock's value. If the investor were to purchase stock index put options, the value of the options would increase if the market declined. The loss on the portfolio as a whole would be offset by the gain on the put option. (The amount offset would depend on how many put options the investor purchased.) As these two cases illustrate, stock index options offer the investor a means to hedge existing portfolios against a decline in the market without having to liquidate the positions and thus incur the capital gains tax liability. By buying or selling the appropriate stock index option, the investor achieved protection of capital without selling the appreciated securities.[10]

No delivery with index options

There is one major difference between stock index options and put and call options on specific stocks. With a call option to buy shares of IBM, the owner may exercise the option and buy the stock. With a put option to sell shares of IBM, the owner may exercise the option by delivering shares of IBM stock. Such purchases or deliveries are not possible with a stock index option. The owner of the call cannot exercise

---

[10] For additional material on hedging, see the appendices to this chapter.

it and receive the index. Instead stock index options are settled in cash. For example, suppose the owner of a call based on the Standard & Poor's 500 index does not sell the option prior to expiration (and thereby closes the position). At expiration the intrinsic value of the option is determined and that amount is paid by the seller of the option to the owner. Of course, if the option has no intrinsic value at expiration, it is worthless and expires. The seller of the option then has no further obligation to the option's owner. In that case the premium paid for the option (i.e., its price) becomes profit for the seller.

In addition to stock index options, there are options on debt instruments (e.g., treasury bonds) and foreign currencies. Each of these options permits the investor (1) to take long or short positions on the underlying assets without actually acquiring them or (2) to establish hedge positions that reduce the risk of loss from price fluctuations. For example, if an investor anticipates declining interest rates, he or she will buy a call option to purchase bonds. If interest rates do fall, the value of bonds will rise, increasing the value of the call option. The call option's price will rise more rapidly than the bond's price because the call offers leverage. However, if the investor were to purchase the call option and interest rates rose, the investor's maximum possible loss would be limited to the cost of the option.

Options on debt instruments

SUMMARY

Calls, like warrants, are options to buy stock at a specified price by a specified date. Puts are options to sell stock at a specified price by a specified date. Puts and calls offer investors who are willing to bear a substantial amount of risk the potential for a large return.

While warrants are issued by firms, puts and calls are issued by individuals. When a call option is exercised, the individual who wrote the call (i.e., the individual who created the call and sold it) must supply the stock and in turn receives the proceeds of the sale. If the individual already owns the stock, that investor has written a "covered" call. However, if the investor does not own the stock, he or she is exposed to a large potential loss should the price of the stock rise dramatically. Such investors are referred to as "naked" option writers.

When a put option is exercised, the individual who wrote the put must buy the stock and supply the funds for the purchase. The owners of put options profit when the price of the stock declines; thus, they have a short position in the stock. The put option offers more potential leverage than a short sale but may result in the investor losing the entire amount invested in the option.

Since the creation of the Chicago Board Options Exchange, put and call options have been traded on organized exchanges. These secondary markets have increased the popularity of put and call options because investors know there are markets in which they can increase or liquidate their positions in the options. The success of option trading has led to the creation of more types of puts and calls, such as stock index options. These are puts and calls based on an aggregate measure of the stock market instead of a specific security. Stock index options offer investors a means to manage their exposure to systematic and unsystematic risk.

Terms to Remember

Call option
Chicago Board Options Exchange
  (CBOE)
Covered option writing

Naked option writing
Put option
Stock index options

Questions

1. What is the source of the leverage in a call option?

2. Why are secondary markets crucial to the popularity of options?

3. What is the difference between covered and naked call writing? Why do some individuals buy calls while others write calls?

4. If an individual buys a call option on a stock and the price of the stock declines, what should happen to the price of the option? What is the maximum amount the investor can lose?

5. In what ways are calls similar to warrants? How do they differ?

6. Explain why each of the following may be a valid strategy if the investor expects security prices to fall:
    a. Sell a naked call.
    b. Buy a put.
    c. Sell a stock index call.

7. Why does the intrinsic value of a call rise with the price of the stock, whereas the intrinsic value of a put declines as the stock's price rises?

8. What should happen to an option's time premium as the option approaches expiration? What happens to an "out of the money" option at expiration?

9. If an individual sells a call option, how may that investor close the position?

Problems

1. What are the intrinsic values and time premiums paid for the following options?

Option	Price of the Option	Price of the Stock
Calls: XYZ, Inc., 30	$7	$34
XYZ, Inc., 35	2½	34
Puts: XYZ, Inc., 30	1¼	34
XYZ, Inc., 35	4¼	34

If the stock sells for $31 at the expiration date of the preceding options, what are the profits or losses for the writers and the buyers of these options?

2. A particular call is the option to buy stock at $25. It expires in six months and currently sells for $4 when the price of the stock sells for $26.
    a. What is the intrinsic value of the call? What is the time premium paid for the call?
    b. What will the value of this call be after six months if the price of the stock is $20? $25? $30? $40?

c. If the price of the stock rises to $40 at the expiration date of the call, what is the percentage increase in the value of the call? Does this example illustrate favorable leverage?

d. If an individual buys the stock and sells this call, what will the profit on the position be after six months if the price of the stock is $20? $26? $40?

e. If an individual sells this call naked, what will the profit or loss be on the position after six months if the price of the stock is $20? $26? $40?

3. A particular put is the option to sell stock at $40. It expires after three months and currently sells for $2 when the price of the stock is $42.

a. If an investor buys this put, what will the profit be after three months if the price of the stock is $45? $40? $35?

b. What will the profit from selling this put be after three months if the price of the stock is $45? $40? $35?

4. The price of a stock is $51. You can buy a six-month call at $50 for $5 or a six-month put at $50 for $2.

a. What is the intrinsic value of the call?

b. What is the intrinsic value of the put?

c. What is the time premium paid for the call?

d. What is the time premium paid for the put?

e. If the price of the stock falls, what happens to the value of the put?

f. What is the maximum you could lose by selling the call covered?

g. What is the maximum possible profit if you sell the stock short?

After six months, the price of the stock is $58.

h. What is the value of the call?

i. What is the profit or loss from buying the put?

j. If you had sold the stock short six months earlier, what would your profit or loss be?

k. If you sold the call covered, what would be your profit or loss?

The existence of many options on the same stock gives the investor numerous possible strategies. For example, the investor may simultaneously buy a put and a call. This position is called a straddle. Problems 5–8 illustrate several possible strategies using puts and calls.

5. Given:

Price of the stock	$50
Price of a six-month call at $50	$5
Price of a six-month put at $50	$3½

The investor buys one put and one call.

a. What is the profit (loss) on the position if by the expiration date of the options the price of the stock rises to $60?

b. What is the profit (loss) if the price of the stock declines over six months to $44?

c. What is the profit (loss) if the price of the stock rises to $60 and subsequently falls to $45 within six months? (To answer, assume that the options sell for their intrinsic values.)

6. Given:

Price of the stock	$26
Price of a six-month call at $25	$4
Price of a six-month call at $30	$2

The investor buys the call with the $25 exercise price and sells the call with the $30 exercise price. What is the profit on the position if at expiration the price of the stock is $20, $25, $26, or $40? (Compare these results with your answers to problem 2d.)

7. Given:

Price of the stock	$15
Price of a nine-month call at $10	$8

a. If the investor buys the stock and sells one call, what is the maximum potential profit and what is the range of stock prices that yields a profit on the position?
b. If the investor buys the stock and sells three calls (one covered and two naked), what is the maximum potential profit and what is the range of stock prices that yields a profit on the position?
(Compare your answers to a. and b. with your answers to problem 3 in Chapter 19.)

8. Given:

Price of the stock	$20
Price of a three-month call at $20	$2
Price of a six-month call at $20	$3½

The investor buys the three-month call and sells the six-month call.
a. What is the profit (loss) if after three months the stock is $20 and after three additional months the price of the stock rises to $25?
b. What is the profit (loss) if after three months the price of the stock is $25 and after three additional months the stock declines to $20?
c. What price behavior would an investor have to expect to establish such a position?

9. Options may be used with other securities to devise various investment strategies. For example, an investor has the following alternative investments and their prices:

Common stock	$50
Six-month call on the stock at $50	$5
Six-month $10,000 U.S. Treasury bill	$9,500

The investor has $10,000 and thus could buy (a) 200 shares of the stock or (b) one call plus the treasury bill. After six months how much profit or loss will the investor have earned on each alternative (excluding commissions) if the price of the stock is $60, $55, $50, $45, or $40? Which alternative is less risky?

10. A stock that is currently selling for $47 has the following six-month options outstanding:

	Strike Price	Market Price
Call option	$45	$6
Call option	50	1
Put option	45	2

a. Which option(s) are "in the money?"

b. What is the time premium paid for each option?

c. What is the profit (loss) at expiration given the following prices of the stock—$30, $35, $40, $45, $50, $55, and $60—if the investor buys the call with the $45 strike price and the put?

d. What is the profit (loss) at expiration given the following prices of the stock—$30, $35, $40, $45, $50, $55, and $60—if the investor buys two of the calls with the $50 strike price and the put?

e. What is the range of stock prices that will generate a profit if the investor sells the stock short and sells the call with the $50 strike price?

Suggested Readings

The risk and returns offered by put and call options are explored in

Hettenhouse, G. W., and D. J. Puglisi. "Investor Experience with Options." *Financial Analyst Journal* (July–August 1975): 53–72.

Reback, Robert. "Risk and Return in Option Trading." *Financial Analyst Journal* (July–August 1975): 42–52.

Strategies using various put and call options are discussed in

Angell, George. *Sure-Thing Options Trading.* Garden City, N.Y.: Doubleday, 1983.

Bookstaber, Richard M. *Option Pricing and Strategies in Investing.* Reading, Mass.: Addison-Wesley, 1981.

McMillan, Lawrence G. *Options as a Strategic Investment.* 2d ed. New York: New York Institute of Finance, 1986.

Nix, William E., and Susan W. Nix. *The Dow Jones-Irwin Guide to Stock Index Futures and Options.* Homewood, Ill.: Dow Jones-Irwin, 1984.

Hedging strategies using warrants are covered in

Thorp, Edward O., and Sheen T. Kassouf. *Beat the Market.* New York: Random House, 1967.

Valuation of options is difficult. The following articles are technical but address the problem of valuation.

Black, Fischer, and Myron Scholes. "The Pricing of Options and Corporate Liabilities." *Journal of Political Economy* (May–June 1973): 637–654.

Black, Fischer. "Fact and Fantasy in the Use of Options." *Financial Analyst Journal* (July–August 1975): 36–41.

Dimson, Elroy. "Instant Option Valuation." *Financial Analyst Journal* (May–June 1977): 62–69.

Dimson, Elroy. "Option Valuation Nomograms." *Financial Analyst Journal* (November–December 1977): 71–75.

For technical explanations of option valuation, see:

Brenner, Menachem. *Option Pricing*. Lexington, Mass.: Lexington Books, 1983.

Jarrow, Robert A., and Andrew Rudd. *Option Pricing*. Homewood, Ill.: Dow Jones-Irwin, 1983.

Appendix   Protective Puts

Purchasing put options may be viewed as a speculative investment strategy. The buyer profits as the value of the underlying stock declines, which causes the value of the put to rise. Since the long-term trend in stock prices is to increase as the economy expands, purchasing a put seems to be betting against the natural trend in a stock's price.

While purchases of puts by themselves may be speculative, they may, when used in conjunction with purchases of the stock, reduce the individual's risk exposure, thus protecting existing profits while permitting the investor to maintain a long position in a stock so the profit may continue to grow. Such a strategy is referred to as a "protective put."

Suppose an individual bought a stock for $25 two years ago, but the price has now risen to $40. The investor has a $15 profit that, if realized, becomes a taxable capital gain. The investor does not want to realize the profit (and thereby generate the tax) but also does not want to lose the gain. One possible way to protect the profit would be to place a limit order to sell the stock if its price fell to $37½. Such a limit order would protect $12.50 of the profit. However, if the price falls sufficiently to cause the limit order to be executed, the taxable gain will be realized and the investor will no longer own the stock. By using the limit order, the investor has protected the profit but may have lost the opportunity for additional profit. This problem will not occur if the investor adopts a protective put strategy.

Instead of placing the limit order, the investor purchases a put. Suppose there is a six-month put with a strike price of $40 that is currently selling for $2½.[11] The put has no intrinsic value, so the investor pays a $2½ time premium for the option. Exhibit 20.7 presents the benefit of buying the put in combination with the stock. The first two columns give the price of the stock and the profit (loss) on the position in the stock based on the original $25 purchase price. The third and fourth columns give the intrinsic value of the put at its expiration and the profit (loss) on the position in the put. The last column gives the net profit (loss), which is the sum of the profits (losses) on the positions in the stock and the put.

As may be seen in the last column of the exhibit, the worst case scenario in this illustration is that the original profit (which occurred when the price of the stock initially rose from $25 to $40) is reduced by $2½ to $12½. This reduction is the result of (and equal to) the time premium paid for the put. No matter how low the price of

---

[11] This strategy requires the existence of a put option on the stock. Obviously it cannot be executed for stocks for which there are no put options.

Price of the Stock	Profit on the Stock	Intrinsic Value of the Put	Profit on the Put	Total Profit
$20	($ 5)	$20	$17½	$12½
25	0	15	12⅕	12½
30	5	10	7½	12½
35	10	5	2½	12½
40	15	0	(2½)	12½
45	20	0	(2½)	17½
50	25	0	(2½)	22½
55	30	0	(2½)	27½
60	35	0	(2½)	32½

Exhibit 20.7
Profit and Loss Resulting from a Long Position in a Stock and a Long Position in a Put to Sell the Stock

the stock falls, the investor is assured of a $12½ profit. This gain is the same profit that can be assured by the use of the limit order to sell the stock at $37½.

If the price of the stock were to rise, the potential profit is not limited. All that would occur by purchasing the put is a reduction in the potential profit equal to the cost of the put, which in this illustration is $2½. This reduction may be seen by comparing columns 2 and 5. What the investor has achieved by purchasing the put is the assurance of a profit of at least $12½ and the reduction of the potential gain by only $2½.

This protective put strategy may be viewed as an alternative to placing the limit order to sell the stock at $37½.[12] The advantage is that the individual is protected from the price of the stock falling, the stock being sold, and the price subsequently rising. Day-to-day fluctuations in the price of the stock have no impact on the protective put strategy. The disadvantage is that the put ultimately expires, while the limit order may be maintained indefinitely. Once the put expires, the investor no longer has the protection and will have to buy another put. Of course, every time the investor purchases an additional put, the cumulative cost of the protection is increased. There are no costs associated with placing the limit order to sell the stock. Thus there is no clear answer as to which strategy is better. The protective put avoids the risk of being sold out by a temporary price decline but requires the investor to pay the cost of the option, which reduces some of the potential profit from the position in the stock.

The Hedge Ratio   Appendix

While the price of a call option moves directly with the price of the underlying stock (and the price of a put option moves inversely with the price of the underlying stock), the absolute price movements are not equal. This was illustrated in Exhibit 20.2 in

---

[12] Investors with short positions in stock may achieve similar protection by purchasing call options.

which the price of the call option rose from $3.00 to $6.00 when the price of the stock rose from $60 to $65. The percentage increase in the call option exceeded the percentage increase in the price of the stock, but the absolute price increase was less. Since absolute price changes are not equal, the investor cannot use one call option to exactly offset price changes in the stock. Thus a hedge position of one call option cannot exactly offset the price movement in 100 shares of the stock.

To exactly offset a stock's price change, the investor must know the "hedge ratio" or the "delta" of the option. This is the ratio of the change in the price of the call option to the change in the price of the stock (i.e., the slope of the line *DE* relating the price of an option to the price of the stock in Figure 19.4). If the ratio is 0.5, this means that the price of the option will rise $0.50 for every $1.00 increase in the price of the stock. Thus, if the investor owns 100 shares of the stock and has written two calls, a $1.00 increase in the stock should generate a $1.00 loss in the options (i.e., a $0.50 increase in the value of each option, which produces a total loss of $1.00 for the individual who has written two options). The gain in one position (e.g., the long position in the stock) is exactly offset by the loss in the other position (e.g., the short position in the option). The entire position is completely hedged.

If an investor or portfolio manager wants to exactly offset price changes by using options, the hedge ratio is crucial information. The reciprocal of the hedge ratio, which is

$$\text{Number of call options for a complete hedge} = \frac{1}{\text{Hedge ratio}},$$

defines the number of call options that should be sold for each 100 shares purchased.[13] Thus, in the previous example, the number of call options sold to construct a complete hedge is

$$\frac{1}{0.5} = 2.$$

The hedger must sell two call options for every 100 shares purchased to have a perfectly hedged position.[14]

For individuals who wish to hedge their entire stock portfolio, the hedge ratio determines the number of stock index call options to sell. For example, suppose an investor is primarily concerned with collecting dividend income from the stock portfolio and wants to reduce the risk of loss from a movement in security prices. The hedge ratio helps achieve that goal by determining the appropriate number of stock index call options to sell to offset decreases (and increases) in the market as a whole.

While the hedge ratio does give the number of call options that must be sold for every 100 shares purchased, the numerical value of the ratio frequently changes. This may be seen by observing the curved line *DE* representing the price of an option in Figure 19.4. The slope of the line changes from being relatively flat for low prices of

---

[13] For short positions in the stock, the ratio indicates the number of calls the individual must buy for every 100 shares sold short.

[14] The hedge ratio may also be viewed as the number of shares of stock that must be purchased for each option sold. In the above example, the hedge ratio of 0.5 implies that 50 shares purchased for every call option sold is a completely hedged position. Either view of the hedge ratio is essentially the same. One view determines the number of shares to buy per call option, while the other determines the number of call options to sell per 100 shares of stock.

the stock to being parallel with the line representing the option's intrinsic value. Since the slope of the line increases with a rise in the stock's price, the numerical value of the hedge ratio also increases. This implies that fewer call options must be sold to construct a perfectly hedged portfolio. To maintain a perfectly hedged position, the individual must frequently adjust the positions in the call options or in the underlying securities. Thus, the use of options to completely erase the risk associated with security price changes may be impractical (if not impossible) to achieve.

Suggested Readings

The hedge ratio is a technical topic that the individual may pursue in the following references:

Bookstaber, Richard M. *Options Pricing and Strategies in Investing*. Reading, Mass.: Addison-Wesley, 1981, 49–53, 144–150, and 163–169.

McMillan, Lawrence G. *Options as a Strategic Investment*. New York: New York Institute of Finance, 1980, 91–98.

Radcliffe, Robert C. *Investment Concepts, Analysis, and Strategy*. Glenview, Ill.: Scott, Foresman, 1982, 360–366.

21

Convertible Bonds and Convertible Preferred Stock

LEARNING OBJECTIVES

After completing this chapter you should be able to

1. Describe the features common to all convertible bonds.
2. Determine the "floor" or minimum price of a convertible bond.
3. List the factors that affect the price of a convertible bond.
4. Identify the two premiums paid for a convertible bond.
5. Explain why the two premiums are inversely related.
6. Compare convertible bonds with convertible preferred stock.
7. Explain the advantage offered by a put bond.

The previous chapters discussed options that offer the investor potential leverage. This chapter considers bonds and preferred stocks with a built-in option. The owner may convert these securities into the issuing firm's common stock. While warrants, calls, and puts may be speculative securities, convertible bonds and convertible preferred stocks are more conservative investments. Generally these convertible securities offer more income (higher interest or higher dividends) than may be earned through an investment in the firm's common stock. In addition, convertible securities have some potential for capital gains if the price of the underlying stock were to rise.

This chapter discusses investing in convertible bonds and convertible preferred stocks. Initially the features and terms of convertible bonds are described, followed by a discussion of their pricing. This includes the premiums paid for convertible bonds, and the relationship between their price and the price of the stock into which they may be converted. The element of safety of convertible bonds is emphasized. The third section is devoted to convertible preferred stock. These shares are similar to convertible bonds but lack the safety implied by the debt element of convertible bonds. Next follows the brief histories of two convertible bonds that illustrate the potential profits and risk associated with investing in them. The chapter ends with a description of a new type of bond with a built-in put option.

478

FEATURES OF CONVERTIBLE BONDS

Convertible bonds are debentures (i.e., unsecured debt instruments) that may be converted at the holder's option into the stock of the issuing company. As was seen in Chapter 9, firms issue a variety of debt instruments to tap funds in the capital markets. Convertible bonds are one means to do so: The conversion feature is granted to bondholders to induce them to buy the debt. Since the firm has granted the holder the right to convert the bonds, these bonds are usually subordinate to the firm's other debt. They also tend to offer a lower interest rate (i.e., coupon rate) than is available on nonconvertible debt. Thus, the conversion feature means that the firm can issue lower quality debt at a lower interest cost. Investors are willing to accept this reduced quality and interest income because the market value of the bond will appreciate *if* the price of the stock rises. These investors are thus trading quality and interest for possible capital gains.

Convertible into stock

Usually subordinate

Convertible bonds have been a popular means for firms to raise funds in the capital markets. A sample of firms and their convertible bonds is presented in Exhibit 21.1. As may be seen in the exhibit, the bonds are not issued just by lower quality firms with poor credit ratings. Some of the country's most prestigious firms, including Xerox and IBM, have issued convertible bonds.

An important source of funds

Since convertible bonds are long-term debt instruments, they have features that are common to all bonds. They are usually issued in $1,000 denominations, pay interest semiannually, and have a fixed maturity date. However, if the bonds are converted into stock, the maturity date is irrelevant because the bonds are retired when they are converted. Convertible bonds frequently have a sinking fund requirement, which, like the maturity date, is meaningless once the bonds are converted.

Debt features

A noteworthy feature of convertible bonds is that they may be called by the issuing firm. The firm uses the call to force the holders to convert the bonds. Once the bond is called, the owner must convert, or any appreciation in price that has resulted from an increase in the stock's value will be lost. Such forced conversion is extremely important to the issuing firm, because it no longer has to repay the debt.

The call feature

Convertible bonds are attractive to some investors because they offer the safety features of debt. The firm must meet the terms of the indenture, and the bonds must be retired if they are not converted. The flow of interest income usually exceeds the dividend yield that may be earned on the firm's stock. In addition, since the bonds

Firm	Coupon Rate of Interest	Year of Maturity	Standard & Poor's Rating
Ashland Oil	4¾	1993	BBB
Black and Decker	4	1992	No rating
Eastern Airlines	11½	1999	CC
Georgia Pacific	5¼	1996	BBB
Greyhound	6½	1990	BBB−
IBM	7⅞	2004	AAA
MGM Grand Hotels	9½	2000	B+
Xerox	6	1995	A+

Exhibit 21.1
Selected Convertible Bonds*

* *Source:* Annual reports and *Standard & Poor's Bond Guide.* January 1986.

may be converted into stock, the holder will share in the growth of the company. If the price of the stock rises in response to the firm's growth, the value of the convertible bond must also rise. It is this combination of the safety of debt and the potential for capital gain that makes convertible bonds an attractive investment, particularly to investors who desire income and some capital appreciation.

Default risk   Like all investments, convertible bonds subject the holder to risk. If the company fails, the holder of a bond stands to lose the funds invested in the debt. This is particularly true with regard to convertible bonds, because they are usually subordinate to the firm's other debt. Thus, convertible bonds are considerably less safe than senior debt or debt that is secured by specific collateral. In case of a default or bankruptcy, holders of convertible bonds may at best realize only a fraction of the principal amount invested. However, their position is still superior to that of the stockholders.

Price fluctuations   Default is not the only potential source of risk to investors. Convertible bonds are actively traded, and their prices can and do fluctuate. As is explained in detail in the next section, their price is partially related to the value of the stock into which they may be converted. Fluctuations in the value of the stock produce fluctuations in the price of the bond. These price changes are *in addition* to price movements caused by variations in interest rates.

During periods of higher interest rates and lower stock prices, convertible bonds are doubly cursed. Their lower coupon rates of interest cause their prices to decline more than those of nonconvertible debt. This, in addition to the decline in the value of the stock into which they may be converted, results in considerable price declines for convertible bonds. Such declines are illustrated in Exhibit 21.2, which gives the high and low prices of several convertible bonds during 1974. During this time period, the Dow Jones industrial average fell from 850 in January 1973 to 607 in September 1974. During the same time period, interest rates on Baa-rated bonds rose from 8.5 percent to 9.8 percent. Thus, the prices of convertible bonds fell sharply. Each bond selected for this exhibit sold for less than half its principal value, and in the case of the Pan American World Airways 4½ 86, the $1,000 bond sold for as little as $130.

The exhibit also includes the prices of the bonds at the end of 1978. As may be seen in that column, each bond's price had risen considerably from the 1974 lows. If these bonds had been purchased in 1974 and sold in December 1978, their rates of

Exhibit 21.2
The High and Low
Prices of Selected
Convertible Bonds in
1974 Compared with
1978, 1981, and 1985
Year-end Prices

			Prices		
				December 31	
Bond	1974 High	1974 Low	1978	1981	1985
Ampex 5½ 94	48½	34	61	74½	Called and converted
Gulf and Western 5½ 93	70	48	78	Called and converted	NA
Pan American World Airways 4½ 86	42½	13	59	46¼	96
Seatrain 6 95	38	20½	56	16	No price quote
TWA 4 92	46⅞	22	47½	43⅛	64⅝

return would have been substantial, because they not only paid interest when due but also appreciated in price.

In addition, the next column of this exhibit shows what ensued after 1978 when interest rates rose once again. This column illustrates the large variety of possible outcomes from investments in convertible bonds. First, the Gulf and Western bond no longer existed because these bonds were called during 1980 and converted into stock. At that time each $1,000 bond was worth over $1,250. At the other extreme, the Seatrain bond's price plummeted because the company went bankrupt and defaulted on its debt obligations. Between these two extremes are the three other bonds. The Pan Am and TWA bonds' prices declined, but the Ampex bond continued to increase in value as the result of Ampex's being absorbed by Signal Company.

The last column of the exhibit brings the bonds' prices to the end of 1985. By then the Ampex bond had been called and converted. The Pan Am bond rose dramatically from its price in 1981 as it approached maturity, and it appeared that Pan Am would be able to redeem the bond at maturity in 1986. The TWA bond had also risen but certainly not as dramatically, as it still had several years to go before it reached maturity in 1992. Seatrain remained in bankruptcy, and no price for the bond was reported in *The Wall Street Journal*.

THE VALUATION OF CONVERTIBLE BONDS

This section considers the valuation of convertible bonds. The value of a convertible bond is related to (1) the value of the stock into which it may be converted and (2) the value of the bond as a debt instrument. Although each of these factors affects the market price of the bond, the importance of each element varies with changing conditions in the security markets. In the final analysis, the valuation of a convertible bond is extremely difficult, because it is a hybrid security that combines debt and equity.

This section has three subdivisions. The first considers the value of the bond solely as stock. The second covers the bond's value only as a debt instrument, and the last section combines these values to show the hybrid nature of convertible bonds. To differentiate the value of the bond as stock from its value as debt, subscripts are added to the symbols used. S will represent stock, and D will represent debt. Although this may make the equations appear more complex, it will clearly distinguish the value of the bond as stock from the value as debt.

The Convertible Bond as Stock

The value of a convertible bond in terms of the stock into which it may be converted (C_s) depends on (1) the face or principal amount of the bond (F), (2) the conversion (or exercise) price of the bond (P_e), and (3) the market price of the common stock (P_s). The face value divided by the conversion price of the bond gives the number of shares into which the bond may be converted. For example, if a $1,000 bond may be converted at $20 per share, then the bond may be converted into 50 shares ($1,000 ÷ $20). The number of shares times the market price of a share gives the value of the bond in terms of stock. If the bond is convertible into 50 shares and the stock sells for $15 per share, then the bond is worth $750 in terms of stock ($15 × 50).

The value of the bond as stock

Exhibit 21.3
The Relationship
between the Price of
a Stock and the Value
of a Convertible Bond

Price of the Stock	Shares into which the Bond is Convertible	Value of the Bond in Terms of Stock
$ 0	50	$ 0
5	50	250
10	50	500
15	50	750
20	50	1,000
25	50	1,250
30	50	1,500

Figure 21.1
The Relationship
between the Price of the
Stock and Conversion
Value of the Bond

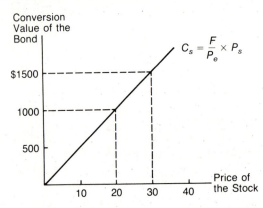

A graphic illustration

This **intrinsic value of the bond as stock** is expressed in Equation 21.1,

$$C_s = \frac{F}{P_e} \times P_s,$$

(21.1)

and is illustrated in Exhibit 21.3. In this example a $1,000 bond is convertible into 50 shares (i.e., a conversion price of $20 per share). The first column gives various prices of the stock. The second column presents the number of shares into which the bond is convertible (i.e., 50 shares). The third column gives the value of the bond in terms of stock (i.e., the product of the values in the first two columns). As may be seen in the exhibit, the value of the bond in terms of stock rises as the price of the stock increases.

This relationship between the price of the stock and the conversion value of the bond is illustrated in Figure 21.1. The price of the stock (P_s) is given on the horizontal axis, and the conversion value of the bond (C_s) is shown on the vertical axis. As the price of the stock rises, the conversion value of the bond increases. This is shown in the graph by line C_s, which represents the intrinsic value of the bond in terms of stock. Line C_s is a straight line running through the origin. If the stock has no value, the value of the bond in terms of stock is also worthless. If the exercise price of the bond and the market price of the stock are equal (i.e., $P_s = P_e$, which in this case is

$20), the bond's value as stock is equal to the principal amount (i.e., the bond's face value). As the price of the stock rises above the exercise price of the bond, the bond's value in terms of stock increases to more than the principal amount of the debt.

As with speculative options, which were discussed in the previous chapter, the market price of a convertible bond cannot be less than the bond's intrinsic value as stock. If the price of the bond were less than its value as stock, an opportunity to arbitrage would exist. Arbitrageurs would sell the stock short, purchase the convertible bond, exercise the conversion feature, and use the shares acquired through the conversion to cover the short sale. They would then make a profit equal to the difference between the price of the convertible bond and the conversion value of the bond. For example, if in the preceding example the bond were selling for $800 when the stock sold for $20 per share, arbitrageurs would enter the market. At $20 per share, the bond is worth $1,000 in terms of the stock (i.e., $20 × 50). Arbitrageurs would then sell 50 shares short for $1,000. At the same time they would buy the bond for $800 and exercise the option. After the shares had been acquired through the conversion of the bond, the arbitrageurs would cover the short position and earn $200 in profit (before commissions).

The intrinsic value sets the minimum price

Arbitrage

As arbitrageurs seek to purchase the bonds, they will drive up their price. The price increase will continue until there is no opportunity for profit. This occurs when the price is equal to or greater than the bond's value as stock. Thus, the intrinsic value of the bond stock sets the minimum price of the bond. Because of arbitrage, the market price of a convertible bond will be at least equal to its conversion value.

However, the market price of the convertible bond is rarely equal to the conversion value of the bond. The bond frequently sells for a premium over its conversion value because the convertible bond may also have value as a debt instrument. As a pure (i.e., nonconvertible) bond, it competes with other nonconvertible debt. Like the conversion feature, this element of debt may affect the bond's price. Its impact is important, for it also has the effect of putting a minimum price on the convertible bond. It is this price floor that gives investors in convertible bonds an element of safety that stock lacks.

The premium paid for convertible bonds

The Convertible Bond as Debt

The **intrinsic value of the convertible bond as debt** (C_D) is related to (1) the annual interest or coupon rate that the bond pays (I), (2) the current interest rate that is paid on comparable nonconvertible debt (i), and (3) the requirement that the principal or face value (F) be retired at maturity (after n number of years) if the bond is not converted. In terms of present value calculations, the value of a convertible bond as nonconvertible debt is given in Equation 21.2.

The value of the bond as debt

$$C_D = \frac{I}{(1 + i)^1} + \frac{I}{(1 + i)^2} + \cdots + \frac{I}{(1 + i)^n} + \frac{F}{(1 + i)^n}.$$ (21.2)

Equation 21.2 is simply the current price of any bond. (The derivation of the equation was discussed in Chapter 10.)

Equation 21.2 may be illustrated by the following example. Assume that the convertible bond in Exhibit 21.3 matures in ten years and pays 5 percent annually. Non-

A bond valuation model

Figure 21.2
The Relationship between the Price of Common Stock and the Value of the Bond as Nonconvertible Debt

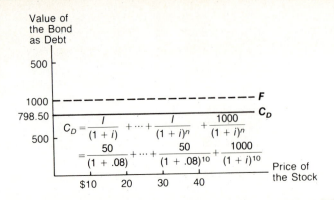

convertible debt of the same risk class currently yields 8 percent. When these values are inserted into Equation 21.2, the value of the bond as nonconvertible debt is $798.50.

$$C_D = \frac{\$50}{(1 + 0.08)^1} + \frac{\$50}{(1 + 0.08)^2} + \cdots + \frac{\$50}{(1 + 0.08)^9}$$

$$+ \frac{\$50}{(1 + 0.08)^{10}} + \frac{\$1,000}{(1 + 0.08)^{10}}$$

$$C_D = \$50(6.710) + \$1,000(0.463) = \$798.50.$$

This equation may be solved by the use of present value tables or a bond table. The 6.710 is the interest factor for the present value of an annuity of $1 for ten years at 8 percent, and 0.463 is the interest factor for the present value of $1 to be received ten years in the future when it is discounted at 8 percent. To be competitive with nonconvertible debt, this bond would have to sell for $798.50.

The relationship between the price of the common stock and the value of this bond as nonconvertible debt is illustrated in Figure 21.2. This figure consists of a horizontal line (C_D) that shows what the price ($798.50) of the bond would be if it were not convertible into stock, in which case the price is independent of the value of the stock. The principal amount of the bond is also shown in Figure 21.2 by the broken line F, which is above line C_D. The principal amount exceeds the value of the bond as pure debt because this bond must sell at a discount to be competitive with nonconvertible debt.

The value fluctuates with changes in the interest rate

The value of the convertible bond as debt varies with market interest rates. Since the interest paid by the bond is fixed, the value of the bond as debt varies inversely with interest rates. An increase in interest rates causes this value to fall; a decline in interest rates causes the value to rise.

The relationship between the value of the preceding convertible bond as debt and various interest rates is presented in Exhibit 21.4. The first column gives various interest rates; the second column gives the nominal (i.e., coupon) rate of interest; and the last column gives the value of the bond as nonconvertible debt. The inverse relation-

Interest Rate	Coupon Rate	Value of a Ten-year Bond
3%	5%	$1,170.50
4	5	1,081.55
5	5	1,000.00
6	5	926.00
7	5	864.20
8	5	798.50
10	5	692.25
12	5	631.70

Exhibit 21.4
The Relationship between Interest Rates and the Value of a Bond

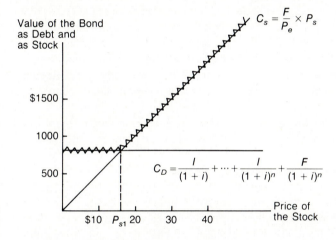

Figure 21.3
The Actual Minimum Price of a Convertible Bond

$$C_s = \frac{F}{P_e} \times P_s$$

$$C_D = \frac{I}{(1 + i)} + \cdots + \frac{I}{(1 + i)^n} + \frac{F}{(1 + i)^n}$$

ship is readily apparent, for as the interest rate rises from 3 percent to 12 percent, the value of the bond declines from $1,170.50 to $631.70.

The value of the bond as nonconvertible debt is important because it sets another minimum value that the bond will command in the market. At that price the convertible bond is competitive with nonconvertible debt of the same maturity and degree of risk. If the bond were to sell below this price, it would offer a more attractive (i.e., higher) yield than that of nonconvertible debt. Investors would seek to buy the bond to attain this higher yield. They would bid up the bond's price until its yield was comparable to that of nonconvertible debt. Thus, the bond's value as nonconvertible debt becomes a floor on the price of the convertible bond. Even if the value of the stock into which the bond may be converted were to fall, this floor would halt the decline in the price of the convertible bond.

Its value as debt sets a price floor

The actual minimum price of a convertible bond combines its value as stock and its value as debt. This is illustrated in Figure 21.3, which combines the preceding figures for the value of the bond both in terms of stock and nonconvertible debt. The

The impact of the bond's value as debt and as stock

bond's price is always greater than or equal to the higher of the two valuations. If the price of the convertible bond were below its value as common stock, arbitrageurs would bid up its price. If the bond sold for a price below its value as debt, investors in debt instruments would bid up the price.

The minimum price of the convertible bond is either its value in terms of stock or its value as nonconvertible debt, but the importance of these determinants varies. For low stock prices (i.e., stock prices less than P_{s1} in Figure 21.3), the minimum price is set by the bond's value as debt. However, for stock prices greater than P_{s1}, it is the bond's value as stock that determines the minimum price.

The Bond's Value as a Hybrid Security

The extreme values

The market price (P_m) of the convertible bond combines both the conversion value of the bond and its value as nonconvertible debt. If the price of the stock were to decline significantly below the exercise price of the bond, the market price of the convertible bond would be influenced primarily by the bond's value as nonconvertible debt. In effect, the bond would be priced as if it were a pure debt instrument. As the price of the stock rises, the conversion value of the bond rises and plays an increasingly important role in the determination of the market price of the convertible bond. At sufficiently high stock prices, the market price of the bond is identical with its conversion value.

These relationships are illustrated in Figure 21.4, which reproduces Figure 21.3 and adds to it the market price of the convertible bond (P_m). For prices of the common stock below P_{s1}, the market price is identical to the bond's value as nonconvertible debt. For prices of the common stock above P_{s2}, the price of the bond is identical to its value as common stock. At these extreme stock prices, the bond may be analyzed as if it were either pure debt or stock. For all prices between these two extremes, the mar-

Prices between the extremes

ket price of the convertible bond is influenced by the bond's value both as nonconvertible debt and as stock. This dual influence makes the analysis of convertible bonds difficult, since the investor pays a premium over the bond's value as stock and as debt.

Figure 21.4
Market Price of a Convertible Bond

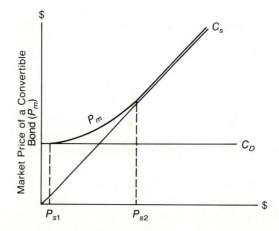

Exhibit 21.5
Premiums Paid for Convertible Debt

Price of the Stock	Shares into which the Bond May be Converted	Value of the Bond in Terms of Stock	Value of the Bond as Non-convertible Debt	Hypothetical Price of the Convertible Bond	Premium in Terms of Stock*	Premium in Terms of Non-convertible Debt[†]
$ 0	50	$ 0	$798.50	$ 798.50	$798.50	$ 0.00
5	50	250	798.50	798.50	548.50	0.00
10	50	500	798.50	798.50	298.50	0.00
15	50	750	798.50	900.00	150.00	101.50
20	50	1,000	798.50	1,100.00	100.00	301.50
25	50	1,250	798.50	1,300.00	50.00	501.50
30	50	1,500	798.50	1,500.00	0.00	701.50

*The premium in terms of stock is equal to the hypothetical price of the convertible bond minus the value of the bond in terms of stock.

[†]The premium in terms of nonconvertible debt is equal to the hypothetical price of the convertible bond minus the value of the bond as nonconvertible debt.

PREMIUMS PAID FOR CONVERTIBLE DEBT

The premiums

One way to analyze a convertible bond is to measure the premium over the bond's value as debt or as stock. For example, if a particular convertible bond is commanding a higher premium than is paid for similar convertible securities, perhaps this bond should be sold. Conversely, if the premium is relatively low, the bond may be a good investment.

The price over the bond's value as stock

The premiums paid for a convertible bond are illustrated in Exhibit 21.5, which reproduces Exhibit 21.3 and adds the value of the bond as nonconvertible debt (column 4) along with hypothetical market prices for the bond (column 5). The premium that an investor pays for a convertible bond may be viewed in either of two ways: the premium over the bond's value as stock or the premium over the bond's value as debt. Column 6 gives the premium in terms of stock. This is the difference between the bond's market price and its value as stock (i.e., the value in column 5 minus the value in common 3). This premium declines as the price of the stock rises and plays a more important role in the determination of the bond's price. Column 7 gives the premium in terms of nonconvertible debt. This is the difference between the bond's market price and its value as debt (i.e., the value in column 5 minus the value in column 4). This premium rises as the price of the stock rises, because the debt element of the bond is less important.

This premium declines as the price of the stock rises

The inverse relationship between the two premiums is also illustrated in Figure 21.5. The premiums are shown by the difference between the line representing the market price (P_m) and the lines representing the value of the bond in terms of stock (C_s) and the value of the bond as nonconvertible debt (C_D).

The premium over the bond's value as debt rises as the price of the stock rises

When the price of the stock is low and the bond is selling close to its value as debt, the premium above the bond's intrinsic value as stock is substantial, but the premium above the bond's value as debt is small. For example, at P_{s1} the price of the stock is $10, the bond's value in terms of stock is $500 (Line *AB* in Figure 21.5), and the premium is $298.50 (Line *BC*). However, the bond is selling for its value as nonconvertible debt ($798.50), and there is no premium over its value as debt. When the

Figure 21.5
**Premiums Paid for
a Convertible Bond**

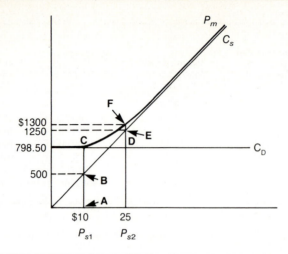

price of the stock is $25 and the bond is selling for $1,300, the premium in terms of stock is only $50 (Line *EF*). However, the bond's premium over its value as nonconvertible debt is $501.50 (Line *DF*).

As these examples illustrate, the premium paid for the bond over its value as stock declines as the price of the stock rises. This decline in the premium is the result of the increasing importance of the conversion value on the bond's market price and the decreasing importance of the debt element on the bond's price.

As the price of the stock rises, the safety feature of the debt diminishes. If the price of the common stock ceased to rise and started to fall, the price of the convertible bond could decline considerably before it reached the floor price set by the nonconvertible debt. For example, if the price of the stock declined from $30 to $15 (a 50 percent decline), the price of the convertible bond could fall from $1,500 to $798.50 (a 46.8 percent decline). Such a price decline would indicate that the floor value of $798.50 had little impact on the decline in the price of the bond.

The probability of a call   In addition, as the price of the stock (and hence the price of the convertible bond) rises, the probability that the bond will be called rises. When the bond is called, it can be worth only its value as stock. The call forces the holder to convert the bond into stock. For example, when the price of the stock is $30, the bond is worth $1,500 in terms of stock. Should the company call the bond and offer to retire it for its face value ($1,000), no one would accept the offer. Instead they would convert the bond into $1,500 worth of stock. If the investor paid a premium over this conversion value (such as $1,600) and the bond were called, the investor would then suffer a loss. Thus, as the probability of a call increases, the willingness to pay a premium over the bond's value as stock declines, and the price of the convertible bond ultimately converges with its value as stock.

*The price of the stock
fluctuates more than the
price of the bond*   This decline in the premium also means that the price of the stock will rise more rapidly than the price of the bond. While options offer investors potential leverage, convertible bonds do not. As may be seen in both Exhibit 21.5 and Figure 21.5, the

market price of the convertible bond rises and falls with the price of the stock, because the conversion value of the bond rises and falls. However, the market price of the convertible bond does not rise as rapidly as the conversion value of the bond. For example, when the stock's price increased from $20 to $25 (a 25 percent increase), the convertible bond's price rose from $1,100 to $1,300 (an 18.2 percent increase). The reason for this difference in the rate of increase is the declining premium paid for the convertible bond. Since the premium declines as the price of the stock rises, the rate of increase in the price of the stock must exceed the rate of increase in the price of the bond. In summary, convertible bonds offer investors the opportunity for some capital growth with less risk.

Because of these advantages, some investors may have the misconception that convertible bonds offer the best of both worlds: high return plus safety. In many cases a convertible bond may prove to be an inferior investment. For example, if the price of the stock rises rapidly, the stock is a superior investment because it will produce a larger capital gain. The stock outperforms the bond because the investor paid a premium for the convertible bond. In the opposite case when the price of the stock does not rise, a nonconvertible bond will outperform the convertible bond because it earns more interest. Thus, the very sources of a convertible bond's attractiveness (i.e., the potential capital growth plus the safety of debt) are also the sources of its lack of appeal (i.e., the inferior growth relative to the stock and the inferior interest income relative to nonconvertible debt). *A common misconception*

For investors, the advantages offered by convertible bonds do not include (1) the potential leverage of options, (2) the potential growth of stock, or (3) the safety and interest income of debt. The advantage is some combination of capital gain, interest income, and the safety of debt. As the previous example illustrated, the investor does receive interest income, and if the price of the stock rises, the price of the bond must also rise. If the stock's price does not rise, the convertible bond must eventually be retired because it is a debt obligation of the firm. Hence, the bond does offer some element of safety that is not available through investments in common stocks as well as some growth potential that is not available through nonconvertible debt. *The advantages*

CONVERTIBLE PREFERRED STOCK

In addition to convertible bonds, many firms have issued **convertible preferred stock**. As its name implies, this stock may be converted into the common stock of the issuing corporation. A sampling of convertible preferred stock is presented in Exhibit 21.6. This exhibit illustrates the diversity of companies that have this security outstanding, including chemical, financial, and consumer products firms. Thus, while nonconvertible preferred stock is primarily issued by utilities, the entire spectrum of firms issues convertible preferred stock. *Convertible preferred stock is similar to convertible debt*

Several of these issues of convertible preferred stock came into existence through mergers. The tax laws permit firms to combine through an exchange of stock, which is not taxable (i.e., it is a tax-free exchange). If one firm purchases another firm for cash, the stockholders who sell their shares have an obvious realized sale. Profits and losses from the sale are then subject to capital gains taxation. However, the Internal Revenue *It may be issued in mergers*

Exhibit 21.6
Terms of Selected Convertible Preferred Stocks as of January 1986

Firm	Dividend Rate	Shares of Common Stock into which Preferred Stock May be Converted	Price of Common Stock	Value of Preferred as Common Stock	Price of Preferred Stock
Allied-Signal	$12.00	2.0265	$46¾	$94.74	$110
Household International	2.375	2.25	42¼	95.06	93¼
Reynolds Metals	4.50	2.13	37¾	80.41	81½
Textron	2.08	1.10	49	53.90	53¾

Source: *Standard & Poor's Stock Guide,* January 1986.

Service has ruled that an exchange of "like securities" is not a realized sale and thus is not subject to capital gains taxation until the investor sells the new shares.

The impact of tax laws   This tax ruling has encouraged mergers through the exchange of stock. In many cases the firm that is taking over (the surviving firm) offers to the stockholders of the firm that is being taken over an opportunity to trade their shares for a new convertible preferred stock. Since the stock is convertible into the common stock of the surviving firm, it is a "like security." Thus, the transaction is not subject to capital gains taxation. To encourage the stockholders to tender their shares, the surviving firm may offer a generous dividend yield on the convertible preferred stock. For this reason many convertible preferred stocks have considerably more generous dividend yields than that which is available through investing in the firm's common stock.

It is equity   Convertible preferred stock is similar to convertible debt; however, there are some important differences. The differences are primarily the same as those between nonconvertible preferred stock and nonconvertible debt. Preferred stock is treated as an equity instrument. Thus, the firm is not under any legal obligation to pay dividends. In addition, the preferred stock may be a perpetual security and may not have to be retired as debt must be. However, many convertible preferred stocks do have a required sinking fund, which forces the firm to retire the preferred stock over a period of years.

Its valuation   The value of convertible preferred stock (like convertible bonds) is related to the price of the stock into which it may be converted and to the value of competitive nonconvertible preferred stock. As with convertible bonds, these values set floors on the price of the convertible preferred stock. It cannot sell for any significant length of time below its value as stock. If it did, investors would enter the market and buy the preferred stock, which would increase its price. Thus, the minimum value of the convertible preferred stock (like the minimum value of the convertible bond) must be equal to the conversion of the stock (P_c). In equation form that is

(21.3)
$$P_c = P_s \times N,$$

where P_s is the market price of the stock into which the convertible preferred stock may be converted, and N is the number of shares an investor obtains through conversion. Equation 21.3 is similar to Equation 21.1, which gave the intrinsic value of the convertible bond as stock.

The convertible preferred stock's value as nonconvertible preferred stock (P_{pfd}) is related to the dividend it pays (D_{pfd}) and to the appropriate discount factor (k_{pfd}), which is the yield earned on competitive nonconvertible preferred stock. In equation form that is

$$P_{pfd} = \frac{D_{pfd}}{k_{pfd}},$$ (21.4)

The impact of dividends and their appropriate discount factor

which is essentially the same as the convertible bond's value as debt except that the preferred stock has no definite maturity date. (Equation 21.4 was derived in Chapter 11.) However, this value does set a floor on the price of a convertible preferred stock because at that price it is competitive with nonconvertible preferred stock.

As with convertible bonds, the convertible preferred stock is a hybrid security whose value combines its worth both as stock and as nonconvertible preferred stock. Convertible preferred stock tends to sell for a premium over its value as stock and its value as straight preferred stock. Figures 21.4 and 21.5, which illustrated the value of the convertible bond at various prices of the stock into which it may be converted, also apply to convertible preferred stock. The only difference is the premium that the preferred stock commands over the value as common stock, which tends to be smaller. The reason for this reduced premium is that the preferred stock does not have the element of debt. Its features are more similar to common stock than are the features of the convertible bond. Thus, its price usually commands less of a premium over its value as stock. This smaller premium is illustrated in Exhibit 21.6 as most of these convertible preferreds are selling near their value, as common stock.

Convertible-Exchangeable Preferred Stock

Convertible-exchangeable preferred stock is a security that includes two options. The holder may convert the shares into the firm's common stock, or the company may force the holder to exchange the shares for the firm's bonds. For example, the Federal Paper Board $2.3125 convertible-exchangeable preferred stock may be converted at the holder's option into 2.51 shares of common stock. However, the firm has the option to exchange each share for $25 worth of the firm's 9¼ percent convertible debentures.

Option to exchange stock for debt

The exchange option gives the firm more control over the preferred stock, as it is a means to force retirement of the shares without an outlay of cash if the value of the common stock rises *or* falls. If the value of the common stock were to rise, the investor may voluntarily convert the preferred stock. However, the firm may exercise its option to exchange the bonds for the preferred stock, thus forcing the stockholder to convert or lose the appreciation in the preferred stock's value. In this case the exchange option operates as a call feature—it forces conversion.

If the value of the common stock were to decline, no one would exercise the option to convert the stock. Without the exchange option, there is nothing the firm could do to retire the stock and rid itself of the required dividend payments except repurchase the shares. However, by having the exchange option, the firm can force the preferred stockholder to exchange the shares for debt. The firm will now have to make interest payments, but these are tax-deductible expenses, while preferred dividends are paid from earnings and are not tax deductible.

SELECTING CONVERTIBLES

Because convertible bonds are a hybrid security, they are more difficult to select than nonconvertible bonds. These securities are debt instruments and pay a fixed flow of interest income, so they appeal to conservative, income-oriented investors. However, since the bonds sell for a premium over their value as debt, investors forgo some of the interest income and safety associated with nonconvertible bonds.

Interest advantage

A convertible bond also offers the potential for capital gains if the value of the stock into which the bond may be converted were to rise. Possible capital gains increase the bond's attractiveness to investors seeking capital appreciation. Since the investor pays a premium over the bond's value as stock, the potential price appreciation is less than is available through an investment in the firm's common stock. However, the investor who purchases the bond does collect the interest, which usually exceeds the dividends paid on an equivalent number of shares into which the bond may be converted.

This interest advantage may be seen by considering the 7½ percent convertible bond issued by The Limited, a retailer with a chain of women's specialty stores. Each bond may be converted into 31.87 shares of common stock. In 1985, the stock paid dividends of $0.16 a share (i.e., the equivalent of $5.09 on 31.87 shares), but the bond paid interest of $75. The bondholder collected $69.91 more in interest income than the stockholder collected on an equivalent number of shares.

Breakeven analysis

This additional flow of income offers one way to analyze the premium paid for a convertible bond. If the bond is held for a sufficient amount of time, the additional income will offset the premium. This time period is sometimes referred to as "years to payback" or the "breakeven time." The following example illustrates how this breakeven time period may be computed.[1] Consider a $1,000 convertible bond with a 7 percent coupon that is convertible into 50 shares of stock. The stock currently sells for $16 a share and pays a dividend of $0.40 a share. In terms of stock the bond is worth $800 (50 × $16), so the premium over the bond's value as stock is $200 ($1,000 − 800). The bondholder receives $70 a year in interest but would receive only $20 ($0.40 × 50) on the stock. Thus purchasing the bond instead of an equivalent number of shares generates $50 in additional income, which offsets the premium over the bond's value as stock in four years ($200/$50 = 4).

This series of calculations may be summarized as follows:

Market value of the bond	$1,000
Minus bond's conversion value	800
Premium over the conversion value	$ 200
Bond's annual income	$ 70
Minus annual income from stock	20
Annual income advantage to bond	$ 50

---

[1] See Michael L. Tennican, *Convertible Debentures and Related Securities* (Boston: Harvard University Press, 1975), 62–67, or Bancroft G. Davis, "Convertible Securities," in *Encyclopedia of Investments*, eds. M. E. Blume and J. P. Friedman, (Boston: Warren, Gorham & Lamont, 1982), 182–184.

$$\text{Payback period} = \frac{\text{Premium over the conversion value}}{\text{Annual income advantage}}$$

$$= \$200/\$50 = 4 \text{ years.}$$

If the additional income offsets the premium paid over the bond's value as stock in a moderate period of time (e.g., three to four years), the convertible bond may be an attractive alternative to the stock. (This, of course, assumes that the stock is also sufficiently attractive and offers the potential for growth.) If the time period necessary to overcome the premium is many years (e.g., ten years), then the bond should not be purchased as an alternative to the stock but should be viewed solely as a debt instrument and analyzed as such.

Quick breakeven is desirable

The individual should realize that this technique is relatively simple and does not consider (1) differences in commission costs to buy bonds instead of stock, (2) possible growth in the cash dividend, which will increase the time period necessary to recapture the premium, and (3) the time value of money. The premium is paid in the present (i.e., when the bond is purchased), but the flow of interest income occurs in the future. However, the technique does permit comparisons of various convertible bonds. If the individual computes the time period necessary to recapture the premium for several bonds, he or she may identify specific convertible bonds that are more attractive potential investments.

Weaknesses in the technique

THE HISTORY OF TWO CONVERTIBLE BONDS

Perhaps the best way to understand investing in convertible bonds is to examine the history of two such bonds. The first is a success story, in that the price of the common stock rose and therefore the value of the bond also rose. The second is a not-so-successful story, for the price of the stock declined and so did the value of the bond. However, the story of this bond is not a tragedy, for the bond was still a debt obligation of the company and was retired at maturity even though it was not converted into stock.

Illustrations of convertible bonds

The American Quasar 7¼ 91

American Quasar is a firm devoted to exploring and drilling for oil and gas. It not only develops known reserves but also drills wells in search of new discoveries. Such wells (called wildcats) can prove to be highly lucrative; however, the majority of such drilling leads only to dry holes (i.e., no oil or gas is found). Because of the nature of its operations, American Quasar is a speculative firm at best. Speculative firms, however, need funds to operate, so the firm issued $17,500,000 in face value of convertible bonds. The coupon rate was set at 7¼ percent, which was quite generous for a convertible bond at that time. The high coupon rate was indicative of the element of risk involved in investing in the security. The exercise price of the bond was $21 (i.e., it was convertible into 47.6 shares), which was a premium of 17 percent over the approximate price of the stock ($18) at the date of issue.

After the bond was issued, American Quasar's stock did particularly well. Perhaps the discovery of some sizable wells in the Midwest and the problems associated with

A success

energy in general helped bolster the firm's stock. Of course, the value of the convertible bond rose as the price of the stock rose. The prices of the bond and the stock moved closely together, and less than two years after being issued the bond was called, which forced conversion of the bond into the stock.

What was the return earned by investors in these securities? Obviously an investment in either the stock or the bond was quite profitable, since the price of the stock rose so rapidly. The bond's price rose from $1,000 to $1,500 during the time it was outstanding. The bond paid $145 in interest. The return earned over the 15 months on an investment in the bond was

$$\frac{\text{Price appreciation + Interest earned}}{\text{Cost}} = \frac{\$1,500 - \$1,000 + \$145}{\$1,000}$$

$$= \frac{\$645}{\$1,000} = 64.5\%.$$

For the stock the return was

$$\frac{\text{Price appreciation + Dividends}}{\text{Cost}} = \frac{\$32 - \$18 + \$0}{\$18} = \frac{\$14}{\$18} = 77.7\%.$$

(It should be noted that the stock did not pay any cash dividends while the bond was outstanding.) As may be seen by these calculations, the returns are both positive. The stock did better because the bond was initially sold for a premium over its value as stock. However, an investor who purchased this convertible bond certainly would have little cause for complaint.

The Pan American World Airways 4½ 86

A poor investment

While the previous example illustrated how the price of a convertible bond may rise as the price of the stock rises, the Pan American World Airways 4½ 86 demonstrates the opposite. When the price of the stock declined, the price of the convertible bond followed it. This bond was issued in 1966, when Pan Am was riding the crest of popularity (which may partially explain why the coupon rate of interest was low on the bond).

Unfortunately for investors purchasing either the stock or the bond, Pan Am's popularity vanished, and with years of continued deficits the price of the stock declined drastically. The decline and its effect on the price of the convertible bond are illustrated in Figure 21.6, which plots the high and low stock and bond prices for 1967 through 1985. Both the stock and the bond fell to "bargain basement" prices in 1974. The market seemed to think that the firm would certainly default on the debt and enter bankruptcy. At that time the bond reached a low of $130 for a $1,000 bond!

After this nadir, the price of both the bond and the stock recovered somewhat so that in June 1978 the stock was selling for $7 per share and the bond was selling for approximately $600. However, both prices were still below the 1966 prices when the bond was initially issued, and after 1978 both the bond's and the stock's price fell once again.

This example illustrates the risk associated with investing in convertible bonds. If the firm becomes financially weak, the price of the convertible bond can fall dras-

Figure 21.6
The Annual Price Range for Pan Am's Stock and 4½ 86 Convertible Bond

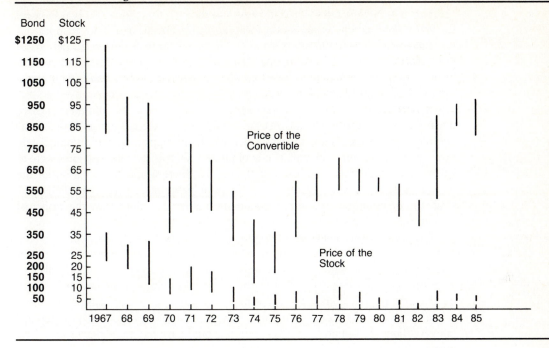

tically. The price of Pan Am stock fell from a high of $36¾ in 1966 to a low of $1¾ in 1974, and the price of the convertible bond fell from $1,221 to $130. However, the bond was still an obligation of Pan Am that had to be retired in 1986. Thus, when Pan Am did redeem the bond in 1986, investors who purchased it initially for $1,000 received their principal back. However, during the many years that the bond was outstanding, there certainly were periods when it appeared that the bond might become worthless.

PUT BONDS

Most of this chapter has been devoted to convertible bonds, which are debt instruments with a built-in call option. If the price of the stock rises, the investor may convert the bond into stock. As with call options the investor profits when the value of the stock rises, making the option to convert more valuable.

During the 1980s, another type of bond was created with a built-in put option. The owner of a put profits if the security's price falls since the security may be sold at the higher price specified in the put. In a similar manner the holder of a **put bond** will profit if interest rates rise (i.e., bond prices fall) because the holder may sell the bond back to the firm. In effect the firm must redeem the bond at a specified date for its principal amount. The investor may then reinvest the funds at the current, higher rate of interest. A typical illustration of a put bond is the Industrial Development Authority

Option to redeem the bond at face value

*Fear of rising
interest rates*

of Richmond, Virginia, put bond due in 2005, which the investor may redeem in 1995 for the principal amount.[2]

Fear that interest rates would increase and thereby inflict losses on bondholders led to the development of put bonds. Firms and governments need long-term financing, but some investors do not want to commit their funds for extended periods of time, especially if they fear rising interest rates. Put bonds permit firms and governments to sell long-term debt to investors who are reluctant to buy bonds with maturity dates 20 to 30 years into the future.

If, after these put bonds were issued, interest rates were to rise and thereby drive down the price of the bonds, the investor would exercise the put option at the specified redemption date. He or she would receive the principal and could immediately invest it at the current (and higher) rate of interest. Of course, if interest rates were to fall, the individual would not exercise the option. There would be no reason for the investor to seek the early redemption of the principal if interest rates have fallen. Instead the investor may sell the bond on the market for more than the principal amount (i.e., for a premium).

*Lower interest costs
to issuer*

Firms and governments are willing to offer investors this put option for much the same reason that they were willing to offer convertibility: lower interest costs. If an investor acquires an option, he or she must pay a price. For regular puts and calls that price (or "premium" as it is called in the jargon of options) is the amount paid to purchase the option. With a convertible bond or a put bond, the option's price is more subtle. Its price is the reduction in interest the investor must forgo to acquire the option.[3] Without the option the bond's coupon would have had to be higher to induce investors to purchase the long-term bond.

Impact on bond's price

The put option's potential impact on the value of a bond as interest rates fluctuate may be seen by the following illustration. A firm issues a bond due in twenty years with a 10 percent coupon. It grants the investor the option to redeem the bond at par at the end of five years. If the option is not exercised, the bond will remain outstanding for an additional fifteen years. (This is a simple illustration with only one future date at which the investor may exercise the put option. Some bonds may grant the bondholder the option to redeem the bond more frequently, such as every five years.)

If the current interest rate is 8 percent, the value of the bond is

$$\$100(9.818) + \$1,000(0.215) = \$1,196.80.$$

9.818 and 0.215 are the interest factors for the present value of an annuity and the present value of a dollar at 8 percent for *twenty* years. Twenty years is the appropriate number of years because, since interest rates have fallen, the investor will not redeem the bond. The option thus has no impact on the increase in the price of the bond.

If the current interest rate is 12 percent, the value of the bond is

$$\$100(3.605) + \$1,000(0.567) = \$927.50.$$

3.605 and 0.567 are the interest factors for the present value of an annuity and the present value of a dollar at 12 percent for *five* years. Five years is the appropriate num-

---

[2] Governments cannot issue convertible bonds because there is no stock into which the bond may be converted. However, they can issue put bonds, and several municipalities and state agencies have issued them.

[3] This price may be expressed in present value terms—it is the difference between the value of the bond with and the value of the bond without the option.

ber of years because if the current rate of interest exceeds 10 percent, the investor will exercise the option and redeem the bond.

The impact of the put option on the value of the bond can be seen by comparing the above value and the bond's value *without* the put option. In that case, if the current interest rate were 12 percent, the value of the bond would be

$$\$100(7.469) + \$1,000(0.104) = \$850.90.$$

7.469 and 0.104 are the interest factors for the present value of an annuity and the present value of a dollar at 12 percent for twenty years. Twenty years is the appropriate number of years because the bond lacks the put option. In this illustration the put option increases the value of the bond by $76.60 ($927.50 − 850.90). Thus the put option affects the value of the bond if interest rates increase. Its impact is to reduce the amount by which the bond's price will decline, because the expected life is the redemption date and not the maturity date.

Since bonds with put options are relatively new securities, one can only speculate as to their future popularity. However, granting the option does alter the interest paid, so one of the participants (i.e., the issuer or the investor) profits from the option. If interest rates remain below the coupon rate, the issuer profits, because the firm (or government) was able to sell a debt instrument with a lower rate than would have been required to sell the bonds without the put option. However, if interest rates rise, investors profit, because they are no longer locked into a debt instrument with an inferior yield. The issuer then will have to pay the higher rates in order to reborrow the funds. Obviously if the investor (1) anticipates rising interest rates or (2) is particularly uncertain as to the direction of future interest rates and wants to hedge against rates increasing, bonds with put options may be attractive alternatives to other types of long-term debt instruments.

SUMMARY

A convertible bond is a debt instrument that may be converted into stock. The value of this bond depends on the value of the stock into which the bond may be converted and on the value of the bond as a debt instrument.

As the value of the stock rises, so does the value of the convertible bond. If the price of the stock declines, the value of the bond will also fall. However, the stock's price will decline faster, because the convertible bond's value as debt will halt the fall in the bond's price.

Since a convertible bond's price rises with the price of the stock, the bond offers the investor an opportunity for appreciation as the value of the firm increases. In addition, the bond's value as a debt sets a floor on the bond's price, which reduces the risk of loss to the investor. Should the stock decline in value, the debt element reduces the risk of loss to the bondholder.

Convertible bonds, like other options, may sell for a premium. For these bonds the premium may be viewed relative to the bond's value as stock or its value as debt. These two premiums are inversely related. When the price of the stock rises, the premium that the bond commands over its value as stock diminishes, but the premium over its value as debt rises. When the price of the stock falls, the premium over the

bond's value as stock rises, but the premium relative to the bond's value as debt declines.

Convertible preferred stock is similar to convertible debt, except that it lacks the safety implied by a debt instrument. Its price is related to its conversion value, the flow of dividend income, and the rate that investors may earn on nonconvertible preferred stock.

A recent innovation in the debt instrument market is the put bond which permits the holder to redeem the bond for its principal amount at some specified time in the future. If interest rates increase, the bondholder may exercise the put option. He or she redeems the bond, receives the principal, and thus is able to reinvest the funds at the higher current rate of interest. However, if interest rates fall, the bondholder will not exercise the option, as there is no reason to redeem the bond prior to maturity. Hence, the advantage put bonds offer investors is protection against being locked into an inferior rate of interest if the rates were to increase in the future.

Terms to Remember

Convertible bond

Intrinsic value as stock

Intrinsic value as debt

Convertible preferred stock

Put bond

Questions

1. What differentiates convertible bonds from other bonds?

2. How is the value of a convertible bond in terms of stock determined? What effect does this value have on the price of the bond?

3. How is the value of a convertible bond in terms of debt determined? What effect does this value have on the price of the bond?

4. Why may convertible bonds be called by the firm? When are these bonds most likely to be called?

5. Why are convertible bonds less risky than stock but usually more risky than non-convertible bonds?

6. Why does the premium over the bond's intrinsic value as stock decline as the value of the stock rises?

7. How are convertible preferred stocks different from convertible bonds?

8. What advantages do convertible securities offer investors? What are the risks associated with these investments?

Problems

1. Given the following information concerning a convertible bond—

Principal	$1,000
Coupon	5%
Maturity	15 years
Call price	$1,050
Conversion price	$37 (i.e., 27 shares)
Market price of the common stock	$32
Market price of the bond	$1,040

answer the following questions:

a. What is the current yield of this bond?

b. What is the value of the bond based on the market price of the common stock?

c. What is the value of the common stock based on the market price of the bond?

d. What is the premium in terms of stock that the investor pays when he or she purchases the convertible bond instead of the stock?

e. Nonconvertible bonds are selling with a yield to maturity of 7 percent. If this bond lacked the conversion feature, what would the approximate price of the bond be?

f. What is the premium in terms of debt that the investor pays when he or she purchases the convertible bond instead of a nonconvertible bond?

g. If the price of the common stock should double, would the price of the convertible bond double? Briefly explain your answer.

h. If the price of the common stock should decline by 50 percent, would the price of the convertible bond decline by the same percentage? Briefly explain your answer.

i. What is the probability that the corporation will call this bond?

j. Why are investors willing to pay the premiums mentioned in parts d. and f.?

2. The following information concerns a convertible bond:

- Coupon 6% ($60 per $1,000 bond)
- Exercise price: $25
- Maturity date: 20 years
- Call price: $1,040

The price of the common stock is $30.

a. If this bond were nonconvertible, what would be its approximate value if comparable interest rates were 12 percent?

b. How many shares can the bond be converted into?

c. What is the value of the bond in terms of stock?

d. What is the current minimum price that the bond will command?

e. If the current market price of the bond is $976, what should you do?

f. Is there any reason to anticipate that the firm will call the bond?

g. What do investors receive if they do not convert the bond when it is called?

h. If the bond were called, would it be advantageous to convert?

i. If interest rates rise, would that affect the bond's current yield?

j. If the price of the stock were $10, would your answer to part i. be different?

3. Given the following information concerning Continental Group $2.00 convertible preferred stock:

- One share of preferred is convertible into 0.33 share of common stock
- Price of common stock: $34
- Price of convertible preferred stock: $17

a. What is the value of the preferred stock in terms of common stock?

b. What is the premium over the preferred stock's value as common stock?

c. If the preferred stock is perpetual and comparable preferred stock offers a divi-

dend yield of 15 percent, what would be the minimum price of this stock if it were not convertible?

d. If the price of the common stock rose to $60, what would be the minimum increase in the value of the preferred stock that you would expect?

4. Two bonds have the following terms:

Bond A	
Principal	$1,000
Coupon	8%
Maturity	10 years

Bond B	
Principal	$1,000
Coupon	7.6%
Maturity	10 years

Bond B has an additional feature; it may be redeemed at par after five years (i.e., it has a put feature). Both bonds were initially sold for their face amounts (i.e., $1,000).

a. If interest rates fall to 7 percent, what will be the price of each bond?

b. If interest rates rise to 9 percent, what will be the decline in the price of each bond from its initial price?

c. Given your answers to a. and b., what is the trade-off implied by the put option in bond B?

d. Bond B requires the investor to forgo $4 a year (i.e., $40 if the bond is in existence for ten years). If interest rates are 8 percent, what is the present value of this forgone interest? If the bond had lacked the put feature but had a coupon of 7.6 percent and a term to maturity of ten years, it would sell for $973.16 when interest rates were 8 percent. What, then, is the implied cost of the put option?

5. Two firms have common stock and convertible bonds outstanding. Information concerning these securities is as follows:

	Firm A	Firm B
Common stock:		
Price of common stock	$46	$30
Cash dividend	none	$1
Convertible bond:		
Principal	$1,000	$1,000
Conversion price	$50	$33⅓
	(20 shares)	(30 shares)
Maturity date	10 years	10 years
Coupon rate	7.5%	7.5%
Market price	$1,100	$1,100

a. What is the value of each bond in terms of stock?

b. What is the premium paid over each bond's value as stock?

c. What is each bond's income advantage over the stock into which the bond may be converted?

d. How long will it take for the income advantage to offset the premium determined in part b.?

e. If after four years firm A's stock sells for $65 and the firm calls the bond, what is the rate of return earned on an investment in the stock or in the bond? (You may wish to review the material on calculating rates of return presented in Chapter 13.)

Suggested Readings

For an elementary discussion of convertible bonds, consult:

Noddings, Thomas. *Investor's Guide to Convertible Bonds*. Homewood, Ill.: Dow Jones-Irwin, 1982.

Techniques used to analyze convertible bonds are discussed in

Baumol, William J., Burton G. Malkiel, and Richard E. Quandt. "The Valuation of Convertible Securities." *Quarterly Journal of Economics* (February 1966): 48–59.

Brigham, Eugene. "An Analysis of Convertible Debentures: Theory and Some Empirical Evidence." *Journal of Finance* (March 1966): 35–54.

Liebowitz, Martin L. "Understanding Convertible Securities." *Financial Analysts Journal* (November–December 1974): 57–67.

Tennican, Michael L. *Convertible Debentures and Related Securities*. Boston: Harvard University Press, 1975.

(The reader should be warned that some of this material requires some understanding of mathematics.)

The fact that the premium paid for convertible bonds may be excessive is discussed in

Weberman, Ben. "The Convertible Bond Scam." *Forbes*, January 19, 1981, 92.

Firms issue convertible securities with the intention of forcing conversion instead of repaying the principal. For a discussion of calling convertible bonds, see:

Dawson, Steven M. "Timing Interest Payments for Convertible Bonds." *Financial Management* (Summer 1974): 14–16.

Miller, Alexander B. "How To Call Your Convertible." *Harvard Business Review* (May–June 1971): 60–70.

A SHORT CASE STUDY FOR CHAPTERS 19–21
A Speculator's Choices

Andrew Patrick is an optimist who likes to speculate. He enjoys watching prices change rapidly and believes that he could make large profits by judiciously taking advantage of price swings. Thus it is easy to see why he is attracted to options whose prices may change rapidly from day to day. He especially likes the securities associated with Thor Construction Corporation, a large building and engineering firm that also has considerable holdings of coal and oil reserves.

Currently the economy is in a recession. Thor is doubly cursed: the recession has resulted in a significant decline in construction, and commodity prices, including oil and gas, are declining. These two factors have reduced Thor's profit margins so that per-share earnings have plummeted from $4.00 to $1.50 during the latest fiscal year. The stock, which at one time had been an outstanding performer, has declined from a high of more than $80 to its current price of $15.

Patrick believes that the stock market has overreacted to the decline in earnings. Furthermore, there are signs that the recession is ending. Retail sales have risen and interest rates are falling. A more robust economy should certainly help Thor's sales and earnings, which Patrick believes would result in a higher stock price. Thor's fundamentals are sound, as its profit margins have historically been among the highest in the industry. However, the firm has a considerable amount of long-term debt outstanding. Even though Thor pays no cash dividends, it has had to issue long-term bonds because retained earnings were insufficient to finance expansion and acquisitions.

Patrick firmly believes that Thor Construction offers an excellent opportunity for profit, but he is very uncertain as to the correct strategy to follow. In addition to the stock, the firm has outstanding a convertible debenture with a 9 percent coupon and an exercise price of $30 (33.33 shares per $1,000 bond). The bond is currently selling for $780 per $1,000 face amount and, like the stock, is actively traded. It is rated double B by one rating service but only single B by another service.

Options on Thor stock are also actively traded. Currently the following options and their prices are available:

Exercise Price	Three-month		Six-month		Nine-month	
	Call	Put	Call	Put	Call	Put
$15	$2	$1½	$3½	$2¼	$5	$3
20	¾	5½	1½	6	2	6¼

To help determine the potential returns from the various alternatives, Patrick decided that answers to the following questions may be useful.

1. What is the current yield offered by the stock, the convertible bond, and the calls and puts?

2. What is the value of the bond in terms of the stock?

3. What is the intrinsic value of each option?

4. What are the premiums paid for the bond and the time premiums paid for each option?

5. What will be the price of each security if after six months the fundamental economic picture is not changed and the price of the stock remains $15?

6. While Patrick considered a further decline in Thor's situation to be unlikely, the possibility does exist that after six months the stock would fall to $10. What impact would that have on the prices of the various securities?

7. Patrick believes that the price of the stock will rise to $25 a share within six months. What impact would such a price increase have on the prices of the various securities?

As an outside financial advisor to Patrick, what course of action would you suggest with regard to Thor's securities? In formulating your answer, consider the pros and cons of each of the alternatives and which conditions favor each security. There is, of course, no one correct strategy.

VI Specialized Investment Alternatives

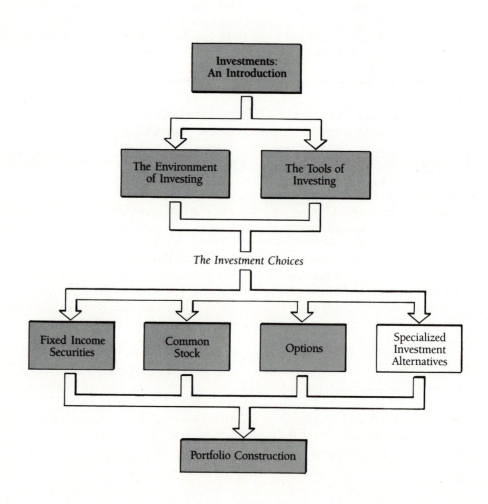

Investments:
An Introduction

The Environment
of Investing

The Tools of
Investing

The Investment Choices

Fixed Income
Securities

Common
Stock

Options

Specialized
Investment
Alternatives

Portfolio Construction

*T*he next part of this text considers a variety of specialized investment alternatives that an individual may acquire instead of traditional stocks and bonds. These alternatives include shares in investment companies, commodity and financial futures contracts, physical assets such as gold and collectibles, real estate, and foreign securities. The poor performance of common stocks and bonds during the 1970s, the impact of inflation, and the need for diversification increased investors' interest in the alternative investments discussed in the next five chapters.

Unfortunately, the novice investor may not recognize the special risks or may lack the necessary information to invest successfully in these assets. While there are illustrations of spectacular returns on the purchase of a specific piece of real estate or a particular art object, such abnormal returns are rare. Since all investors compete against each other, it is not possible for everyone to achieve abnormally large returns by acquiring these specialized investment alternatives. However, they may reward the patient individual who takes the time to learn how these investments may be used as part of a total investment strategy.

The first chapter in Part Six considers the purchasing of shares in investment companies such as mutual funds. With these investments the individual turns over the supervision of the specific securities to the managers of the investment companies. Chapter 23 considers a sharply contrasting approach—investing in commodity contracts. These contracts for the future delivery of commodities such as wheat or financial assets such as U.S. Treasury bills may be very speculative. Commodity contracts can produce large and sudden profits or losses, and they require that the individual actively participate in the day-to-day management of the investments. Chapters 24 and 25 consider investments in a variety of nonfinancial (i.e., physical) assets: Chapter 24 is devoted to collectibles such as art works and precious metals such as gold, and Chapter 25 is devoted to real estate, especially home ownership. Chapter 26 adds international investments. The inclusion of the material in Part Six broadens the investor's perception of the portfolio.

22 Investment Companies

LEARNING OBJECTIVES

After completing this chapter you should be able to

1. Differentiate between closed-end and open-end investment companies.

2. Define *net asset value*.

3. Identify the costs of investing in mutual funds and closed-end investment companies.

4. List the advantages offered by investment companies.

5. Distinguish among the types of mutual funds.

6. Identify hidden capital gains and losses.

7. Differentiate between before- and after-tax rates of return.

8. Distinguish between loading fees, exit fees, and 12b-1 plans.

9. Adjust returns for risk.

*B*ecause many investors find managing their own portfolios to be difficult or time-consuming or both, they purchase shares in investment companies. The managements of these companies then invest the funds primarily in a diversified portfolio of stocks and bonds. Since the individual owns shares in the investment company, it owns a claim on the diversified portfolio. Thus the saver can achieve the advantage of diversification while investing only a modest amount. Investment companies have been a popular vehicle for many investors, and they play a significant role in security markets.

There are two general types of investment companies: closed-end and open-end. The open-end investment company is commonly referred to as a mutual fund and is by far the more popular. This chapter discusses both types of investment companies, the mechanics of buying and selling their shares, the costs associated with these investments, and the potential sources of profit. Also included in the discussion are the various specialized investment companies, such as stock index funds or junk bond funds, that have recently developed and that

offer investors a broad spectrum of investment alternatives to the direct purchase of stocks and bonds through brokers.

The chapter also discusses factors to consider when investing in mutual funds. These include hidden capital gains and losses, the age and size of the fund, and its previous performance. The chapter ends with a discussion of returns from investments in mutual funds. Special emphasis is given to (1) the difference in the reported returns and the after-tax return the investor realizes, (2) the impact of fees in addition to sales fees, called loading charges, that the investor pays when the shares are purchased, and (3) differences in risk among the various mutual funds.

INVESTMENT COMPANIES: ORIGINS AND TERMINOLOGY

Investment companies are not a recent development but were established in Britain during the 1860s. Initially, these investment companies were referred to as trusts because the securities were held in trust for the firm's stockholders. These firms issued a specified number of shares and used the funds that were obtained through the sale of the stock certificates to acquire shares of other firms. Today the descendants of these companies are referred to as **closed-end investment companies** because the number of shares is fixed.

Investment companies started over a century ago

While the first trusts offered a specified number of shares, the most common type of investment company today does not. Instead, the number of shares varies as investors buy more shares from the trust or sell them back to the trust. This **open-end investment company** is commonly called a **mutual fund.** Such funds started in 1924 when Massachusetts Investor Trust offered new shares and redeemed (i.e., bought) existing shares on demand by stockholders.

Mutual funds

The rationale for investment companies is very simple and appealing. The firms receive the funds from many investors, pool them, and purchase securities. The individual investors receive (1) the advantage of professional management of their money, (2) the benefit of ownership in a diversified portfolio, (3) the potential savings in commissions, as the investment company buys and sells in large blocks, and (4) custodial services (e.g., the storing of certificates and the collecting and disbursing of funds).

The rationale for investment companies

The advantages and services help to explain why both the number of mutual funds and the dollar value of their shares have grown since the 1940s. This growth is illustrated in Figure 22.1, which presents mutual funds' net sales and total assets from 1960 through 1984.[1] (Net sales are gross sales minus redemptions, which are shares sold back to the mutual fund.) During the 1970s the growth in mutual funds stopped as redemptions exceeded sales for several years. The redemptions, plus the general decline in the market, produced a 23 percent decline in mutual funds' total assets during 1974. However, during the 1980s sales of shares plus the general increase in security prices has dramatically increased mutual funds' total assets.[2]

---

[1] The assets of money market mutual funds are excluded.

[2] The value of closed-end investment companies has also grown, but the total value of their assets is less than one-tenth the value of mutual funds' assets.

Figure 22.1
**Mutual Funds' Total
Assets and Net Sales,
1960–1984**

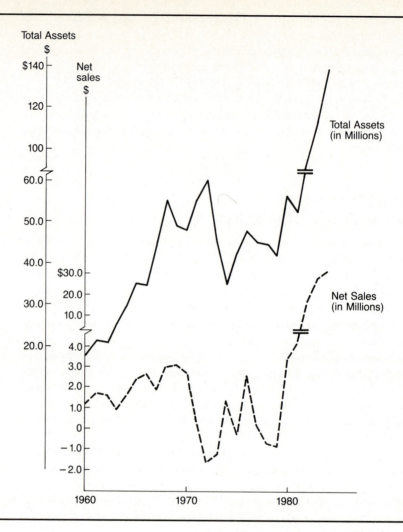

Special tax treatment

Investment companies receive special tax treatment. Their earnings (i.e., dividend and interest income) and capital gains are exempt from taxation at the corporate level. Instead, these profits are taxed through their stockholders' income tax returns. Dividends, interest income, and capital gains realized (whether they are distributed or not) by the investment companies must be reported by their shareholders, who pay the appropriate income taxes.

Their income and gains
are distributed

For this reason, income that is received by investment companies and capital gains that are realized are usually distributed. The companies, however, offer their stockholders the option of having the firm retain and reinvest these distributions. While such reinvestments do not erase the stockholders' tax liabilities, they are an easy, convenient means to accumulate shares. The advantages offered by the dividend reinvestment plans of individual firms that were discussed in Chapter 15 also apply to the dividend reinvestment plans offered by investment companies. Certainly the most

important of these advantages is the element of forced savings. Since the stockholder does not receive the money, there is no temptation to spend it. Rather, the funds are immediately channeled back into additional income-earning assets.

One term frequently encountered in a discussion of an investment company is its **net asset value**. The net asset value of an investment company is the total value of its stocks, bonds, cash, and other assets minus any liabilities (e.g., accrued fees). The net value of any share of stock in the investment company is the total net asset value of the fund divided by the number of shares outstanding. Thus, net asset value may be obtained as follows:

The net asset value

Value of stock owned	$ 1,000,000
Value of debt owned	+1,500,000
Value of total assets	$ 2,500,000
Liabilities	− 100,000
Net worth	$ 2,400,000
Number of shares outstanding	1,000,000
Net asset value per share	$2.40

The net asset value is extremely important for the valuation of an investment company, for it gives the value of the shares should the company be liquidated. Changes in the net asset value, then, alter the value of the investment company's shares. Thus, if the value of the firm's assets appreciates, the net asset value will increase, which may also cause the price of the investment company's stock to increase.

CLOSED-END INVESTMENT COMPANIES

As was explained in the previous section, the difference between open-end and closed-end investment companies is the nature of their capital structure. The closed-end investment company has a set capital structure that may be composed of all stock or a combination of stock and debt. The number of shares and the dollar amount of debts that the company may issue are specified. In an open-end investment company (i.e., a mutual fund), the number of shares outstanding varies as investors purchase and redeem them. Since the closed-end investment company has a specified number of shares, an individual who wants to invest in a particular company must purchase existing shares from current stockholders. Conversely, any investor who owns shares and wishes to liquidate the position must sell the shares. Thus, the shares in closed-end investment companies are bought and sold in the open market, just as the stock of IBM is traded. Shares of these companies are traded on the New York Stock Exchange (e.g., Adams Express), on the American Stock Exchange (e.g., Realty Income Trust), and in the over-the-counter markets (e.g., American Equity REIT[3]). Sales and prices of these shares are reported in the financial press along with the shares of other firms.

The fixed capital structure

The market value of these shares is related to the potential return on the investment. The market price of stock in a closed-end company, however, need not be the net asset value per share; it may be above or below this value, depending on the de-

The premium and the discount

---

[3] Many AMEX and OTC closed-end investment companies are real estate investment trusts.

Exhibit 22.1
Net Asset Value and
Market Prices of
Selected Closed-end
Investment Companies
as of December 31, 1985

Company	Price	Net Asset Value	Discount or (Premium) as a Percentage of Net Asset Value
Adams Express	$19⅜	$20.31	4.6%
Drexel Bond-Debenture Trust	21⅞	20.26	(7.4)
General American Investors	19¼	20.42	6.1
The Japan Fund	13⅝	15.28	10.8
Tri-Continental	29⅜	29.49	nil

Source: *Standard & Poor's Stock Guide,* Year-end Issue, 1985.

mand and the supply of stock in the secondary market. If the market price is below the net asset value of the shares, the shares are selling for a **discount.** If the market price is above the net asset value, the shares are selling for a **premium.**

The cause of the discount   These differences between the investment company's net asset value per share and the stock price are illustrated in Exhibit 22.1, which gives the price, the net asset value, and the discount or the premium as of the end of 1985 for five closed-end investment companies. Three of the shares sold for a discount (i.e., below their net asset values) and only one sold for a premium. The cause of this discount is not really known, but it is believed to be the result of taxation. The potential impact of capital gains taxation on the price of the shares is illustrated in the following example.

A closed-end investment company initially sells stock for $10 per share and uses the proceeds to buy the stock of other companies. If transaction costs are ignored, the net asset value of a share is $10, and the shares may trade in the secondary market for $10. The value of the firm's portfolio subsequently rises to $16 (i.e., the net asset value is $16). The firm has a potential capital gain of $6 per share. If it is realized and these profits are distributed, the net asset value will return to $10 and each stockholder will receive $6 in capital gains, for which he or she will pay the appropriate capital gains tax.

Suppose, however, that the capital gains are not realized (i.e., the net asset value remains $16). What will the market price of the stock be? This is difficult to determine, but it will probably be below $16. Why? Suppose an investor bought a share for $16 and the firm then realized and distributed the $6 capital gain. After the distribution of the $6, the investor would be responsible for any capital gains tax, but the net asset value of the share would decrease to $10.

Obviously this is not advantageous to the buyer. Individuals may only be willing to purchase the shares at a discount that reduces the potential impact of realized capital gains and the subsequent capital gains taxes. Suppose the share had cost $14 (i.e., it sold for a discount of $2 from the net asset value), and the firm realized and distributed the gain. The buyer who paid $14 now owns a share with a net asset value of $10 and receives a capital gain of $6. Although this investor will have to pay the appropriate capital gains tax, the impact is reduced because the investor paid only $14 to purchase the share whose total value is $16 (the $10 net asset value plus the $6 capital gain).

The discount or the   Since the shares may sell for a discount or a premium relative to their net asset
premium may change   value, it is possible for the market price of a closed-end investment company to fluctu-

ate more or less than the net asset value. For example, the net asset value of Adams Express (presented in Exhibit 22.1) rose from $14.51 to $20.31 (a 40 percent increase), but the stock increased 58 percent (12¼ to 19⅜) as the discount fell from 15.6 to 4.6 percent. Since the market price can change relative to the net asset value, an investor is subject to an additional source of risk. The value of the investment may decline not only because the net asset value may decrease but also because the shares may sell for a larger discount from their net asset value.

Some investors view the market price relative to the net asset value as a guide to buying and selling the shares of a closed-end investment company. If the shares are selling for a sufficient discount, they are considered for purchase. If the shares are selling for a small discount or at a premium, they are considered for sale. Of course, determining the premium that will justify the sale or the discount that will justify the purchase is not simple.

Sources of Profit from Investing in Closed-end Investment Companies

Profits are the difference between costs and revenues. Investing in closed-end investment companies involves several costs. First, since the shares are purchased on the open market, there is the brokerage commission for the purchase and for any subsequent sale. Second, the investment company charges a fee to operate the assets. This fee is subtracted from any income that the firm's assets earn. These management fees range from 1 to 2 percent of the net asset value. Third, when the investment company purchases or sells securities, it also has to pay brokerage fees, which are passed on to the investor.

Other investments may not involve these costs

The purchase of shares in closed-end investment companies thus involves three costs that the investor must bear. Some alternative investments, such as savings accounts in commercial banks, do not involve these costs. Although commission fees are incurred when stock is purchased through a broker, the other expenses associated with a closed-end investment company are avoided. However, the investment company does relieve the individual of some of the cost of storing securities and keeping the records necessary for the preparation of tax papers.

The sources of profit

Investors in closed-end investment companies may earn profits in a variety of ways. If the investment company collects dividends and interest on its portfolio of assets, this income is distributed to the stockholders in the form of dividends. Second, if the value of the firm's assets increases, the company may sell the assets and realize profits. These profits are then distributed as capital gains to the stockholders. Third, the net asset value of the portfolio may increase, which will cause the market price of the company's stock to rise. In this case the investor may sell the shares in the market and realize a capital gain. Fourth, the market price of the shares may rise relative to the net asset value (i.e., the premium may increase or the discount may decrease); the investor may then earn a profit through the sale of the shares.

These sources of profit are illustrated in Exhibit 22.2, which presents the distributions and price changes for Lehman Corporation from December 31, 1981, through December 31, 1985. As may be seen from this exhibit, the firm distributed cash dividends of $0.495 and capital gains of $1.085 in 1985. The net asset value rose from $14.67 to $16.78 and the price of the stock likewise rose (from $15 to $16 at 12/31/

Exhibit 22.2
Annual Returns on an Investment in Lehman Corp., a Closed-end Investment Company

Distributions and Price Changes	1985	1984	1983	1982	1981
Per-share income distributions	$0.495	0.545	0.625	0.71	0.72
Per-share capital gains distributions	$1.085	2.44	1.365	2.01	2.04
Year-end net asset value	$16.78	14.67	18.25	16.64	15.56
Year-end market price	$16.00	15.00	18.625	17.375	14.875
Annual return based on prior year's market price					
a. Dividend yield	3.3%	2.9	3.6	4.8	4.5
b. Capital gains yield	7.2%	13.1	7.9	13.5	16.8
c. Change in price	6.7%	(19.5)	7.2	16.8	(7.0)
Total return	17.2%	(3.5)	18.7	35.1	10.3

The potential for loss

85). An investor who bought these shares in December 1984 and sold them in December 1985 earned a return of 17.2 percent on the investment.

The potential for loss is also illustrated in Exhibit 22.2. If an investor bought the shares on December 31, 1983, he or she suffered a loss during 1984. While Lehman distributed $0.545 per share in income and $2.44 in capital gains, the net asset value and the price of the stock decline sufficiently to more than offset the income and capital gains distributions.

UNIT TRUSTS

A variation on the closed-end investment company is the fixed-unit investment trust, commonly referred to as a **unit trust**. These trusts, which are formed by brokerage firms and sold to investors in units of $1,000, hold a fixed portfolio of securities such as federal government or corporate bonds, municipal bonds, or mortgage loans. An example of such a trust is Merrill Lynch's Government Securities Income Fund, which invested solely in U.S. Treasury securities and other obligations backed by the full faith and credit of the federal government.

Frozen assets

A unit trust is a passive investment, as its assets are not traded but are frozen. The trust collects income (e.g., interest on its portfolio) and, eventually, the repayment of principal. The trust is also self-liquidating because as the funds are received, they are not reinvested but are distributed to stockholders. Since the trust's portfolio is fixed and not altered, operating expenses are low. Such trusts are primarily attractive to investors such as retirees who seek a steady, periodic flow of payments. If the investor needs the funds earlier, the shares may be sold back to the trust at their current net asset value.

MUTUAL FUNDS

Open-end investment companies

Open-end investment companies, which are commonly called mutual funds, are similar to closed-end investment companies. However, there are some important differences. The first concerns their capital structure. Shares in mutual funds are not traded

Exhibit 22.3
**Loading Charges for
Selected Mutual Funds**

American Balanced Fund	8.5%
American Growth Fund	8.5
Dean Witter High Yield Fund	5.5
Eagle Growth Fund	8.5
Franklin Group Gold Fund	7.3
Lord Abbott Government Securities	6.7
Merrill Lynch Basic Value Fund	6.5

like other stocks and bonds. Instead, an investor who wants a position in a particular mutual fund purchases shares directly from the company. After receiving the money, the mutual fund issues new shares and purchases assets with these newly acquired funds. If an investor owns shares in the fund and wants to liquidate the position, the shares are sold back to the company. The shares are redeemed, and the fund pays the investor from its cash holdings. If the fund lacks sufficient cash, it will sell some of the securities it owns to obtain the money to redeem the shares. The fund cannot suspend this redemption feature except in an emergency, and then it may be done only with the permission of the Securities and Exchange Commission (SEC).

Loading fees

A second important difference between open-end and closed-end investment companies pertains to the cost of investing. Mutual funds continuously offer to sell new shares, and these shares are sold at their net asset value plus a sales fee, which is commonly called a *loading charge*. When the investor liquidates the position, the shares are redeemed at their net asset value. For most funds no additional fees are charged for the sale.

The loading fee may range from zero for **no-load mutual funds** to between 5 and 9.3 percent for **load funds**. Exhibit 22.3 presents the loading fees for ten mutual funds. Although these fees vary, 8.5 percent is the most common figure.

The fees may vary with the amount invested

If the individual makes a substantial investment, the loading fee is usually reduced. For example, the American Balanced Fund offers the following schedule of fees:

Investment	Fee
$ 25,000	6%
50,000	4.5
100,000	3.5
250,000	2.5

The investor should be warned that mutual funds state the loading charge as a percentage of the *offer* price. The effect of the fee being a percentage of the offer price and not a percentage of the net asset value is an increase in the effective percentage charged. If the loading charge is 8 percent and the offer price is $10, then the loading fee is $0.80. However, the net asset value is $9.20 ($10 minus $0.80). In this example, the loading charge as a percentage of the net asset value is 8.7 percent ($8.0\%/[1 - 0.08]$ $= 8.0/0.92 = 8.7\%$), which is higher than the stated 8 percent loading charge.

No-load funds

It is immediately apparent which funds are no-load funds by the way in which mutual fund prices are quoted. Exhibit 22.4, which reproduces a quotation of mutual

Exhibit 22.4
Offer price and Net
Asset Value (NAV) for
Selected Mutual Funds

MUTUAL FUNDS

Thursday, January 2, 1986
Price ranges for investment companies, as quoted by the
National Association of Securities Dealers. NAV stands for
net asset value per share; the offering includes net asset
value plus maximum sales charge, if any.

	NAV	Offer NAV Price Chg.			NAV	Offer NAV Price Chg.
AARP Invest Program:				Constlatn	21.62	N.L.− .17
Cap Grw	19.12	N.L.− .09		Copley Fd	9.35	N.L.− .03
Gen Bnd	15.76	N.L.− .01		Coutry Cap	17.74	19.18− .16
Ginnie M	15.95	N.L.+ .01		**Criterion Funds:**		
Gro Inc	19.13	N.L.− .05		Cm IncS	10.11	11.05− .02
TxFr Bd	15.62	N.L.+ .05		Inv Qual	10.42	10.91+ .01
TxF Shrt	15.26	N.L.+ .07		Lowry M	9.71	10.61− .07
ABT Midwest Funds:		......		Pilot Fd	9.37	10.24− .10
Emrg Gr	15.43	16.86− .07		Qlty TF	10.46	10.95+ .01
Growth I	12.30	13.44− .04		Sunblt G	16.18	17.68− .13
Int Govt	10.48	N.L. ...		US Govt	10.27	11.01− .01
LG Govt	10.90	11.35 ...		**Dean Witter:**		
Sec Inc	10.95	11.97+ .01		Cal TxFr	11.42	N.L.+ .01
Util Inc	16.37	17.89− .05		Convrt	10.48	N.L.− .03
Acorn Fnd	37.65	N.L.− .17		DevlGr r	8.77	N.L.− .03
Adtek Fd	10.88	N.L.+ .01		Div Grw	16.28	N.L.− .07
Afuture Fd	13.32	N.L.− .06		High Yld	13.70	14.50− .01
AIM Funds:				Ind Val r	12.61	N.L.− .06
Conv Yld	12.28	13.13+ .01		Nat Resr	7.35	N.L.− .02
Grnway	10.11	10.81− .07		NY TxFr	10.58	N.L.+ .01
HIYld Sc	10.00	10.70 ...		Option In	10.09	N.L.− .03
Summit	6.45	(z) − .04		Sears Tx	11.42	N.L.+ .02
American Funds Group:				**Drexel Burnham:**		....
Am Bal	11.60	12.68− .05		DB Fund	21.80	22.59− .15
Amcap F	9.54	10.43− .06		Drexl Gv	xd10.59	N.L.− .28
Am Mutl	xd16.59	18.13− .29		Drxl Opt	xd10.21	N.L.− .35
Bnd FdA	14.02	15.32+ .01		ST Grow	xd11.27	N.L.− .53
Eupac	18.74	20.48+ .10		ST Emrg	d13.18	N.L.− .21
Fund Inv	14.26	15.58− .10		**Dreyfus Group:**		
Govt	14.78	15.52+ .02		A Bonds	x14.48	N.L.− .13
Gth FdA	14.44	15.78− .07		CalT Ex	14.16	N.L.+ .03
Inc FdA	x11.55	12.62− .23		Dreyf Fd	13.84	15.13− .03
I C A	13.43	14.68− .08		Dreyf Lv	18.07	19.75 ...
Nw Econ	19.43	21.23− .11		GNMA	x15.59	N.L.− .14
Nw Prsp	9.08	9.92− .02		Growth	11.64	N.L.+ .05
Tax Ex	10.51	11.03+ .01		Insr TE	16.95	N.L.+ .09
Wash Mt	10.96	11.98− .08		Intrmd	13.18	N.L.+ .02

Source: The Wall Street Journal, January 3, 1986, p. 22. Reprinted by permission of *The Wall Street Journal,*
© Dow Jones & Company, Inc. 1986. All Rights Reserved.

fund prices from *The Wall Street Journal,* illustrates this difference. The publication
reports the net asset value (NAV), the offer price, and any change in the asset value
from the previous day. If the offer price and the net asset value are the same (i.e., if the
fund has no loading charge), "N.L." is printed in the offer price column. For example,
the Acorn Fund has a net asset value of $37.65, and "N.L." appears in the offer col-
umn. Thus, these shares may be bought and sold from the company at their net asset
value.

The quotation of funds with loading fees includes the net asset value and the offer
price. For example, American Balanced Fund has a net asset value of $11.60 per share
and an offer price of $12.68. It is a load fund. The buyer pays $1.08 ($12.68 − 11.60)
to purchase a share worth $11.60. Such a charge is 8.5 percent of the asking price and
9.3 percent of the net asset value.

In addition to loading charges, investors in mutual funds have to pay management fees, which are deducted from the income earned by the fund's portfolio. The
fund also pays brokerage commissions when it buys and sells securities. The total cost
of investing in mutual funds may be substantial when all of the costs (the loading

POINTS OF INTEREST
Dollar Cost Averaging and Mutual Funds

One of the advantages offered investors by mutual funds is dollar cost averaging. As was explained in Chapter 13, an individual may make equal, periodic investments. With such a strategy, the investor acquires fewer shares when prices rise but more shares when prices fall. The larger purchases reduce the average cost of a share, and, if the value of the stock subsequently rises, the low-cost stock generates more capital gains.

While the individual may follow such a strategy by purchasing stock through brokers, transaction fees reduce the attractiveness of dollar cost averaging, especially if the individual is investing a modest amount (e.g., less than $500). Transaction costs may be eliminated or at least reduced

through the use of mutual funds. While avoidance of fees is obvious in the case of no load funds, reduction in costs may also apply to load funds. Consider a load fund that charges 8½ percent. If an individual seeks to invest $300 a month, the load fee will be $25.50. Many brokers may not execute such a small order. If they do buy $300 worth of stock, brokerage firms (including discount brokerage firms) will charge the minimum commission, which is generally $30 to $40. Thus even with loading fees, mutual funds can still offer investors with modest sums a cheaper means to achieve the advantage associated with dollar cost averaging.

charge and management and brokerage fees) are considered. Of course, the cost of investing is substantially reduced when the individual buys shares in no-load funds. The investor, however, must still pay the management fees and commission costs.

Sources of profit

The third difference between closed-end and open-end investment companies is the source of profits to the investor. As with closed-end investment companies, individuals may profit from investments in mutual funds from several sources. Any income that is earned from the fund's assets in excess of expenses is distributed as dividends. If the fund's assets appreciate in value and the fund realizes these profits, the gains are distributed as capital gains. If the net asset value of the shares appreciates, the investor may redeem them at the appreciated price. Thus, in general, the open-end mutual fund offers investors the same means of earning profits as the closed-end investment company does, with one exception. In the case of closed-end investment companies, the price of the stock may rise relative to the net asset value of the shares. The possibility of a decreased discount or an increased premium is a potential source of profit that is available only through closed-end investment companies. It does not exist for mutual funds because their shares never sell at a discount.[4] Hence, changes in the discount or premium are a source of profit or loss to investors in closed-end but not in open-end investment companies.

Sources of risk

While purchases of shares in investment companies may generate profits, they also subject the investor to risk. In Chapters 1 and 8 several sources of risk were discussed. These included the risk associated with investments in the securities of a par-

---

[4] Load funds are actually sold at a premium (i.e., the loading fee).

ticular firm (e.g., the stocks and bonds issued by AT&T). Since investment companies construct diversified portfolios, the impact of a particular investment on the outcome of the portfolio as a whole is reduced. Thus, the risk associated with an individual firm's securities is small (if not nonexistent).[5]

Systematic risk

Other sources of risk, however, cannot be eliminated through the purchases of shares of investment companies. If security prices in general rise (or fall), the value of the investment company's portfolio will probably also rise (or fall). The managements of investment companies cannot consistently predict changes in the market and adjust their portfolios accordingly. The value of investment companies' portfolios and the value of their shares tend to move systematically with the market as a whole. Thus the risk associated with movements in the market is not eliminated through the purchase of shares in investment companies.

Purchasing power risk

Inflation is also another source of risk that cannot be eliminated by acquiring shares in investment companies. If the return these firms earn is insufficient (i.e., is below the rate of inflation), their stockholders experience a loss of purchasing power. It is even possible that the value of the investment company's stock may decline while inflation continues, in which case the investors are worse off than if they had held a regular savings account with a commercial bank.

The Portfolios of Mutual Funds

Income funds

The portfolios of investment companies may be diversified or very specialized, but most may be classified into one of four types: income, growth, special situations, and balanced. Income funds stress assets that produce income; they buy stocks and bonds that pay generous dividends or interest income. The Value Line Income Fund is an example of a fund whose objective is income. Virtually all of its assets are income stocks, such as those of utilities, which pay generous dividends and periodically increase them as their earnings grow.

Growth funds

Growth funds stress appreciation in the value of the assets, and little emphasis is given to current income. The portfolio of the Value Line Fund is an example of a growth fund. The majority of the assets are the common stocks of companies with potential for growth. These **growth stocks** include the shares of very well known firms as well as those of smaller firms that may offer superior growth potential.

Even within the class of growth funds there can be many differences. Some stress riskier securities in order to achieve larger returns and faster appreciation in their investors' funds. For example, the 44 Wall Street Fund seeks capital appreciation by investing in riskier securities including new issues, over-the-counter stocks, and warrants. Other growth funds, however, are more conservative. The Delaware Fund is a growth fund emphasizing larger companies that still are considered to offer capital appreciation.

Special situations

Special situation investment companies specialize in more speculative securities that, given the "special situation," may yield large returns. These investment companies are perhaps the riskiest of all the mutual funds. The portfolio of Value Line Special Situation Fund illustrates this element of risk. The stocks in this portfolio tend

---

[5]The investor still must bear the unsystematic risk associated with the individual investment company. This source of risk is reduced by investing in several investment companies.

to be in small companies or companies that have fallen on bad times but whose course may be changing. Investments in special situation securities can be very rewarding but some do not fulfill their potential return.

Balanced funds own a mixture of securities that sample the attributes of the assets of other mutual funds. A balanced fund, such as the Sentinel Group Balanced Fund, owns a variety of stocks, some of which offer potential growth while others are primarily income producers. A balanced portfolio may include short-term debt (such as U.S. Treasury bills), long-term debt, and preferred stock. Such a portfolio seeks a balance of income from dividends and interest and capital appreciation. *Balanced funds*

Many investment companies manage a wide spectrum of mutual funds. Each fund has a separate goal and hence has a different portfolio designed to achieve the fund's purpose. As may be seen in Exhibit 22.4, the American Funds Group offers investors the choice among numerous different mutual funds covering a wide spectrum of investment alternatives. The individual may choose any combination of these funds. For example, an investor who seeks income may acquire shares in the equity income fund, the government securities fund, and the bond fund. Such investments would give that individual a diversified portfolio of income-earning assets.

In addition to offering a variety of funds from which to choose, companies that manage several mutual funds may permit the investor to shift investments from one fund to another fund without paying any fees. For example, an individual who is currently employed may seek capital appreciation and invest in a growth-oriented fund but on retirement may shift the proceeds to a bond fund to collect a flow of interest income. Such a shift could be achieved by converting the shares in the growth fund into shares of the bond fund. In many cases this switch may be made without the investor paying any commissions on the transaction. *Shifting among funds*

The Portfolios of Specialized Mutual Funds

Investment trusts initially sought to pool the funds of many savers and to invest these funds in a diversified portfolio of assets. Such diversification spread the risk of investing and reduced the risk of loss to the individual investor. While a particular investment company had a specified goal, such as growth or income, the portfolio was still sufficiently diversified so that the element of unsystematic risk was reduced. *Diversification and the distribution of risk*

Today, however, a variety of funds have developed that have moved away from this concept of diversification and the reduction of risk. Instead of offering investors a cross section of American business, many funds have been created to offer investors specialized investments. For example, an investment company may be limited to investments in the securities of a particular sector of the economy or particular industry, such as gold (e.g., ASA, Limited). There are also funds that specialize in a particular type of security, such as bonds (e.g., American General Bond Fund). *Special investment companies*

During the 1970s the scope of some investment companies became even narrower. For example, the Dreyfus Merger and Acquisition Fund, which originated in 1978, seeks to identify firms that are potential candidates for merger or take-over by other firms. Such mergers and take-overs often result in substantial profits for the stockholders of the target firms. These profits can be even larger if two firms seek to take over a third company and a bidding war erupts. The management of the Dreyfus Merger and Acquisition Fund tries to identify the stocks of companies that appear to

be underpriced and that may be bought out at substantial premiums over their current prices. Obviously, this is a very specialized fund, and its investors bear two considerable risks not borne by investors in the traditional mutual fund. These risks involve (1) the ability of the fund's management to identify take-over candidates and (2) the possibility that the mergers and take-overs will not actually occur. If a stock is underpriced but no one seeks to take over the firm, then the stock may remain underpriced for a long period of time![6]

Perhaps the extreme in specialized funds arose in October 1978, when the shares of Gaming Funds Incorporated were registered with the SEC. This fund specializes in gaming and sports investments. The securities it purchases may even include stocks for which there is no secondary market. Furthermore, the fund employs speculative techniques, such as short selling and the use of financial leverage. Obviously such a fund does not offer the advantages of diversification and risk reduction that are offered by traditional mutual funds.

Specialized mutual funds

In addition to these speculative funds, several specialized investment companies have been established that offer real alternatives to the traditional types of mutual funds. For example, money market mutual funds, which were discussed in Chapter 2, provide the individual with a means to invest indirectly in money market instruments such as treasury bills and negotiable certificates of deposit. Funds that acquire foreign securities offer the individual a means to invest in stocks of companies located in Europe and Asia. (The discussion of these funds is deferred to Chapter 26.) Other specialized funds include index funds and tax-exempt funds.

Index funds

The purpose of an **index fund** is almost diametrically opposed to the traditional purpose of a mutual fund. Instead of identifying specific securities for purchase, the managements of these funds seek to duplicate the composition of an index, such as Standard & Poor's 500 stock index. Such funds should then perform in tandem with the market as a whole. Although they cannot generally outperform the market, neither can they underperform the market. In a sense, these funds have a defeatist attitude: Because they cannot beat the market, they try to avoid earning a return less than that of the market as a whole. Part of the popularity of such funds has been attributed to the poor performance of mutual funds in general in the past. (The returns earned by mutual funds will be discussed later in this chapter.) While these funds cannot overcome any risk associated with price fluctuations in the market as a whole, they do eliminate the risk associated with the selection of specific securities.

Tax-exempt funds

Another recently introduced specialized mutual fund is the investment company whose portfolio is devoted to tax-exempt bonds. Until 1976, open-end mutual funds were legally barred from this market. However, with the passage of enabling legislation, mutual funds were permitted to own tax-exempt bonds, and several funds were immediately started that specialize in tax-exempt securities. These funds offer investors, especially those with modest funds to invest, an opportunity to earn tax-free income and maintain a diversified portfolio. Since municipal bonds are sold in minimum units of $5,000, a sizable sum is required for an individual investor to obtain a diversified portfolio. Ten bonds of ten different state and local governments

---

[6] The efficient market hypothesis suggests that such undervaluations will quickly disappear. If a firm were a take-over candidate, its price should already discount that information.

would cost about $50,000.[7] The advantages of tax-free income and a reduction in risk were virtually impossible for most investors.

However, mutual funds that specialize in tax-exempt bonds offer small investors both of these advantages. The funds are sold in smaller denominations. For example, $1,000 may be the minimum initial investment, and additional investments may be made for as little as $100. The ability to buy in small denominations means that modest investors may buy shares in these funds. Since the firms pool the funds of many investors, small investors also obtain the advantage of diversification.

SELECTING MUTUAL FUNDS

Selecting a mutual fund requires matching the goals of the investor and the objectives of the fund. The individual's need for custodial services, diversification, and professional management also affect the selection. In addition, there are several subtle factors that can have an impact on the decision to acquire the shares of a particular mutual fund, including taxation, the maturity of the fund and its management, and rates of return. These considerations may affect not only the decision to purchase mutual funds instead of other investments but also the decision to purchase a particular fund instead of another competing fund.

There are several hundred mutual funds from which to choose. Obviously the investor cannot buy shares in all of them but must select among the alternatives. Thus, while investment companies may relieve individuals from selecting particular stocks and bonds, they do not relieve investors from having to select among the mutual funds that meet the individual's financial goals (e.g., growth or income).[8]

The need to choose

The choice is not easy. The individual should obtain a fund's prospectus, which states the fund's goals, current portfolio, and recent performance, the services offered, and fees charged. Funds with loading fees also have sales staffs who are a source of information concerning the funds (although the investor will be subjected to a certain degree of sales pressure). No-load funds do not have sales staffs, so information concerning these funds may be obtained by directly writing to the fund.

Obtain the prospectus

The investor can obtain addresses and a substantial amount of information concerning all investment companies by reading the publications of Wiesenberger Service, Inc. This firm annually publishes a summary of investment company performance and illustrates the growth in the fund under the assumption that the individual reinvests income and capital gains distributions. Wiesenberger publications are standard references on investment companies and should be available in local libraries. The securities held by each investment company may be found in *Moody's Investment Company Manual,* which is published annually. *Forbes* and *Barron's* also publish annual summaries of investment company results. The investor, however, should remember that past performance need not be indicative of future performance.

Published material

---

[7] Like all debt instruments, tax-exempt bonds may sell for a discount, so the investor may be able to acquire $50,000 face amount for less than a $50,000 cash outlay.

[8] There are mutual funds that specialize in acquiring the shares of other funds. Their managements seek to identify which funds will perform best under varying economic conditions. These funds relieve the investor from selecting among the various funds, but he or she in effect pays two management fees for the selection of assets.

Hidden Capital Gains

Sources of taxation

As was explained earlier, investment companies receive favorable tax treatment—they pay no federal income tax. They are a conduit through which income and capital gains are passed to stockholders. The investor ultimately has to pay any applicable taxes on the profits earned on the investment or by the fund. If the value of the shares increases and the investor sells them for a profit, he or she will have to pay any applicable capital gains taxes. If the mutual fund earns income, the individual stockholder pays the appropriate income tax on those earnings. If the mutual fund realizes capital gains on its portfolio, the investor must pay any capital gains taxes.

Taxes can have an important impact on the individual's selection of a particular fund. Besides creating problems for tax planning, taxation alters the net return the investor earns. As is explained in the section on rates of return, taxation reduces the individual's ability to compare his or her return on money invested in the fund with the performance claimed by the fund's management. Taxation may even offer the investor an opportunity for profit by investing in funds with tax losses. However, the main concern is that even though the fund's objectives are consistent with those of the individual the fund's management still may not follow a policy that is in the best interests of the individual investor's tax strategy.

Hidden capital gains

The individual mutual fund can have built into its portfolio the potential for a considerable tax liability that may not be obvious to the investor. In some cases this liability may fall on investors who do not experience the gains. This potential tax liability is the result of the fund experiencing paper profits on its portfolio (i.e., profits that have not been realized). As long as the gains are not realized, there will be no taxation, which only occurs once the investment company sells the appreciated assets and thus realizes the capital gain.

This potential tax liability is perhaps best seen by a simple illustration. If a mutual fund is started by selling shares for $10, (excluding costs) the net asset value of a share is $10. The fund invests the money in various securities, which appreciate in value during the year. At the end of the year the net asset value of a share is now $14. Since the fund has not sold any of its holdings, its stockholders have no tax liability.

This fund is a going concern and like all mutual funds offers to redeem its shares and sell additional shares to investors. Suppose an original investor redeems shares at the net asset value of $14. This individual has a capital gain because the value of the shares rose from the initial offer price of $10 to $14. Such a capital gain is independent of whether or not the fund realizes the capital gain on its portfolio, because the investor realizes the gain.

Suppose, however, this individual had not redeemed the shares but continued to hold them. The fund then realizes the $4 per share profit and distributes the capital gain. Once again this investor must pay the appropriate capital gains tax. These two cases are exactly what the investor should expect. If the investor redeems the shares and realizes the gain or if the fund realizes the gain, the individual stockholder is responsible for the taxes.

Taxation of distributions

It is, however, possible for an investor to be responsible for the tax without experiencing the capital gain. Suppose the individual purchases shares at the current net asset value of $14 for a cost basis of $14. On the next day the management of the fund realizes the profits on the portfolio (i.e., sells its securities) and distributes the capital gain. The investors who purchased the initial shares at $10 have earned a profit and

must pay any appropriate capital gains tax. The individual who has just purchased the shares for $14 also receives a capital gain distribution and thus is also subject to the capital gains tax. Even though this investor paid $14 per share, that individual is the holder of record for the distribution and thus is responsible for the tax.

When the capital gain distribution is made, the value of the stock declines. In this illustration the net asset value of the shares declines by $4 (i.e., the amount of the distribution) to $10. The investor who bought the shares for $14 could offset the $4 distribution by redeeming the shares. Since the shares cost $14 but are now worth only $10, this investor sustains a $4 loss. Such a sale offsets the distribution, and thus the stockholder no longer has any tax obligation. However, the original purchase, the redemption, and any subsequent reinvestment may involve transaction costs that this investor must bear. So the stockholder loses either through having to pay the capital gains tax or having to absorb the fees associated with the redemption designed to offset the tax necessitated by the distribution.

Could the individual have anticipated this potential tax liability? The answer is "Yes" when the investor realizes that the source of the tax is the unrealized capital gains embodied in the mutual fund's net asset value. If a fund's portfolio has risen in value, the fund has unrealized capital gains. When the gains are realized, they accrue to the shareholders to whom they are distributed. These shareholders are not necessarily the stockholders who owned shares when the appreciation occurred. If the individual were to determine the cost basis of the fund's portfolio and the current value of that portfolio, any unrealized capital gains would be apparent. If, for example, the fund has $100,000,000 in assets that cost only $60,000,000, there is $40,000,000 in unrealized gains. If these profits are realized, they will create tax liabilities for current stockholders, not former stockholders.[9]

Unrealized capital gains

Hidden Capital Losses

While the existence of unrealized gains implies the potential for future tax liabilities, the existence of unrealized capital losses offers the possibility of tax-free gains. Suppose a mutual fund started with a net asset value of $10 but as the result of a declining market currently has a net asset value of $6. Any individual who originally bought the shares at $10 and now has redeemed them for $6 has sustained a capital loss, and he or she will use that loss to offset other capital gains or income (up to the limit allowed by the current tax code).

Unrealized capital losses

If, however, an individual purchases shares at the current net asset value of $6, the value of the portfolio could rise without necessarily creating a tax liability for that investor. Suppose the portfolio's net asset value rises back to $10, at which time the mutual fund sells the securities. Since the cost basis to the fund of the sold securities is $10, the fund has no capital gain. The shareholder has seen the net asset value rise from $6 to $10 without there being any tax liability created by the mutual fund.

If the net asset value continues to rise to $12 and the fund sells the securities, it realizes a $2 gain ($12 − $10). The investor who bought the shares at $6 will only be

---

[9]This tax problem could also be avoided by purchasing the shares after the distribution and the decline in the net asset value. Obviously, ascertaining when the shares may be purchased exclusive of the distribution may save the investor considerable tax expense over a period of years.

subject to capital gains tax on the $2, because the fund's cost basis is $10. The investor has seen his or her investment rise from $6 to $12 but is only subject to tax on the appreciation from $10 to $12. As long as this investor *does not redeem the shares acquired for $6,* the tax on the $4 appreciation from $6 to $10 is deferred even if the mutual fund sells the securities. Thus, if the fund has unrealized losses, this may offer the individual an opportunity for tax savings just as the unrealized capital gains may create future tax liabilities.

The investor should realize that a fund with unrealized losses is not necessarily an attractive investment. The losses may be the result of inept management, and if such performance continues, the fund will generate larger losses. However, if the investor believes that the fund will be acquired or will turn around and perform well so that its net asset value increases, the unrealized tax losses embodied in the fund's portfolio can magnify the after-tax return the investor earns.

Tax Swapping

Acquiring pairs of funds

The ability to take tax losses on an investment in a mutual fund offers another possible strategy to increase the individual's return. Unlike the previous strategy, in which the shares of funds with tax losses were acquired, in this strategy the investor purchases shares in two similar funds (e.g., two modest-sized growth funds). If the shares of one of the funds decline in value, the shares are sold and the proceeds of the sales are then used to acquire additional shares in the fund that has not declined in value. Since the investor continues to hold the original position in the second fund, there is no tax obligation. The loss, however, is used to offset other capital gains or ordinary income.

This strategy is then repeated. The investor always acquires similar pairs of mutual funds and sells the inferior performer. The investor does not sell the shares of the fund that have appreciated in the same year in which the losses are taken, because under current laws capital losses and capital gains are netted out. The object of the strategy is to take losses to offset income from other sources and to increase the investor's position in the better performing mutual fund.[10]

Mature versus New Funds

Track records

All funds had to be created. Those that have been successful have grown as the value of their portfolio has appreciated and as investors have purchased additional shares. Should an investor purchase the shares of new funds or those with the advantage of established track records? *Forbes* annually publishes performance ratings of mutual funds and separates performance into rising and declining markets. Thus, the investor can learn how well a fund has performed when security prices rose and how well the fund protected capital during a period of declining security prices.

---

[10] Such a strategy is referred to by Gerald Perritt as "semi-active trading." Perritt suggests that for individuals in the higher marginal tax brackets, such a strategy significantly increases the after-tax return earned by portfolios. (See Gerald W. Perritt, "Semi-active Trading: A Strategy for a Taxing Problem," *American Association of Individual Investors Journal,* (November 1984), 24–26.) It should be noted that such a strategy may work for the selection of individual stocks in which the investor purchases the shares of two similar companies, subsequently weeds out the poorer performer, and invests the proceeds in the better performing stock.

A fund's performance record is also a record of its management. While the fund has an indeterminant life, portfolio managers change with the passage of time. The individuals who guided the fund during the period of its initial success and growth may no longer be associated with the fund. A change in a fund's management may reduce continuity and alter investment philosophy. The investor should not assume that new management will be able to match a prior management's record.

Over time mutual funds grow by issuing new shares. As the fund expands, its capacity to perform may decline. It is easier for a small fund to move in and out of the market when it buys or sells in modest-sized blocks. As the fund's portfolio increases, this flexibility decreases. A large fund may be unable to quickly establish a position in an attractive security or to rapidly liquidate a position if the fund is buying or selling large blocks of stock.

Small versus large fund

Even if the fund is able to establish a position, the market makers may require the fund to pay a higher-than-market price to purchase a large block or to accept a lower-than-market price to sell a large block. The effect is to increase transaction costs. Even if the fund negotiates smaller brokerage commissions on the purchase or sale, the total cost, which includes brokerage commissions, the spread between the bid and ask prices, and any price concessions necessary to execute the transactions, may exceed that which an individual investor pays to buy and sell securities.[11]

Large funds may also have difficulty sustaining growth. It is harder to increase by 20 percent the value of a portfolio worth $2,000,000,000 than a portfolio worth $200,000,000. The base for the former portfolio is so large that a decent performance in the value of one of the fund's holdings may have little impact on the fund's total value.

A smaller and newer fund may not have these problems. The fund's size permits it to readily establish a position in a given security or to liquidate the position. It is small enough that a major move in the market or selected holdings is readily discernible in the fund's net asset value. And the young management may have an aggressiveness (or incentive) that generates more growth and success.

Unfortunately a new fund does not have a track record, and investors do not know how well management will perform under varying conditions in the securities markets. The fund may have been created during a bull market and thus management would not have been tested during a period of declining prices. There is also the possibility that only funds that perform well are taken public. For example, a fund may be initially sold privately. If the management is unsuccessful, the shares are never offered to the public, but if it succeeds and the value of the portfolio appreciates, the fund is offered publicly. Management has a record of success that will be detailed in the fund's prospectus. Obviously such previous success will help market the shares.[12] Whether management will be able to sustain the growth once the fund is public and its total assets are larger is not known when the initial public offering of the shares is made.

New versus old fund

---

[11] See Gerald W. Perritt and L. Kay Shannon, *The Individual Investor's Guide to No-Load Mutual Funds* (Chicago: American Association of Individual Investors, 1984), 2–30.

[12] See Randall Smith, "Mutual Funds are Popular Again, Fueled by Strong Marketing," *The Wall Street Journal,* July 13, 1984, 21.

In addition, some funds are created to take advantage of a particular fad or investment opportunity. For example, a fund may be created to invest in high technology stocks or gambling stocks at the height of speculative fever. The investor who purchases shares in the funds is, in effect, paying top dollar for the underlying securities. When the fad ends or these stocks are unable to sustain their previous growth, the net asset value of the fund declines, inflicting losses on its initial investors.

THE RETURNS EARNED ON INVESTMENTS IN MUTUAL FUNDS

The advantages of investment companies

As was previously explained, the securities of investment companies offer individuals several advantages. First, the investor receives the advantages of a diversified portfolio, which reduces risk. Some investors may lack the resources to contruct a diversified portfolio, and the purchase of shares in an investment company permits these investors to own a portion of a diversified portfolio. Second, the portfolio is professionally managed and under continuous supervision. Many investors may not have the time and expertise to manage their own portfolios and, except in the case of large portfolios, may lack the funds to obtain professional management. By purchasing shares in an investment company, individuals buy the services of professional management, which may increase the investor's return. Third, the administrative detail and custodial aspects of the portfolio (e.g., the physical handling of securities) are taken care of by the management of the company.

The disadvantages

Although investment companies offer advantages, there are also disadvantages. The services offered by an investment company are not unique but may be obtained elsewhere. For example, the trust department of a commercial bank offers custodial services, and leaving the securities with the broker and registering them in the broker's name relieves the investor of storing the securities and keeping some of the records. In addition, the investor may acquire a diversified portfolio with only a modest amount of capital. Diversification does not require 100 different stocks. If the investor has $10,000, a reasonably diversified portfolio may be produced by investing in the stock of eight to ten companies in different industries. One does not have to purchase shares in an investment company to obtain the advantage of diversification.

Investment companies do offer the advantage of professional management, but this management cannot guarantee to outperform the market. A particular firm may do well in any given year, but it may do very poorly in subsequent years. Several studies have been undertaken to determine if professional management results in superior performance for mutual funds.

The returns earned

The first study, conducted for the SEC, covered the period from 1952 through 1958.[13] This study found that the performance of mutual funds was not significantly different from that of an unmanaged portfolio of similar assets. About half the funds outperformed Standard & Poor's indices, but the other half underperformed these aggregate measures of the market. In addition, there was no evidence of superior performance by a particular fund over a number of years.

---

[13] See Irwin Friend et al., *A Study of Mutual Funds* (Washington, D.C.: U.S. Government Printing Office, 1962).

These initial results were confirmed by later studies.[14] When the loading changes are included in the analysis, the return earned by investors tends to be less than that which would be achieved through a random selection of securities.

These results are easy to misinterpret. They do not imply that the managements of mutual funds are incompetent. The findings do give strong support for the efficient market hypothesis that was discussed in Chapter 8. In an efficient market, only competent managers would be able to match the market over a period of years. The incompetent would be forced out by their inferior results.

Managements are not incompetent

What these findings do imply is that mutual funds and other investment companies may offer investors a means to match the performance of the market and still obtain the advantages of diversification and custodial services. For some, these are sufficient reasons to invest in the shares of investment companies instead of directly in stocks and bonds. These investors do not have to concern themselves with the selection of individual securities.

A means to match the market

Impact of Taxes on Rates of Return

While returns to mutual funds in the aggregate do not consistently outperform the market, the investor purchases shares in individual funds; thus he or she should compare the individual fund's performance. One method for doing this is to compare them in rising and declining markets. For example, in its annual issue devoted to mutual funds, *Forbes* ranks the funds with regard to their performance in up markets and in down markets.

Sources of comparisons

Another source of comparison is to answer the following question: If $10,000 were invested in the fund, how much would the investor have after five years or ten years, assuming dividends and capital gains distributions were reinvested? *Barron's* publishes the answer to that question in its periodic reviews of mutual fund performance.

While comparisons of funds are possible, the rate of return earned by the fund may not be useful for computing the rate of return earned on an individual's investment in the fund. One important problem concerning calculating the individual's realized rate of return pertains to federal income taxation. For example, suppose a fund has a net asset value of $10. During the year it earns $1 per share in income, which it distributes as dividends. For the individual who owns 100 shares and who participates in the dividend reinvestment plan, the $100 in dividends is used to purchase additional shares. The amount invested in the fund now rises to $1,100. The initial investment has appreciated by 10 percent, but the investor must pay income tax on the distribution. The amount of the tax depends on the individual's marginal tax bracket. If the tax rate is 28 percent, the investor must pay $28. There are essentially two choices—liquidate part of the holdings in the fund or pay the taxes with funds from other sources.

Individual's return may not be comparable to fund's return

If this individual wants to maintain the full investment in the fund, he or she must finance the tax payment from another source. In effect, the investor must commit more funds to maintain the investment, making the net return less than the gross

---

[14] See, for instance, William F. Sharpe, "Mutual Fund Performance," *Journal of Business,* special supplement, 39 (January 1966): 119–38, and Michael C. Jensen, "The Performance of Mutual Funds in the Period 1945–64," *Journal of Finance* 23 (May 1968): 389–416.

return. The mutual fund, however, cannot be expected to know its stockholders' tax brackets and thus reports returns on a before-tax and not on an after-tax basis.[15]

In the previous illustration, the distribution was income (i.e., dividends). If the fund's net asset value increased by $1 per share through appreciation in its portfolio, the fund could realize and distribute the capital gain. Once again the participant in the dividend reinvestment plan would have these funds plowed back into additional shares. The number of shares obtained would be the same, since $100 of reinvested income and $100 of reinvested capital gains would purchase the same number of additional shares.

The distribution of the capital gain has the same implication for taxes as the distribution of the income. In either case, the investor must pay federal income tax on the return. If the investor wants to reinvest the full amount of the capital gain distribution, he or she must finance the tax payment from another source. Once again the investor should realize that the return earned is reported by the fund on a before-tax basis, but the investor only has the after-tax return to use.

Calculating the after-tax return earned on an investment in a mutual fund is difficult because of several variables that affect this return. These include (1) the individual's marginal income tax rate, (2) the increase in the fund's net asset value, (3) the fund's distributions, and (4) whether the individual sells some shares to pay the applicable taxes or pays the taxes out of pocket and thus forgoes the alternative uses for that money.[16]

Impact of Fees on Rates of Return

The return earned by the investor is also affected by the fund's fees (e.g., management fees, commissions to brokers, and sales fees called loading charges). Perhaps the most visible are the loading charges, which may be levied when the investor purchases the shares (i.e., the fund is front-loaded) or may be assessed when the shares are redeemed (i.e., the fund is back-end loaded). As with taxes, loading fees make it more difficult to compare the performance reported by the funds and the returns actually realized by the investor.

Fees reduce realized return

Consider a front-loaded mutual fund that charges 8.5 percent of the amount invested. If the net asset value of the fund is $10, the investor must remit $10.93 to purchase a share.[17] The fund during the year earns $1, so the net asset value grows to $11. The fund's management reports a return of 10 percent, but the individual investor has certainly not earned 10 percent. Instead the actual amount invested ($10.93)

---

[15] This problem, of course, applies to all investments subject to income taxation. However, the general existence of the problems does not erase the fact that it reduces the comparability of the individual's realized after-tax return and the before-tax return reported by the mutual fund.

[16] One method has been suggested for the individual to compute his or her after-tax, realized return on an investment in a mutual fund. (See Alan Pope, "Distributions: A Taxing Effect on Mutual Fund Returns," *American Association of Individual Investors Journal* (October 1984), 15–18.) The calculation assumes the investor reinvests all distributions but liquidates sufficient shares to pay the taxes. The suggested technique permits the individual investor to determine the after-tax growth in the value of his or her holdings after adjusting for (1) the individual's tax bracket, (2) fund's distributions out of income, and (3) capital gain distributions.

[17] This cost of the share is determined as follows:

$$\$10/(1 - 0.085) = \$10/0.915 = \$10.93.$$

The loading fee is $0.93, which is 8.5 percent of the amount invested ($10.93 × 0.085 = $0.93). As was discussed earlier in this chapter, loading fees are figured on the amount invested and not on the net asset value.

has grown to $11, an increase of less than 1 percent. Over a period of years the loading fee significantly reduces the return. For example, if the fund were to earn 12 percent compounded annually for seven years, its net asset value would grow from $10 to $22.11. However, the investor's return would be only 10.6 percent as the actual amount invested ($10.93) rises to $22.11.

The return is further decreased if the fund has a deferred exit fee (or nuisance fee) that applies if shares are redeemed within a specified time period. For example, the Dean Witter Natural Resources Fund has a 5 percent redemption fee even though it is considered to be a no-load fund. Several of the Fidelity funds have both a loading fee and a redemption fee.[18] Such fees may be designed to reduce switching investments and cover the costs to the funds of handling withdrawals. Such deferred fees reduce the return and make comparisons of the fund's stated return and the individual's realized return more difficult.

Exit fees

This problem of comparisons created by fees is considerably lessened for a no-load mutual fund if (1) the management fees of the no-load fund are no higher than the management fees of the load fund and (2) the no-load fund does not have an exit fee. Some no-load funds assess a sales charge when the investor redeems the shares (i.e., a load fee in reverse). Since the fund lacks a traditional front-end load fee, it may refer to itself as a no-load fund.

The impact of a back-end load fee can be considerable even though the charge may be expressed as a modest 2 or 3 percent. Consider the preceding illustration in which the net asset value grew from $10 to $22.11 in seven years for a 12 percent annual increase. If the fund assesses a 3 percent back-end fee, the investor receives $21.44, so the realized return is reduced from 12 percent annually to 11.5 percent.

If the fund has both a front-end and back-end load, the investor's return is reduced even further. To continue the preceding example, the individual spends $10.93 to acquire a share with a net asset value of $10. The net asset value then compounds at 12 percent for seven years to $22.11, and the fund assesses a 3 percent back-end load. The investor receives $21.44, so that individual has in effect invested $10.93 to receive $21.44 over seven years. This is a return of 10.1 percent annually, which is almost two percentage points below the 12 percent that the fund can report as the growth in the net asset value.

Actually, the impact on the terminal value of an investment in the fund is the same for a back-end and a front-end loading fee as long as the percentages are the same. For example, fund A charges a 3 percent front-end load fee while fund B charges a 3 percent exit fee. The initial net asset value of each is $10, which grows annually at 12 percent for 12 years. The terminal value of fund A is

Exit fee may have same impact as the loading fee

$$\$10 - 0.30 = \$9.70,$$
$$\$9.70(3.8960) = \$37.79.$$

The terminal value of fund B is

$$\$10(3.8960) = \$38.96,$$
$$\$38.96 - 0.03(\$38.96) = \$37.79.$$

In both cases the terminal value is $37.79.[19]

---

[18] See Gerald W. Perritt, "Playing the Sector Game: Big Wins and Big Losses," *Barron's*, November 11, 1985, 59–63.

[19] 3.8960 is the interest factor for the future value of $1 at 12 percent for 12 years.

The impact of these differences in loading fees is substantial when the dollar amount of the investments is substantial and when the rate differences are compounded over many years. Consider a $50,000 investment in a fund that is left to compound at 12 percent for 20 years. The $50,000 grows to $482,314. However, if the fund had charged an initial load fee of 8.5%, the investor would have only $45,350 actually invested by the fund. At 12 percent compounded annually for 20 years, the terminal value would be $437,459. This is $44,855 less than would be earned with the no-load fund.

Suppose the investor had purchased shares in a no-load fund with an exit fee of 3 percent. In this case the investor receives $467,845 ($482,314 − $14,469). If the investor had purchased a load mutual fund with an 8½ percent front load and a 3 percent back-end load, this individual would have netted only $424,335, or $57,979 less than the no-load fund with no exit fee. Obviously the loading fees can have a considerable impact on the net return the investor ultimately earns, even though the net asset value increased by the same percentage in each case!

Impact of loading fee is not reduced over time

While it should be obvious from the preceding illustrations, the investor should not view the load as a one-time fee whose impact is reduced over time as it is spread over an ever increasing investment. Instead the opposite is true. The longer the investor holds the shares, the greater the absolute differential will be between the terminal values of the load and no-load funds. The funds not lost to the load fee are being compounded over a longer period of time; thus, the terminal value of the no-load fund becomes even larger.

While this discussion suggests that investors should purchase no-load mutual funds in preference to those with load fees, the investor still needs to be aware of an expense some no-load funds charge that may prove over a period of time to be more costly than the loading fees. The purpose of the loading fee is to compensate those individuals who sell the fund's shares. No-load funds do not have a sales force and thus do not have this expense. They may, however, use other marketing devices, such as advertising, that must be paid for.

12b-1 plans may be annual fees

Some no-load funds have adopted an SEC rule that permits management to use the fund's assets to pay for these marketing expenses. These funds have adopted a **12b-1 fee**, which is named for the number of the SEC rule that enables funds to assess what is, in effect, an on-going charge that stockholders pay. For example, E.F. Hutton's Investment Series Growth Fund's 12b-1 fee in 1985 was 0.85 percent of total assets and its Government Series Fund charged 0.90 percent of total assets. Unlike a front load fee, which is charged when the shares are purchased, this 12b-1 fee can be a continuous annual fee. Thus over a number of years, investors in no-load funds assessing this charge may pay more than they would have paid in loading fees.

Over a period of years 12b-1 fees can significantly reduce the return the investor earns, since the fee is paid not only in good years but also in years when the fund experiences losses and a decline in its net asset value. The investor needs to be aware of 12b-1 fees when selecting a mutual fund, since the growth in the fund's net asset value will be reduced by the fee. Suppose one fund charges a fee that averages 1.0 percent of total assets while another fund does not assess the fee. Both funds earn 12 percent on assets before the fees, so after the fee is paid the returns are 12 percent for the fund without the fee but 11 percent for the fund with the 12b-1 fee. Obviously the stockholder's return is reduced, and over time the impact of this reduction can be

surprisingly large. Consider an initial investment of $1,000. After 20 years the $1,000 grows to $9,643 in the fund without the fee but only grows to $6,728 in the fund with the fee. The difference ($2,915) is, of course, the result of the 12b-1 fee. Thus unless the fees lead to higher investment returns, they must reduce the return earned by the investor.[20]

Risk Adjustments for Comparing Rates of Return

Even if the investor is able to determine the rates of return various funds have earned, these rates may still not be comparable. Different funds with the same goal (such as capital appreciation) may not be equally risky. From the investor's viewpoint a return of 15 percent achieved by a low-risk portfolio is preferred to 15 percent earned on a very risky portfolio. If the investor compares absolute rates of return, he or she is implicitly assuming that both funds are equally risky.

One way to standardize returns for risk is to use beta coefficients. As was explained in Chapter 8, a beta coefficient is an index of systematic risk that measures the volatility of the fund's returns relative to the market as a whole. A beta of 1.0 indicates that the volatility of the fund's return is the same as that of the market. A beta of greater than 1.0 indicates that the fund is more volatile and a beta of less than 1.0 indicates the fund is less volatile.

Standardizing for risk

To standardize for risk, divide the individual fund's return by its beta coefficient. That is, the risk-adjusted return is

$$\text{Risk-adjusted return} = \text{Return on the fund/beta.}$$

If fund A has a return of 15 percent and a beta of 1.4 while fund B has a return of 15 percent and a beta of 0.8, their risk-adjusted returns are

$$\text{Risk-adjusted return for A} = 0.15/1.4 = 10.7\%.$$
$$\text{Risk-adjusted return for B} = 0.15/0.8 = 18.75\%.$$

Obviously the investor would prefer fund B, whose risk-adjusted return is superior.

If the investor wants to determine whether or not the fund has outperformed the market, the risk-adjusted return is compared to the return on the market. This comparison may be achieved in two ways. The return on the market may be subtracted from the individual fund's risk-adjusted return. For example, if a fund's risk-adjusted return is 13.6 percent and the market return is 12.4 percent, the fund outperformed the market by 1.2 percent (13.6 − 12.4). The second method is to divide the risk-adjusted return by the return on the market. Using the numbers of the previous illustration, the calculation is

Compare risk adjusted return with return on the market

$$13.6/12.4 = 1.097.$$

Either calculation gives essentially the same information. The latter procedure, however, standardizes each fund's return and may make it easier to compare several funds' risk-adjusted rates of return. All funds with a score of greater than 1.0 outperformed the market while all with a score of less than 1.0 underperformed the market on a risk-adjusted basis.

---

[20] See Laura R. Walbert, "Bark Watchdogs," *Forbes,* June 16, 1986, 174, for a discussion of the impact of 12b-1 fees.

Whether the investor should purchase individual mutual funds on the basis of management's outperforming the market is open to debate. Previous performance may not be indicative of future performance, and the efficient market hypothesis suggests that it is extremely difficult to outperform the market consistently. The word *consistent* is exceedingly important, since it requires that the fund's management do well in both rising and falling markets. The individual investor may be better off remembering the implications of the efficient market hypothesis than concentrating on the past performance. Even if past performance is repeated, it still may not indicate the return the individual investor earns once the impact of fees, taxes, and risk are considered.

SUMMARY

Instead of directly investing in securities, individuals may buy shares in investment companies. These firms, in turn, invest the funds in various assets, such as stocks and bonds.

There are two types of investment companies. A closed-end investment company has a specified number of shares that are bought and sold in the same manner as the stock of firms such as AT&T. An open-end investment company (i.e., a mutual fund) has a variable number of shares sold directly to investors. Investors who desire to liquidate their holdings sell them back to the company.

Investment companies offer several advantages, including professional management, diversification, and custodial services. Dividends and the interest earned on the firm's assets are distributed to stockholders. In addition, if the value of the company's assets rises, the stockholders profit as capital gains are realized and distributed.

Mutual funds may be classified by the types of assets they own. Some stress income-producing assets, such as bonds, preferred stock, and common stock of firms that distribute a large proportion of their income. Other mutual funds stress growth in their net asset values through investments in firms with the potential to grow and generate capital gains. There are also investment companies that specialize in special situations, particular sectors of the economy, and tax-exempt securities. There are even mutual funds that seek to duplicate an index of the stock market.

Although investment companies are professionally managed, the returns that mutual funds have earned over a period of years have not consistently outperformed the market. This result is consistent with the efficient market hypothesis.

To select a mutual fund, the individual should match his or her objectives with those of the fund. The age and size of the fund, its past performance, and the potential for hidden tax liabilities should also be considered. The investor should realize that it is difficult to compare the returns earned on different mutual funds with the return the individual investor may earn. Differences in the volatility of the funds' returns; differences in loading charges, exit fees, and 12b-1 plan expenses; and differences in taxes on ordinary income and unrealized capital gains further complicate comparing the growth in the fund's net asset value and the individual investor's return on money invested in the mutual fund.

Terms to Remember

Closed-end investment company   Unit trust
Open-end investment company   No-load fund
Mutual fund   Load fund
Net asset value   Growth stock
Premium and discount (from net asset   Index fund
     value)   12b-1 fees

Questions

1. What is the difference between a closed-end and an open-end investment company?

2. Are mutual funds subject to federal income taxation?

3. What custodial services do investment companies provide?

4. What is a loading charge? Do all investment companies charge this fee?

5. Why may the small investor prefer mutual funds to other investments?

6. What is a specialized mutual fund? How is it different from a special situation fund?

7. Should an investor expect a mutual fund to outperform the market? If not, why should the investor buy the shares?

8. What are the differences among loading fees, exit (or nuisance) fees, and 12b-1 plans?

9. How can an investor determine if a mutual fund has hidden capital gains? What impact may these gains have on the return of an investor who currently buys the shares?

10. What advantages may small funds offer over large funds? What advantages may an older fund offer over a new fund? Why may it be important to determine if a mutual fund's management has recently changed?

11. Why may the annual growth in a fund's net asset value not be comparable to the return earned by an individual investor?

12. How may beta coefficients be used to standardize returns for risk to permit comparisons of mutual fund performance?

Problems

1. What is the net asset value of an investment company with $10,000,000 in assets, $790,000 in current liabilities, and 1,200,000 shares outstanding?

2. If a mutual fund's net asset value is $23.40 and the fund sells its shares for $25, what is the load fee as a percentage of the amount invested?

3. If an investor buys shares in a no-load mutual fund for $31.40 and the shares appreciate to $44.60 in two years, what would be the rate of return on the investment? If the fund charges an exit fee of 1 percent, what would be the rate of return on the investment?

4. An investor buys shares in a mutual fund for $20. At the end of the year the fund distributes a dividend of $0.58, and after the distribution the net asset value of a share is $23.41. What would be the investor's return on the investment?

5. Fund A experienced a return of 14.5 percent while fund B experienced a return of only 13.2 percent. If their beta coefficients were 1.2 and 0.86, respectively, which fund achieved the superior performance?

SUGGESTED READINGS

For essential information on investment companies (e.g., address, purpose, dividend distributions, price performance, and so on), consult:

Investment Companies. New York: Wiesenberger Services, Inc. Published annually.

For similar information that is limited to no-load funds, consult:

The Individual Investor's Guide to No-Load Mutual Funds. Chicago: American Association of Individual Investors. Published annually.

Quarterly data concerning the performance of mutual funds is reported in *Barron's* in a section entitled "Barron's/Lipper Gauge—A Quarterly Survey of Mutual Fund Performance."

General books that discuss the merits of investing in mutual funds include:

Anderson, Carl E. *Anderson on Mutual Funds.* Glenview, Ill.: Scott, Foresman, 1984.

Rugg, Donald D., and Norman B. Hale. *The Dow Jones-Irwin Guide to Mutual Funds.* Revised ed. Homewood, Ill.: Dow Jones-Irwin, 1983.

While many mutual funds have not outperformed the market, they may reduce risk relative to the return that the individual investor may achieve by purchasing individual securities. For a discussion of this advantage offered by investment companies, see:

Levy, Haim, and Marshall Sarnat. "Investment Performance in an Imperfect Securities Market and the Case for Mutual Funds." *Financial Analysts Journal* (March–April 1972): 77–81.

For a comparison of returns earned by investment companies and the returns earned by other financial institutions (trust departments of commercial banks, investment counselors, and insurance companies), see:

Bogle, John C., and Jan M. Twardowski. "Institutional Investment Performance Compared: Banks, Investment Counselors, Insurance Companies, and Mutual Funds." *Financial Analysts Journal* (January–February 1980): 33–41.

A discussion of the factors that affect the discounts or premiums paid for the shares of closed-end investment companies can be found in:

Malkiel, Burton G. "The Valuation of Closed-End Investment Company Shares." *Journal of Finance* (June 1977): 847–959.

Mendelson, Morris. "Closed-end Fund Discounts Revisited." *The Financial Review* (Spring 1978): 48–72.

For discussion of mutual funds whose portfolios seek to match broad indices of the market (i.e., the so-called "index" funds), consult:

Calderwood, Stanford. "The Truth About Index Funds." *Financial Analysts Journal* (July–August 1977): 36–47.

A guide to a mutual fund's prospectus is given in:

Perritt, Gerald W. "Fund Literature: A Guide to the Essentials," *AAII Journal* (March 1986): 22–24.

For an interview with Peter Lynch, portfolio manager of the Fidelity Magellan Fund, one of the few funds that has consistently outperformed the market from 1975 through 1985, see:

"Blending Conservative, Growth and Cyclical Stocks Into a Winning Strategy." *AAII Journal* (September 1985): 5–8.

During 1985, the largest sales of new mutual fund securities were the shares of bond and income funds. Yields, however, tend to be overstated after considering loading fees and 12b-1 plans as well as nonrecurring gains generated during a period of lower interest rates and higher bond prices. For a discussion of the potential bias in yields reported by income funds, see:

Sloan, Allan, and Laura R. Walbert. "The Game Is Getting Out of Hand." *Forbes,* March 24, 1986, 30–34.

23 Commodity and Financial Futures

LEARNING OBJECTIVES

After completing this chapter you should be able to

1. Define *futures contract*.

2. Differentiate between the long and short positions in a commodity futures contract.

3. Contrast the role of margin in the stock market with its role in the commodity futures markets.

4. Identify the sources of leverage in commodity futures.

5. Distinguish speculators from hedgers and describe the role played by each in the futures markets.

6. Identify the forces that determine the price of a commodity futures contract.

7. Explain how speculators may earn profits or suffer losses in financial and currency futures.

Do you want excitement and rapid action? Would you prefer to speculate in pork bellies (i.e., bacon) instead of investing in the stock of Swift or Armour? Then investing in commodity futures may satisfy this speculative desire. These futures contracts are among the riskiest investments available, as prices can change rapidly and produce sudden losses or profits.

There are two participants in the futures markets, the speculators who establish positions in anticipation of price changes and the hedgers who seek to employ futures contracts to reduce risk. The hedgers are growers, producers, and other users of commodities. They seek to protect themselves from price fluctuations, and by hedging they pass the risk of loss to the speculators. The price of a futures contract ultimately depends on the demand for and supply of these contracts by the hedgers and speculators.

This chapter is an elementary introduction to investing in contracts for the future delivery of commodities. The chapter describes the mechanics of buying and selling the contracts,

the role of margin, the speculators' long and short positions, and how the hedgers use the contracts to reduce risk. The chapter concludes with a discussion of financial futures, since commodity contracts are not limited just to physical assets. There are also futures contracts for the purchase and sale of financial assets and foreign currencies. There are even futures based on the Standard & Poor's 500 stock index or the New York Stock Exchange composite index. The last part of this chapter provides an explanation of these newest futures contracts.

WHAT IS INVESTING IN COMMODITY FUTURES?

A commodity may be purchased for current delivery or for future delivery. Investing in commodity futures refers to the buying or the selling of a contract to deliver a commodity in the future. For this reason these investments are sometimes referred to as "futures." A **futures contract** is a formal agreement between a buyer or seller and a commodity exchange. In the case of a purchase contract, the buyer agrees to accept a specific commodity that meets a specified quality in a specified month. In the case of a sale, the seller agrees to deliver the specified commodity during the designated month.

A futures contract

Investing in commodity futures is considered to be very speculative. For that reason investors should participate in this market only after their financial obligations and goals have been met. There is a large probability that the investor will suffer a loss on any particular purchase or sale of a commodity contract. Individuals who buy and sell commodity contracts without wanting to deal in the actual commodities are generally referred to as **speculators,** which differentiates them from the growers, processors, warehousers, and other dealers who also buy and sell commodity futures but really wish to buy or sell the actual commodity.

Commodities are very speculative

The primary appeal of commodity contracts to speculators is the potential for a large return on the investment resulting from the leverage inherent in commodity trading. This leverage exists because (1) a commodity contract controls a substantial amount of the commodity and (2) the investor must make only a small payment to buy or sell a contract (i.e., there is a small margin requirement). These two points are discussed in some detail later in this chapter.

The potential leverage

THE MECHANICS OF INVESTING IN COMMODITIES

Like stocks and bonds, commodity futures may be purchased in several markets. One of the most important is the CBT, the Chicago Board of Trade, which executes contracts in agricultural commodities such as wheat, soybeans, and livestock. Other commodities are traded in various cities throughout the country. Over 50 commodities are traded on 10 exchanges in the United States and Canada. As may be expected, the markets for some commodity futures are close to the area where the commodity is produced. Thus, the markets for wheat are located not only in Chicago but also in Kansas City and Minneapolis. The market for several commodity futures is in New York. Cocoa, coffee, sugar, potatoes, and orange juice are bought and sold there. This geographical diversity does not hamper commodity traders, who may buy and sell commodity contracts in any market through their brokers.

How they are purchased

The role of brokers

Commodity contracts are purchased through brokers just as stocks and bonds are. The broker (or a member of a brokerage firm) owns a seat on the commodity exchange. Membership on each exchange is limited, and only members are allowed to buy and sell the commodity contracts. If the investor's broker lacks a seat, then that broker must have a correspondent relationship with another broker who does own a seat.

The broker acts on behalf of the investor by purchasing and selling contracts through the exchange. Each commodity exchange has a clearinghouse that watches the various buy and sell orders. The investor opens an account by signing an agreement that requires the contracts to be guaranteed. Since trading commodity contracts is considered to be speculative, some brokers will open accounts only after the investor has proved the capacity both to finance the account and to withstand the losses.

A commodity order

Once the account has been opened, the investor may trade commodity contracts. These are bought and sold in much the same way as stocks and bonds. A commodity order specifies whether the contract is a buy or a sell (i.e., whether the investor will take delivery or make delivery), the type of commodity and the number of units, and the delivery date (i.e., the month in which the commodity is to be delivered). The speculator can request a market order and have the contract executed at the current market price, or he or she may place orders at specified prices. Such orders may be for a day or until the investor cancels them (i.e., the order is good till canceled). Once the order is executed, the broker will provide the speculator with a confirmation statement of the purchase or sale and statements of the investor's positions in the various commodities.

Fees

The broker will also charge a fee or commission for executing the orders. This fee tends to be modest. For example, one broker charges $80 per contract, and the fee covers *both the purchase and subsequent sale* of the contract. Perhaps the reduction in paperwork partially explains the modest fees. An investment in commodity futures relieves the broker and the investor of handling dividend checks, the certificates from stock splits and stock dividends, proxies and votes, and other custodial matters associated with an investment in stocks and bonds.

Commodity Positions

The long position

The investor may purchase a contract for future delivery. This is the **long position**, in which the investor will profit if the price of the commodity and hence the value of the contract rise. The investor may also sell a contract for future delivery. This is the **short position**, in which the seller agrees to make good the contract (i.e., to deliver the goods) sometime in the future. This investor will profit if the price of the commodity and hence the value of the contract decline. These long and short positions are analogous to the long and short positions that the investor takes in the security market. Long positions generate profits when the value of the security rises, whereas short positions result in profits when the value of the security declines.

The short position

The source of profits

The way in which each position generates a profit can be seen in a simple example. Assume that the **futures price** of wheat is $3.50 per bushel. If a contract is purchased for delivery in six months at $3.50 per bushel, the buyer will profit from this long position if the price of wheat *rises*. If the price increases to $4.00 per bushel, the buyer can exercise the contract by taking delivery and paying $3.50 per bushel.

The speculator then sells the wheat for $4 per bushel, which produces a profit of $0.50 per bushel.

The opposite occurs when the price of wheat declines. If the price of wheat falls to $3.00 per bushel, the individual who bought the contract for delivery at $3.50 suffers a loss. But the speculator who sold the contract for the delivery of wheat (i.e., who took the short position) earns a profit from the price decline. The speculator can then buy wheat at the market price (which is referred to as the **spot price**) of $3.00, deliver it for the contract price of $3.50, and earn a $0.50 profit per bushel.

The "spot" price is the current price

If the price rises, the short position will produce a loss. If the price increases from $3.50 to $4.00 per bushel, the speculator who sold a contract for delivery suffers a loss of $0.50 per bushel, because he or she must pay $4.00 to obtain the wheat that will be delivered for $3.50 per bushel.

Actually, the preceding losses and profits are generated without the goods being delivered. Of course, when a speculator buys a contract for future delivery, there is always the possibility that this individual will receive the goods. Conversely, if the speculator sells a contract for future delivery, there is the possibility that the goods will have to be supplied. However, such deliveries occur infrequently, because the speculator can offset the contract before the delivery date. This is achieved by buying back a contract that was previously sold or selling a contract that is owned.

The delivery need not occur

This process of offsetting existing contracts is illustrated in the following example. Suppose a speculator has a contract to buy wheat in January. If the individual wants to close the position, he or she can sell a contract for the delivery of wheat in January. The two contracts cancel each other, as one is a purchase and the other is a sale.[1] If the speculator actually received the wheat by executing the purchase agreement, he or she could pass on the wheat by executing the sell agreement. However, since the two contracts offset each other, the actual delivery and subsequent sale are not necessary. Instead, the speculator's position in wheat is closed, and the actual physical transfers do not occur.

The process of offsetting a contract

Correspondingly, if the speculator has a contract for the sale of wheat in January, it can be canceled by buying a contract for the purchase of wheat in January. If the speculator were called upon to deliver wheat as the result of the contract to sell, the individual would exercise the contract to purchase wheat. The buy and sell contracts would then cancel each other, and no physical transfers of wheat would occur. Once again the speculator has closed the initial position by taking the opposite position (i.e., the sales contract is canceled by a purchase contract).

Because these contracts are canceled and actual deliveries do not take place, it should not be assumed that profits or losses do not occur. The two contracts need not be executed at the same price. For example, the speculator may enter a contract for the future purchase of wheat at $3.50 per bushel. Any contract for the future delivery of comparable wheat can cancel the contract for the purchase. But the cost of the wheat for future delivery could be $3.60 or $3.40 (or any conceivable price). If the price of wheat rises (e.g., from $3.50 to $3.60 per bushel), the speculator with a long position earns a profit. However, if the speculator has a short position (i.e., a contract to sell wheat), this individual sustains a loss. If the price declines (e.g., from $3.50 to $3.40 per bushel), the short seller earns a profit, but the long position sustains a loss.

---

[1] This process is analogous to the writer of an option buying back the option. In both cases the investor's position is closed.

Exhibit 23.1
Selected Commodities,
Their Markets, and
Their Units of Trading

Commodity	Market	Unit of One Contract
Corn	Chicago Board of Trade	5,000 bushels
Soybeans	Chicago Board of Trade	5,000 bushels
Barley	Winnipeg Commodity Exchange	20 metric tons
Cattle	Chicago Mercantile Exchange	30,000 pounds
Coffee	New York Coffee and Sugar Exchange	37,500 pounds
Copper	Commodity Exchange, Inc., of New York	25,000 pounds
Platinum	New York Mercantile Exchange	50 troy ounces
Silver	Commodity Exchange, Inc., of New York	5,000 troy ounces
Lumber	Chicago Mercantile Exchange	100,000 board feet
Cotton	New York Cotton Exchange	50,000 pounds

The Units of Commodity Contracts

The uniformity of contracts

To facilitate trading, contracts must be uniform. For a particular commodity the contracts must be identical. Besides specifying the delivery month, the contract must specify the grade and type of the commodity (e.g., a particular type of wheat) and the units of the commodity (e.g., 5,000 bushels). Thus, when an individual buys or sells a contract, there can be no doubt as to the nature of the obligation. For example, if the investor buys wheat for January delivery, there can be no confusion with a contract for the purchase of wheat for February delivery. These are two different commodities in the same way that AT&T common stock, AT&T preferred stock, and AT&T bonds are all different securities. Without such standardization of contracts there would be chaos in the commodity (or any) markets.

The units of trading

The units of trading vary with each commodity. For example, if the investor buys a contract for corn, the unit of trading is 5,000 bushels. If the investor buys a contract for eggs, the unit of trading is 22,500 dozen. A list of selected commodities, the markets in which they are traded, and the units of each contract are given in Exhibit 23.1. While the novice investor may not remember the units for a contract, the experienced investor is certainly aware of them. As will be explained later, because of the large units of many commodity contracts, a small change in the price of the commodity produces a considerable change in the value of the contract and in the investor's profits or losses.

Reporting of Futures Trading

Reports in the financial press

Commodity futures prices and contracts are reported in the financial press in much the same way as stock and bond transactions are. This is illustrated in Exhibit 23.2, which was taken from *The Wall Street Journal*. As may be seen in the exhibit, wheat is traded on the Chicago Board of Trade (CBT). The unit for trading is 5,000 bushels, and prices are quoted in cents per bushel. The opening price for December delivery was 262¢ ($2.62) per bushel, while the high, low, and closing (i.e., the "settle") prices were 262½¢, 258½¢, and 259¢, respectively. This closing price was 1¢ lower than the closing price on the previous day. The high and low prices (prior to the previous day

Exhibit 23.2
Selected Futures Prices

FUTURES PRICES

Wednesday, June 11, 1986.

Open Interest Reflects Previous Trading Day.

	Open	High	Low	Settle	Change	Lifetime High	Lifetime Low	Open Interest
-GRAINS AND OILSEEDS-								
CORN (CBT) 5,000 bu.; cents per bu.								
July	235¾	236¼	233¼	234¼	− 2¼	286	215½	33,301
Sept	201¼	201¾	200½	200¾	− ½	270	197	16,379
Aug	148.70	149.10	148.20	149.00	+ 1.00	163.50	135.50	7,832
Sept	147.00	147.00	145.70	146.70	+ .20	160.50	137.50	3,565
Oct	144.80	144.80	143.50	144.30	+ .40	162.10	136.00	5,799
Dec	147.50	147.50	145.50	146.20	.20	162.10	136.00	12,103
Jan87	149.00	149.00	147.10	147.20	− .30	163.10	136.10	2,048
Mar	151.00	151.00	149.70	149.70	.80	163.10	146.50	1,021
May	153.00	153.40	153.00	153.40	+ 1.40	169.70	149.50	578
Est vol 11,000; vol Tues 12,258; open int 50,620, +614.								
SOYBEAN OIL (CBT) 60,000 lbs.; cents per lb.								
July	16.93	17.04	16.89	16.95	+ .09	25.25	16.60	19,390
Aug	17.15	17.20	17.07	17.15	+ .11	25.15	16.75	10,664
Sept	17.35	17.35	17.21	17.25	+ .12	24.05	16.95	5,754
Oct	17.35	17.40	17.28	17.30	+ .10	22.80	17.05	5,429
Dec	17.74	17.75	17.62	17.66	+ .06	22.50	17.35	14,414
Jan87	17.80	17.88	17.78	17.78	+ .08	22.35	17.65	2,577
Mar	18.20	18.20	18.05	18.05	+ .05	20.25	17.85	1,140
May	18.40	18.45	18.39	18.39	+ .09	20.90	18.22	545
Est vol 12,000; vol Tues 15,170; open int 59,938, +121.								
SOYBEAN OIL (CBT) 60,000 lbs.; cents per lb.								
July	16.93	17.04	16.89	16.95	+ .09	25.25	16.60	19,390
Aug	17.15	17.20	17.07	17.15	+ .11	25.15	16.75	10,664
Sept	17.35	17.35	17.21	17.25	+ .12	24.05	16.95	5,754
Oct	17.35	17.40	17.28	17.30	+ .10	22.80	17.05	5,429
Dec	17.74	17.75	17.62	17.66	+ .06	22.50	17.35	14,414
Jan87	17.80	17.88	17.78	17.78	+ .08	22.35	17.65	2,577
Mar	18.20	18.20	18.05	18.05	+ .05	20.25	17.85	1,140
May	18.40	18.45	18.39	18.39	+ .09	20.90	18.22	545
Est vol n.a.; vol Tues 15,170; open int 59,938, +121.								
WHEAT (CBT) 5,000 bu.; cents per bu.								
July	254	256½	252	252½	+ ½	310	241	15,815
Sept	255	255¼	251	252¼	....	299	242	11,074
Dec	262	262½	258½	259	− 1	309	251	7,500
Mar87	262	262	257½	258	....	308	251	1,597
May	250	250½	247½	247¾	− ¼	300	244	455
July	240	240	236½	236½	− 1½	250	236	179
Est vol 8,000; vol Tues 7,829; open int 36,620, +937.								
WHEAT (KC) 5,000 bu.; cents per bu.								
July	248	248¾	245	245¼	− 1	298½	237½	9,807
RYE (WPG) 20 metric tons; Can. $ per ton								
July	106.20	106.40	105.90	106.30	+ .40	130.00	95.50	945
Oct	108.00	108.50	108.00	108.30	+ .80	127.50	97.70	1,526
Dec	108.80	109.20	108.80	109.20	+ 1.10	127.40	99.00	625
Est vol 360; vol Tues 187; open int 3,146, −25.								
-LIVESTOCK & MEAT-								
CATTLE-FEEDER (CME) 44,000 lbs.; cents per lb.								
Aug	56.15	56.50	55.75	56.35	− .02	68.70	53.35	3,969
Sept	54.20	54.60	53.80	54.57	− .12	64.25	52.40	1,948
Oct	54.50	54.87	54.25	54.57	− .02	64.10	52.85	2,561
Nov	55.55	55.95	55.45	55.70	....	64.35	54.15	798
Jan87	57.20	57.35	57.10	57.35	− .17	63.00	56.25	221
Est vol 1,476; vol Tues 1,622; open int 9,561, +96.								
CATTLE-LIVE (CME) 40,000 lbs.; cents per lb.								
June	53.35	53.40	52.75	53.05	.60	66.60	52.42	5,937
Aug	50.25	50.50	49.85	50.32	− .65	61.75	49.85	24,833
Oct	50.10	50.10	49.75	49.90	− .57	60.60	49.50	12,472
Dec	52.20	52.32	51.85	52.27	− .15	61.75	51.60	9,403
Feb87	52.25	52.37	51.92	52.37	− .12	60.50	51.70	2,308
Apr	53.70	53.75	53.30	53.70	− .27	59.00	53.30	452
Est vol 15,050; vol Tues 15,687; open int 55,436, +684.								
HOGS (CME) 30,000 lbs.; cents per lb.								
June	51.80	52.10	51.70	51.97	− .20	52.50	39.80	3,884
July	48.50	49.00	48.35	48.85	.20	49.85	40.45	9,442
Aug	45.60	45.95	45.30	45.90	− .05	48.00	39.27	5,833
Oct	41.50	41.75	41.35	41.70	− .10	42.60	36.50	3,325
Feb87	60.05	60.05	57.85	58.20	− 1.65	62.60	56.40	1,633
Est vol 5,397; vol Tues 5,162; open int 10,403, −276.								
-FOOD & FIBER-								
COCOA (CSCE) 10 metric tons; $ per ton.								
July	1,797	1,797	1,760	1,763	− 22	2,429	1,691	4,244
Sept	1,852	1,852	1,815	1,818	− 21	2,430	1,755	6,904
Dec	1,905	1,905	1,876	1,877	− 17	2,425	1,805	4,756
Mar87	1,945	1,947	1,923	1,923	10	2,385	1,865	2,426
May	1,980	1,980	1,975	1,958	10	2,184	1,900	1,529
July	2,005	2,005	1,986	1,991	− 2	2,200	1,935	1,217
Sept	2,025	2,025	2,025	2,018	− 2	2,055	1,955	1,783
Est vol 3,739; vol Tues 3,329; open int 22,859, −123.								
COFFEE (CSCE) 37,500 lbs.; cents per lb.								
July	180.50	185.00	177.60	178.05	− 5.04	278.38	135.50	5,458
Sept	184.75	188.00	182.30	182.48	− 4.22	282.78	137.50	5,686
Dec	191.00	193.25	187.00	187.00	− 6.00	287.10	138.00	2,651
Mar87	193.00	194.50	190.55	190.55	6.00	290.33	156.75	1,253
May	195.50	196.00	193.75	193.75	− 6.00	291.83	188.00	392
July	196.00	196.00	196.00	196.00	− 6.00	266.25	201.00	181
Est vol 4,900; vol Tues 5,738; open int 15,671, −281.								
COTTON (CTN) 50,000 lbs.; cents per lb.								
July	67.24	67.44	66.75	66.80	− .63	70.05	56.05	5,324
Oct	33.45	34.10	33.45	33.60	+ .12	65.50	33.00	2,625
Dec	33.85	34.53	33.85	34.07	+ .24	59.25	33.37	13,213
Mar87	34.70	35.22	34.70	34.75	+ .05	49.50	34.20	1,349

	Open	High	Low	Settle	Change	Lifetime High	Lifetime Low	Open Interest
May	35.50	35.90	35.50	35.60	....	52.75	35.20	445
July	36.20	36.65	36.20	36.22	− .08	46.80	36.18	502
July	6.90	7.00	6.85	6.96	+ .10	9.50	3.79	16,904
Sept	7.05	7.06	7.00	7.05	+ .09	9.42	4.05	481
Oct	7.23	7.33	7.15	7.27	+ .06	9.40	4.02	46,734
Jan87	7.36	7.36	7.32	7.44	+ .09	9.50	5.65	217
Mar	7.69	7.79	7.62	7.74	+ .08	9.64	6.03	20,102
May	7.85	7.92	7.85	7.91	+ .08	9.82	6.75	5,707
July	7.98	8.05	7.96	8.05	+ .10	9.92	7.77	3,295
Oct	....	....	....	8.23	+ .10	9.60	8.05	981
Est vol 9,986; vol TTues 20,533; open int 94,421, −1,164.								
SUGAR-DOMESTIC (CSCE)-112,000 lbs.; cents per lb.								
Sept	20.95	21.00	20.95	21.00	....	21.95	19.70	2,591
Nov	20.70	20.70	20.70	20.70	− .03	21.70	20.40	1,724
Jan87	....	....	....	20.84	− .09	21.31	20.42	245
Mar	20.70	20.70	20.70	20.73	....	21.40	20.50	914
July	....	....	....	20.90	....	20.96	20.65	286
Est vol 9; vol Tues 7; open int 5,813, −390.								
-METALS & PETROLEUM-								
COPPER (CMX)-25,000 lbs.; cents per lb.								
June	63.95	63.95	63.95	64.00	+ .25	67.45	62.40	1
July	64.05	64.20	63.85	64.10	+ .10	72.55	60.35	29,829
Sept	64.20	64.40	64.05	64.30	+ .15	70.90	60.90	23,864
Dec	64.55	64.75	64.45	64.65	+ .20	70.30	61.60	12,760
Mar87	64.90	64.95	64.90	64.95	+ .20	70.00	62.55	2,306
May	65.25	65.25	65.05	65.20	+ .20	70.00	62.90	451
July	65.25	65.45	65.35	65.40	+ .20	69.95	63.25	310
Dec	....	....	....	66.00	+ .20	69.50	64.80	102
Est vol 5,500; vol Tues 5,135; open int 69,768, −70.								
GOLD (CMX)-100 troy oz.; $ per troy oz.								
June	348.10	351.20	347.50	348.60	+ .50	433.50	320.50	3,269
Aug	351.30	354.20	350.50	351.70	+ .50	427.50	328.00	49,760
Oct	354.50	357.60	354.10	355.10	+ .50	395.70	331.50	7,899
Dec	358.80	361.50	357.50	358.70	+ .50	392.00	336.50	15,897
Feb87	362.50	364.50	361.80	362.60	+ .50	397.50	337.30	8,885
Apr	367.10	368.00	367.10	366.40	+ .50	405.00	346.30	8,357
June	372.00	372.00	372.00	370.30	+ .50	409.00	350.50	9,039
Aug	376.50	376.50	376.50	374.60	+ .50	408.50	356.00	6,972
Oct	381.50	381.50	378.50	378.90	+ .50	420.00	361.00	5,104
SILVER (CBT)-1,000 troy oz.; cents per troy oz.								
June	532.0	545.0	532.0	536.0	+ 1.0	765.0	483.0	377
Aug	538.0	554.0	537.0	541.0	+ 1.0	765.0	491.0	2,613
Oct	547.0	557.0	546.7	549.0	+ 2.0	720.0	500.0	385
Dec	553.0	568.0	552.0	555.0	− .50	727.5	504.0	7,295
Feb87	560.0	572.0	560.0	562.0	....	725.0	510.0	294
Apr	568.0	580.0	568.0	569.0	....	660.0	520.0	1,097
June	574.0	590.0	573.0	576.0	....	694.0	525.0	791
Est vol 3,000; vol Tues 2,750; open int 12,965, +15.								
CRUDE OIL, Light Sweet (NYM) 42,000 gal.; $ per bbl.								
July	12.72	13.59	12.65	13.49	+ .93	27.53	10.15	27,382
Aug	12.68	13.48	12.57	13.42	+ .89	27.23	10.30	33,602
Sept	12.70	13.50	12.70	13.46	+ .86	27.00	10.60	12,977
Oct	12.77	13.55	12.77	13.50	+ .83	26.73	10.80	9,014
Nov	13.00	13.60	13.00	13.56	+ .80	26.60	11.01	4,932
Dec	13.00	13.74	13.00	13.62	+ .77	26.20	11.20	11,217
Jan87	13.00	13.50	13.00	13.55	+ .70	26.30	12.10	2,035
Feb	13.38	13.65	13.38	13.52	+ .67	24.90	11.35	1,483
Mar	13.50	13.50	13.50	13.50	+ .65	17.90	11.35	405
Apr	13.40	13.40	13.40	13.48	+ .63	14.65	11.55	177
May	....	....	....	13.46	+ .61	14.75	12.50	103
Est vol 38,538; vol Tues 22,661; open int 103,331, −1,797.								
HEATING OIL NO. 2 (NYM) 42,000 gal.; $ per gal.								
July	.3640	.3890	.3630	.3835	+ .0233	.7400	.3140	9,485
Aug	.3710	.3861	.3700	.3861	+ .0200	.7415	.3200	14,287
Sept	.3815	.3945	.3815	.3945	+ .0200	.7250	.3280	7,756
Est vol 12,909; vol Tues 11,561; open int 48,493, +486.								
GAS OIL (IPEL) 100 metric tons; $ per ton								
July	114.00	118.75	113.50	118.00	+ 3.50	240.00	105.25	4,676
Aug	115.75	120.25	115.00	119.50	+ 3.75	230.00	107.50	2,810
Sept	118.00	122.50	116.50	122.25	+ 4.75	208.00	112.00	1,758
Oct	120.00	124.25	119.50	123.25	+ 3.25	165.00	118.75	985
Nov	125.75	125.75	125.75	125.75	+ 5.75	137.50	120.75	253
Dec	....	....	....	129.50	....	137.00	125.00	171
Actual Wednesday; vol 3,023; open int 10,653, −818.								

ACC–Amex Commodities Corp.; CBT–Chicago Board of Trade; CME–Chicago Mercantile Exchange; CMX–Commodity Exchange, New York; CRCE–Chicago Rice & Cotton Exchange; CSCE–Coffee, Sugar & Cocoa Exchange, New York; CTN–New York Cotton Exchange; IPEL–International Petroleum Exchange of London; IMM–International Monetary Market at CME, Chicago; KC–Kansas City Board of Trade; LIFFE–London International Financial Futures Exchange; MCE–MidAmerica Commodity Exchange; MPLS–Minneapolis Grain Exchange; NYFE–New York Futures Exchange, unit of New York Stock Exchange. NYM–New York Mercantile Exchange; PBOT–Philadelphia Board of Trade; WPG–Winnipeg Commodity Exchange.

	Open	High	Low	Settle	Change	Lifetime High	Lifetime Low	Open Interest
NY GASOLINE, leaded reg. (NYM) 42,000 gal.; $ per gal.								
July	.4100	.4360	.4080	.4283	+ .0232	.7880	.3390	8,430
Aug	.4030	.4197	.4010	.4197	+ .0200	.7820	.3370	8,575
Sept	.4020	.4100	.4000	.4100	+ .0200	.7350	.3325	3,488
Oct	.3800	.3980	.3800	.3980	+ .0200	.4625	.3730	1,493
-FINANCIAL-								
BRITISH POUND (IMM)-25,000 pounds; $ per pound								
June	1.5240	1.5340	1.5210	1.5270	+ .0095	1.5525	1.1530	22,607
Sept	1.5140	1.5250	1.5110	1.5175	+ .0095	1.5430	1.3240	12,486
Dec	1.5045	1.5150	1.5045	1.5085	+ .0090	1.5360	1.3250	505
Est vol 11,635; vol Tues 13,568; open int 35,611, +1,509.								
CANADIAN DOLLAR (IMM)-100,000 dlrs.; $ per Can $								
June	.7202	.7204	.7193	.7199	−.0004	.7360	.6845	6,248
Sept	.7172	.7174	.7162	.7170	−.0004	.7305	.6809	5,415
Dec	.7140	.7148	.7140	.7140	−.0005	.7285	.6790	1,327
Mar87		....	....	.7109	−.0007	.7256	.6770	318
Est vol 2,020; vol Tues 2,650; open int 13,345, −265.								
JAPANESE YEN (IMM) 12.5 million yen; $ per yen (.00)								
June	.6016	.6032	.5997	.6010	+.0010	.6245	.4220	21,898
Sept	.6053	.6069	.6033	.6048	+.0010	.6280	.4690	18,157
Dec	.6091	.6102	.6075	.6086	+.0008	.6320	.4720	1,077
Mar87	.6145	.6145	.6135	.6142	+.0017	.6032	.5850	262
Est vol 19,073; vol Tues 26,073; open int 41,394, +2,981.								
SWISS FRANC (IMM)-125,000 francs-$ per franc								
June	.5480	.5502	.5460	.5471	−.0011	.5580	.4190	13,886
Sept	.5515	.5537	.5492	.5503	−.0011	.5625	.4790	14,998
Dec	.5555	.5575	.5530	.5539	−.0016	.5660	.4878	685
Est vol 21,673; vol Tues 24,898; open int 29,574, +540.								
W. GERMAN MARK (IMM)-125,000 marks; $ per mark								
June	.4517	.4533	.4509	.4517	+.0005	.4648	.3335	30,120
Sept	.4550	.4564	.4538	.4546	+.0005	.4675	.3762	17,675
Dec	.4579	.4585	.4568	.4576	+.0005	.4703	.4090	464
Est vol 28,918; vol Tues 34,844; open int 48,271, −1,119.								
EURODOLLAR (LIFFE)-$1 million; pts of 100%								
June	92.93	92.94	92.91	92.92	− .02	93.72	87.64	4,443
Sept	92.82	92.83	92.74	92.76	− .03	93.78	89.06	9,573
Dec	92.66	92.67	92.61	92.62	....	93.67	90.20	4,492
Mar87	92.42	92.43	92.39	92.39	+ .02	93.46	90.80	2,483
June	92.10	92.10	92.10	92.07	+ .02	93.15	90.85	634
Sept		....	....	91.78	+ .02	92.95	91.65	223
Dec		....	....	91.52	+ .02	....	....	108
Est vol 3,058; vol Tues 5,156; open int 22,061, −249.								
Est vol 800; vol Tues 1,614; open int 2,806, −61.								
The index: High 112.95; Low 112.43; Close 112.80 −.18								
TREASURY BONDS (CBT)-$100,000; pts. 32nds of 100%								
June	92-31	93-25	91-19	93-25	+ 32	8.660	− .112	21,978
Sept	92-05	93-01	90-24	92-31	+ 31	8.751	− .110	167,156
Dec	91-07	92-05	89-31	92-03	+ 30	8.850	− .108	15,550
Mr87	90-12	91-09	89-11	91-09	+ 30	8.944	− .110	5,052
June	89-02	90-17	88-12	90-16	+ 29	9.035	− .108	2,997
Sept	88-13	89-26	87-31	89-26	+ 29	9.116	− .109	2,206
Dec	87-25	89-06	87-11	89-06	+ 29	9.191	− .110	1,271
Mr88	87-10	88-20	86-25	88-20	+ 29	9.259	− .111	1,132
June	86-11	88-03	86-11	88-03	+ 29	9.324	− .112	698
Sept	....	....	....	87-20	+ 29	9.382	− .113	207
Dec	....	....	....	87-07	+ 29	9.432	− .114	111
Est vol 260,000; vol Tues 246,199; open int 218,358, −381.								
TREASURY NOTES (CBT)-$100,000; pts. 32nds of 100%								
June	97-21	98-16	97-06	98-16	+ 24	8.223	− .113	7,866
Sept	96-22	97-20	96-05	97-18	+ 25	8.365	− .119	66,077
Dec	95-28	96-24	95-12	96-23	+ 25	8.493	− .121	2,384
Mr87	....	....	....	95-29	+ 25	8.619	− .122	263
Est vol 24,000; vol Tues 31,389; open int 76,590, +3,559.								
TREASURY BILLS (IMM)-$1 mil.; pts. of 100%								
	Open	High	Low	Settle	Chg	Discount Settle	Discount Chg	Open Interest
Sept	93.81	93.81	93.67	93.80	....	6.20	....	25,639
Dec	93.70	93.71	93.59	93.70	+ .01	6.30	− .01	6,523
June	90-12	90-12	89-21	90-09	....	103-17	79-10	3,094
Sept	89-15	89-21	88-24	89-19	+ 5	103-01	79-10	7,147
Est vol 5,000; vol Tues 3,806; open int 10,244, −175.								
The index: Close 90-06; Yield 8.67.								
S&P 500 INDEX (CME) 500 times index								
June	239.00	241.50	238.65	240.70	+ 1.40	250.40	183.90	56,007
Sept	240.80	243.00	240.30	242.30	+ 1.50	252.70	187.00	41,324
Dec	242.75	244.90	242.30	244.40	+ 1.60	254.80	209.50	1,180
Est vol 80,025; vol Tues99,927; open int 98,602, +1,149.								
The index: High 241.13; Low 239.21; Close 241.13 +1.55								
NYSE COMPOSITE INDEX (NYFE) 500 times index								
June	137.40	138.65	137.05	138.20	+ .75	143.95	106.90	8,448
Sept	138.45	139.75	138.15	139.35	+ .80	145.40	108.10	5,425
Dec	139.75	140.75	139.75	140.45	+ .80	146.55	121.10	952
Mar87	140.90	141.85	140.90	141.55	+ .80	147.70	139.90	246
Est vol 10,099; vol Tues 11,725; open int 15,071, −623.								
The index: High 138.58; Low 137.57; Close 138.58 +.88								
KC VALUE LINE INDEX (KC) 500 times index								
June	238.90	241.20	238.20	240.15	+ 1.05	248.80	197.00	9,438
Sept	239.90	242.30	239.20	241.50	+ 1.40	250.35	199.45	4,756
Est vol 3,000; vol Tues 3,531; open int 14,375, −357.								
The index: High 241.12; Low 239.84; Close 241.12 +1.29								
MAJOR MKT INDEX (CBT) $250 times index								
June	348.50	351.00	347.30	349.90	+ 1.40	359.25	255.75	5,470
July	350.00	351.75	348.40	350.90	+ 1.50	360.00	332.60	370
Est vol 7,500; vol Tues 8,221; open int 5,903, −138.								
The index: High 350.83; Low 347.37; Close 350.77 +2.10								

Source: *The Wall Street Journal*, June 12, 1986, p. 50. Reprinted by permission of *The Wall Street Journal*,

Figure 23.1
**Spot and Futures Prices
and Open Interest for
a September 19x2
Contract for Kansas
City Wheat**

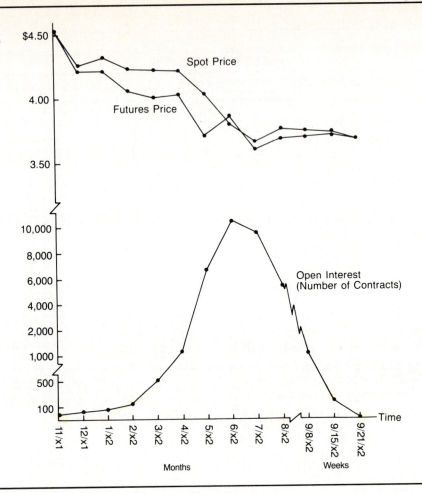

The open interest

of trading) for the lifetime of the contract were 309¢ and 251¢, respectively. The **open interest**, which is the number of contracts in existence, was 7,500.

This open interest varies over the life of the contract. Initially, the open interest rises as buyers and sellers establish positions. It then declines as the delivery date approaches and the positions are closed. This changing number of contracts is illustrated in Figure 23.1, which plots the spot and futures prices and the open interest for a September contract to buy Kansas City wheat. When the contracts were initially traded in late 19x1, there were only a few contracts in existence. By June 19x2 the open interest had risen to over 10,000 contracts. Then, as the remaining life of the contracts declined, the number of contracts fell as the various participants closed their positions. By late September only a few contracts were still outstanding.

Spot and futures prices

Figure 23.1 also shows the spot price (i.e., the current price) and the futures price for Kansas City wheat. In this case the futures price was generally less than the

spot price. Usually the futures price exceeds the spot price, but the reverse may occur if investors believe the price of the commodity will decline in the future. These investors seek to sell contracts now to lock in the higher prices so they may buy back the contracts at a lower price in the future. This selling of the futures contracts drives the futures price down below the spot price.

If investors anticipate higher prices for wheat in the future, they would seek to buy contracts for the future delivery of wheat. The anticipation of inflation and the cost of storing commodities usually drive up the futures price relative to the spot price. The value of the futures contract would then exceed the current price of the commodity.

The futures price must converge with the spot price as the expiration date of the contract approaches. As with options such as puts and calls, the value of the futures contract can be worth only the value of the underlying commodity at the expiration date. This pattern of price behavior is also illustrated in Figure 23.1. In March, April, and May there was a considerable differential between the two prices. However, in late September the futures and spot prices converged and erased the differential.

The Regulation of Commodity Markets

The commodity exchanges, like stock exchanges, are subject to regulation. Federal laws pertaining to commodity exchanges and commodity transaction laws are enforced by the Commodity Exchange Authority, which is a division of the Department of Agriculture. As with the regulation of security transactions, the regulations do not protect investors or speculators from their own folly. Instead, the regulations establish uniform standards for each commodity. The regulatory authority also has control over trading procedures, the hours of trading, and the maximum allowable daily price movements.

LEVERAGE

Commodities are paid for on delivery. Thus, a contract for future delivery means that the goods do not have to be paid for when the contract is executed. Instead, the investor (either a buyer or a seller) provides an amount of money, which is called **margin**, to protect the broker and to guarantee the contract. This margin is not to be confused with the margin that is used in the purchase of stocks and bonds. In the trading of stocks and bonds, margin represents the investor's equity in the position, whereas margin for a commodity contract is a deposit to show the investor's good faith and to protect the broker against an adverse change in the price of the commodity.

Margin—a good faith deposit

In the stock market, the amount of margin required varies with the price of the security, but in the commodity markets the amount of margin does not vary with the dollar value of the transaction. Instead, each contract has a fixed minimum margin requirement. These margin requirements for selected commodities are given in Exhibit 23.3. Thus, an investor who purchases a futures contract for cocoa must put up $1,000. These margin requirements are established by the commodity exchanges, but individual brokers may require more.

Exhibit 23.3
Margin Requirements
for Selected Commodity
Contracts

Commodity	Margin Requirement
Broilers	$ 500
Cocoa	1,000
Cotton	1,000
Hogs	800
Lumber	1,200
Potatoes	500
Soybeans	1,500
Wheat	1,000

The margin requirements are only a small percentage of the value of the contract. For example, the $1,000 margin requirement for cocoa gives the owner of the contract a claim on 10 metric tons of cocoa. If cocoa is selling for $1,400 a metric ton, the total value of the contract is $14,000. The margin requirement as a percentage of the value of the contract is only 7.14 percent ($1,000/$14,000). This small amount of margin is one reason why a commodity contract offers so much potential leverage.

A major source of leverage

The potential leverage from speculating in commodity futures may be illustrated in a simple example. Consider a contract to buy wheat at $3.50 per bushel. Such a contract controls 5,000 bushels of wheat worth a total of $17,500 (5,000 × $3.50). If the investor buys this contract and the margin requirement is $1,000, he or she must remit $1,000. An increase of only $0.20 per bushel in the price of the commodity produces an increase of $1,000 in the value of the contract. This $1,000 is simply the product of the price change ($0.20) and the number of units in the contract (5,000). The profit on the contract if sold is $1,000.

What is the percentage return on the investment? With a margin of $1,000 the return is 100 percent, because the investor put up $1,000 and then earned an additional $1,000. An increase of less than 6 percent in the price of wheat produced a return on the speculator's money of 100 percent. Such a return is the result of leverage that comes from the small margin requirement and the large amount of the commodity controlled by the contract.

Leverage works both ways

Leverage, of course, works both ways. In the previous example if the price of the wheat declines by $0.10, the contract will be worth $17,000. A decline of only 2.9 percent in the price reduces the investor's margin from $1,000 to $500. To maintain the position, the investor must deposit additional margin with the broker. The broker's request for additional funds is referred to as a **margin call.** Failure to meet the margin call will result in the broker's closing the position. Since the contract is supported only by the initial margin, further price declines will mean that there is less collateral to support the contract. Should the investor default on the contract, the broker becomes responsible for its execution. The margin call thus protects the broker.

Maintenance margin

Actually, there are two margin requirements. The first is the minimum initial deposit, and the second is the maintenance margin. The **maintenance margin** specifies when the investor must deposit additional funds with the broker to cover a decline in

the value of a commodity contract. For example, the margin requirement for wheat is $1,000 and the maintenance margin is $750. If the investor owns a contract for the purchase of wheat and the value of the contract declines by $250 to the level of the maintenance margin ($750), the broker makes a margin call. This requires the investor to deposit an additional $250 into the account, which restores the initial $1,000 margin. This additional deposit protects the broker, since the value of the contract has declined and the investor has sustained a loss.

Maintenance margin applies to both buyers and sellers. If, in the previous example, the price of wheat were to rise by $250, the speculators who had sold short would see their margin decline from the initial deposit of $1,000 to $750. The broker would then make a margin call, which would require the short sellers to restore the $1,000 margin. Once again this protects the broker, since the value of the contract has risen and the short seller has sustained the loss.

These margin adjustments occur daily. After the market closes, the value of each account is totaled. In the jargon of futures trading, each account is "marked to the market." If the account does not meet the margin requirement, the broker issues a margin call that the individual must meet or the broker will close the position.

Marked to the market

Margin requirements are set by the commodity exchanges, but they cannot be below the minimums established by the Commodity Exchange Authority. These requirements are designed to protect brokers from the losses incurred by speculators. Individual brokers may further protect themselves from price fluctuations by requiring larger amounts of margin for commodity contracts.

While commodity futures prices can and do fluctuate, limits are imposed by the markets on the amount of price change per day. There are two types of limits—the daily limit, and the daily range. The **daily limit** establishes the maximum permissible price increase or decrease from the previous day. The **daily range** establishes the maximum permissible range in the commodity's futures price for the day. These limits may be the same, or the daily range may be twice as large as the daily limit. In this latter case the price can rise and fall by the amount of the daily limit. However, if the daily limit and the daily range are the same, the futures price of the commodity can rise but cannot fall (or vice versa) by the amount of the limit.

Price limits

These limits are illustrated in the following example. Suppose a commodity's futures price is $4.00, and the daily limit is $0.10. Accordingly, the price could increase to $4.10 or decline to $3.90. However, if the maximum daily range is also $0.10, then the price could rise to $4.10 but then could not fall below $4.00. Or the price could fall to $3.90 but then could not rise above $4.00. The price could range from $4.10 to $3.90 only if the daily range is twice the daily limit (i.e., a daily range of $0.20 in this example).

The daily limit and the daily range illustrated

Once the price of the futures contract rises by the permissible daily limit, further price increases are not allowed. This does not mean that trading ceases, because transactions can still occur at the maximum price or below should the price of the commodity weaken. The same applies to declining prices. Once the daily limit has been met, the price cannot continue to fall, but transactions can still occur at the lowest price and above should the price of the contract strengthen. These limits help to maintain orderly markets and to reduce the potentially disruptive effects from large daily swings in the price of the futures contract.

POINTS OF INTEREST

The Pig and the Pyramid of Gold—A Fable for Our Times

Once upon a time, way back at the start of 1979, a pig chanced to meet a wizard, who told him: "The world is going to hell. This means that the price of gold must rise."

"How much will it rise?" the pig asked.

"Before we greet the next new year," the wizard replied, "it shall have doubled."

The pig believed him. Being smart and bold, but a bit short on cash, the pig set out to make his fortune by leveraging and pyramiding in the gold futures market. He could buy a contract for later purchase of 100 ounces of gold with a tiny down payment. As the price of gold rose, so would the value of his contract. With his profits he could buy more contracts without stopping until he was very, very rich. Gold was then $227 an ounce, and the wizard had *assured* him it would double. And so this little pig went off to the gold futures market.

On Jan. 5, the pig bought his first contract—the right to buy 100 ounces of gold in October at $241.50 an ounce. It cost him just $750. At that price, an increase of only $7.50 an ounce would double the pig's money. A decline of $7.50 would wipe him out, of course, but it is not in a pig's nature to think negative thoughts. For a few weeks he was a happy pig, indeed. By Feb. 23, in fact, having pyramided all his paper profits into additional contracts, his $750 was worth nearly $40,000. Alas, on Apr. 12, gold fell and the pig was wiped out.

Undaunted, the pig bided his time. In mid-May, when the U.S. Treasury decided to reduce the amount of gold it sold monthly, he moved again. For a $1,000 deposit, he picked up one contract at $269.60. With scarcely a hitch, pyramiding again, his equity soared. On July 27, with gold at

$311.60, he had 318 contracts worth $373,000 and blessed the day he had run into the wizard. But after some good news on U.S. trade balances, gold fell, and by Aug. 3 the pig was wiped out again.

Still undaunted, and having heard rumors that "the Arabs are buying," the pig anted another $1,000 on Aug. 24 for a contract at $314.40 and was soon off on another giddy ride. By Oct. 1, pyramiding again, and with gold at $416, his equity had soared to almost $124,000. But he had been richer than that before, on paper, and he held out for more. By Oct. 4, gold had fallen back

to $370 and the pig once more was wiped out. Moral: Wizards don't always tell you that in any market, but especially in commodity futures, the shortest distance between two points is almost never a straight line.

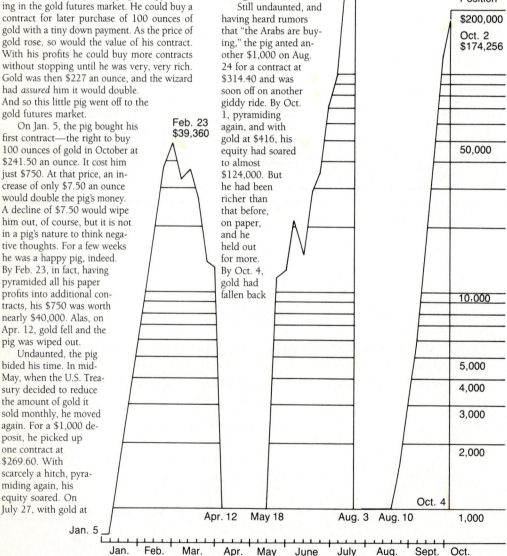

Net Cash Position

Source: Forbes, October 29, 1979. Reprinted by permission. Copyright 1979, Forbes, Inc.

HEDGING

One of the major reasons for the development of commodity futures markets was the desire of producers to reduce the risk of loss through price fluctuations. The procedure for this reduction in risk is called **hedging**, which consists of taking opposite positions at the same time.[2] In effect, a hedger simultaneously takes the long and the short position in a particular commodity.

Hedging reduces the risk of loss

Hedging is best explained by illustrations. In the first example, a wheat farmer expects to harvest a crop at a specified time. Since the costs of production are determined, the farmer knows the price that is necessary to earn a profit. Although the price that will be paid for wheat at harvest time is unknown, the current price of a contract for the future delivery of wheat is known. The farmer can then sell a contract for future delivery. Such a contract is a hedged position, because the farmer takes a long position (the wheat in the ground) and a short position (the contract for future delivery).

Such a position reduces the farmer's risk of loss from a price decline. Suppose the cost to produce the wheat is $2.50 per bushel and September wheat is selling in June for $2.75. If the farmer sells wheat for September delivery, a $0.25 per bushel profit is assured, because the buyer of the contract agrees to pay $2.75 per bushel on delivery in September. If the price of wheat declines to $2.50, the farmer is still assured of $2.75. However, if the price of wheat rises to $3.10 in September, the farmer still gets only $2.75. The additional $0.35 gain goes to the owner of the contract who bought the wheat for $2.75 but can now sell it for $3.10.

The risk from price declines

Is this transaction unfair? Remember that the farmer wanted protection against a decline in the price of wheat. If the price had declined to $2.40 and the farmer had not hedged, the farmer would have suffered a loss of $0.10 (the $2.40 price minus the $2.50 cost) per bushel. To obtain protection from this risk of loss, the farmer accepted the modest profit of $0.25 per bushel and relinquished the possibility of a larger profit. The speculator who bought the contract bore the risk of loss from a price decline and received the reward from a price increase.

Users of wheat hedge in the opposite direction. A flour producer desires to know the future cost of wheat in order to plan production levels and the prices that will be charged to distributors. However, the spot price of wheat need not hold into the future, so this producer buys a contract for future delivery and thereby hedges the position. This is hedging because the producer has a long position (the contract for the future delivery of wheat) and a short position (the future production of flour, which requires the future delivery of wheat).

The risk from price increases

If the producer buys a contract in June for the delivery of wheat in September at $2.75 per bushel, the future cost of the grain becomes known. The producer cannot be hurt by a price increase in wheat from $2.75 to $3.10, because the contract is for delivery at $2.75. However, the producer has forgone the chance of profit from a decline in the price of wheat from $2.75 to $2.40 per bushel.

Instead, the possibility of profit from a decline in the price of wheat rests with the speculator who sold the contract. If the price of wheat were to decline, the speculator

---

[2] Hedging cannot erase risk and may even increase it. For a discussion of how such an increase may occur, see Richard J. Teweles, Charles V. Harlow, and Herbert L. Stone, *The Commodity Futures Game—Who Wins? Who Loses? Why?* (New York: McGraw-Hill, 1974), 35–43.

could buy the wheat in September at the lower price, deliver it, and collect the $2.75 that is specified in the contract. However, this speculator would suffer a loss if the price of September wheat rose over $2.75. The cost would then exceed the delivery price specified in the contract.

Speculators take opposite positions of hedgers

These two examples illustrate why growers and producers hedge. They often take the opposite side of hedge positions. If all growers and producers agree on prices for future delivery, there would be no need for speculators; but this is not the case. Speculators buy or sell contracts when there is an excess or an insufficient supply. If the farmer in the preceding example could not find a producer to buy the contract for the future delivery of wheat, a speculator would buy the contract and accept the risk of a price decline. If the producer could not find a farmer to supply a contract for the future delivery of wheat, the speculator would sell the contract and accept the risk of a price increase.

Of course, farmers, producers, and speculators are simultaneously buying and selling contracts. No one knows who buys and who sells at a specific moment. However, if there is an excess or a shortage of one type of contract, the futures price of the commodity changes, which induces a certain behavior. For example, if September wheat is quoted at $2.75 per bushel, but no one is willing to buy at that price, the price declines. This induces some potential sellers to withdraw from the market and some potential buyers to enter the market. By this process, an imbalance of supply and demand for contracts for a particular delivery date is erased. It is the interaction of the hedgers and the speculators that establishes the price of each contract.

THE SELECTION OF COMMODITIES FUTURES CONTRACTS

The technical approach

As with the selection of securities, there are two basic methods for the selection of commodities futures contracts: the technical approach and the fundamental approach. The technical approach uses the same methods that are applied to the selection of securities. Various averages, point-and-figure charts, and bar graphs and their patterns are constructed for various commodities and are used to identify current price movements and to predict future price movements. Since this material was covered previously in Chapter 18, it is not repeated here.[3]

The fundamental approach

The fundamental approach is primarily concerned with those factors that affect the demand for and the supply of the various commodities. While the approach is similar to the selection of securities in that it uses economic data, the specifics are different. The price of a commodity depends on the supply of that commodity relative to the demand. Since the commodities are produced (e.g., wheat) or mined (e.g., silver), there are identifiable sources of supply. Correspondingly, there are identifiable sources of demand. However, there is also a variety of exogenous factors that may affect the supply of or the demand for a particular commodity, and these factors can have a powerful impact on the price of a specific commodity.

---

[3] The investor who is interested in the application of technical analysis to commodity selection should consult Richard J. Teweles, Charles V. Harlow, and Herbert L. Stone, *The Commodity Futures Game—Who Wins? Who Loses? Why?* (New York: McGraw-Hill, 1974), Chapter 7.

POINTS OF INTEREST
Commodity Mutual Funds

An alternative to investing directly in futures contracts is to acquire shares in a commodity mutual fund such as the Commodity Growth Fund, the Commodity Trend Timing Fund, or the Commodity Venture Fund. Purchases of commodity funds are similar to traditional investments. The individual buys the fund's shares, and the fund invests in futures contracts. Since the fund holds positions in a variety of contracts, the portfolio is diversified. This diversification is a major advantage of a commodity fund. Since diversification requires an individual to acquire positions in several commodities and since following positions in many commodities is very difficult, diversification may be virtually impossible for the individual investor to achieve in the futures markets.

To illustrate these points, consider a basic commodity such as wheat. It takes several months for wheat to be produced. It has to be planted, grown, and harvested. The amount of wheat that is planted is known because statistics are kept by the Commerce Department of the U.S. government. Such statistics are necessary for government forecasts of the economy, and this information is certainly available to those firms and individuals concerned with the size of the wheat crop.

The size of the crop that is planted and the size that is harvested, however, may be considerably different. The actual harvest depends on other factors. Particularly important is the weather, which can increase or decrease the yield. Good weather at the appropriate time can result in a bountiful harvest. A larger than anticipated supply of wheat should depress its price. On the other hand, bad weather, be it drought or excess rain, will have the opposite effect and will significantly reduce the anticipated supply. A reduction in supply should increase the price of wheat.

Demand, like supply, depends on both predictable and unpredictable forces. The demand for wheat depends on the needs of the firms that use the grain in their products. The producers of flour and cereals are obvious potential customers for wheat. However, the total demand also includes exports. If a foreign government enters the market and buys a substantial amount of wheat, this may cause a significant increase in its price.

Such government intervention in the market is not limited to foreign governments. The U.S. federal government also buys and sells commodities. Sometimes it buys to absorb excess supplies of a commodity and thus supports the commodity's price. In other cases the federal government may sell from its surplus stocks of a given commodity. This, of course, has the opposite impact on the price of the commodity. The increased supply tends to decrease the price or at least to reduce a tendency for the price to rise. These exogenous forces in the commodity markets are just another source of risk with which the speculator must contend.

Government intervention

Obviously the speculator seeks to identify shifts in demand or supply before they occur in order to take the appropriate position. Anticipation of a price increase indicates the purchase of a futures contract, whereas an anticipated price decline indicates

the sale of a futures contract. Unfortunately, the ability to consistently predict changes in demand and supply is very rare. This should be obvious! If an individual could predict the future, he or she would certainly make a fortune not just in the commodity futures markets but in any market. Mortals, however, lack such clairvoyance, which leaves them with fundamental and technical analysis as a means to select commodity futures for purchase.

The need to limit losses   Whether an investor uses technical or fundamental analysis, there is an important strategy for trading futures. The speculator should seek to limit losses and permit profits to run. Successful commodity futures trading requires the speculator's ability to recognize bad positions and to close them before they generate large losses. Many speculators, especially novices, do the exact opposite by taking small profits as they occur but maintaining positions that sustain losses. Then, when price changes produce margin calls, the speculator is forced either to close the position at a loss or to put up additional funds. If the speculator meets the margin call by committing additional funds, that individual is violating the strategy. Instead of taking the small loss, this investor is risking additional funds in the hope that the price will recover.

FINANCIAL AND CURRENCY FUTURES

In the previous discussion commodity contracts meant futures contracts for the delivery of physical goods. However, there are also **financial futures**, which are contracts for the future delivery of securities such as treasury bills, and **currency futures**, which are contracts for the future delivery of currencies (e.g., the British pound or the German mark). Several financial futures are illustrated in Exhibit 23.2 under the heading "Financial." The market for financial futures, like the market for commodity futures, has two participants: the speculators and the hedgers. It is the interaction of their demands for and supplies of these contracts that determines the price of a given futures contract.

The hedgers   While any speculator may participate in any of the financial or currency futures markets, the hedgers differ from the speculators because they also deal in the currency itself. The hedgers in currency futures are primarily multinational firms that make and receive payments in foreign moneys. Since the value of these currencies can change, the value of payments that the firms must make or receive can change. Firms thus establish hedge positions to lock in the price of the currency and thereby avoid the risk associated with fluctuations in the value of one currency relative to another.

As interest rates and bond prices change, the yields from lending and the cost of borrowing are altered. To reduce the risk of loss from fluctuations in interest rates, borrowers and lenders may establish hedge positions in financial futures to lock in a particular interest rate.

The speculators   Speculators, of course, are not seeking to reduce risk but reap large returns for taking risks. The speculators are bearing the risk that the hedgers are seeking to avoid. The speculators try to correctly anticipate changes in the value of currencies and the direction of changes in interest rates and to take positions that will yield profits. The return they earn (if successful) is then magnified because of the leverage offered by the small margin requirements necessary to establish the positions.

How financial futures may produce profits for speculators may be illustrated with an example using a futures contract for the delivery of U.S. Treasury bonds. Suppose a speculator expects interest rates to fall and bond prices to rise. This individual would *buy* a contract for the delivery of treasury bonds in the future (i.e., the *long* position). If interest rates do fall and bond prices rise, the value of this contract increases because the speculator has the contract for the delivery of bonds at a lower price (i.e., higher yield). If, however, interest rates rise, bond prices fall and the value of this contract declines. The decline in the value of the contract inflicts a loss on the speculator who bought the contract when yields were lower.

If the speculator expects interest rates to rise, that individual *sells* a contract for the future delivery of treasury bonds (i.e., establishes a *short* position). If interest rates do rise and the value of the bonds decline, the value of this contract must decline, but the speculator earns a profit. This short seller can buy the bonds at a lower price and deliver them at the price specified in the contract. Or the speculator may simply buy a contract at the lower value, thereby closing out the position at a profit. Of course, if this speculator is wrong and interest rates fall, the value of the bonds increases, inflicting a loss on the speculator, who must now pay more to buy the bonds to cover the contract.

The same general principles apply to currency futures. Suppose the price of the British pound is $2. A speculator who is bullish and anticipates that the price of the pound will rise establishes a long position in the pound. This individual buys a contract for the future delivery of pounds. The futures price may be $2.02 or $1.96. It need not necessarily equal the current or spot price. (If many speculators expect the price of the pound to rise, they will bid up the futures price so that it exceeds the current price. If speculators expect the price of the pound to fall, they will then drive down the futures price of the pound.) If this speculator buys the futures contract for $2.02 and is correct (i.e., the price of the pound rises), that individual makes a profit. If, for example, the price of the pound were to rise to $2.20, the value of the contract may rise by $0.18 per pound (i.e., $2.20 − $2.02).[4] Of course, if the speculator who bought the contract is wrong and the price of the pound declines to $1.80, the value of the contract also declines, and the speculator suffers a loss.

If the speculator had been bearish and anticipated a decline in the value of the pound, that individual would establish a short position and sell contracts for the future delivery of pounds. If the speculator is right and the value of the pound declines, the speculator may close the position for a profit. Since pounds are now worth less, the speculator may buy the cheaper pounds and deliver them at the higher price specified in the contract.[5] If the speculator had been wrong and the price of the pound had risen, that individual would have suffered a loss, as it would have cost more to buy the pounds to make the future delivery required by the contract.

Financial and currency futures, like all futures contracts, offer the speculator an opportunity for profit from a change in prices. While such securities are not suitable

Financial futures—

1. Long position

2. Short position

Currency futures—

1. Long position

2. Short position

---

[4]At expiration the futures and spot prices must be equal. Thus, if the pound is $2.20 on the expiration date, the value of the contract must be $2.20 per pound.

[5]Actually the speculator would close the short position by buying an opposite contract (a contract for the future delivery of pounds).

POINTS OF INTEREST
The Variety of Financial Futures

While the text discussion features U.S. Treasury bonds and NYSE Composite Index futures, there are a variety of financial futures available to the investor. These contracts and their respective markets include those in the table below.

In addition to financial futures, there are options available on U.S. Treasury securities. Put and call options on treasury bonds are traded on the Chicago Board of Trade, and put and call op-tions on treasury notes and bills are traded on the American Stock Exchange. And in 1983, put and call options on financial futures were created and commenced trading. The investor may now pur-chase a put or a call option based on Standard & Poor's 500 futures contracts. For an explanation of these options, see "The New Options on S&P 500 Futures," *The Outlook* (February 23, 1983), 908–909.

Contract	Market
U.S. Treasury bonds	Chicago Board of Trade
U.S. Treasury notes	Chicago Board of Trade
U.S. Treasury bills	International Monetary Market at the Chicago Mercantile Exchange
Bank CDs	International Monetary Market at the Chicago Mercantile Exchange
Standard & Poor's 500 Index futures	Chicago Mercantile Exchange
NYSE Composite futures	New York Futures Exchange
KC Value Line Futures	Kansas City Board of Trade
Major Market Index	Chicago Board of Trade
Muni Bond Index	Chicago Board of Trade
Eurodollar	International Monetary Market at the Chicago Mercantile Exchange
British Pound	International Monetary Market at the Chicago Mercantile Exchange
Canadian Dollar	International Monetary Market at the Chicago Mercantile Exchange
Japanese Yen	International Monetary Market at the Chicago Mercantile Exchange
Swiss Franc	International Monetary Market at the Chicago Mercantile Exchange
West German Mark	International Monetary Market at the Chicago Mercantile Exchange

for the portfolios of most individuals, they do offer more sophisticated investors an opportunity for large returns. Whether the returns justify the large risks is, of course, a decision that each individual investor must make.

Hedging against an increase in interest rates

While most individuals think of futures contracts as a means to speculate on price changes, financial futures may be used to reduce the risk of loss from an increase in interest rates. Consider an investor who desires a flow of income and has constructed a large portfolio of bonds. The portfolio's market value would decline if interest rates rose. To offset the potential loss, the investor could hedge using financial futures. Since the individual has a long position in the bonds, the investor must take a short position in the futures. Therefore, the investor sells contracts for the future delivery of bonds. If interest rates rise (and therefore cause the value of the bonds to fall), the value of the futures contracts also falls. Since the investor has a short position in the contracts, the

individual profits from the rising interest rates. The profits on the futures contracts then offset the decline in the value of the bonds.[6]

STOCK MARKET FUTURES

During 1982, a new type of futures contract based on an index of the stock market (e.g., the Value Line stock index, the Standard & Poor's 500 stock index, or the New York Stock Exchange Composite Index) started trading. These **stock index futures** contracts offer speculators and hedgers opportunities for profit or risk reduction that are not possible through the purchase of individual securities. For example, the NYSE Composite Index futures contracts have a value that is 500 times the value of the NYSE Index. Thus, if the NYSE Index is 140, the contract is worth $70,000. By purchasing this contract (i.e., by establishing a long position), the holder profits if the market rises. If the NYSE Index were to rise to 145, the value of the contract would increase to $72,500. The investor would then earn a profit of $2,500. Of course, if the NYSE Index should decline, the buyer would experience a loss.

The sellers of these contracts also participate in the fluctuations of the market. However, their positions are the opposite of the buyers (i.e., they are short). If the value of the NYSE Index were to fall from 140 to 135, the value of the contract would decline from $70,000 to $67,500, and the short seller would earn a $2,500 profit. Of course, if the market were to rise, the short seller would suffer a loss. Obviously if the individual anticipates a rising market, that investor should buy the futures contract. Conversely, if the investor expects the market to fall, that individual should sell the contract.

These contracts may also be bought and sold by professional money managers who are not speculating on price movements but who seek to hedge against adverse price movements. For example, suppose a portfolio manager has a well-diversified portfolio of stocks. If the market rises, the value of this portfolio appreciates. However, there is the risk of loss if the market were to decline. The portfolio manager can reduce this risk by selling a NYSE Composite Index futures contract. If the market declines, the losses experienced by the portfolio will at least be partially offset by the appreciation in the value of the short position in the futures contract.

The hedgers are professional money managers

NYSE Index futures contracts are similar to other futures contracts. The buyers and sellers must make good faith deposits (i.e., margin payments). As with other futures contracts, the amount of this margin is modest, only $3,500 per contract. Thus, these contracts offer considerable leverage. If stock prices move against the investor and his or her equity in the position declines, the individual will have to place additional funds in the account to support the contract. Since there is an active market in the contracts, the investor may close a position at any time by taking the opposite position. Thus, if the investor had purchased a contract, that long position would be closed by selling a contract. If the investor had sold a contract, that short position would be closed by buying a futures contract.

The margin requirement

---

[6] To determine the exact number of contracts that should be sold to offset the potential loss, see Nancy H. Rothstein, *The Handbook of Financial Futures* (New York: McGraw-Hill, 1984), 262–264.

POINTS OF INTEREST
The Triple Witching Hour

Four times a year, on the third Friday in March, June, September, and December, Wall Street experiences the "triple witching hour." This hour occurs on the last day of trading in (1) a set of futures contracts on stock indexes, (2) options on stock indexes, and (3) options on specific individual stocks. This confluence of several expiring options and futures contracts sometimes generates considerable price volatility as professional traders complete maneuvers generated by programmed trading.

With programmed trading, computers are used to identify differentials in the prices of options and the underlying securities. If, for example, the index options are selling slightly below their intrinsic value, the professional traders will purchase the index options and simultaneously sell the stocks in the index. Since all the transactions are effectuated very rapidly, price changes can be sudden and dramatic. For example, on March 21, 1986, the Dow Jones industrial average declined over 35 points, most of which occurred in the last few minutes of trading when frantic sell orders dramatically drove down security prices.

The possibility of such volatility has both its detractors and supporters. Critics suggest that computer-driven programmed trading and the resulting increased volatility drive away small investors who perceive the stock market as becoming riskier. The supporters of programmed trading contend that such trades increase market efficiency by erasing price differentials.

No physical delivery of securities

There is one important difference between stock market futures and other futures contracts. Settlement at the expiration or maturity of the contract occurs in cash. There is no physical delivery of securities as could occur with a futures contract to buy or sell wheat or corn. Instead gains and losses are totaled and are added to or subtracted from the participants' accounts. The long and short positions are then closed.

SUMMARY

Investing in commodity futures involves the buying or selling of contracts for future delivery. The speculator may take a long position, which is the purchase of a contract for future delivery, or a short position, which is the sale of a contract for future delivery. The long position generates profits if the commodity's price rises, while the short position results in a gain if the price falls.

Commodity contracts are purchased through brokers who own seats on commodity exchanges. The contracts are supported by deposits, which are called margin, that signify the investor's good faith. The margin requirement is only a small fraction of the value of the contract, and this produces considerable potential for leverage. A small change in the price of the commodity produces a large profit or loss relative to the small amount of margin. For this reason, commodity contracts are considered very speculative.

Hedging plays an important role in commodity futures markets. Growers, miners, and other users of commodities often wish to reduce their risk of loss from price fluctuations and thus hedge their positions. Growers sell contracts for future delivery, and producers buy contracts for future delivery. Frequently, it is the speculators who are buying and offering the contracts sought by the hedgers. In this way the risks that the hedgers seek to reduce are passed on to the speculators.

The price of a commodity, and thus the value of a futures contract, is related to the supply of and the demand for the commodity. Speculators may use technical or fundamental analysis to help forecast supply, demand, and price movements. Unfortunately, many exogenous factors, such as the weather or government intervention, make accurate forecasting difficult. These forces also contribute to the price fluctuations experienced in the commodity markets and are a major source of the risk associated with investing in commodity futures.

Besides commodity futures there are financial futures, currency futures, and stock market futures. Financial futures are contracts for the delivery of financial assets such as U.S. Treasury bills and bonds. Currency futures are contracts for the future delivery of foreign moneys such as German marks or British pounds. Stock market futures are based on a broad measure of the market (e.g., the New York Stock Exchange Composite Index). Speculators who anticipate movements in interest rates, foreign currencies, or the stock market can speculate on these anticipated price changes by taking appropriate positions in futures contracts. As with all commodity contracts, the potential return may be quite large, but the risk of loss is also large. Speculating in commodity futures is probably best left for those few investors who understand these potential risks and can afford to take them.

Terms to Remember

Futures contracts	Margin call
Speculators	Maintenance margin
Long position	Daily limit
Short position	Daily range
Futures price	Hedging
Spot price	Financial futures
Open interest	Currency futures
Margin	Stock index futures

Questions

1. What is a futures contract? What is the spot price and the futures price of a commodity?

2. Why is investing in commodity futures considered to be speculative?

3. What is the difference between a long and a short position in a commodity future?

4. What is margin and why is it a source of leverage? What is a margin call?

5. Why do farmers and other users of commodity futures hedge their positions?

6. If an investor anticipates a decline in a commodity's price, which futures position should he or she take?

7. How may government intervention affect commodity prices? Are commodity futures markets subject to government regulation?

8. What is a financial futures contract? If you expect interest rates to rise, should you buy a financial futures contract?

9. If you anticipated that the price of the British pound would rise and wanted to speculate on that increase, should you sell or buy a contract for the delivery of pounds?

10. What is the difference between the long and the short positions in a contract for the future delivery of U.S. Treasury bonds?

Problems

1. This problem is designed to illustrate hedging with currency futures. The subsequent questions lead you, the student, through the process of hedging. While this material was not explicitly covered in the text material, your instructor may use this problem to show how hedging may reduce the risk of loss from fluctuations in the price of a foreign currency.

You expect to receive a payment of 1,000,000 British pounds after six months. The pound is currently worth $1.60 (i.e., £1 = $1.60), but the six-month futures price is $1.56 (i.e., £1 = $1.56). You expect the price of the pound to decline (i.e., the value of the dollar to rise). If this expectation is fulfilled, you will suffer a loss when the pounds are converted into dollars when you receive them six months in the future.

    a. Given the current price, what is the expected payment in dollars?

    b. Given the future price, how much would you receive in dollars?

    c. If, after six months, the pound is worth $1.35, what is your loss from the decline in the value of the pound?

    d. To avoid this potential loss, you decide to hedge and sell a contract for the future delivery of pounds at the going futures price of $1.56. What is the cost to you of this protection from the possible decline in the value of the pound?

    e. If, after hedging, the price of the pound falls to $1.45, what is the maximum amount that you lose? (Why is your answer different than your answer to part c.?)

    f. If, after hedging, the price of the pound rises to $1.80, how much do you gain from your position?

    g. How would your answer be different to part f. if you had not hedged and the price of the pound had risen to $1.80?

2. You expect the stock market to decline, but instead of selling a stock short, you decide to sell a stock index futures contract based on the New York Stock Exchange Composite Index. The index is currently 138, and the contract has a value that is 500 times the amount of the index. The margin requirement is $3,500 and the maintenance margin requirement is $1,000.

    a. When you *sell* the contract, how much must you put up?

    b. What is the value of the contract based on the index?

c. If after one week of trading the index stands at 140, what has happened to your position? How much have you lost or profited?

d. If the index rose to 144, what would you be required to do?

e. If the index declined to 136.6 (approximately 1 percent from the starting value), what is your percentage profit or loss on your position?

f. If you had purchased the contract instead of selling it, how much would you have invested?

g. If you had purchased the contract and the index subsequently rose from 138 to 144, what would be your required investment?

h. Contrast your answers to parts d. and g.?

Suggested Readings

For general but detailed descriptions of commodity futures trading and hedging, consult:

Gould, Bruce G. *Dow Jones-Irwin Guide to Commodities Trading.* Revised ed. Homewood, Ill.: Dow Jones-Irwin, 1981.

Teweles, Richard J., Charles V. Harlow, and Herbert L. Stone. *The Commodity Futures Game— Who Wins? Who Loses? Why?* New York: McGraw-Hill, 1974.

The more recent financial futures and currency futures are covered in:

Loosigian, Allan M. *Foreign Exchange Futures.* Homewood, Ill.: Dow Jones-Irwin, 1981.

Loosigian, Allan M. *Interest Rate Futures.* Homewood, Ill.: Dow Jones-Irwin, 1980.

Schwarz, Edward W. *How To Use Interest Rate Futures Contracts.* Homewood, Ill.: Dow Jones-Irwin, 1979.

For a detailed guide to financial futures that includes the mechanics of futures markets, the role of clearinghouses, trading in international currencies, hedging, speculative and hedging strategies, fundamental and technical analysis, and regulation, see:

Rothstein, Nancy H. *The Handbook of Financial Futures.* New York: McGraw-Hill, 1984.

For information on stock index futures, consult:

Smith, Courtney D. *How to Make Money in Stock Index Futures.* New York: McGraw-Hill, 1985.

Weiner, Neil S. *Stock Index Futures.* New York: John Wiley & Sons, 1984.

The exchanges also publish a considerable amount of material. For example, see:

Chicago Board of Trade. *Options on U.S. Treasury Bond Futures for Institutional Investors.*

Chicago Board of Trade. *Interest Rate Futures for Institutional Investors.* 1985.

The reader should be warned that none of this material is inherently easy and that these books require concentrated and serious reading.

24 Investing in Nonfinancial Assets: Collectibles and Gold

LEARNING OBJECTIVES

After completing this chapter you should be able to

1. Compare the sources of risk from investing in collectibles and other physical assets with the sources of risk from investing in financial assets.

2. Define *income-in-kind* and illustrate how it applies to investments in some physical assets.

3. Explain the role of auctions in investing in collectibles.

4. Explain why the valuation of art is exceedingly subjective.

5. List the possible mediums for investing in gold.

6. Describe the relationship between inflation and the price of gold.

7. Explain why an investment in gold may result in a loss.

S*ome individuals start accumulating objects (e.g., baseball cards, stamps, or dolls) when they are young. While these collections may have only been youthful hobbies, they may stimulate the appetite for collecting. Many individuals who invest in collectibles and other nonfinancial assets have done so for years. However, the inflation of the 1970s and early 1980s increased the general public's interest in collectibles and other physical assets. In the mid-1980s this interest in collectibles abated as inflation declined, but a collection constructed with thoughtfulness and foresight can still be both satisfying and serve as a store of value.*

Investing in collectibles and other nonfinancial assets is essentially no different from investing in financial assets. The investments are made now and the returns are earned in the future. The returns consist of income or services generated by the physical asset plus any capital gains. In order to realize capital gains, the asset must be sold. Hence, a market must exist for the asset. Realized gains are subject to capital gains taxation. And, as with any investment, there is the element of risk.

While investing in physical assets is similar to investing in financial assets, there are important differences. Nonfinancial assets have their own markets, and investing in them requires specialized knowledge, which is considerably different from the knowledge used in the selection of financial assets. An entire lifetime may be spent learning the fine points that make an individual an expert in a particular type of asset, such as art or real estate.

This chapter briefly covers investing in two general classes of physical assets: collectibles (including art, Oriental rugs, and antiques), and gold. It can be only a cursory survey of the field. The emphasis will be placed on the elements most similar to those associated with investing in financial assets: the potential returns, an asset's marketability, and the risks involved. Implicit throughout the discussion is the assumption that the individual needs specialized information to know and understand these investments. Such information can best be obtained through careful and extensive study of the particular physical assets of interest to an individual.

While the chapter primarily uses art and gold to illustrate investments in collectibles, these do not exhaust the possibilities. Many physical assets that people accumulate have the characteristics of investments. Old baseball cards, antique furniture, bisque dolls, stamps, and autographs can serve as potential stores of value. They may prove to be excellent investments that yield substantial returns for individuals who take the time to learn what differentiates the wheat from the chaff and who judiciously acquire quality representations of these collectibles.

RETURNS, MARKETS, AND RISK

Investing in physical assets requires that the investor have a broad definition of markets, returns, and risk. A market brings together buyers and sellers in order to transact the exchange of goods and services. When a mutually acceptable price is determined, the goods are transferred from the seller to the buyer. This is obviously what occurs in the organized security markets such as the New York Stock Exchange (NYSE). Sellers and buyers of securities are brought together, and they trade securities for money.

Many securities, however, are bought and sold in that informal market called the over-the-counter market. There is no centralized place where transactions in the over-the-counter market are consummated. It exists wherever a buyer and a seller can trade cash for securities.

The market is informal

The market for art and other collectibles is also an informal market that is similar to the over-the-counter market for securities. There is no organized center such as the NYSE for the transfer of these physical assets. While there may be certain centers, such as the diamond district in New York, the market is geographically dispersed and not formally organized.

Because there is no formal market, there are none of the advantages offered by such formality. For example, price quotations (i.e., bid and ask prices) are not readily available. The volume of transactions is generally not recorded, and when it is, this information is not widely disseminated as are reports of security trades, which are published in the financial press. Specialized publications may report some of this information, but these are frequently not well known to the investor and may not be readily available.

Furthermore, there is little or no regulation of these informal markets. While the Securities and Exchange Commission may work to reduce fraud and to assure the

There is less regulation

timely disclosure of pertinent financial information that may affect the value of a firm's securities, no such government organization exists to protect the buyers of many physical assets. It is a case of "let the buyer beware," and the unsuspecting investor is certainly an easy target for the forger or any other shady dealer who can prey on the individual's desire to find an asset that will offer an exceptional return.

The return

The return offered by an investment in a physical asset such as gold comes from the same sources as the gain from an investment in a financial asset: the potential for price appreciation and the flow of income. The return earned through price appreciation is the difference between the net sale price and the purchase price. The net sale price is the realized price minus any commissions or fees necessary to make the sale. While the commissions for buying and selling stock may be only 2 or 3 percent of the price, the commissions for buying and selling physical investments may be considerably more. These fees vary with the different types of assets, but they can consume a substantial portion of any profit earned through price appreciation.

Other expenses

In addition to commissions, other expenses may be incurred with an investment in physical assets that are not incurred with financial assets. The investor may take out special insurance to cover insurable risks. For example, insurance may be desirable for investments in art, which are subject to theft and fire. Or the investor may rent space (e.g., a safe deposit box) to store the assets. This certainly would apply to valuable stamps, coins, and gold. These additional expenses reduce the return earned by the investment.

Income-in-kind

Besides the return earned through price appreciation, the investor may receive a return through income received. Many physical assets that are held as investments offer **income-in-kind** (i.e., a nonmonetary form of income). Oriental rugs may be functional; art works are decorative, and housing provides shelter and space. These flows of income-in-kind may not be considered income by the typical investor, but they should be because they are part of the return earned by the investment. Actually, the potential flow of services offered by some physical assets should be the prime reason for buying them. It is not so much the potential for price appreciation but the flow of income-in-kind that makes some investments attractive. This concept will be developed further when it is applied to several specific investments that are subsequently discussed.

Sources of risk

Investing in art and collectibles subjects the investor to the same basic risks associated with investing in financial assets. These are the elements of risk attributable to the market (i.e., the risk associated with price changes of a class of assets) and the risk associated with a particular company or asset.[1] In addition, the investor must face the risk of loss from inflation and the problems associated with theft and fraud.

Price fluctuations

The markets for physical assets vary over time. Prices do fluctuate and not always upward. Presumably, if prices in general move in a particular direction, the value of specific assets will move accordingly. Hence, if the price of gold rises, then the value of gold coins will rise. Conversely, if the price of gold declines, the value of gold coins will fall. The investor who buys gold and gold coins cannot avoid this market risk, which applies to all physical assets.

The investor must bear the risk associated with the specific investment. Changes in taste alter the public's demand for specific goods. For example, if the demand for

---

[1] In Chapter 8 these sources of risk were called systematic and unsystematic, respectively.

POINTS OF INTEREST
Insuring Your Collectibles

If the investor has a sizable collection of collectibles, it may be desirable to insure it against loss from fire, theft, and other perils. Before purchasing this insurance, the investor should consider the costs and benefits of such coverage. Special insurance may not be necessary since the investor's homeowner's policy generally covers the contents of the house up to one-half the value of the home. There may, however, be a limit on the coverage of a particular item or class of items.

The investor may remedy this limitation by adding a floater to the policy to cover specific items. This will require that the investor and the insurance company agree on the value of each specific item. Instead of a floater, the investor may buy a specialized policy (e.g., a fine arts policy). This also requires enumeration and valuation of specific items. Such coverage should be updated annually.

Insurance is not free, and for sizable collections (e.g., over $100,000) the insurance company will probably require a security system. The investor should never overinsure, since the companies will pay only the market value of the item. Claim adjusters are not fools and will not accept inflated claims. Overinsurance is a waste of funds that may be used more profitably elsewhere.

Oriental rugs increases, the value of most Oriental rugs also will appreciate. However, even within this group some will appreciate more than others. The rugs that are popular today will not necessarily be those that are popular tomorrow. Thus, the investor may experience losses on specific investments even though the market as a whole moves upward in price.

A major reason for purchasing physical assets as an investment is that they may help the individual beat inflation. The value of financial assets such as stocks and bonds often decline when the inflation rate increases. This was illustrated earlier in Figure 13.5, which showed the sharp declines in the Dow Jones industrial average during inflationary periods. However, the value of physical assets may keep pace with the rate of inflation, as individuals seek to buy them in preference to financial assets, thus driving up their prices.

The investor should realize that for this above strategy to work, he or she must anticipate inflation in order to purchase physical assets before the price increases. In addition, even if inflation were to occur, it is not necessarily true that the price of all physical assets will rise. Their prices can rise, fall, or remain the same. Inflation inflicts a loss of purchasing power on any investor whose particular portfolio does not keep pace with the rate of inflation. While some physical assets have appreciated in price (e.g., housing), this is not true for all physical assets. For example, the price of gold fell during 1981, but the inflation rate during the same period was approximately 9 percent. Obviously, the rate of inflation exceeded the rate of return on an investment in gold during that particular period.

The last sources of risk are theft and fraud. Although financial assets such a stocks and bonds can be left with custodians (e.g., brokers), that is not necessarily the case

Theft and fraud

with physical assets. One's house is not left with the real estate broker. The investor in Oriental rugs or art will want to use these items or at least display them in order to enjoy them. The coin and stamp collector probably enjoys looking at the collection and does not leave it with coin and stamp dealers. While coins, gold, stamps, art, and Oriental rugs may be stored with a dealer or in a safe deposit box when the investor cannot care for them, most of the time these items are kept at home, where they are subject to theft and fire. Although the individual may seek to protect these investments with insurance, adequate protection will require detailed records to verify the asset's value.

Finally, the investor must bear the risk of fraud. Fakes and misrepresentations are frequently sold to unsuspecting buyers who lack the knowledge to appraise them properly. This applies not only to novices but also to sophisticated professionals who, on occasion, have been completely deceived. The possibility of fraud, or at least of excessive pricing, truly makes investing in art and collectibles areas in which the novice should move with caution.

Some practical advice

This suggests several practical steps for investing in these assets. First, investors should buy only after doing their homework. They should know what they are looking at and what to look for. Second, investors should seek to specialize in those particular physical assets that appeal to them. For example, one should not buy Oriental rugs because they are Oriental rugs but should collect them because they can be enjoyed and are very functional. Third, one should invest in art and collectibles only after sufficient financial assets have been accumulated to meet financial emergencies and contingencies. Physical assets offer little, if any, liquidity. Fourth, the investor should be willing to lose the entire investment in the art object or other collectible. Under these circumstances the investor will not be deluded into thinking that the asset will offer extraordinary gains. Such gains rarely, if ever, accrue to the novice, and investors in art and other collectibles are competing with professionals who have a lifetime of experience on which to base decisions.

ART, ORIENTAL RUGS, AND ANTIQUES [2]

Past returns

During the 1970s, perhaps no investments performed better than those in art (i.e., paintings, sculpture, and graphics). One art expert, Willi Bongard (who is also an economist), has estimated that the value of the works of leading modern artists increased 18 percent compounded annually in the period from 1965 to 1975.[3] That is the equivalent of $1.00 growing to $5.25 after ten years. Such a return compares very favorably with the Dow Jones industrial average or Standard & Poor's 500 stock index. During the same period, the stock market declined according to these two price indices! Such comparisons, however, can be misleading, because stocks are homogeneous and their values are easily measured. Art works are very difficult to compare (i.e., each is unique), and their values can only be approximated.

---

[2] The general concepts in this section apply to other collectibles, such as gems or even baseball cards and beer cans.

[3] D. McConathy, "Art as Investment," *Artscanada* (Autumn 1975): 46.

The Market for Collectibles

Art objects may be purchased in a variety of ways. The primary means is through dealers, many of whom make a market in the items. Such dealers sell as well as buy. Why do they do both? The art and security markets are very similar in that they are primarily secondhand markets. Since van Gogh and Rembrandt are no longer producing, sales of their work can only be secondary transactions. The same applies to many Oriental rugs and to antiques. Any exchanges after the initial sale are in the secondary markets. In order for dealers to have these items for sale (i.e., inventory), many either acquire them or hold them on consignment. Dealers who purchase art, antiques, and Oriental rugs hold them in inventory for future sale. They may not be able to operate solely on new output, especially since the most valuable works of art and Oriental rugs and all antiques are those already in existence.   *How to buy collectibles*

Since some dealers make markets, they, in effect, establish bid and ask prices. While such prices may not be readily known to the investor, any dealer who is willing to buy used rugs, antiques, or art is offering a bid. Of course, the offer to sell establishes an asking price.   *Market makers*

Since the volume of transactions is low and the number of dealers in these specialized areas is relatively small, the spread between the bid and the ask will be substantial. The buyer may be paying the retail price but only receiving the wholesale price, which will certainly consume a substantial amount of any price appreciation. For example, a dealer in Oriental rugs may be willing to repurchase a rug (in acceptable condition) at the original sale price, in which case the individual has had the use of the rug but has not realized any price appreciation.   *Large spread between bid and asked prices*

Instead of repurchasing the rug, the dealer may offer to hold it on consignment. The title remains with the owner while the dealer tries to sell the rug. If a sale occurs, the dealer receives a set percentage of the price. This commission can be as high as 30 or 40 percent of the sale price. Obviously, the price of collectibles must rise substantially for the owner to recoup the cost, pay the commission, and still net a profit.

The second major market for valuable art, Oriental rugs, and antiques is the auction. While the word *auction* may imply the Saturday afternoon sale of an estate, many major works are sold through auctions. The important auction houses of the world (e.g., Sotheby Parke-Bernet or Christie's, both of which have offices in New York and London) hold auctions that handle many valuable art treasures.   *Auctions*

Such auction houses permit the owners of valuable art, antiques, and Oriental rugs to offer them for sale, but the sale price that will be realized is unknown in advance. Although the auction house places an estimated value on the item, the realized price can be higher or lower than the estimate. After the sale, the auction house takes its fee or commission from the realized price. This fee can be as high as one-third of the sale price for small dollar amounts. The percentage charged often declines as the realized value increases.   *Fees*

Buyers as well as sellers may have to pay a fee for items bought at an auction. Both Christie's and Sotheby Parke-Bernet add a premium that the buyer must pay of up to 10 percent of the cost of the purchase. This charge is in addition to their fees charged the seller, which range from 2 to 10 percent of the proceeds of the sale.

Although the fees for selling art, antiques, and Oriental rugs are substantial, there is a secondary market for these goods. Although the investor can seek to avoid the costs by directly marketing the items, the dealers and auction houses may be able to

realize a better price than the individual could. These specialists have a better idea of the value of a specific item and hence may price it more realistically than, and perhaps more profitably for, the seller.

The Return on Collectibles

Sources of return

The return on investments in art, antiques, or Oriental rugs comes from two sources: price appreciation and the flow of services generated by the investment (i.e., income-in-kind). It is obvious how price appreciation generates a return, since it is the difference between the net proceeds of the sale (the sale price minus the commissions) and the purchase price. As has already been discussed, the commissions may consume a substantial portion of any gross profits.

Income-in-kind

The second source of the return, income-in-kind, is also obvious, since art, many antiques, and Oriental rugs are functional. Some individuals may not view these services as a flow of income, but they are. The services of Oriental rugs and antiques and the aesthetic pleasure of art generate nonmonetary income.

The flow of services

An Oriental rug, antique, or painting may offer a superior total return when both the flow of services and price appreciation are considered. For example, if the investor compares the cost of wall-to-wall carpeting with the cost of an Oriental rug, the return offered by the Oriental rug will probably be superior. The wall-to-wall carpeting depreciates and cannot be readily moved if the investor changes homes. The Oriental rug performs the same service, may not depreciate and may even appreciate in value, and is easily moved. No wonder such rugs are viewed by some individuals as excellent investments, because these rugs generate many years of service and offer the potential for price appreciation.

The same applies to art works and many antiques. Paintings, lithographs, and sculpture all generate a flow of service. The owner derives pleasure from them, which is part of the total return on the investment. Of course, calculating this flow of income is probably impossible, so the true return on an investment in these items cannot be determined.

The Valuation of Collectibles

Value is related to scarcity

What gives art, antiques, or Oriental rugs their value? The answer to this question is both simple and complex. The obvious answer is scarcity relative to demand. There are only so many paintings by a master, and certainly this scarcity enhances their value.

Although there is a paucity of works by major artists, there is an abundance of what passes for art. This abundance (or an abundance relative to the demand) has resulted in very low prices for the vast majority of paintings, graphics, and poor quality Oriental rugs. But scarcity alone does not explain value.

The work's creator and quality

The valuation of art objects actually depends on many factors.[4] Value is affected by the reputation of the artist and quality of the work as well as by many other factors, including attributes of the work itself and exogenous factors.

---

[4] See Richard H. Rush, "Art as an Investment," in L. Barnes and S. Feldman, *Handbook of Wealth Management* (New York: McGraw-Hill, 1977), 37–1 through 37–16.

The creator of the work and its quality are the easiest attributes to isolate. The paintings of old and modern masters are readily identified, and the quality of their work is well known. However, the cost of their works frequently exceeds $100,000 and may reach into millions of dollars. Such prices virtually exclude all but a handful of collectors and museums.

Even many lesser-name artists are readily identifiable, and an investor may determine the quality of their work through reading, studying, and viewing the art first-hand. A minor name in art history is usually minor for a reason. Investments in this type of art may appreciate (especially if art prices rise in general), but the probability of a large increase in value is small.

In addition to the artist and the quality of the work, value depends on several factors that are both inherent in and external to the specific piece. Factors indigenous to the work itself include the medium and the subject matter. For example, oil paintings tend to cost more than watercolors by the same artist. Landscapes command higher prices than portraits. Dark or somber scenes may be less valuable than brightly colored and cheerful ones.

Additional factors that affect value

Factors affecting value that are independent of the piece itself include the condition of the work, the former owners, the museums or shows in which the work was previously exhibited, and the seller.

Condition obviously affects value. As one would expect, a damaged painting or antique or a badly worn Oriental rug commands a lower price. However, the owner may be able to have damaged works restored (for a price). Such restoration should help increase the value of the work. Just the cleaning of an old painting or an Oriental rug will bring out the colors and perhaps make the piece both more attractive and marketable.

Who has previously owned the work, where it has been exhibited, and who is selling it may also affect the value of an art object. If a painting has passed through the collection of an important museum or major collector, its value is enhanced. In a sense, previous owners and exhibitions are like a pedigree. They establish authenticity and credibility that can enhance the value of a particular art object.

As the preceding discussion suggests, the valuation of art is very subjective. Professionals (e.g., art dealers and museum curators) know this and are capable of making reasonably accurate appraisals. When a piece is offered at an auction, these professionals know approximately how much the work should bring. If it appears that such a price will not be obtained, these professionals may enter the bidding and purchase the piece for their own galleries or collections. For this reason the novice investor should not expect to acquire quality art, antiques, or Oriental rugs at bargain prices. Those in the know will outbid such a naive investor.

The valuation is subjective

The Selection of Collectibles

How does the investor tackle the problem of selecting among the works of art or other collectibles that are available? Essentially the choice is either to buy the works of known artists or to try to identify the artists that will gain acceptance in the future. In a sense, this is similar to buying stock issued by IBM or AT&T, which are known firms in excellent financial condition, versus buying stock in the over-the-counter market that is issued by some small company that offers promise for the future. The works of

The problem of choice

Exhibit 24.1
**Confirmation for the
Sale of a Painting**

*Unknown versus
known artist*

*Quality and reputable
dealers*

Avoid copies

the known artists, of course, will cost more. However, even the works of minor names in art may command high prices, and the investor, in essence, must decide whether to bite the bullet and pay the price or to select the works of the unknown artists.

The works of an unknown artist will, of course, tend to be inexpensive, and if the artist subsequently acquires a "name," his or her works will appreciate in value. However, the probability of this occurring is small, in which case the investor will probably be lucky to recoup even the meager cost of the investment.

There are, however, several things that the investor can do to help increase the chance of earning a positive return on an investment in a painting or an Oriental rug. First, the investor should buy from reputable dealers. Although prices from dealers will tend to be higher, their reputation verifies the authenticity of the work. Exhibit 24.1 presents the confirmation statement from a dealer for the sale of a painting. In addition to the title of the work and the medium (oil), the statement presents the year of the painting's execution (1974) and the work's identifying number (58). Such a statement is not only proof of purchase but also serves to authenticate the work.

Buying from known dealers or through major auction houses will also aid in any subsequent sale. Dealers often specialize in the work of particular artists and are thus aware of the market for these artists. Should the investor want to sell the piece, the dealer may be a major source of information regarding the market and may even be able to execute the sale.

Second, the investor should avoid buying prints and other objects that masquerade as potential investments. Unsigned prints and reproductions may be an excellent means to decorate a room and to learn about art, but they are not originals, nor are they unique. Generally, unsigned prints and reproductions are not investments, and the individual should realize this fact and not be deluded into believing that such items will appreciate in value.[5]

---

[5]In the past, print makers (e.g., Dürer) did not sign their works, but these unsigned original prints are potential investments. However, prints and reproductions of these originals should not be considered to be investments.

Third, the investor should develop a specialty. Just as one cannot learn about all *Develop a specialty*
possible firms and their securities, the individual cannot know everything concerning
all forms of art. The best strategy, then, is to develop an area of expertise that will
permit the investor to learn which factors affect the value of particular art objects. In
this way the investor can accumulate a collection that is decorative and that serves as a
store of value.

GOLD [6]

Gold has held a specific fascination for centuries. It has been minted into coins and *Gold as a medium*
used as a medium of exchange. Its color and durability have made it a popular metal *of exchange*
for jewelry. Gold is also a very popular store of value. Some investors, who are frequently referred to as gold bugs, consider it to be among the best investments available. A few investment advisory services even recommend that investors hold a substantial proportion of their portfolios in some form of gold.

The main reason for investing in gold is a belief that it is the best insurance *Its universal*
against inflation. The universal acceptability of gold makes it the one commodity to *acceptability*
own during a period of rapid inflation. The price of gold tends to mirror fears of inflation. If the rate of inflation rises, purchases of gold will increase along with its price.
Conversely, during periods of declining inflation, the price of gold tends to decrease.
This is illustrated in Figure 24.1, which plots the price of an ounce of gold and the
rate of inflation. As may be seen in the figure, the price of gold does seem to respond
to the inflation rate.

Figure 24.1 also points out another fact: Investors can lose money by buying *The profit is not assured*
gold. As with any other investment, there is always the risk of loss. Holders of gold not
only forgo income, such as dividends and interest, but also have to store the metal and
bear the risk of fraud and capital loss from declining prices. From February 1975
through August 1976, the price of an ounce of gold declined by nearly one half—
from $180 to $110. Obviously, investors who purchased gold in January 1975 (when
it was first legal for Americans to own gold bullion) learned an essential lesson: Buying
gold can be as risky as buying stocks and bonds. However, those investors who
bought gold in August 1976 may have earned a substantial return, as the price of gold
rose to over $800 in 1980. Of course, if those investors chose not to realize their paper
profits, they watched the profits melt away, as the price of gold has steadily declined
since it reached those historic highs in 1980.

There are several mediums for investing in gold: jewelry, coins, bullion (which is *The variety of potential*
usually in the form of gold bars), stocks of mining companies, and futures contracts. *investments*
As an investment gold jewelry is a poor choice, because the cost of the jewelry includes not only the cost of the gold but also the cost of the copper used to strengthen
the gold and the wages of the craftspeople who design and construct the jewelry.
There may be excellent reasons for buying gold jewelry, but it is not a good choice as
an investment. (Jewelry, especially rare gems, may prove to be an acceptable investment. However, the individual is primarily buying the gems instead of the gold, and
such investments are very illiquid and produce no monetary income.)

---

[6]While this section is devoted to investing in gold, much of the material also applies to investing in silver and other precious metals.

Figure 24.1
Price of Gold and the Annual Percentage Change in the Consumer Price Index

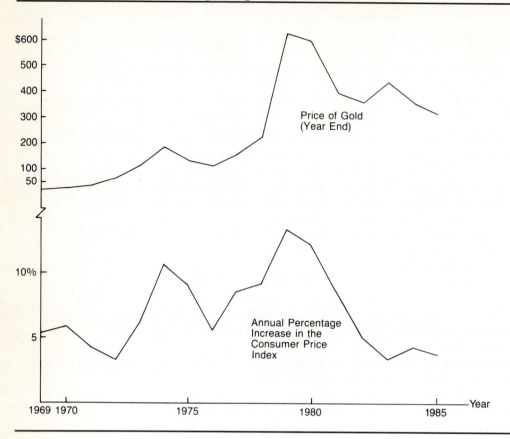

Gold Coins

Coins

Gold coins are a better vehicle than jewelry for investing in gold. These coins initially came into existence as currency, but in the United States they no longer serve as a medium of exchange. Many coins still exist from the past and may be purchased through coin dealers and at auctions.

The numismatic value

Like jewelry, gold coins have a serious weakness as an investment. Their price is related to two things: the bullion content and the coin's numismatic value. The bullion value of a coin depends on the gold content and the price of gold. This price, in turn, depends on the market's demand for and supply of gold. Gold is used in various products (e.g., jewelry) and is continually being mined. The demand for gold in its various uses (including investments) relative to the supply that is offered determines the market price of gold bullion.

The value of gold coins depends not only on the value of bullion but also on the numismatic value of the coin. Some coins are much scarcer than others and hence are more valuable as collector's items. For example, the value of an uncirculated ten dollar

POINTS OF INTEREST
What Goes Up Must Come Down

The market for collectibles, like the markets for stocks, options, and commodities, is not immune to speculation fever. The late 1970s and 1980 was such a period when prices of art work, coins, stamps, and other collectibles rose dramatically. As with other speculative binges, the bubble ultimately burst and prices declined dramatically. By 1982 rare stamps and coins had declined 40 to 50 percent; diamonds that had sold for over $50,000 sold for $15,000. Gold declined from over $800 an ounce in 1980 to $300 in early 1982. In some cases the markets entirely dried up, as there were few buyers and owners were re-luctant to sell at distress prices. The causes of this dramatic price decline included the reduction in the rate of inflation during 1982, the high rates of interest that could be earned on investments in short-term securities and money market funds, and the recession. This period taught investors in collectibles a lesson that investors in securities already know (but must periodically relearn): Speculative excesses ultimately correct themselves and prices fall. Unfortunately the lesson can be expensive for those investors who are sucked in when prices reach their peaks.

gold piece minted in the United States in 1861 rose from $37.50 in 1946 to $200 in 1974, but an uncirculated three dollar piece minted in 1889 rose in value from $25 to $1,100 during the same period.[7] The difference, of course, is the result of the scarcity of three dollar gold pieces. This gives it great numismatic value in addition to its value as gold.

If the investor is concerned only with accumulating gold, then numismatic rarities may be of little interest because the investor pays more for the same amount of gold. The premium paid over the bullion value can be substantial; the investor, therefore, is really gambling on the coin as a collector's item and not on its gold content.

Coin rarities

Investors who wish to acquire both coin collections and gold bullion may prefer such rarities. These will probably increase in value more rapidly than the more common gold coins. In general, it is the rarer items that appreciate the fastest. Collectors of gold coins (and stamps, antiques, and other collectibles) may find that the best strategy is to buy a few expensive, high-quality representations instead of trying to amass large collections of less rare and cheaper specimens.

One coin of particular interest to gold collectors is the **Canadian Maple Leaf**, which is issued by the Canadian government. After the Union of South Africa, Canada is the free world's main producer of gold. It mints the Canadian Maple Leaf to sell to gold collectors.[8] While the coin may be used as money, it is not circulated, for such use would scar the coins and reduce their value.

The Canadian Maple Leaf

---

[7] See Q. David Bowers, *Collecting Rare Coins for Profit* (New York: Harper & Row, 1975), 303–304.

[8] The Union of South Africa also mints a coin to sell to collectors, the Krugerrand. Importation of Krugerrands in the United States was banned on October 11, 1985. Investors, however, may still buy and sell Krugerrands that were imported prior to the ban.

The primary attractiveness of the Canadian Maple Leaf is that the coin is issued in exactly one troy ounce of fine gold. This uniformity of metal content increases its marketability in the secondary markets. In addition, the coin sells for a modest premium over the value of the gold bullion in the coin. Other gold coins, especially commemorative coins or limited foreign edition coins, are frequently sold (at least initially) at a considerable premium over their value as bullion. The investor runs a substantial risk in that the price of these commemorative coins may decline relative to the value of the gold bullion in the secondary markets. This potential price decline, however, does not apply to Canadian Maple Leafs.

Gold Bullion

Gold bars

Until January 1, 1975, gold coins and jewelry offered Americans the only legal means to own gold. However, Americans can now own gold bullion in the form of gold bars. These may be bought through gold dealers and brokerage firms. Once the investor purchases the gold, he or she may take possession of it or leave it with the dealer or broker. Leaving the gold with the broker involves storage and insurance costs, which increases the price of the investment.

The investor may take delivery

The investor may take delivery and store the gold in a presumably safe place. The gold ingots should be stamped and numbered by the refiner, who also supplies correspondingly numbered certificates. These must be delivered with the gold should the investor ever sell the ingots. If the certificates are lost, the ingots will have to be **assayed** to prove their gold content. This expense must be paid by the investor to ensure the marketability of the gold bars. Even if the documentation is not lost, the investor may have to have the gold assayed because taking possession results in a loss of the guarantee of the gold's quality, and this guarantee can only be restored by having the gold assayed.

The problem of fraud

The need to assay the metal points out a major problem with investing in gold: fraud. Coins and bars can be passed off as gold with fake numbers and fake documentation. By purchasing gold bullion from a reputable dealer or through a brokerage firm, the investor can substantially reduce the possibility of fraud. Certainly, no investor should buy unassayed gold that is offered at a discount from the price of gold bullion. Such a purchase will certainly prove to be a bad investment.

Gold Mining Stocks

Mining companies

The investor may also buy the shares of gold mining companies. This, of course, is not owning gold. Instead, the firm may own gold mines and mining equipment. Presumably, the value of the shares is related to the value of the gold, but it is possible for the price of gold to rise while the price of the mining company's stock declines. Various factors, such as a strike or a fire, can affect the value of the mining firm and its securities, but such events may have no impact on the price of gold.[9]

---

[9] The investor may reduce the impact of such events by purchasing the shares of an investment company that specializes in the securities of gold mining companies. For example, American-South African Investment Company (or ASA) is a closed-end investment company whose shares are traded on the New York Stock Exchange. ASA specializes in the stocks of South African gold mining firms.

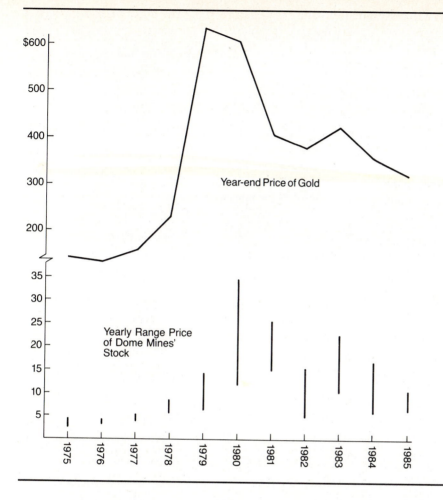

Figure 24.2
**Price of Gold and
Dome Mines Stock**
(December 1975–
December 1985)

Year-end Price of Gold

Yearly Range Price
of Dome Mines'
Stock

These exogenous factors (especially political forces) are particularly important in the valuation of gold mining stocks. The primary producers of gold are the Union of South Africa and the Soviet Union. The Union of South Africa alone accounts for about two-thirds of the world's output of newly mined gold. The political climate in the Union of South Africa is somewhat unstable, and this instability can have an impact on the value of gold mining shares in South African companies.

Political forces

The investor may avoid these political problems by limiting purchases to shares in gold mining companies in the United States and Canada (e.g., Dome Mines, Campbell Red Lakes) whose values tend to follow closely the price of bullion. This is illustrated in Figure 24.2, which shows the price performance of shares of Dome Mines (a Canadian firm) and the price of gold. As may be seen in the figure, the price of these shares moved in tandem with the price of gold. Thus, shares of American and Canadian gold mining companies may offer the investor a viable alternative to owning gold bars. Such shares not only avoid the costs of storage, insurance, and assaying but also may pay dividend income, which is not possible from any other form of investment in gold.

*U.S. and Canadian
gold stocks*

Gold Futures and Options

Gold as a commodity

In addition to gold coins, gold bullion, and gold mining shares, the investor may speculate in gold futures and gold options.[10] Like many other commodities, there exists an active market in contracts for the future delivery of gold. This market is a recent development; it came into existence only after it became legal for Americans to own gold bullion. The principal markets for these gold futures are the Chicago International Monetary Market and the New York Commodity Exchange (COMEX).

Considerable leverage

As with other commodity contracts, the appeal of gold futures is in the great leverage that they offer investors. A contract for the future delivery of gold is for 100 troy ounces. At $350 an ounce, the contract has a face value of $35,000. If the margin requirement were $3,500, the speculator would have a claim on $35,000 worth of gold for an outlay of only $3,500. If the price were to rise by only $10 per ounce, the value of the contract would rise by $1,000 to $36,000. The speculator would then make $1,000 on an investment of only $3,500. Of course, if the price of gold were to fall by only $10 per ounce, the speculator would lose $1,000. Since gold prices can and do fluctuate rapidly, there exists considerable potential for large profits and losses, which is a primary reason for the attractiveness of gold futures to speculators.

The special risks

While all forms of investing in gold involve several sources of risk, gold futures involve a special source of risk. Government and international agencies participate in the market for gold. For example, the U.S. Treasury periodically sells gold, and this additional supply tends to reduce its price. In addition, the International Monetary Fund of the United Nations sells gold to raise currency for its international transactions. This also tends to reduce the price of gold. These sales make investing in gold futures more risky, as they alter the supply and demand of the metal.

Gold futures options

The New York Commodity Exchange also offers gold futures options, which are put and call options to sell and buy gold futures contracts. While they are not options to buy and sell gold, their prices move with the price of gold. As with other put and call options, the reason for purchasing them is the potential leverage they offer. Suppose the investor pays $1,000 for a call option to purchase a gold futures contract for 100 ounces at $320. The value of the call option will rise as the price of gold (and the futures price) rises above $320. For example, if the price of gold rose to $350 by the expiration date of the call, the option would be worth $3,000. This $3,000 is the $30 difference between the current price ($350) and the price specified in the call option ($320) times 100, since the option is the right to buy a contract for 100 ounces. Thus, in this illustration the price of gold rose less than 10 percent (from $320 to $350), but the value of the option tripled from $1,000 to $3,000. If the investor had purchased the option for $1,000, this individual would have earned a $2,000 profit on the transaction.

If the price of gold were to decline, the value of the call option would also decline. If the price of gold fell to $300, then the call option to buy the gold futures contract at $320 would become worthless. No one would exercise the option to buy at $320 what could be purchased elsewhere for $300. In that case the investor would lose the $1,000 invested in the call option.

---

[10] Refer to Chapter 23 for a general discussion of investing in commodity futures and Chapters 19 and 20 for a discussion of options.

While both futures contracts and put and call options are means to lever one's position when speculating on changes in the price of gold, the gold option offers one major advantage over the futures contract. With a futures contract, the investor could lose a substantial amount if there were a large and sudden change in the price of the commodity. This is because the investor has not purchased anything but has entered into a contract to buy (or sell) gold at a specified price. If the price moved against the investor, that individual could sustain a large loss in order to fulfill the contract. However, with a put or a call option the investor actually owns something (i.e., the option). Thus, the maximum amount that may be lost is the cost of the option. This limit reduces the risk associated with speculating in the movements of the price of gold.

SUMMARY

The poor performance of stocks during the 1970s and the continuation of inflation have increased investor interest in various collectibles and other physical assets. Art objects, Oriental rugs, antiques, stamps, coins, gold, and silver have attracted the attention of some investors as alternatives to the more traditional investments (i.e., stocks and bonds).

These physical assets offer investors potential price appreciation and, in some cases, income from services. They may be purchased from dealers or at auctions, and while these assets are not purchased on organized exchanges, secondhand markets exist in which the investor can sell the assets.

Investors who acquire physical assets, like investors who acquire financial assets, bear the risk of loss. This risk is due to fluctuations in the prices of the assets in general and of the specific assets, inflation, theft, and fraud. To help overcome these risks, the investor needs to be well informed and to specialize in a particular type of physical asset.

Art and gold were used in this chapter to illustrate two types of possible investments in physical assets. The valuation of art objects is extremely subjective, because it depends not only on the work and its creator but also on several intangibles. However, art objects can be very decorative, and they do suggest to others the taste of the investor.

Gold may be acquired in a variety of forms, including jewelry, coins, and bullion. The investor can also buy the stock of gold mining companies, futures contracts, and gold options. Gold jewelry is the poorest means to invest in gold, and a futures contract is the riskiest. Most investors prefer gold coins and bullion as their vehicles for an investment in gold.

Like any investment, acquiring gold subjects the investor to risk. The price of gold, like the price of other assets, can fall and has done so in the past. This, plus the fact that gold must be stored, insured, and assayed, reduces the potential return on the investment. A positive return on gold, as on all other investments, cannot be assured.

Terms to Remember

Income-in-kind
Canadian Maple Leaf
To assay

Questions

1. How are collectibles and gold bought and sold?

2. Why is it important to have specialized knowledge when investing in physical assets such as art or gold?

3. What are the sources of risk from investing in collectibles and gold?

4. What is income-in-kind and how does it apply to investments in art and Oriental rugs?

5. Why have the prices of selected art objects risen? Is there a secondary market for art objects? What are the special costs associated with investing in art?

6. What are the sources of return from an investment in art and other collectibles?

7. What are the mediums for investing in gold? What are the special costs associated with these investments?

8. Why may gold bullion have to be assayed? Why may individuals who desire to invest in gold prefer bullion to gold coins?

9. What is the relationship between the rate of inflation and the price of gold?

Suggested Readings

There is a dearth of substantive material written on investing in art and collectibles. Much of what is available falls into one of two categories: (1) how to make a fortune by investing in . . . or (2) a description of past investment performance. For a sampling of readings written by individuals with a financial background, see:

Bongard, Willi. "Wall Stocks." *Across the Board* (November 1977): 42–57. "Magic Carpets?" *Forbes,* Oct. 1, 1975, 54.

O'Hanlon, D. "Limited Edition Lithography: Buyer Beware!" *Forbes,* July 10, 1978, 65–67.

Schonfeld, Robert. "Forum: Investing in Art." *American Artist* (February 1980): 18+.

The Schonfeld is must reading for anyone considering investing in art. Other readings of interest that are not necessarily written by individuals with a background in finance include:

Bowers, Q. David. *Collecting Rare Coins for Profit.* New York: Harper & Row, 1975.

"Investor's File," a monthly column in the *Connoisseur.*

McConathy, D. "Art as Investment." *Artscanada* (Autumn 1975): 46.

Shapiro, Cecile, and Lauris Mason. *Fine Prints: Collecting, Buying, and Selling.* New York: Harper & Row, 1976.

Trucco, T. "Art Market," a monthly column in *Artnews.*

Much of what has been written on gold suggests that gold is the only safe and certain investment. This, of course, is not true, as the decline in gold's price during the early 1980s proves. Like collectibles there is a dearth of financial analysis applied to investing in gold. For a sampling of descriptive readings, see:

Dreyfus, Patricia A. "A Gold Buyer's Guide." *Money,* November 1979, 87–88.

Hoppe, Donald J. *How to Invest in Gold Stocks and Avoid the Pitfalls.* New Rochelle, N.Y.: Arlington House, 1972.

"Investing in Gold." *Business Week,* Feb. 5, 1979, 96–98.

"The Gold Rush of '79." *Newsweek,* Oct. 1, 1979, 48–54.

Understanding Gold Futures Trading. Chicago: International Monetary Market Division of the Chicago Mercantile Exchange, 1974.

While the major non-Communist producers of gold are primarily located in the Union of South Africa, for descriptions of North American gold companies and the advantages they offer, consult:

Jackson, Robert S. *North American Gold Stocks*. Chicago: Probus Publishing, 1986.

For an excellent source of basic information on many collectibles, see:

Blume, Marshall E., and Jack P. Friedman, eds. *The Encyclopedia of Investments*. Boston: Warren, Gorham & Lamont, 1982.

The book contains chapters devoted to art nouveau and art deco, books, coins, folk art, gemstones, motion pictures, paintings, furniture, photographs, porcelain, prints, rugs, sculpture, and stamps. In general each chapter covers the basic characteristics of the asset, its attractive features and the potential risks, special factors to consider when investing in the collectible, and custodial care. Each chapter also has a glossary and suggested readings.

25

Investing in Real Estate

LEARNING OBJECTIVES

After completing this chapter you should be able to

1. Explain how income-in-kind applies to investments in homes.
2. Illustrate the tax advantages of home ownership.
3. Explain why home ownership may be the best hedge against inflation.
4. Compare the sources of funds to finance the purchase of a home.
5. Differentiate among the alternatives to home ownership for an investment in real estate.
6. Explain how financial leverage and tax deductions affect the cash flow and return from an investment in real estate.
7. Forecast the cash flow from an investment in real estate.
8. Distinguish among the types of real estate investment trusts.
9. Apply the dividend-growth valuation model to the shares of real estate investment trusts.

*H*ome ownership is a very distinctive American characteristic. It is almost synonymous with the American dream of prosperity. Over fifty million residential units are owner-occupied. More individuals own homes than directly own stock.[1] Home ownership, however, is not the only way to invest in real estate. The individual may also own land, income properties, or shares in real estate partnerships and real estate investment trusts. This chapter is an overview of these investments in real estate.

The first section is devoted to home ownership, including the tax advantages of home ownership and the various types of mortgage loans available to finance the purchases of homes. Next follows a discussion of investments in both unimproved and improved land, in-

---

[1] Many investors may indirectly own stock through pension plans and employee savings programs.

cluding limited partnerships that acquire and operate income-earning properties. Emphasis is placed on the determination of the property's cash flow and the uncertainties associated with investments in rental properties.

The chapter ends with a discussion of real estate investment trusts (REITs). REITs are a type of investment company that specializes in real estate. The types of trusts, their methods of financing, the risks, and the potential returns associated with this particular investment are covered. The chapter ends with a discussion of how the dividend-growth valuation model presented in Chapter 14 may be applied to shares in REITs.

HOME OWNERSHIP

Every person must live somewhere. This obvious fact differentiates home ownership from all other investments. People must secure living space. Their choices are either to rent the property or to own it and, in effect, rent the space to themselves. If they rent, the individuals are consuming space. If they own, they are simultaneously consuming space and making an investment.

People must secure living space

There are many reasons for owning a home instead of renting. These include the psychic income that comes with the pride of owning a place that can be called one's home. Home ownership also offers a very pragmatic advantage over renting: It is a means to force saving. Every payment on a mortgage loan represents interest and principal. The amount that the individual has invested in the home increases with each mortgage payment. These payments become a convenient means to force oneself to save. In addition, any repairs and improvements made in the property accrue to the owner and not to the landlord.

There are two major financial reasons for home ownership. The first pertains to the tax benefits, and the second is the potential return on the investment. Of course, this return depends partially on the tax shelters generated by home ownership. These tax breaks are rarely referred to as tax shelters, but they are because they either reduce taxable income or defer tax payments. The tax shelters or tax advantages of home ownership are (1) the deductions from income that the home owner who itemizes is able to take, (2) the possible deferment or even avoidance of capital gains taxes when the property is sold, and (3) the tax-free income generated by the living space.

The tax benefits and the potential return

Income Tax Deductions

The vast majority of homes are purchased through the use of mortgage loans. The interest paid is a tax-deductible expense. If the home owner itemizes deductions, the deduction of interest reduces taxable income and thus results in a tax savings. This savings can be substantial. If the home owner is carrying a $50,000 mortgage at 12 percent, the approximate interest charge is $6,000 in the first year of the mortgage. Itemization of this interest expense reduces taxable income by $6,000.

Mortgage financing

The effect of this deduction is a reduction in the true or effective cost of a mortgage loan. The individual's true cost of a mortgage is related to (1) the interest rate and (2) the marginal income tax rate. If an investor borrows funds and pays 12 percent, the *before-tax* interest rate is 12 percent, but the true cost of the loan is less.

The effective interest cost

A simple example illustrates how the deduction reduces the effective cost of the debt. If an investor has a marginal tax rate of 28 percent and borrows funds at

12 percent interest, then the effective cost of the mortgage is 8.64 percent. The effective **cost of debt** is

$$\text{Cost of debt} = \text{Before-tax interest rate } (1 - \text{Marginal tax rate}).$$

For this individual the calculation is

$$\text{Cost of debt} = 0.12(1 - 0.28) = 8.64\%.$$

This effective cost of debt (i_e) is expressed in symbolic form in Equation 25.1:

(25.1)
$$i_e = i(1 - t).$$

The effective cost of debt (i_e) is simply the product of the stated interest rate (i) and the tax effect $(1 - t)$, where t represents the investor's marginal income bracket. Obviously, the higher the individual's marginal tax rate, the lower is the true cost of borrowing.

The deduction of property taxes

The home owner is also permitted to deduct from taxable income the property taxes that are paid on the home. As with the interest deduction, the home owner must itemize expenses in order to receive the benefit of the deduction. The effect of itemizing property taxes is a reduction in the individual's taxable income and therefore a reduction in the federal income tax liability. Since the property tax charged by some local governments amounts to over $1,000 on even moderately valued homes (e.g., $70,000 to $100,000 homes), the property tax deduction can result in substantial savings on income taxes for middle-income home owners.

Renters cannot take advantage of these deductions

Owing to these deductions, several important expenditures or cash outlays associated with home ownership come from *before-tax* dollars. Most expenditures made by individuals come from *after-tax* dollars. Renters, who cannot take advantage of these deductions, pay rent with after-tax dollars. If an individual is in the 28 percent tax bracket, that person must earn $1,042 to make $750 in rental payments. However, that same individual could reduce taxes by $28 for every $100 paid in interest or property taxes on a house.

Capital Gains Deferment

Realized capital gains may be deferred

In addition to the previous deductions, a home owner may receive a tax break when the home is sold. If the owner sells for a profit and reinvests the funds in another home within 24 months, any realized capital gains may be deferred. Thus, if a home owner bought a house for $20,000 in 1960 and sold it for $100,000 in 1986 the $80,000 capital gain is not realized for federal income tax purposes as long as the home owner buys a new house that costs at least $100,000. Instead of a capital gain, the cost basis of the initial house is transferred to the new home.[2]

If the price of the new house were $105,000, its cost basis would be $25,000, which is the $20,000 cost of the original house plus the $5,000 difference between the purchase price of the new house and the sale price of the old house. If the price of the new house were $95,000, then the cost would be less than the proceeds of the sale by $5,000 ($100,000 − $95,000). This $5,000 must be reported to the Internal Revenue Service as a capital gain. However, the tax on the remaining $75,000 in profit is de-

---

[2] This tax benefit applies only to a primary residence; it does not apply to a vacation home.

ferred, and the cost basis of the new house becomes $20,000 (i.e., the cost basis of the original house).

Legislation was passed in 1981 that gives some home owners an even larger tax break. This legislation exempts a capital gain of up to $125,000 from taxation provided the individual is over 55 years old. The investor is allowed this tax break only once. Under this legislation, a home owner who bought a house for $20,000 in 1955 and upon retirement in 1985 at the age of 65 sold it for $145,000 could completely avoid taxation on the capital gain.

A special exemption

Income-in-Kind

Individuals either rent space or own it and "rent" it to themselves. The money that home owners do not pay to a landlord may be viewed as rent that they pay to themselves. The home owner receives income-in-kind (just as the owner of an Oriental rug or an art work does). Such income is not subject to federal income tax. While home ownership generates a tax-free flow of services, renting does not. Tax-free services, like deductions that reduce taxable income, increase the attractiveness of investing in a house or a condominium. While the importance of this tax-free income varies with the financial situation and income level of the investor, it generally is more advantageous to own than to rent as the individual's income and tax bracket rise.

The flow of services

In light of these tax advantages, it is not surprising to find that many individuals invest in homes. The ability to reduce taxable income by certain deductions, the capital gains deferment, and tax-free income-in-kind all favor investments in residential homes. In addition, the individual may obtain mortgage money at an effective cost (i.e., after the tax adjustment) that is less than the rate of inflation. Since the tax laws favor the home owner, investments in houses may offer the individual one of the best possible investments.

These reasons for home ownership also apply to **condominiums.** A condominium is similar to an apartment, but instead of renting, the individual owns the "apartment." The grounds and general facilities belong to all of the owners of the condominiums, who pay a fee for their maintenance.[3] The portion of the building that the individual owns may be subsequently sold, and the seller may earn a capital gain if the property is sold for a profit. In addition, since the individual owns and does not rent the space, the tax advantages of home ownership apply. Thus, in some ways ownership of a condominium is no different from ownership of a home; a condominium may be treated as an investment just as a home is.

Condominiums

The condominium is particularly attractive to people who have little need or desire for lawns and shrubs. The maintenance of a home and the grounds can be expensive in terms of both time and money. While the condominium owner does not avoid the monetary cost of this maintenance, he or she may not have to expend the effort. If the individual lacks the time or the inclination for home maintenance, the condominium may offer the best of both worlds: the convenience of renting and the advantages of home ownership.

---

[3] The investor should read carefully the agreement that specifies what is covered by the maintenance fee. Some managements have defaulted and not fulfilled their part of the contracts, which leaves condominium owners with additional obligations that must be met to comply with local health and fire regulations.

Risks and Returns

A hedge against inflation

Many people believe that residential homes are among the best investments. The appreciation in the value of the home acts as a hedge against inflation, and at the same time the investor receives the services of the home.

The rate of price appreciation in residential homes is presented in Figure 25.1.[4] The graph also presents the Dow Jones industrial average for the same time period. As is obvious from the graph, during the 1970s the prices of residential homes appreciated while the Dow Jones industrial average fluctuated but showed no pattern of steady growth. This tends to confirm the belief that during the last decade home ownership was a superior investment to the purchase of common stocks.

During 1981 to 1986, however, this perception may have changed. Home prices tended to stagnate or at least not to rise as rapidly as in the immediate past, and the security markets moved sharply higher. For example, during 1985, the Dow Jones industrial average increased over 29.2 percent. Both the NYSE composite index and the Standard & Poor's 500 index rose over 27 percent, and the NASD composite index of over-the-counter stocks rose almost 32 percent. Even bond prices staged significant increases in response to declining interest rates. Whether financial assets will continue to outperform home ownership as an investment during the 1980s is open to speculation. There are, however, good reasons to expect the value of homes will continue to rise even if the rate of increase is slower.

The increased cost of construction

Part of the explanation for the increase in home values is the increased cost of construction. The rising building costs of new homes translate into increased values for old homes. Old and new homes are substitutes for each other. If the cost of one rises relative to the cost of the other, buyers will seek to purchase the cheaper home. As the cost of new homes rises, some individuals will seek to purchase existing homes. This, in turn, will drive up the prices of older homes to keep them in line with the prices of newly constructed homes.

The increased demand

Another explanation for the increased value of homes is the continued increase in demand for them. Conventional wisdom suggests that home ownership is a good investment. This belief encourages individuals to buy homes even though they may have to take on more financial obligations than is prudent for their capacity to service the debt. As is subsequently discussed, the tendency on the part of some home owners to use excessive amounts of debt financing (i.e., excessive financial leverage) is a major source of risk of investing in homes. However, to the extent that these individuals are willing and able to obtain this mortgage money, they increase the demand for homes and hence help to increase their prices.

The realized returns

Is an investment in a home really one of the best hedges against inflation? One study found that *only* private residential real estate offered complete protection against inflation.[5] Other investments, such as debt instruments, were a successful hedge against anticipated inflation, because their yields adjusted for the anticipated rate of inflation. However, these assets did not protect against unanticipated inflation. Only

---

[4] Figure 25.1 presents both the average price and the median price of a single-family residential home. Since the average price is raised by the sales of a few expensive homes, the median price may be more representative of the cost of a home to the typical buyer.

[5] Eugene F. Fama and G. William Schwert, "Asset Returns and Inflation," *Journal of Financial Economics* 5 (November 1978): 115–146.

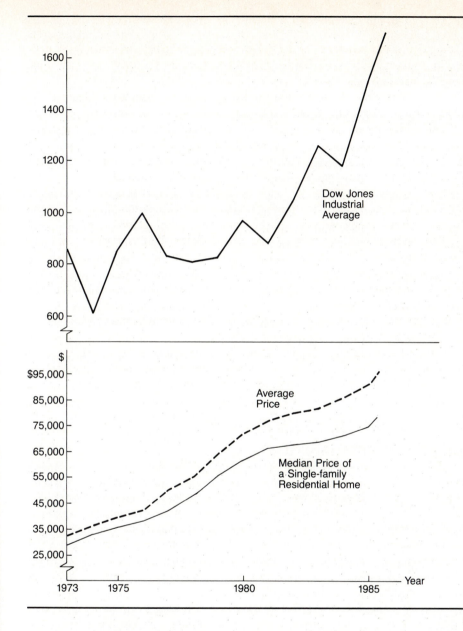

Figure 25.1
Dow Jones Industrial Average and the Average and Median Price of a Single-family Residential Home, 1973–March 1986

private residential real estate provided a safeguard against both expected and unexpected inflation. This study thus supports the conventional wisdom that home ownership is one of the best investments available, especially during inflationary times.

   Although in the aggregate home ownership has been a successful hedge against inflation, it does not follow that there are no risks or that home ownership is desirable for everyone. Home ownership can produce many headaches for the individual. Owners are responsible for maintenance, which (even if the cost is recouped when the

There are risks

home is sold) still requires a current outlay of cash and may require considerable effort. In addition, the cost of running a home rises with the rate of inflation. The increased costs of insurance, energy, and various other expenses (which are not deductible from taxable income) may strain the individual's budget if personal income does not rise as rapidly. Even though the resale value of the house may be increasing, that is not cash currently received. But it is current cash that is necessary to meet the expenses associated with running the home.

The excessive use of financial leverage

Another source of risk is the use of debt financing to acquire the home.[6] Carrying the mortgage is a fixed monthly expense that must be met, or the holder of the mortgage may seize the home (through a court proceeding) and sell it to recoup the funds lent to the home owner. Investors thus run considerable risk of loss should they be unable to maintain mortgage payments. Some individuals purchase expensive homes and anticipate that home values and their salaries will rise while mortgage payments remain constant, only to find that the mortgage payment becomes a real burden when adversity strikes (e.g., the loss of a job or an extended illness).

The different rates of price appreciation

The last source of risk is due to the fact that not all real estate values increase at the same rate. During the 1970s suburban homes appreciated in value more rapidly than city properties. However, pockets within some cities have appreciated very rapidly since 1975. If the individual had the foresight to buy in an area where home values subsequently appreciated, the home has also served as a hedge against inflation. But many individuals do not have this foresight (or are not so lucky), and while their homes may have appreciated in value, the return need not have kept pace with the rate of inflation.

SOURCES OF MORTGAGE MONEY

One problem facing the individual seeking to buy a home is financing. Few individuals have sufficient funds to pay the entire purchase price and hence must borrow to finance the purchase. Prior to the high interest rates experienced during the early 1980s, borrowed funds were obtained through mortgage loans from a financial intermediary such as a commercial bank or a savings and loan association. There were basically two types of mortgage loans: conventional loans and loans backed by an agency of the federal government.

Conventional mortgage

With a **conventional mortgage loan** the individual buys the house with a down payment and borrows the balance. The loan is retired over a period of years by payments (usually monthly) that pay the interest and retire the principal. The amount of the periodic payment is fixed, and the interest is determined on the balance owed. Exhibit 25.1 presents parts of a mortgage schedule for a loan of $50,000 at 12% for 25 years. Each monthly payment is $526.62, which consists of an interest payment and a principal repayment. The first column of the table gives the number of the payment. These range from 1 to 300 because the loan requires 12 monthly payments for 25 years for a total of 300 payments. The second column presents the interest payment, and the third column gives the amount of principal repayment. The balance of

---

[6] Various types of mortgage loans are covered in the next section.

Number of Payment	Interest Payment	Principal Repayment	Balance of Loan
1	$500.00	$ 26.62	$49,973.38
2	499.73	26.89	49,946.49
3	499.46	27.16	49,919.34
—	—	—	—
—	—	—	—
—	—	—	—
148	411.69	114.93	41,053.64
149	410.54	116.08	40,937.56
150	409.38	117.24	40,820.32
—	—	—	—
—	—	—	—
—	—	—	—
298	15.34	511.28	1,023.11
299	10.23	516.39	506.72
300	5.07	506.72	0.00

Exhibit 25.1
Selected Payments from a Repayment Schedule for a $50,000 Mortgage Loan at 12% for 25 Years (Monthly payment: $526.62)

the loan is given in the last column. Since the amount of interest is determined on the balance owed, the amount of interest remitted with each payment declines, and the amount of the payment used to retire the principal rises. For example, the amount of interest in the third payment is $499.46, but in payment number 148 interest is $411.69. Since the amount of interest declines, the principal repayment increases from $27.16 in payment number 3 to $114.93 in payment number 148. Payments during the early years of the mortgage loan primarily cover the interest owed, but payments near the end of the life of the loan primarily reduce the balance owed.

The periodic payment required to cover the interest and retire the loan is determined through the use of present value calculations presented in Chapter 6. The following simple example illustrates this calculation. An individual borrows $10,000 for ten years and agrees to make annual payments that retire the loan and pay 12 percent interest on the declining balance owed. What is the annual payment? The answer is

$$\$10,000 = \frac{x}{(1 + 0.12)^1} + \cdots + \frac{x}{(1 + 0.12)^{10}}.$$

Since the periodic payments will be equal, this equation may be solved by the use of the present value of an annuity table. The problem collapses to

$$\$10,000 = x \text{ times the interest factor for the present value}$$
$$\text{of an annuity at 12\% for 10 years}$$

$$\$10,000 = x(5.650)$$

$$x = \$10,000/5.650 = \$1,769.91.$$

Annual payments of $1,769.91 for ten years will retire the loan and pay 12 percent on the declining balance owed. This illustration is an oversimplification because payments are made annually only; however, adjustments can be readily made to deter-

Government guarantees

mine monthly payments.[7] The basic principle remains the same. The given rate of interest and the amount initially borrowed are used in conjunction with the present value of an annuity table to determine the amount of each monthly payment.

If the borrower defaults and does not make the monthly payment, the lender may seize the property through a legal process called foreclosure. The property then may be sold to recoup the principal and interest owed. Banks and other lenders thus consider the amount of the down payment and the borrower's capacity to service the debt as conditions for granting the mortgage loan.

To broaden the market for homes, the federal government has followed a policy of encouraging mortgage loans. While the government does not originate mortgage loans, it may guarantee them through insurance issued by the **Federal Housing Administration (FHA)**. FHA-insured loans started during the 1930s. This insurance reduces the element of risk to the lender because if the borrower defaults, the FHA will make good the loan. The effect of this guarantee has been to make mortgage money available to low- and middle-income individuals who lack the necessary down payment or who may not be able to meet other requirements necessary to obtain conventional mortgage financing.

A similar program was started in 1944 by the **Veterans Administration (VA)** when the VA began to guarantee mortgage loans made to veterans. As with FHA-insured loans, VA-guaranteed loans reduce the risk of loss to the lender and hence encourage the flow of funds into the mortgage market. The requirements for veterans to obtain the guarantees are less than with conventional, noninsured mortgages, especially the amount of the initial down payment required to obtain mortgage financing.

With the increase in interest rates in general during the late 1970s and early 1980s, the market for mortgage loans became very unsettled. Interest rates on mortgage loans rose, as is illustrated in Figure 25.2. This figure shows the sudden and rapid increase during 1980 through 1981 in the interest rate charged for conventional mortgage loans. While the cost of such loans was around 9 percent in 1978, the interest rate rose to about 16 percent in 1981. This increase meant that a $50,000 mortgage at 16 percent for 25 years required annual payments of about $8,200, but the same loan at 9 percent would require annual payments of about $5,000. Obviously the cash payments necessary to service the 16 percent loan are significantly higher, which means fewer people would be able to afford the higher interest rates.

In addition to higher interest rates, lending institutions became increasingly unwilling or unable to make conventional mortgage loans. When a commercial bank or savings and loan institution makes a conventional mortgage loan, it ties up its funds for many years. As with all long-term debt obligations, the value of the mortgage loans

---

[7] To obtain monthly payments (i.e., compounding monthly), divide the interest rate by 12 months and multiply the number of periods by 12. In this case that is

$$\$10,000 = \frac{x}{\left(1 + \frac{0.12}{12}\right)} + \cdots + \frac{x}{\left(1 + \frac{0.12}{12}\right)^{10 \times 12}}$$

$\$10,000 = x$ times the interest factor for the present value of an annuity at 1 percent for 120 time periods

$\$10,000 = x(69.698)$
$x = \$143.48.$

The monthly payment is $143.48. Notice that this amount is less than $1,769.91/12 months = $147.49 per month. Since the loan is being retired more rapidly (i.e., every month the principal is reduced), the effect is to reduce the total amount of interest paid and thus decrease the total monthly payment.

Figure 25.2
Interest Rates on Conventional Mortgage Loans, 1974–March 1986

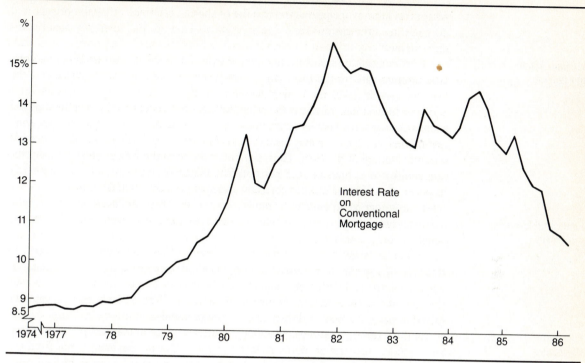

is reduced when interest rates rise, inflicting losses on the lenders. This problem is exacerbated when the banks and thrift institutions must pay higher rates of interest to attract deposits. The years 1981 and 1982 were particularly painful for savings and loan associations, since the bulk of their assets were mortgage loans that carried much lower interest rates than they had to pay to obtain deposits. In addition, many depositors withdrew funds and invested them in money market mutual funds, so savings and loan associations had fewer funds to invest in mortgage loans even if they could have earned higher interest rates. The result of the plight of the savings and loans was a reduction in the amount of funds available for mortgage loans, even for individual home buyers who were willing and able to pay the high interest rates.

High interest rates and the shortage of mortgage money led to nontraditional *Creative financing* sources of funds and to variations on the conventional mortgage loan. These new loans are frequently referred to as **creative financing**, as buyers and sellers of homes seek to find ways to finance the purchases of houses.

One possible source of creative mortgage financing is the seller of the property. *Seller financing* Some sellers are willing to accept the mortgage loan as a means to sell the house. The buyer makes a down payment and the seller accepts the mortgage loan for the balance of the purchase price. The seller may even charge several percentage points below the going rate in order to sell the house. The original mortgage may remain outstanding because the seller has not received the cash necessary to retire the original loan. However, the seller may earn more interest than is being paid on the initial mortgage. In effect what occurs is that the buyer pays funds to the seller, who in turn is retiring the

initial mortgage on the home. It should be noted, however, that the terms of the original mortgage may preclude such a pass-through. Then the seller will be willing to accept this kind of arrangement only if he or she can retire the original mortgage and does not need the cash to make other payments (such as the down payment on another home).

Variable interest rate mortgages

One variation on the conventional mortgage has been the substitution of a **variable interest rate** for the fixed rate. As interest rates vary, the rate of interest on the loan changes. In 1979 the Federal Home Loan Bank Board, which oversees savings and loan associations in much the same way that the Federal Reserve supervises the actions of commercial banks, permitted savings and loan associations to offer variable-rate mortgages. The rates may change ½ percent each year with a limit of 2½ percent over the lifetime of the loan. Thus, if a borrower obtained funds for 14 percent, the rate could rise as high as 16.5 percent. The length of the loan was still long-term, however; if the lender did not correctly anticipate the direction of change in interest rates, the lender could own in the future a mortgage note that offered an inferior yield.

Renegotiable rate mortgages

This problem plus the existence of some conventional mortgage financing resulted in only a modest amount of home financing through variable-interest-rate mortgages. In 1980 another variation developed: **renegotiable-rate mortgages.** In this type of loan the terms may be renegotiated at specified intervals. For example, while the term of the mortgage may be twenty-five years, the lender may renegotiate the interest rate every three to five years. If interest rates rose, the borrower would be forced to pay the higher and then current rate of interest.

Graduated-payment mortgages

A third variation on the conventional mortgage is the **graduated-payment mortgage.** Under this type of mortgage loan the amount of the payment is not fixed (although the rate of interest may be fixed) but rises during the lifetime of the loan. Such loans may be beneficial to home owners who anticipate rising incomes that can service the higher mortgage payments over time. However, such loans could prove to be disastrous if the borrower's income does not rise or if other expenses consume any increase in income. Then the burden of the debt would obviously increase, and since the loan is secured by the home, default could lead to the borrower losing the property.

Besides variable interest rate, renegotiable-rate, and graduated-payment mortgage loans, shorter term mortgage loans have developed. With this type of loan, the borrower has the funds for a short time, such as three years, pays the interest for the term of the loan, but then refinances the loan at the end of the time period. Such an arrangement obviously protects the lender from being locked into a lower rate if interest rates increase. However, these loans place borrowers in a precarious position, because they may not be able to find new financing when the loan becomes due.

Equity participation

Even with creative financing, it may be difficult to find financing during a period of high interest rates. Some lenders are now seeking and obtaining equity participation in the real estate they fund. In return for lower interest payments, these lenders receive a share in the appreciation of the value of the real estate. If inflation continues to increase the value of homes, these creditors, as well as the owners, will participate in the appreciation. This, of course, reduces the attractiveness of home ownership as an investment, because the owners will receive a lower return on their equity in the properties. However, if this is the only means to obtain financing, borrowers may have to agree to such equity participation as a means to obtain the funds necessary to buy the properties.

LAND AND RENTAL PROPERTIES

An alternative means to invest in real estate is to purchase land and/or rental properties. Land is either unimproved or improved. **Unimproved land** is raw land, whereas
improved land has curbs and sewers, has buildings constructed on it, or has been
cleared for farming or other agricultural uses. Unimproved land is a passive investment that may require little action on the part of the investor. However, improved land
may require considerable attention from the investor.

Leverage and Tax Write-offs

The primary appeal of investing in real estate is, of course, the potential return on the   *The potential return*
investment. This return is enhanced by the ability to use substantial amounts of finan-
cial leverage and to obtain advantageous tax write-offs, which may be seen in the following simple example. A piece of land costs $100,000. It may be purchased with a
20 percent down payment, with the balance being financed through a mortgage loan
at 12 percent annual interest rate. The individual's investment out of pocket is only
$20,000.

Land cost	$100,000
Loan	80,000
Equity	20,000

The tax write-offs

Several of the costs of carrying this investment (e.g., interest and property taxes)
are tax-deductible. If the property tax rate is 3 percent, then the deductible expenses are

Interest	$ 9,600
Property tax	+3,000
	$12,600

If the individual is in the 28 percent tax bracket, the effective cost of carrying the land
is reduced to

$$\$12,600(1 - 0.28) = \$8,640.$$

There is a tax savings of $3,960 ($12,600 − $8,640). For an initial cash outlay of
$20,000 and an annual cash outlay (after adjusting for taxes) of $8,640, the individual
has control of over $100,000 worth of land.

If the land were to appreciate in one year by 20 percent, the investor would realize a $20,000 gross profit (excluding commissions). This gross profit is reduced to
$11,360 by the after-tax cash outlays for property taxes and interest ($20,000 −
$8,640). But this net profit still means that the investor earned a return of 56.8 per-
cent ($11,360 ÷ $20,000).[8] The small down payment plus the deduction of interest
and property taxes from taxable income significantly increased the return on the investor's funds.

---

[8] The 55.9 percent is the rate of return only if the property were held for one year.

A substantial amount of financial leverage

The ability to use a large amount of borrowed funds and the capacity to write off certain (and important) expenses against taxable income increase the attractiveness of speculating in nonresidential real estate. Although the use of debt financing is not limited to investments in real estate, the ability to apply leverage is greater. The investor's capacity to use leverage in investments in stocks and bonds is subject to the margin requirements set by the Federal Reserve. And these requirements are considerably higher than the down payments required to purchase real estate.

Risk

Of course, the use of a substantial amount of leverage does increase the element of risk. However, many investors believe that the continuation of inflation will tend to increase real estate values. The potential for loss is viewed as being smaller than the potential for profits, which justifies bearing the risk that results from the use of a large amount of financial leverage.

Unimproved Land

No flow of income

Unimproved land by itself produces nothing and hence cannot generate a flow of income. Any income generated is the result of using the land for some activity, such as farming or mining. Even cutting down trees for sale as firewood requires expenditures of labor and tools. Since unimproved land cannot by itself generate income, the primary source of the return on such an investment is the potential for price appreciation.

Land must have some potential for use

For land to appreciate in value, it must have some potential for use in the future, such as lots for building, acreage for farming, or rights for mining. For the investment to earn a return commensurate with the risk, the investor must acquire land with potential for future value. Such future value may be difficult to foresee, as it depends on location, zoning requirements, road frontage or access to roads, and proximity to population centers. These factors can and do vary. Zoning laws may change, or the owner may be able to obtain a variance. New roads are built and the population moves. All of these factors affect the value of land and in some cases even cause its value to decline.

Factors that reduce the return

The potential return on an investment in unimproved land may be reduced by several other factors. First, many state and local governments tax land as well as other real estate investments. Second, land may be difficult to sell. Although the title can be readily transferred, finding a buyer may take several months or even years. Third, real estate commissions on the sale of land may be as high as 10 percent of the sale price. Therefore, the price of the land must appreciate sufficiently to recoup these commissions plus any other fees that may be associated with the sale (e.g., lawyer's fees) and still earn a profit.

To be a good investment, land must have the traits of other investments: marketability, income, and the potential for capital appreciation. Land offers little income, may be very difficult to sell, and has varying potential for future use. The investor should not be swayed by ads claiming "Buy land; they aren't making it any more!" There are still many acres of undeveloped land, but only that land which has the potential for future use will prove to be a desirable investment today. For example, there are undeveloped acres in the middle of Maine that could be very valuable for timber. However, if there is no access to the land and the trees, they are of little value.

The valuation

The valuation of land, then, is essentially no different than the valuation of any investment. The estimated future cash flow is discounted back to the present at the appropriate discount rate. Therein lies the clue to the problem of investing in un-

improved land. The future cash flows are very uncertain, and the discount factor is quite subjective. For most investors, raw, undeveloped land is a poor investment. However, for those knowledgeable individuals who are willing to wait, forgo current income, and even pay out cash to carry the land, the return may be considerable if economic trends alter the unimproved land's potential.

Improved Land

The investor may buy improved land, which includes land on which buildings, such as apartments, are constructed, or land with other improvements, such as curbs and sewers. Such purchases are alternatives to investments in financial assets, but they may also be viewed as business ventures. As with any business venture, the management of improved land requires special knowledge that differs markedly from the knowledge employed in the selection of financial assets. The investor needs to know such things as zoning and other land-use laws, the laws regulating the relationship between landlord and tenant, and the management of accounts receivable (i.e., rent owed). *A business venture*

    This does not mean that the individual should avoid purchasing and managing improved land as a viable investment. Obviously the investor must select among options that include both financial assets and business ventures. Investing in improved real estate is a possible alternative, but so are many other business ventures, which may range from becoming a dealer in collectibles to the raising of champion dogs or publishing books. Ultimately, each individual must decide how to allocate his or her savings among the many possible alternatives. These investments may offer superior returns if the investor has the specialized knowledge and capacity to manage them. However, many individuals lack either the knowledge or the inclination to risk their savings on business ventures and thus select financial assets. While business ventures are beyond the scope of this book, the individual should realize that such ventures offer alternatives to investments in financial assets. *An investor must select among alternatives*

    For those investors who are willing to invest in rental property, the potential benefits are illustrated in Exhibit 25.2. This exhibit projects the cash flow estimates for an investment in a rental property and illustrates several facets of investing in such properties: the initial tax savings, the reinvestment of the cash flow generated by the property, and the appreciation of the rental property's value. The benefits of such an investment require time. This particular example has a 20-year time horizon. While the investor may sell the property at any time (assuming that a buyer can be found), rental properties should be viewed as long-term investments whose returns are a combination of initial tax advantages, annual flows of cash, and potential long-term growth in property values. *Cash flow projections*

    In the example in Exhibit 25.2, the investor purchases a rental property for $100,000. The purchase is financed with a $20,000 down payment and a conventional loan for $80,000 at 12 percent for 20 years. To simplify the analysis, the loan is amortized (i.e., retired) in 20 equal annual installments of $10,710.30 (column 7). The breakdown of this annual payment into interest and principal repayment is given in columns 8 and 9, respectively, in the exhibit.

    The first two columns give the year and the annual rental income. Rents are assumed to increase annually by 5 percent. Thus rental income is $12,000 in the first year but grows to $30,323.40 during the twentieth year. The third and fourth col-

Exhibit 25.2
Cash Flow Projections for a Real Estate Investment

Year (1)	Rents (2)	Depreciation (3)	Cost basis (4)	Value (5)	Maintenance (6)	Mortgage payment (7)
1	$12,000.00	$5,000.00	$95,000.00	$105,000.00	$2,000.00	$10,710.30
2	12,600.00	5,000.00	90,000.00	110,250.00	2,100.00	10,710.30
3	13,230.00	5,000.00	85,000.00	115,762.50	2,205.00	10,710.30
4	13,891.50	5,000.00	80,000.00	121,550.63	2,315.25	10,710.30
5	14,586.08	5,000.00	75,000.00	127,628.16	2,431.01	10,710.30
6	15,315.38	5,000.00	70,000.00	134,009.56	2,552.56	10,710.30
7	16,081.15	5,000.00	65,000.00	140,710.04	2,680.19	10,710.30
8	16,885.21	5,000.00	60,000.00	147,745.54	2,814.20	10,710.30
9	17,729.47	5,000.00	55,000.00	155,132.82	2,954.91	10,710.30
10	18,615.94	5,000.00	50,000.00	162,889.46	3,102.66	10,710.30
11	19,546.74	5,000.00	45,000.00	171,033.94	3,257.79	10,710.30
12	20,524.07	5,000.00	40,000.00	179,585.63	3,420.68	10,710.30
13	21,550.28	5,000.00	35,000.00	188,564.91	3,591.71	10,710.30
14	22,627.79	5,000.00	30,000.00	197,993.16	3,771.30	10,710.30
15	23,759.18	5,000.00	25,000.00	207,892.82	3,959.86	10,710.30
16	24,947.14	5,000.00	20,000.00	218,287.46	4,157.86	10,710.30
17	26,194.50	5,000.00	15,000.00	229,201.83	4,365.75	10,710.30
18	27,504.22	5,000.00	10,000.00	240,661.92	4,584.04	10,710.30
19	28,879.43	5,000.00	5,000.00	252,695.02	4,813.24	10,710.30
20	30,323.40	5,000.00	0.00	265,329.77	5,053.90	10,710.30

umns give the depreciation expense on the property and the resulting cost basis of the property. To simplify the analysis, the property is depreciated by an equal annual amount ($5,000) for 20 years. Thus the cost basis declines annually by $5,000, so that at the end of the 20 years, the cost basis has been reduced to $0. (In reality the asset could not be completely depreciated because there would be some residual value, such as the value of the land, that cannot be depreciated. The rate at which the asset may be depreciated and the time period over which it is depreciated is established by the tax laws. Under tax reform residential is depreciated over 27.5 years and other real estate is depreciated over 31.5 years.) While the asset is being depreciated, its market value may increase. In this example the value is assumed to increase by 5 percent annually, so the property that initially cost $100,000 is worth $265,329.77 at the end of 20 years.

Determination of net income

To determine the net income generated by the property, all expenses must be deducted from the rental income. These expenses include depreciation (column 3), interest (column 8), and maintenance expenses (column 6). This last expense includes all the operating expenses (e.g., insurance) and repair expenses associated with the building. This expense rises by 5 percent annually to adjust for increases in the running expenses that tend to occur over time. The total expenses are subtracted from the rental income to determine taxable income (column 10).

The tax paid on the income is given in column 11. A tax rate of 40 percent is assumed in this example, but the actual tax that would be paid would depend on the rates set by Congress plus any taxes established by state legislatures. After the taxes have been paid, net earnings are determined (column 12). In this illustration the operation generates a loss during the first seven years. The investor uses these losses

Year (1)	Interest (8)	Principal Repayment (9)	Earnings before Taxes (10)	Taxes (11)	Net Earnings (12)	Cash Flow (13)	Cumulative Cash Flow (14)
1	$9,600.00	$1,110.30	$−4,600.00	$−1,840.00	$−2,760.00	$1,129.70	$1,129.70
2	9,466.76	1,243.54	−3,966.76	−1,586.70	−2,380.06	1,376.40	2,641.67
3	9,317.54	1,392.76	−3,292.54	−1,317.02	−1,975.52	1,631.72	4,590.38
4	9,150.41	1,559.89	−2,574.16	−1,029.66	−1,544.50	1,895.61	7,036.84
5	8,963.22	1,747.08	−1,808.16	−723.26	−1,084.89	2,168.03	10,049.29
6	8,753.57	1,956.73	−990.75	−396.30	−594.45	2,448.82	13,704.02
7	8,518.76	2,191.54	−117.80	−47.12	−70.68	2,737.78	18,086.28
8	8,255.78	2,454.52	815.22	326.09	489.13	3,034.61	23,291.25
9	7,961.23	2,749.07	1,813.32	725.33	1,087.99	3,338.92	29,425.13
10	7,631.34	3,078.96	2,881.94	1,152.78	1,729.17	3,650.21	36,606.35
11	7,261.87	3,448.43	4,027.08	1,610.83	2,416.25	3,967.82	44,966.93
12	6,848.06	3,862.24	5,255.33	2,102.13	3,153.20	4,290.96	54,653.92
13	6,384.59	4,325.71	6,573.97	2,629.59	3,944.38	4,618.67	65,831.06
14	5,865.50	4,844.80	7,990.99	3,196.40	4,794.59	4,949.79	78,680.58
15	5,284.13	5,426.17	9,515.19	3,806.07	5,709.11	5,282.94	93,405.19
16	4,632.99	6,077.31	11,156.29	4,462.52	6,693.78	5,616.47	110,230.28
17	3,903.71	6,806.59	12,925.04	5,170.01	7,755.02	5,948.43	129,406.35
18	3,086.92	7,623.38	14,833.26	5,933.31	8,899.96	6,276.58	151,211.69
19	2,172.11	8,538.19	16,894.08	6,757.63	10,136.45	6,598.26	175,955.35
20	1,147.53	9,562.77	19,121.97	7,648.79	11,473.18	6,910.41	203,980.41

to offset income from other sources and thus to reduce taxes paid on the other income. These initial losses are an important tax shelter that reduce the investor's total taxes. For example, this tax shelter reduces taxes by $1,840 in year 1 and continues to reduce taxes for the next seven years. However, eventually the property earns income and requires the investor to pay taxes.

Importance of cash flow

The individual who invests in rental property is more concerned with cash flow than with net earnings. Cash flow may be used for reinvestment purposes and is the sum of net earnings plus depreciation minus principal repayment (column 12 plus column 3 minus column 9 = column 13). Depreciation is added back to net income because it is a *non-cash* expense that allocates the cost of the investment over a period of time. Since it is a non-cash expense, it is a source of funds that may be reinvested. Principal repayment is subtracted because it is a cash outlay that has not been previously subtracted. All other cash outlays were tax-deductible expenses (e.g., interest and maintenance) and therefore were deducted from the rental income to determine taxable income. Principal repayment is not a tax-deductible expense; thus, to determine the cash flow generated by the operation, this repayment must be subtracted from the sum of net income plus depreciation.

Uses of cash flow

The investor may use the cash flow generated in each year. For example, if the investor were a retiree, the cash flow may be used to finance retirement. In this example, the cash flow is reinvested in other assets that earn 12 percent annually. It is presumed that the investor can earn at least 12 percent because if other alternatives were not available, the mortgage loan could be paid off more rapidly. Since the loan has an interest rate of 12 percent, it is reasonable to assume that the cash flow can be reinvested at this rate. Column 14 presents the cumulative cash flow. At the end of

20 years, the investor will have accumulated $203,980.41 by reinvesting the cash flow received each year.

Earnings may exceed cash flow

The investor should note that in this illustration net earnings start to exceed cash flow in year 15. The principal repayments have risen sufficiently that they exceed depreciation. Thus while the operation now appears profitable, the investor has a large principal repayment that (1) is not tax deductible and (2) consumes cash. Unlike the early years when the cash generated exceeded earnings, earnings now exceed the cash being generated.[9]

If the individual holds the property to the end of the time period, the investor has $203,980.41 through the reinvestment of the cash flow plus property worth $265,329.77. Thus, the original $20,000 investment has grown to $469,310.18. Of course, the individual over time has invested a total of $100,000 in the property as the mortgage is retired. However, while the total investment is $100,000, the final value of the investor's assets (before tax)[10] is $469,310.18—the $100,000 invested in the property, plus the assets acquired through the reinvestment of the cash flow, plus the appreciation in the property's value. Of course, for this result to occur in this example, the value of the property and the rental income must increase annually by 5 percent. Changes in the growth rate of expenses, changes in the tax laws, and the inability to earn 12 percent annually on the accumulated cash flow will also affect the return ultimately earned on the investment in the rental property.

Uncertainties and Investing in Real Estate

While Exhibit 25.2 illustrated the fundamentals to include when determining a real estate investment's cash flow, it also highlights the major factors to consider when acquiring income-earning properties. Forecasting the cash flow is crucial to real estate investments, but this cash flow is very uncertain because so few of the pieces of the analysis are fixed in the present and because the time dimension is so long. The major factors that may be fixed include the cost of the investment, the depreciation schedules, and the cost of financing the mortgage loan.[11] Even the mortgage loan payment could vary if the loan has a variable interest rate.

Variations in occupancy rates

All the other factors in the analysis are subject to change. For example, rental income could (and probably will) vary with changes in occupancy rates. Rental properties rarely remain 100 percent occupied. Instead, rental income will fluctuate even though the long-term trend in rents is positive (they increase when prices in general rise).

Fluctuations in expenses

Operating expenses may also fluctuate. Certainly inflationary (and deflationary) pressures will have an impact on expenses. Maintenance and repairs, property taxes, and management expenses will tend to rise over time. Some expenses (e.g., insurance and especially liability coverage) may rise erratically and perhaps dramatically. Such

---

[9] It is possible that the taxes owed on the income will exceed the cash being generated. See, for instance, year 20 in Exhibit 25.2.

[10] The illustration does not assume that any tax has been paid on the earnings generated by the reinvestment of the cash flow. Nor does it consider any capital gains tax on the property if it were sold.

[11] Even though Congress may change depreciation schedules for new investments, investments made under previous depreciation schedules would not be adversely affected.

fluctuations in expenses, along with fluctuations in rental income, make forecasting cash flow many years into the future extremely difficult. Current estimates of cash flow must be viewed as tentative at best.

The individual must also realize that other factors may affect real estate investments. The political climate may change. For example, rent control or rent stabilization can be imposed. While such laws generally are usually not applied to commercial properties, they may be applied to residential apartment buildings.

Rental properties are obviously long-term investments and may generate cash flow for many years. They are certainly not liquid assets, and they may also lack marketability. While title to the property may be transferred, such transfers require a buyer. It may take a considerable amount of time and expense (e.g., real estate brokerage commissions, legal fees, and transfer taxes) to sell rental properties. This will be particularly true during periods of high interest rates, low occupancy rates, or political uncertainty. Of course, accepting a lower price will facilitate the sale.

This discussion suggests that real estate investments are fraught with uncertainty. However, they can play an important role in an individual's well-diversified portfolio. While such investments cannot meet financial goals by providing funds for emergencies, real estate may be an excellent means to generate cash flow plus appreciation through the growth in the value of the property.

LIMITED PARTNERSHIPS

Investing in and managing rental property is a business enterprise. It is virtually impossible for the investor to participate passively in such real estate ownership.[12] However, the investor may buy shares, called "units," in limited **partnerships** that own and manage real estate. Like the rental property discussed in the previous illustration, these partnerships offer investors a possible return from cash flows and from appreciation in real estate values.

Units in partnerships

In a real estate partnership there are two types of partners: the general partners who manage the real estate and the limited partners. The limited partners provide the funds to acquire the properties but are passive owners who do not manage the real estate. Unlike the general partners, the limited partners have limited liability. Since the business is a partnership and not a corporation, the limited partners directly reap the benefits of any profits earned.

In the initial years of the partnership (when the properties are being developed), the partnership generally operates at a loss. After the buildings are completed, the partnership may still generate losses from depreciation expenses. Once again this depreciation expense is a non-cash expense (i.e., it does not require a disbursement of funds) that allocates the cost of investment in the properties over a period of time. While the buildings are being depreciated, these properties may generate cash that, when distributed to the limited partners, is a return of their capital invested in the project. Such return of capital is *not* income and hence not subject to income taxes. Instead the partners' cost basis in the investment is reduced.

---

[12] The investor may employ a real estate agent to handle the properties, but this, of course, will consume part of the return earned by the properties.

Partnership losses offset partnership income

The initial operating losses and the depreciation expense shelter cash payments to the limited partners from income taxation. The losses may also be used to offset income from limited partnerships that are profitable. After a period of years, the cost of the investment will be recouped through the depreciation expenses. When the properties are sold, any appreciation in value of the properties will be treated as capital gains.

The tax laws pertaining to investing in limited partnerships and the tax shelters associated with them are exceedingly complex. These investments are primarily of interest to sophisticated investors. Investors with only modest sums to invest or who are in lower tax brackets should probably choose a home or condominium as a means to invest in real estate.

REAL ESTATE INVESTMENT TRUSTS

REIT—a type of investment company

One way to invest indirectly in real estate is to buy shares in **real estate investment trusts** (commonly called **REITs**). These real estate trusts are another type of closed-end investment company. They receive the special tax treatment granted other investment companies (e.g., mutual funds). As long as a REIT derives 70 percent of its income from real estate (e.g., interest on mortgage loans and rents) and distributes at least 95 percent of the income as cash dividends, the trust is exempt from federal income tax. Thus, REITs, like mutual funds and other closed-end investment companies, are conduits through which earnings pass to the shareholders.

Shares are traded like other stocks

Shares of REITs are bought and sold like the stocks of other companies. Some are traded on the New York Stock Exchange (e.g., HRE Properties), while others are traded on the American Stock Exchange (e.g., Washington REIT) and in the over-the-counter markets (e.g., Old Dominion REIT). The existence of these markets means that the shares of REITs may be readily sold. This ease of marketability certainly differentiates shares of REITs from other types of real estate investments.

The income is distributed

Real estate investment trusts also differ from some forms of investments in real estate because they offer the potential for monetary income. Most trusts distribute virtually all of their earned income to maintain their tax status. This often results in significant dividend yields on investments in these shares. Selected dividend yields are illustrated in Exhibit 25.3, which presents the prices of the stock of five REITs, their dividends, and the dividend yield (i.e., the dividend divided by the price of the stock). In many cases this yield exceeds 8.5 percent annually.

The dividends fluctuate

Whereas other firms may seek to maintain stable dividends and increase them only after there has been an increase in earnings that management anticipates will continue, the dividends of REITs often fluctuate from year to year. This is because tax regulations require the distribution of earnings in order to maintain the trust's tax status. Thus, as earnings fluctuate, so do the dividends that are distributed. This fluctuation in earnings and hence in dividends is illustrated in Figure 25.3, which presents the dividends per quarter for Realty ReFund. As may be seen in the exhibit, the dividends vary almost every quarter. Shares of REITs, therefore, may not be desirable investments for individuals who need steady and stable sources of income. These investors may find such fluctuations in dividends undesirable and probably would prefer other stocks that offer high yields, such as those of utilities.

Firm	Price of the Stock as of 1/1/86	Annual Dividend	Dividend Yield
HRE Properties	$24¼	$2.28	9.4%
Pennsylvania REIT	26¼	2.00	7.6
Santa Anita REIT	23½	1.94	8.3
United Dominion REIT	13⅜	0.96	7.2
Washington REIT	18⅝	1.28	6.9

Exhibit 25.3
Selected REITs and
Their Dividend Yields

Source: Annual reports and Standard & Poor's *Stock Guide,* various issues.

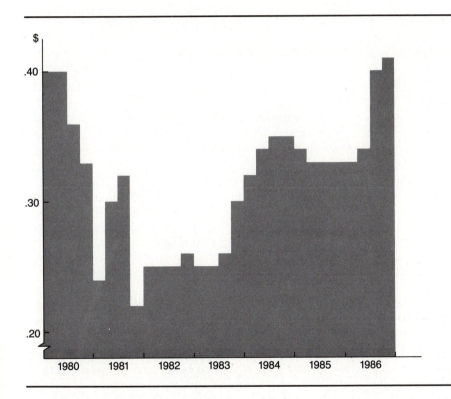

Figure 25.3
**Quarterly Dividends
for Realty ReFund (for
fiscal years ending
January 31)**

Classification of REITs

REITs may be grouped according to either the types of assets they acquire or their capital structure. **Equity trusts** own property and rent it to other firms (i.e., they lease their property to others). **Mortgage trusts** make loans to develop property and finance buildings. There is a considerable difference between these two approaches to investing in real estate. Loans to help finance real estate, especially developmental loans, can earn high interest rates, but some of these loans can be very risky. Contractors may be unable to sell or lease the completed buildings, which may consequently cause them to default on their loans. In addition, any inflation in the value of the property cannot be enjoyed by the lender, who owns a fixed obligation.

Mortgage trusts

Equity trusts

In an equity trust the REIT owns the property and rents space. This can also be risky because the properties may remain vacant. Unleased property, of course, does not generate any revenue, but the owner still has expenses, such as insurance, maintenance, and depreciation. Like any operation with few variable costs and many fixed expenses, there can be large fluctuations in the earnings of equity trusts. However, should there be an increase in property values, the trust may experience capital appreciation.

The varying use of debt financing

The second method for differentiating REITs is according to their capital structure or the extent to which they use debt financing. Some trusts use virtually no debt financing, while others use a large amount of leverage. The latter can be very risky investments, because the trusts borrow from one group either to lend or to invest directly in real estate. If their loans turn sour and the borrowers default or if the properties remain unrented, the trusts that use extensive financial leverage will have difficulty meeting their own debt obligations.

These differences among REITs are illustrated in Exhibit 25.4, which lists eight trusts that were earning profits as of December 1985. The exhibit is constructed in two parts. The top half shows equity trusts whose primary assets are real estate. The second half presents trusts whose primary assets are mortgages. The entries in each section are listed in descending order according to their debt ratios (column 3). Thus, IRT Properties is an equity trust with a modest amount of debt, while Realty ReFund uses a great deal of leverage because over 80 percent of its assets are financed by debt.

In addition to equity trusts and mortgage trusts there are finite life REITs (called FREITs). Regular REITs have an indefinite life, but FREITs do not. Their real estate assets will be liquidated within a specified time period, and the funds will be distributed to stockholders. For example, EQK Realty Investors I was sold to the public in 1985 and will be liquidated after 12 years. Of course, such forced sales of the properties could prove to be deleterious to stockholders if the market for real estate is weak when the sales must be made.

Exhibit 25.4
Selected REITs by Types of Assets and Capital Structures (as of end of fiscal year 1985)

Firm	Real Estate Owned as a Percent of Total Assets	Debt Ratio (Debt to Total Assets)
BankAmerica Realty Investors	56.1%	37.5%
HRE Properties	72.4	21.6
IRT Properties	45.2	19.7
Washington Real Estate Investment Trust	71.7	19.2

Firm	Mortgages as a Percent of Total Assets	Debt Ratio (Debt to Total Assets)
Realty ReFund	97.8%	81.5%
Wells Fargo Mortgage and Equity Trust	61.8	70.0
Lomas and Nettleton Mortgage	95.2	57.6
MONY	84.7	50.6

Source: Annual reports.

Returns Earned by Investments in REITs

Initially REITs were very popular, and several hundred came into existence. Many were financed with substantial amounts of debt. Commercial banks were only too happy to lend them funds because the loans were very profitable for the banks. Not only did the banks lend money to REITs, but they also formed advisory services and received management fees from the trusts. *REITs were popular*

While interest was being received and properties were leased, the extensive use of financial leverage posed no problems. However, when short-term interest rates rose to record heights in 1973 and 1974, many trusts found that they were unable to collect the interest owed them. Partially completed buildings were left unfinished, as there was virtually no demand for the properties. Those properties that did sell often went for prices that produced losses for the builders, who in turn defaulted on loans from the trusts. The trusts were then unable to meet their own interest payments. A substantial number defaulted on their debt. Some creditors seized properties, and a long period of reorganization for the trusts followed. *REITs fell on hard times*

Today REITs are considerably different. Those that weathered the storm are much healthier firms today than was the industry as a whole in the mid-1970s. However, this past experience does suggest that an individual should invest in REITs cautiously. The investor should prefer those trusts with proven records of performance. Obviously the properties must be consistently leased to generate income, so fluctuations in occupancy rates suggest the trust will experience fluctuating revenues and income. The investor should also examine the fees charged to manage the properties, especially to learn if these expenses are related to the properties' performance. In addition, the trust should use only a modest amount of debt financing, and its properties should be diversified with regard to type and/or location. If the trust uses a substantial amount of financial leverage or if it invests in only one type of property (e.g., apartments) or only one location (e.g., California), that will tend to increase the trust's (and the investor's) risk exposure. *Today REITs are financially sounder*

The Valuation of Shares in REITs

The valuation of shares in REITs is essentially the same as the valuation of any other security. The valuation model for common stocks that was presented in Chapter 14 also applies to the shares of REITs. According to that model, the value of stock depends on the dividends that the firm will pay in the future brought back to their present value at the appropriate discount rate. However, the application of this model is particularly difficult with regard to the shares of REITs.

First, there is the problem of estimating future earnings and dividends. Although many firms grow and their dividends follow a steady pattern of growth in response to higher earnings, the dividends of REITs fluctuate from quarter to quarter. In many cases the dividend cannot grow because the earnings are not retained but are distributed. *Estimating future earnings and dividends*

Earnings and dividends may be increased if the firm successfully increases its use of financial leverage. But this may also increase the element of risk, which may offset the value of the increased dividends. This suggests a second important problem in the valuation of the shares of REITs: the determination of the appropriate discount factor. *Accounting for risk*

POINTS OF INTEREST
Real Estate at a Discount?

Real estate tends to appreciate in value with inflation; however, for tax purposes the cost of the property may be depreciated. Thus, the value of real estate on a firm's balance sheet (i.e., the book value) may be less than the replacement cost or current market value of the property. In addition, since REITs must distribute their earnings, these stocks may be sensitive to changes in interest rates. If interest rates rise, the value of REIT stocks tends to fall. When this occurs, the price of the stock may sell below its per-share equity value, which in turn may be understated because of the understated book value of the REIT's properties.

Since REIT shares may sell below their equity per share, should investors consider these REITs attractive? The answer is "Not necessarily." If a REIT's shares are selling for less than the equity per share, that alone is insufficient justification to purchase the stock. The investor should determine the cash flow (profits plus depreciation) generated by the properties. If the properties are generating sufficient cash flow, the REIT may be considered attractive. However, if the cash flow is insufficient, the shares are unattractive even if they sell at a discount from equity per share.

If the REIT is truly undervalued, the stock may be tailor-made for a takeover. The company taking over will be obtaining property at less than current cost. It may then sell the pieces of the REIT's property individually at their current market value. Since the pieces are more valuable than the sum of the parts, this strategy earns profits for the aggressive firm doing the takeover.

Many REITs are very risky firms. Some have issued a substantial amount of debt, and others own real estate that may lie unrented. Risk is inherent in both sides of a REIT's balance sheet. For many of these firms, the type of assets they own and the sources from which they obtain financing may result in a substantial amount of both business risk and financial risk.

If the investor can account for these risks and estimate future dividends, the valuation of the stock becomes straightforward. This is illustrated in the following example, which uses the security valuation model presented in Chapter 14 and the shares of Washington REIT. Washington REIT is an equity trust so its earnings and dividends can grow as rents increase. From 1966 to 1985 its dividends grew annually by 10 percent, and its current dividend is $1.28 a share. If the investor seeks a return of 15 percent and expects the firm to continue to grow annually at 10 percent, the value of a share is

$$V = \frac{D_0(1 + g)}{r - g}$$

$$= \frac{1.28(1 + 0.1)}{0.15 - 0.1}$$

$$= \$29.44.$$

Any price below $29.44 produces a yield in excess of 15 percent, and any price above $29.44 produces a yield less than 15 percent.

It must be emphasized that the value that any investor places on the shares through the use of this model is simply the result of the dividends that have been forecast and the application of the appropriate discount rate. This valuation model can only be as good as its inputs. Forecasting the future dividends of a REIT and determining the appropriate discount rate may be extremely difficult. However, the efficient market hypothesis suggests that the current price of a share in a publicly held REIT does appropriately value the future prospects of the firm.

The need for accurate forecasts

SUMMARY

The poor performance of stocks during the 1970s and the increase in the rate of inflation resulted in investors' broadening their portfolios to include physical assets such as real estate. This chapter has been devoted to three types of real estate investments: home ownership, land and rental properties, and real estate investment trusts (REITs).

In recent years home ownership has been a particularly attractive investment. Since the individual must live somewhere, it may be more advantageous to own than to rent, especially if the cost of housing continues to rise. The federal income tax laws encourage investments in homes. In addition to untaxed income-in-kind, several expenses (e.g., interest and property taxes) are allowed as deductions in the determination of the individual's taxable income. Under some circumstances, capital gains taxes on the sale of a home may be deferred or even avoided.

Homes may be financed by mortgage loans that are secured by the property. Conventional mortgage loans are retired through monthly payments that include both interest and principal repayment. The federal government has followed a policy of encouraging investments in homes by guaranteeing some mortgage loans. These insurance programs are administered by the Federal Housing Administration and the Veterans Administration. The high interest rates of the late 1970s and early 1980s altered the supply of mortgage money and the terms under which it was obtained. Many mortgage loans now may use creative financing involving variable interest rates, graduated payments, or renegotiable interest rates. These features are designed to protect lenders from further increases in interest rates and thus encourage them to make loans that they would not make under conventional terms.

Investors may also buy land and rental properties. The potential return on such investments is also enhanced by the income tax laws, which permit the deduction of several expenses from taxable income. Unimproved land may appreciate in value if there is potential use for the land in the future. An investment in rental properties is essentially a business venture and may earn a return from the cash flow generated by the properties and the potential for capital appreciation.

Real estate investment trusts (REITs) offer investors an alternative means to invest in real estate. These trusts are a type of investment company, and stockholders enjoy the same tax benefits given to the stockholders of other closed- and open-end investment companies. Real estate investment trusts either make loans to firms that develop and manage real estate or own properties and lease them.

The valuation of the shares of REITs is essentially the same as the valuation of any stock: Future dividend payments are brought back to the present value at the appropriate discount rate. However, estimating future dividends and determining the appropriate discount rate may be extremely difficult.

Terms to Remember

Cost of debt

Condominium

Conventional mortgage loan

Federal Housing Administration (FHA)

Veterans Administration (VA)

Creative financing

Variable-interest-rate mortgage loan

Renegotiable-rate mortgage loan

Graduated-payment mortgage loan

Unimproved and improved land

Partnership

Real estate investment trust (REIT)

REIT: equity trust

REIT: mortgage trust

Questions

1. What are the sources of risk and return from investing in a home?

2. What are the special tax advantages associated with home ownership? Do these advantages apply to renters or owners of condominiums?

3. Has an investment in a home been a good hedge against inflation?

4. What are several expenses associated with owning real estate?

5. What is financial leverage and how does it apply to investments in real estate?

6. What are the differences among conventional mortgages, VA-insured mortgages, and variable-interest-rate mortgages?

7. Why may a seller of a home accept a mortgage loan in partial payment?

8. What are real estate investment trusts? Why are they similar to closed-end investment companies?

9. What differentiates a mortgage REIT from an equity REIT? Which should prove to be the better investment during a period of high interest rates and rising prices?

10. What is the cash flow associated with an investment in real estate? What impact will each of the following have on a rental property's cash flow?
    a. Increase in depreciation expense
    b. Decrease in rental income
    c. Increase in principal repayment
    d. Decrease in interest rates

11. What are the risks associated with investing in real estate? In what ways are they similar to the risks associated with investments in financial assets? Why may an investment in real estate be more risky than an investment in a stock or a bond?

Problems

1. Determine the annual repayment schedule for the first two years (i.e., interest owed, principal repayment, and balance owed) for each of the following. (Assume that only one payment is made annually.)
    a. a $60,000 conventional mortgage for 25 years at 10 percent
    b. a $60,000 conventional mortgage for 20 years at 10 percent
    c. a $60,000 conventional mortgage for 25 years at 8 percent
    d. a $50,000 conventional mortgage for 25 years at 10 percent

Compare the total annual payment and the amount of interest in the first year of each of the above.

2. What is the expected cash flow and tax liability (or savings) for the first two years for an investment in an apartment building given the following information?

Cost of the building	$800,000
Cost of the land	200,000
Required down payment	25%
Interest on balance owed	10%
Annual principal repayment	20,000
Annual operating expenses	30,000
Rent, year 1	120,000
Rent, year 2	140,000
Annual depreciation expense	40,000
Individual owner's income tax rate	30%

Suggested Readings

General textbooks that cover the area of real estate (e.g., financing, valuation, land use, and development) include:

Beaton, William R. *Real Estate Finance,* 2nd ed. Englewood Cliffs, N.J.: Prentice Hall, 1982.

Floyd, Charles F. *Real Estate Principles.* New York: Random House, 1981.

Unger, Maurice A., and George R. Karvel. *Real Estate: Principles and Practice,* 7th ed. Cincinnati: South-Western Publishing Co., 1983.

For an excellent book written for laymen and investors in real estate, consult:

Mader, Chris, and John Bortz. *The Dow Jones-Irwin Guide to Real Estate Investing,* revised ed. Homewood, Ill.: Dow Jones-Irwin, 1983.

For an excellent guide to the laws governing real estate, consult:

Corley, Robert N., Peter J. Shedd, and Charles F. Floyd. *Real Estate and the Law.* New York: Random House, 1982.

The history of REITs before their collapse during 1973–1974 is chronicled in

Hall, John T., ed. *REITs: The First Decade.* Mequon, Wis.: John T. Hall, Inc., 1974.

While many REITs have folded, those that remain may be interesting investments. See, for instance:

Rudnitsky, Howard. "Speculating in White Elephants." *Forbes* (Dec. 1, 1977), 79–86.

During the 1980s REITS again became popular. See, for instance:

Sanger, Elizabeth. "Red-Hot REITs." *Barron's,* April 15, 1985, 15, 18, and 22.

Rudnitsky, Howard. "REITs Redux." *Forbes,* April 22, 1985, 44.

Information concerning investing in REITs may be obtained from the National Association of Real Estate Investment Trusts, 1101 17th Street NW, Suite 700, Washington, DC, 20036.

For a discussion of builders (e.g., U.S. Homes), how they operate, and an economic analysis of the industry, consult:

Eichler, Ned. *The Merchant Builders.* Cambridge, Mass.: The MIT Press, 1982.

Investing in undeveloped land is generally more speculative than acquiring rental properties. For a discussion of factors to consider when acquiring land, see:

Sheerin, James J. *The Complete Guide to Buying, Selling and Investing in Undeveloped Land.* Chicago: Probus Publishing, 1986.

26

Investing in Foreign Securities

LEARNING OBJECTIVES

After completing this chapter you should be able to

1. Enumerate the advantages offered by foreign investments.

2. Differentiate American bonds, Euro-bonds, and foreign bonds.

3. Define American depository receipts (ADRs), foreign exchange, and foreign exchange rates.

4. Explain how and why ADRs came into existence.

5. Contrast devaluation and revaluation.

6. Identify the special risks associated with foreign investments.

7. Explain how hedging with currency futures may be used to reduce the risk associated with fluctuations in exchange rates.

8. Determine the advantages offered by shares in international investment companies.

The development of many foreign economies and the rapid growth experienced by many foreign firms has resulted in some American investors taking a more global view of investment alternatives. Europeans, Asians, and other people throughout the world have held such a view for many years, as they have invested in assets located in nations foreign to them, such as the United States. American firms have also invested abroad for many years. However, interest in international investments has only recently grown among Americans, who now perceive such investments as a means to obtain increased returns or to diversify their portfolios.

This chapter is concerned with such foreign investments. It initially covers the foreign investments that are available to Americans, the method by which the individual acquires the assets, and the sources of return from these investments. Next follows a discussion of fluctua-

tion in the prices of foreign exchange (i.e., foreign currencies), which represents a major source of risk associated with acquiring foreign securities. While foreign investments subject the investor to the same risks associated with domestic securities, they also add risks associated with the political climate and fluctuations in the prices of foreign currencies. Political risk cannot be avoided if the investor acquires assets in politically unstable countries, but the risk associated with fluctuating exchange rates can be managed through hedging with futures contracts. The chapter ends with a discussion of the advantages offered by investing in foreign securities and the acquisition of shares in mutual funds that specialize in foreign investments.

FOREIGN SECURITIES

Foreign stock exchanges

Foreign companies, like American companies, issue a variety of securities as a means to acquire funds. These securities subsequently trade on foreign exchanges or foreign over-the-counter markets. For example, there are stock exchanges in London, Paris, Tokyo, and other foreign financial centers. Unless Americans and other foreigners are forbidden to acquire these securities, Americans can buy and sell stocks through these exchanges in much the same way that they purchase domestic American stocks and bonds. Thus, foreign securities may be purchased through the use of American brokers who have access to trading on these exchanges. In many cases this access is obtained through a correspondent relationship with foreign security brokers.

Foreign securities may differ significantly from American securities. For example, terminology differs. In Britain a debenture is secured by the firm's assets, while in the United States a debenture is an unsecured, general obligation of the firm. Foreign dividends are usually paid semiannually or annually, and the amount is expressed as a percent of par and not as an amount, as is done in the United States (e.g., 10% of $2 par instead of $0.20). Foreign investors such as Americans may be limited to acquiring only nonvoting shares, and the unit of trading may be greater than the 100 share round lot used in the U.S. This is especially true in Japan, where frequent stock splits and stock dividends are used to reduce the security's price.

There are also differences in business practices. For example, Japanese firms use more financial leverage than is customary in the United States. It is not unusual for more than three-fourths of a Japanese firm's assets to be financed with debt. Accounting practices such as the consolidation of subsidiaries' balance sheets or the depreciation of assets differ from generally accepted American accounting practices. Such differences make comparisons of foreign and American accounting data exceedingly difficult.

Foreign stocks listed on NYSE and AMEX

By far the easiest way to buy foreign stocks is to purchase the shares of firms that are traded on American exchanges or through American over-the-counter markets (i.e., through NASDAQ). To be eligible for such trading, the foreign securities must be registered with the SEC. About 100 foreign stocks are listed on the New York and American stock exchanges and more than 250 trade through NASDAQ.

Exhibit 26.1 enumerates several foreign firms whose shares are traded in the United States. The exhibit gives the company, its country of origin, its primary industry, and where the shares are traded. As may be seen in the exhibit, many foreign stocks, such as SONY and Royal Dutch Petroleum, are traded on the New York Stock Exchange. Others, such as Dunlop Holdings, trade on the American Stock Exchange,

Exhibit 26.1
Selected Foreign
Securities Traded on
the New York Stock
Exchange, on the
American Stock
Exchange, and
through NASDAQ

Firm	Country of Origin	Primary Industry	Where Traded in the United States
Alcan Aluminum	Canada	Aluminum	NYSE
Campbell Red Lakes	Canada	Gold mining	NYSE
Dunlop Holdings	Britain	Tires, sporting goods	AMEX
Hitachi	Japan	Electronics	NYSE
Imperial Group	Britain	Tobacco, food	AMEX
Japan Airlines	Japan	Airline	NASDAQ
KLM Royal Dutch Airlines	Netherlands	Airline	NYSE
Kloof Gold Mines	South Africa	Gold mining	NASDAQ
Plessey	Britain	Electronics equipment	NYSE
SONY	Japan	Electronics	NYSE
TDK	Japan	Electronics	NYSE
Volkswagenwerk	Germany	Automobiles	NASDAQ

Receipts for foreign securities

and many others trade through NASDAQ.[1] The majority of the firms whose securities are actively traded in the U.S. are either Japanese or Canadian.

These domestic markets do not actually trade the foreign shares but trade receipts for the stock called **American Depository Receipts** or **ADRs.** Such receipts are created by large financial institutions such as commercial banks. The ADRs are then sold to the American public and continue to trade in the United States.

There are two types of ADRs. "Sponsored" ADRs are created when the firm wants the securities to trade in the U.S. The firm employs a bank to perform the paperwork to create the ADRs and to act as transfer agent. In this case the costs are absorbed by the firm. All ADRs listed on the NYSE and AMEX are sponsored ADRs. "Unsponsored" ADRs come into existence when a brokerage firm believes there will be sufficient interest in a stock or bond to make a market in the security. The brokerage firm buys a block of securities and hires a commercial bank to create the ADRs and to act as transfer agent. However, fees for this service and for converting dividend payments from the foreign currency into American dollars will be paid by the stockholders, not the issuing firm.

ADRs facilitate trading

The creation of ADRs greatly facilitates trading in foreign securities. First, ADRs reduce the risk of fraud. If the investor purchased a foreign stock issued by a Japanese firm, the stock certificate would be written in Japanese. It is highly unlikely that the American investor could read the language, and thus he or she could become prey to bogus certificates. ADRs erase that risk, since the certificates are in English and their authenticity is certified by the issuing agent. The investor is assured that the receipt is genuine even though it is an obligation of the issuing agent. The ADR represents only the underlying securities held by the agent and is not an obligation of the firm that issued the stock.

Besides reducing the risk of fraud, ADRs are convenient. Securities do not have to be delivered through international mail; prices are quoted in dollars; and dividend

[1] Foreign stock exchanges may also list American securities. The London Stock Exchange is the most liberal and actually encourages foreign listings.

payments are received in dollars. The ADR can represent any number of foreign shares. For example, Japanese stocks traditionally trade for low prices; such stocks would be considered penny stocks in the United States. To make the prices comparable to U.S. security prices, an ADR may represent ten or fifteen Japanese shares. Thus, if a Japanese share is worth $2.00, that will translate into $20 if the ADR represents ten shares.

If there are no ADRs issued for the stock the investor seeks to purchase, then the actual foreign securities will have to be acquired. The individual instructs his or her broker to purchase the foreign stock in the appropriate foreign market. As with any other security purchase, the shares or bonds are acquired through exchanges or over the counter from dealers who make a market in the security. The trading practices followed by foreign exchanges need not coincide with American practices. For example, after a stock is purchased, a settlement date is established at which time payment is due. This settlement date may not coincide with the American practice of payment due after five business days. However, such differences are more a matter of detail than substance and are diminishing with increased global investing. After the purchases are completed, the investor may choose to leave the securities registered with the broker or may take delivery.

The prices of a number of foreign stocks are given daily in the American financial press. For example, *The Wall Street Journal* gives prices for selected securities traded on several exchanges. Exhibit 26.2 reproduces a sample of the prices reported in *The Wall Street Journal*. As may be seen in the exhibit, the information is limited to prices—there is no reporting of volume of transactions, dividends, or P/E ratios. However, the number of foreign stock prices reported in the American press is small. If the investor seeks to track the prices of many foreign stocks, that will require access to a foreign publication such as the *Financial Times*, a British newspaper that is comparable to *The Wall Street Journal*.

Reporting of prices

In addition to stocks, Americans may also acquire bonds sold in foreign countries. There are basically three general types: (1) bonds issued by foreign firms; (2) bonds issued by foreign governments; and (3) bonds issued in foreign countries by American firms. Bonds issued by foreign firms and foreign governments are similar to American bonds. Foreign firms can default, but foreign governments have the power to tax and create money. Thus, bonds issued by foreign governments, like those issued by the U.S. federal government, have an element of safety that is not applicable to the debt of foreign firms. (Whether the funds received by the repayment of principal will buy anything in the United States when the funds are repatriated is a different issue and will be addressed later in this chapter.)

Foreign bonds

Bonds issued abroad by American firms are basically of two types, depending on the currency in which they are denominated. The American firm can sell bonds denominated in the local currency (e.g., British pounds or French francs), or the firm can sell abroad bonds denominated in American dollars called **Euro-bonds**. This term applies even though the bonds may be issued in, say, Asia instead of Europe. When a firm issues a Euro-bond, the American firm promises to make payments in dollars. In this case the American investor will not have to convert the payments from the local currency (e.g., British pounds) back into dollars. While there is an obvious convenience factor, the importance of the currency used to denominate the payments will be explained later in this chapter.

Bonds denominated in dollars

Exhibit 26.2
Selected Closing Prices
for Foreign Securities

FOREIGN MARKETS

Wednesday, March 5, 1986

LONDON (in pence)

	Close	Prev. Close
Allied Lyons	306	295
Babcock	189	183
Barclays Bk	497	499
B A T Indust	373	356
Bass Ltd	693	685
BOC Group	353	339
British GE	208	202
BTR PLC	448	433
Cable&Wi	678	665
Cadbury Sch	166	165
Charter Con	250	248
Coats Patons	254	150
Consol Gold	477	462
Dalgety	275	270
Distillers Co	633	628
Glaxo	993	978
Grand Metro	420	413
Guest Keen	337	331
HansonTrust	166	162
Johnson Mat	173	175
Legal Gen	782	772
Lonrho	249	251
Lucas Indust	635	626
MIM Hold	119	122
Nat'l WestBk	734	734
Nrthrn Food	290	286
Racal Elect	194	194
Redland	415	409
Reed Int'l	819	814
Rio Tinto	632	609
STC	118	120
Tate&Lyle	598	595
TaylrWoodrw	538	536
Thorn EMI	464	452
Trust House	163	162
T I Group	453	429
Ultramar	211	210
Utd Biscuit	232	224
Vickers	433	418

SWITZERLAND (in Swiss francs) Zurich

Brown Bov	1,710	1,695
Ciba-Geigy	3,950	3,875
Credit Suisse	3,750	3,700
Nestle	8,625	8,475
Sandoz	11,000	10,500
Sulzer	450	460
Swissair	1,975	1,950
Swiss Alum	735	735
Swiss Bancp	558	546
Union Bank	4,900	4,820

Basel

vHoffmn-LaR	12,775	12,525
Pirelli Intl	428	425

v-1/10 share.

South African Mines (in U.S. currency)

Bracken	2.25	2.25
Deelkraal	2.60	2.60
Doornfontein	12.00	12.00
DurbanDeep	9.25	9.25
East Rand	5.88	5.75
Elandsrand	7.63	7.38
Elsburg	2.60	2.60
Ergo	5.56	5.63
General Mng	c10.00	c10.00
Grootvlei	5.00	4.88
Harmony	13.50	13.50
Hartebeest	4.35	4.40
Johannesb C	c80.00	c79.00
Kinross	16.25	16.13
Leslie	2.10	2.00
Libanon	18.00	18.13
Loraine	5.15	5.20
Randfontein	9.35	9.40
Rustnbg Plat	11.00	11.00
Southvaal	42.00	42.25
Stilfontein	7.88	8.00
Unisel	7.75	7.88
West Areas	4.00	3.90
Winkelhaak	21.75	21.25

c-In British pounds.

MILAN (in Lire)

Buitoni	6,500	6,399
Ciga	12,390	12,545
Fiat	9,800	9,635
Generali	93,910	92,400
La Rinas	1,270	1,200
Mont Ed	3,770	3,560
Olivetti	12,600	11,800
Pirelli	4,590	4,550
Snia Visc	6,794	6,699

STOCKHOLM (in Swedish krona)

AGA	183	180
Alfa Laval b	260	265
Electrolux b	260	255
Svenska Cel b	188	189

PARIS (in French francs)

AirLiq	622	616
Aquitaine	217	221.50
BSNGrD	3,235	3,235
Club Med	466	462.50
Imetal	88	84.30
L'Oreal	3,035	3,017
Hachette	1,780	1,701
LafargeCoppee	980	940
Machines Bull	64	61
Michelin	2,210	2,185
MoetHen	2,005	1,947
PeugtCtn	895	865
Source Perrier	520	522
Total CFP	312	315

TOKYO (in yen)

	Close	Prev. Close
Ajinomoto	1,310	1,340
Asahi Chem	788	799
Bk of Tokyo	734	730
BridgestnTire	548	538
C. Itoh	441	448
Daiwa House	937	960
Daiwa Secur	947	956
Eisai	1,500	1,480
Fuji Bank	1,560	1,550
Fujitsu	999	985
Isuzu Mot Ltd	365	363
Kajima Corp	550	564
Kansai Elec	2,250	2,300
Komatsu Ltd	470	470
MaruiDeptStr	1,800	1,800
Marubeni	329	335
Mazda	373	376
MitsubishiEst	1,240	1,240
MitsubishiInd	380	387
Mitsui & Co	435	436
MitsuiRealE	1,110	1,110
Nikko Secur	755	750
NipponKogaku	1,060	1,030
NipponGakki	1,420	1,450
NipponSteel	164	167
NomuraSecur	1,270	1,260
Ricoh	938	922
Sekisui House	909	925
SumitomoBk	1,700	1,710
SumitomoCh	262	261
Taisei Const	361	364
Takeda Chem	1,150	1,130
Teijin	482	485
Tokyo Elec	3,100	3,160
Toshiba	360	358
YamaichiSec	749	750
Yasuda M&F	582	582

FRANKFURT (in marks)

AEG-Tele	325.70	318.50
Allianz Vers	2,240	2,235
BASF	315.50	317
Bayer AG	330	331.80
BMW	535	510
Cont'l Gummi	219.50	214.80
Commerzbnk	297	303
Daimler-Benz	1,268	1,242
Degussa	464.80	462
Deutsche Bk	807	799
Dresdner Bk	399	397.50
Hoechst AG	322.50	324
Lufthansa	288	275
RWE	234	237
Schering AG	543	529
Siemens	740	728
Thyssen-Hut	175	170.50
Veba	294	290.50
Volkswagen	553.50	529.50

AMSTERDAM (in guilders)

AKZO	162.40	159.60
Ahold	76.40	75.70
Algemene Bk	570	558
Amst-Rot Bk	104.80	101.30
Elsevier-NDU	174	162.50
Fokker	86.50	86
Heineken's	224.50	221
Holec	292	265
Hoogovens	87.40	85.20
Nation Neder	77.10	73.70
Nedlloyd	178.50	177.50
Robeco	86	85.30
Rolinco	73.40	72.40
Rorento	48.50	48.30
Wessanen	252	247.50

a-Ex-dividend.

HONG KONG (in Hong Kong dollars)

Bk of East Asia	19.80	20.10
Cheung Kong	19.40	19.80
Hang Seng Bk	44.50	45.25
Hong Kong El	8.55	8.65
Hong Kong Lnd	6.25	6.30
HongkongShBk	7.80	7.80
Hutchsn Whmp	26.20	26.60
Jardine Mathsn	12.40	12.50
SunHungKaiP	10.90	11.40
Swire Pacific	31.75	33
World Intl	2.35	2.40

z-Not quoted.

BRUSSELS (in Belgian francs)

ARBED	3,000	3,000
Gevaert	6,840	6,600
GB-Inno-Bm	6,300	6,270
GrpBrLambrt	3,000	3,020
Metal Hobokn	7,250	7,120
Petrofina	6,570	6,570
SocGenerale	2,515	2,560
Solvay	8,110	8,070

SYDNEY (in Australian dollars)

ANZ Bk Grp	5.36	5.26
Central Norse	7.40	7.30
Coles GJ	4.44	4.40
CRA	5.90	5.82
CSR	2.95	2.96
LeightonHld	0.70	0.65
Natl Aust Bk	5.46	5.30
News Corp	12.85	12.70
RensnGoldFlds	5.46	5.40
Repco	1.75	1.65
Santos	3.88	3.90
SouthrnPacPet	0.17	0.17
Westrn Mining	3.50	3.50
Westpac	5.46	5.36
Woodside Pete	1.02	1.05
Woolworth Ltd	3.65	3.65

Source: The Wall Street Journal, March 6, 1986. Reprinted by permission of *The Wall Street Journal*, © Dow Jones & Company, Inc., 1986. All Rights Reserved.

RETURNS ON FOREIGN INVESTMENTS

As with other investments, the American investor in foreign securities earns a return through the receipt of dividends or interest and price appreciation. These sources of return are complicated by the fact that the returns received in foreign funds must be converted back to dollars before the investor may use the funds in this country. Obviously the investor who receives dividends in British pounds can spend the funds in London.

If the investor receives dividends or interest, those payments may be subject to *Local taxation*
local taxation. Just as the U.S. government taxes dividend income, foreign governments may also tax dividend and interest payments. To facilitate the collection of the
funds, these taxes are usually withheld before the American investor receives the
money. For example, if the withholding rate is 15 percent and a British firm distributes a cash dividend of 100 pounds, then 15 pounds are withheld and 85 pounds
are remitted to the American holder, who must convert the pounds into dollars. If the
American investor owns ADRs instead of the actual British stock, the bank that is the
transfer agent receives the payment, converts the pounds into dollars, and remits
the funds to the holder of the ADR. As was previously explained, the bank collects a
fee for this service. However, since the bank exchanges large amounts of foreign currency, any fee charged will probably be less than the individual investor would have to
pay to have the pounds converted into dollars.

The dividends (and interest) received from this foreign investment are also sub- *U.S. tax credits*
ject to income taxation in the United States. If the investor in the previous illustration
is in the 28 percent federal income tax bracket, then 28 percent of the 100 pounds is
subject to tax. To facilitate the illustration, assume a pound is worth $2.50, so the
dividend is $250 ($2.50 × 100). The federal income tax would be $70 ($250 × 0.28).
This tax is in addition to the 15 pounds ($32.50) that the British government has
already withheld. The U.S. federal government permits the American investor to take
a foreign tax credit for the amount of the foreign tax. Thus, the net amount owed by
the American investor to the U.S. federal government is $38.50 ($70.00 − $32.50).

The second source of return is capital gains, which occur when the value of an
asset appreciates and it is sold for a profit. This appreciation may occur because the
value of the asset rises or because the value of the currency in which it is denominated
rises. Since capital appreciation is related not only to the price of the asset but also to
the value of the currency, it is possible for the price of the asset to rise but for this
price increase to be offset by a decline in the value of the currency. It is also possible
for the price of the asset to decline but for the price decline to be offset by an increase
in the value of the currency.

These possibilities are illustrated in Figures 26.1, 26.2, and 26.3. In each case the *Impact of changes in*
investor buys British stock, so its price is quoted in pounds. This price, which is given *currency values*
in the first row of figures, rises from £20 to £30 in Figure 26.1, falls from £20 to £10
in Figure 26.2, and remains stable at £20 in Figure 26.3. The value of the stock to an
American depends on both the value of the shares in pounds and the value of the
pound in dollars. The second row of graphs shows the value of the pound in terms of
dollars. To illustrate the potential for loss, the dollar price of the pound declines from
$2.00 to $1.00 in the left-hand panels. To illustrate the potential for gain, the dollar
price of the pound rises from $2.00 to $3.00 in right-hand panels. The important set
of figures for the American investor is, of course, the value of the stock in dollars. This
"bottom line" is the third row of graphs in each figure.

In Figure 26.1, in which the price of the stock rises, the value of the shares in
dollars rises dramatically when the price of the pound also rises. On the right-hand
side of the figure, the stock rises from £20 to £30 while the pound rises from $2 to $3.
Thus, the value of the stock rises from $40 to $90. If both the value of the stock and
the pound decline, as in the left-hand side of Figure 26.2, the value of the shares in
terms of dollars falls dramatically. In this illustration the price of the stock declines
from £20 to £10 and the pound declines from $2 to $1. Thus, the dollar value of the

Figure 26.1
**Value of British Stock in
Terms of Dollars—Stock
Price Appreciating**

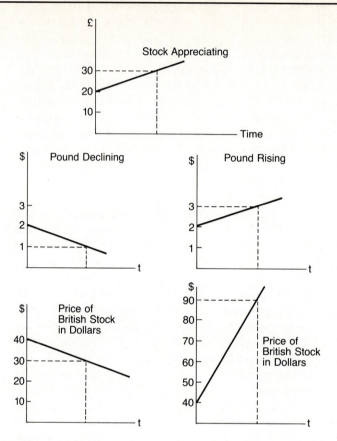

stock falls from $40 to $10. These two cases illustrate that when the value of the pound and the price of the stock move in the same direction, the fluctuation in the stock's value in terms of dollars is magnified.

If the price of the pound moves against the price of the stock, the two price fluctuations tend to offset each other. This is illustrated in the left-hand side of Figure 26.1, in which the value of the stock rises from £20 to £30 but the value of the pound in terms of dollars falls from $2 to $1. While the value of the stock was initially $40, it is now worth only $30. This case shows that correct security selection (i.e., choosing a stock whose price rises) can be negated by the decline in the value of the currency.

In the right-hand side of Figure 26.2, the price of the stock falls from £20 to £10 while the dollar value of the pound rises from $2 to $3. Thus, the dollar value of the stock, which initially cost $40, is now $30. This case illustrates that an investment mistake (i.e., choosing a stock whose price declines) is offset (at least partially) by the increase in the value of the currency.

The last examples in Figure 26.3 illustrate what happens when the price of the stock is stable. Under those circumstances the bottom line depends only on what hap-

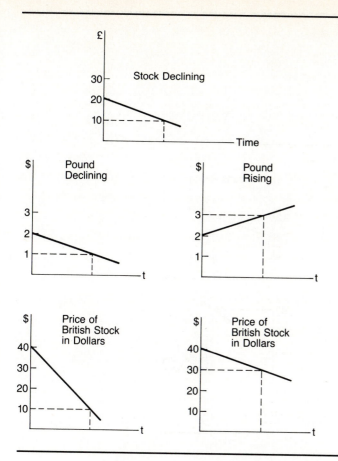

Figure 26.2
**Value of British Stock in
Terms of Dollars—Stock
Price Declining**

pens to the value of the currency. If the currency rises from $2 to $3 (as shown on the right-hand side), the value of the shares in terms of dollars also increases (from $40 to $60). If the price of the currency declines from $2 to $1, the value of the shares in terms of dollars also falls (from $40 to $20). Of course, of all three of these illustrations, case 3 is the least likely to occur because the value of the stock is assumed to be stable. This is highly unlikely, since the prices of both stocks and currencies literally vary each day.

As these illustrations indicate, the value of foreign currencies becomes crucial to investing in foreign assets. Fluctuations in the value of currencies can enhance or reduce the return earned on such investments, thus affecting the risk associated with investing in foreign assets. This risk is in addition to the usual risks the investor must bear: the unsystematic risk associated with the particular asset and the systematic risk associated with fluctuations in market prices, fluctuations in interest rates, and loss of purchasing power through inflation. Foreign investments thus require that the investor bear an additional source of nondiversifiable (systematic) risk—fluctuations in currency values.

Figure 26.3
**Value of British Stock in
Terms of Dollars—Stock
Price Stable**

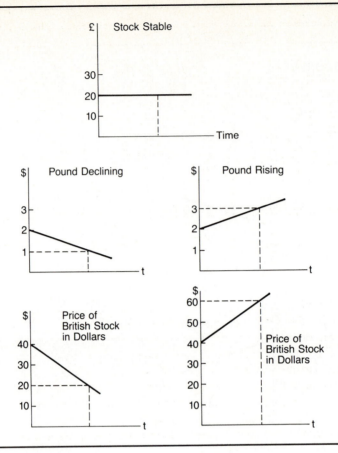

FLUCTUATIONS IN EXCHANGE RATES

Demand for currencies

The demand for foreign investments (as well as foreign goods and services) is also a demand for foreign money. To acquire these funds, buyers must exchange their currency for the foreign currency. For example, if Americans want to purchase stocks and bonds denominated in British pounds, they must exchange dollars for pounds. The opposite is true when British citizens seek to purchase securities denominated in American dollars. These investors must exchange pounds for dollars.

The market for foreign currencies is called the **foreign exchange market.** The price of one currency in terms of another is referred to as the **exchange rate.** Currencies are traded daily, and the prices of major currencies are reported in the financial press. While these prices change daily, such reporting gives the investor a close indication of the currencies' current prices.

Exhibit 26.3, a clipping from *The Wall Street Journal,* gives the exchange rates for selected currencies as of March 5, 1986. At that time the price of a British pound was $1.447 and the French franc was $0.1432. This exhibit also expresses the value of each currency in terms of a dollar. Thus, $1.00 purchased 0.6911 pounds or 6.9855

FOREIGN EXCHANGE

Wednesday, March 5, 1986

The New York foreign exchange selling rates below apply to trading among banks in amounts of $1 million and more, as quoted at 3 p.m. Eastern time by Bankers Trust Co. Retail transactions provide fewer units of foreign currency per dollar.

Country	U.S. $ equiv. Wed.	Tues.	Currency per U.S. $ Wed.	Tues.
Argentina (Austral) ...	1.2484	1.2484	.801	.801
Australia (Dollar) ...	.7015	.6950	1.4255	1.4388
Austria (Schilling) ...	.0633	.06460	15.79	15.48
Belgium (Franc)				
Commercial rate ...	.02182	.02212	45.84	45.21
Financial rate ...	.02168	.02200	46.13	45.47
Brazil (Cruzeiro) ...	.00007262	.00007262	13770.00	13770.00
Britain (Pound) ...	1.4470	1.4620	.6911	.6840
30-Day Forward ...	1.4410	1.4506	.6940	.6894
90-Day Forward ...	1.4306	1.4457	.6990	.6917
180-Day Forward ...	1.4180	1.4325	.7052	.6981
Canada (Dollar) ...	.7092	.7037	1.4100	1.4210
30-Day Forward ...	.7060	.7004	1.4164	1.4277
90-Day Forward ...	.7021	.6964	1.4243	1.4360
180-Day Forward ...	.6981	.6921	1.4325	1.4448
Chile (Official rate) ...	.005426	.005426	184.29	184.29
China (Yuan) ...	.3125	.3125	3.1999	3.1999
Colombia (Peso) ...	.005634	.005634	177.48	177.48
Denmark (Krone) ...	.1200	.1229	8.3300	8.1400
Ecuador (Sucre)				
Official rate ...	.01504	.01504	66.48	66.48
Floating rate ...	.00613	.00613	163.00	163.00
Finland (Markka) ...	.1953	.1980	5.1200	5.0500
France (Franc) ...	.1432	.1480	6.9855	6.7575
30-Day Forward ...	.1422	.1470	7.0305	6.8050
90-Day Forward ...	.1408	.1454	7.1005	6.8775
180-Day Forward ...	.1398	.1443	7.1530	6.9275
Greece (Drachma) ...	.007220	.007299	138.50	137.00
Hong Kong (Dollar) ...	.1281	.1281	7.8060	7.8070
India (Rupee) ...	.08170	.08218	12.24	12.17
Indonesia (Rupiah) ...	.0008857	.0008857	1129.00	1129.00
Ireland (Punt) ...	1.3600	1.3690	.7353	.7305
Israel (Shekel) ...	.6725	.6725	1.487	1.487
Italy (Lira) ...	.0006545	.0006667	1528.00	1500.00
Japan (Yen) ...	.005517	.005590	181.25	178.90
30-Day Forward ...	.005525	.005599	181.00	178.63
90-Day Forward ...	.005544	.005619	180.36	177.98
180-Day Forward ...	.005577	.005652	179.31	176.94
Jordan (Dinar) ...	2.9481	2.9481	.3392	.3392
Kuwait (Dinar) ...	3.5224	3.5224	.2839	.2839
Lebanon (Pound) ...	.05102	.05102	19.60	19.60
Malaysia (Ringgit) ...	.3979	.4002	2.5135	2.4990
Malta (Lira) ...	2.5221	2.5221	.3965	.3965
Netherland (Guilder) ...	.3948	.4017	2.5330	2.4895
New Zealand (Dollar) ...	.5170	.5200	1.9342	1.9231
Norway (Krone) ...	.1410	.1433	7.0900	6.9775
Pakistan (Rupee) ...	.06258	.06310	15.98	15.85
Peru (Inti) ...	.07171	.07171	13.945	13.945
Philippines (Peso) ...	.04535	.04535	22.05	22.05
Portugal (Escudo) ...	.006780	.006682	147.50	146.50
Saudi Arabia (Riyal) ...	.2739	.2740	3.6515	3.6505
Singapore (Dollar) ...	.4622	.4643	2.1635	2.1540
South Africa (Rand)				
Commercial rate ...	.5040	.6392	1.9841	1.5646
Financial rate ...	.3750	.3715	2.6666	2.6917
South Korea (Won) ...	.001131	.001131	884.50	884.50
Spain (Peseta) ...	.007092	.007192	141.00	139.05
Sweden (Krona) ...	.1381	.1406	7.2400	7.1400
Switzerland (Franc) ...	.5214	.5348	1.9180	1.8700
30-Day Forward ...	.5232	.5367	1.9112	1.8632
90-Day Forward ...	.5268	.5402	1.8984	1.8512
180-Day Forward ...	.5318	.5456	1.8805	1.8330
Taiwan (Dollar) ...	.02563	.02563	39.01	39.01
Thailand (Baht) ...	.03788	.03788	26.40	26.40
United Arab (Dirham) ...	.2723	.2723	3.673	3.673
Uruguay (New Peso)				
Financial ...	.007526	.007526	132.87	132.87
Venezuela (Bolivar)				
Official rate ...	.13333	.13333	7.50	7.50
Floating rate ...	.05450	.05450	18.35	18.35
W. Germany (Mark) ...	.4396	.4545	2.2740	2.2000
30-Day Forward ...	.4527	.4559	2.2090	2.1935
90-Day Forward ...	.4434	.4584	2.2551	2.1815
180-Day Forward ...	.4471	.4623	2.2367	2.1631
SDR	1.15583	1.15708	0.865180	0.864246
ECU	0.968041	0.974486		

Special Drawing Rights are based on exchange rates for the U.S., West German, British, French and Japanese currencies. Source: International Monetary Fund.
ECU is based on a basket of community currencies.
Source: European Community Commission.
z-Not quoted.

Exhibit 26.3
Selected Foreign
Exchange Rates

francs. (These amounts may be derived by dividing $1 by the dollar price of the foreign currency. For example, $1/1.447 = 0.6911 units of the British pound.)

An imbalance in the demand for or supply of a currency causes its price to change. Excess demand generates a higher price while excess supply depresses the price. Such price changes are often referred to as devaluations and revaluations. With a **devaluation**, the price of one currency declines relative to all other currencies. A **revaluation** is an increase in the price of one nation's currency relative to all other currencies.

Daily fluctuations

Under the current international monetary system such devaluations and revaluations occur daily, for the prices of currencies are permitted to fluctuate. If the demand for a particular currency rises so that the demand exceeds the supply, the price of that currency rises relative to other currencies. If the supply of the currency exceeds the demand, the price falls. There are continual devaluations of some currencies and revaluations of others as their prices vary daily in accordance with supply and demand.

Trends in currency values

While day-to-day fluctuations in currency values may not be important, longer term trends are. Currency values can rise or fall over an extended period of time. Such trends are illustrated in Figure 26.4, which plots the price of the British pound in terms of American dollars from 1975 through 1985. As may be seen in this graph, the pound's price fluctuated considerably during the time period, from a high of more than $2.40 in 1975 to below $1.10 in 1985. This fluctuation in the dollar value of the British pound (or any currency) is, of course, a major source of risk from investing in securities not denominated in the currency of the investor's country.

RISK REDUCTION THROUGH HEDGING

Fluctuations in exchange rates—an additional source of risk

The American investor who acquires foreign stocks and bonds has to bear a special risk that is unique to foreign securities—the risk associated with fluctuations in exchange rates. If the dollar declines relative to other currencies, those currencies can buy more dollars. As was explained previously, the American investor can earn a

Figure 26.4
Dollar Value of the British Pound, 1975–1985

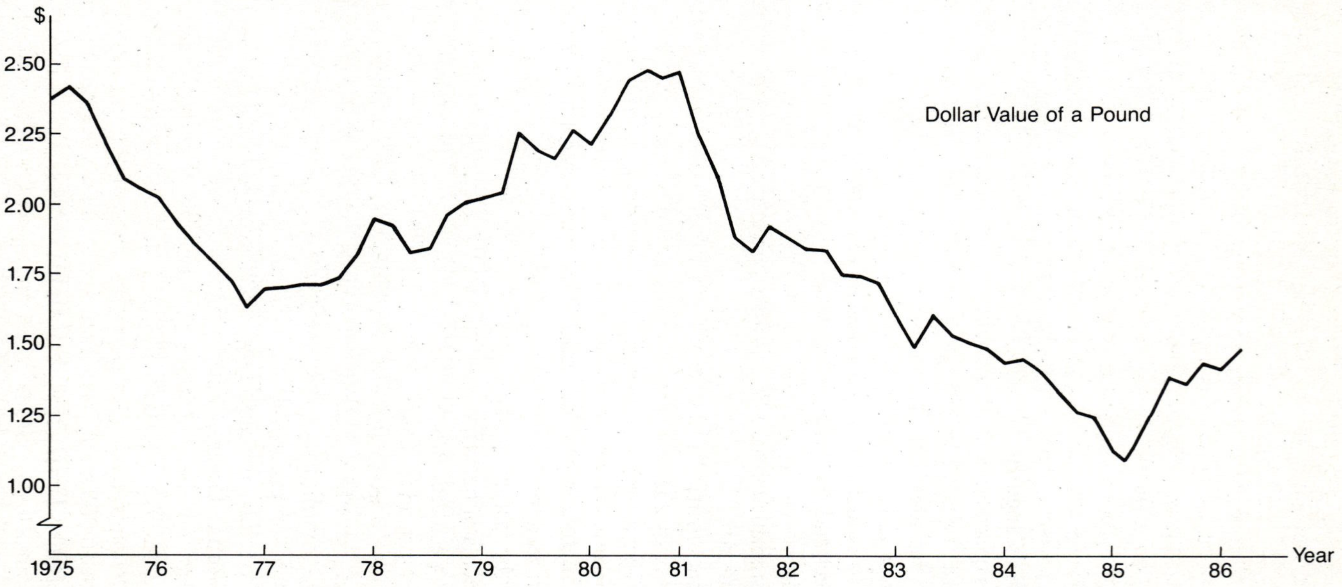

Dollar Value of a Pound

$
2.50
2.25
2.00
1.75
1.50
1.25
1.00

1975   76   77   78   79   80   81   82   83   84   85   86   Year

profit on a foreign investment even if its price declines as long as the decline in the dollar's value more than offsets the decline in the value of the particular asset. The converse is also possible. The value of the particular asset can appreciate, but if the value of the currency falls, the American investor can still sustain a loss. And if the value of the dollar rises sufficiently, it can more than offset the gain in the value of the foreign security.

If the prices of currencies were stable, there would be little risk associated with currency price fluctuations. However, this is not the case, as was illustrated in Figure 26.4. There we see that the price of the pound ranged from over $2.40 in 1975 to below $1.10 in 1985, for a fluctuation in excess of 50 percent. The question then arises: Can the investor reduce the risk associated with the variability in the price of foreign exchange? The answer is "Yes," as the investor may reduce the risk of loss by hedging with futures contracts. Of course, for such risk reduction to occur there must be speculators who are willing to accept that risk.

Risk reduction with currency futures

As with all futures contracts, speculators buy and sell foreign exchange futures in order to take advantage of changes in exchange rates. If a speculator anticipates that the value of the British pound will rise relative to the American dollar, he or she enters into a contract to buy pounds (i.e., supply dollars) in the future. The investor has a long position in pounds (which may also be viewed as a short position in dollars). If the speculator is correct and the price of the pound rises, the value of the contract rises, and the speculator earns a profit. As with other futures trading, the margin requirement is so modest relative to the value of the contract that the percentage earned on the margin is substantial.

Speculators anticipate price changes

If the speculator anticipates that the value of the British pound will fall relative to the American dollar, he or she enters into a contract to deliver pounds (i.e., buy dollars) in the future. The investor has a short position in pounds (which may also be viewed as a long position in dollars). If the speculator is correct and the price of the pound falls, the value of the contract declines and the speculator earns a profit. Once again, since the margin requirement is modest relative to the value of the contract, the percentage earned on the margin can be substantial.

Of course, the speculator bears the risk that the currency's value may move in the wrong direction. To a speculator who has a long position in the British pound, a decline in the value of the pound inflicts a substantial loss. (Of course, speculators with short positions profit.) If the speculator has a short position in the British pound and the value of the pound rises, then this individual sustains a loss. (Conversely, speculators with long positions profit.) The willingness of speculators to accept the risk associated with fluctuations in exchange rates means that other investors are able to hedge their positions to reduce the risk of loss from exchange rate fluctuations.

Speculators bear risk

Individuals who acquire foreign securities purchase them for the returns offered by the investments, not for the potential return offered by correctly anticipating changes in exchange rates. For example, an American purchases $16,000 worth of stocks and/or bonds denominated in German marks. If the value of the mark is $0.40, the securities are worth 40,000 marks. Should the value of the mark rise, this investor could experience a profit on the price increase. If the value of the mark were to fall, the investor could sustain a loss on the decline in the mark's value. To reduce this risk, the American investor constructs a hedge position. Since the investor has a long position in the German securities, he or she establishes a short position in marks by entering into a contract for the delivery of marks in the future. If the value of the mark does

Hedge positions are simultaneous long and short positions

POINTS OF INTEREST
Forward Contracts and Futures Contracts

Hedging may be achieved through the use of "futures" contracts or "forward" contracts. Conceptually these two types of contracts are the same, but their features differ. A futures contract is a standardized contract that specifies the amount of the currency and the delivery date. Since it is standardized, it may be bought and sold. A for-

ward contract is tailor-made for each transaction, which makes it adaptable to the specific needs of the respective parties. While a forward contract specifies the amount and delivery date, the uniqueness of its features means that the contract is not negotiable (i.e., there is no secondary market in forward contracts).

decline, the resulting loss on the investment in German securities is offset by the profit on the futures contract.

To see how this works, continue the example started above. Assume that the current price (i.e., the spot price) of the mark is $0.40 ($1.00 = 2.5 marks) and that the futures price of the mark is $0.405. (In this example the futures price of the mark exceeds the spot price. The converse, in which the spot price exceeds the futures price, is also possible.) The investor enters into a contract for the future sale of marks—for example, the delivery of 40,000 marks at $0.405 per mark. The value of this contract is almost the same as the value of the German securities acquired by the investor ($16,200 versus $16,000). Suppose the value of the mark then declines to $0.38. The securities are now worth $15,200 (40,000 marks × $0.38), and the investor has sustained a loss of $800 ($16,000 − 15,200). However, this investor can buy marks at $0.38 and deliver them at the $0.405 specified in the futures contract. The investor thus makes $0.025 per mark on the short position in the currency futures. The total profit is $1,000 (40,000 marks × $0.025), which more than offsets the loss from the decline in the value of the security denominated in marks.

A German investor who acquires American securities would follow an opposite strategy. That individual has a long position in American securities and thus would take a long position in German marks (i.e., a short position in dollars). If this individual acquires $16,000 worth of American stocks for 40,000 marks, he or she would sustain a loss if the value of the mark rises. For example, if the mark's value were to rise to $0.42 (i.e., $1.00 = 2.39 marks), the value of this investment would be $38,240 (16,000 × $2.39) in terms of marks. The investor would thus sustain a loss of $1,780 ($40,000 − $38,200). To protect against this loss, the investor enters into a futures contract for the purchase of marks. Such a contract would rise in value if the value of the dollar were to decline. If the investor acquired a futures contract for the delivery of 40,000 marks at $0.0405 a mark, that investor would gain $0.015 per mark when the price of the mark rose from $0.405 to $0.42. This price increase would generate a profit of $600 (0.015 × 40,000), which would partially offset the loss resulting from the decrease in the value of the dollar relative to the mark.

Positions may not be completely hedged   It should be noted that in both of these examples, the investors did not completely hedge their positions. In the first example the investor profited by the change

in the value of the currency, while in the second case there was a net loss. This inability to hedge completely results from (1) differences between futures prices and spot prices and (2) differences between the size of contracts and the amounts invested in the foreign securities. However, the inability to hedge completely and to exactly offset the potential loss does not mean that a substantial amount of the risk associated with exchange rate fluctuations cannot be eliminated through the use of futures contracts in hedge positions.

THE POLITICAL CLIMATE

The political climate of the foreign nation may also create risks for investors. The fact *Changes in* that governments and political systems do change is a major concern of American *political systems* businesses seeking to expand their markets through foreign operations. Many firms with foreign investments have experienced their nationalization and expropriation. These firms may or may not be compensated for the seized assets. For example, Cuba did not offer compensation when Fidel Castro came to power and nationalized the facilities of American firms.[2] However, when Venezuela nationalized Exxon's oil investments in that country, it did agree to compensate Exxon for the seized assets.

Individuals seeking to invest funds in foreign countries can significantly reduce the risk associated with the political climate by limiting purchases to assets in countries with stable political climates. For example, even when the Labour Party is in power, Great Britain is still politically very stable when compared with other countries. Because of political unrest in South Africa or in regions such as the Middle East or parts of Asia, the investor bears more risk when buying the stocks of foreign companies headquartered in these countries or the securities of these foreign governments. Of course, such political risks are avoided when the investor does not purchase securities of firms located in politically unstable countries.

ADVANTAGES OFFERED BY FOREIGN SECURITIES

Investing in foreign securities offers three major advantages. The first is the obvious *Potential growth* advantage associated with investing in economies and firms experiencing rapid economic growth. The other two advantages, however, may be even more important for an individual's portfolio, since economic growth is not unique to foreign firms and economies. Many American firms (e.g., IBM) have exhibited superior earnings and dividend growth for many years.

The other advantages of foreign investment are diversification and possible excess returns. As was explained in Chapter 8 on risk analysis, constructing a diversified portfolio reduces unsystematic risk (i.e., the risk associated with the specific asset). However, combining the shares of two telephone utilities does not achieve significant diversification, since the returns on the two assets will be similar. Diversification re-

---

[2] Besides nationalizing assets held by American firms, Cuba also repudiated debts it owed. To this day, Cuban bonds (and bonds of other communist countries such as Czechoslovakia) are still outstanding. Perhaps even more surprising is that some of these bonds are still traded. For example, an issue of Cuban bonds that was due in 1977 traded in 1985 from as high as 17⅜ to as low as 10 for $100 face amount of the debt. Even though the bond is past maturity and has not paid interest for years, there is still a market for it. Presumably, investors who purchase this bond are speculating on an improvement in political relations between the United States and Cuba that might result in repayment of some of the debt.

Figure 26.5
Relative Performance of
International Stock
Markets

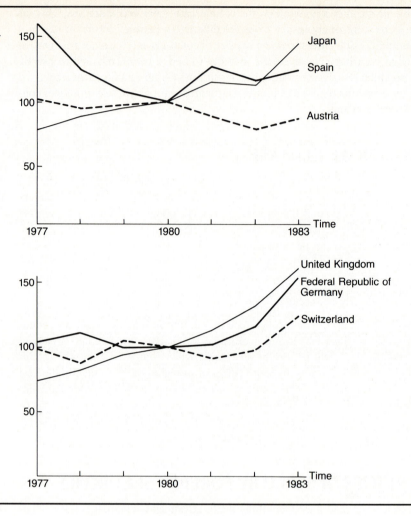

quires that the returns from the two assets not have high positive correlation, and negative correlation is desirable. The more negatively correlated the returns from the two assets, the greater the reduction in risk that is achieved by combining the securities in a portfolio.

Diversification   Foreign investments may help achieve diversification because the returns earned on foreign securities need not be positively correlated with those earned on domestic securities. While global economies are interrelated and security prices on various international stock markets may move together, there can be considerable variation in these movements. This may be seen in Figure 26.5, which presents the relative performance of several foreign stock markets. To facilitate comparisons, the International Monetary Fund data expresses all the stock markets in terms of a base year (i.e., 1980 = 100). As is evident from the figure, some of the stock prices have moved together (e.g., British and West German security prices during 1982 to 1983). However, some stock prices moved in opposite directions (e.g., Austrian and Spanish stocks during 1978 to 1982). Since foreign security prices are not perfectly correlated, combining

securities from various countries should tend to reduce the individual investor's risk exposure from fluctuating security prices in a particular market.[3]

In addition, global investing may offer the possibility of higher returns. As was also explained in Chapter 8, the rapid dissemination of new information and the intense competition among investors produces efficient American financial markets. If new information becomes available that implies a security is undervalued (or overvalued), its price changes rapidly. The opportunity to profit from such misvaluation disappears before most investors learn the new information. Unless the investor is able to anticipate new information and to adjust his or her positions before it becomes generally available, the individual cannot expect to outperform the market consistently. Thus, according to the efficient market hypothesis, higher returns can then be achieved only by bearing more risk (i.e., by purchasing assets whose returns tend to be more volatile than the market as a whole).

Efficient markets

Foreign financial markets need not be so efficient. Less analysis is applied to foreign securities, and the results of the analysis are not widely disseminated. This suggests that the astute investor may be able to isolate securities that are under- or overvalued. If this is true, the opportunity for an excess return would exist. Foreign investments thus may offer individuals a means to increase the return on their portfolios that is generally not available with domestic investments.

Foreign markets may be less efficient than American markets

Of course, obtaining information on which to base foreign investment decisions may be difficult. While foreign firms with securities traded on American exchanges must meet SEC disclosure requirements, this reporting does not apply to non-listed securities. In general, foreign firms do not publish as much information as American firms. For example, some firms do not publish quarterly operating results. Even obtaining an annual report may be difficult.

Problem of obtaining information

For this reason many investors prefer to acquire the shares of mutual funds that specialize in foreign stocks and bonds. If foreign financial markets are inefficient, the successful managers of these funds should be able to take advantage of these inefficiencies. Thus, the individual investor is relieved of the actual security selection but must instead select the mutual fund whose management is best able to exploit any market inefficiencies.

MUTUAL FUNDS WITH FOREIGN INVESTMENTS

From an American perspective, there are basically three types of mutual funds with international investments. **Global funds** invest in foreign and American securities. Many American mutual funds are global, as they maintain some part of their portfolios in foreign investments. While these funds do not specialize in foreign securities, they do offer the individual investor the advantages associated with foreign investments: returns through global economic growth, diversification from assets whose returns are not positively correlated, and possible excess returns from inefficient foreign financial markets.

Mutual funds with foreign investments

In addition to global funds, there are **international funds**, which invest solely in foreign securities and hold no American securities, and **regional funds**, which spe-

---

[3] The investor still has the risk associated with fluctuating exchange rates and political instability, but the former may be reduced through hedging and the latter avoided by not purchasing securities issued in politically unstable countries.

POINTS OF INTEREST
European Options

Put and call options are not unique to American financial markets but are also available in some foreign security markets. However, these put and call options can differ significantly from American options. Specific differences vary from country to country but revolve around the duration of the option and the existence of secondary markets. For example, the duration of the traditional British option is three months. Six-month and nine-month options are not available.

Some secondary markets do exist, but not for all foreign puts and calls. For example, there is no secondary market for the traditional three-month British option. Once purchased, the option cannot be sold. The investor must either exercise the option at a specified time or let it expire. Thus the most important difference between an American option and a so-called European option is the requirement that the investor must exercise the European option to realize any gain achieved through appreciation in the option's value.

Exhibit 26.4
Types of Funds

Global Funds
  Dean Witter World Wide
  Paine Webber Atlas
  Templeton World
  United International Growth

International Funds
  Fidelity Overseas
  International Fund
  Kemper International
  Transatlantic Fund

Regional Funds (International)
  First Australia Prime
  France Fund
  Japan Fund
  Merrill Lynch Pacific Fund
  Scandinavia Fund

Regional Funds (Domestic)
  North Star Fund (seven upper midwest states)
  Sunbelt Growth Fund
  Washington Area Growth Fund

---

cialize in a particular geographic area, such as Asia. (There are also mutual funds that specialize in a particular geographic area within the United States.) While the regional funds obviously specialize, the international funds may also specialize during particular time periods. For example, in 1985 the FT International Fund had over a quarter of its portfolio invested in Japanese stocks. A selected list of investment companies

that represent global, international, and regional funds is given in Exhibit 26.4. (The objectives and types of more than 900 funds may be obtained from *Barron's/Lipper Gauge,* published quarterly.)

American investors may also acquire shares in foreign investment companies, *Foreign mutual funds* such as the British mutual funds called "unit trusts." Thus, if an American investor cannot find an acceptable domestic fund, the search may be extended to a foreign fund. However, since these securities are not registered with the SEC, some foreign funds will not sell shares directly to Americans, as these funds believe such sales are illegal. In other cases purchases may be made for a fee through foreign banks with branches in the U.S. However, the individual should probably ask himself or herself if the potential return is worth the additional expense required to acquire the shares.

SUMMARY

Americans are beginning to take a global view of investing and to acquire stocks and bonds issued in foreign countries. These include the securities of foreign firms, foreign governments, and American firms that have issued securities abroad. These assets may be bought and sold through American brokers in much the same way investors acquire domestic securities. American depository receipts (ADRs) representing the foreign securities have been created to facilitate trading in foreign stocks and bonds. These ADRs are denominated in dollars, their prices are quoted in dollars, and their units of trading are consistent with the units of trading used in the U.S.

Foreign investments involve several sources of risk in addition to the usual sources of unsystematic and systematic risk. Investors in foreign securities must bear the risk associated with unstable political climates and fluctuations in exchange rates. The values of foreign currencies (i.e., foreign exchange) fluctuate daily with the demand for and supply of each currency. When foreign securities are sold and converted back into American dollars, the value of the dollars may have risen or declined, depending on what has happened in the foreign exchange markets.

The investor may reduce the risk of loss from fluctuations in exchange rates by constructing a hedge position using currency futures. For example, if the individual acquires a long position in foreign securities, he or she can hedge against loss by selling contracts for the future delivery of the currency. The investor thus has a long position in the securities and a short position in the currency, which reduces the risk resulting from fluctuations in the dollar value of the foreign currency.

Foreign investments offer the individual several advantages. Since the returns on foreign securities are not perfectly correlated with returns on domestic securities, such investments are a means to diversify the individual's portfolio. In addition, foreign security markets may not be as efficient as American security markets. Such inefficiencies suggest that foreign investments may offer astute investors an opportunity to increase the return earned on their portfolios.

Obtaining information on foreign securities may be difficult. Thus American investors may prefer to acquire shares in mutual funds that make foreign investments. Many American funds maintain a portion of their assets in foreign securities. Other mutual funds invest exclusively abroad while others specialize in particular countries or geographic regions. Such investment companies relieve the investor of having to

select individual foreign securities but still offer the advantages of global diversification and possible increased returns through investments in less efficient markets.

Terms to Remember

American Depository Receipts (ADRs)	Revaluation
Euro-bonds	Global funds
Foreign exchange market	International funds
Exchange rate	Regional funds
Devaluation	

Questions

1. If IBM were to issue a bond in Europe due in 1999, how might that bond differ from one issued in the United States?

2. What is foreign exchange and the foreign exchange market? What causes the prices of currencies to fluctuate?

3. What are the sources of risk associated with foreign investments? What can the individual investor do to manage those risks?

4. Would an American investor who owned foreign securities prefer a devaluation or revaluation of the American dollar?

5. Why do Americans purchase ADRs in preference to the actual securities? How do ADRs come into existence?

6. If a British investor who purchased French securities anticipates that the value of the franc may fall but does not wish to sell the securities, what should this investor do?

7. Why may the addition of foreign securities to an American's portfolio reduce this individual's risk exposure?

8. Why may investing in mutual funds with foreign investments be preferable to purchasing foreign stocks?

Problems

1. What is the cost of $1.00 in each of the following currencies?
   - pound—$1.75
   - franc—0.24
   - mark—0.46
   - yen—0.01

2. If you purchase 100,000 lira for $5,000, what is the price of a lira?

3. You purchase 100 ADRs of British Oil for $12 per ADR. What is the value of the shares in dollars given the following information?

Time	Price of the Stock in Pounds	Dollar Price of the Pound
1/1/x0	£ 6.00	$2.00
4/1/x0	7.80	2.10
7/1/x0	9.30	1.85
10/1/x0	10.20	1.70
1/1/x1	14.00	1.65

Compare the returns earned by an American and by a British investor.

4. You anticipate buying a German car in six months for $30,000. Currently the spot price of the mark is $0.50 and the six-month futures price is $0.505. You anticipate that the value of the dollar relative to the mark will decline. What course of action should you take and how much will it cost you (excluding brokerage commissions)?

5. A portfolio manager owns a bond worth £2,000,000 that will mature in one year. The pound is currently worth $1.45, while the one-year futures price is $1.40. If the value of the pound were to fall, the portfolio manager would sustain a loss. If the value of the pound were to rise, the portfolio manager would experience a profit.

    a. What is the expected payment based on the current exchange rate?

    b. What is the expected payment based on the futures exchange rate?

    c. If, after a year, the pound is worth $1.33, what is the loss from the decline in the value of the pound?

    d. If, after a year, the pound is worth $1.62, what is the gain from the increase in the value of the pound?

    e. To avoid the potential loss in part c., the portfolio manager hedges by selling futures contracts for the delivery of pounds at $1.40. What is the cost of the protection from a decline in the value of the pound?

    f. If, after hedging, the price of the pound falls to $1.33, what is the maximum amount the portfolio manager can lose? Why is this answer different from the answer to part c. above?

    g. If, after hedging, the price of the pound rises to $1.62, what is the maximum amount the portfolio manager can gain? Why is this answer different from the answer to part d. above?

Suggested Readings

For a general text on international financial management, see:

Shapiro, Alan C. *Multinational Financial Management,* 2d ed. Boston: Allyn and Bacon, 1986.

Descriptions of the major foreign financial markets are given in:

Warfield, Gerald. *How to Buy Foreign Stocks and Bonds.* New York: Harper & Row, 1985.

The impact of international diversification is discussed in:

Solnik, Bruno H. "Why Not Diversify Internationally Rather Than Domestically?" *Financial Analysts Journal,* (July–August 1974): 48–54.

Obtaining information on international firms can be exceedingly difficult. However, a data base is being developed by the Center for International Financial Analysis and Research, Inc. When the data base is completed, it will have financial statements and stock price data on over 3,000 non-American firms. For further information, write the center at Princeton Professional Park, 601 Ewing Street, Princeton, NJ 08542.

A SHORT CASE STUDY FOR CHAPTERS 22–26
Collectibles Are Not Commodities

Paul Sifford is a bachelor who has accumulated a substantial sum, primarily through periodic investments in savings accounts at a commercial bank ($80,000), shares in a mutual fund ($95,000), and a pension plan ($68,000). Sifford has also been a life-long philatelist. Ever since receiving a stamp album for his twelfth birthday, he has been fascinated with collecting stamps. As a child Sifford collected any and all stamps, but for the last 20 years he has devoted his efforts to the stamps of Great Britain and her colonies. Sifford has now obtained a reputation for expertise in this area and has accumulated a sufficiently large collection to have received recognition from a regional stamp organization.

The value of Sifford's stamp collection is unknown, and it has never been insured. Sifford believes that over the years he has spent at least $25,000 on the collection. Unfortunately the exact cost of many of the items is lost in time, as Sifford did not keep records of his early purchases made during the late 1950s and early 1960s. Some of these acquisitions have proven to be among the most valuable stamps in the collection.

Sifford has become increasingly concerned with the performance and quality of his financial assets. He realizes the funds in the savings account are insured by the FDIC, but the shares in the mutual fund are not insured. In addition, the fund has not performed well during the preceding year, as it rose less than the Dow Jones industrial average. Except for his pension (which he cannot withdraw until retirement), he believes the portfolio needs changing. Sifford knows very little about stocks and bonds and tends to distrust things he cannot touch. He recently read an advertisement that suggested commodities offered large potential returns. Sifford thought he could buy commodities like silver and hold them for subsequent sale in much the way he has acquired and held the stamps. He has also thought about a purchase of real estate, especially lots slightly out of town. Sifford believes that such property would have to appreciate in value as the town expands.

To finance these purchases, Sifford expects to sell his shares in the mutual fund or some of his stamp collection. Sifford's brother David (who is an accountant) was distressed when he learned of Paul's ideas. David suggested that they have lunch with his stockbroker, Jerry Walmsley. At that time Walmsley could explain some of the features, risks, and potential return associated with Paul's proposed portfolio changes. Paul agreed to the lunch, which David arranged for the next week. David also privately suggested to Walmsley that he should at a minimum discuss the following:

1. The differences between collecting and investing in stamps and investing in commodities.

2. The risks and liabilities associated with owning the lots.

3. The tax implications (if any) of redeeming the mutual fund shares, closing the bank account, or selling the stamps.

4. The need to insure the stamp collection.

5. Any need to diversify the mutual fund holdings.

6. Alternatives to the savings account with the bank.

If you were Walmsley, how would you respond to each of these considerations? What course(s) of action would you recommend?

VII Portfolio Construction

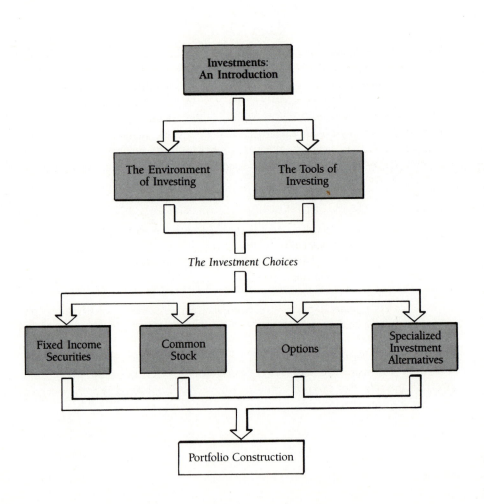

Investments:
An Introduction

The Environment
of Investing

The Tools of
Investing

The Investment Choices

Fixed Income
Securities

Common
Stock

Options

Specialized
Investment
Alternatives

Portfolio Construction

Benjamin Britten in his Young Person's Guide to the Orchestra describes and illustrates the instruments of the symphony orchestra. Then Britten reconstructs the orchestra one instrument at a time and ends the work with a glorious fugue that combines all the instruments. The preceding chapters of this text have described and illustrated individual investments: bonds, preferred stock, common stock, options, shares in investment companies, commodity futures, physical assets, collectibles, and real estate. In a manner similar to Britten's fugue, the investor combines the individual assets to construct a portfolio. The individual acquires assets one at a time, and they are blended together into a portfolio designed to meet the investor's financial goals.

Portfolio construction, then, is a process in which the individual specifies financial goals, identifies financial resources and obligations, and acquires a diversified portfolio designed to meet the goals within the investor's constraints. Of course, this process is affected by the economy (e.g., expectation of inflation), changes in the tax laws, the deregulation of financial markets, and the speed of technological change. In addition, changes in the individual's economic or family environment can have an important impact on financial planning and the resulting portfolio.

The process of financial planning and portfolio construction is not an easy task; it requires considerable analytical thought and extensive calculations. There are so many assets from which to choose; the economic environment can be so dynamic; the tax code is complex; and individuals' obligations and resources change throughout their lives. But the difficulty of the task is no reason to avoid planning one's financial future and constructing a well-diversified portfolio that offers as high a return as possible consistent with the individual investor's willingness to bear risk.

27

Portfolio Construction in an Efficient Market Environment

LEARNING OBJECTIVES

After completing this chapter you should be able to

1. Differentiate the three forms of the efficient market hypothesis.
2. Identify financial goals.
3. Enumerate the features of investment alternatives.
4. Match types of assets with individual financial goals.
5. Construct an individual's balance sheet.
6. Construct an individual's cash budget.
7. Explain the importance of financial planning in an efficient market context.

All the previous chapters have considered pieces of the investment puzzle. Pages have been devoted to describing various investment alternatives and how they may be analyzed. The mechanics of acquiring and liquidating positions, each investment's risks and sources of return, the tax implications, and the process of valuation have been covered in detail. However, the individual does not acquire just one asset but accumulates a portfolio of assets. Thus, all the pieces of the puzzle must ultimately fit together into a whole, a portfolio that is designed to meet some purpose or set of goals.

This chapter puts the pieces together. It commences with a review of the efficient market hypothesis and a summary of empirical evidence in support of the hypothesis. Since the efficient market hypothesis concludes that in most cases the individual investor cannot expect to consistently outperform the market (after adjusting for the amount of risk the investor bears), the emphasis in this chapter shifts to financial planning in an efficient market context.

Financial planning is a process in which the investor (a) specifies financial goals; (2) considers the possible investment alternatives, individual resources, the tax environment, and willingness to bear risk; and (3) constructs a diversified portfolio designed to meet these goals. After the portfolio is constructed, the individual continues to monitor the individual assets to determine that they are contributing to the portfolio. Underperforming assets or

assets whose risk/return characteristics have adversely changed are culled from the portfolio. Of course, changes in the tax laws, the expected economic environment, or the individual's goals or resources will also necessitate changes in the portfolio.

THE EFFICIENT MARKET HYPOTHESIS REVIEWED

The discussion of the efficient market hypothesis in Chapter 8 suggested that financial markets are very efficient. The competition among investors, the rapid dissemination of information, and the swiftness with which security prices adjust to this information produce efficient financial markets in which an individual cannot expect to consistently outperform the market. Instead the investor can expect to earn a return that is consistent with the amount of risk he or she bears.

In previous discussions risk was subdivided into systematic and unsystematic risk. Unsystematic risk, which applied to the individual asset, was significantly reduced, if not eliminated, through the construction of a diversified portfolio. Thus, the investor was left with deciding how much systematic risk he or she was willing to bear. Once this was determined, the next step was to construct an optimal portfolio that offered the most return for the given level of risk. Of course, the portfolio was composed of assets that were bought and sold in the efficient financial markets.

While the investor may know that financial markets are efficient, that does not   *Degree of efficiency* tell him or her how efficient they are. The degree of efficiency is important, because it determines the value the individual investor places on various types of analysis to select securities. If financial markets are inefficient, then many techniques may aid the investor in selecting securities that may produce superior investment results. However, as the markets become more efficient and the various tools of analysis become well known, their usefulness for security selection is reduced, since they will no longer produce superior results.

Forms of the Efficient Market Hypothesis

The investor may believe that the financial markets are weakly efficient, semi-strongly   *Weak form* efficient, or strongly efficient. The *weak form* of the efficient market hypothesis suggests that the fundamental analysis discussed in Chapters 16 and 17 may produce superior investment results but that the technical analysis discussed in Chapter 18 will not. Thus, studying past price behavior and other technical indicators of the market will not produce superior investment results. For example, if a stock's price rises, the next change cannot be forecasted by studying previous price behavior. According to the weak form of the efficient market hypothesis, technical indicators do not produce returns on securities that are in excess of the return consistent with the amount of risk borne by the investor.

The *semi-strong form* of the efficient market hypothesis asserts that the current   *Semi-strong form* price of a stock reflects all of the public's information concerning the company. This knowledge includes both the firm's past history and the information learned through studying a firm's financial statements, its industry, and the general economic environment. Analysis of this material cannot be expected to produce superior investment results. Notice that the hypothesis does not state that the analysis cannot produce superior results. It just asserts that superior results should not be expected. However,

there is the implication that even if the analysis of information produces superior results in some cases, it will not produce superior results over many investment decisions.

This conclusion should not be surprising to anyone who thinks about the investment process. Many investors and analysts study the same information. Their thought processes and training are similar, and they are in competition with one another. Certainly, if one perceives a fundamental change in a particular firm, this information will be readily transferred to other investors, and the price of the security will change. The competition among the potential buyers and the potential sellers will result in the security's price reflecting the firm's intrinsic worth.

As may be expected, the investment community is not particularly elated with this conclusion. It implies that the fundamental analysis considered in Chapters 16 and 17 will not produce superior investment results. Thus, neither technical nor fundamental analysis will generate consistently superior investment performance. Of course, if the individual analyst is able to perceive fundamental changes before other analysts do, that individual can outperform the market as a whole. However, few, if any, individuals should be able to *consistently* perceive such changes. Thus, there is little reason to expect investors to achieve consistently superior investment results.

Inside information

There is, however, one major exception to this general conclusion of the semi-strong form of the efficient market hypothesis. If the investor has access to *inside information,* that individual may consistently achieve superior results. In effect, this individual has information that is not known by the general investing public. Such privileged information as dividend cuts or increments, new discoveries, or potential takeovers may have a significant impact on the value of the firm and its securities. If the investor has advance knowledge of such events and has the time to act, he or she should be able to achieve superior investment returns.

Of course, most investors do not have access to inside information or at least do not have access to information concerning a number of firms. An individual may have access to privileged information concerning a firm for which he or she works. But as was previously pointed out, the use of such information for personal gain is illegal. To achieve continuous superior results, the individual would have to have a continuous supply of correct inside information and to use it illegally. Probably few, if any, investors have this continuous supply, which may explain why both fundamentalists and technical analysts watch sales and purchases by insiders as a means to glean a clue as to the true future potential of the firm as seen by its management.

Strong form

The *strong form* of the efficient market hypothesis asserts that the current price of a stock reflects all known (i.e., public) information *and* all privileged or inside information concerning the firm. Thus, not even access to inside information can be expected to result in superior investment performance. Once again, this does not mean that an individual who acts on inside information cannot achieve superior results. It means that these results cannot be expected and that success in one case will tend to be offset by failure in other cases, so over time the investor will not achieve superior results.

This conclusion rests on a very important assumption: Inside information cannot be kept inside! Too many people know about the activities of a firm. This information is discerned by a sufficient number of investors, and the prices of the firm's securities adjust for the informational content of this inside knowledge. Notice that the conclusion that the price of the stock still reflects its intrinsic value does not require that all investors know this additional information. All that is necessary is for a sufficient

number to know. Furthermore, the knowledge need not be acquired illegally. It is virtually impossible to keep some information secret, and there is a continual flow of rumors concerning a firm's activities. Denial by the firm is not sufficient to stop this spread of rumors, and when some are later confirmed, it only increases the credibility of future rumors as a possible means to gain inside information.

Although considerable empirical work has been designed to verify the forms of the efficient market hypothesis, these tests generally support only the weak and semi-strong forms.[1] The use of privileged information may result in superior investment performance, but the use of publicly known information cannot be expected to produce superior investments. Thus, neither technical nor fundamental analysis may be of help to the individual investor, because the current price of a stock fully incorporates this information.

Empirical Evidence for the Efficient Market Hypothesis

As a general statement, empirical evidence tends to support the concept of efficient financial markets. This is particularly true with regard to the weak form. If the weak form were not true, investors could devise systems that would analyze historical data and predict future stock prices with such accuracy that these investors would earn superior returns. However, the evidence suggests that successive price changes are random. The correlation between stock prices is virtually nil, and thus past price behavior provides little useful information for predicting future stock prices.[2]

Support for efficient market

Most empirical evidence also suggests that the semi-strong version of the efficient market hypothesis is valid. This hypothesis, which suggests that fundamental analysis is futile, is a very strong statement. Empirical tests of strategies that use publicly available information such as the data found in a firm's financial statements have concluded that this information does not produce superior results.[3] Prices change very rapidly once information becomes public, and thus the security's price embodies all known information. If an investor could anticipate the new information and act before the information becomes public, that investor may consistently outperform the market, but public information rarely can be analyzed in such a way that generates superior investment results.

Semi-strong version seems valid

There are, however, a few chinks in this general conclusion. Some empirical results do suggest there may be some inefficiencies in the market that, if exploited, could generate superior investment results. For example, one study suggested that stocks that performed poorly in December (perhaps as the result of tax-loss selling) tended to outperform the market in January.[4] This, of course, suggests that investors

Some market inefficiencies may exist

---

[1] This evidence is discussed in the next section.

[2] For a summary of this empirical work, see James H. Lorie and Mary T. Hamilton, *The Stock Market: Theories and Evidence* (Homewood, Ill.: Richard D. Irwin, 1973), 70–97.

[3] For several studies that test the semi-strong form of the efficient market hypothesis, see the section on market efficiency in James Lorie and Richard Brealey, eds., *Modern Developments in Investment Management* (New York: Praeger Publishers, 1972). The student should be warned that most of this material requires considerable knowledge of statistics.

[4] Ben Branch and Cornelius Ryan, "Tax Loss Trading: An Inefficiency Too Large to Ignore," *The Financial Review* (Winter 1980): 20–29. Other studies that have found evidence of seasonality in returns include D. B. Keim, "Size-related Anomalies and Stock Return Seasonality: Further Empirical Evidence," *Journal of Financial Economics* (June 1983): 13–32, and A. Berges, J. J. McConnell, and G. C. Schlarbaum, "An Investigation of the Turn-of-the-Year Effect, the Small Firm Effect and the Tax-Loss Selling Pressure in Canadian Stock Returns," *Journal of Finance* (March 1984): 185–192.

should purchase these stocks in late December with the intention of selling them in January. Other studies suggest that if reported per-share earnings differ significantly from expected per-share earnings, the market price adjustment occurs over several weeks and thus may offer an opportunity for abnormal returns.[5] There is also evidence that portfolios consisting of stocks with low price-earnings ratios (low P/E ratios) or the stocks of small companies may tend to generate returns in excess of what would be anticipated by the risk borne by the investor.[6] The market may be underpricing small companies or low P/E stocks, which implies that investors who construct portfolios consisting of stocks with low P/E ratios or whose total market value is small may earn abnormally large returns.

The results of these studies, however, should not lead investors to conclude that financial markets are inefficient. Most empirical evidence supports the semi-strong form of the efficient market hypothesis. While these exceptions do suggest that opportunities for excess returns may exist, the magnitude of these returns may be modest. This is particularly true after the investor considers the commission costs associated with establishing and subsequently changing the composition of the investor's portfolio.

Less support for the strong form

The evidence in support of the strong form of the efficient market hypothesis is mixed. While there is evidence that even access to inside information will not produce superior investment returns, these results have been disputed by other studies.[7] It is probably safe to assert that until the strong form is verified or at least has more empirical support, there will be reason to analyze the purchases and sales of securities by those most likely to know the true fundamentals of the firm, the insiders.

Implications of the Efficient Market Hypothesis

It is particularly important that the individual investor understand the efficient market hypothesis and several of its implications. The first implication is that the market is efficient because investors and financial analysts are using this known information in a rational way. This information is being digested, and its implications for the future performance of the firm are being properly discounted back to the present. Thus, the individual cannot use public information for superior investment results because the investment community is using it! If the investment community did not use this information and the correct valuation models, the individual could achieve superior investment results. It is the very fact that financial analysts and investors are competent and are trying to beat each other that helps to produce the efficient market.

[5]See Charles P. Jones and Robert H. Litzenberger, "Quarterly Earnings Reports and Intermediate Stock Price Trends," *Journal of Finance* (March 1970): 143–148; Stewart L. Brown, "Earnings Changes, Stock Prices and Market Efficiency," *Journal of Finance* (March 1978): 17–28; and R. Rendleman, C. P. Jones, and H. A. Latané, "Empirical Anomalies Based on Unexpected Earnings and the Importance of Risk Adjustments," *Journal of Financial Economics* (November 1982): 269–287.

[6]See S. Basu, "Investment Performance of Common Stocks in Relation to Their Price-Earnings Ratios: A Test of the Efficient Market Hypothesis," *Journal of Finance* (June 1977): 663–694; S. Basu, "The Relationship between Earnings Yield, Market Value and Return for NYSE Common Stocks," *Journal of Financial Economics* (June 1983): 129–156; T. J. Cook and M. S. Rozeff, "Size and Earnings/Price Ratio Anomalies: One Effect or Two?" *Journal of Financial and Quantitative Analysis* (December 1984): 449–466; David Dreman, *The New Contrarian Investment Strategy* (New York: Random House, 1980); and M. C. Reingsum, "Portfolio Strategies Based on Market Capitalization," *Journal of Portfolio Management* (Winter 1983): 29–36.

[7]See, for instance, Joseph E. Finnerty, "Insiders and Market Efficiency," *Journal of Finance* (September 1976): 1141–1148 and the references given in this article.

POINTS OF INTEREST
The Money Masters

The efficient market hypothesis suggests that few, if any, investors will outperform the market for an extended period of time. Nine individuals who seem to have achieved that feat are highlighted in a fascinating book, *The Money Masters,* by John Train (Harper and Row, 1980). In this book Train explores the ideas and strategies of these nine portfolio managers who achieved extraordinary records of capital appreciation for a period of at least ten years.

The strategies and characteristics of these nine individuals have common threads. They sought undervalued securities and tended to avoid stocks that were currently popular. They avoided new ventures, well-known firms (the so-called "blue chips"), and gimmicks such as options. They made realistic appraisals and favored stocks that tended to sell below book value. Each of these investors was patient and willing to wait until the prices of his stocks rose to reflect the securities' true value.

These nine men (there were no women) tended to be loners. While they were obviously very well informed concerning Wall Street, they were geographically dispersed and not necessarily located in New York City. While their success could be interpreted to refute the efficient market hypothesis, the opposite inference is more correct. The paucity of individuals who have achieved such success is strong support for the hypothesis that few individuals will achieve superior returns over an extended period of time.

The second implication is that while security markets are efficient, they are not necessarily equally efficient. The hypothesis applies primarily to the large firms with securities listed on organized exchanges. There may be small over-the-counter securities that are fundamentally sound but that may not be accurately priced. Perhaps the individual investor may be able to identify these undervalued smaller firms.

The hypothesis need not apply to all assets

Although most securities are purchased in an efficient market, the investor may not buy and sell nonfinancial assets in such a market. This means that the current price need not reflect the intrinsic value of the asset, that is, the price may not reflect the asset's potential flow of income or price appreciation. If the markets for assets other than financial assets are dispersed and all transactions are, in effect, over-the-counter, the dissemination of information and prices is limited. This tends to reduce the efficiency of markets and to result in prices that can be too high or too low. While such a situation may offer excellent opportunities for the astute and the knowledgeable, it can also spell disaster for the novice.

Nonfinancial markets may be inefficient

The third and perhaps most important implication of the efficient market hypothesis applies to an individual's portfolio. The efficient market hypothesis seems to suggest that the individual investor could randomly select a diversified portfolio of securities and earn a return consistent with the market as a whole. Furthermore, once the portfolio has been selected, there is no need to change it. The strategy, then, is to buy and hold. Such a policy offers the additional advantage of minimizing commissions.

The problem with this naive policy is that it fails to consider the reasons an investor saves and acquires securities and other assets. The goals behind the portfolio are disregarded, and different goals require different portfolio construction strategies. Fur-

The need to match the portfolio with the investor's goals

thermore, goals and conditions change, which in turn requires changes in an individual's portfolio. Altering the portfolio for the sake of change will probably result in additional commissions and not produce superior investment returns. However, when the investor's goals or financial situation change, the portfolio should be altered in a way that is consistent with the new goals and conditions.

The investor should earn a return consistent with the market

The importance to the individual investor of the efficient market hypothesis is not the implication that investment decision making is useless. Instead, it brings to the foreground the environment in which the investor must make decisions. The hypothesis should make the investor realize that investments in securities may not produce superior returns. Rather, the investor should earn a return over a period of time that is consistent with the return earned by the market as a whole and the amount of risk borne by the investor. This means that individual investors should devote more time and effort to the specifications of their investment goals and the selection of securities to meet those goals than to the analysis of individual securities. Since such analysis cannot be expected to produce superior returns, it takes resources and time away from the important questions of why we save and invest.

THE PROCESS OF FINANCIAL PLANNING

Establish financial goals

In order to construct an optimal portfolio, the investor should start by defining its purpose. There has to be some goal (or goals) to guide the selection of the assets that should be included. After specifying realistic financial objectives, the next step is determining which assets are appropriate to meet the goals. There are many possible assets, and the individual must choose among these alternatives. This requires knowledge of the assets' features, including the sources of return, sources of risk, and tax implications.

Identify appropriate assets

Assess financial environment

After establishing investment goals and identifying assets that may meet the goals, the investor should analyze his or her environment. Environments obviously vary with individuals and change over an individual's lifetime. The investor needs to be aware of the resources and sources of income with which he or she has to work. The investor then will construct a financial plan designed to fulfill the investment goals within these environmental and financial constraints.

The Specification of Investment Goals

Reasons for saving

The purpose of investing is to transfer purchasing power from the present to the future. A portfolio is a store of value designed to meet the individual investor's reasons for postponing the consumption of goods and services from the present to the future. Several reasons for saving and investing were offered in the introductory chapter. These goals included

1. the capacity to meet financial emergencies;
2. the desire to finance specific future purchases, such as the down payment for a home;
3. the need for additional current income;
4. the desire to leave a sizable estate to heirs or to charity;

5. the inclination to speculate or the enjoyment derived from accumulating and managing wealth.

These are not all the possible reasons for deferring current consumption, but they indicate several motives for constructing a portfolio. However, not every asset is appropriate for each of the above goals. Matching the goals with the assets requires knowing the features of the specific assets, which are reviewed in the subsequent section.

The Investment Alternatives

The investor has a large variety of assets from which to choose, and within each type of asset there is an almost unlimited number of choices. However, each of the assets have common characteristics: liquidity, marketability, potential income and/or capital gains, risk, and tax implications. Exhibit 27.1 lists the major classes of assets covered in this text and summarizes their characteristics. The exhibit reviews the various assets in the order in which they appear in the text, starting with money and bank deposits and ending with foreign securities.

Common characteristics of assets

The first characteristic reviewed in Columns two and three is the asset's liquidity and marketability. Liquidity is the ease of converting the asset into cash with little risk of loss. NOW accounts, savings accounts, shares in money market mutual funds, and treasury bills are very liquid assets, since there is virtually no chance of loss of principal. However, only treasury bills are also marketable. There is no secondary market for NOW and savings accounts because the saver simply withdraws the funds on demand, and shares in money market mutual funds are redeemed (i.e., sold back to the fund).

Many assets that are marketable are not truly liquid, as there is the potential for loss. Without the existence of secondary markets, there would be no means by which the investor could convert the asset back to cash. These markets may be very well developed and organized, such as in the case of stock traded on the New York Stock Exchange, or poorly developed and very informal, as in the secondary market for collectibles.

Every asset offers a potential return that comes either through income, such as interest or dividends, or through capital gains. Capital gains offer a modest tax advantage, since the tax is deferred until the gain is realized. The sources of an asset's return are reviewed in Columns four and five in Exhibit 27.1. The next column presents the federal income tax status of each asset. The returns earned by most assets are taxable at the federal level, but there are major exceptions, such as the interest earned on municipal bonds. Other assets (such as real estate) also permit the deferral of tax, as the funds generated by the investment are sheltered from income taxes by expenses such as noncash depreciation charges.

Sources of return

The last column reviews the sources of risk. Since the future is uncertain, the investor must bear risk to earn a return. Unsystematic risk applies only to the specific asset, and for firms it covers the nature of the operation (business risk) and how the firm is financed (financial risk). Since unsystematic risk is reduced through the construction of diversified portfolios, systematic risk is by far the more important source of risk. Sources of systematic risk include market risk, interest rate risk, and purchas-

Sources of risk

Importance of diversification

Exhibit 27.1
A Summary of Investment Alternatives and Their Characteristics

Asset	Liquidity	Marketability	Return: Possible Income	Return: Possible Capital Gains	Tax Status	Sources of Risk
Money	Complete	None	No	No	None	Purchasing power risk
NOW and savings accounts	High	None	Yes	No	Taxable	Meager purchasing power risk (risk free up to $100,000)[1]
Certificates of deposit	High	None	Yes	No	Taxable	Meager purchasing power risk (risk free up to $100,000)
Money market mutual funds	High	None	Yes	No	Taxable	Meager purchasing power risk (virtually risk free)[1]
Quality corporate bonds	Moderate	Yes	Yes	Yes[2]	Taxable	Business/financial/ interest rate/ purchasing power risk
Lower-rated corporate bonds	Moderate to little	Moderate	Yes	Yes[2]	Taxable	Business/financial/ interest rate/ purchasing power risk
Preferred stock	Moderate	Moderate	Yes	Yes	Taxable	Business/financial/ interest rate/ purchasing power risk
Treasury bills	High	Yes	Yes	No	Taxable[3]	Meager purchasing power risk (virtually risk free)[1]
Treasury bonds	Moderate	Yes	Yes	Yes	Taxable[3]	Purchasing power/ interest rate risk
EE and HH bonds	High	None	Yes	No	Taxable[3]	Purchasing power risk[1]
Federal agency bonds	Moderate	Yes	Yes	Yes[2]	Taxable[3]	Purchasing power/ interest rate risk
Municipal bonds	Moderate to little	Yes	Yes	Yes[2]	Nontaxable[4]	Purchasing power/ interest rate risk

ing power risk. Those assets whose returns tend to fluctuate with fluctuations in the market as a whole have market risk. Assets whose prices are sensitive to changes in interest rates have interest rate risk.

Virtually all assets subject the investor to purchasing power risk, since the realized return may be less than the rate of inflation. For example, when an individual purchases a fixed-income security such as a long-term corporate or municipal bond, the investor locks in a particular return. If inflation increases, the fixed return may be insufficient to compensate for the rate of inflation. Of course, if the rate of inflation declines, the real purchasing power of the fixed return is increased.

An investor seeking to avoid loss of purchasing power should not acquire fixed-income securities but instead should purchase variable-income securities. For ex-

Exhibit 27.1
Continued

Asset	Liquidity	Marketability	Return: Possible Income	Possible Capital Gains	Tax Status	Sources of Risk
Quality common stock	Moderate	Yes	Yes	Yes	Taxable	Business/financial/market/purchasing power risk
Speculative common stock	Little	Moderate	In selective cases	Yes	Taxable	Business/financial/market/purchasing power risk
Options: warrants, puts, calls	Low to nil	Moderate	None[5]	Yes	Taxable	Business/financial/market/purchasing power risk
Closed-end investment companies	Moderate	Moderate	Yes	Yes	Taxable	Market/purchasing power risk
Mutual funds	Moderate	None (shares redeemed)	Yes	Yes	Taxable[6]	Market/purchasing power risk
Futures	Low to nil	Moderate	No	Yes	Taxable	Business/market risk
Collectibles	Low to nil	Low	No	Yes	Taxable	Market risk
Gold	Moderate	Yes	No	Yes	Taxable	Market risk
Homes	Low	Low to moderate	No	Yes	Tax deferred	Market/interest rate risk
Real estate	Low	Low	Yes	Yes	Tax shelter or tax deferred	Business/financial/interest rate risk
Foreign investments (bonds, stocks)	Low	Low to moderate	Yes	Yes	Taxable[7]	Business/financial/market/purchasing power/political/exchange rate risk

[1] Yields may adjust to offset purchasing power risk.

[2] Capital gains do not apply to zero coupon bonds, bonds sold initially at a discount, or bonds issued after July 18, 1984, and bought at a discount.

[3] Interest is not taxable at the state and local level.

[4] Interest on nontaxable bonds may be taxable at the state and local level.

[5] Writers of options earn income.

[6] Mutual funds that invest in state and local government securities are tax-exempt.

[7] Foreign securities may be taxable both abroad and domestically.

ample, the return earned on investments in money market mutual funds, money market bank accounts, or any short-term asset that is rapidly retired is not fixed. The rapid turnover of these assets permits yields to quickly adjust, allowing the individual to reinvest the funds at the higher short-term rates. Thus, these assets are among the best means to reduce purchasing power risk.

The diversity of alternative investments available to the individual investor should be immediately apparent from Exhibit 27.1. Obviously not all of these investments are appropriate to meet specific investment goals. Also, some of them would not be appropriate for an individual with modest resources or one who is very risk averse. Since each individual's financial goals, resources, aversion to risk, and tax environment vary, there are many possible portfolios that different individuals can construct.

Diversity of alternatives

Active versus passive management

However, each portfolio should seek to obtain the maximum possible return given the investor's resources and willingness to bear risk.

In addition, the individual must decide whether or not he or she wants to manage the portfolio actively or passively. Some individuals have neither the time nor the inclination to oversee their portfolios and thus employ the services of others (e.g., financial planners, stockbrokers, portfolio managers in trust departments, or the managers of mutual funds). However, individual investors must still select who will administer their assets and, of course, suffer any losses that result from poor management of the funds. Ultimately it is the saver who bears the risk and reaps the reward from the portfolio whether the funds are managed by that individual or by others.

The Analysis of the Individual's Environment and Resources

The need to be aware of one's resources

As mentioned before, individuals should be aware of their environment and financial resources. These differ from person to person, and what may be the correct investment strategy for one individual may not be correct for another. While this seems self-evident, many individuals do not recognize their environment and the resources they have.

Environments differ

One's environment includes such factors as age, health, employment, and family. A young bachelor in good health who is securely employed does not need the same portfolio as a young man with a family, even if his health is excellent and his employment is secure. The more current obligations an individual has (be they debt or family), the greater the need for a conservative portfolio of assets. Such assets should stress safety and liquidity so that short-term obligations may be met as they occur. In contrast, the young bachelor could afford to bear more risk in the selection of a portfolio.

Enumerate what one owns and owes

In addition to the individual's environment, the investor should take an accurate account of resources. This may be done by constructing two financial statements. The first one enumerates what is owned and owed, and the other enumerates cash receipts and disbursements. The former is, of course, a balance sheet, whereas the latter is a cash budget.

The entries for an individual's balance sheet are given in Exhibit 27.2. It lists all of the individual's assets and liabilities. The difference between these assets and liabilities is the individual's net worth (which would be the estate if the individual were to die at the time the balance sheet is constructed). For clarity, the individual should list short-term assets and then long-term assets, and the same should be done with liabilities. In effect, an individual's balance sheet is no different from a firm's balance sheet presented in Chapter 7.

Projected financial statements

The entries for the balance sheet given in Exhibit 27.2 consider the individual's financial position as of the present and as of some specified time in the future (e.g., at retirement). For the purpose of financial planning, it is advisable to construct one's current financial position as well as to project what that position will be at some time in the future. Such a projection is often referred to as a **pro forma financial statement**. The construction of a pro forma balance sheet will require that the individual make assumptions concerning (1) his or her ability to accumulate assets and retire liabilities and (2) the rate of growth or rate of return that will be achieved by the assets. While the resulting projections will depend on the assumptions, the projec-

	As of Now	At Retirement	Exhibit 27.2 An Individual's Balance Sheet and the Determination of Net Worth

CURRENT ASSETS

1. Bank deposits
   a. Cash, checking accounts
   b. Savings accounts
   c. Certificates of deposit
   d. Money market accounts
   e. Credit union accounts
   f. Other
   Subtotal

2. Liquid financial assets
   a. Money market mutual funds
   b. Treasury bills
   c. Series EE and HH bonds
   d. Amounts owed and payable on demand
   e. Tax refunds and other payments owed
   f. Cash value of life insurance
   Subtotal

3. Retirement and savings plans
   a. IRA accounts
   b. Keogh accounts
   c. Lump sum distributions and/or IRA rollover accounts
   d. Employee savings and investment plan:
      Before tax
      After tax
   e. Employee stock ownership plan
   f. Deferred compensation due
   g. Company options
   Subtotal

4. Financial assets
   a. Treasury notes and bonds
   b. Corporate bonds
   c. Corporate stock
   d. Municipal bonds
   e. GNMAs and other federal agency debt
   f. Mutual funds
   Subtotal

5. Tangible assets
   a. Real estate
      1. Home
      2. Vacation properties
      3. Other
   b. Collectibles
   c. Cars
   d. Personal tangible property (e.g., furs, silver, furniture, jewelry, boats)
   Subtotal

Total Assets

continued

**Exhibit 27.2
Continued**

LIABILITIES

1. Short-term
   a. Current portion of mortgage owed   _____   _____
   b. Current portion of car payments   _____   _____
   c. Personal debts   _____   _____
   d. Credit card balances   _____   _____
   e. Miscellaneous   _____   _____

   Subtotal   _____   _____

2. Long-term
   a. Mortgage balance owed   _____   _____
   b. Balance owed on car or other tangible
      assets   _____   _____
   c. Bank loans, amount borrowed on life
      insurance   _____   _____
   d. Other long-term debts   _____   _____

   Subtotal   _____   _____

Total Liabilities   _____   _____

SUMMARY

Total assets   _____   _____
Total liabilities   _____   _____
Net worth (Value of estate) (Assets minus liabilities)   _____   _____

tions often bring into sharp focus the individual's future financial needs. Such projects then can prove to be helpful in establishing current investment strategies.

The balance sheets in Exhibit 27.2 are more detailed than is necessary for most individuals. Few individual investors will have entries for each asset or liability enumerated in the exhibit. For example, many investors may not be eligible for Keogh accounts or have deferred compensation owed them. Also, some of the entries may not apply now but may apply in the future. For example, if the individual has not started an IRA but intends to, this should be included in the projected balance sheet even though it is not applicable to the current balance sheet.

Problem of valuation   The mechanics of constructing a balance sheet are relatively easy. The difficult part is enumerating the assets and placing values on them. Such valuation is easy for publicly traded securities such as stocks and bonds. The problem concerns placing values on tangible personal assets such as collectibles or real estate. Since the purpose of constructing a balance sheet is to determine the individual's financial condition, it is advisable to be conservative in estimating the value of these assets. If, for example, the individual had to sell antiques to finance living expenses, it would be better to underestimate than to overestimate the prices for which these assets may be sold. Such underestimation cannot lead to disappointment.

Cash budget enumerates receipts and disbursements   After the individual enumerates what is owned and what is owed and thereby determines his or her net worth, the next step is to analyze the flow of receipts and disbursements. This is done by constructing a **cash budget**. Exhibit 27.3 enumerates the entries needed for the construction of a cash budget. It lists all of the individual's sources of receipts (e.g., salary, interest, and rental income) and all of the disburse-

	Present	At Retirement

Exhibit 27.3
An Individual's Cash
Budget for One Year

CASH RECEIPTS

Salary (after deductions) _____ _____
Social security _____ _____
Pension _____ _____
Interest from savings _____ _____
Dividends on stock _____ _____
Commissions & bonuses _____ _____
Royalties, fees _____ _____
Distributions from businesses _____ _____
Rental income _____ _____
Veterans benefits _____ _____
Annuity payments _____ _____
Distributions from trusts _____ _____
Mortgage payments received _____ _____
Distributions from IRA, Keogh, and IRA rollover
accounts _____ _____
Other receipts _____ _____
Total Receipts _____ _____

CASH DISBURSEMENTS

1. Housing
   a. Mortgage payments _____ _____
   b. Rent _____ _____
   c. Maintenance _____ _____
   d. Utilities _____ _____
   e. Fuel _____ _____
   f. Property taxes _____ _____
2. Food and personal expenditures
   a. Dining at home _____ _____
   b. Dining out _____ _____
   c. Personal care _____ _____
   d. Clothing _____ _____
   e. Recreation and travel _____ _____
   f. Furniture, appliances _____ _____
   g. Hobbies _____ _____
3. Transportation
   a. Automobile expense _____ _____
   b. Car replacement _____ _____
   c. Public transportation _____ _____
4. Medical
   a. Insurance _____ _____
   b. Deductibles paid _____ _____
   c. Miscellaneous expense _____ _____
5. Insurance
   a. Life insurance _____ _____
   b. Homeowner's insurance _____ _____
   c. Automobile insurance _____ _____
   d. Other _____ _____
6. Estimated taxes _____ _____
7. Other disbursements
   a. Gifts _____ _____
   b. Contributions _____ _____
   c. Miscellaneous _____ _____
Total Disbursements _____ _____

SUMMARY

Total receipts _____ _____
Total disbursements _____ _____
Difference between receipts and disbursements _____ _____

ments (e.g., mortgage payments, living expenses, and taxes). As with the balance sheet, the cash budget may be constructed for the present or projected for a specific time in the future (e.g., at retirement). Exhibit 27.3 thus provides for both a current annual cash budget and a pro forma cash budget. While the cash budget illustrated in this exhibit is for one year, cash budgets may be constructed to cover other time periods, such as monthly receipts and disbursements.

As with the balance sheet in Exhibit 27.2, the entries in Exhibit 27.3 are probably too detailed for many individuals. Obviously, not everyone receives veterans' benefits or royalty payments. However, such completeness is desirable, for it brings to the foreground the variety of possible sources and uses of funds. If the individual's receipts exceed disbursements, the excess receipts become a source of funds that should be profitably invested to meet future financial needs. It is quite possible that after constructing such a cash budget, the individual will perceive ways to increase receipts and decrease disbursements and thus generate additional funds for investment.

The Establishment of Financial Plans

Establish a financial strategy

After specifying goals and analyzing one's financial position, the investor can establish a **financial plan** or course of action. This plan is the strategy by which the investor will fulfill the financial goals. While plans will vary among individuals, the importance of such a plan applies to all. It is the means to the end—the means to financial success and security.

Establish priorities

Plans require the establishment of priorities. Those financial goals that are most important should be fulfilled first. After investments have been made to satisfy these needs, the next most important goals should be attacked. In this way the investor systematically saves and invests to meet the specified goals. For example, an individual may determine the following goals and their priority:

- funds to meet financial emergencies
- funds to finance a child's education
- funds to finance retirement
- funds for an estate

The initial goal, then, is sufficient liquid assets to cover emergencies (e.g., unemployment or extended illness). After this goal has been met, the investor proceeds to save and accumulate assets designed to finance the child's college education. The process is continued until all of the goals have been met.

Liquidity and safety are stressed

The capacity to meet financial emergencies. While this financial goal can be well defined, planning to have funds to meet financial emergencies involves considerable uncertainty. The investor does not know when (or even if) the money will be needed. While long-term securities may be used to meet a financial goal that has an identifiable time period, they would probably be inappropriate to meet the goal of having sufficient funds to deal with emergencies. Assets that are very liquid (i.e., that are easily converted into cash without a loss) should be chosen to fulfill this investment goal. These include savings accounts, high-quality short-term debt, series EE bonds, and money market mutual funds.

Savings accounts, money market accounts, and certificates of deposit with short maturities may be readily converted into cash. While their yields may be lower than would be available from debt with a longer maturity, these liquid assets offer the important advantages of the safety of the principal and the ease of conversion into cash.

Short-term debt instruments, such as treasury bills and commercial paper, are also excellent investments for funds that are being held for emergencies. Although such investments may not maximize the investor's yield, they are more productive than leaving the money in a checking account. If the investor lacks sufficient funds to buy treasury bills, money market mutual funds offer a viable alternative. Of course, the problem of the amount of the minimum unit of purchase does not apply to series EE bonds, and they offer the additional advantage of deferring income taxes until the funds are needed and the bonds redeemed.

The desire to finance identifiable future purchases, such as a child's education. By the nature of emergencies, it is impossible to know when the funds will be needed, but this need not apply to other future purchases of goods and services. The desire to purchase a specified good or service often has a known time dimension. Financing an education and planning for retirement are both examples of expenditures that will occur at a particular time in the future. Individuals know approximately when their children will be in college or when they will retire. While there may be some deviation in the time of the actual occurrence, the investor knows approximately when these events will happen and can plan now to have the funds to finance the purchase.

Consider the financing of a child's college education. If the child is currently eight years old, the funds for a college education will be needed in approximately ten years.[8] What assets are desirable to meet this particular financial goal? The answer to the question is primarily long-term but relatively safe assets. They should be long-term because the funds will not be needed for many years, and such investments tend to offer a superior yield to short-term assets. They should be relatively safe because one should not want to gamble with funds earmarked for this education. What assets are long-term and relatively safe? There are many, including

Long-term assets and safety are stressed

- conservative growth stocks
- high-yielding utility stocks
- long-term bonds

Long-term growth stocks offer possible appreciation in the investor's capital. Since the emphasis is on the need for funds many years in the future, steady long-term growth is one means to meet this goal. In effect, this strategy suggests that the investor select known growth stocks, such as IBM, rather than riskier stocks that may offer a higher return but require that the investor bear more risk.

Growth stocks

Utility stocks that offer a high dividend yield may also earn a considerable amount of money over time. Stocks with an 8 to 10 percent annual dividend yield may double an investment in less than seven years. However, the investor cannot spend the divi-

Utilities with generous dividends

---

[8]Although the exact future cost of the education is unknown, the parents can systematically accumulate assets to begin to meet this anticipated expense.

dends as they are received or the amount of savings will not grow. This forced saving may be achieved by opting for the dividend reinvestment plans that many utilities offer their stockholders. Since the investor never receives the cash dividends, they cannot be spent. Hence, such plans offer a painless means to save for a specified goal.

Long-term bonds

Long-term bonds are also an excellent means to save for a certain time period. Since the bonds mature at specified times, the investor can purchase an issue that will be redeemed at the desired time in the future. For example, if the funds are needed after ten years, the investor may buy bonds that mature after ten years. If the investor knows when the money will be needed, a portfolio of bonds may be constructed that matches the maturity dates of the bond and the time when the funds will be required.

Each of the aforementioned alternatives requires that the investor choose an individual asset for purchase. The investor may avoid this decision by purchasing shares in a mutual fund that meets the specific investment goal. Investment companies that specialize in growth or in high-yielding securities offer another means to accumulate funds designed to finance a specific expenditure in the future, such as a college education. Obviously, investment companies that specialize in risky securities or special situations do not meet this investment goal and should be avoided.

Although the preceding discussion used the financing of a college education as the investor's goal, other similar goals could have been used. For example, the accumulation of funds to help finance retirement is a similar goal. Once again, the investor knows approximately when the event (i.e., retirement) will occur. The portfolio should then be constructed with assets that can be converted into cash at a specified time in the future. This general principle actually applies to any portfolio whose purpose is to meet a goal whose time dimension is known with some degree of certainty.

Safety and income

The need for additional future income and financial independence at retirement. Some investors save and purchase assets so that they may have an increased flow of income in the future. These investors are not particularly concerned with capital appreciation, but they are concerned with the general safety of principal and the flow of income. This is especially true if this investment income is to be a primary source of the individual's total income. Although such investors may receive supplemental income, their investment income is extremely important to their well-being. Such investors should choose assets that offer generous income and assure to some extent the safety of the principal. These include

- preferred stock
- bonds
- federal government securities

All of these assets tend to offer generous yields and the relative safety of the principal. The safest is, of course, the long-term debt of the federal government, but these bonds offer returns that are less than those that may be earned on high-quality corporate debt, such as bonds issued by AT&T. Preferred stocks are the riskiest of the alternatives listed but may offer the highest yield. The bonds and preferred stock are easily sold should the investor need immediate cash.

Stocks with a history of dividend increments

This investor should also consider common stocks with generous dividends or with a history of dividend increments. While the aforementioned securities may be

safer than corporate stock, they do not offer the possibility of growth in income. Such growth may be very desirable, especially during periods of inflation, because without an increase in income, the investor's purchasing power would be diminished. Common stocks do offer the possibility of increased dividends, and some companies (e.g., telephone utilities) have a history of annual dividend increments. Such common stocks offer the investor who is primarily concerned with income and the safety of the principal a means to obtain some increment in income for accepting only a modest degree of risk.

The desire to accumulate an estate. The desire to accumulate a substantial estate may be fullfilled by virtually any of the assets discussed in this text. However, there is less emphasis on liquidity and a current flow of income. Instead, the portfolio should stress assets whose values tend to appreciate over time. These may include

Less need for liquidity and safety

- growth stocks
- art objects and various collectibles
- real estate
- convertible bonds

Growth stocks and convertible bonds place emphasis on price appreciation, but they also generate some flow of income. Collectibles and art work produce no income in cash but do offer income-in-kind. The quantifiable yield on such investments is limited to price appreciation. Real estate may be particularly attractive, since it may offer current tax advantages while it appreciates. Although the time of one's death is unknown, an estate portfolio still places emphasis on those assets with potential for long-term growth. Many of these assets would not be appropriate in a portfolio stressing safety and liquidity.

Potential growth is stressed

While the above goals are the ones most frequently specified for the purposes for saving, individuals may have other reasons for investing. These may include the enjoyment associated with managing one's own funds or the desire to speculate. The success of casinos or state lottery games suggests that some individuals do enjoy gambling. No doubt others enjoy the game associated with speculating. Of course, prudence dictates that financial goals such as planning for emergencies or retirement should take precedence, but after accumulating sufficient assets to meet emergencies and other financial goals, the individual may seek to increase the return earned by bearing more risk.

Many assets are available that may satisfy an investor's desire to speculate. These include

A large potential return is stressed

- poor-quality debt
- stocks of small and risky companies
- options
- commodities
- collectibles

Poor-quality bonds offer higher potential return as compensation for the additional risk. Debentures, income bonds, even bonds in default may produce speculative gains should the company improve its financial position, which will improve the

Additional risk

quality of the bonds. There certainly have been many bonds that at one time fell on bad times, yet returned to respectability and rewarded those willing to bear the risk.

Small growth firms

All large companies were small at one time. Although purchasing the shares of small or risky companies may often result in substantial losses (especially if the firm should fail, as many do), the rewards can be substantial if the firm succeeds. Investors who purchased the shares of Coca-Cola, IBM, or Johnson & Johnson when these firms were small and just emerging were well rewarded for bearing this risk. Of course, hindsight is considerably better than foresight; it is extremely difficult to identify which of today's small but growing companies will be the success stories of tomorrow. But it is the possibility of such success that stimulates speculators' willingness to bear the risk and purchase the shares of emerging companies.

Options and commodities

Options and commodity contracts may offer the speculator the greatest satisfaction. While it may take years for poor-quality debt to improve or for small companies to grow, the action with options and commodity contracts is very rapid. Both are a means to apply leverage to one's position. The potential for large and sudden price changes is substantial. If the price of the underlying stock changes, the resulting change in the price of the option will be magnified. The same applies to the value of commodity contracts. The small margin requirement magnifies the potential return (or loss) on the speculator's funds. This potential for fast action and larger percentage gains increases the appeal of these very risky assets to investors who seek to speculate.

Collectibles

Although not all speculators will invest in collectibles, these assets offer special appeal to some investors who are willing to bear substantial risk. Investing in these assets requires specialized knowledge, and the possibility of buying a collectible at a minimal price and then seeing one's appraisal of the asset's potential value prove to be correct should appeal to some investors who are willing to accept the risk for the possibility of a large return.

MONITORING AND REVALUATION

Changing financial conditions

While financial planning is the backbone of portfolio construction, the individual must realize that goals and financial conditions do change. Such changes may alter the general financial plan. The birth of a child, the death of a spouse, a promotion, or a new job are just some of the many possible events that shape our lives and alter our financial goals. The individual must be willing to adjust financial plans accordingly. If a financial plan becomes outmoded, the investor should act rapidly to change the portfolio. This requires that investors be continually aware of (1) their financial environment, including their sources and uses of funds, (2) the composition of their portfolios, and (3) conditions in the financial markets.

Changes in individual assets

Firms also change, so their securities may no longer be appropriate for a particular individual's portfolio. For example, AT&T is a different firm today than it was prior to divestiture. While previously it may have been considered a conservative firm that paid stable and slowly growing dividends, such a description may no longer apply now that it is not a regulated utility. If the individual included the common stock of AT&T in a portfolio primarily as an income vehicle, that investor should no longer hold this stock but should acquire some alternative.

Changes in financial markets

Financial markets are certainly not static. For example, the deregulation of the banking system has had a profound impact on financial markets. Intense competition

among financial intermediaries has led to a blurring of distinctions among the various savings institutions. Such was not the case prior to deregulation. Also, new financial products such as stock index futures and bonds with put options have been created. Thus, financial markets are dynamic markets with an expanding array of investment alternatives.

One of the most important facets of investing—taxation—is also subject to change. Taxes alter the environment in which investment decisions are made. Some changes encourage investing or favor specific securities that the individual may acquire. Changes in the tax laws can have a profound impact on the individual's portfolio and thus require the investor to reassess the composition of the portfolio and make appropriate adjustments. It is only possible to conjecture as to what future changes in the tax code may be enacted, but certainly the investor should be aware of current tax laws and the impact that any proposed changes may have on the portfolio.

Finally, the investor must be willing to realize that not all investments will achieve their anticipated return or serve the purpose for which they were acquired. That is the nature of risk; the future is uncertain. If a particular asset is no longer appropriate or the anticipated return has not been realized, the investor should be willing to liquidate that asset and acquire an alternative. This does not mean that the individual should continuously turn over the portfolio. Such a course of action may be counterproductive and perhaps may even reduce the return as the investor pays the fees associated with the sale of one asset and the purchase of another. However, the investor should not become so enamored with particular assets that they are an end unto themselves instead of a means to meet specified financial goals.

Expected return may not be realized

Portfolio planning and management are not easy tasks that can be performed casually and infrequently. It is for this reason that many investors employ others who are more versed in the subject to do their financial planning and construct their portfolios. Trust departments of commercial banks, financial planning consultants, and the managers of investment companies partially relieve the individual of making investment decisions. Such professional help is not free. The fees may reduce the return the investor earns, but that is the price the investor must pay for giving up some of the responsibilities of investment decision making.

SELECTING A MONEY MANAGER OR FINANCIAL PLANNER

Since the management of assets requires specialized knowledge and can be time consuming, some individuals prefer to use the services of a money manager or financial planner. Financial planning is an emerging profession, so the terms "money manager" or "financial planner" can be both broad and vague. Many individuals may offer financial counsel. For example, the accountant who completes the investor's income tax forms may be a natural source for financial advice. The same applies to insurance salespeople, bankers, and stockbrokers. Any of these individuals can (and often do) offer financial advice as part of the usual services they provide.

With individuals in a specific area of finance, one must question whether their advice is self-serving. For example, an insurance salesperson or stockbroker may recommend purchasing specific investments. While these investments can be valuable as

Potential conflicts of interest

part of the individual's portfolio, their purchase may not necessarily be in the best interests of the investor.

To avoid this problem, the individual may seek the services of an independent financial planner, who develops financial plans for clients. Unlike bankers, brokers, or insurance salespeople who may be compensated through sales commissions, independent financial planners are compensated for constructing the financial plan and not for its execution. In effect, there are no sales commissions for the planning service. The individual will, however, have to pay appropriate commissions when the plan is executed. Thus, if a fee-only financial planner suggests the individual sell selected securities and replace them with other assets, the sales will generate brokerage commissions.

The selection of a money manager/financial planner is a highly individual decision. In some cases the choice may have been forced upon the individual. For example, a spouse may have inherited an estate that is managed by the trust department of a commercial bank. Someone, however, had to initially select that trust department to manage the assets. Since financial planning and money management is an emerging field, it may be difficult to identify competent asset managers.

The selection of a money manager/financial planner is not made easier when the individual realizes that financial planning requires access to very personal information. As a medical doctor may require confidential, personal information, so too will a money manager/financial planner require information that many individuals do not care to disclose. One's sources of income, the value of one's assets and outstanding debts, or relationships with one's family are illustrative of the information that a money manager may need. Before an investor seeks the help of a money manager or professional financial planner, it is desirable for the individual to determine his or her willingness to reveal personal financial information.

Several considerations should enter the selection of a knowledgeable money manager. Financial planning is a broad area requiring breadth of knowledge in the various investment alternatives as well as risk management through insurance, tax planning, retirement, and estate planning. While it is difficult to measure an individual's breadth and depth of knowledge, credentials such as academic background, previous experience, and professional designations such as CFP (Certified Financial Planner) or ChFC (Chartered Financial Consultant) help indicate the level of knowledge. References and word of mouth can also be an excellent way to learn about specific individuals. In addition, membership in professional associations such as the International Association for Financial Planning and the Institute of Certified Financial Planners is desirable, as these associations establish codes of ethics to which their members must subscribe.

Finally, the money manager/financial planner and the individual must concur on the individual's financial goals and willingness to bear risk. If the individual believes that he or she can bear more risk than the money manager/financial planner believes is prudent, there may be inherent conflicts. There must be a meeting of the minds between the money manager/financial planner and the client for the process to be successful. Also, without rapport and respect, the individual may not be willing to divulge information necessary for the construction of realistic financial plans.

The individual must realize that the establishment of financial goals and the selection of professional help remains his or her responsibility. In addition, the individual must realize that professional money managers and financial planners cannot perform

miracles. These professionals make decisions in efficient financial markets and cannot be expected to be one of the very rare individuals whose financial plans outperform the market consistently.

SUMMARY

Investment decisions are made in efficient financial markets, but how efficient the financial markets are is open to debate. The weakest form of the efficient market hypothesis asserts that technical analysis of a stock's past price behavior (as discussed in Chapter 18) will not lead to superior performance. Empirical evidence supports the weak form of the efficient market hypothesis.

The semi-strong form of the efficient market hypothesis suggests that analysis of publicly known information, such as a firm's financial statements and data concerning the economic environment, will not lead to superior investment results. While the empirical evidence generally supports the semi-strong form, there are exceptions, such as the evidence that low P/E stocks tend to do better than the market as a whole. To the extent that the market is inefficient, the use of the fundamental analysis discussed in Chapters 16 and 17 may lead to somewhat superior investment results.

The strong form of the efficient market hypothesis states that even access to inside information will not provide consistently superior investment performance. Since empirical evidence does not offer as much support for the strong form of the efficient market hypothesis as it does for the weak and semi-strong forms, efforts designed to track the purchases and sales of insiders are given some credibility.

Because investments are made in efficient financial markets, it is very difficult for an individual investor to outperform the market consistently. However, this does not imply that securities or other assets should be acquired randomly. Instead the investor should have a financial plan. First, financial goals are defined and priorities determined. Next, the individual should analyze his or her financial position. This may be achieved through the use of two financial statements—a personal balance sheet that enumerates what the individual owns and owes and his or her net worth, and a cash budget that enumerates the individual's cash receipts and disbursements. These financial statements may be created for the present or may be projected for some time in the future.

After specifying the financial goals and analyzing the financial environment, the investor should construct a diversified portfolio designed to meet these goals. Diversification reduces (and perhaps eliminates) the unsystematic risk associated with each asset; the remaining systematic risk cannot be reduced through diversification. If the individual is willing to bear more systematic risk, he or she may achieve a higher return.

Not all assets are appropriate for every goal, so a diversified portfolio will contain various types of assets, each of which plays a role in the portfolio as a whole through its impact on risk and its capacity to meet specific financial needs.

After the portfolio has been constructed, the individual must continue to make investment decisions. Financial needs change; the individual's resources and environment change; financial markets and the economic environment change; and certainly the performance of individual assets changes. The investor should view the portfolio as a dynamic entity requiring frequent surveillance. When appropriate, adjustments

in the composition of the portfolio should be made. Professional financial planners can provide assistance in managing a portfolio, but the individual is ultimately responsible for determining financial goals and bearing the risk of investment decisions.

Terms to Remember

Pro forma financial statement
Cash budget
Financial plan

Questions

1. What are the different forms of the efficient market hypothesis and their implications for security analysis and portfolio construction?

2. Is the efficient market hypothesis supported by empirical evidence?

3. Do the implications of the efficient market hypothesis suggest that professional money managers are incompetent?

4. Does the efficient market hypothesis apply to nonfinancial assets?

5. Why should investors specify financial goals?

6. What types of assets are appropriate to meet financial emergencies?

7. What are the steps for constructing a financial plan?

8. What is a pro forma balance sheet? A cash budget?

9. Which of the following should be part of a balance sheet and which should be part of a cash budget?
    a. mortgage owed
    b. principal payments made
    c. dividends received
    d. Social Security payments
    e. IRA account
    f. gifts to children
    g. mutual fund shares
    h. interest owed
    i. antiques
    j. credit card balances

10. After constructing a financial plan and executing it, does financial planning cease to be important?

Suggested Readings

Now that you have completed this text, you may expand your knowledge of investments by several approaches. For instance, you could read a more advanced text. Two possibilities are

Radcliffe, Robert C. *Investment Concepts, Analysis, and Strategy,* 2nd ed. Glenview, Ill.: Scott, Foresman, 1986.

Sharpe, William F. *Investments,* 3rd ed. Englewood Cliffs, N.J.: Prentice-Hall, 1985.

Several references on investments have been compiled into books of readings. The following collections complement the material in this text.

Aby, Carroll D., Jr., and Donald E. Vaughn. *Investment Classics*. Santa Monica, Calif.: Goodyear Publishing Co., 1979.

Fabozzi, Frank J. *Readings in Investment Management*. Homewood, Ill.: Richard D. Irwin, 1983.

Financial planning is an integral part of portfolio management. The following books discuss planning and include material on budgeting, taxes, estate planning, and insurance.

Scott, Carole Elizabeth. *Your Financial Plan*. New York: Harper & Row, 1979.

Van Caspel, Venita. *The Power of Money Dynamics*. New York: Simon & Schuster, 1985.

Planning may be devoted to a specific topic, such as retirement. For instance, see

Hakala, Donald, and Michael M. Delaney. *Financial Planning for Retirement*. Newton, Mass.: Allyn and Bacon, 1983.

Leonetti, Michael E. "Retirement Planning: A Step-by-Step Approach." *AAII Journal* (April 1986): 17–22.

The American Association of Individual Investors (AAII), in conjunction with the accounting firm Deloitte, Haskins & Sells, annually publishes a personal tax and financial planning guide. For information, write the association at 612 North Michigan Avenue, Chicago, IL 60611.

A SHORT CASE STUDY FOR CHAPTER 27
Goals and Portfolio Selection

William Galleher is a very successful self-employed freelance writer of romantic novels. He has a reputation for writing rapidly and is able to complete at least six books a year, which net after expenses $10,000 to $15,000 per book per year. With this much income, Galleher is concerned with both sheltering income from taxes and planning for retirement. Currently he is 40 years old, he is married, and his only child is entering high school. Galleher anticipates sending the child to a quality college to pursue a degree in computer sciences.

While Galleher is intelligent and well informed, he knows very little about finance and investments other than general background material he has used in his novels. Since he does not plan to write prolifically into the indefinite future, he has decided to obtain help in financial planning from Steven Raysor, a certified financial planner (CFP). Raysor had served as an accountant and financial advisor before becoming a financial planner. In his present position he specializes in retirement and estate planning.

At their first meeting, Raysor suggested that Galleher establish a tax-sheltered retirement plan and consider making a gift to his child, perhaps in the form of future royalties from a book in progress. Both of these ideas intrigued Galleher, who thought that funds were saved, then invested to accumulate over time, and then transferred to heirs after death. While Galleher wanted to pursue both ideas, he thought approaching one at a time made more sense and decided to work on the retirement plan first. He asked Raysor for several alternative courses of action. Raysor offered the following possibilities:

1. An IRA with a bank with the funds deposited in a variable rate account.
2. A self-directed Keogh account with a major brokerage firm.
3. A Keogh account with a major mutual fund.
4. An account with a brokerage firm to accumulate common stocks with substantial growth potential but little current income.

Galleher could not immediately grasp the implications of these alternatives and asked Raysor to clarify several points:

1. What assets would be owned under each alternative?
2. What are the current and future tax obligations associated with each choice?
3. What amount of control would he have over the assets in the accounts?
4. How much personal supervision would be required?

If you were Raysor, how would you reply to each question? Which course(s) of action would you suggest that Galleher pursue?

How would each of the following alter Raysor's advice?

1. Galleher's wife is not employed and has a record of poor health.

2. Galleher would like to write less and perhaps teach creative writing at a local college.

3. Galleher has expensive tastes and finds saving to be difficult.

Appendix A The Future Sum of One Dollar

$$P_o(1 + i)^n = P_n \qquad \text{Interest factor} = (1 + i)^n$$

Period	1%	2%	3%	4%	5%	6%	7%
1	1.010	1.020	1.030	1.040	1.050	1.060	1.070
2	1.020	1.040	1.061	1.082	1.102	1.124	1.145
3	1.030	1.061	1.093	1.125	1.158	1.191	1.225
4	1.041	1.082	1.126	1.170	1.216	1.262	1.311
5	1.051	1.104	1.159	1.217	1.276	1.338	1.403
6	1.062	1.126	1.194	1.265	1.340	1.419	1.501
7	1.072	1.149	1.230	1.316	1.407	1.504	1.606
8	1.083	1.172	1.267	1.369	1.477	1.594	1.718
9	1.094	1.195	1.305	1.423	1.551	1.689	1.838
10	1.105	1.219	1.344	1.480	1.629	1.791	1.967
11	1.116	1.243	1.384	1.539	1.710	1.898	2.105
12	1.127	1.268	1.426	1.601	1.796	2.012	2.252
13	1.138	1.294	1.469	1.665	1.886	2.133	2.410
14	1.149	1.319	1.513	1.732	1.980	2.261	2.579
15	1.161	1.346	1.558	1.801	2.079	2.397	2.759
16	1.173	1.373	1.605	1.873	2.183	2.540	2.952
17	1.184	1.400	1.653	1.948	2.292	2.693	3.159
18	1.196	1.428	1.702	2.026	2.407	2.854	3.380
19	1.208	1.457	1.754	2.107	2.527	3.026	3.617
20	1.220	1.486	1.806	2.191	2.653	3.207	3.870
25	1.282	1.641	2.094	2.666	3.386	4.292	5.427
30	1.348	1.811	2.427	3.243	4.322	5.743	7.612

Appendix A   The Future Sum of One Dollar *(Continued)*

Period	8%	9%	10%	12%	14%	15%	16%
1	1.080	1.090	1.100	1.120	1.140	1.150	1.160
2	1.166	1.188	1.210	1.254	1.300	1.322	1.346
3	1.260	1.295	1.331	1.405	1.482	1.521	1.561
4	1.360	1.412	1.464	1.574	1.689	1.749	1.811
5	1.469	1.539	1.611	1.762	1.925	2.011	2.100
6	1.587	1.677	1.772	1.974	2.195	2.313	2.436
7	1.714	1.828	1.949	2.211	2.502	2.660	2.826
8	1.851	1.993	2.144	2.476	2.853	3.059	3.278
9	1.999	2.172	2.358	2.773	3.252	3.518	3.803
10	2.159	2.367	2.594	3.106	3.707	4.046	4.411
11	2.332	2.580	2.853	3.479	4.226	4.652	5.117
12	2.518	2.813	3.138	3.896	4.818	5.350	5.936
13	2.720	3.066	3.452	4.363	5.492	6.153	6.886
14	2.937	3.342	3.797	4.887	6.261	7.076	7.988
15	3.172	3.642	4.177	5.474	7.138	8.137	9.266
16	3.426	3.970	4.595	6.130	8.137	9.358	10.748
17	3.700	4.328	5.054	6.866	9.276	10.761	12.468
18	3.996	4.717	5.560	7.690	10.575	12.375	14.463
19	4.316	5.142	6.116	8.613	12.056	14.232	16.777
20	4.661	5.604	6.728	9.646	13.743	16.367	19.461
25	6.848	8.623	10.835	17.000	26.462	32.919	40.874
30	10.063	13.268	17.449	29.960	50.950	66.212	85.850

Appendix B   The Present Value of One Dollar

$$P_o = \frac{P_n}{(1 + i)^n} \qquad \text{Interest factor} = \frac{1}{(1 + i)^n}$$

Period	1%	2%	3%	4%	5%	6%	7%	8%	9%	10%	12%	14%	15%
1	0.990	0.980	0.971	0.962	0.952	0.943	0.935	0.926	0.917	0.909	0.893	0.877	0.870
2	0.980	0.961	0.943	0.925	0.907	0.890	0.873	0.857	0.842	0.826	0.797	0.769	0.756
3	0.971	0.942	0.915	0.889	0.864	0.840	0.816	0.794	0.772	0.751	0.712	0.675	0.658
4	0.961	0.924	0.889	0.855	0.823	0.792	0.763	0.735	0.708	0.683	0.636	0.592	0.572
5	0.951	0.906	0.863	0.822	0.784	0.747	0.713	0.681	0.650	0.621	0.567	0.519	0.497
6	0.942	0.888	0.838	0.790	0.746	0.705	0.666	0.630	0.596	0.564	0.507	0.456	0.432
7	0.933	0.871	0.813	0.760	0.711	0.665	0.623	0.583	0.547	0.513	0.452	0.400	0.376
8	0.923	0.853	0.789	0.731	0.677	0.627	0.582	0.540	0.502	0.467	0.404	0.351	0.327
9	0.914	0.837	0.766	0.703	0.645	0.592	0.544	0.500	0.460	0.424	0.361	0.308	0.284
10	0.905	0.820	0.744	0.676	0.614	0.558	0.508	0.463	0.422	0.386	0.322	0.270	0.247
11	0.896	0.804	0.722	0.650	0.585	0.527	0.475	0.429	0.388	0.350	0.287	0.237	0.215
12	0.887	0.788	0.701	0.625	0.557	0.497	0.444	0.397	0.356	0.319	0.257	0.208	0.187
13	0.879	0.773	0.681	0.601	0.530	0.469	0.415	0.368	0.326	0.290	0.229	0.182	0.163
14	0.870	0.758	0.661	0.577	0.505	0.442	0.388	0.340	0.299	0.263	0.205	0.160	0.141
15	0.861	0.743	0.642	0.555	0.481	0.417	0.362	0.315	0.275	0.239	0.183	0.140	0.123
16	0.853	0.728	0.623	0.534	0.458	0.394	0.339	0.292	0.252	0.218	0.163	0.123	0.107
17	0.844	0.714	0.605	0.513	0.436	0.371	0.317	0.270	0.231	0.198	0.146	0.108	0.093
18	0.836	0.700	0.587	0.494	0.416	0.350	0.296	0.250	0.212	0.180	0.130	0.095	0.081
19	0.828	0.686	0.570	0.475	0.396	0.331	0.276	0.232	0.194	0.164	0.116	0.083	0.070
20	0.820	0.673	0.554	0.456	0.377	0.312	0.258	0.215	0.178	0.149	0.104	0.073	0.061
25	0.780	0.610	0.478	0.375	0.295	0.233	0.184	0.146	0.116	0.092	0.059	0.038	0.030
30	0.742	0.552	0.412	0.308	0.231	0.174	0.131	0.099	0.075	0.057	0.033	0.020	0.015

Appendix B The Present Value of One Dollar (Continued)

Period	16%	18%	20%	24%	28%	32%	36%	40%	50%	60%	70%	80%	90%
1	0.862	0.847	0.833	0.806	0.781	0.758	0.735	0.714	0.667	0.625	0.588	0.556	0.526
2	0.743	0.718	0.694	0.650	0.610	0.574	0.541	0.510	0.444	0.391	0.346	0.309	0.277
3	0.641	0.609	0.579	0.524	0.477	0.435	0.398	0.364	0.296	0.244	0.204	0.171	0.146
4	0.552	0.516	0.482	0.423	0.373	0.329	0.292	0.260	0.198	0.153	0.120	0.095	0.077
5	0.476	0.437	0.402	0.341	0.291	0.250	0.215	0.186	0.132	0.095	0.070	0.053	0.040
6	0.410	0.370	0.335	0.275	0.227	0.189	0.158	0.133	0.088	0.060	0.041	0.029	0.021
7	0.354	0.314	0.279	0.222	0.178	0.143	0.116	0.095	0.059	0.037	0.024	0.016	0.011
8	0.305	0.266	0.233	0.179	0.139	0.108	0.085	0.068	0.039	0.023	0.014	0.009	0.006
9	0.263	0.226	0.194	0.144	0.108	0.082	0.063	0.048	0.026	0.015	0.008	0.005	0.003
10	0.227	0.191	0.162	0.116	0.085	0.062	0.046	0.035	0.017	0.009	0.005	0.003	0.002
11	0.195	0.162	0.135	0.094	0.066	0.047	0.034	0.025	0.012	0.006	0.003	0.002	0.001
12	0.168	0.137	0.112	0.076	0.052	0.036	0.025	0.018	0.008	0.004	0.002	0.001	0.001
13	0.145	0.116	0.093	0.061	0.040	0.027	0.018	0.013	0.005	0.002	0.001	0.001	0.000
14	0.125	0.099	0.078	0.049	0.032	0.021	0.014	0.009	0.003	0.001	0.001	0.000	0.000
15	0.108	0.084	0.065	0.040	0.025	0.016	0.010	0.006	0.002	0.001	0.000	0.000	0.000
16	0.093	0.071	0.054	0.032	0.019	0.012	0.007	0.005	0.002	0.001	0.000	0.000	0.001
17	0.080	0.060	0.045	0.026	0.015	0.009	0.005	0.003	0.001	0.000	0.000		0.001
18	0.069	0.051	0.038	0.021	0.012	0.007	0.004	0.002	0.001	0.000	0.000		0.000
19	0.060	0.043	0.031	0.017	0.009	0.005	0.003	0.002	0.000	0.000			0.000
20	0.051	0.037	0.026	0.014	0.007	0.004	0.002	0.001	0.000	0.000			0.000
25	0.024	0.016	0.010	0.005	0.002	0.001	0.000	0.000					
30	0.012	0.007	0.004	0.002	0.001	0.000	0.000	0.000					

Appendix C　The Future Sum of an Annuity of One Dollar for N Periods

$$CS = I(1 + i)^0 + I(1 + i)^1 + \cdots + I(1 + i)^{n-1} \qquad \text{Interest factor} = \sum_{t=1}^{n} (1 + i)^{n-t}$$

Period	1%	2%	3%	4%	5%	6%
1	1.000	1.000	1.000	1.000	1.000	1.000
2	2.010	2.020	2.030	2.040	2.050	2.060
3	3.030	3.060	3.091	3.122	3.152	3.184
4	4.060	4.122	4.184	4.246	4.310	4.375
5	5.101	5.204	5.309	5.416	5.526	5.637
6	6.152	6.308	6.468	6.633	6.802	6.975
7	7.214	7.434	7.662	7.898	8.142	8.394
8	8.286	8.583	8.892	9.214	9.549	9.897
9	9.369	9.755	10.159	10.583	11.027	11.491
10	10.462	10.950	11.464	12.006	12.578	13.181
11	11.567	12.169	12.808	13.486	14.207	14.972
12	12.683	13.412	14.192	15.026	15.917	16.870
13	13.809	14.680	15.618	16.627	17.713	18.882
14	14.947	15.974	17.086	18.292	19.599	21.051
15	16.097	17.293	18.599	20.024	21.579	23.276
16	17.258	18.639	20.157	21.825	23.657	25.673
17	18.430	20.012	21.762	23.698	25.840	28.213
18	19.615	21.412	23.414	25.645	28.132	30.906
19	20.811	22.841	25.117	27.671	30.539	33.760
20	22.019	24.297	26.870	29.778	33.066	36.786
25	28.243	32.030	36.459	41.646	47.727	54.865
30	34.785	40.568	47.575	56.085	66.439	79.058

Appendix C   The Future Sum of an Annuity of One Dollar for N Periods (*Continued*)

Period	7%	8%	9%	10%	12%	14%
1	1.000	1.000	1.000	1.000	1.000	1.000
2	2.070	2.080	2.090	2.100	2.120	2.140
3	3.215	3.246	3.278	3.310	3.374	3.440
4	4.440	4.506	4.573	4.641	4.770	4.921
5	5.751	5.867	5.985	6.105	6.353	6.610
6	7.153	7.336	7.523	7.716	8.115	8.536
7	8.654	8.923	9.200	9.487	10.089	10.730
8	10.260	10.637	11.028	11.436	12.300	13.233
9	11.978	12.488	13.021	13.579	14.776	16.085
10	13.816	14.487	15.193	15.937	17.549	19.337
11	15.784	16.645	17.560	18.531	20.655	23.044
12	17.888	18.977	20.141	21.384	24.138	27.271
13	20.141	21.495	22.953	24.523	28.029	32.089
14	22.550	24.215	26.019	27.975	32.393	37.581
15	25.129	27.152	29.361	31.772	37.280	43.842
16	27.888	30.324	33.003	35.950	42.753	50.980
17	30.840	33.750	36.974	40.545	48.884	59.118
18	33.999	37.450	41.301	45.599	55.750	68.394
19	37.379	41.446	46.018	51.159	63.440	78.969
20	40.995	45.762	51.160	57.275	72.052	91.025
25	63.249	73.106	84.701	98.347	133.334	181.871
30	94.461	113.283	136.308	164.494	241.333	356.787

Appendix D The Present Value of an Annuity of One Dollar

$$PV = \sum_{t=1}^{n} \frac{1}{(1+i)^t} \qquad \text{Interest factor} = \sum_{t=1}^{n} \frac{1}{(1+i)^t}$$

Period	1%	2%	3%	4%	5%	6%	7%	8%	9%	10%
1	0.990	0.980	0.971	0.962	0.952	0.943	0.935	0.926	0.917	0.909
2	1.970	1.942	1.913	1.886	1.859	1.833	1.808	1.783	1.759	1.736
3	2.941	2.884	2.829	2.775	2.723	2.673	2.624	2.577	2.531	2.487
4	3.902	3.808	3.717	3.630	3.546	3.465	3.387	3.312	3.240	3.170
5	4.853	4.713	4.580	4.452	4.329	4.212	4.100	3.993	3.890	3.791
6	5.795	5.601	5.417	5.242	5.076	4.917	4.766	4.623	4.486	4.355
7	6.728	6.472	6.230	6.002	5.786	5.582	5.389	5.206	5.033	4.868
8	7.652	7.325	7.020	6.733	6.463	6.210	5.971	5.747	5.535	5.335
9	8.566	8.162	7.786	7.435	7.108	6.802	6.515	6.247	5.985	5.759
10	9.471	8.983	8.530	8.111	7.722	7.360	7.024	6.710	6.418	6.145
11	10.368	9.787	9.253	8.760	8.306	7.887	7.499	7.139	6.805	6.495
12	11.255	10.575	9.954	9.385	8.863	8.384	7.943	7.536	7.161	6.814
13	12.134	11.348	10.635	9.986	9.394	8.853	8.358	7.904	7.487	7.103
14	13.004	12.106	11.296	10.563	9.899	9.295	8.745	8.244	7.786	7.367
15	13.865	12.849	11.938	11.118	10.380	9.712	9.108	8.559	8.060	7.606
16	14.718	13.578	12.561	11.652	10.838	10.106	9.447	8.851	8.312	7.824
17	15.562	14.292	13.166	12.166	11.274	10.477	9.763	9.122	8.544	8.022
18	16.398	14.992	13.754	12.659	11.690	10.828	10.059	9.372	8.756	8.201
19	17.226	15.678	14.324	13.134	12.085	11.158	10.336	9.604	8.950	8.365
20	18.046	16.351	14.877	13.590	12.462	11.470	10.594	9.818	9.128	8.514
25	22.023	19.523	17.413	15.622	14.094	12.783	11.654	10.675	9.823	9.077
30	25.808	22.397	19.600	17.292	15.373	13.765	12.409	11.258	10.274	9.427

Appendix D   The Present Value of an Annuity of One Dollar (*Continued*)

Period	12%	14%	16%	18%	20%	24%	28%	32%	36%
1	0.893	0.877	0.862	0.847	0.833	0.806	0.781	0.758	0.735
2	1.690	1.647	1.605	1.566	1.528	1.457	1.392	1.332	1.276
3	2.402	2.322	2.246	2.174	2.106	1.981	1.868	1.766	1.674
4	3.037	2.914	2.798	2.690	2.589	2.404	2.241	2.096	1.966
5	3.605	3.433	3.274	3.127	2.991	2.745	2.532	2.345	2.181
6	4.111	3.889	3.685	3.498	3.326	3.020	2.759	2.534	2.339
7	4.564	4.288	4.039	3.812	3.605	3.242	2.937	2.678	2.455
8	4.968	4.639	4.344	4.078	3.837	3.421	3.076	2.786	2.540
9	5.328	4.946	4.607	4.303	4.031	3.566	3.184	2.868	2.603
10	5.650	5.216	4.833	4.494	4.193	3.682	3.269	2.930	2.650
11	5.988	5.453	5.029	4.656	4.327	3.776	3.335	2.978	2.683
12	6.194	5.660	5.197	4.793	4.439	3.851	3.387	3.013	2.708
13	6.424	5.842	5.342	4.910	4.533	3.912	3.427	3.040	2.727
14	6.628	6.002	5.468	5.008	4.611	3.962	3.459	3.061	2.740
15	6.811	6.142	5.575	5.092	4.675	4.001	3.483	3.076	2.750
16	6.974	6.265	5.669	5.162	4.730	4.033	3.503	3.088	2.758
17	7.120	6.373	5.749	5.222	4.775	4.059	3.518	3.097	2.763
18	7.250	6.467	5.818	5.273	4.812	4.080	3.529	3.104	2.767
19	7.366	6.550	5.877	5.316	4.844	4.097	3.539	3.109	2.770
20	7.469	6.623	5.929	5.353	4.870	4.110	3.546	3.113	2.772
25	7.843	6.873	6.097	5.467	4.948	4.147	3.564	3.122	2.776
30	8.055	7.003	6.177	5.517	4.979	4.160	3.569	3.124	2.778

Glossary

accelerated depreciation the writing off of plant and equipment in such a way that most of the cost is recovered in the early years of an asset's life (chapter 5).

account receivable an account that arises from credit sales and has not been collected (chapter 7).

accrued interest interest that has been earned but not received (chapter 9).

acid test current assets excluding inventory divided by current liabilities; a measure of liquidity (chapter 17).

ADRs American Depository Receipts; receipts issued for foreign securities held by a trustee (chapter 26).

AMEX American Stock Exchange (chapter 3).

annual report a financial report sent yearly to a publicly held firm's stockholders (chapter 4).

annuity a series of equal annual payments (chapter 6).

annuity due a series of equal annual payments with the payments made at the beginning of the year (chapter 6).

anticipation note a short-term liability that is to be retired by specific expected revenues (e.g., expected tax receipts) (chapter 12).

arbitrage the simultaneous buying and selling of an asset in two markets to take advantage of price differences (chapter 19).

arrearage cumulative preferred dividends that have not been paid (chapter 11).

assay a process by which metallic content is determined (chapter 24).

assets what a firm or individual owns (chapter 7).

auditor's opinion the opinion of the certified public accountant who analyzes a firm's financial statements for their conformity to generally accepted accounting principles (chapter 7).

average collection period the number of days required to collect accounts receivable (chapter 17).

balance sheet a financial statement that enumerates at a point in time what an economic unit owns and owes and its net worth or equity (chapter 7).

balloon payment the large final payment necessary to retire a debt issue (chapter 9).

bar graph a graph indicating the high, low, and closing prices of a security (chapter 18).

Barron's confidence index an index designed to identify investors' confidence in the level and direction of security prices (chapter 18).

bearer bond a bond with coupons attached or a bond whose possession denotes ownership (chapter 9).

bearish expecting that prices will decline (chapter 3).

best efforts agreement an agreement with an investment banker who does not guarantee the sale of a security but who agrees to make the best effort to sell it (chapter 2).

beta coefficient an index of risk; a measure of the systematic risk associated with a particular stock (chapter 8).

bid and ask prices at which a security dealer offers to buy and sell stock (chapter 3).

"big board" the New York Stock Exchange (chapter 3).

bond a long-term liability with a specified amount of interest and specified maturity date (chapter 9).

book value a firm's total assets minus its total liabilities; equity or net worth (chapter 7).

broker an agent who handles buy and sell orders for an investor (chapter 3).

bullish expecting that prices will rise (chapter 3).

business risk the risk associated with the nature of the business (chapter 1).

buy, sell, or hold a brokerage firm's recommendations as to investment strategy for a particular security (chapter 4).

bylaws a document specifying the relationship between a corporation and its stockholders (chapter 14).

call option an option sold by an individual that entitles the buyer to purchase stock at a specified price within a specified time period (chapter 20).

call feature the right of an issuer to retire a debt issue prior to maturity (chapter 9).

call penalty a premium paid for exercising a call feature (chapter 9).

Canadian Maple Leaf a Canadian gold coin issued in units of one troy ounce of gold (chapter 24).

capital asset pricing model (CAPM) a risk-adjusted valuation model that may be applied to corporate stock (chapter 14).

capital gain an increase in the value of a capital asset such as a stock (chapters 1, 5).

capital loss a decrease in the value of an asset such as a stock or a bond (chapter 5).

cash budget a financial statement enumerating cash receipts and cash disbursements (chapter 27).

CBOE Chicago Board Options Exchange; the first organized secondary market in puts and calls (chapter 20).

certificate of deposit (CD) a time deposit with a specified maturity date (chapter 2).

certificate of incorporation a document creating a corporation (chapter 14).

charter a document specifying the relationship between a firm and the state in which it is incorporated (chapter 14).

closed-end investment company an investment company with a fixed number of shares that are bought and sold in the secondary security markets (chapter 22).

commercial paper unsecured short-term promissory notes issued by the most creditworthy corporations (chapter 2).

commissions fees charged by brokers for executing orders (chapter 3).

common stock a security representing ownership in a corporation (chapter 14).

compounding the process by which interest is paid on interest that has been previously earned (chapter 6).

condominium an apartment that is owned instead of rented (chapter 25).

confirmation statement a statement received from a brokerage firm detailing the sale or purchase of a security and specifying a settlement date (chapters 3, 9).

consolidated balance sheet a parent company's balance sheet, which summarizes and combines the balance sheets of the firm's various subsidiaries (chapter 7).

conventional mortgage loan a standard loan to finance real estate (and secured by the property) in which the loan is periodically retired and the interest paid is figured on the declining balance owed (chapter 25).

convertible bond a bond that may be exchanged for (i.e., converted into) common stock (chapters 9, 21).

convertible preferred stock preferred stock that may be exchanged for (i.e., converted into) common stock (chapter 21).

cost of debt the interest rate paid adjusted for any tax savings (chapter 25).

coupon rate the specified interest rate or amount of interest paid by a bond (chapter 9).

coupon bond a bond with coupons attached that are removed and presented for payment of interest when due (chapter 9).

covered option an option for which the seller owns the securities (chapter 20).

covering the purchase of securities or commodities to close a short position (chapter 19).

credit rating systems classification schemes designed to indicate the risk associated with a particular security (chapter 9).

creative financing the use of nonconventional mortgages to finance the acquisition of real estate (chapter 25).

cross-sectional analysis an analysis of several firms in the same industry at a point in time (chapter 17).

cumulative preferred stock a preferred stock whose dividends accumulate if they are not paid (chapter 11).

cumulative voting a voting scheme that encourages minority representation by permitting the stockholder to cast all of his or her votes for one candidate for the firm's board of directors (chapter 14).

currency futures contract for the future delivery of foreign exchange (chapter 23).

current asset an asset that should be converted into cash within 12 months (chapter 7).

current liability a liability that has to be paid within the next 12 months (chapter 7).

current ratio current assets divided by current liabilities; a measure of liquidity (chapter 17).

current yield annual income divided by the current price of the security; annual return (chapters 9, 10).

cyclical industry an industry whose sales and profits are sensitive to changes in the level of economic activity (chapter 16).

daily limit the maximum daily change permitted in a commodity future's price (chapter 23).

daily range the maximum daily range permitted in a commodity future's price (chapter 23).

date of record the day on which an investor must own shares in order to receive the dividend payment (chapter 15).

day order an order placed with a broker that is canceled at the end of the day if it is not executed (chapter 3).

dealers over-the-counter market makers who buy and sell securities for their own accounts (chapter 3).

debenture an unsecured bond (chapter 9).

debt ratio the ratio of debt to total assets; a measure of the use of debt financing (chapter 17).

default the failure of a debtor to meet any term of a debt's indenture (chapter 9).

deficit spending government expenditures exceeding government revenues (chapter 16).

depreciation the allocation or writing off of the cost of a fixed asset over a period of time (chapter 7).

devaluation a decrease in the value of one currency relative to other currencies (chapter 26).

dilution a reduction in earnings per share due to the issuing of new securities (chapter 15).

director a person who is elected by stockholders to determine the goals and policies of the firm (chapter 14).

discount the sale of anything below its stated value (chapter 9).

discount (from net asset value) the extent to which the price of a closed-end investment company's stock sells below its net asset value (chapter 22).

discount broker a broker who charges lower commissions on security purchases and sales (chapter 3).

discount bond a bond that is sold for less than its face amount or principal (chapter 10).

discounting the process of determining present value (chapter 6).

discount rate the rate of interest charged by the Federal Reserve when banks borrow reserves from the Fed (chapter 16).

dispersion deviation from the average (chapter 8).

distribution date the day on which a dividend is paid to stockholders (chapter 15).

diversification the process of accumulating different securities to reduce the risk of loss (chapter 8).

dividend a payment to stockholders that is usually in cash but may be in stock or property (chapter 15).

dividend-growth valuation model a valuation model that deals with dividends and their growth properly discounted back to the present (chapter 14).

dividend reinvestment plan a plan that permits stockholders to have cash dividends reinvested in stock instead of received in cash (chapter 15).

dollar cost averaging the purchase of securities at different intervals to reduce the impact of price fluctuations (chapter 13).

Dow Jones industrial average an average of the stock prices of 30 industrial firms (chapter 13).

Dow theory a technical approach based on the Dow Jones averages (chapter 18).

duration the average time it takes to collect a bond's interest and principal repayment (chapter 10).

earnings per preferred share the total earnings divided by the number of preferred shares outstanding (chapter 11).

earnings per share (EPS) the total earnings available to common stock divided by the number of common shares outstanding (chapter 7).

efficient market hypothesis a theory that security prices correctly measure the firm's future earnings and dividends (chapter 8).

efficient portfolio the portfolio that offers the highest expected return for a given amount of risk (chapter 8).

8-K report a document filed with the SEC that describes a change in a firm that may affect the value of its securities (chapter 4).

EPS earnings per share (chapter 7).

equilibrium price a price that equates supply and demand (chapter 3).

equipment trust certificate a serial bond secured by specific equipment (chapter 9).

equity assets minus liabilities; net worth; investment in a firm by its stockholders (chapter 7).

equity trust a real estate investment trust that specializes in acquiring real estate for subsequent rental income (chapter 25).

estate tax a tax on the value of a deceased individual's assets (chapter 5).

Euro-bonds bonds denominated in American dollars but issued abroad (chapter 26).

exchange rate the price of a foreign currency in terms of another currency (chapter 26).

ex dividend stock that trades exclusive of any dividend payment (chapter 15).

ex dividend date the day on which a stock trades exclusive of any dividends (chapter 15).

exercise price (strike price) the price at which the investor may buy or sell stock through an option (chapter 19).

expected return the sum of the anticipated dividend yield and capital gains (chapter 8).

expiration date the date by which an option must be exercised (chapter 19).

extra dividend a dividend that is in addition to the firm's regular dividend (chapter 15).

face amount the amount of a debt; the principal (chapter 9).

federal agency bonds debt issued by agencies of the federal government (chapter 12).

Federal Deposit Insurance Corporation(FDIC) a federal government agency that supervises commercial banks and insures commercial bank deposits (chapter 2).

Federal Housing Administration (FHA) an agency of the federal government that will insure mortgages granted to qualified recipients (chapter 25).

Federal Reserve the central bank of the United States (chapter 16).

financial futures contract for the future delivery of a financial asset (chapter 23).

financial intermediary a financial institution such as a commercial bank that borrows from one group and lends to another (chapter 2).

financial leverage the use of borrowed funds to acquire an asset; the use of debt financing (chapter 14).

financial plan the programs designed to meet financial goals (chapter 27).

financial risk the risk associated with a firm's sources of financing (chapter 1).

fiscal policy taxation, expenditures, and debt management of the federal government (chapter 16).

fixed asset turnover ratio of sales to fixed assets; tells how many fixed assets are needed to generate sales (chapter 17).

fixed flow of income the annual flow of interest paid by a bond; the coupon (chapter 10).

flat a description of a bond that trades without accrued interest (chapter 9).

forecasting the process of predicting the future (chapter 16).

foreign exchange market market for the buying and selling of currencies (chapter 26).

foreign exchange rate the price of foreign moneys or currencies (chapter 26).

401(k) plan See Supplementary retirement account.

full disclosure laws the federal and state laws requiring publicly held firms to disclose financial and other information that may affect the value of their securities (chapter 3).

future sum of an annuity compound value of a series of equal annual payments (chapter 6).

futures contract an agreement for the future delivery of a commodity at a specified date (chapter 23).

futures price the price for a contract for the future delivery of a commodity (chapter 23).

general obligation bond a bond whose interest does not depend on the revenue of a specific project; government bonds supported by the full faith and credit of the issuer (chapter 12).

Ginnie Mae mortgage pass-through bond issued by the Government National Mortgage Association (chapter 12).

global funds mutual funds whose portfolio includes securities of firms with international operations that are located throughout the world (chapter 26).

good-till-canceled order an order placed with a broker that remains in effect until it is executed by the broker or canceled by the investor (chapter 3).

graduated-payment mortgage loan a mortgage loan in which the periodic payments rise over time (chapter 25).

growth stock the shares of a company whose earnings are expected to grow at an above average rate (chapter 22).

head-and-shoulder pattern a tool of technical analysis; a pattern of security prices that resembles a head and a shoulder (chapter 18).

hedging simultaneous buying and selling to reduce risk (chapters 19, 20, 23).

hidden asset an asset that has appreciated in value but is carried on the balance sheet at a lower value such as its acquisition cost (chapter 7).

holding period return income plus price appreciation during a specified time period; this total return divided by the cost of the investment (chapter 13).

improved land land that has been cleared or that includes improvements such as curbs, gutters, or buildings (chapter 25).

income the flow of money or its equivalent produced by an asset; dividends and interest (chapter 1).

income bond a bond whose interest is paid only if it is earned by the firm (chapter 9).

income-in-kind nonmonetary income, such as services received instead of cash (chapter 24).

income statement a financial statement that summarizes revenues and expenses for a specified time period; a statement of profit or loss (chapter 7).

indenture the document that specifies the terms of a bond issue (chapter 9).

individual retirement account   see IRA

inefficient portfolio   a portfolio whose return is not maximized given the level of risk (chapter 8).

index fund   a mutual fund whose portfolio seeks to duplicate an index of stock prices (chapter 22).

inheritance tax   a tax on what an individual receives from an estate (chapter 5).

inside information   privileged information concerning a firm (chapter 4).

interest   payment for the use of money (chapter 9).

interest rate risk   the uncertainty associated with changes in interest rates; the possibility of loss resulting from increases in interest rates (chapter 1).

internal rate of return   the discount rate that equates the cost of an investment with the cash flows generated by the investment (chapter 13).

international funds   American mutual funds whose portfolios are limited to non-American firms (chapter 26).

intrinsic value   what an asset is worth (chapter 19).

intrinsic value as debt   a convertible bond's value if it lacked the conversion feature (chapter 21).

intrinsic value as stock   the value of stock embodied in a convertible bond (chapter 21).

inventory   raw materials, goods-in-process, and finished goods; what a firm has available to sell (chapter 7).

inventory turnover   the speed with which inventory is sold (chapter 17).

investment (in economics)   the purchase of plant, equipment, or inventory (chapter 1, 7).

investment (in lay terms)   acquisition of an asset such as a stock or a bond (chapter 1).

investment banker   an underwriter; a firm that sells new issues of securities to the general public (chapter 2).

investment club   a club whose members make contributions for the purpose of investing (chapter 4).

investment tax credit   a direct reduction in taxes owed resulting from investment in plant or equipment (chapter 5).

investments (on balance sheet)   corporate securities (e.g., stock) held by a firm (chapter 7).

IRA   a retirement plan that is available to workers (chapter 5).

irregular dividends   dividend payments that either do not occur in regular intervals or vary in amount (chapter 15).

Keogh account (HR-10 plan)   a retirement plan that is available to self-employed individuals (chapter 5).

leverage   magnification of the potential return on an investment (chapter 19).

liabilities   what an economic unit owes (chapter 7).

limit order   an order placed with a broker to buy or sell at a specified price (chapter 3).

liquidation   the process of converting assets into cash; dissolving a corporation (chapter 15).

liquidity   moneyness; the ease with which assets can be converted into cash with little risk of loss of principal (chapter 1).

listed security   a security that is traded on an organized exchange (chapter 3).

load fund   a mutual fund that charges a fee to purchase its shares (chapter 22).

long position   owning assets for their income or possible price appreciation (chapters 3, 19, 23).

long-term asset   an asset that is expected to last (or to be held) for more than one year, such as plant and equipment (chapter 7).

long-term debt   debt that becomes due after more than one year (chapter 7).

long-term liability   an obligation that is due to be retired after the fiscal year (chapter 7).

M-1   sum of demand deposits, coins, and currency (chapter 16).

M-2   sum of demand deposits, coins, currency, and savings accounts at banks (chapter 16).

maintenance margin   the minimum level of funds in a margin account that triggers a margin call (chapter 23).

margin the amount that an investor must put down to buy securities on credit (chapter 3); the good faith deposit made when purchasing or selling a commodity contract (chapter 23).

margin call a request by a broker for an investor to place additional funds or securities in an account as collateral against borrowed funds or as a good faith deposit (chapter 23).

marginal tax rate the tax rate paid on an additional last dollar of taxable income; an individual's tax bracket (chapter 5).

marketability the ease with which an asset may be bought and sold (chapter 1).

market order an order to buy or sell at the current market price or quote (chapter 3).

market risk systematic risk; the risk associated with the tendency of a stock's price to fluctuate with the market (chapter 1).

maturity date the time at which a debt issue becomes due and the principal must be repaid (chapter 9).

money market instruments short-term securities such as treasury bills, negotiable certificates of deposit, or commercial paper (chapter 2).

money market mutual fund a mutual fund that specializes in short-term securities (chapter 2).

moral backing nonobligatory support for a debt issue (chapter 12).

mortgage bond a bond that is secured by property (chapter 9).

mortgage trust a real estate investment trust that specializes in loans secured by real estate (chapter 25).

moving average an average in which the most recent observation is added and the most distant observation is deleted before the average is recomputed (chapter 18).

municipal bond a tax-exempt bond; a bond issued by a state or one of its political subdivisions (chapter 12).

mutual fund an open-end investment company (chapter 22).

naked option an option that is sold for which the seller does not own the underlying securities (chapter 20).

naked option writing the selling (i.e., writing) of an option without owning the underlying security (chapter 20).

NASDAQ National Association of Security Dealers Automatic Quotation system; quotation system for over-the-counter securities (chapter 3).

negotiable certificate of deposit a certificate of deposit in which the rate and the term are individually negotiated between the bank and the lender and which may be bought and sold (chapters 2, 22).

net asset value the asset value of a share in an investment company; total assets minus total liabilities quantity divided by the number of shares outstanding (chapter 22).

net profit margin the ratio of earnings after interest and taxes to sales (chapter 17).

New York Stock Exchange (NYSE) the largest organized exchange; market for the purchase and sale of listed securities (chapter 3).

no-load fund a mutual fund that does not charge a fee for buying or selling its shares (chapter 22).

noncumulative preferred stock preferred stock whose dividends do not accumulate if the firm misses a dividend payment (chapter 11).

NOW account a bank account that earns interest and against which negotiable orders of withdrawal may be written (chapter 2).

NYSE composite index New York Stock Exchange index; an index of prices of all the stocks listed on the New York Stock Exchange (chapter 13).

odd lot a unit of trading that is smaller than the general unit of sale, such as 22 shares (chapter 3).

odd lot theory a technical approach to the stock market that purports to predict security prices on the basis of odd lot sales and purchases (chapter 18).

open-end investment company a mutual fund; an investment company from which investors buy shares and to which they resell them (chapter 22).

open interest the number of futures contracts in existence for a particular commodity (chapter 23).

open market operations the buying and selling of government securities by the Federal Reserve (chapter 16).

operating profit margin percentage earned on sales before deducting interest expense and taxes (chapter 17).

option the right to buy or sell something at a specified price within a specified time period (chapter 19).

ordinary annuity a series of equal periodic payments in which the payments are made at the end of each time period (chapter 6).

organized exchange a formal market for buying and selling securities or commodities (chapter 3).

originating house an investment banker that makes an agreement with a firm to sell a new issue and that forms the syndicate to sell the securities (chapter 2).

over-the-counter market (OTC) the informal secondary market for unlisted securities (chapter 3).

paper profits price appreciation that has not been realized (chapter 5).

partnership an unincorporated business owned by two or more individuals (chapter 25).

payout ratio the ratio of dividends to earnings (chapter 15).

P/E ratio the ratio of the price of a stock to the firm's per-share earnings (chapter 3).

perpetual bond a debt instrument with no maturity date (chapter 10).

point and figure chart See X-O chart.

portfolio an accumulation of assets owned by the investor and designed to transfer purchasing power to the future (chapter 1).

portfolio risk the total risk associated with owning a portfolio; the sum of systematic and unsystematic risk (chapter 8).

preemptive rights the right of current stockholders to maintain their proportionate ownership in the firm (chapter 14).

preferred stock a class of stock (i.e., equity) that has a prior claim to common stock on the firm's earnings and assets in case of liquidation (chapter 11).

preliminary prospectus (red herring) initial document detailing the financial condition of a firm that must be filed with the SEC to register a new issue of securities (chapter 2).

premium the market price of an option (chapter 19).

premium (of a bond) the extent to which a bond's price exceeds the face amount of the debt (chapter 10).

premium (over net asset value) the extent to which the price of a closed-end investment company's stock exceeds the share's net asset value (chapter 22).

present value the current worth of an amount to be received in the future (chapter 6).

present value of an annuity the present worth of a series of equal payments (chapter 6).

primary market the initial sale of securities (chapter 1).

principal the amount owed; the face value of a debt (chapter 9).

private placement the non-public sale of securities to a financial institution (chapter 2).

pro forma financial statement a projected or forecasted financial statement (chapter 27).

progressive tax a tax whose rate increases as the tax base increases (chapter 5).

project note a short-term tax-exempt note issued through the Department of Housing and Urban Development to finance urban renewal (chapter 12).

property tax a tax levied against the value of real or financial assets (chapter 5).

proportionate tax a tax in which the tax rate remains constant as the tax base changes (chapter 5).

prospectus a document filed with the Securities and Exchange Commission to register securities for sale to the general public (chapter 2).

purchasing power risk the uncertainty that future inflation will erode the purchasing power of assets and income (chapter 1).

put option an option to sell stock at a specified price within a specified time period (chapter 20).

put bond a bond that the holder may redeem at a specified price within a specified time period (chapter 21).

quarterly report a financial report sent every three months to a firm's stockholders (chapter 4).

quick ratio see acid test.

rate of return the annual percentage return realized on an investment (chapters 1, 13).

real estate investment trust see REIT.

recapitalization an alteration in a firm's sources of finance, such as the substitution of long-term debt for equity (chapter 15).

receivables turnover the speed with which a firm collects its accounts receivable (chapter 17).

recession a period of rising unemployment and declining national output (chapter 16).

red herring the preliminary prospectus (chapter 2).

refunding the act of issuing new debt and using the proceeds to retire existing debt (chapter 9).

regional fund a mutual fund that specializes in a particular geographical area (chapter 26).

registered bond a bond whose ownership is registered with the commercial bank that distributes interest payments and principal repayments (chapter 9).

registered representative a person who buys and sells securities for customers; a broker (chapter 3).

registration the process of filing information with the Securities and Exchange Commission concerning a proposed sale of securities to the general public (chapter 2).

regressive tax a tax whose rate declines as the tax base increases (chapter 5).

regular dividends steady dividend payments that are distributed at regular intervals (chapter 15).

REIT real estate investment trust; a closed-end investment company that specializes in real estate or mortgage investments (chapter 25).

REIT: equity trust See equity trust.

REIT: mortgage trust See mortgage trust.

renegotiable-rate mortgage loan a mortgage loan in which the parties have the option to renegotiate the interest rate charged on the loan (chapter 25).

repurchase agreement a security sale and agreement to buy back the security at a specified price at a specified future date (chapter 2).

required rate of return the expected return necessary to induce the investor to purchase an asset (chapters 8, 14).

reserve requirement the percentage that banks must hold in reserve against their deposit liabilities (chapter 16).

reserves deposits at the Federal Reserve held by banks against their deposit liabilities (chapter 16).

retained earnings earnings of a firm that have been retained instead of distributed as dividends to stockholders (chapter 7).

return the sum of income plus capital gains earned on an investment in an asset (chapter 1).

return on assets the ratio of earnings to total assets (chapter 17).

return on equity the ratio of earnings to stockholders' equity (chapter 17).

revaluation the increase in the value of one currency relative to other currencies (chapter 26).

revenue bond a bond whose interest is paid only if the debtor earns sufficient revenue (chapter 12).

rights an option given to stockholders to buy additional shares at a specified price during a specified time period (chapter 19 appendix).

rights offering sale of new securities to existing stockholders (chapter 14).

risk the possibility of loss; the uncertainty of future returns (chapters 1, 8).

round lot the general unit of trading in a security, such as 100 shares (chapter 3).

secondary market a market for buying and selling previously issued securities (chapter 1).

Securities and Exchange Commission (SEC) the federal government agency that enforces the federal security laws (chapter 2).

Securities Investor Protection Corporation See SIPC.

semiannual compounding the payment of interest twice a year (chapter 6).

semilogarithmic paper graph paper on which one axis is expressed in logarithms (chapter 13).

serial bond an issue of bonds in which specified bonds mature each year (chapter 9).

series E and EE bonds savings bonds issued in small denominations by the federal government (chapter 12).

series H and HH bonds income bonds issued by the federal government (chapter 12).

settlement date the date on which an investor must pay for a security purchase or receive payment for a security sale (chapter 3).

share averaging a system for the accumulation of shares in which the investor periodically buys the same number of shares (chapter 13).

short position owing assets for possible price deterioration; being short in a security or a commodity (chapters 19, 23).

short sale the sale of borrowed securities in anticipation of a price decline; a contract for future delivery (chapter 19).

sinking fund a series of periodic payments to retire a bond issue (chapter 9).

SIPC Security Investors Protection Corporation, which insures investors against failures by brokerage firms (chapter 3).

specialist a market maker on the New York Stock Exchange who maintains an orderly market in the security (chapter 3).

speculation an investment that offers a potentially large return but that is also very risky; a reasonable probability that the investment will produce a loss (chapters 1, 23).

speculator an individual who is willing to accept substantial risk for the possibility of a large return (chapter 23).

spot price the current price of a commodity (chapter 23).

spread the difference between the bid and ask prices (chapter 3).

Standard & Poor's 500 stock index a value-weighted index of 500 stocks (chapter 13).

statement of changes in financial position a financial statement that highlights a firm's sources and uses of funds (chapter 7).

statement of retained earnings a financial statement that highlights whether a firm distributed or retained its earnings (chapter 7).

stock dividend a dividend paid in stock (chapter 15).

stockholders' equity equity; stockholders' investment in a firm; the sum of stock, paid-in capital, and retained earnings (chapter 7).

stock index futures a contract based on an index of security prices (chapter 23).

stock index options rights to buy and sell based on an aggregate measure of stock prices (chapter 20).

stock repurchases the buying and retiring of stock by the issuing corporation (chapter 15).

stock split recapitalization that affects the number of shares outstanding, their par value, the earnings per share, and the price of the stock (chapter 15).

stop loss order a purchase or sell order designed to limit an investor's loss on a position in a security (chapter 3).

straightline depreciation the allocation of the cost of plant and equipment by equal annual amounts over a period of time (chapter 5).

street name the registration of securities in the broker's name instead of in the buyer's name (chapter 3).

strike price see exercise price.

supplementary retirement account (401k plan or SRA) tax-deferred retirement account that is in addition to the worker's pension plan (chapter 5).

supply of money see M-1 and M-2 (chapter 16).

syndicate a selling group assembled to market an issue of securities (chapter 2).

systematic risk risk associated with fluctuations in security prices; market risk (chapters 1, 8).

tax credit a credit against one's tax liabilities, that reduces the amount of tax owed (chapter 5).

tax-deferred annuity a contract sold by an insurance company in which the company guaran-

tees a series of payments and whose earnings are not taxed as they are earned but are taxed when distributed (chapter 5).

tax-exempt bond   a bond whose interest is excluded from federal income taxation (chapters 5, 12).

tax shelter   an asset or investment that defers, reduces, or avoids taxation (chapter 5).

technical analysis   an analysis of past volume and/or price behavior to identify assets and the best time to purchase them (chapter 18).

10-K report   a required annual report filed with the Securities and Exchange Commission by publicly held firms (chapter 4).

10-Q report   a required quarterly report filed with the Securities and Exchange Commission by publicly held firms (chapter 4).

thin issue   an issue of securities with either a small number of securities in the hands of the general public or a small volume of transactions (chapter 3).

third market   over-the-counter market for securities listed on an exchange (chapter 3).

time premium   the amount an option's price exceeds the option's intrinsic value (chapter 19).

time-series analysis   an analysis of a firm over a period of time (chapter 17).

times-dividend-earned ratio   earnings divided by preferred dividend requirements (chapter 11).

times-interest-earned   ratio of earnings before interest and taxes divided by interest expense; a coverage ratio that measures the safety of debt (chapter 17).

total return   the sum of dividend yield and capital gains (chapter 14).

trader   an investor who frequently buys and sells (chapter 3).

treasury bills   the short-term debt of the federal government (chapters 2, 12).

treasury bonds   the long-term debt of the federal government (chapter 12).

treasury notes   the intermediate-term debt of the federal government (chapter 12).

trust department   a division of a financial institution that manages individuals' investments (chapter 4).

trustee   a commercial bank that is appointed to uphold the terms of a bond's indenture (chapter 9).

12b-1 fees   fees that a no-load mutual fund may charge to cover marketing and advertising expenses (chapter 22).

undercapitalized   having insufficient equity financing (chapter 17).

underwriting   the guaranteeing of the sale of a new issue of securities (chapter 2).

unimproved land   land that has not been cleared and that lacks improvements, such as curbs and gutters (chapter 25).

unit trust   a passive investment company with a fixed portfolio of assets that are self-liquidating (chapter 22).

unsystematic risk   the risk associated with individual events that affect a particular security (chapters 1, 8).

valuation   the process of determining the current worth of an asset (chapter 1).

value   what something is worth; the present value of future benefits (chapter 1).

variable interest rate bond   a long-term bond with a coupon rate that varies with changes in short-term rates (chapter 9).

variable-interest-rate mortgage loan   a mortgage loan in which the interest rate periodically changes to reflect current interest rates (chapter 25).

Veterans Administration (VA)   an agency of the federal government that will guarantee mortgages granted to qualified veterans (chapter 25).

voting rights   the rights of stockholders to vote their shares (chapter 14).

warrant   an option issued by a corporation to buy stock at a specified price within a specified time period (chapter 19).

working capital   current assets minus current liabilities (chapter 7).

X-O chart   a chart composed of Xs and Os that is used in technical analysis to summarize price movements (chapter 18).

yield curve the relationship between time to maturity and yields for debt in a given risk class (chapter 9).

yield to call the yield earned on a bond from the time it is acquired until the time it is called and retired by the firm (chapter 10).

yield to maturity the yield earned on a bond from the time it is acquired until the maturity date of the bond (chapters 9, 10).

zero coupon bond a bond on which interest accrues and is paid at maturity, and is initially sold at a discount (chapter 9).

Index